NOT HOME FOR CHRISTMAS

NOT HOME FOR CHRISTMAS

A Day in the Life of the Mighty Eighth

Collected and Compiled by
JOHN MEURS

Copyright ©2009 John Meurs

All Rights Reserved

No part of this book may be reproduced or utilized in any form without written permission from the publisher.

Library of Congress Cataloging-in-Publication Data

Not home for Christmas : a day in the life of the Mighty Eighth / collected and compiled by John Meurs. -- 1st ed.
   p. cm.
 ISBN-13: 978-1-934193-31-0
 ISBN-10: 1-934193-31-3
1. United States. Army Air Forces. Air Force, 8th—History. 2. World War, 1939-1945—Aerial operations, American. 3. World War, 1939-1945—Personal narratives, American. 4. United States. Army Air Forces—Airmen—Biography. 5. Bombing, Aerial—Germany—History—20th century. I. Meurs, John.
 D790.228th .N68 2009
 940.54'4973--dc22   2009014950

ISBN-13: 978-1-934193-31-0 • ISBN-10: 1-934193-31-3

Design by Cyndi Clark

Cover illustration ©1999 Gil Cohen / Knightsbridge Press.
Please send all print inquires to gilcoart@verizon.net

Printed in the United States of America

First edition, July 2009

Quail Ridge Press
P. O. Box 123 • Brandon, MS 39043
info@quailridge.com • www.quailridge.com

DEDICATION

This book is dedicated to
all the brave young men of the 8th USAAF
who lost their lives over Europe
in World War II.

CONTENTS

Publisher's Note 9
Preface 11
Roll of Honor 15
Bombers Lost 23
Introduction 25

1. 351st Bomb Group, 511th Bomb Squadron (Boettcher) 37
2. 388th Bomb Group, 563rd Bomb Squadron (Daniels) 45
3. 398th Bomb Group, 601st Bomb Squadron (Rolfe) 83
4. 398th Bomb Group, 600th Bomb Squadron (Douglas) 97
5. 398th Bomb Group, 600th Bomb Squadron (Pope) 109
6. 91st Bomb Group, 324th Bomb Squadron (Flint) 115
7. 91st Bomb Group, 323rd Bomb Squadron (Stevens) 131
8. 91st Bomb Group, 324th Bomb Squadron (Miller) 217
9. 305th Bomb Group, 365th Bomb Squadron (Schmid) 231
10. 303rd Bomb Group, 358th Bomb Squadron (Jameson) 239
11. 381st Bomb Group, 532nd Bomb Squadron (Smith) 255
12. 390th Bomb Group, 568th Bomb Squadron (Meyer) 269
13. 487th Bomb Group, 839th Bomb Squadron (Davidson) 277
    Ringmasters, Misburg 287
14. 491st Bomb Group, 853rd Bomb Squadron (Hite) 297
15. 491st Bomb Group, 853rd Bomb Squadron (Stevens) 303
16. 491st Bomb Group, 853rd Bomb Squadron (Cloughly) 311
17. 491st Bomb Group, 853rd Bomb Squadron (Bennett) 319

Contents

18. 491st Bomb Group, 853rd Bomb Squadron (Moore) 329
19. 491st Bomb Group, 853rd Bomb Squadron (Stewart) 347
20. 491st Bomb Group, 853rd Bomb Squadron (Butler) 369
21. 491st Bomb Group, 853rd Bomb Squadron (Budd) 401
22. 491st Bomb Group, 853rd Bomb Squadron (Ecklund) 413
23. 491st Bomb Group, 854th Bomb Squadron (Simons) 425
24. 491st Bomb Group, 854th Bomb Squadron (Meuse) 437
25. 491st Bomb Group, 854th Bomb Squadron (Warczak) 449
26. 491st Bomb Group, 854th Bomb Squadron (Wynn) 457
27. 491st Bomb Group, 854th Bomb Squadron (Weitz) 463
28. 491st Bomb Group, 854th Bomb Squadron (Vukovich) 469
29. 445th Bomb Group, 701st Bomb Squadron (Boykin) 475
30. 445th Bomb Group, 701st Bomb Squadron (Barringer) 481
31. 445th Bomb Group, 703rd Bomb Squadron (Harris) 491
32. 445th Bomb Group, 703rd Bomb Squadron (Snow) 493
33. 445th Bomb Group, 703rd Bomb Squadron (McPartland) 507
34. 389th Bomb Group, 566th Bomb Squadron (Hicks) 525
    Epilogue 537
    About the Author 541

PUBLISHER'S NOTE

I am the brother of one of the airmen whose tragic story is one of the many included in this book (Chapter 17). Raymond was the oldest of six in our family, and I was the youngest. He was born October 14, 1919; I was born on October 16th, eighteen years later. Our home was a small farm near Folsom, Louisiana.

I have very few memories of my brother but I distinctly remember the day my mother received the telegram bringing the news that Raymond was missing in action. Our father had died a few years earlier of a heart attack, and our family had moved to Baton Rouge. We were visiting in the country when the telegram arrived at our house in Baton Rouge. Since we were not home our neighbor contacted my aunt who called my two sisters who worked for Esso (Exxon). They were given gas rations to travel the sixty miles to bring the sad news to our mother.

I had been playing in my grandmother's yard and was fascinated by an old workshop in the back. When I returned to the house, a pall had fallen over the adults in the room, and I sensed right away it was news about Raymond...and not good news.

In 1948, Raymond's remains were shipped home. The initial burial had been in a cemetery in Oerie, Germany, but his remains were later re-interred in a military cemetery in Baton Rouge. This day stands out in my mind because so many relatives came to the memorial service. It was only then that I fully realized...Raymond was not coming back.

The son my brother never knew, Raymond, Jr., was born in April of

Raymond and Barney McKee

Publisher's Note

1945. It was my nephew who John Meurs eventually located in his research, and how I became aware of this book. I was immediately impressed and appreciative of the tremendous task he had undertaken to pay tribute to the Americans who had given so much to liberate his country. John's book has enabled me to gain some understanding of what these young men experienced. Try as I might, I still cannot fathom what it was like to be in a metal cylinder at 30,000 feet with the noise, wind, and cold of an open plane while being shot at from below and all around.

Although the small publishing company I own publishes primarily regional books and cookbooks, it was an honor to offer publishing assistance to John so that *Not Home for Christmas* could be recorded and made available to the many families of the crew members.

All revenue received from the sale of this book will be used to pay the manufacturing cost plus expenses related to fulfillment and shipping. Although he has not requested any kind of royalty or other compensation, any remaining revenue will go to John for his years of dedicated effort to research and record the stories included in his book.

As John noted in his Preface, English is his second language and some of his words or phrases may seem a bit awkward; I did not find this to be distracting. To give the book an extensive copy-editing process would have caused a considerable delay in its completion. I also think the book would have lost some of the uniqueness of his presentation.

John and I have exchanged many emails and have come to know each other to some degree. I would like to meet him in person, but, at our advanced age, this may not happen. I, therefore, would like to take this opportunity to express my deepest gratitude and thanks to him for compiling this book, and the tribute it represents.

I'm sure I speak for the many families and friends of the other crew members as well.

Thanks, John.

Barney McKee
Quail Ridge Press

PREFACE

On a sunny Sunday late in November 1944 in Apeldoorn, Holland, when the Meurs family was having their meagre lunch, the B-17 bomber called "Little Guy" of the 381st Bomb Group, came rumbling low over their roof. So low that they had the impression it would take their roof away. The sound was overwhelming; it made the cups on the table dance on their saucers: then followed the deafening sound of the final crash.

They ran to their rear window and saw, half a mile behind their house, a large ink black cloud billow to the sky, followed by the noise of gun shells exploding in the fire. The Meurses and their neighbours ran in the direction of the crashed bomber but were stopped by nervous German soldiers, who had come speeding out of the schoolhouse where they were billeted.

It soon became known that the bomber, with three engines dead, had approached Apeldoorn at a very low altitude. The crew had bailed out over the centre of the village, but the pilot, Kyle "Scott" Smith of Albany, Ohio, had stayed behind the controls and had kept the plane in the air, long enough to avoid the built-up area of the village. He had managed to ditch his aircraft in the open air swimming pool, killing himself in the crash. The other crew members were fired upon by Germans soldiers, who had come running out of a café on the market square. The ball-turret gunner Gustavo "Gus" Contreras was killed and the tail-gunner Francis "Bob" DeLange, was seriously wounded. He was brought to the German field hospital near Apeldoorn from where, two months later, he escaped with the help of the underground. He spent some time with a family, living on the same street where the author and his family had their home.

I visited the crash site as soon as the Germans had cleared out. What was left of the bomber lay straddling the canoe pond of the swimming pool complex.. The almost intact tail-piece stuck out

Preface

high on the island in the middle of the circular ditch, where in better times the burghers of Apeldoorn had paddled their canoes. The fuselage was lying in the water. Debris of the cockpit, engines and wings were spread out on the bank. The typical stench of a burned-out airplane lingered in the air. A few machine guns, their perforated barrels twisted by the impact were lying there, next to yellow painted, portable oxygen tanks. A strange, quiet atmosphere reigned over the wreck, as if the brutal impact had chased all the noise away. The body of Scott Smith had meanwhile been removed and buried in the local cemetery.

I was deeply impressed, when I saw the heap of twisted, burned out aluminium, the remnants of a Flying Fortress, that had flown with a crew of nine inside, all the way from England to this peaceful play-ground in the middle of Holland.

I was so impressed that after my retirement about sixty years later, I decided to research the fate of all thirty-four heavy bomber crews of the 8th USAAF who had not returned to their bases in England on that Sunday, November 26, 1944. The bombers that crash landed behind allied lines are not included.

The Thanksgiving Sunday 1944 mission, had been "business as usual" for the Mighty Eighth. They had sent 1137 B-24's and B-17's into the air escorted by 732 fighter planes. Targets were the synthetic fuel plant at Misburg near Hannover, the rail road viaducts of Altenbeken and Bielefeld and the marshalling yards of Osnabrück and Hamm. All targets were in Germany.

The top brass of the 8th Air Force had decided to try a ruse that day to fool the German Fighter Command. The greatest part of this flying armada would cross the Dutch border at Egmond, fly over the IJssel Lake, which had been called the Zuider Zee before the Dutch closed if off from the North Sea, and fly east in the direction Berlin. By giving the German Luftwaffe the impression that the Third Reich's capital was the target-of-the-day, they assumed that the German fighters would be held back to defend Berlin. Then, all of a sudden, the bomber stream would make a sharp turn to the south and fly back to Hannover and Misburg. They would attack the target on the way home.

Unfortunately the ruse only worked partially. Due to various cir-

Preface

cumstances, the bombers arrived twenty minutes late over Misburg and the German fighters, rushing in from Berlin, met the tail-end of the attacking force: the 491st and the 445th Bomber Groups. Within minutes the sky was filled with burning and exploding bombers, with airmen dangling under the white canopies of their parachutes and with blazing German fighters. The 491st lost fifteen bombers that day. These being the heaviest losses the group sustained on one day during the whole war, they have rightfully called that Sunday in November 1944 "Bloody Sunday" ever since.

An official report of the 8th Air Force HQ comments:

> " . . . Now became apparent an unfortunate deviation in our timing as flown: there was supposed to have been a time difference of 12 minutes between the heads of the 1st and 2nd Task Forces; but the 1st Task Force was now 5 minutes early while the 2nd Task force was 11 minutes late. Hence, as the enemy concentrations hurried westward as expected, instead of being too late to catch the bombers, they caught the 2nd Division with only 2 groups of escort just after they had bombed Misburg. A force of some 350 to 400 enemy aircraft swamped our 5 groups of escort and got through to our bombers with some 150 fighters. Making a skilful attack on the trailing squadron, they wiped out all 9 B-24s. Then overtaking the next squadron which had cut across course, they destroyed 6 of the 10 bombers in this unit. Proceeding up the line, the continued their destruction until they had accounted for a total of 20 B-24s.
>
> . . . Our plan only missed to being a brilliant success by the deviations in timing of the 1st and 2nd Task Forces. But our losses relative to our bombing and the loss inflicted on the enemy still make this a highly successful mission for us . . ."

A last word: this book contains contributions from a wide variety of people. Most of them live in the States, some of them in Germany or in the Netherlands. I did my best to check on spelling errors but left any mistakes in the grammar, this to make to make sure that these contributions remain authentic.

English is not my mother tongue so please accept my apologies for any sins I may have committed against your beautiful language.

John Meurs, June 2009

ROLL OF HONOR

Members of the 8th USAAF (heavy bonbers)
Missing in Action on
Sunday, November 26, 1944

Name	Rank	BG	BS	Pos.	Status*	Serial	Chapter
Chester Adkins	2Lt.	491	854	CP	KIA	0-925956	27
Harry N. Alexander	1Lt.	389	566	CP	KIA	0-767721	34
Dale E. Allan	T/Sgt.	491	854	E	POW	37501911	25
Harold L. Anderson	2Lt.	445	703	N	POW	0-723529	31
Laverne G. Anderson	T/Sgt.	491	853	E	KIA	17154654	19
Randolph D. Anderson	1Lt.	398	600	N	POW	0-703920	4
Robert T. Anderson	Sgt.	91	323	BT	POW	37623990	7
Vernon D. Anderson	2Lt.	398	601	N	KIA	0-926286	3
Thomas Arnold	Sgt.	381	532	WG	POW	16173436	11
Irving Aschendorf	FO	390	568	N	POW	T-127406	12
Walter M. Bagot	1Lt.	398	600	CP	POW	0-679020	5
Herbert E. Bailey	2Lt.	445	701	N	KIA	0-712477	29
Joseph W. Barbieri Jr.	T/Sgt.	445	703	E	POW	32781916	32
Mabry D. Barker	T/Sgt.	91	323	B	EVD	39705634	7
John D. Barringer Jr.	1Lt.	445	701	P	KIA	0-763904	30
John L. Bartram	S/Sgt.	390	568	E	POW	38559818	12
Herman C. Bauer	1Lt.	491	853	N	KIA	0-718214	20
Clarence R. Becker	Sgt.	487	839	E	POW	39117134	13
Elmer H. Bemis	T/Sgt.	491	853	RO	KIA	31261913	21
Roland J. Bender	Sgt.	303	358	BT	POW	16116162	10
David N. Bennett Jr.	1Lt.	491	853	P	KIA	0-686214	17
Gordon L. Benson	Sgt.	445	703	WG	POW	31417427	33
William B. Bigham	S/Sgt.	491	854	E	POW	14177872	27
David L. Bishop Jr.	2Lt.	91	324	CP	POW	0-927629	6
Joseph F. Black	S/Sgt.	445	701	E	KIA	39414426	30
Willard J. Blanchard	2Lt.	487	839	N	POW	02065938	13
Robert N. Blazey	2Lt.	303	358	CP	POW	0-819250	10
Jessie F. Blount	2Lt.	491	853	CP	KIA	0-710548	17
Frank P. Boettcher	2Lt.	351	511	P	KIA	0-927075	1
William R. Boling	S/Sgt.	491	854	NG	KIA	34766825	25
Frederick F. Borger Jr.	S/Sgt.	491	853	WG	KIA	33623530	18
Thomas A. Bottomley Jr.	2Lt.	91	324	N	POW	2065500	8
Joseph L. Boyer	T/Sgt.	491	853	E	KIA	37261239	15
William L. Boykin Jr.	2Lt.	445	701	P	KIA	0-772784	29

*KIA: Killed in Action; POW: Prisoner of War; EVD: "Evaded" (hidden by the Dutch underground)

Roll of Honor

Name	Rank	BG	BS	Pos.	Status	Serial	Chapter
Robert J. Brennan	2Lt.	491	854	B	KIA	0-716708	25
Douglas C. Brink	2Lt.	487	839	CP	POW	0-774505	13
Vernon R. Brock	T/Sgt.	491	853	E	KIA	36458670	21
Norman F. Brunswig	2Lt.	445	701	B	KIA	0-722691	30
Daniel C. Budd	1Lt.	491	853	P	KIA	0-797459	21
Wayne H. Buhrmann	2Lt.	389	566	N	POW	0-719833	34
Donald T. Burke	2Lt.	491	854	B	KIA	02061423	28
Alfred W. Burkhart	2Lt.	390	568	CP	POW	0-776228	12
Robert J. Burnett	S/Sgt.	491	854	TG	KIA	15313690	23
Ralph J. Butler	1Lt.	491	853	P	POW	0-706122	20
Hartwell P. Byrnes	S/Sgt.	491	854	TG	KIA	34872984	24
Victor E. Callicrate	S/Sgt.	491	853	WG	POW	37332584	20
William L. Carlisle	T/Sgt.	491	853	RO	KIA	17115091	16
Lawrence H. Carmichael	Sgt.	491	854	BT	KIA	35898770	26
Ashley J. Carswell	2Lt.	445	703	B	POW	0-780294	31
Joseph R. Caruso	S/Sgt.	491	854	WG	KIA	36876521	24
Robert E. Cloughly	1Lt.	491	853	P	POW	0-700599	16
Dennis C. Cole	S/Sgt.	491	853	TG	POW	16115245	22
Jesse W. Cole	S/Sgt.	491	853	WG	KIA	34854210	16
Lester F. Colson	Sgt.	381	532	RO	POW	32941940	11
John F. Conboy	Sgt.	445	703	WG	POW	13152336	31
Walker E. Conrad	S/Sgt.	491	854	WG	POW	38511840	25
Gustavo E. Contreras	Sgt.	381	532	BT	KIA	39863258	11
James W. Cook	F/O	491	854	B	KIA	T-004607	27
Richard J. Cook	Sgt.	351	511	TG	POW	13094540	1
Ovila S. Corbiere	T/Sgt.	398	600	E	POW	11038403	5
George H. Corona	S/Sgt.	491	853	WG	KIA	39122650	19
James B. Coulson	Sgt.	398	601	BT	KIA	37484766	3
Otis D. Craig	S/Sgt.	445	701	TG	KIA	32956491	29
Thomas R. Crane	S/Sgt.	491	853	TG	KIA	32757283	21
Americo A. Crespolini	S/Sgt.	445	701	WG	KIA	33609563	29
Charles F. Cumings	Sgt.	91	324	E	KIA	36817724	6
Wayne W. Daniels	2Lt.	388	563	P	POW	0-770591	2
Burr E. Davidson	2Lt.	487	839	P	POW	0-394117	13
Joseph P. Dechaine	T/Sgt.	491	853	RO	POW	31315932	15
Francis R. DeLange	Sgt.	381	532	TG	POW	17144240	11
Russell D. Dennis	T/Sgt.	491	854	RO	POW	36745822	24
Roy R. DeNure	2Lt.	487	839	B	POW	0-780298	13
Dewey A. Deweber	T/Sgt.	491	854	RO	KIA	38436457	26
George E. Diamond	Sgt.	445	703	NG	POW	38389221	33
Joseph Di Filippo	T/Sgt.	491	854	E	KIA	32952888	26
Joseph W. Dory	Sgt.	487	839	TG	POW	39918335	13
Gene L. Douglas	Capt.	398	600	Cd.P	POW	0-798637	4
Paul E. Doyle	2Lt.	398	601	CP	KIA	0-775831	3
Harvey B. Duncan	S/Sgt.	491	854	WG	KIA	35572587	23

Roll of Honor

Name	Rank	BG	BS	Pos.	Status	Serial	Chapter
Donald B. Dykstra	S/Sgt.	445	703	RO	POW	32834490	33
Charles J. Ecklund	1Lt.	491	853	P	POW	0-772320	22
John W. Eldridge	T/Sgt.	491	854	E	KIA	32935514	24
George H. Engel	2Lt.	491	853	N	KIA	0-723332	17
Dan W. Finlayson	2Lt.	390	568	B	POW	0-681880	12
John T. Fithen	S/Sgt.	389	566	WG	POW	35457526	34
Robert J. Flint	1Lt.	91	324	P	POW	01012030	6
William R. Foster	Sgt.	445	703	TG	POW	32756416	33
Robert L. Francis	2Lt.	351	511	B	POW	02061112	1
Alfred H. Fromm	S/Sgt.	389	566	WG	POW	16088667	34
William H. Fulkerson	S/Sgt.	491	854	E	KIA	17045556	28
Gordon B. Fuller	S/Sgt.	491	853	WG	KIA	39131096	20
Michael A. Gallo	S/Sgt.	491	854	WG	POW	15076689	24
Paull C. Garrett	Major	389	566	Obs.	KIA	0-388758	34
Carl L. Geppert	2Lt.	491	854	CP	KIA	02058157	28
Gerald M. Greer	2Lt.	491	853	CP	POW	0-768523	16
Carl W. Groshell	S/Sgt.	491	854	TG	POW	39037332	25
Walter O. Grotz	T/Sgt.	445	703	E	POW	37566220	33
Edward C. Guerry	T/Sgt.	491	853	E	POW	39281104	22
Joe A. Gutowsky	S/Sgt.	445	701	NG	KIA	36262079	29
Ferdinand P. Haevers	T/Sgt.	303	358	B	POW	36232827	10
Glenn W. Hall	T/Sgt.	303	358	E	POW	06561676	10
Joseph J. Hanzock	2Lt.	445	703	N	POW	2056795	33
Clarence W. Harris	2Lt.	445	703	P	POW	0-696462	31
Francis S. Hawkins	T/Sgt.	491	853	E	KIA	12122898	18
Kenneth B. Hawkins	S/Sgt.	398	600	BT	POW	10600497	5
John N. Heib	T/Sgt.	491	853	RO	KIA	39203497	22
Harold E. Henley	S/Sgt.	491	854	WG	POW	33657770	25
Keith D. Hereford	Sgt.	305	365	TG	POW	37726165	9
Carl J. Hert	1Lt.	445	703	CP	KIA	0-887066	33
Robert A. Hicks	1Lt.	389	566	P	POW	0-696772	34
Daniel V. Hiner	S/Sgt.	91	324	B	KIA	15354958	6
Norman F. Hirsch	1Lt.	491	853	N	KIA	0-709375	21
John P. Hite	2Lt.	491	853	P	KIA	0-448833	14
Charles E. Hixson	S/Sgt.	491	853	WG	KIA	34505462	17
Howard D. Hole	S/Sgt.	303	358	RO	POW	10100320	10
William L. Hoots	S/Sgt.	303	358	TG	POW	16073336	10
Earl R. Hoppe Jr.	S/Sgt.	491	854	RO	POW	18110446	25
Thomas G. Horger	S/Sgt.	305	365	E	POW	16160898	9
Ross S. Houston	1Lt.	491	853	N	POW	0-886618	18
Robert F. Hudson	2Lt.	445	703	N	POW	02056798	32
William S. Hurtley	Sgt.	91	324	WG	POW	39723469	8
Frank Iaconis	S/Sgt.	398	601	RO	KIA	32987202	3
Wilbur A. James	Sgt.	388	563	RO	POW	33422508	2
Chet H. Jameson	1Lt.	303	358	P	POW	0-451979	10

Roll of Honor

Name	Rank	BG	BS	Pos.	Status	Serial	Chapter
Robert S. Jarois	Sgt.	351	511	RW	POW	36872940	1
Thaddeus C. Jarosz	S/Sgt.	491	853	WG	POW	31362327	21
Burton A. Johns	S/Sgt.	491	853	WG	POW	39290817	22
Woodrow G. Johnson	1Lt.	491	853	N	KIA	0-702443	19
Stanley F. Johnston	2Lt.	91	323	CP	EVD	0-759017	7
Elmer R. Jones	T/Sgt.	491	853	E	POW	14056943	20
Robert Jordan	Sgt.	445	703	TG	POW	42101534	32
Paul J. Juliano	F/O	445	701	N	KIA	T-106230	30
John T. Jurcyk	FO	398	600	N	POW	T-129691	5
Edwin E. Kamarainen	T/Sgt.	491	853	RO	POW	36249633	20
John S. Kendall	Sgt.	91	324	RO	KIA	11038499	6
Joseph R. Kerr	S/Sgt.	398	600	WG	POW	12048880	5
Thomas E. Kincade	S/Sgt.	91	324	E	POW	33784337	8
Glenn C. Knudson	Sgt.	91	324	TG	POW	37584237	8
Norman E. Kottke	1Lt.	398	600	B	POW	0-762637	4
Michael Krivonak	2Lt.	491	854	CP	KIA	0-720867	26
Richard W. Kuerten	Sgt.	390	568	TG	POW	37487968	12
Aaron Kuptsow	2Lt.	398	600	RN	POW	0-710276	4
Eugene A. LaLanze	T/Sgt.	389	566	E	KIA	33684980	34
Melvin A. LaLuzerne	FO	381	532	N	POW	T-128460	11
Thomas W. Lattimore Jr.	Sgt.	305	365	WG	POW	17134062	9
Leo R. Lehr	S/Sgt.	491	853	NT	KIA	11034382	16
Robert D. Levy	2Lt.	445	701	CP	KIA	0-825915	30
Delmont E. Lewis	S/Sgt.	398	600	RO	POW	15041705	5
Richard G. Lipinski	2Lt.	491	854	CP	POW	0-823139	24
Benjamin W. Long	1Lt.	445	703	CP	POW	0-705725	31
Alton Lowe	S/Sgt.	91	324	B	POW	16051876	8
Glenn P. Lynch	Sgt.	91	324	WG	POW	11058136	6
Roland C. Lyons Jr.	Sgt.	445	701	WG	KIA	33543987	30
Paul W. Manter	T/Sgt.	491	853	E	KIA	31321694	16
Sheldon P. Markham	Sgt.	491	854	TG	KIA	33710884	28
Andrew Marko	Sgt.	491	853	WG	KIA	31409763	14
Stanley J. Maronski	Sgt.	445	703	WG	POW	42029120	32
Johnnie H. Martin Jr.	T/Sgt.	491	854	E	KIA	18201716	23
Raymond W. Maul	Sgt.	390	568	BT	POW	37358750	12
Owen L. Mayberry	2Lt.	305	365	CP	EVD	0-778879	9
Charles A. McBride	Sgt.	487	839	BT	POW	37675484	13
Philip J. McCaffrey	Sgt.	388	563	W	KIA	39137896	2
David W. McCarty	1Lt.	491	853	N	POW	0-702065	15
Henry M. McCormack Jr.	S/Sgt.	389	566	NG	KIA	18232463	34
Maurie S. McDade Jr.	2Lt.	303	358	N	POW	0-712301	10
Melvin L. McDaniel	Sgt.	491	854	RO	KIA	35806187	27
Richard K. McDonnell	1Lt.	491	853	NG	POW	0-754752	18
Walter C. McFadden	S/Sgt.	445	701	WG	POW	33679986	29
Donald F. McGurk	2Lt.	381	532	CP	POW	02058845	11

Roll of Honor

Name	Rank	BG	BS	Pos.	Status	Serial	Chapter
Malcolm R. McInnes	Sgt.	388	563	TG	KIA	18175715	2
Robert D. McIntyre	1Lt.	491	853	CP	POW	0-699618	18
John D. McJimsey Jr.	S/Sgt.	491	853	WG	POW	38387667	15
Raymond O. McKee	S/Sgt.	491	853	BT	KIA	38309651	17
Ernest M. McKim	T/Sgt.	445	703	RO	POW	32903189	32
Lee E. McPartland	2Lt.	445	703	P	KIA	0-823508	33
Terrence F. Messing	2Lt.	305	365	N	POW	2066012	9
George A. Meuse	1Lt.	491	854	P	POW	0-820799	24
Gilbert A. Meyer	1Lt.	390	568	P	POW	0-767602	12
Aaron E. Mickelson	Sgt.	390	568	WG	POW	16116167	12
William Millard	Sgt.	487	839	RO	POW	39100980	13
Adolph P. Miller Jr.	2Lt.	91	324	P	POW	0-767604	8
Charles D. Miller	2Lt.	491	854	CP	POW	0-771091	25
Robert J. Miller	FO	91	324	N	POW	T-128773	6
Leonard U. Mitchell	2Lt.	351	511	N	POW	0-739045	1
Owen W. Monkman	Sgt.	91	324	TG	KIA	39622026	6
William H. Mooney	1Lt.	491	854	N	POW	01995888	23
Mitchell H. Moore	S/Sgt.	491	854	WG	KIA	14137474	28
Warren C. Moore	1Lt.	491	853	P	POW	0-547092	18
Henry K. Mosley Jr.	S/Sgt.	491	853	TG	POW	15140725	19
Daniel D. Moynihan Jr.	S/Sgt.	91	324	R	POW	12121342	8
John P. Murray	S/Sgt.	491	853	WG	KIA	12193506	18
Carl Negrin	Sgt.	491	853	WG	KIA	32823090	14
Harry Nelson	Capt.	398	600	N	POW	0-669422	4
Thomas R. O'Brien	2Lt.	491	853	N	KIA	02062692	14
Paul C. Odell	2Lt.	491	854	B	KIA	0-772993	26
Robert G. Ostrander	1Lt.	491	853	CP	POW	0-715802	20
Noel A. Oury	2Lt.	491	853	CP	KIA	01998532	21
Pete Patrick Jr.	T/Sgt.	491	853	RO	KIA	33741746	17
George K. Patten	1Lt.	491	853	B	KIA	0-754761	18
Lester R. Pearson	Sgt.	91	324	BT	POW	39217230	8
Kenneth M. Peiffer	S/Sgt.	491	854	TG	POW	13158746	26
Eldon R. Personette	Sgt.	445	701	WG	KIA	37568985	30
William F. Phelps	1Lt.	491	853	B	KIA	0-706899	21
Gasper Pizzolato Jr.	S/Sgt.	303	358	WG	POW	38488490	10
Harry H. Pollak	T/Sgt.	491	853	RO	POW	12093803	19
Walter W. Poole Jr.	1Lt.	398	600	B	POW	0-734383	5
Kermit R. Pope	1Lt.	398	600	P	POW	0-677562	5
Robert K. Porter	Sgt.	381	532	E	POW	13032669	11
Thomas S. Pozder	S/Sgt.	398	601	TG	KIA	39619814	3
Rene P. Pratt	T/Sgt.	91	323	RO	POW	31296553	7
Joseph M. Price Jr.	S/Sgt.	398	601	TT	KIA	34037612	3
Junius C. Price	T/Sgt.	445	701	E	POW	34644499	29
Milton O. Price	Sgt.	487	839	WG	POW	33000932	13
Richard E. Prunty	2Lt.	91	324	CP	KIA	0-774763	8

Roll of Honor

Name	Rank	BG	BS	Pos.	Status	Serial	Chapter
Roger C. Randles	2Lt.	388	563	B	KIA	02063196	2
Theodore Raybould	S/Sgt.	491	854	NG	KIA	35876057	23
Quilla D. Reed	T/Sgt.	91	323	E	EVD	14107991	7
William L. Reese	1Lt.	491	853	NG	KIA	0-703016	19
Francis M. Reffner	Sgt.	491	854	WG	KIA	37535928	27
Walter W. Reichenau	S/Sgt.	491	853	WG	POW	38366875	19
William E. Reutener	S/Sgt.	491	853	WG	KIA	15140449	16
Robert Richards	S/Sgt.	491	854	WG	KIA	06564934	23
Bernard G. Rieth	2Lt.	388	563	CP	POW	0-827966	2
Joseph F. Rimassa	T/Sgt.	491	853	RO	POW	32159109	18
Richard W. Rimmer	S/Sgt.	398	601	B	KIA	36769929	3
Frank B. Rivera	Sgt.	491	854	TG	KIA	11110234	27
Herman E. Roberts Jr.	2Lt.	491	854	N	KIA	02058550	26
Theodore E. Roblee	Sgt.	305	365	B	EVD	36827301	9
Frank C. Roe	F/O	491	854	N	KIA	T-129192	27
J. B. Rogers	S/Sgt.	445	703	WG	POW	38346476	32
Benjamin G. Rolfe	1Lt.	398	601	P	KIA	0-768682	3
Donald U. Romberger	S/Sgt.	491	854	RO	KIA	33187130	23
Samuel S. Rosenfield	S/Sgt.	491	853	WG	POW	12075010	22
Opher E. Rumney	T/Sgt.	398	600	E	POW	11067317	4
Troy L. Ryan	S/Sgt.	491	853	B	KIA	34622806	15
Richard M. Sagers	T/Sgt.	389	566	TG	KIA	39318635	34
Harold R. Saunders	Sgt.	388	563	TT	POW	33641766	2
Walter O. Schatzel	Sgt.	491	854	WG	KIA	42091484	27
Henry D. Schmid	2Lt.	305	365	P	POW	0-770801	9
Arthur P. Schmidt	S/Sgt.	398	601	RW	KIA	37683661	3
Charles M. Scott	2Lt.	491	854	CP	POW	0-713561	23
Joseph D. Shaffer	Sgt.	388	563	BT	KIA	16130512	2
Elmore W. Shepherd	S/Sgt.	491	853	WG	KIA	32755264	15
Warren K. Simmons	2Lt.	491	854	N	KIA	02061423	28
Horace R. Simms Jr.	2Lt.	491	853	B	POW	0-773343	22
Robert W. Simons	1Lt.	491	854	P	POW	0-699455	23
John H. Singley	2Lt.	491	853	B	KIA	0-707445	16
Cletus A. Sisley	S/Sgt.	445	703	WG	POW	36832348	33
Edward F. Sloane	Sgt.	491	854	RO	KIA	32786393	28
Kyle S. Smith	2Lt.	381	532	P	KIA	0-771565	11
Daniel W. Snow	2Lt.	445	703	P	POW	0-690264	32
Harry W. Sonntag	1Lt.	491	854	B	POW	0-752785	24
Alfred Y. Soo	2Lt.	388	563	N	POW	02064348	2
Frank A. Spady Jr.	1Lt.	491	853	CP	POW	0-815007	19
Harvey Spiegel	2Lt.	445	703	CP	POW	0-834053	32
Irving B. Starr	S/Sgt.	491	853	NG	KIA	32995257	17
Charles H. Steele	S/Sgt.	398	600	TG	POW	17107576	5
Charles W. Stevens Jr.	1Lt.	491	853	P	POW	0-811461	15
John R. Stevens	1Lt.	91	323	P	EVD	0-757319	7

Roll of Honor

Name	Rank	BG	BS	Pos.	Status	Serial	Chapter
Henry M. St. George	S/Sgt.	91	323	TG	EVD	32845187	7
Elmer Steinman	S/Sgt.	491	853	TG	KIA	32775794	15
Russell C. Stewart	S/Sgt.	491	853	TG	KIA	35892782	16
Wayne E. Stewart	Capt.	491	853	P	KIA	0-811152	19
Charles E. Stoetzer	Sgt.	445	703	TG	POW	35758101	31
Phern Stout	S/Sgt.	398	600	TG	POW	37007793	4
Henry P. Stovall	S/Sgt.	491	853	TG	KIA	35869219	17
James C. Strafford	T/Sgt.	398	600	RO	POW	15195342	4
Marvin E. Strohl	2Lt.	491	853	CP	POW	0-720957	22
Eugene J. Sullivan	S/Sgt.	445	701	RO	KIA	11069588	30
Bill H. Sutton	2Lt.	491	853	B	KIA	0-780466	14
Glenn T. Swanby	S/Sgt.	491	854	WG	KIA	39276091	26
Brice E. Thornburg	1Lt.	491	853	CP	POW	0-813609	15
Thomas S. Tolin	2Lt.	491	854	B	KIA	0-570547	23
Richard A. Trombley	S/Sgt.	91	323	WG	EVD	11056622	7
Robert V. Trombly	S/Sgt.	491	853	TG	POW	11085782	20
Gene S. Trumpower	Sgt.	445	703	WG	POW	33901743	31
Gary V. Tubergen Jr.	2Lt.	445	701	CP	KIA	0-821812	29
Edward B. Tykarsky	Sgt.	491	853	E	KIA	13108280	14
George A. Valashovic	1Lt.	491	853	B	POW	0-886529	19
Biaggio R. Valore	Sgt.	445	703	NG	POW	35924434	32
William L. Vance Jr.	Sgt.	445	701	TG	KIA	34778642	30
Frank Verbovsky	S/Sgt.	491	853	WG	POW	32911685	21
Warren H. Voelz	Sgt.	445	703	E	POW	39206592	31
Morris J. Volden	2Lt.	491	853	CP	KIA	0-689416	14
George K. Voseipka	2Lt.	491	853	N	POW	02056649	22
Matthew Vukovich Jr.	2Lt.	491	854	P	KIA	0-714786	28
Harold R. Wagers	Sgt.	491	853	TG	KIA	35872381	14
Fred M. Wakeman	S/Sgt.	491	854	WG	KIA	19188580	26
Floyd A. Walker Jr.	2Lt.	491	853	N	KIA	02058592	21
Edward L. Walota	FO	351	511	CP	KIA	T-003087	1
John S. Warczak Jr.	1Lt.	491	854	P	KIA	0-696926	25
Norman G. Warford	T/Sgt.	491	853	E	KIA	35703424	17
Byron F. Wear	S/Sgt.	381	532	B	POW	16154134	11
Kenneth F. Weible	Sgt.	491	853	RO	KIA	37356037	14
John C. Weisgarber	1Lt.	91	323	N	POW	0-717544	7
Floyd I. Weitz	2Lt.	491	854	P	POW	0-557979	27
Donald N. Welch	T/Sgt.	445	701	RO	POW	35549094	29
Francis E. Welter	Sgt.	445	703	RO	POW	37657028	31
Robert B. Westcott	Sgt.	351	511	BT	POW	33901808	1
Dale T. Westell	S/Sgt.	390	568	RO	POW	37672307	12
Buford Wilhoit	M/Sgt.	351	511	TT	POW	15061962	1
James R. Williams Jr.	S/Sgt.	398	600	WG	POW	14105594	4
Marshall E. Williams	S/Sgt.	491	853	TG	KIA	18219340	18
Fred V. Willis Jr.	2Lt.	491	854	N	POW	0-716564	24

Roll of Honor

Name	Rank	BG	BS	Pos.	Status	Serial	Chapter
Robert E. Willson	S/Sgt.	305	365	RO	POW	34612804	9
Leonard C. Wloczewski	Sgt.	305	365	BT	POW	13187676	9
Robert E. Wombold	Sgt.	351	511	RO	POW	35804837	1
Kenneth C. Wylie	S/Sgt.	389	566	RO	KIA	31261735	34
James J. Wynn	1Lt.	491	854	P	KIA	0-771205	26
Richard F. Yergey	Sgt.	491	854	WG	KIA	33831532	28
Stanley A. Yergey	1Lt.	491	853	B	KIA	0-717010	20
Samuel Yuzwa	S/Sgt.	491	854	NG	KIA	06716563	24
Bartolomeo Zanotto	S/Sgt.	91	324	BT	KIA	36854602	6
Charles E. Zimmer	1Lt.	398	600	P	POW	0-814622	4

BOMBERS LOST

8th USAAF losses on November 26, 1944.
Heavy bombers only

BG	BS	Type	Serial Nr.	MACR	Pilot	Chapter
351	511	B17G-65-BO	43-37571	11203	Boettcher	1
388	563	B17G-60-DL	44-6626	11207	Daniels	2
398	601	B17G-55-BO	42-102565	11147	Rolfe	3
	600	B17G-30-VE	42-97740	11146	Douglas	4
	600	B17G-70-BO	43-37846	11144	Pope	5
91	324	B17G-20-BO	42-31515	10836	Flint	6
	323	B17G-75-BO	42-37913	10837	Stevens	7
	324	B17G-30-DL	42-38128	10838	Miller	8
305	365	B17G-75-BO	43-37955	11202	Schmid	9
303	358	B17G-40-VE	42-97972	11200	Jameson	10
381	532	B17G-35-DL	42-106994	11205	Smith	11
390	568	B17G-50-DL	44-6491	11209	Meyer	12
487	839	B17G-80-BO	43-38141	10758	Davidson	13
491	853	B24H-15-DT	41-28884	10762	Hite	14
		B24H-15-CF	41-29464	10763	Stevens	15
		B24J-150-CO	44-40212	11158	Cloughly	16
		B24J-145-CO	44-40073	10764	Bennet	17
		B24J-150-CO	44-40205	10765	Moore	18
		B24J-5-FO	42-51530	10767	Stewart	19
		B24J-55-CF	44-10485	10760	Butler	20
		B24J-140-CO	42-110167	10768	Budd	21
		B24J-60-CF	44-10534	10761	Ecklund	22
491	854	B24J-150-CO	44-40172	11157	Simons	23
		B24J-155-CO	44-40271	10766	Meuse	24
		B24J-1-DT	42-51253	11108	Warczak	25
		B24H-20-FO	42-95007	11159	Wynn	26
		B24J-145-CO	44-40117	11156	Weitz	27
		B24J-145-CO	44-40108	11155	Vukovich	28

Bombers Lost

BG	BS	Type	Serial Nr.	MACR	Pilot	Chapter
445	701	B24H-20-FO	42-94940	10754	Boykin	29
	701	B24J-40-CF	42-50467	11214	Barringer	30
	703	B24J-5-FO	42-51549	11218	Harris	31
		B24J-1-FO	42-50756	11217	Snow	32
		B24J-1-FO	42-50729	11216	McPartland	33
389	566	B24J-65-CF	44-10579	11208	Hicks	34

INTRODUCTION

For John Meurs, a nine year old schoolboy living in Nazi-occupied Holland, the Big War had been a very exciting episode. In May 1940 he had seen the Germans march through the wide avenue where he lived with his mother, his brother and two sisters. He was the Benjamin of the family: ten years separated him from his brother and eight years from his youngest sister.

His home town Apeldoorn, reckoned in square miles the largest village in the country, is situated smack in the geographical centre of the Netherlands. In the late nineteen thirties it was a rather sleepy town of seventy thousand inhabitants, dominated by the presence of one of the royal palaces. Many retired people used to live there, enjoying the quiet atmosphere and the pure air of the surrounding woodlands. Paper was the main industry then, using the clear water that was pumped up through the sand on which Apeldoorn was built. Farmers from all around would come and do their shopping in the village. It counted two hospitals and a number of good secondary schools but no museums to speak of and no theatre. Religion was there and then in line with the split-up of the total country; 40% catholic, 60% protestant.

Queen Wilhelmina, who did not like the hustle and bustle of The Hague, used the palace as her permanent residence. Her presence in Apeldoorn attracted a large group of people connected with the court. An important detail of the 'Marechaussee' guarded the palace; some sort of military police but commanded by the minister of justice. Quite a few shops in the village carried the royal coat of arms, indicating them as purveyor to Her Majesty the Queen. Once a year, on the queen's birthday, the children of the village would gather in front of the palace to sing their tribute, with Queen Wilhelmina standing on the flight of steps of her residence and waving at the hundreds of kids who were each carrying an orange ribbon.

Introduction

The war ended that pleasant picture. On Friday, May 10, 1940, Hitler invaded Holland and shattered the Dutch dream about neutrality. German paratroops quickly conquered the bridges leading to the big cities in the Western part of the country, and the Luftwaffe had no trouble in annihilating the pitifully few fighters of the Dutch Air Force. The Dutch resisted for five days, but when the Germans had heavily bombed Rotterdam and threatened to do the same with Amsterdam and Utrecht, they recognised that continuing the hostilities was without sense and they capitulated before the overpowering enemy. Queen Wilhelmina and her government fled to England, together with what had remained of the Royal Dutch Navy in Holland. The greater part of the fleet however, including most of the submarines, was stationed in the Dutch East Indies and thus escaped the German attack.

On Saturday morning May 11, John, then almost five years old, stood on his favourite look-out post; one of the red brick pillars that fenced off the front-garden of his home. There he stood and waited for the German army. The word war meant nothing to him, but the way his family discussed the Germans made it clear that they were an evil bunch of people, out to make life difficult for everybody in Holland and in particular for the Meurs family.

He was to be disappointed. The advancing German 227th infantry division did not pass through Apeldoorn via the street where he lived, but used another thorough-fare to push on to the city of Amersfoort; thirty miles to the west.

John saw his first Germans late that afternoon, in the woods behind the secondary school one block from where he lived. They looked and sounded like beings from another world to him. Clad in their dull grey uniforms with their weapons nearby, they stood grooming their steaming horses. John was not overly afraid of these soldiers. They looked friendly enough and even tried to start a conversation with him. Some of them sat on the ground eating chunks of dark bread and munching enormous sausages. He listened to their guttural speech that sounded familiar, but was at the same time incomprehensible for him.

An officer beckoned the boy and gave him a piece of chocolate: dark with a yellow filling. John took it home running and showed

Introduction

it to his mother, who after consultation with her two daughters and after some deliberations, came to the conclusion that it was not poisoned and gave it free for consumption. John ate it. His first encounter with the German army had turned out to be positive.

John's first experience with the invader from the East corresponded indeed with the first view of the Dutch population. The Wehrmacht treated the civilians correctly. When entering a shop they paid for what they took and if possible, did not damage civilian property. This with the big exception: the bombardment of Rotterdam's city centre.

The Austrian Arthur Seys-Inquart, appointed by Adolf Hitler as his deputy in the Netherlands, had a complicated job. The Dutch were slowly but surely to be indoctrinated with the national socialistic dogmas of the Third Reich, and all aspects of daily life in the Netherlands had to be influenced in order to reach a political and economical liaison with Germany. Newspapers and radio broadcasts came under close German control together with the labour unions, the youth organisations, the cultural performances and even the charitable institutions. The official Dutch government; the Head-of-State Queen Wilhelmina and her ministers, was in London. Parliament was dissolved. Seys-Inquart ruled the country by means of the various department heads of the ministries who had stayed in the country when their ministers moved to England.

As the war dragged on, Holland was getting poorer. Stocks of almost all goods were confiscated by the Germans and disappeared over the Eastern border. Shops became empty. Distribution systems had to be set up. Certain items in the normal food basket became scarce: butter, cheese, meat, soap, oil for cooking. Supply of textiles was limited, furniture was hard to obtain. Coffee and tea had disappeared completely: people started to grow their own tobacco for cigarettes. Coal was strictly rationed.

***

The first important group of Jews came to the Netherlands in the late fifteen hundreds. They arrived from Spain, chased away by Ferdinand and Isabella and settled mostly in Amsterdam. There they could freely practice their religion in a country that had just lib-

Introduction

erated itself from Spanish rule for exactly the same reason: freedom of faith. There they could build their synagogues, maintain their own cemeteries and live without ghettos. They were joined a century later, in 1655, by Jews driven from the Ukraine. These spoke Yiddish and were poorer than their religious fellows from Spain. In 1796 all Jews received civil rights; making them fully equal citizens with the rest of the Dutch population.

When the war broke out in 1940, Holland counted about 140,000 Jews, who were living peacefully next to their Christian fellow countrymen, but the German tyrant changed all that. In January 1941 it became forbidden for Jews to visit cinemas. Jews were excluded from the universities in February of the same year. Jewish doctors and dentists were not allowed to treat non-Jewish patients. Jewish musicians were banned from the various orchestras throughout the country. Swimming pools were closed for Jews and so were all public primary and secondary schools.

They were no longer permitted to visit restaurants, libraries, theatres, zoo's, museums and other pubic facilities. All these measures were meant to isolate the Jews from the rest of the Dutch population and to make the mass deportations that were to follow later, easier. Holocaust was on his way, also in Holland.

***

Starting early in the war, the first clandestine newsletters began to appear. The Dutch knew that the 'official' coverage they received via the dailies and the piped-in broadcast system was heavily censored by the Germans. Not only censored: the media were told what to print and what to broadcast. So the Dutch turned to the transmissions from the BBC in London to get the real picture. This, however, was not without danger as all wireless radio sets had been confiscated by the Germans in the early years of the war and listening to 'London' could easily land you in a concentration camp. Quite a few Dutchmen, however, had hidden their radio, transcribed and multiplied the BBC news transmissions and passed these impromptu mini-newspapers on to friends and neighbours. Next to these garden variety kind of papers, professionalized edited and printed 'underground', dailies appeared with a circulation that covered the

Introduction

whole country. All these illegal publications were passed on from hand to hand to trustworthy friends and neighbours.

The Meurs family had one favourite illegal newsman. This son of a neighbour would stealthily find his way in the dark to their backdoor, one hand in the pocket where he had hidden the forbidden pamphlet. He would knock on the door with a pre-arranged signal and silently hand over the paper, but not before having looked right and left to see if the coast was really free. All this to the amusement of mother Meurs and her kids who treated the danger involved much more lightly.

In addition to these illegal newspapers, the occupied Dutch also received pamphlets dropped by the Royal Air Force. The Dutch edition of these, a small booklet called 'De Wervelwind' (Whirlwind) was extremely popular as it presented a tangible token of the free outside world. John and his brother Hans used to make long walks in the woods looking for these pamphlets dropped the previous night. After reading they were passed on to others.

Apart from pamphlets printed in Dutch, did the RAF regularly drop over Holland propaganda material printed in German. Although this material was intended for the people of the Third Reich, the British pilots often released the 'propaganda bombs' already over the Netherlands as some kind of bonus. One of these made a vivid impression on the then eight years old John. It depicted the horrors the German soldiers had met during the siege of Stalingrad with photographs of corpses with frozen off limbs and pulverised skulls. John learned at that early age that the real side of war is not something romantic with laughing soldiers riding impressive armoured vehicles but something very ugly and cruel.

***

The allied bombers became very good friends of the Dutch as they passed over their heads on their way to Berlin or the Ruhr Valley. They were, at least until the allied invasion of Normandy on D-Day, for the people in the occupied countries the only evidence of the Anglo-American war effort against Hitler Germany. Based mainly in East-Anglia, those big American birds of freedom overflew Holland almost on a daily basis on their way to Germany. The

Introduction

British came at night and passed over the Meurs house between nine and ten o'clock. In John's ears they sang a lullaby: he was nestling in bed next to his mother and listened to the soft dark friendly and continuous murmur made by good friends watching over his sleep. It gave him such a feeling of well being that he would remember this sound for the rest of his life.

Around four hours later the RAF returned. The Meurs family then woke up and listened attentively for that different irregular tone that meant that one or more of the bombers had engine trouble and was losing height trying fervently to reach the English coast.

One night in February 1943 their bedrooms were brightly lit by a burning Lancaster, that a few moments later exploded some ten miles behind their house. After the crash, a red glow coloured the winter sky for some hours. The Meurses fell silent. In the middle of the night mother Meurs and her four children kneeled down on the steps of their staircase and said the rosary to accompany the dead airmen on their way to that big airfield in the sky.

The next morning John's youngest sister and some of her friends went to the site of the crash. The bomber had come down on a field, part of the holdings of the royal palace. In the cockpit the dead pilot could be seen, still sitting behind his controls. He wore a bright white pullover; one that John's sister would have loved to posses. She came home carrying a heavy leather flyer's glove she had found near the debris of the bomber.

***

The Dutch resistance towards the German occupying force started early in the war and became stronger, better organised and more specialised over the years. It is not the intention of the author to give a detailed narrative about the "underground" in Holland, but as it played an important role in John's wartime years and as the reader is possibly not familiar with this episode in Dutch history, a few words may be called for. For this purpose the author borrowed heavily from Professor Louis de Jong's standard work: 'The Kingdom of the Netherlands in the Second World War'.

Holland during the war was full of people who had to hide themselves from the Germans. The Dutch word for these people

Introduction

in hiding was 'onderduiker' (someone who disappears under the surface). The peak was reached around 1944 when more than half a million Dutchmen between eighteen and fifty-five became 'onderduikers.' Many of them stayed with farmers in the polders (land recently reclaimed from the sea) but quite a few lived with friends or neighbours.

A huge highly illegal organisation appeared on the scene, 'De Landelijke Organisatie voor Hulp aan Onderduikers' or the National Organisation for the Assistance of Onderduikers. The 'LO', as the organisation was named, started on a very small scale. A protestant clergyman, Frits Slomp, went in hiding in the Eastern part of Holland and met there an inspired housewife Helena Kuipers who persuaded him to travel illegally from pulpit to pulpit and to convince people to take up 'onderduikers'. It worked: Frits 'The Wanderer' as he was nicknamed, managed to set up local committees to gather addresses of people willing to cooperate in this matter. 'Exchanges' appeared where offer and demand met each other: formed by groups in the big cities looking for hiding places versus committees in rural areas offering safe havens. Small camps appeared hidden in the forest but these proved to be too dangerous. It was safer in Holland to hide people among people.

In 1944 the LO had grown into an organisation with 12,000 co-workers divided over 100 districts. Over a thousand female couriers served this vast network, plodding from town to town with their messages hidden in the frame of their bicycles. It was impossible to hide such a big movement completely from the Germans. Meetings were raided, arrests were made and people vanished into the dungeons of the German Sicherheits Dienst. But others replaced them, the work continued. Falsified identity papers were produced by the thousands in specialized workshops. One of these had a collection of over two thousand counterfeited German stamps nicely arranged in wooden boxes.

The Underground Movement in Holland was like an octopus with each tentacle covering a special facet of active resistance. There was the underground press, the assistance to downed allied airmen, the assistance to people in hiding. Falsifying units produced identity papers and ration cards. There were groups specialised in

Introduction

espionage, armed groups for liberating prisoners, groups helping Jews. The people active in the Underground were not even very numerous. Fifty thousand is an estimate, but they were the living proof that Holland was not willing to bend before the German terror. They lived a dangerous life, because when arrested. they faced almost always death by string or bullet after days of torture.

On the Dutch side the players came from all aspects of life; farmers, teachers, housewives, priests, artists, students. Facing these amateurs were the specialists of the German Gestapo, Sicherheits Dienst, or the Abwehr. For security reasons the underground was organised in small groups, the smaller the safer.

Then autumn 1944 came with two occurrences that, almost sixty years later, would bring John Meurs to compile this book.

The first occurrence actually started on April 29, 1944, after a US 8th Army Air Force mission to Berlin. A B-17 bomber, called "Karen B" of the 452nd Bomb Group, had lost two engines over the target and was falling behind the formation.

After the war Navigator Noyes Richey recalls:

> "I plotted courses to both Sweden and England, but we opted for England. We were flying at about 10,000 feet, because that's where the cloud cover was, and we wanted to avoid German fighters. When the cloud cover dissipated, we knew that we had to go down to tree level to avoid fighters."
>
> "At this point the pilot said, "It looks shaky, if anyone wants to bail out, go ahead."
>
> "One member of the crew bailed out. The rest of us stayed with the plane. We were flying on two engines. Just after we crossed into Holland the third engine went out. A B-17 won't fly on one engine! We crash landed safely."
>
> "On hitting the ground we were met by the Dutch Underground who took us to a place of hiding. For almost a year we were hidden in barns, haystacks, cellars, attics, sewers, just anywhere that would keep the Germans from capturing us."

The boyfriend of John's eldest sister Els, Joop Bitter, was a member of one of the groups in the underground, specialised in helping bailed-out allied air-crews find their way back to their bases in England. Headed by a colonel in the Dutch army, they were a bunch of around ten well-meaning, enthusiastic but hopelessly in-

Introduction

---

experienced partisans, trying to find their way in that jungle called active resistance.

Joop lived four houses down the road from John's home.

Early September 1944, the Tail-Gunner of the "Karen B" bomber, Bob Zercher, who originated from York in Pensylvania, came via a couple of other addresses to the house where Joop Bitter and his mother lived. There he joined the twenty-one year old Englishman Kenneth Ingram, who two months earlier had bailed out of his Lancaster bomber after a mission to Gelsenkirchen in Germany.

One night of one of the last days of September 1944, the Meurs family woke up with a start by loud voices and a running car engine in their street. It was long after curfew. Looking out of their sleeping-room window, they heard men shouting in German and saw people coming out of one of the houses further up the road, entering a waiting car and driving of. When nothing further happened, the Meurses went back to their warm beds and fell asleep again.

About two hours later, John's ten years elder brother Hans, who had his bedroom at the back of the house, woke up by a light tapping on the door that lead to a small balcony. Looking out of his window he saw Joop standing in the dark. He opened the door, Joop slipped in and briefly told Hans what had happened.

"We have been raided by the Sicherheits Dienst. When I woke up, one of the Jerries was already standing next to my bed. He told me to get up and get dressed. When I had put some clothes on, the SD-man turned to look into the drawer of my nightstand. I kicked him in the bottom. He fell with his head through the mirror on the stand, and I managed to run down two flights of stairs and to escape via the kitchen door, through the back garden, and into the woods behind our house."

"I ran through the woods for about a mile, scaled the fence of the municipal swimming park and hid myself there in one of the changing-booths. I waited until I was certain that nobody had followed me, sneaked out of the park again, climbed a rain pipe to get to your room and here I am."

Hans went to his sisters' bedroom and whispered; "Joop is here."

John's youngest sister Miep, half awake, replied; "Oh, that's

Introduction

nice," and went back to sleep again. Joop said; "Not so nice, our house has been raided by the SD." Then John and his mother woke up and joined the whispered conversation. Joop told Els where his revolver was hidden in his room and asked her to try and fetch it the next day, when and if the coast would be clear.

Els found her boyfriend's house deserted when she tip-toed the following morning through the backdoor and up to the bedroom were the weapon was concealed. She found it and brought it home where Joop was waiting. "No trace of your mother," she told him, "and the bottle of wine she had saved to celebrate the liberation, lies on the garden-path, empty."

Joop and John's family discussed the next step to be taken. They reasoned that the SD would quickly find out that Joop had a girlfriend and could possibly come to question Els. John's mother was afraid that the SD would arrest Els and use her as a hostage in forcing Joop to give himself up. That meant not only that Joop had to leave the Meurs's house immediately, but also that Els had to move to another address. Joop left without telling where he was going and Els moved to friends a few houses further on the road.

News reached the Meurses later that day that all members of this resistance group had been arrested the previous night, with the exception of Joop and one other member. Joop's mother was taken to the SD headquarters, together with the two airmen she had hidden in her house.

The following morning people of Apeldoorn found, at various intersections in the village, the dead bodies of the male members of the group, including the two airmen. All carried a carton notice board on their chest on which the word "terrorist" was scrawled.

After the war, a Belgian member of the German SD Sicherheits Dienst, who had attended the execution, made the following statement:

> " . . . On the 30th of September 1944 several persons of the underground movement at Apeldoorn were arrested. Among them were two allied airmen. On the evening of the 1st of October, the commander of the SD unit, Hauptsturmführer Carl Filietz, gave me the order to come early next morning with my car. Early next morning the prisoners were loaded in

my car and we brought them to the Apeldoornsche Bos (*a wood south of Apeldoorn – John Meurs*). Then we all knew already that two of the prisoners were allied airmen. One of us spoke fluent English.

"When we came to the Apeldoornsche Bos, an execution platoon of about eight men was already drawn up. The commanding officer was already there. The prisoners were lined up with their backs to a bunker, while before them, at a distance of about 6-7 meters, the firing squad was drawn up. Filietz then told the prisoners, amongst them were the two airmen, that they were to be executed because they were found guilty of the possession of forbidden arms and anti Nazi propaganda. Then he gave the prisoners over to the commander of the execution platoon.

"One of the condemned, a former colonel of the Royal Dutch Army, started to sing the Dutch national anthem in which he was followed by some of the other prisoners. Then the order to shoot was given. The prisoners were not dead at once and several final shots had to be given. I saw that Filietz looted the bodies of the victims after they were shot, and put their valuables and identity papers in his pocket. Then Filietz gave me the order to drive my car backwards to the place where the bodies were shot, gave one of them a push with his foot and said: "Away with them" (in German; "Weg damit"). We then put the bodies into the car and deposited them on several places in Apeldoorn which were pointed out by Filietz, whereupon Filietz himself put a sign on which the word "Terrorist" was written around their neck."

CHAPTER 1

351ST BOMB GROUP 511TH BOMB SQUADRON

Aircraft Type: B17G, Serial: # 43-37571,
"Dottie's Taxi", MACR: 11203
Airbase: Polebrooke

"They were the best crew anywhere."

—From a letter from Larry Gore, the original navigator of this crew, to the wife of ball-turret gunner Robert Westcott.

Pilot: 2Lt Frank P. Boettcher (KIA) New York NY

Co-Pilot: FO Edward L. Walota (KIA) Irvington NJ

Navigator: 2Lt Leonard U. Mitchell (POW) Evansville IN

Bombardier: 2Lt Robert L. Francis (POW) Bismarck ND

Top-Turret: M/Sgt Buford Wilhoit (POW) Bagdad KY

Radio-Operator: Sgt Robert E. Wombold (POW) Bradford OH

Ball-Turret: Sgt Robert B. Westcott (POW) Baltimore MD

Waist-Gunner: Sgt Robert S. Jarois (POW) Detroit MI

Tail-Gunner: Sgt Richard J. Cook (POW) Coatesville PA

Total: 2 KIA, 7 POW

Target: Synthetic fuel plant Misburg, near Hannover, Germany

NOT HOME FOR CHRISTMAS

The Group Narrative of this mission mentions:

"The oil refinery at Misburg was the next target. The three squadrons found the target area free of cloud, but had to bomb using pathfinder methods, because of haze and smoke screens. Intense accurate flak shot down one plane, 43-37571, piloted by Lt. Boettcher, and damaged six others"

This was the sixth mission of this crew. Previous missions included Hamburg, Frankfurt, Merseburg, Eschwiller and Metz.

During debriefing, immediately after this mission, a certain 1Lt. Robert Kasper wrote the following eyewitness account:

"I was flying as pilot of a/c # 43-38650 on a mission to Misburg, Germany, November 26, 1944. Lt. Boettcher was flying in front of me and on my right. About fifteen minutes after bombs away I noticed that he had fallen out of his position. I could not see him, but I heard over the VHF that heavy flak over the target had knocked out two engines and they were both feathered. He called for fighter support, of which was plenty nearby and said he had fallen back into the formation directly behind us. He intended to make France. I saw no parachutes and heard nothing more."

Bombardier **Robert Francis'** story as told by his son Steve:

"Robert Francis was born on September 23, 1920 in Bismarck, the son of Stanley and Nevada (McDonald) Francis. He was raised and educated in Bismarck and graduated from Bismarck high school. After high school Bob attended Bismarck State College.

"On Sunday, November 26, 1944 Dad and his crew did not have an assigned aircraft and ground crew. The plane they flew on their 7th mission was one they were apparently unfamiliar with. Dad believed the engines were 'improperly timed' when they took off as they had difficulty taking off and holding formation with the rest of the group. Dad's opinion was that the pilot had grounds to abort and probably should have done so due to equipment malfunctions but he also said that aborting a mission was grounds for court martial and was done only under extreme circumstances.

"I don't recall Dad talking about the initial damage the plane took. I only know the details just prior to the plane crashing. They had been hit by intense anti-aircraft fire and had lost three of the four engines. They had

Bombardier 2Lt. Robert L. Francis

dumped everything they could from the aircraft to reduce weight and try to hold altitude but were not able to do so. At this point they were on their own and were flying an erratic path trying to avoid the flak. Dad believed that their rapid drop in altitude saved most of the crew as the anti-aircraft gunners were unable to reset the altitude fuses quickly enough to destroy the aircraft. Then the aircraft took a direct hit to the remaining engine from what Dad believed was an 88 mm cannon. It rocked the entire aircraft and the crew immediately began to abandon the aircraft. The navigator jumped but held on to the hatch by his fingers. Dad stepped on his fingers to get him to let go and then jumped himself. As he left the plane, the co-pilot was next to him tying his shoes and preparing to jump.

"Dad was knocked unconscious, either from the shock of the parachute opening or possibly from the plane exploding. He regained consciousness laying in a field with a German soldier pointing a gun at him. This was the only mission where Dad did not carry a side arm. He was dazed and said that he would have tried to shoot the German solder if he were armed. He felt that not carrying the side arm on the mission saved his life.

"Dad told me that he had been hit by shrapnel in the elbow and initially thought his entire arm had been blown off as there was no sensation.

"Dad and the rest of the crew were extremely impressed with their pilot: Frank P. Boettcher. He had immigrated to the US in the 1930s from Germany and they bombed cities where his relatives lived. My Dad had absolutely no doubts about his patriotism and felt completely safe with him flying the plane. Dad was very fatalistic and was glad that Frank died in the crash rather than ending up in the hands of the Gestapo. The pilot was superstitious of being photographed and refused to be in any pictures.

"After the war my father enrolled in the University of North Dakota. Graduated in chemistry and engineering. He returned to Bismarck as a chemist of the North Dakota Health department. After 38 years of service he retired as Assistant Director of the Division of Water Supply and Pollution Control.

"Bob married Jewell McBee in 1953 and raised three sons. He had many interests and talents. He loved to travel, read and to do carpentry projects. Robert "Bob" Leroy Francis, 83, died on December 18, 2003 in Bismarck.

From ball-turret gunner **Robert Westcott's** handwritten notes:

"Nov. 26, 1944. 6th Mission, target Misburg - 6 miles south of Hannover, Germany. Weather clear. Ship B17G, bomb load twelve 500 lbs.

"We took off as per schedule, nos. 2 + 3 three engines did not come up to 2600 R.P. Mis. Upon take-off and no. 1 engine developed an oil leak soon after take-off. Everything went fairly well until about ten minutes before we got to target. Then an oil leak in no. 1 engine caused it to catch fire. This engine had to be feathered and we fell behind our formation. No. 4 engine also developed an oil leak about this time.

"A call came over V.H.F. that bandits were in the area. Our co-pilot Ed Walota set up the superchargers and un-feathered no. 1 engine in order to try to catch up to our formation. About this time and upon the signal from the lead ship the bombardier dropped our bombs upon the target.

"No. 1 engine again caught fire and had to be feathered. No. 4 engine also caught fire. Our Pilot Frank Boettcher tried to feather this engine but due to lack of oil he could not do so. This wind milling prop caused the whole ship to vibrate. Everyone put on their chutes in preparation to jump. The pilots pulled the ship up and then dropped it into a steep dive. Finally they were able to toss off the prop. Everyone felt much better after this, but we had lost about ten thousand feet of altitude. No. 2 and 3 engines were half burnt out and only turning over about twelve hundred R.P. mis. This was not enough to keep the ship up in the air so we were fast losing altitude. This is not good. The lower you go the better the flak gunners get.

"Boettcher ordered everything thrown out of the ship in order to lighten it. This was done and also the ball-turret was salvoed. All the guns and the flak suits were thrown out. Frank got a heading from the Navigator Leonard Mitchell. Leonard was flying his first mission with us but this

351st Bomb Group, 511th Bomb Squadron

was his thirty-fourth mission in total. He gave a heading of one hundred and seventy degrees, this was a direct course to Brussels, which we hoped to make.

"We were down to about three thousand feet of altitude. With two engines out and the other two only turning over twelve hundred this was so high an altitude as the ship could maintain.

"The compass was way off so we could not maintain a true course for Brussels. We flew over a heavy concentration of flak. Due to our low altitude, the flak gunners hit our ship repeatedly, but not in a vital place. The bombardier Lt. R. Francis was hit on the elbow but did not break his skin. We passed out of this flack concentration safely. We flew on for about five minutes and then hit another flack concentration, which was worse than the previous one.

"Tail-gunner Richard Cook and myself were crouched against the armour in the waist. The radio man Robert Wombold was in his position, waist-gunner Robert Jarois was up on the flight deck with our top-turret gunner Buford Wilhoit and the two pilots. The bombardier Lt. R. Francis and navigator Lt. Mitchell were in the nose.

"The flak really hit the ship this time and we were in range of 20 mm and also the fifty calibres besides the eighty-eights. A big shell hit in the back of No. 3 engine in the main gas tank and flak hit No. 2 engine and stopped it.

"This was the end of the ship.

"Cook bailed out of the waist door with myself right behind him, Wombold the radio operator came right behind me. Wilhoit and Jarois went out of the nose hatch followed by Mitchell and Francis. The whole ship was on fire from the gas tank being hit. Robert Wombold, the radio operator, was badly burnt about the face. I received small burns on the face and feet which later got infected. The ship after it got hit went into a gentle bank to the right and went into the ground, upon crashing it exploded. There was little left of it: it looked like burnt paper spread over a wide area.

"After I bailed out of the ship and had opened my chute, I had time to count seven chutes. I landed right in the arms of German soldiers, as did the rest of the crew that bailed out. I found out later on that the pilot and co-pilot never bailed out, why we will never know. The only reason we can think of is that they tried to crash land the ship. The last words I heard the co-pilot speak were "Co-pilot to crew hang on, co-pilot to crew hang on". Later on a German flak gunner told me that their bodies were found in the wreckage of the plane.

NOT HOME FOR CHRISTMAS

Robert passed away in 1995.

Waist-gunner **Robert S. Jarois** as told to his grandson Ryan Jarois:

"For this particular mission the crew was assigned a new navigator, Mitchell, because Larry Gore was assigned to radar school. This was Mitchell's last mission in his tour.

"While in route to the target two of the four engines on the B-17 died. Ground fire near Cologne struck the B-17 catching it on fire. The pilots nursed the plane down to 4000 feet then they all bailed out. A statement by my grandfather states that he recalls he was the third one out the front hatch, one more followed and then the plane exploded with both pilots still in the cockpit. He also recalls that one his buddies' parachute failed to open. I'm not sure who this was. He safely parachuted to the ground only to become entangled in some power lines and picked up by German soldiers. He later found out that they had only landed 10 miles behind enemy lines.

"He was taken prisoner by the Luftwaffe and transferred to Stalag Luft 4. He remained there until March 4, 1945, when the Russian army advancing in from the East, forcing the Germans to move the prisoners back west. My grandfather then spent the next 87 days marching across German occupied territory. They marched on foot over a total of 1200 miles always staying just ahead of the advancing Russians. My grandfather recalled one day the Germans all ran off and left the prisoners by themselves. An hour later the British came and said they were liberated.

"My Grandfather later became a police officer for the City of Detroit. At the age of 24 he met another fellow officer Gerald P. DeVine and began talking about their war experience. DeVine had been a Mustang fighter pilot in the war during the same period. As they talked Devine then realized that my grandfather's story sounded all too familiar. On the same day Devine had tracked down my grandfather's B-17 and covered them down in their last moment of flight and during their descent back to the ground. I found this little bit of info very interesting."

The bomber crashed about twenty miles south-west of Cologne in Germany.

German records mention that six crew members were taken to Dulag Luft-West as POW's and that the wounded Wombold was taken to a nearby hospital.

The two pilots were found in the wreck of the bomber and re-interred after the war in the American Military Cemetery near Margraten in the Netherlands. As they could not be individually identified they received at a later stage a Group Burial in the Long Island National Cemetery in Farmingdale, NY: probably because the pilot came from the State of New York.

*****

Acknowledgements:
Steve Francis, son of bombardier Robert Leroy Francis
Robert Wombold, radio-operator
Ryan Jarois, grandson of waist-gunner Robert S. Jarois
Gayle Westcott, daughter-in-law of waist-gunner Robert B. Westcott
Jan Hey of Hengelo in the Netherlands, for his summary of the Missing Air Crew Report.

CHAPTER 2

388TH BOMB GROUP 563RD BOMB SQUADRON

Aircraft Type: B-17G, Serial # 44-6626,
"Thunderbird", MACR 11207
Airbase: Knettishall

"The next thing I recall was that I found myself in the wreckage of the cockpit, semi-reclined and still in what remained of my seat, flight boots under the rudder bar, instruments dancing on their cables in the open air; clouds rotating meaning upside down and spinning! The silence and peace of a near-death experience; I was an observer in a bizarre world."

—Pilot Wayne W. Daniels in the unpublished story
"The Death of The Thunderbird"

Pilot: 2Lt Wayne W. Daniels (POW) Peoria IL

Co-Pilot: 2Lt Bernard G. Rieth (POW) Syracuse NY

Navigator: 2Lt Alfred Y. Soo (POW) Berkley CA

Bombardier: 2Lt Roger C. Randles (KIA) Concord CA

Top Turret: Sgt Harold R. Saunders (POW) Portsmouth PA

Radio: Sgt Wilbur A. James (POW) New Eagle PA

Ball Turret: Sgt Joseph D. Shaffer (KIA) Wyandote MI

Waist Gnr.: Sgt Philip J. McCaffrey (KIA) Vallejo CA

Tail Gunner: Sgt Malcolm R. McInnes (KIA) Austin TX

Total: 4 KIA, 5 POW

Target: Marshalling Yard at Hamm, Germany

NOT HOME FOR CHRISTMAS

Mission Report, # 228, of the 388th Bomb Group:

"The 8th Air Force again going up in strength dispatched the 1st Division to Altenbeken and Misburg with the 2nd Division going to Bielefeld and Misburg. The 3rd Air Division, for which the 388th furnished the lead and high Groups in the 45th A Combat Wing, attacked Hamm, Germany.

"23 a/c plus 3 PFF a/c were airborne between 0830 and 0850 hours. Assembly was accomplished with the briefed route to the target followed. The weather was about 8/10 cloud coverage but PFF method was used in bombing. Bombs were away at 1218 hours from 25,700 feet. The high Groups mickey equipment failed on the bomb run, so they dropped on the lead Group.

"Meagre to moderate flak was encountered in the target area with one of our crews (Lt. Daniels) being shot down. 11 of our a/c received battle damage. Two jet a/c were seen near the target but did not attack. 2 a/c failed to drop their bombs due to mechanical problems.

"25 a/c returned safely to base by 1442 hours.

"Lt. Daniels in a/c 44-6626 "Thunderbird", was hit by flak on the bomb run and left the formation. With the cockpit filled with smoke, in anticipation of an explosion, the pilot sounded the bail-out alarm. The plane exploded and surviving crew members were apparently blown from the plane. The following group bombed through the parachutes, apparently taking one crew member down with them.

After the war radio-operator **Wilbur James,** together with other crew members, wrote the following unpublished story of the "Thunderbird"

Wilbur James about himself;

"I was born in New Eagle, Pennsylvania on June 3, 1923. Upon graduation, at age 18, from the Monongahela High School, I worked in a steel mill for three months, and at the encouragement of my mother, took an office job, for less pay than I was currently earning and longer hours, with the Mississippi Glass Company, and mostly did what others didn't want to do. I worked there until my enlistment and was happy to get out of an office setting. I wanted excitement and action, and as this history will reveal, I found more than I bargained for."

388th Bomb Group, 563rd Bomb Squadron

Wilbur James, July 2002

Pilot **Wayne W. Daniels** recalls:

"To step back quickly, I began the process of entering the US Army Air Corps on my 18th birthday, over the objections of my mother who had been widowed three years earlier when my father had drowned in a futile attempt to save my brother and sister from drowning. I mention this because the sense of responsibility I carried for the welfare of my mother was to be triggered by later events.

"I had wanted to become a military pilot since long before WWII, and was also taken up in the overwhelming support of the war effort by everyone I knew. (It has been suggested that this was our last popular war). Now, I was an eager enlistee, assuring my mother that I would not be killed in the war and would return to take care of her.

"Enlisted as a Private in the Army Air Corps Reserve, I waited three months for call to active duty, meanwhile flying as an observer for the Civil Air Patrol on Gulf Patrol to spot German submarines. It was to be June, 1943 before I took the tests for Aviation Cadets and was selected for pilot training. Then things moved at a quicker pace and in March, 1943, I finished Multi-engine Advance School and was commissioned. Three months of intensive pilot training followed on the B-17, and this led to the assembly of a crew for combat training, the beginning of my duties as Pilot of Crew 155.

NOT HOME FOR CHRISTMAS

"A few words about that experience through over 100 hours of flying together, I found that we were a compact, dedicated and skilled group of young men. With the final addition of **Al Soo** in the navigator position, we were a top-flight team, headed for the biggest air battle ever staged.

"Of the ten young men who began as crew 155 and the nine who flew the "Thunderbird," only three of us remain at the time of this writing. It is both a privilege and a duty for us to leave a record of those days together and to note something of our lives after the traumatic end of that crew. The focus is on our wartime experiences, but the drama of those days made a lasting impression on the minds of the survivors, and shaped our approach to the lives we were granted to live beyond the war.

Wilbur James remembers:

"After three months at Tampa I found myself on a military train heading for Gulfport, Mississippi. I had been assigned to Daniels crew, along with Daniels and eight others. As we rode along, quite a few guys were wandering up and down the train aisle trying to find their assigned crew mates. Some of our crew members found me. As I recall, one was our co-pilot; Lt. Bernard G. Rieth, from Syracuse, N. Y. Rieth came across as friendly and I liked him from the start.

"I also met top-turret gunner Harold R. "Ray" Saunders. We finally arrived at Gulfport Army Air Force Base, Gulfport, Mississippi, around July 10, 1944. We got assigned to our barracks and for the first time, really had time to meet our other crew members. We bunked close to each other and our tail gunner, Malcolm McGinnis, from Austin, Texas, took the lower bunk and I took the top bunk.

"Mac was seventeen years old and lied about his age, to enlist as an aerial gunner. Joseph "Don" Schaffer, from Wyandotte, Michigan was our ball turret gunner and I believe that he, also, was seventeen. He and Mac became very close buddies. Harold "Ray" Sunders, from Portsmouth, Virginia, was our engineer and top turret gun operator. George Mendenhall, from the Missoula, Montana area, was our left waist gunner. Philip J. McCaffrey, from Vallejo, California, was our armament man and right waist gunner. I was the radio operator/mechanic and radio gunner.

"The officers of our crew were assigned to barracks in the officers' quarters, which were the same style wooden buildings, as provided for the enlisted men, but were just in a different area. Lt. Wayne W. Daniels, from Peoria, Illinois was our pilot in command; Lt. Bernard G. Rieth, from Rochester, New York, was our co-pilot; Lt. Roger C. Randles, from

Concord, California, was our bombardier and while we had another navigator for a short time, we permanently were assigned, Lt. Alfred Y. Soo, from Berkley, California.

"We had a very young crew. I was twenty-one, Daniels, nineteen, Rieth was about twenty-five, McCaffrey, twenty-six, Shaffer and McInnis both seventeen, and I believe Mendenhall was about twenty.

"Lt. Rieth was older than Lt. Daniels, and was chafed somewhat in his position as second-in-command to the pilot. Wayne called him by his initials, "B.G." - which also could be interpreted as an abbreviation for Brigadier General. Wayne states that he deliberately encouraged Bernie to become the "father figure" to the crew. In this he was successful because we all looked up to Rieth.

"Daniels and Rieth pressured the "system" to get Al Soo assigned to our crew. He was an unknown quantity; gone on emergency leave to the funeral of his brother, who was a marine killed in the Pacific. It was to become a splendid decision, as Al was a perfect match with the crew and Wayne trusted him completely. We were all relieved to have such a competent crew member keeping us on course.

"Our three months of combat flight training now started, with a serious tone. We were kept very busy with introductory courses, lectures, physical training, physical exams, specialized courses and much flying. Before the completion of our combat training, we would be flying those mammoth Flying Fortresses about 150 hours, most of which would be at high altitudes.

"The B-17G Flying Fortress was appropriately named. It literally was a flying fortress. All of its guns were 50 calibre, air cooled machine guns. Starting from the front of the plane, it had a twin chin turret mounted under the extreme front of the plane which was operated by Lt. Randles, our Bombardier. Our Navigator, Lt. Soo, operated two hand held guns, one mounted on each side of nose of the plane. Overhead, behind the Pilot and Co-pilot, Cpl. Saunders, our engineer, operated the twin fifties mounted in the upper turret. In the radio room, I operated a single, hand held, gun that protruded from the overhead canopy, of the radio room. Before we went overseas, the radio gun was removed and I was responsible for the right waist gun.

"Behind the radio room, in the belly of the Fort, was the twin fifties (ball turret) operated by Don Shaffer. Behind the ball turret, on the sides of the plane was the left waist, hand held gun, operated by Mc Caffrey. Across the aisle from him, in a staggered position, so they wouldn't interfere with each other, was the right hand held, waist gun, operated by

NOT HOME FOR CHRISTMAS

Mendenhall. Finally, in the tail position were twin fifties, operated by McGinnis.

"In all, there were thirteen guns in each Fort and about half of them could be brought to bear on any attacking plane. Later, the radio room gun was removed, reducing the total fifties to twelve.

"In combat there were twelve Forts in each squadron, each with twelve fifties, and three squadrons formed on each other to comprise a group, so it meant that an enormous and awesome fire power could be directed at the attacking enemy planes. To be exact, there were 432 fifty calibre machine guns in just one group, plus those in the other nearby groups.

"At 25,000 feet, your life span without oxygen is not very long. You would lose consciousness in only a few minutes. This is the reason we had small walk around oxygen bottles to use, if we moved about the plane. We'd disconnect from the central system and plug our oxygen hose into the portable bottle. We kept close tabs on each other to be sure no one had a problem due to lack of oxygen.

"We looked like men from Mars, all dressed up in our flight gear. A helmet with goggles covered our head. From the helmet, wires were strung, that were plugged into the central communications system, to become our "intercom." Our face was covered with an oxygen mask, with its dangling hose plugged into the central oxygen system. Over our heated flight suit was our "Mae West" deflated life jacket and over it was our parachute harness. We wore thick flying boots and equally thick gloves to protect us from the severe cold encountered in all high altitude flying.

"Sometime during the summer, Malcolm McInnis told us that his girl friend was coming to visit him. As I understood it, she was a college student and was boarding at his mother's house. I believe that she was en route from her hometown, in New York State, to Malcolm's home, in Austin, Texas, via Gulfport. Upon her arrival at Gulfport, Malcolm went on pass and they got married

"Mac was a great young man and a straight shooter. He loved his country enough to enlist, at barely seventeen years of age, to serve as an aerial gunner. We all liked Mac very much and he and Don Shaffer were especially good buddies. I'm sure that their comparable ages had a great deal to do with it.

"Bernie Rieth's wife, Peg, came to visit him at Gulfport and we easily befriended her. Somebody suggested that the crew go horse back riding, which we did. Rieth and Peg joined us and we had a great time. I remember that Ray Saunders rode very well, as he had a horse back home, in Portsmouth. Rieth was very well liked by the enlisted men of our crew. He didn't pay much attention to rank, as required by protocol, and the guys appreciated it. Our crew would know when Rieth was landing the plane and it didn't matter, if it was a smooth landing or a bouncy one, we all clapped and cheered just to tease Wayne. Rieth hadn't flown a B-17 prior to joining our crew and had to be trained by Daniels. Wayne was one of the youngest members of our crew, but he took his "Pilot in Command" responsibilities very seriously and sometimes appeared to be a little stern or stiff. He did have a great responsibility, for the safety of the entire crew, and he handled it well. He was an excellent pilot and we all had great confidence in him, as he did in us.

"Our crew had decided that we were going to name our Fortress, "The Thunderbird." The reason for choosing this name was that Wayne had graduated from Air Cadets, at Thunderbird Field.

"Ray Saunders was an exciting person. He was short in stature but big in spirit. When he talked to you, he would look you straight in the eyes and talk with his eyes. His eyes just sparkled, as he told you a story. I guess Ray's friends back home paid some attention to his nose too, as they called him "Nose." He was always in a good mood and lots of fun. When it came to flying that Fortress, he was serious, highly competent and took his engineering and gunnery very serious. He was all business, when on the job.

"Ray used to brag a little, but we didn't pay much attention to him, as he described his house back at Portsmouth, Virginia. When I visited Ray and his family, after the war, and we drove up to the front of the Civil War era mansion, situated on Portsmouth Bay, I realized that all of Ray's stories about it, were true. It was breathtaking and beautiful.

"We rode up to the giant B-17G Flying Fortress, # 43-38680, and it was a sight to behold. Her aluminium body was glistening in the sun and it indeed looked like a Fortress, with those twelve fifties protruding from the gun ports. What a sight! Here was a war machine that really looked indestructible. It gave us great confidence.

"On October 18, 1944 we arrived at Valley in the United Kingdom.

"As we completed our landing roll at Valley, I saw, what appeared to be hundreds of B-17 Flying Fortresses parked anywhere that they could be fitted in. We were instructed to park the bomber, that we ferried across the stormy Atlantic, and it was quite a chore to find a slot and even more difficult, to manoeuvre the plane into her position. The ground was soaked and muddy and there just wasn't sufficient room to easily park it.

"Wales was the location of the main B-17 modification center, where even brand new airplanes were altered to incorporate the latest changes to make them combat ready. We were later to pick-up one of these newly modified airplanes to become the "Thunderbird."

"On October 20, 1944, we received our shipping orders and after breakfast, we loaded all of our gear into a military truck and were transported up some very narrow roads, steep hills, over open country roads and finally arrived at a train station at a large town called Holyhead, Wales.

"We boarded the train and knew that we were being shipped to an Army Air Force Replacement Depot at Stone, England. The train ride to Stone was a pleasant one and we enjoyed seeing the Welsh and English countryside, en route. It was all part of our big adventure and we enjoyed it. After what seemed to be a long train ride, we arrived in Stone, England.

"On October 24, 1944 we were packing our gear again, for departure to our final base: Knettishall, England. It wasn't much longer before our truck pulled up in front of the headquarters building where we could see a sign that said "Welcome to the 388th. Bombardment Group."

"Lt. Daniels delivered our shipping papers and orders to the desk sergeant, who made it official that we were assigned to the 388th. Bombardment Group (Heavy), 563rd. Bombardment Squadron, 3rd Bomb Division, 8th Air Force.

"The barracks that we were assigned to, were former British permanent barracks, constructed of bricks. They were fairly large and quite an improvement over the Nissen huts that we stayed in, en route overseas. The barracks were nestled besides a small village and had a path leading to it. The village was called Barningham. It had a small pub called "White Swan Pub" and a small store.

"When we were taken to our barracks, we picked the only empty cots available. The empty cots formerly belonged to another B-17 crew that got shot down over Germany and we were their replacements. The long barracks were heated by a very small stove at the far end of the barracks and didn't put out enough heat to make much difference.

"Knettishall is just a little hamlet, consisting of a few stone houses, in the rolling country side of East Anglia, England. The closest town of any size is Thetford and not much farther is Bury St Edmunds. About 60 miles Northeast is Norwich and about 30 miles South West, is Cambridge. London is about 100 miles southwest. The whole of East Anglia is beautiful rolling country side, almost completely used to grow sugar beets, cabbage, and various grains. This farm land was converted into air fields for the British and Americans.

"The following is a clipping that I read that I thought was a good description of the area which we were to call home:

"The flatlands of East Anglia, east of Cambridge were like a giant aircraft carrier late in the war, dotted with dozens of relatively primitive airfields from which British and American bombers and fighters flew. More than 50,000 airmen were killed or lost on operations launched from this country. The Madingley cemetery holds 3,812 graves, arranged in concentric arcs, in addition to the lists of those missing in action. An inscription in the memorial chapel speaks of those who, "from these friendly isles, flew their final flight."

"Behind our barracks was a farmers' fence, lined by oak trees and brush. In the field was a large pile of sugar beet, harvested before our arrival. I recall taking a walk, down the narrow path, to Barningham to see what was there. The White Swan Pub, sometimes called "The Bloody Duck", was an attractive brick building bearing an impressive sign. This was the center of attraction, for the local farmers and residents, as they took a break from their mid-day work and stopped at the pub for a pint of beer and a little game of darts.

"Across the narrow road from the pub was a small store that had been built into a house. When I looked into the big plate glass window, I saw a few cans of Heinz products and it made me homesick. The Heinz Company headquarters was back home in Pittsburgh. Due to rationing, there wasn't much that we could buy in the store, but I enjoyed going to it anyhow. It reminded me of Hoskin's Store back home, when I was a kid.

"Back in the States, one of the big treats in life was a nice hot shower, at least once a day. At our base, a hot shower became a "non frequent event." It was about a mile to the shower room from our barracks and was shared by the airmen from the other Bomb Squadrons. The shower room was always cold and depending on when you arrived there, so was the water. It really wasn't much fun and as a result, we usually struggled through about one shower per week.

"Our 563rd Bomb Squadron was one of the few squadrons, housed in permanent structures. Our barracks was made of tile or bricks, and overall was much better than the Nissen Huts that housed others. Our quarters were always cold. In the far end of the barracks, from my bunk, was a small steel, coal stove. Its fire chamber was too small to hold much coal, which resulted in it generating very little heat and being out most of the time. Coal was rationed, and kept in a barbed wire enclosure, to protect it.

NOT HOME FOR CHRISTMAS

"The English children were deprived of many things that we took for granted back home. A primary deprivation was candy and various other sweets. To remedy this, a large barrel was placed in the Mess Hall for the purpose of those who cared to do so, to put their candy ration, or part of it, for later distribution to these children. It was a great gesture and created lots of good will with the English children and their parents. Many children visited the barracks and became friends of the Yank airmen. In some cases some became lifetime friends.

"During a Bomb Group reunion, in 1988 I believe, I was standing in front of St. Mary's Church, when an Englishman came up to me and asked if "Lt James Godwin" was with the group. I told him that he was and was just coming out the door. He ran up to Jim and said - "Do you remember me?" Jim, with a puzzled look on his face, said - "No, I don't believe so." The Englishman said - "I'm the little boy that used to come to your barracks and do things for you." Immediately Jim remembered him and they embraced in a very touching hug.

"Our ball-turret gunner Don Shaffer and I learned that there was a practice ball turret set up in a hangar, and decided to use it mainly for Don to practice getting out of its small enclosure, during an emergency, and for me assisting him. Don would crawl down in it, and I could communicate with him with the inter-com. He practiced rolling the ball to different positions, and practiced how I could get him out if he was wounded.

"Don knew the risks of flying the ball turret in combat, and wanted to take every step possible to increase his odds of getting out of it under emergencies, such as, power failure, where I could use the emergency crank to roll the ball to a position that put his escape door to the top, providing entrance into the waist position. I could do likewise if Don was disabled, and couldn't use the controls to escape.

"I took specialized radio operator training. Since our crew was destined to become a lead crew someday, because we had a bombardier and navigator (not all crews did) I had to learn special radio techniques and standardized reports. One that I specifically recall, was the S T R I K E report.

"Each letter in the word strike was an abbreviation for something. I was trained to send a STRIKE report, as soon as the bombs were dropped and the results known. The bombardier was trained on the data that he was to submit to the radio operator, who would put it in a strike report, and transmit it in Morse code to the bomber base headquarters. In this manner, the guys back at home base knew the results of the raid in advance of us returning to the base.

"Another item that I was trained for was to activate the IFF (Identification Friend or Foe) equipment upon word from the pilot as we left our base, so that the American & British Radar units would identify us properly. I had to shut it off as we approached enemy territory, so that they couldn't home on it, and then turn it back on, as we neared allied territory on our return from a raid, so our friends wouldn't shoot at us.

"If we weren't assigned to some special duty, or on alert to fly a mission the next day, we could go to a pre-designated place, and hitch a ride, on a G.I. truck or bus, to nearby Bury St. Edmunds. It was a fairly good sized town, and we usually ended up at a pub where most of the airmen loafed. It was a very friendly atmosphere and was a welcome break from military life at the base. I can still remember the old English gentlemen, playing darts. This was a favourite game in the pubs, and some of these people got very good at hitting the bull's eye.

"Of the five squadrons in the 388th Bombardment Group, three were expected to fly when the Group was posted for a mission. Normally, if enough planes were left from previous missions, the 388th would put up 21 bombers - 7 from each squadron. Two lead crews led the 388th formation. One would be primary and the other, secondary. The second lead plane took over in the event that the first lead plane had to abort, due to engine or other problems, or got shot down.

"A composite group of planes were also in the air, in the event any of the original group had to turn back during the initial part of the mission. This would usually occur before reaching the English Channel. If the composite planes weren't needed, they returned to the base.

"As the day progressed, the crewmen would keep their eyes on the headquarters office to see what kind of a light was shining. If it was "green" -- no missions would be posted and it was considered ok to drink. If the light was "red" -- that was the alert that a mission would be posted -- no drinking, get lots of rest. In due time the crew names, on alert, would be posted, and it was early to bed.

"Our first mission; November 5, 1944.

"To see our crew's name posted on the headquarters bulletin board, being alerted to fly a combat mission the next day, was electrifying to say the least. It seemed unreal. Our time had come and all of that thorough flight training was going to be put to use and we were going to start paying back Uncle Sam for all the money he advanced to educate us in the "arts of killing and spreading destruction upon the enemy."

"The 563rd Bomb Squadron headquarters had a listing of each airman and where his bunk was located, so that they could easily locate us, and get us up when it was time to prepare for a mission.

NOT HOME FOR CHRISTMAS

"The orderly slipped quietly into our hut, about 4:00 a.m., lightly tapped each of our enlisted crew members, in an attempt not to awaken the crews who weren't scheduled. Some awakened anyhow, chatted quietly with us, as we slipped our clothes over our long underwear, and securely tied our shoe strings. They always wished us luck, and then started to worry about us and "sweat us out."

"I had learned that most of the combat crew members didn't take their .45 cal. revolver with them on a mission, because they felt that it might just get them in trouble with the Germans, in the event that they got shot down, and were trying to escape. Since I hadn't practiced with mine, as yet, I decided to let it in my foot locker. I had planned on going out and shooting stumps with it, but I never got around to it.

"Daniel's crew slipped out of the hut, made a quick stop at the latrine, and joined the officers at the awaiting G.I. truck, and was soon on our way to the Mess Hall, for an early breakfast. The breakfast provided, before a mission, always included fresh eggs. This was a treat. We were always given the best of food, and even though we were supposed to eat foods that weren't inclined to create lots of "gas" at high altitude, we usually just ate what we wanted. As soon as breakfast (chow) was over, we were driven to the Briefing Room.

"The briefing room was about thirty feet long and twenty feet wide. It has a middle aisle, with rows of chairs on both sides. At the rear of the room was an elevated platform, and on the rear wall was a large map of Europe, that was covered with a cloth, to hide the target for to-day.

"As we anxiously awaited the arrival of the briefing officers, we would chat with those near us, and while some smiled and joked, it was apparent that everybody was concerned, anxious, and nervous.

"Suddenly, somebody from the front entrance of the briefing room shouted - " Ahh TENSHUN!" Everyone leaped to their feet and stood at attention, as the briefing officers hurried down the aisle, towards the platform, and said - "at ease men". Without further ado, the chief briefing officer, walked over to the covered map on the wall, removed the covering, and with his pointer tapping at a spot on the huge map, exclaimed - "Your target for today is the Benzol Plant at Duisburg. The secondary target is the Rheydt Marshalling Yards." The map was clearly marked with coloured cord, showing the route to Duisburg from Knettishall, and return.

"The target briefer, pointed to areas in which we could expect anti-aircraft fire (flak), and the most likely places that we'd encounter enemy fighters, the estimated number of enemy fighters and the number of fighters we'd have for escort. We were told that the en route and exit routes had been chosen, to avoid, as much as possible, heavy concentrations of anti aircraft batteries.

"There being no questions asked, the weather briefer proceeded to tell us about the kind of weather that we could expect, and where we'd find it. The Chaplain was then called upon, and he offered a prayer for our safe guidance and return. Most airmen listened reverently.

"The officer in charge told us to get ready to "hack our watches" and as he called off the seconds, followed by "HACK" we all pressed our watch button and our watches were all synchronized, reading the exact same time.

"We were then dismissed to go to our individual specialty briefings and I headed off to join the other radio operators who would be flying with the 388th this day. We weren't briefed on anything particularly new for this mission, but were reminded to activate the IFF equipment and deactivate it at proper times; given our secret radio code books; reminded of ditching procedures and dismissed.

"Our crew rendezvoused and was driven to the locker rooms and equipment shop. Here we emptied our pockets of all personal items, like our wallets, etc; picked up all of our flight gear, our .50 calibre machine guns, parachute harnesses, Mae West Life jackets, and proceeded down the hall to the parachute shop. As we walked down the line in the parachute shop, we were given the type of parachute that best suited our position. For example, the pilot and co-pilot were given back packs, and the remainder of the crew was given chest chutes. Back packs were in short supply, but may have been issued to the Bombardier and Navigator if requested.

"Once again, our entire crew met at the awaiting truck, which transported us across the airport to our awaiting B-17.

"As we jumped down from the truck bed, heavily laden with all of the required equipment, we were greeted by the ground crew that was responsible for keeping this particular bomber in good flying order. The bombs were already hanging on their racks in the bomb bay, the fuel tanks were filled, oil checked, the gasoline operated generator was running and its cable was attached to the plane to assist in the cold start.

"Each crew member climbed aboard with their equipment, to put it near the place that they would be working for the next six or seven hours. Those of us who had gunner responsibilities, installed our .50s, checked them to be sure that they were operating; checked the ammunition boxes to be sure that they were full; and we'd then lift the belt of shells and insert the first one in the guns breech, so it would be ready to insert in the

NOT HOME FOR CHRISTMAS

chamber on the first pull.

"McCaffrey, our left waist gunner and armament man, was more highly trained than us, and we counted on him to assist us with anything that we couldn't fix. He was our best trained gunner.

"My next duty was to check out all of my radio equipment, test it, insert the correct frequency module, based on my briefing, and zero beat the transmitter and receiver to the frequency meter. Once this was completed, I could be pretty sure that everything would work satisfactory in flight. I would also hit the switch for the "trailing wire antennae ball" to be sure that it was giving power. In flight, to get the best possible reception, I would let out a long string of antenna wire, weighted down by the heavy ball attached to it, until I got the best reception. Without it, my radios wouldn't be nearly as effective.

"I completed all of my technical checks, and then walked through the waist to the door on the right side, not far from the tail, and exited the plane, and joined the other crew members who were finished with their checks. Ray Saunders, as Engineer and Top Turret Gunner and I, as Radio Operator/Mechanic/Gunner, had more to check out that most of the other crew members, except of course, the pilot and co-pilot, who had many switches, gauges, etc. on their "to do list."

"Wayne Daniels then instructed us to start winding the props through, to limber up the engines, on this brisk November morning. After having done this, we started putting on our flight gear.

"The electric suits were pulled over our wool clothing and zipped up. We put on our heated boots and plugged their wires into the suit wires. Our Mae West Life Jacket was put on and the narrow canvas straps adjusted, until the jacket was snug to our bodies. Our parachute harness was put on and snuggled up around our legs and buckled near our belt line. The flight helmet with goggles was put on, leaving the goggles ride on the forehead for the time being, and the chin strap was snapped. We checked to be sure that our flak suit (like a bullet proof vest) lay near our position, so we could hurriedly put it on, as we entered the combat zone. It weighed about 40 pounds, and we didn't need anymore weight, considering every thing else we had to wear. The entire crew had flak helmets, similar to infantry helmets, with flaps on the sides to permit the entry and exit of wires to the earphones in the normal flying helmet.

"While the pilot and co-pilot put their back pack chutes on before sitting down at their positions, most of us laid our parachutes on the floor, near us, confident that we could pick it up quickly, and snap it on, during an emergency. We snapped our "throat Mike" (micro-phone) around our

388th Bomb Group, 563rd Bomb Squadron

throats, and plugged it into the head set wires. We then connected our wires to the master radio wires, that put us on inter-com, so that we could communicate with the other crew members. Our oxygen mask was fastened securely to our flight suit, and left to dangle, until we'd need it later, as we passed through 10,000 ft. of elevation. Our electric suit wires were attached to the central electric system after we were airborne.

"Lt. Wayne Daniels, Pilot in Command, notified the crew to go to their takeoff stations, as he'd soon be cranking the engines through. Most of the crew members assembled with me, in the radio room, sitting at their assigned spots on the floor. During takeoff, nobody was permitted in the tail, waist, or nose of the plane.

"As dawn was just about to start breaking, Daniels and Rieth saw the flare, arching through the sky from the control tower, which was the signal to "start engines."

"One by one those mighty engines started to belch acrid smoke, assisted by the auxiliary power from the gasoline generators, and as the ground crew stood by, with the fire extinguishers in ready position, the rumble of the engines began to get smoother, as the earth shook, from all 20 Fortresses starting at the same time. Records indicate that only part of the full compliment of the 388th BG aircraft was scheduled on this and other missions. If all had flown, a complete group would have been 36 airplanes.

"With the engines running smoothly, the ground crews removed the umbilical cord from our power supply, and removed the chocks from the wheels, that held our plane in place, during the run up.

"I was busy getting my radios ready, when I glanced to my left and right about forehead level, I saw a flak hole about as big as a nickel! This flak hole came from a previous mission, and the ground crew hadn't covered it yet. This really brought the reality of war to me, and I knew that the enemy wasn't playing games. They were playing for keeps. I wondered if it wounded or killed the radio man who sat in the seat now occupied by me, on that last flight.

"Rieth spotted the next flare, arching up from the control tower that signalled all planes to taxi to their take off position. Our Fort started twisting out of our hard stand and creaking and groaning with its heavy load, as we slowly taxied across the field, and lined up with the others of the 388th, getting ready to take off for assembly, high in the heavens.

"Finally, our pilots spotted the final flare, fired by the air controller, and each Fort reacted to this take off signal. The lead plane rumbled down the runway, engines at high RPM, developing full power, flaps down, as the pilot eased back on the yoke, as the runway distance shortened,

NOT HOME FOR CHRISTMAS

and the mighty bomb laden war machine, lifted and slowly climbed out straight, maintaining its runway heading.

"Daniels stated that take-off in England in November 1944 was always into fog, and required that the pilot fly instruments from the moment the throttles were opened until breaking out above the clouds. The co-pilot watched the runway lights whiz by on the right side and called out to the pilot, if he appeared to drifting across the runway. The full length of the runway was needed to lift the heavy birds, and there was little room for error. More than one Fortress crashed on take-off and few airmen ever survived these crashes.

"About every 30 seconds, each and every Fortress followed the lead plane, until all twenty of them were in the sky, circling slowly around the radio signal. As they climbed, when possible, they kept the flares of their lead plane in sight, so that they could form on it. They continued to climb to the assigned altitude, to form up with the 388th lead plane.

"To keep spacing between airplanes on the climb out, airspeed and rate-of-climb were to be maintained precisely. Often the bombardier and tail positions blinked "biscuit guns" with orange lens to warn other aircraft if they were getting too close.

"Once our Fort was in the air, each crew member went to his assigned station, connected up his electric and radio wires, and attached his oxygen hose to the central oxygen system. The tail, waist, ball and upper turret gunners could now act as observers, and report anything unusual to the pilot.

"As we continued to climb, each crew member pulled his goggles down over his eyes. Among other things, the goggles gave the eyes some protection against an explosion and flash fire.

"Pilot to crew; "we're ascending through 10,000 feet, so put on your oxygen masks, and check to be sure your system is operating properly. Make sure that your 'walk around oxygen bottle is filled."

"These were important instructions, since unconsciousness would occur quickly and death was a possibility within minutes if oxygen was not administered, at our assigned altitude.

"The lead plane had now picked up the formations of the other bomb groups assigned to bomb Duisburg, and carefully approached them, slipping our seventeen aircraft into our assigned position. The three backup planes weren't needed, so these banked west and headed back to the base.

"At zero hour (the exact time that the lead plane takes its course to the target) the lead plane turns to the assigned course, en route to the target; Duisburg synthetic fuel plant, Germany.

"We were now approaching our assigned altitude of 26,500 ft. and were starting across the English Channel. Through breaks in the clouds, you could see the water glistening below.

"Pilot to crew, we're over the English Channel now, so test fire your guns, but be careful of the other planes."

"I removed my oxygen hose from the central oxygen system, and inserted it into a walk around oxygen bottle, and headed for the right waist gun position. In just moments, the bomber vibrated from the concussion of thirteen fifty calibre machine guns, being fired, in short bursts, at the same time. I pulled back on the charging handle on my gun, which put the first brass cartridge in the chamber, sighted down into the channel and shot a few short bursts. In a way, it felt and sounded good. That was the first firing for any of us, since we left Gulfport in September.

"Pilot to crew, we're approaching the coast of Belgium, so be on the look out for bandits"

"Pilot to crew; 'Keep on the alert for bandits, and keep the chatter on the inter-com down. Just report important things.'

"As we pass over the coast of enemy territory, burst of flak are reported, but none seemed to be a threat to our planes. Hopefully, the designated course to the target will keep us away from intense flak areas.

"After about two and one half hours of high altitude flying, and numerous radio checks, and following the designated course, we start approaching the target area.

"Pilot to crew - in a short time we'll be starting the bomb run. Bandits are reported in the area. Gunners, be alert. I can see heavy flak concentrations ahead on our course. Be sure that your iron helmets and flak suits are on you now and secured."

"Pilot to crew, we're at the I.P [initial point] and have commenced our bomb run."

"Had we been the lead plane, the pilot would have turned control of the aircraft over to Randles, our bombardier. Since we were not in the lead, the control of the airplane remained with the pilot and the bombardier [if he had a bombsight installed] operated it as a back-up to the lead airplane. It would be dangerous for the wingman to move around independently of the lead airplane, where the bombardier was flying that airplane.

"The bomb run is one of the most vulnerable times of a combat mission, as the flight path has to be straight and level, and no evasive action can be taken from flak bursts.

"Bombardier to crew, bomb bay doors open."

"As the bomb bay doors open, it affects the drag of the plane, and the crew can feel the change.

NOT HOME FOR CHRISTMAS

"At 1031 hours, the inter-com crackles as Randles calls out; "bombs away"

"As the bombs leave our bomb bay, screaming down to the benzol plant, five miles below, the reduction of weight causes our B-17 to lurch upward, and we have to be extra careful not to collide with the planes near us.

"It was a great feeling to have our first bombs away, after all the training we had, learning how to do it. The 388th lead plane started the turn away from the smoking target area and started the long flight back to our base.

"By this time, the bombardier of the lead plane was calling his report to the radio operator, who was putting it into the STRIKE format, and sending it back to "1TL," our headquarters back at Knettishall.

Lt. Cunliffe in a/c 42-31996 "War Weary", was hit by flak over the target and was forced to crash-land in Belgium after they had lost three engines. They came down in a cabbage patch near Gazelles, Belgium. Four of the crew had bailed out.

"PFF" equipment, commonly called "Mickey" was a rather new method of bombing unseen targets, using the new science called radar. Visual bombing was still preferred, but "PFF" enabled missions to proceed, when the target was covered by cloud cover, and while it was not always accurate, it did a pretty good job overall.

"After being in the air, according to my flight log, for 5:25 hours, we were finally circling home base, and made a safe landing. Taxing back to our hard stand was uneventful, and we were all relieved to take off our heavy flight gear, especially the oxygen masks, and jump out of the plane. The ground crew welcomed us back with much appreciated smiles, congratulations and hand shakes.

"Our entire crew was assigned an officer, who would de-brief us. First, he offered each of us a shot of whiskey, to warm us up and to relax us a bit. Some didn't accept it, and some other airman was glad to have two. We all sat around a table, with the de-briefer at the head, and informally discussed the mission. He wanted to know if we saw any German fighters; how much flak we encountered and where; did we see anything unusual; sight any aircraft going down; where, etc.

"The de-briefing officers often secured some very valuable information, during the de-briefing sessions, and often could pin point where crews bailed out, how many parachutes were spotted, etc. which gave them a pretty good idea, of how many got killed in the ailing fortress, and how many became POWS. They were particularly interested in learning whether we had seen any enemy jet fighters.

"Our tired, weary, elated crew got on the truck again, and was driven to the mess hall, where we had a good warm meal awaiting us. We could have all we wanted, and usually the G.I. coffee was a big hit.

"After chow, we walked the mile or so back to our huts, where we were greeted by our new found friends, who were sweating us out. Nobody had to coax us to go to bed that night, and we slept!

The Longest Day.
Target for today - Hamm Marshalling Yards
Sunday, November 26, 1944
Wilbur James recalls:

"It was a fitful night. I was restless all night, had short sleeps and nightmares. I can't honestly say that I had a premonition, but it was a very bad night.

"The crew members received the slight touch on the shoulder, which meant that it was time to get up, and we quietly dressed in our warm gear, headed for the latrine, and were soon off to the Mess Hall.

"We did the usual thing of going to the supply room to pick up our combat gear, including going to the parachute shop. We each picked up our chute.

"I recall some of the briefing, being told that our target for the day was the Hamm Marshalling Yards, in Northwest Germany, part of the Ruhr Valley complex, and while we'd heard of it before, and that it had heavy flak concentrations, we didn't seem particularly concerned about it.

"The briefer told us that the purpose of the mission was to try to destroy the huge rail yard, and at the same time catch the heavy concentration of German troops that were funnelling through it to attack our troops in Holland. I believe that the concentration of the German troops was the main purpose of the mission.

"We were reunited with the *Thunderbird*. This was the first time that McGinnis, McCaffrey, Randles, and Shaffer saw "our own plane."

"Having finished our own check up, we got out of the *Thunderbird*, and started winding the props through. The weather wasn't very nice, and was foggy and hazy, which wasn't unusual in England.

"After winding through the props, we boarded the plane, and upon signal from the tower, Daniels and Rieth stated the engines, one by one, as the ground safety man stood by with a fire extinguisher.

"During the early part of the take off and climbing around the splasher beacon, most of the crew was sitting in the radio room and waist section of the plane. As we gained altitude, the individual crew members, moved

NOT HOME FOR CHRISTMAS

to their respective flight positions.

Daniels recalls: "The climb out was uneventful, with the exception that it took us from nearly zero to 20,000 feet on instruments. We had a brand new airplane, it was unnamed and we decided to call it the *"Thunderbird."* We hadn't painted it, since we had been a new crew, and had not been assigned our own airplane. Until this time, we flew other peoples' airplanes.

"We exited the overcast very rapidly, and the sky was full of airplanes. In fooling around trying to get out of the overcast for a few extra minutes, we were out of position, so we had a little trouble figuring out where our own formation was, since there were so many airplanes up there.

"We pulled in on a formation, sort of in a tail chase, and they were lining up. They were exiting across the English Channel, and the bomber stream had started. When we pulled into the formation, we realized that the position that we were assigned was filled with another airplane, and not only that, we were in the wrong formation. The airplanes had a different marking on them. So, then we moved on to the formation in front of that formation, and it turned out that, this was the 388th. We were late in joining our formation, and another B-17 has taken our position. It was ordered to move to another position, and the *Thunderbird* snuggled in close to the lead, as briefed. Everyone was in their proper place, and the state was set.

"The Thunderbird was equipped with a small tube in the left side of the floor of the radio room, within easy reach of my seat. When the pilot so advised me, I was to remove the many packs of chaff, which looked exactly like Christmas tinsel, from the many cases that were on the floor, around my seat. The chaff was to flutter to earth, creating thousands of reflections on the enemy radar, and making it unlikely that they could track us or plot our position. I pulled the boxes of chaff closer to me, not only to make it easy to reach when I got the command, but to offer me some protection from the enemy flak.

Long after the war, the various crew members recall:

DANIELS - "We entered the bomb-run, the bomb bay doors were opened, and the plane was turned over to Randles, the bombardier, for the bomb run. The pilots were simply monitoring the flight of the airplane, while he was steering it. Since we were high on the left wing, the co-pilot had the best viability of the lead plane to our right and had his hands on the wheel. I was probably not even touching the controls - I was looking around. I do remember the upper turret rotating around and saw the shadow of the guns coming across the windshield, a couple of times."

JAMES - "When we started the bomb-run, I started throwing the chaff out the floor tube as fast as I could throw it. Every once in awhile, I could feel the plane lift and that was probably due to nearby flak bursts. Even though it was 55 degrees below zero, I began to sweat, and was considering shutting off my electric suit, or turning it down. I'm sure that the sweating was mostly caused by excitement and fear. We were so helpless against flak. If we were attacked by the enemy fighters, at least we could fight back, but with flak, you just had to stay there and take it. It was a very long bomb run. I seem to recall hearing that it was about twenty minutes, and it seemed every bit that long to me."

"Bombardier Randles to radio: 'We have about one minute until bombs away, and I'm getting a reading on the bomb bay door lights, that the bomb bay isn't opened properly. Could you check it out?'

JAMES - "Immediately upon Randles' request, I quit throwing out chaff, stood up, turned around, and opened the bomb bay door that was behind me. I looked at the doors on both sides of the bay, and they looked normal to me. I turned around, and called the Bombardier.

"Radio to Bombardier, over."

RANDLES - "Ok Radio, this is the Bombardier, Go ahead."

JAMES - "I checked the bomb bay doors, and they are ok. Over."

RANDLES - "Bombardier to Radio. Ok"

Those were probably the last words that Randles uttered.

DANIELS - "We were very close to bombs away and the first jolt of a near miss is followed closely by a second, lifting the aircraft. It came up again, but it was without the pilots help. Then came a third burst that destroyed the *Thunderbird* and decided the lives of the nine members of its crew. It was approximately 30 seconds to bombs away. Here our individual experiences begin."

RIETH - "Since our flight position required us to stay in close to the plane to our right, I was flying the plane, trying to keep a tight formation. The flak was getting more intense and I could see the black bursts out in

NOT HOME FOR CHRISTMAS

front of us and knew that we were going to get hit, but I couldn't alter our course. I was praying."

Bombs away at 12.18 hours

DANIELS – "Then there was a violent explosion! The cockpit filled with smoke. I was convinced that the aircraft would explode, initiated a bank to the left, and attempted to activate the bail-out alarm. The next thing I recall was that I found myself in the wreckage of the cockpit, semi-reclined and still in what remained of my seat, flight boots under the rudder bar, instruments dancing on their cables in the open air; clouds rotating meaning upside down and spinning! The silence and peace of a near-death experience; I was an observer in a bizarre world. Then, detachment quickly shifted to thought of the consequences of my death to my mother - of my responsibilities to her and to the crew. Sensation returned, and I looked across the cockpit - nothing but a wall of red - Bernie blown to bits? No top to the cockpit and no upper turret - has Ray suffered the same fate? I quickly turned away as an oxygen bottle exploded, sending flame shooting over me.

"Now clearly convinced I was very much alive and with the smell of burned hair in my nostrils, I knew I had only seconds to escape. Sensing the possibility of suction over the cockpit I struggled to get up but realized that my seat belt was securely fastened across my legs. I released the belt, and as I pushed myself into the slip stream, I was suddenly airborne with wreckage whizzing by. I instinctively rolled into a ball, then sensing I was losing consciousness; I reached for the parachute release and the curtain lowered on the most memorable moments in my life.

"The next scene opened with boots swinging into and out of view over a white back ground. I had to force rational thought and regained consciousness, hanging in my parachute, my boots swinging over the clouds far below. I looked above to see a canopy of rips and burn holes.

"I received the first evidence that other crew members may have escaped when I saw four chutes several thousand feet above, so high they seemed above the approaching formation of B-17s, and one chute moving closer, its occupant hanging motionless. That these were the chutes of fellow crew members seemed confirmed as I believe I recognized Roger Randles although James later said that Randles definitely did not have his chute on and probably went out of the fortress without a chute.

"Suddenly, death reappeared in the form of bombs falling from the formation above. My chute swung with an impact and then the bombs arched away, trailing a strange screaming sound. The other chute and

388th Bomb Group, 563rd Bomb Squadron

its occupant had disappeared, apparently swept away with the bombs. Now the possible survivors numbered five. I had lost all sense of time and checked my watch. Approximately ten minutes had elapsed since our scheduled bombs-away on that Sunday in November, 1944.

"I checked the pockets in my flight suit and tore up the notes from our pre-mission briefing. I came down through the overcast. I checked to see what was in my pockets, and didn't dispose of my escape kit, because I recalled it wasn't necessary to do so. I got rid of the secret code information, which was in my pocket, and had a lot of roaring sounds in my ears.

"I happened to land in a small tree. I first ducked under some bushes and checked my escape kit, but I was confused, and I couldn't follow the map.

"I felt as though I had to get away from the area quickly, and the best I could do was to figure out the directions, the compass was on the top of the escape kit, and I used it to head west, which I did and was able to evade the Germans for about two hours.

"A humorous incident occurred, possibly after an hour or so went by. I began to feel pain and discomfort. I saw that my arm was cut pretty severely, and I recalled in training that we were to take sulpha tablets from our escape kit, to counteract infection. I proceeded to do so, and it was the awfullest tasting thing that I have ever tasted. I spit it out, and either at that time, or later, in looking at the escape kit again, I realized that I tried to swallow an iodine heliozoan tablet. I had tried to swallow the purification of a gallon of water, instead of a sulpha tablet.

"You are supposed to put the sulpha on the wound, but it was a tablet in our escape kits, not powder. I didn't bother with it anymore after that, but just kept going, and was captured by farmers. They took me to a small town nearby, where *Thunderbird* had crashed and people showed me pieces of the airplane, including the master compass.

"I must have come down close to the airplane. I was kept in the local jail for a few days, and developed a high fever, and became delirious. Then I took the sulpha with some water that they gave me. It was a very small amount of liquid, and later I was told that I had developed a reaction to the sulpha.

"I was put in jail in the city of Hamm, in what appeared to be a prison. I was then taken to the train station that we had bombed, threatened by the local people for a while, put on a train and left that area. I endured the first of many experiences of spending air raids with Germans in train stations or air raid shelters. My guards protected me from lynching or attack by civilians on several occasions.

"I was then taken to a Luftwaffe Station, guarded by two Wehrmacht officers, and turned over to the Luftwaffe. They assigned one guard to me and took me to Frankfurt for interrogation.

SAUNDERS - "The only thing I knew is that one moment I was flying and everything was good, and then the next minute I was in the air and falling."

"JAMES recalls: "Major Harris, who was flying near our bomber, later said that when our Fortress blew up, the fire was so intense, that it lit up his cockpit, and he thought that his plane was on fire, and was just about to ring the bail out signal, when he looked back and saw our disintegrated, burning aircraft.

"Carmen Romeo, a Radio Operator, that I met and befriended at the 388th Bomb Group Reunion at Seattle, WA, wrote the following in his letter of August 1986 to me from Ft. Lauderdale, Fl.

"Yes I was with the 563rd Bomb Squadron, 388th Bomb Group. As a matter of fact I flew on the mission you were shot down. I remember one of our crew calling that a B-17 was falling out of formation and a moment later calling that it had exploded."

RIETH - "There was a terrific explosion and everything went black. I though that I was dead, and just kept on praying. Suddenly, it got very cold, and I opened my eyes. I was outside the airplane and falling. I looked down and saw that I still had the steering controls in my hands. I released them, and pulled the rip cord on my back pack parachute. It didn't open! I started fighting my back pack, and somehow I got it to open. Then I felt this heavy weight on my legs, and looking down, I saw that I was still strapped into my pilot seat! I released the safety belt, and the seat disappeared below me."

JAMES - "As I started to bend down, to throw chaff once again, there was a deafening explosion! My legs flew up in the air and everything went black. I'll never forget the sound of that explosion - it was a very brassy rattling sound - like a galvanized roof vibrating violently. I said - `She's exploded - I'm done for!"

"Immediately I experienced my body tumbling; what felt like a suction, and, like Rieth, I felt intense cold, and opened my eyes. I was cannon balling through space, and barely missed the propeller of a Fortress, that looked like it was in about a 45 degree angle of descent. I'll never forget the sound of that prop, as it screamed past me. I came so close to being struck by it, and torn apart in pieces.

"I remember the explosion very well, and I don't really believe that I was ever unconscious. It was black, everything seemed black to be, but it seemed like my mind was functioning, and I knew that I was in trouble; that I was hit and had to do something about it. I did not get out of the plane on my own. I was just pulled out of it, blown out, or sucked out of it, or something.

"I stopped my tumbling, straightened my self up, and realized that my parachute was attached to the chest harness by only one snap. I looked down, to try to snap it, and the chute was laying in perfect position across my chest. I started working on the snap, but was working on the wrong side. I guess I was groggy. I recall saying that it was snapped, but it wasn't, and reached for the red handle on the rip cord. I didn't have any trouble seeing it. I pulled it hard, and the small chute in it hit my face, and immediately the big chute opened over my head, and gave me a very hard jolt. It amazes me that it didn't break my back.

"I noticed right away, that I was hanging in the chute side ways, since only one iron ring was holding me, and the chute was full of flak holes. I observed that there was blood on my flight suit, on my left leg, below the knee. I knew that I was severely wounded, and couldn't escape, so I reached down to the pocket in my flight suit leg, found my escape kit, and threw it down, so the Germans couldn't get it, and make use of it. It disappeared so quickly that it made me nauseous. I knew that if that one iron ring didn't hold, I would go crashing to earth."

SAUNDERS - "I heard the explosion, and that's when I pushed the mike button, but I was in the air, and I didn't realize what had happened. I didn't know that I was in the air. I didn't do anything to help myself out."

JAMES - "It appears that we were hit on the left side of the plane, based on the position where I was sitting, and the location of my wounds. My wounds were all from the rear, as I was hit in eleven places - left arm, left shoulder, and both legs."

DANIELS - "It would seem to me that the fellows who didn't get out of the airplane, probably didn't survive for the simple reason that they did not have access to their parachutes."

"I exited the airplane later than the other crew members. I counted three, and possibly four chutes above me. I saw airplanes approaching, that I thought at first they were actually lower than the parachutes. The parachutes were really quite high in relation to me; several thousand feet."

"I saw another parachute not in that group. That group stayed up there and never did approach me. I actually moved away from them, but one chute seemed to be travelling down a little faster than the other parachutes. It was not very far away and above me, and that parachute had an unconscious person under it. I would almost swear that it was Randles, as everything looked like Randles to me. He was unconscious or dead, hanging in his very severely damaged parachute. He was falling fairly rapidly, and passed me at a very steady rate."

"I remember that I had a very severely damaged ear, and have the recollection that my ears were very cold. I was frostbitten. My boots were still on, but I had lost my headgear, one glove, and, of course, my flak suit and May West. One leg of my flying suit was ripped off to the knee with the seam still attached to the leg pocket that contained my escape kit."

"Later, in a little jail in a town in Germany, where I was first locked up, some people came in and talked to me. One was a young lady who could speak a little bit of English. She said that there were three bodies at the wreckage of the bomber, and another one not far away. She used German that I didn't understand, and I asked her two or three times, and she realized that she couldn't convey what she was saying, so she borrowed a handkerchief from a man, and then repeated it in German, whatever it was, and demonstrated a parachute that was collapsed. I believe the woman was trying to convey to me that there were four people dead."

JAMES - "After getting my parachute opened, I got very cold. The explosion blew off my iron helmet, flying helmet and goggles, flak suit, Mae West, heated gloves, and while I'm not sure, possibly my boots. I still had my silk gloves on, and I covered my ears with my hands. As it was reported to be 55 degrees below zero, my hands, ears, face and feet got frost bite."

"As I descended it was very quiet; all that I could hear were cracking of the parachute shrouds. I kept looking around and it seemed that I was miles above the undercast. There were no planes in sight. All that I saw was the three parachutes, very far below me. The fact that they were so far below me, always led me to believe that I was one of the first to pull the rip cord, and was the highest person in the sky."

"I knew that I was wounded badly, and didn't have much chance of escaping. I needed medical attention. I thought about becoming a prisoner of war, but it didn't seem to bother me too much. I suppose I was suffering from shock, but still had the survivor instinct."

"After I descended quite a distance, I realized that the Germans were shooting at me. There were no planes around that they'd be shooting at, and I could hear, what I believe were 88 millimetre anti-aircraft shells crackling past me, with a very loud swoosh. I felt sure that I'd be hit, and I just closed my eyes. After awhile it stopped. I'll never forget the total silence of descending from such a high altitude, and nothing around me."

"After awhile, I became conscious of the fact that I was getting down near the under-cast. Then it seemed to be rushing up at me. I went down through it quickly, and could then see that the ground wasn't very far below me. I was in farm land, and I always remembered that the ground had snow on it.

"The earth was rushing up at me now. My rate of descent became very real. I could see that I was falling towards a farm house, and I was kicking like mad to miss it. I drifted over it, and came very close to a big tree, about the size of a huge oak tree. I slid past it, and saw that I was going to hit a fence. Somehow, I missed it, and hit the ground very hard.

"When I hit the ground, my left leg cracked like a rifle shot. It broke, probably because it was all shot up from flak, and the bone was probably already cracked. The wind caught my chute on the ground, and started to drag me, across what I thought was snow, and I was skidding, with a broken leg, very fast across the ground. I did everything that I could to spill the chute, but was dragged quite a way, until finally I was successful.

"I saw some people coming out of the farm house, that I almost hit, and they were running towards me. My left foot was laying 90 degrees to the left, broken very badly. In a short time a man came running to me, dressed in some sort of a military uniform: quite different than I later saw the Germans wearing. He bent over me and said, in perfect English, that he'd try to help me, and wanted to get me into the house quickly.

"I remember seeing people coming across the fields from all directions. A heavy set woman ran up to me, and I saw that she was wearing wooden shoes. I said to her - `Hollanda!' She replied - `Nix Hollanda, heil Hitler.' What a shock! I thought perhaps the wind had carried me into Holland."

"By this time, I released my parachute snap, and let it fall to the ground. There were all kinds of people around me by this time. I was in shock and had very severe pains, all over my body. I decided to give myself a shot of morphine, to end the terrible pain. I reached for the first aid kit that was strapped on my parachute harness, and some people dove on me, took it off, and away from me. I often wondered if they might have thought that it was a hand grenade."

NOT HOME FOR CHRISTMAS

"Then some of the German women got into a fight over my parachute. I guess that they wanted the silk very badly. I'm laying there dying, and they're fighting over my chute."

"The man that first came to me, faded away in the crowd. There was lots of talking in German, but I don't know what the multitude was talking about."

"After what seemed forever, I could see a man coming, with a cart pulled by an ox. He pulled up pretty close to me, as the crowd moved back, and some of the people gently lifted me into the straw covered Ox cart. At that time, the man that I saw at first, in the uniform, came up to me, bent over, and said - "Here, you lost your pencil." My pencil must have fallen out of one of the pockets in the flight suit."

"I've always been curious about that man. I have an idea that if my landing hadn't been detected by other people, that somehow he would have tried to help me."

"For what seemed a long time, the oxen driver, directed the cart or wagon, down a very narrow bumpy road. It was more like a single lane than a road. Every bump brought severe pain to me. My broken leg was jiggling around, and every wound started to hurt very badly. I'm sure that I was also hurting from the severe shock of the parachute opening at a speed of about 150 - 180 miles per hour. Wayne said that the wind was 60 knots, from our tail, so we must have been whistling down that bomb run."

"As we rode along, I looked up and saw a formation of planes, which I felt were heading back to England. There were only twelve in the formation, and at that time I felt that it was our formation, going home without me. It was a very lonely feeling, being left behind, and not knowing how many of my buddies were now dead."

"I realized later, that the formation that I saw couldn't have been mine, as it would have been long gone. I still felt lonely."

"The ox cart finally stopped in front of a small hospital, and the driver went inside. Two Catholic Sisters, who must have been nurses, came out of the hospital with the man, and somehow they put me on a litter and took me into what appeared to be an operating room. There weren't any doctors around, just the two sisters. Very carefully, they cut open my flight suit left leg, to expose the wounded, broken leg. They gave me a shot of something, which helped relieve the pain. I was in shock, but watched everything that they did. They cleaned up the wounds somewhat, and then made a cast for the lower part of my leg, to keep my broken leg in its correct posture."

"I couldn't understand anything that they said, but I could feel the compassion that they had for my suffering. When they finished, I reached into one of my pockets, and pulled out a pack or two of chewing gum. I handed it to them and extended my thanks for their kindness. At first they didn't want to take it from me, but I kept pushing it their way, and finally they accepted it."

"That's the last thing that I remember about being with them. Sometime later, I don't know why I awakened, but it was dark, and I was in a very little room, that as near as I can remember had the bed or cot that I was laying on, another one across from me, on which Rieth was laying, and near me, and I believe sitting on a chair, at my feet, was Saunders. Now I knew of at least two others that survived."

"Saunders kept calling me Staff Sergeant. I didn't understand why he was doing that, and then I realized that we were put in for a promotion to Staff Sergeant, and the more rank we had, the better off we'd be in the hands of the Germans. We didn't admit knowing each other, and didn't chat too much. I knew that Rieth was seriously wounded, and I could see that Saunders had a very big black eye, and his face was all bruised, worse that he would have gotten in a big fight that he lost."

"Sometime later that night, the three of us was put into an unheated German ambulance. Again, Rieth was laying on a litter across the narrow aisle from me, and Saunders was sitting, probably on my litter, close to my bare feet."

"As we started riding along, I was very groggy, and I'm sure that Rieth and Saunders were likewise. It was winter, and my bare feet were very cold. I said to Saunders, pretending not to know him - "Fellow, could you pull my blanket down over my feet? They're cold." He tried, but he was so stiff and sore, that he couldn't do it. I just suffered with the cold for the rest of the ride to Eickelborn Reserve hospital. It was a former lunatic asylum, converted to a war time hospital."

"Later, the Germans told me that Rieth had parachuted into a swamp, and when they found him, he was sitting there, making scarves out of the silk of his parachute. They got him up, put him in a car, and two German officers guarded him, one sitting on each side of him. As they rode along, he tried to disarm them, but they just humoured him, and didn't do anything to him. My opinion is that Rieth was suffering from severe shock, and didn't remember anything about it."

"Rieth got severely wounded. He had a real big chunk of flak in his butt, and got hit in the leg, which later caused him problems in holding his foot up. He may have been wounded elsewhere, also."

NOT HOME FOR CHRISTMAS

SAUNDERS - "I landed in an open field, and there wasn't any snow. A little girl came that was about twelve years old. She could speak perfect English, as she was from Detroit, and got caught over there, before they could get back."

"We went up to a farm house; a great big farm house where I was interrogated. They wanted to know the names of the other crew members. I lied, and told them that I didn't know any of us. I told them that I was awakened in the morning, and was told that they needed me to fill in for a crew member who couldn't fly. At this, they hit me, knocking me over against a hot stove and I got badly burned."

JAMES - "When Rieth, Saunders and I arrived, during the night, at the Eickelborn Hospital, I vividly remember being in the operating room. I was on a litter, or perhaps the operating table, and was running a high fever, and was in severe pain. There were people stirring around in the room, but the only two that I recall very well, was the German Doctor Lorent, who was a Captain, and an arrogant SS. officer."

"I was burning up with fever, and pleading for water. After awhile, somebody got me a container of water to drink, from the faucet, and I later learned that all the water in the lines was contaminated. I drank it, and was thankful for it."

"The German SS. officer started to interrogate me, and all that I'd tell him was name, rank and serial number. "I'm Sergeant Wilbur A. James, and my serial is 33422508." He wanted to know what kind of a plane I was in; where I flew from; and plenty of other questions. I just kept repeating my name, rank and serial number."

"The S.S. officer spied the rings on my fingers and kept trying to pull them off. Even though I was groggy, suffering from fever and shock, I was stronger than he was, and kept snapping my hands closed. The rings were my high school graduation ring, and a cheap Air Force ring. I kept pointing to my high school ring, and saying "Mother," trying to communicate to him that my mother brought that ring for me, and I wanted to keep it. He kept prying my hands open, pulling at the ring, and I kept snapping my hands closed, making a tight fist."

"This went on and on. Finally, He grabbed his officers' hat off his head, slammed it on the floor, and started screaming at me. I couldn't understand a word of it. Dr. Lorent was standing close by, and he kept gesturing to my rings, and shouting to the doctor. They appeared to be arguing, and sometime later, the doctor told me that the SS Officer ordered him to cut the rings from my fingers, and he told him that he was a doctor, and not a butcher. That took lots of courage, because the S.S. Officers were an elite group, very loyal to Hitler, and had power to do anything that they wanted. They were feared by the German military and civilians alike."

"Most of what happened the next several days was not remembered by me, as I was suffering much pain, and had a high fever. I assume that for the most part, I was delirious, and kept going from consciousness to unconsciousness. I hurt and pained all over, and my left leg, below the knee was swelling in the cast that the Sisters put on it, and it was killing me. I remember, time and time again, crying out – 'Nurse, Nurse, Nurse.' My cries were to deaf ears because nobody showed up."

"I was in bed in a narrow room, which had a very high ceiling. There were no windows, except a very small one, above the door. The room was Spartan; just my bed. I don't know how long I was in that room, but I got very little attention. I figured that I was in solitary confinement, but didn't know why. I just kept crying out for a nurse to help me."

"Finally, Dr. Felix Lorent showed up and after examining me, ordered the nurse, a Catholic Sister to bring me something to drink for my fever. She brought in a small glass of apple juice, and I gulped it down. It tasted so cool and wonderful. I'll never forget it. Dr. Lorent started to talk to me, trying to be friendly, but I didn't trust him, and generally didn't respond. I later realized that he was trying to learn some English. He asked me what they called the drink that I just had, in America. I didn't reply. He then said "Apple squeezings?" I didn't reply."

"Dr. Felix Lorent told me that during World War I, the American soldiers occupied his parents' house, were gentlemen, and treated his family well. He said that despite all of the propaganda that he heard, he believed that the Americans were still gentlemen, and that he would try to help me in every possible way. The doctor's comments were nice to hear, and I later found out that he was sincere and trustworthy, but at that time, I didn't trust anyone. I was now starting to get occasional visits by the Sisters, who would check up on me, and bring me some small quantity of food; mostly a light broth, with a few potatoes in it. Sometimes it included a slice of black bread that I couldn't eat."

"It may have been a week before I started to comprehend what was really going on, and how bad I was wounded. I hurt so badly all over. All of my clothes, my navigation watch, flight suit, - everything was taken from me, except the top part of my long G.I. Undershirt. I was constantly cold and hungry."

"I finally noticed blood marks on my leg, below the right knee, and down to my heel. Upon examination, I learned that I'd been wounded on the back of my right leg, at about ankle height. Then I found where flak fragments were in the muscle, on the left side of my right leg, below the knee, and had started to heal. A few months later, a piece of flak worked itself through the skin, and the opening healed."

"My left arm and shoulder hurt all the time. Every time I'd try to move a little, they would hurt. I finally realized that I'd been wounded in the left arm, above the elbow, and pieces of flak were still in there. Every time I moved a little bit, my shoulder would just kill me. Days later I realized that I had a big wound in my left shoulder, and the puss from the infection had hardened into my undershirt, and that's why it hurt so bad to move. After a fashion, I gradually separated the undershirt from the wound, and after a long fashion, it healed, leaving the large piece of flak in my shoulder."

"Every place that weren't protected by my helmet and flak suit had been hit. Even to the extent of the shoulder wound being where the flak suit flapped over to make room for me to attach the parachute snap to the harness. If it hadn't been for the helmet, flak suit, armour in the back of my seat, and perhaps the frequency meter under my seat, I doubt seriously that I would have survived the explosion."

SAUNDERS - "In hospital I stayed in a room by myself. I don't know how long, both feet and my both hands were as big as boxing gloves, and already turned black, and cracked open. My left eye was shot out, and both ears were frozen. I had shrapnel in both legs. What gave me my most trouble were my hands. Both of my eyes were black. Aw, they pushed me around. I don't know why they didn't give me any medical treatment. I don't think they liked my attitude. They did pull the shrapnel out of my legs, and wrapped crepe paper around it. They kept my hands wrapped."

***

In 1948 Wilbur James married his former military nurse, Lt. Hannah "Virginia" Jones.

He graduated from the Robert Morris College, Pittsburgh, PA and in 1954 he joined the staff of Fox Grocery Company where he became Vice President - Finance and a Member of the Board of Directors. He retired from the company in 1988 but continued to serve on a consulting basis.

He was active in civic affairs in the Monongahela Valley, and, to mention a few, he was Director and Chairman of the New Eagle School District; President of the Mon Valley United Fund and Vice Chairman & Director of the Mon Valley Hospital, Inc.

He's was member of the Riverview Baptist Church where he's served as Deacon, Trustee and Sunday School Teacher.

He became a private pilot in 1971 and flew his own Cessna 182 Skylane. Writing, hunting, fishing, trail riding, camping and travelling became his hobbies.

Wilbur Albert James, died Saturday, April 12, 2003, at the age of 79 while visiting relatives in Merthyr Tydfil, South Wales, UK

Apart from his wife for many years, Wilbur left three children; Linda, Keith and Virginia, and two grandchildren, Todd and Brandy Joy.

In 2001, Wilbur wrote the author:

"Randles, Mc Caffrey and Mc Innis' family didn't care to communicate, so I finally lost touch with them.

"I found Al Soo, our navigator, by going through the phone information while on a business trip to San Francisco, and we remained in touch ever since - phone calls - letters and meeting at various 388th BG Reunions all over the U.S.

Re Daniels, I started communicating with him early on and we always kept in touch - same as Soo.

"I located B.G. Rieth years ago, by a lead that Al Soo found in a magazine article, which he showed me when I visited him the first time, and I located him through a phone call to his attorney, who was mentioned in the article, living in Washington, D.C. He reluctantly gave me Rieth's phone number, in Buffalo, N. Y. and I called him and when he answered I said "Sprecken ze Duetch." His reply was - "Is that you, James?" I then arranged to see Rieth and his lovely wife, Peg, in Buffalo, while returning through there from a business flight to Toronto, Canada. Later, I had business in Buffalo, and I flew my plane there and again we had a wonderful reunion. Rieth was a very wonderful man - loved his wife and children above all else. He was the most popular man on our crew. "

***

In June, 2002, Rita Kreienfeld of Hamm, Germany, the target of "Thunderbird, sent the following e-mail to Wilbur:

NOT HOME FOR CHRISTMAS

"I got your address from Mr. John Meurs, who sent me a part of your book "Fate of the Thunderbird".

"I was very impressed. John asked me to find out what happened to the aircraft, where it crashed and where you and your friends came down by parachutes. I found the site and an eyewitness who saw the plane crashing into a field near his house, only ten meters from the farmhouse, where he lived and still lives. He was then a boy of 14. He saw the three dead airmen in a part of the plane near the edge of the nearby forest. And he saw three or four parachutes gliding to the east.

"A year later he found together with his father the body of another American soldier in the forest.

"I'm now trying to find the site where you came down. It is not so easy, because my questions bring back all the trouble that happened during the war and elder people don't like to remember. Maybe the hospital with the two catholic sisters was in Heessen, that's my hometown. I am a teacher of 52 years and I am interested in history.

"Years ago we found out where a British Lancaster Bomber crashed in a nearby wood. We put a memorial on the site. Every second year a group of Englishmen come to visit the site. It's always very moving. To find out what happened to the crew of the Lancaster was easier, because we found it out twenty years ago. But I will not give in. Next week we will put the story into our local paper, maybe people remember the incidents.

"The war in the air as seen by the population of Hamm, Germany" By Rita Kreienfeld

"Hamm was a primary air attack target and was at the beginning of the war the most frequently attacked city in the industrial region. The strategic importance of the Hamm area was not only caused by the marshalling yards (the largest in Europe) and the canal but also by the presence of four military barracks and the for the economy of the city so important wire factories, where for instance military important goods were manufactured such like wire for the in Peenemünde assembled V-rockets.

"Starting in 1940, eleven over ground bunkers were built, who still deface the picture of the city, together with 30 public shelters. The over ground bunkers even resisted direct bomb impacts and have saved many Hammers their lives.

"When America entered World War II in 1941, the position of the civilian population became more hazardous. In 1943 the allies started saturation bombing and "bombing around the clock", i.e. during the day the Americans came with their "Flying Fortresses" and at night the British Lancaster bombers drove the people out of their beds and into the bomb shelters. The first heavy day-time attack came on March 4, 1943 on the industrial area west of the city and caused 154 deaths.

"In the evening of April 22, 1944, came the first heavy attack on the city itself and the surroundings of Hamm. Seven hundred and fifty bombers and a few hundred fighters dropped 8000 bombs and 3500 incendiary bombs that turned the city within a couple of hours into a sea of flames and a desert of rubble.

"On May 31, 1944 another heavy attack caused with 205 deaths, 151 of them were forced labourers and POW's, for the greater part from the Soviet Union.

"Three big series of attacks followed in autumn of the same year on the city and vicinity. Especially the raid of December 5 caused heavy damages. About 400 bombers dropped 2000 bombs, 10'000 incendiary bombs and 40 bombs with retarded action then on the centre of the city. In less than five minutes 92 buildings were totally destroyed during this attack, 113 others buildings - among them the barracks and a the military hospital - were partially destroyed, 115 medium and 800 slightly damaged.

"On April 6, 1945, Hamm was occupied by the Americans. Until that date, 1029 people in Hamm had lost their lives due to bombardments. Fifty of them belonged to the Wehrmacht, 746 were civilians and 233 of them foreign forced labourers and POW's.

"The city was fully destroyed. Compared with the number of inhabitants she belonged to the most damaged cities in Germany. The railroad viaduct, prime target of the bombers, remained intact. Even now you can distinguish the bomb craters in the Lippewiesen.

"Every quarter of the year, since the end of the war, unexploded bombs are retrieved in Hamm. Every time people are evacuated, the bomb is disarmed and life goes on. It's nothing special in Hamm and appears regularly. With every building project the bomb disposal squad comes first. American aerial pictures are used to locate unexploded bombs as the situation becomes more critical as the detonators could rust through and could cause an explosion. That's why in the year 2002 we are still engrossed with the war.

"Those who suffered most under these aerial attacks were women, children, adolescents and old men. Late December most people were waiting for the end of the war, most of them waiting for the liberation of the Nazis. As the Americans entered the city from the north they were in the suburbs cheerfully greeted by many people. Especially by those who had suffered most under the terror of the Nazis; the social democrats and the communists, many Catholics, labour union members, Jews who had survived, they all were indeed relieved.

"Many however remained in their cellars. They were afraid that the Americans would cut their throats. The Nazi propaganda was still rooted. Many Hammers saw for the first time coloured people. Children and adolescents befriended the GI's regardless of the anti-fraternisation policy, and swapped swastikas and pistols against food and cigarettes. Many people had thrown their weapons in the lake. Now kids dived them up while they meant to a certain extend survival. The kids were sad when the Americans departed and the Englishmen came, the "Tommies", who were obviously less well off than the Americans. Hamm belonged to the English zone of occupation: their troops were housed in the former barracks. When the years went by friendship was built with the British.

"The town archives were destroyed during one of the severe attacks on Hamm. Since then we are a city without history as many irreplaceable and very old documents together with more recent documents had found a place in these archives. Also the Town Hall was annihilated and so were lists of prisoners and documents concerning captured American airmen.

***

In September 2006, pilot Wayne Daniels paid a visit to Hamm:

"Al Soo was unable to travel to this event. I travelled with my wife, Anita, and two of her relatives. We were met by Rita Kreinfeld at our hotel, and she remained our contact throughout the short visit. We met for several hours in a restaurant in Heessen, at a location near where I may have been taken after my capture, and then went to the farm to meet Theo Wickford, who was 14 years old when he witnessed the crash of the "Thunderbird"..

"Without exception, every person I met and talked with was very cordial, and this included Rita's husband and son, Seigfried Paul and his wife, Theo Wickford and his wife, and a former anti-aircraft gunner from the Hamm defences. They were very interested in the particulars of the B-17, my crew, and impressions of my experience as a German POW. Siegfried showed me photos of the destruction of the marshalling yard and the city of Hamm by our bombers. The anti-aircraft gunner told me of his experience as a young man who was assigned the job of operating an optical sighting device used to derive the altitude of the bombers. I also met another historian and writer, Anneliese Beeck. She wrote an article for a local newspaper about my visit, which I will try to copy and send to you separately.

"Theo provided information concerning the wreckage of the aircraft which landed on his parent's farm on November 26, 1944. It was in at least three sections, spread apart along a path of perhaps a quarter of a mile. The portion that was closest to the farmhouse was the center section, consisting of what remained of the wings and perhaps the cockpit. The bodies of three crewmen were located in what remained of the rear section of the fuselage, in a field at some distance from the farmhouse. What may have been the nose section was located at some distance on the other side of the farmhouse, in a field which was underwater due to recent flooding. The engines landed separately, and were retrieved many years after the war.

"Nothing remains of the wreckage at the crash site, and they know of no existing photographs. Rita informed me that any official records of that incident perished, along with all of the other records of that period, in a bombing raid. I was able to secure the permission of Theo to place a reminder of this event on his property, and Rita suggested that, since this is a remote area unlikely to be seen by others, it might be possible to place a memorial in the town of Heessen. I will follow-up on this. I'm glad I made the pilgrimage, met many generous people, will continue my contacts, and plan to record a more thorough account of my impressions in my own writings.

***

Acknowledgements:
Official Report of the November 26, 1944 mission.
Source: The 388th Bombardment Group at War
By: Edward J. Huntzinger, Secretary
388th Bombardment Group Association
Pilot Wayne Daniels
"Thunderbird"; an unpublished book by Wilbur James in cooperation with other crew members.
Rita Kreienfeld, "The war in the air as seen by the population of Hamm."

CHAPTER 3

398ᵀᴴ BOMB GROUP 601ˢᵀ BOMB SQUADRON

Aircraft Type: B-17G, Serial # 42-102565,
"Ugly Duckling", MACR 11147
Airbase: Nuthampstead

"Which one is it?"

—Top-turret gunner Joe Price's mother when the Western Union car drove into her back yard. She had three sons serving overseas

Pilot: 1Lt Benjamin G. Rolfe (KIA) Lark UT

Co-Pilot: 2Lt Paul E. Doyle (KIA) Shellsburg WI

Navigator: 2Lt Vernon D. Anderson (KIA) Seattle WA

Bombardier: S/Sgt Richard W. Rimmer (KIA) Cook County IL

Top-Turret: S/Sgt Joseph M. Price Jr. (KIA) Forest City NC

Radio Operator: S/Sgt Frank Iaconis (KIA) Richmond Hill NY

Ball-Turret: Sgt James B. Coulson (KIA) Sioux City IA

R. Waist-Gunner: S/Sgt Arthur P. Schmidt (KIA) Osaga IA

Tail-Gunner: S/Sgt Thomas S. Pozder (KIA) Great Falls MT

Total: 9 KIA

Target: Synthetic fuel plant Misburg, Germany

NOT HOME FOR CHRISTMAS

Operations Officer's Report of Mission on 26 November 1944.
(TRANSCRIPTION)

HEADQUARTERS
Aaf Station 131
APO 557, U.S. Army

27 November 1944

SUBJECT: Operations Officer's Report of Mission on 26 November 1944.

To: Commanding General, First Bombardment Division, APO 557
Commanding General, 1st Combat Bombardment Wing, APO 557

1. SUMMARY OF OPERATIONS:

A. Data:
(1) Date of Mission:	26 November 1944
(2) Target assigned:	MISBURG, GERMANY
(3) Target attacked:	MISBURG, GERMANY
(4) Units Participating:	37 A/C of this group including 2 PFF A/C formed the first "C" GHG
(5) Returned early:	42-97338
(6) Failed to Take-Off:	None
(7) Lost:	43-97740 PFF, 42-102565, 43-37846

2. NARRATIVE:

Lead squadron, 1ST "C" CBG

Take-off was normal consisting of 2 PFF and 35 regular aircraft.

Assembly was as briefed and actual assembly was good. Departed point A 3 minutes early.

Control Point was was reached thirty seconds early. Had to S for some time in Division assembly line before the group could get into proper position.

Started climbing at control point one and continued until bombing altitude was reached.

398th Bomb Group, 601st Bomb Squadron

No persistant contrails at 20'000 feet and above.

Formation was good.

Followed flight plan as briefed to the target.

Individual squadrons took interval and bombed by squadrons. Target was visual. Interval of squadrons on the bomb run was extremely good. For two or three minutes before bombs away the lead squadron was under fire by heavy flak. Just after bombs away the group lead and deputy group lead aircraft were knocked out of formation. The deputy group aircraft returned alone and landed at an airfield near Leiston.

Flak was heavy, intense and very accurate.

Fighter support was good.

No enemy aircraft were sighted.

Weather was worse than briefed on return.

Strike report was sent in as unobserved by the deputy lead because of smoke from preceeding bombing.

Low Squadron, 1st "C" CBG

Take-off normal and on time. Assembly of entire group normal and very satisfactory. All aircraft believed to be in position at departure from assembly point. Left on course in time.

Climb on course very good with normal account of "S" ing by groups to take interval. Bit of difficulty encountered holding proper position on lead squadron caused by unnecessary lagging of low and low low elements of lead squadron.

Course and control points made good entire route. Formation really became good and tight when "bandits" were reported to be in area on route in.

Squadrons took good interval at I.P. and proceeded down bomb run being notified by lead aircraft that run would be started as PFF with good possibility of turning visual. Bombardier notified to this effect, but smoke screen and damage from preceeding groups prevented visual run by this squadron. Bombed approximately 30 to 40 seconds after lead squadron on lead aircraft smoke marker. Damage by flak to lead aircraft caused him to diving turn to left. Lead squadron started to follow until apparent that it was in trouble and then entire squadron seemed to break up. Low squadron continued evasive action on briefed route off target until about six aircraft of lead squadron "spotted" trying to reform. Low Squadron proceeded to intercept high and lead squadron regaining position in formation. Reforming by squadron considered very good.

Necessary for high squadron to take over lead of group on return. Two

85

NOT HOME FOR CHRISTMAS

flak areas, one being uncharted, crossed with light but accurate enemy opposition encountered. Evasive action taken by all squadrons.

Group broke up into individual squadron formations over North Sea and returned to base. Weather difficulties encountered in trying to land.

Group formation for flight was good. Very good fighter protection on flight. Flak was heavy, accurate and tracking over target.

High Squadron, 1st "C" CBG

Take off and assembly was as briefed. Departed from Debdon on course and on time with thirty seven aircraft. Control point was made on course on time. Route in to target was as briefed. Control point 3 group was 2 minutes late. At the I.P. the group CA fired a red flare and announced whether the run would be visual or not, which message was not received by high squadron. Group's deputy stated the message could be presumed that target looked visual. The high squadron bombed on the smoke marker of the deputy group lead, the group lead having been knocked out about ten seconds before deputy released.

Twelve aircraft composed high squadron at bombs away, one aircraft having aborted over the channel. Reformation of a group after bombs away was confusing because both group lead and deputy lead were casualties, although this fact was not realised until about ten minutes after the target since six of the lead squadron aircraft were in formation and generally on course. When loss of both group leaders was discovered, the low squadron and remainder of lead squadron fell in formation on high squadron for return. The route out was south of briefed course up to Zwolle, when division formation was effected. Contact with cycle relay suggested 1st down over channel to below overcast, which was done.

Weather en route over continent was much better than briefed, over England it was worse.

Fighter support was superior. Flak at target was moderate and very accurate, at Zwolle meagre and inaccurate. No enemy fighter observed although reported.

Returned early

A/C 42-97338 – not a pathfinder, left formation and returned to base due to leak in oxygen line in camera well. Not a sortie. Mechanical.

                              Edwin b. Daily
                              Lt. Col. Air Corps
                              Operations Officer
                              (signed)

On the return leg, after having accomplished the mission, the "Ugly Duckling" was hit by flak over Zwolle in the Netherlands. Hit in one engine the bomber drifted out of formation.

Briefed after the mission, the following statement was made by Henry A Skubik, co-pilot of a/c # 43-36558:

"Our formation was hit by flak around Zwolle, Holland. I saw one burst of flak directly beneath Rolfe's left wing. Immediately after the burst he peeled off and to the left of the formation. There was no visible fire or smoke. The next I heard, he was calling on VHF stating that he had a runaway prop and he could not feather it. And he would try to make Belgium or France. When our crew last sighted him he was about the same altitude but dropping behind and to the left."

The Mission Summary Report of the 359th Fighter Group mentions: "A straggling B-17 escorted after eight chutes came from it over Zuider Zee. Bomber seen to go into North Sea about 75 miles from base on compass course of 140 degrees".

The whole crew bailed out and perished in the icy water of the IJssel Lake in Holland. Only several months later were eight of the nine bodies recovered.

Pilot **Benjamin G. Rolfe** was born on November 27, 1919 in Hunter, Utah as the son of William Benjamin Rolfe and Mary Ellen Anderson Rolfe. Benjamin was married to Fern Crump Rolfe.

His widow remembers:

"I met Ben while working with his sister at Camp Kearns. His family lived at Hunter just north of the camp. Ben was home on a survivors leave after he being in a mid air collision; the other pilot was killed but

NOT HOME FOR CHRISTMAS

Ben was able to eject. I was decorating the glass case with the valentines when he came in to ask if Mabel was there, it so happened she was off that day. The next day Mabel asked me if I would go on a dinner date with her brother. I said I really couldn't as I was engaged at the time. She laughed and said I am not asking you to marry him, just to spend an evening with him.

"I can only say that it was love at first sight on our first date. He took me to the Rainbow for dinner and dancing. Ben was the best dancer I had ever danced with and his personality was perfect. He loved to laugh and was a real tease: his sense of humour was endless. After taking me home and saying goodnight he asked me if I was busy the next night. I eagerly replied no and he said; "I wish I wasn't as I have a date". I was so disappointed. The next day he came to the store and asked me if I was still not busy as he had broken his date. We went dancing again and spent the next couple of days together whenever it was possible. Needless to say I soon returned my ring and broke my engagement.

"Ben called from New Mexico daily and also wrote letters, we knew we really wanted to get married but didn't make any firm plans. His sisters told me his mother wanted to meet me so we made plans and all went to dinner. It was there that they gave me the engagement ring from Ben. You have to realize that things were different during the war. Everything was so uncertain and we made decisions much faster than at peace time. Arrangements were made and his Mom and mine went with me by bus to Roswell, New Mexico on the 31st of March. We were getting married on April 1st. The date was significant as everything in our lives was on holidays; Ben was born on Thanksgiving, I was born on July 4th and surely April Fools Day would be a perfect date for our marriage. Ben had an apartment rented so we all stayed there that night. The next morning we went to the county court house to get our license and as they handed it to Ben he turned and handed it to me and said April Fools and walked away. For a minute I was shocked but then realized it was his usual sense of humour.

"We were married that afternoon at the camp chapel with the crossed sword and all. My life had totally changed in a matter of two months from our first date. It was a story book love story and we were living it.

"Ben was stationed at the Air Force base in Roswell where he was training in B-17 bombers. Our best friends there were Ralph and his wife Raine who lived in the same apartment complex. Actually it was a house divided into rooms with a bath and bedroom; that was the way young couples lived during the war. The summer went by so fast, we went home on leave in June to stay with his mother, prior to being transferred to Lincoln, Nebraska. I really learned to love her. She was just as angelic as Ben had said.

"We were stationed there for a while and then were sent to Rapid City, South Dakota where they received their final training before being sent overseas. While training there they were assigned their crew members who would be with them when they left to go to war. Ben was the pilot and was very protective and so determined to see that they all returned safely. We became very close to the crew and their wives, we were all nervous about them going into fighting, but were all so certain that they would return. Ben and I had planned my pregnancy so that the baby would be born about the time he would complete his missions and return. I went to Lincoln to be with him until he was to fly out: he had been ill for a couple of days and was running a fever, but refused to report in sick because he didn't want to be separated from his crew. Ben really loved all of them and felt they had to stay together.

"The last time I saw him was at the base airport when he walked out to get into his plane. He stopped and turned around blew me a kiss and waved. He left for England on the 1st of October 1944. I received letters daily until the 1st of December when they stopped. His last letter was the night before his birthday and he said they were flying a night mission over Germany. He asked if I could still love an old man of twenty-five. When the letters stopped I reasoned that it was the Christmas mail and I would probably get a bunch all at once. The morning after Christmas two service men came to the door with the telegram stating that Ben was missing in action since the mission he flew the night before his birthday. All the telegrams had been held up until the day after Christmas and the front page of the newspaper was totally filled with pictures of the missing and dead service men. Grandma Rolfe stayed with me that night at my parents' home. I had cried so much and had an inner ear infection causing a lot of pain, but nothing compared to the pain in my heart.

"I received a letter from Ben's squadron that gave me hope. He said they had bombed Hannover, Germany and had encountered strong enemy flak. Ben's plane had been hit. Ben reported that that no one was hurt but they had lost one engine and were having trouble keeping up with the squadron and felt it would be best to head for allied controlled territory, they were near Holland.

"Time went by and life was so hard; one day I would be sure he was all right and then I would go into total fear that he was dead. All the families of the crew kept in constant contact with each other. After many months I

NOT HOME FOR CHRISTMAS

Daughter Bennie Lynn with her father's photo.

received a letter from Joe Price's wife Cassie stating that she was informed her husband was buried in Belgium. Cassie and Joe had been especially close and loved each other so much. Little by little we learned that all the crew members were buried there. The only thing that could have happened is that they were attacked by fighter planes, the crew bailed out and were killed, the officers stayed with the plane. The war in Europe ended and I waited breathlessly for news that Ben was a prisoner of war; it didn't happen.

"On March, 14th, 1945, Bennie was born at the Camp Kearns hospital. She wasn't a boy, but I named her Bennie Lynn after her father thinking when he came home he would think it was great to have a little girl. She was a joy and a comfort for me even though I was full of sadness.

One day someone mentioned that there was a man from Holland who worked at the church office and may be he could give me some information on what might have happened to Ben. I went to Frank I. Kooyman's office and gave him all the information I had. He said he would write to his friends and burgomasters (mayors), to see what they might know about what happened to the plane and Ben. In less than a month I had Ben's dog tags, his watch, wedding ring and pictures of his burial in a small church yard in Urk, Holland. The bodies of the three officers had been picked up by a fisherman on March 18, 1945 (his mother's birthday and four days after Bennie's birth) in the Zuider Zee; a body of water that fed off the North Sea so their bodies were well preserved. They had buried them and kept all the personal items waiting for an enquiry from our government. We then had closure and could mourn our loss, although I had dreams for many years that he came home. Now all my hopes were gone.

"We had a memorial service at the Hunter Ward on April 28, 1946. I say again that Ben's mother was so good to me; it was very obvious why Ben had adored her. Grandma Rolfe had been a widow since she was thirty-seven years old. Ben was her baby and only son with four sisters. He was only seven when his father died. They lived on a farm and Grandma raised her family and ran the farm with her children. She was a truly great lady who was greatly loved by her children.

On May 3rd, 1945 I was sealed to Ben by proxy in the Salt Lake Temple."

Ben's body was retrieved from the IJssel Lake (Netherlands) on March 17, 1945 by the fisherman Albert Koffeman from Urk and buried the next day in the local cemetery there.

Almost a year after the war, the Mayor of Urk wrote to the American Consulate in Amsterdam:

".....Rolfe has been buried with all honours due to one of our allies. I send you herewith the ring found on him as a last memento. I also enclose some pictures to give you an impression of such a funeral...."

On January 15, 1948, Benjamin's mother requested the government to bring his remains over to Utah to be re-interred in the Wasath Lawn Cemetery in Salt Lake City, UT.

About a month after the end of the war in Europe, co-pilot **Paul Eugene Doyle**, washed ashore near Urk, Holland. A Dutch couple were present at the funeral and wrote to Paul's parents:

"Hereby I send you some snapshots which I have taken of the funeral of your son. He is buried on Urk, Holland, a little island where people with a total number of 4000 are living from fishing.

June 1945, Funeral of co-pilot Paul Doyle in Urk, Netherlands

"It was by accident. I was staying there for I made a cruising trip with a yacht. Urk is now connected by a dam to the mainland.

"Your son was drifted ashore on Saturday, June 10, 1945 and people thought he perished eight or nine weeks before. I can tell you the funeral was very solemn and the Dutch people looked with tears in their eyes. The coffin was carried by members of the Dutch Internal Forces and behind the coffin walked two officers of the RAF. A Dutch clergyman spoke at the graveside and talked of the supreme sacrifice of your son's life which was given also for our liberation. There were many flowers and the weather on that afternoon was good.

"The cemetery is a civil one and lies beside the church. In the corner where your son is buried, with some other militaries, you can see the sea and this position is about 60 feet above the sea level. In the immediate neighbourhood there is a lighthouse whose rays of light are shining over the cemetery."

Ball-turret gunner **James B. Coulson** was found on April 23, 1945 on the beach of the IJsel Lake by soldiers of the 1st Canadian Infantry Division during the liberation of the Netherlands. He was initially buried in the village called Ermelo (Netherlands) but found his final place of rest in the American Military Cemetery in Neuville-en-Condroz in Belgium.

Jim's sister, Kathy Coulson Deignan, in a letter to the author:

"Needless to say, it was with amazement and shock to have received your letter and to learn the details concerning Jim's last mission. After so many years of not knowing the details concerning Jim's death, this past week has been one of great reflection for all of us. You will never know how thankful we are to you for sharing your information with us. Some of us have tried to do research concerning the mission but were not successful in our attempts. One of my

Ball-Turret Gunner Sgt. James B. Coulson of Sioux City, IA, with sister Janice and brother Bill

sisters did have the opportunity to visit Jim's grave in Ardennes Military Cemetery, which is his final place of rest. My parents did not have him returned to the States as they felt he had endured too much already and they just wanted him to rest in peace."

Waist-gunner **Arthur P. Schmidt** washed ashore on April 6, 1945 and was buried in the historical small town of Elburg in the Netherlands.

Arthur Schmidt was born on July 23, 1924 on a farm near Osage, Iowa on July 23, 1924. He was the youngest of a family of eight: seven boys and one girl. His farmer was a farmer and his mother had a full time job caring for the family.

He attended all twelve grades at the Mitchell Consolidated School, and graduated from High School there. As a young boy, he worked on his father's farm. Arthur was a happy individual and looked on the bright side of life. After having graduated from High School he rented a farm and worked it for a while. However, he finally decided to enlist in the Army Air Corps. Arthur was engaged to be married when he enlisted.

Waist-gunner Arthur Paul Schmidt

Arthur's body was not returned to Osage, Iowa. He is buried in the American Military Cemetery in Margraten, Holland.

The body of top-turret gunner **Joseph "Joe" Price** was brought ashore by fishermen on the IJssel Lake and initially buried in Harderwijk.

His sister, Wynelle Price McDaniel, remembers:

"Joseph (Joe) Madison Price was born in North Carolina on a large farm in Rutherford County. He grew up in the small rural community of Mt. Pleasant, Forest City. There were five share croppers on the farm, four African American families and one white family, all with many children. There was no problem with segregation during those years. They all worked and played side by side. The farm had fifteen mules, two horses and fifteen cows. We ran a dairy and delivered milk and butter to the textile community.

"Joe attended a country elementary school. The school sessions were out during the summer for the children to help work the crops. There was plenty of work to be done with the crops and farm chores.

"Joe graduated from Tri-Hi School. He played the trumpet and played taps on many occasions. Now I can hardly bear to hear "taps" at funerals.

"One teacher wrote this about Joe: "Some boys come to school to study: some come for a good time: Joe comes for both, as may easily be ascertained by his scholastic record and popularity.

Joe truly believes that "to have a friend is to be one." We can wish Joe no better luck than a pleasant journey along the highway of life; with dashes of romance for spice".

"After high school Joe went to work at Hotel Charlotte (in the largest city in North Carolina). He met Cassy Wagnon, they married and went to Washington D.C. to work. He was drafted but joined the Air Force in order to get the type of service he wanted. Things happened fast. He went to Shepherd Field, Texas for his training. Cassie stayed with him there. After training, he came home for two days. This was our only visit with Joe after his joining the Air Force before he was sent overseas. In our last letter from Joe after his eighteenth mission he wrote; "By the grace of God I made one more. When I make twenty-four I will get to come home."

"On December 22, 1944 the government declared him missing. As I remember, it was several months before they declared him dead. I will never forget that day. My son Buddy was born on December 23. Mama saw the Western Union car drive into our back yard. I will always remember her scream "Which one is it?" She had three sons serving overseas.

"The fisherman that found Joe wrote to Cassie and sent her the things they found on his body. Cassie identified his watch and rings. He told her that Joe was buried at a church cemetery in Urk, Holland and later moved to Belgium to a national cemetery.

"When this cemetery was disposed of, the government asked if we wanted him sent home. We requested that he come home. At this time our beloved Cassie had remarried. When the train bearing Joe's body passed through Washington, D.C., Cassie and her husband William (Bill) Crouch boarded the train and made the trip home with Joe's body. A memorial service for Joe was held with full military rites. Joe is buried in the family plot in Mt. Pleasant Baptist Church cemetery.

Tail-gunner **Thomas S. Pozder** was born March 7, 1925, in Great Falls, Montana. He graduated from Great Falls High School. During his high school years and up, until he enlisted in the service, he worked for a leather company called Victor Airo. He was a saddle maker. People would ask for him, even at that young age, to do the work when they ordered a new saddle.

Thomas Pozder, washed ashore near Bunschoten. On March 26, 1945 he was buried in the Rusthof Cemetery in Amersfoort, Netherlands. After the war he was re-interred in the Netherlands American Cemetery near Margraten in the southern part of the Netherlands.

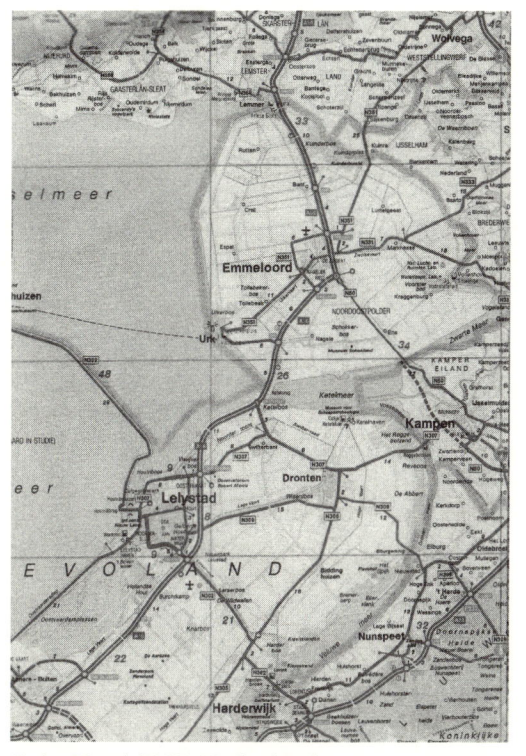

Lake IJssel 2007, Netherlands

Radio-Operator **Frank Iaconis'** body was never found. He is mentioned on the Wall of the Missing on the American Netherlands Cemetery in Margraten (Holland).

His brother John wrote:

"Our parents and our older sister were born in a village in Calabria in southern Italy. Mary, Frank and I were born in Clarksburg, West Virginia, and Peter in New York.

"My brother Frank was probably the brightest child in the family and his scholastic record confirmed that. He graduated from Queens College at age 19 and was drafted soon after on July 17, 1943.

"Frank was Chemical Engineer but never got further than an offer from DuPont when he was called to duty. He was always a top student in his class. The day he was killed he was one month away from his 21st birthday, December 26th 1944. You can see that he never got to live a very long life, much to our regret.

Navigator **Vernon Anderson,** was recovered from the IJssel Lake on June 29, 1945 by the fisherman S. Hopman. He was initially buried in the cemetery of the fishermen's village Elburg and after the war re-interred in the Netherlands American Cemetery near Margraten in the southern part of the Netherlands.

Bombardier **Richard W. Rimmer**, found on the dike from Urk to Kampen on June 17, 1945. He was buried in the cemetery of Urk. Richard was Canadian.

***

Acknowledgements:
"Ugly Dickling" www.398th.org
NARA, Filmroll B5005, document 1216.
Fern Rolfe Nelson, for pilot Benjamin Rolfe
Wynelle Price McDaniel, for top-turret gunner Joseph "Joe" Price
Steve Pozder for tail-gunner Thomas Pozder
John Iaconis for radio-operator Frank Iaconis.

CHAPTER 4

398ᵀᴴ BOMB GROUP 600ᵀᴴ BOMB SQUADRON

Aircraft Type: B17G, Serial Nr.: # 42-97740,
MACR: 11146
Airbase: Nuthampstead

"I had the premonition that we weren't coming back from this one. I wasn't scared in the sense of being scared, but I knew we were pushing our luck."

—Lead bombardier 1Lt. Norman Kottke in an interview with the "The News" – Buffalo Lake, October 1976

Command-Pilot: Capt. Gene L. Douglas (POW) Washington DC
Pilot: 1Lt Charles E. Zimmer (POW) Flushing NY
Lead Navigator: Capt Harry Nelson (POW) Milwaukee WI
Check Navigator: 1Lt Randolph D. Anderson (POW) Worcester MA
Radar Navigator: 2Lt Aaron Kuptsow (POW) Philadelphia PA
Lead Bombardier: 1Lt Norman E. Kottke (POW) Gibbon MN
Fl. Eng. and TT: Sgt Opher E. Rumney (POW) Manchester Depot VT
Radio & Gunner: Sgt James C. Strafford (POW) Portsmouth OH
Waist Gunner: Sgt James "Dick" R. Williams Jr. (POW) Eufaula AL
Tail Gunner: S/Sgt Phern Stout (POW) Lockwood MO

Total: 10 POW
Target: Synthetic fuel plant Misburg, near Hannover, Germany

NOT HOME FOR CHRISTMAS

Radar navigator **2Lt. Aaron Kuptsow** recalls:

"As for my recall of the events of that morning - I had been alerted the evening before that I would be part of the mission. I never knew which crew I would be flying with. I was sort of a 'specialist' As a radar-navigator-bombardier, I always flew in a Pathfinder or lead plane. I worked out of a "pool" and was assigned to whichever plane was going to lead the group that morning.

"As was the custom, I was awakened very early, usually about 4:30, got dressed in my flying outfit, went to breakfast and then to the briefing room. I did have a sense of foreboding about the flight. Four of the officers that lived in my barracks had been killed the day before. Their plane had been badly damaged, had flown back but crashed before getting to our base. This created a degree of fear in me.

"Anyhow, at the briefing, we learned that the target was to be Misburg. I had been on a mission there before and it had not been too bad so I was hoping for a repeat. After the briefing, I went out to the assigned plane and met the crew. Most of the NCO's apparently were on their last mission before returning to the States. I settled myself at the radar station and got out my information in preparation for the flight. We took off, had a rendezvous of the group and headed in to Germany. The flight in was uneventful until we reached Initial Point from where we started the bomb run.

"A lot of flak was coming up at us. The radar was working well and I was able to give the pilot the heading into the target. Just before we dropped our bombs, we heard that the deputy lead plane, on our left, had been hit and had dropped out of formation. We dropped our bombs and turned to get away as soon as possible. Just at that moment, our plane was hit by several blasts. I felt something fly by over my head. The pilot announced that we had lost two engines and that the cockpit windshield had been blown out and most of the instruments were damaged.

"He would try to keep the plane up and head for friendly territory. Not too long after, he announced that it was impossible and that we should abandon ship. It was my responsibility to destroy the tubes in the radar, since at that time, radar was considered a secret weapon. I took the top off the equipment and used my GI shoes to smash the tubes, then hooked up my chute, tied my GI shoes to the parachute harness and went to the escape door. The only other person in the plane at that time was the tail gunner. He went out first and then I followed.

"I pulled the rip cord immediately, then remembered that I was supposed to count to ten. Anyhow, the chute opened and I was clear of the plane. When the chute opened, there was a terrific jolt and my GI shoes were gone. The ride down did not take long. I landed in a field, got out of my chute harness and prepared to run. As I recall, I saw men running toward me and I thought I heard shooting. I put up my hands and surrendered.

"In the meantime, I had pulled off my dog tags and thrown them away in the field. You see, the tags had an "H" on them, signifying that I was Jewish and we had been advised to dispose of them if facing capture. The men who got me seemed to be farmers. They marched me out to the road where we were joined by police on bicycles. They escorted me for a

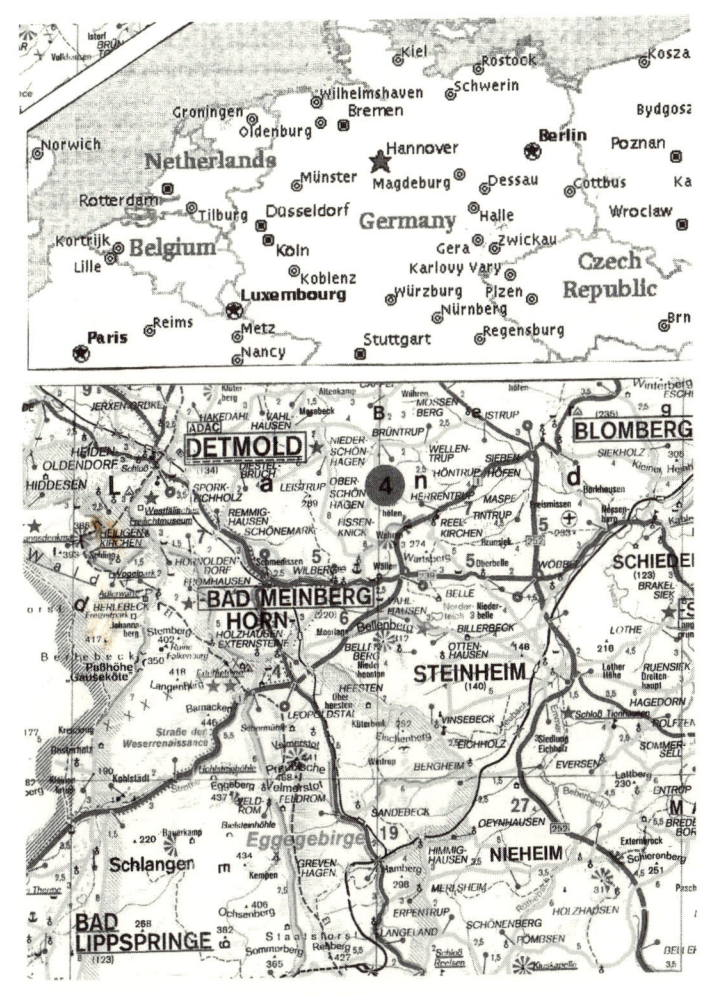

Crash Site (4) E of Oberschönhagen, 5 Km. from Estate Forest, Germany

NOT HOME FOR CHRISTMAS

distance along the road and we hooked up with the remainder of my crew members. Since I was the only one without dog tags they kept accusing me of being a spy. A short time later, a farmer came walking up with my dog tags. He must have seen me throw them away and retrieved them.

"They then realized that I was Jewish. One of the men yelled "Jude", balled up his fist and struck me on the left side of my face.

"They then started to march us toward Detmold. The only shoes I had were the fleece lined flying boots which were much too large for me. As we marched along, my feet were killing me. I wanted to stop for a rest but they prodded me with a machine gun and made me realize that I would be shot if I did not continue.

"As we marched, I seem to recall seeing a sign that said 17 KM to Detmold. That gave me incentive to keep on walking. By the time we reached that town, my feet were a mess. They herded us into a large room where I was finally able to sit down on a cot and take off the boots. My feet were blistered and bleeding. One of the guards saw that, went out and got me a pan of cold water. It felt so good that I have often said that I could have kissed him for his thoughtfulness. By this time, darkness had set in and we were kept in that room overnight with instructions that we were not to talk to each other. That's the end of the story as I recall it pertaining to the day of November 26, 1944.

Check navigator **Randy D. Anderson** of Worcester, MA, in an e-mail to Mary Smith, daughter of waist-gunner Dick Williams:

"I'm sorry to say that I didn't know your father very well - I only met him the morning of November 26, 1944, and only briefly at that. In fact, I didn't know any of the crew that day with the exception of Capt. Gene Douglas, who was the commander of all aircraft from our 398th Bomb Group (flying in the right hand seat or co-pilot's seat as leader of the group (36 ships) that day and Capt. Harry Nelson, lead navigator for the flight. Both were close buddies as well as Nissen hut mates of mine. I'll try, as best I can from the best of memory of nearly 55 years ago, to put the details of the days' mission in some sort of narrative form.

"Mission #110 commenced with lead aircraft (Zimmer/Douglas) taking off successfully at 08:22 hrs and departing for the Debden Buncher (a radio beacon), around which the lead aircraft was to fly a rectangular pattern while each successive plane formed or latched on it. The last aircraft took off at 08:50. When the assembly was completed (09:44 hours) all aircraft were in correct position in the formation i.e. 600th Squadron

398th Bomb Group, 600th Bomb Squadron

as lead squadron, 601st Squadron in the high position, and 602 Sq. in the low position. Entire assembly was as briefed and was considered good. Departed Debden on time and headed for Glaston on the English coast to effect the 1st. Division Assembly.

"The 1st Division (one of the 3 Divisions forming the 8th Air Force Heavy Bomber Force) was composed of 3 or more Combat Wings, each wing composed of 3 or more groups, thus the official designation of our 398th Bomb Group was - 398th Bomb Group, 1st Combat Wing, 1st Air Division, 8th Air Force. The 8th Air Force had as many as 38 to 40 Bomb Groups each consisting of usually 4 squadrons with each squadron having up to 18 combat crews (12 of which flew at any one time) unless the mission called for Maximum Effort, when all 4 squadrons instead of the usual 3 actually flew. The squad that rested was considered "Stood Down".

"Back to the Division Assembly, 1st Division assembly was effected with only minor difficulty at 10:04 hrs and the Strike Force (1st. Div.) left the English coast shortly thereafter, about two minutes early. Had to "S" (zig-zag) the Division to kill a couple of minutes to effect proper position in the total strike force. We reached enemy coast at 10:55 hrs on time and on course. All other check points reached on time and on course.

"As the group left the I.P. (Initial Point) and started on the Bomb Run, we were on a Magnetic Compass leading of 250 degrees. The indicated air speed was 160 MPH and the air temperature was approx. - 45 degrees Fahrenheit. Moderate flak started coming up toward us. Very soon the moderate flak (anti-aircraft fire) became moderately heavy flak, then tracking flak. The enemy gunners had their sights on us! About 20 seconds before "Bombs Away" we took our first near direct hit which took out #2 engine and damaged #1.

"The shrapnel spray sent some jagged pieces of hot metal over the navigators head. Ten seconds later we took a hit on the left wing, destroying the control surfaces (aileron) and finishing off #1 engine. Almost simultaneously another hit blew out the pilots' windshield, destroying many of the flight instruments and the super charger of one of the right side engines. There was no panic - we just calmly went ahead and completed the bomb run as best we could - with 1 and 1/2 engines operating. There was no time to hand the flight over to the deputy leader.

"Immediately after the signal indicating "Bombs Away" we made a sharp diving turn to the left to get out of the way of the rest of the formation - with limited engine power there was no way to maintain altitude and air speed and to avoid a catastrophe it was the prudent thing to do.

NOT HOME FOR CHRISTMAS

Armed with a new compass heading, we headed toward the nearest Allied front lines.

"Less than about 5 minutes later, I think every member of our crew realized it was not to be - we would not be sleeping in Nuthampstead, England, but would be Adolph Hitler's guests instead. We had done all we could - we had jettisoned everything we could, including our guns and map cases to lighten the ship, yet we were still losing altitude fast and now the wing was shaking rather badly. We were in the Minden, Germany area when the "Bail Out" bell was sounded. The time was approximately 12:55 hours, less than 10 to 15 minutes after we had dropped our bombs (12:24 hours).

"The Home Guard (old men, farmers and others unfit to serve in the Wehrmacht) quickly picked us up after the usual greetings of "American Gangsters", "Baby Killers" and the obligatory "For you die Var ist over."

"Luftwaffe guards were summoned from a small base not far distanced. We were all in pretty good shape other than a sprained ankle or two and bruises and cuts suffered in rough landing. The guards were a welcome sight since we knew we'd be protected from any very angry citizens we'd encounter as we were marched (in our bulky flying boots and carrying our bulky, unfolded parachutes) about 10 to 15 kilometres to a guard house of the Luftwaffe base in Detmold. Stayed there overnight, tried to catch a little sleep, but the all wood beds and elevated pillow (wood too) wasn't conducive to much rest. No talking between prisoners was allowed during the march or train rides - only when we were in a permanent POW camp. One of the guards brought us a semblance of a meal (rutabagas and a piece of black, heavy bread which tasted as if it were half sawdust) along with water."

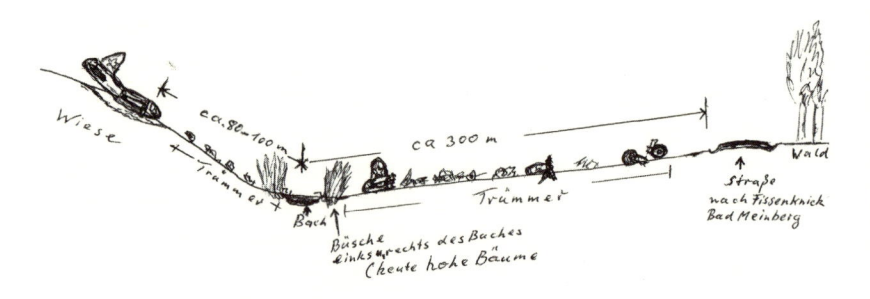

Sketch of the Crash Site by Mr. Friedhelm Dux. Wiese = Meadow, Trummer = Debris, Bach = Stream, Büsches = Bushes (now tall trees)

Lead bombardier **Norman E. Kottke** of Gibbon, MN, from an interview published in the "The News" of Buffalo Lake, Minnesota of October. 7, 1976:

> It started out well enough, that late November day in 1944. The 398th Bomb Group, stationed 40 miles north of London was screaming with the sounds of B-17 bombers going to and returning from runs over Germany.
>
> This was to be 1st Lt. Norman Kottke's last bombing run. His transfer had come through the night before. The eleven men that made up the crew of the bomber went to briefing the night before and received instruction.
>
> As the men walked back to barracks late that night Kottke felt very uneasy.
>
> "Knowing this was to be my last bombing run, and that all the others were successful, I had the premonition that we weren't coming back from this one. I wasn't scared in the sense of being scared, but I knew we were pushing our luck."
>
> "Kottke had been on thirty-two successful missions in his thirteen months of military duty. He recalls bombing oil refineries, railroad yards, and shipping lanes in Hamburg, Cologne, Munich and Berlin.
>
> "Sure it's a terrible thing to bomb cities, but in time of war, you do what they tell you, that's your job!"
>
> "Early that Sunday morning the B-17 was high over cloud-covered England headed for Germany with a full load of 500 pound bombs.
>
> "Kottke was the bombardier of the craft and was strapped in at his station in the glass enclosed nose of the plane. All the instruments checked out and the 33rd bombing mission was a "go".
>
> "A normal run takes 8 or 9 hours, so Kottke and his men settled back for idle talk while they headed for enemy territory... "We were up at around 26,000 feet, the routine altitude for a bombing run, almost 5 miles above the earth, cruising at just under 150 miles an hour. Our radar device, which was a brand new addition to warfare at the time, was designed to pick up large amounts of steel below and was giving a good read-out of our target."
>
> "In briefing, crews are familiarised with what they were going to strike. Using binoculars over clear skies, they pick out tell-tale signs such as a large smoke stack or railroad tracks converging together below. In the event of cloud cover, their radar finds the site for them.
>
> "We were headed downwind for our target when we noticed that right above it was this huge hole in the clouds about twenty miles in diameter, looking straight and clear to Germany! We had to fly right through them to release our load.

NOT HOME FOR CHRISTMAS

"Just as we dropped the last rack of bombs, a terrific blast hit us, shattering all glass in the pilot's cockpit. That stuff up there is 3/4 inch thick and supposedly shatterproof, but it busted like fine China!"

"There was no panic in the plane," reported Kottke, "nobody lost their cool, but we all knew that what we learned in survival training was gonna be put to good use from then on!"

"All the pilot's instruments were rendered useless, the ailerons were flapping in the breeze, and our radio was knocked out of commission. Our intercom fortunately was working so the first thing we did was to check and make sure everyone was okay, which we were.

In my compartment I had an altimeter and an airspeed indicator, so my job became reporting our altitude every minute"

The other planes saw Kottke's drop out of formation and reported back to base that they were still under control, they weren't spinning wildly or anything, there was no fire and nobody bailed out.

"They expected that we would make it back by the way our plane looked, and we might have done so had we two good engines to fly by. Our bomber had close to 150 miles to make it back to United States controlled France, but we were dropping at better than 700 feet per minute. It was then that we realized we wouldn't make it."

"Gliding at 130 miles per hour from 26.000 feet, the bomber returned about 60 miles from bombing site. The pilot was now faced with the decision either to stay with the plane or to bail out.

"We were flying into a heavy cloud bank at the time and we didn't know how far the clouds extended to the ground. The pilot decided it was time."

"I happened to be one of the first out of the plane. I had this little escape hatch under me so I opened it and pushed out with al my might. They say if you don't clear the plane you'll get cut in half by the gun turret on the belly of the plane. I didn't feel like taking any chances."

"It's quite a feeling jumping out of a wrecked plane for the first time in your life doing 130 miles an hour, 7000 feet over Germany. The roar of the huge whining engines is deafening at first and an instant later it's perfectly calm, almost peaceful."

"Kottke was just about to pull his ripcord when an impulse hit him.

"Norman, I said, as long you're up here 7000 feet with nothing better to do why don't you try free fall? And be damned if I didn't! It worked beautifully. You put out an arm and your body goes one way, put out the other arm and you drift over the other way. It works great, but probably a stupid thing to be doing while dropping unexpectedly into enemy territory."

"I drifted through the clouds and right over a small town. There were half a dozen houses, a church and a beer joint. The kids were playing outside on a crisp Sunday afternoon. It was a breathtaking site to see from the air."

"I watched the adults as they ran around pointing up at me. I came down in a wheat field a few hundred feet from the village, ditched my parachute and started to run."

"Two men and a woman began chasing me, so I headed for a small wood to hide in. My luck had been going so great all day long, I guess it was bound to continue. Here the woods I was heading for was completely bare. No place to hide! The only thing left to do was lay down in the tall grass, so I pulled up some roots to cover myself with. The wait seemed to last forever."

"The two men headed right for the grove, like they should, but this darn woman came right for me. I could hear her walking closer and closer, and was just waiting for her to peer down at me over the grains of wheat!"

Kottke laughed, saying "And to this day I've never trusted women."

"Well, the jig was up. I was caught. But to this day I wonder what would've happened to me if she hadn't found me."

"The military picked us up and marched us all night to some kind of holding camp, a place they keep you until they decide what they're going to do with you. The rest of the crew was rounded up by this time and we were re-united in that basement room."

Waist gunner **James "Dick" R. Williams Jr.** of Eufaula, AL, from a letter his daughter Mary Smith sent to Friedhelm Dux, who as a twelve years old German school boy witnessed the crash of the bomber:

"I would like to tell you a little bit about my father. His name was James Richard "Dick" Williams, Jr. and he was from a small town (population 6,000) in south Alabama called Eufaula. He had probably never been outside of Eufaula much when he joined the service and went for training in the Army Air Corps and then off to England. His family owned and operated a laundry and dry cleaning business and he was an only child.

"He met and married my mother after he returned from the war. They had four children: three girls and a boy.

"He was a kind and gentle man who had many friends. He was the type who never lost his temper, always had a smile and a kind word and never complained no matter how hard times could get. When he died

NOT HOME FOR CHRISTMAS

unexpectedly in June 1979, the stores in his hometown closed so that the people that worked in them could attend his funeral. This was the first and only time I know of that being done."

Tail gunner **Phern Stout** of Lockwood, MO, enlisted in the Army Air Force on June, 1941 at Ft. Leavenworth in Kansas. He graduated from Aerial Gunnery School in Las Vegas and was sent as a tail gunner to England where he joined the 379th Bomb Group.

When flying a mission to Stuttgart, his Flying Fortress called "Judy" was hit by enemy fire. Manual flight controls were lost and the plane flew on automatic. The left waist-gunner was knocked out by shrapnel fire in head and knee. The other waist-gunner was wounded in his right arm but continued to fire his machine gun with his left hand.

Over France on the way back home, the crew refused to bail out as the left wait gunner would not be able to pull the rip cord. The bomber landed safely on a RAF field.

He completed the then required twenty-five missions and returned to the States.

After six months in the States as an instructor in Florida he was sent again to Europe. He dreaded to go and before leaving Lockwood he mentioned to one of his friends: "A man can never be that lucky twice".

Back in England he was assigned to the 398th Bomb Group, again as a tail-gunner.

After the war Phern returned to Lockwood and married Lela Arft. They had no children. Together with his brother Harry he managed a local service station. He died in 1971.

Crash Site.

In October 2001, the author received the following letter from Friedhelm Dux of Blomberg in Germany;

> "On that particular day, I was almost twelve years old, I was near the house of my parents in the village Brüntrup, when all of a sudden an enormous plane dived with screaming engines straight through the clouds and seemed to head directly for the village.
>
> "The plane arrived at a height of about 300 - 500 meters when it pulled up again and disappeared in the clouds again. As far as I remember she

made a curve to the left after which she crashed coming from the east or south-east. I don't recall the sound of the crash but I am of the opinion that I saw to the south-west a cloud of dust.

"At the same time my father and I saw various parachutes float down between Brüntrup and the village Cappel. My father, frightened by the screaming engines, had come running out of the house. As far as I recall I saw six or seven chutes but according to you it must have been nine.

"The parachutes with the clearly visible airmen drifted off in the direction of the hill called "Mossenberger Himmel" and disappeared behind the woods. I did not see them landing but they came down between the wood and the village Mossenberg, at about 1.5 - 2 kilometres as the crow flies from were I was standing.

"A little bit later a single parachute jumper could be seen coming from the west. He drifted in the direction of the village and came down immediately afterwards at the edge of the village on a field behind a barn near a farm. I could not see him landing as he was hidden by the high roof of the barn and some big oak trees.

"When the last parachute had landed my father took his bicycle to go to the site. When he returned (he had forbidden me to go there also) I learned that some men and women were already there and that the airman had already been arrested on the farm near by, waiting for the military that had been summoned from Detmold.

"As I already mentioned I assumed the crash site to be situated in western direction. Quickly it became known that the aircraft had crashed in Oberschönhagen. That village consisted only of a few farms and fields (with a few hundred meters between them) on the left side of the road to Fissenknick/Bad Meinberg.

"The next day my friend (same age as me) and I tried to get near the crash site but were turned away by German soldiers guarding the wreck. However, during the following days we could get near the no longer guarded wreck that we could thoroughly study.

"The aircraft had come down on a steep meadow between two farms. She had made a deep gully in the slope. Only small fragments could be found between the gully and a small stream that ran in the valley. The fuselage, the wings (the tail was broken off), the engines and, nearer to the road, the big wheels were lying behind the stream on a farmer's field that went again slightly up. Smaller fragments could be found between these parts.

"As all boys in our age did, we took cartridges, an oxygen mask and a strong magnet of about eight kilos home.

NOT HOME FOR CHRISTMAS

"Some weeks later we visited the site again. All parts of the wreck had been collected (presumably by the German military) and the whole field had been ploughed again. For years the gully the plane had made was still visible from the road. Later this gully seems to have been filled by the owner of the meadow. When I visited the site about 8 days ago I could easily (and within a couple of meters exactly) find the meadow, the stream, the field and the crash site, but the gully has disappeared.

***

Acknowledgements:
Aaron Kuptsow
Mary Smith
Dwight Kottke
Friedhelm Dux.
"The News" of Buffalo Lake, Minnesota

CHAPTER 5

398ᵀᴴ BOMB GROUP 600ᵀᴴ BOMB SQUADRON

Aircraft Type: B17G, Serial Nr. # 43-37846,
"Phoney Express", MACR 11144
Airbase: Nuthampstead

I'm positive if it wasn't for Lt. Bagot's action I wouldn't be writing this letter.

—Engineer Ovila Corbiere, about the crash landing in Nazi-occupied Holland

---

Pilot: 1Lt Kermit R. "Rudy" Pope (POW)*

Co-Pilot: 1Lt Walter M. Bagot (POW)*

Navigator: F/O John T. Jurcyk (POW)*

Bombardier: 1Lt Walter W. Poole Jr. (POW)*

Engineer: T/Sgt Ovila S. Corbiere (POW)*

Tail-Gunner: S/Sgt Charles H. Steele (POW)*

Ball Turret: S/Sgt Kenneth B. Hawkins (POW)*

Waist-Gunner: S/Sgt Joseph R. Kerr (POW) Flemington NJ

Radio Operator: S/Sgt Delmont E. Lewis (POW)*

* Hometown not available

Totalt: 9 POW

Target: Synthetic fuel plant at Misburg, Germany

NOT HOME FOR CHRISTMAS

The waist-gunner **Joseph R. Kerr**, recalls in a letter to the author dated May. 2001:

"I will start by telling you a little background information as to how I happened to be on that flight. I graduated from Flemington High School, Flemington, New Jersey, USA in June of 1942 and enlisted in the US Army ten days later. After training as a gunner, I arrived in England in June 1943 and assigned to the 91st Bomb Group at Bassingbourn as a ball turret gunner. After flying seven missions, our crew was reassigned to the 482nd Pathfinder Group at Alconbury, England. Our duty at that time was to lead all raids when the targets were cloud-covered as we had the only radar at that time. Eventually, all groups were supplied with radar equipment and our group was doing mostly training after March of 1944.

"In November, some of the men were getting anxious to finish our tour of duty and with others we formed crews and transferred out to the 398th Bomb Group - which is how we were flying the "Phoney Express". This was our first mission with the 398th. I can remember it had been raining that night and, as I was getting into my flying equipment, I stepped into a puddle of water and soaked my stockings which I had worn on every raid and considered them to be my "lucky charm" so I had to change to new stockings. That was the start of one sad day.

"Now, to give you some details of the flight as I remember them. Our mission was to bomb the synthetic oil plant at Misburg, Germany. Everything was going well until we got over the target. At that point we were struck by flak which knocked out an engine forcing us to leave the formation. Our bombardier was very badly wounded. I can't relate too much as to what went on in the cockpit but we were losing altitude. We were throwing everything overboard to lighten the plane. Finally a second engine went out and another was on fire. The pilot had to land in a freshly-ploughed field after hitting the chimney of a small farmhouse. Everyone managed to get out of the plane but we didn't know where we were.

"I walked over to the farmhouse to ask where we were and found out we were in Holland in German-occupied territory. My close buddy had a broken leg and I decided I might be able to help him evade. We started out with me carrying his weight. It was a struggle as I had injured my back in the crash. I can remember there were a few people who had gathered but were leaving the area as we started out. We made it to a couple of fields away when the Germans arrived.

"A soldier on a motorcycle with a sidecar picked us up and took us back to the plane where a German truck was waiting. My first night in captivity, I spent in a nearby prison and eventually ended up in Stalag Luft IV in Gross Lychow, Poland.

Pilot **Kermit Pope** wrote the author in May, 2001:

". . . We were hit by flak at "bombs away". In fact, one bomb would not release. I never knew whether the release malfunctioned or if it was shot out. At any rate, we were never able to get rid of the bomb and carried it with us through our subsequent crash lading.

"Minutes after being hit we lost the # 1 engine and had to leave the formation, trying to stay close for protection, but rapidly falling behind. About ten minutes later we lost # 4. About an hour and forty five minutes after being hit we lost the # 2 engine.

"Visibility was not too good and the horizon ahead seemed to be clouded with trees. I could see a farm field located at about two-o'clock that was big enough for a belly landing. My bombardier was badly injured and I didn't trust "Phoney Express" to fly on one engine. So I elected to set her down.

"It so happened that a German Wehrmacht unit was located in the immediate vicinity and several of us were taken prisoner within minutes. The others managed to escape capture for a matter of hours. . . . ..

Navigator **John T. Jurcyk** recalls in March, 2005:

"On November 26, 1944 as our aircraft approached the target we received a burst of flak slightly below our nose, during bombs away. The shrapnel penetrated the forward part of the aircraft and seriously injured our bombardier Lt. Walter Poole. I received a cut on my head. As we left the target area, we were on our own due to engine failure.

"I directed the aircraft heading toward friendly lines. It learned that a bomb failed to release at bombs away.

"I elected to enter the bomb bay, with screw driver in hand, to release the bomb manually. The release was impossible due to a damaged shackle. I returned to my position in the forward of the bomber. When the order was given to take crash landing position, I dragged Lt. Poole as far away from the nose of the aircraft.

"After the aircraft came to rest in a ploughed field I left the aircraft as fast as I could. Lt. Pope and my self decided to re-enter the plane to carry Lt. Poole out of the aircraft. In doing so we gave the Germans time to capture us. I notice many people streaming toward the aircraft, as well as the Germans.

NOT HOME FOR CHRISTMAS

Engineer **Ovila S. Corbière** remembers:

"Pope did not land that plane. Rudy Pope was hit by flak in his upper right arm and he could not use his arm. Lt. Bagot took control of the plane right away.

"I was the flight engineer and administrated first aid to Lt. Poole. As he was unconscious I dragged him from his position to the hatchway below the pilot and co-pilot. When we got to 5000 ft., Lt Bagot ordered the crew to get in the radio room as we were going to crash land. We had two engines out at this time. He asked me if I would stay in the cockpit to assist him and try to protect Lt. Poole because I couldn't get him to the radio room. When the 3rd engine went out Lt. Bagot asked me to put my weight on Lt. Poole and assist him using the pilot's control. I'm positive if it wasn't for Lt. Bagot action I wouldn't be writing this letter.

"Lt. Bagot, Chas. Steele, Joe Kerr and myself were members of Capt. Wine's crew in the 482th which was not going on missions at that time. Capt. Wine was Squadron Commander so the four of us asked him to be transferred to an operational group and Lt. Bagot was to be our pilot. Rudy Pope and Lt. Poole were in the 398th before so Rudy Pope pulled his seniority on Lt. Bagot and was made pilot of this new crew.

"During the crash Joe Kerr got hit in his back by the ball turret that came lose. Chas Steele's knees were injured. I am service connected for a broken neck, broken right elbow, broken right ankle and severe trauma to both knees due to this crash-landing.

"Joe Kerr and I have kept in contact since we were discharged. We also kept in contact with Chas. Steele until his death. We never heard about Jurcyk, Lewis or Hawkins. Joe and I met Lt. Poole in Florida before his death. I met Rudy Pope in Orlando, Florida about 1995.

***

Acknowledgements:
Joseph R. Kerr
Kermit Pope
Ovila Corbiere

398th Bomb Group, 600th Bomb Squadron

* PHONY EXPRESS *

On Nov. 26, 1944 we were on a mission to Misburg. As we dropped our bombs we were hit by flax in the front of the fuselage on the # 2 engine side. We immediately went into a dive. I was in the top turret and the centrifugal force was holding me in the turret so I put my guns pointing up and used the butts of the guns to push myself out. The pilot's right arm was badly injured and could not use it so I helped Lt. Walter M Bagot the co-pilot to pull the plane out of the dive. At that time we lost our # 2 engine. About ten minutes later we lost the # 3 engine.

After losing altitude Lt. Bagot informed the crew to bail out if they wanted to as it was evident we were going to crash land. Lt. Bagot asked me to stay in the cockpit (standing up between the pilot and co-pilot) to assist him. When our # 4 engine gave out, we started to come down sideways and the tip of our right wing hit the chimney of a house and we landed in plowed farm land. I fractured my Cervical Spine, Right Ankle, Right Elbow and injured both knees. Joseph Kerr was in the radio room at the time of the crash and was injured by the ball turret coming loose. One 500 lb bomb could not be dropped due to a malfunction caused by the flax and was still in the bombay when we crash landed. Joseph Kerr carried me on his back to the house to inquire where we were. He then carried me about one half mile on plowed farm land to a ditch and there we were taken prisoners.

Recently I was on the Internet and researching the 8th Air Force and I found this picture of the plane we crash landed in Holland. Note that the chimney of the house has been knocked out, the top turret guns are still in the same position I left them and the plowed farm land.

T/Sgt Ovila S. Corbiere Flight Engineer *Ovila S Corbiere* 3/19/02

S/Sgt Joseph R Kerr Ball Turret Operator *Joseph R. Kerr* 3/22/0.
To : John Meurs

Narrative of engineer Ovila S. Corbière and waist-gunner Joseph R. Kerr

CHAPTER 6

91ˢᵀ BOMB GROUP
324ᵀᴴ BOMB SQUADRON

Aircraft Type: B17G, Serial Nr.: 43-31515, "The Wild Hare", MACR: 10836
Airbase: Bassingbourn

"If God should ever grace me with a son, I pray he will never have to go to war."

—From a letter of radio-operator John S. Kendall to his mother

---

Pilot: 1Lt Robert J. Flint (POW) Cincinnatti OH

Co-Pilot: 2Lt David L. Bishop Jr. (POW) Spartenburg SC

Navigator: F/O Robert J. Miller (POW) Nevada MO

Bombardier: S/Sgt Daniel V. Hiner (KIA) Toledo OH

Tailgunner: Sgt Owen W. Monkman (KIA) Bynum MT

Ball Turret: S/Sgt Bartolomeo Zanotto (KIA) Detroit MI

Waistgunner: Sgt Glenn P. Lynch (POW) Union Bridge MD

Radio: Sgt John S. Kendall (KIA) New Port VT

Engineer: Sgt Charles F. Cumings (KIA) Neenah WI

Total: 5 KIA, 4 POW

Target: Altenbeken rail-road viaduct

NOT HOME FOR CHRISTMAS

Jan Hey of Hengelo of the Netherlands, who has summarized a huge quantity of the 8th Air Force's MACR's, wrote about this aircraft:

> "The formation was attacked by about seventy-five fighters when five minutes before the I.P. The B-17 was hit in # 3 engine which was set on fire, dropped back and lost altitude. Then nosed downward, exploded and broke in two pieces.

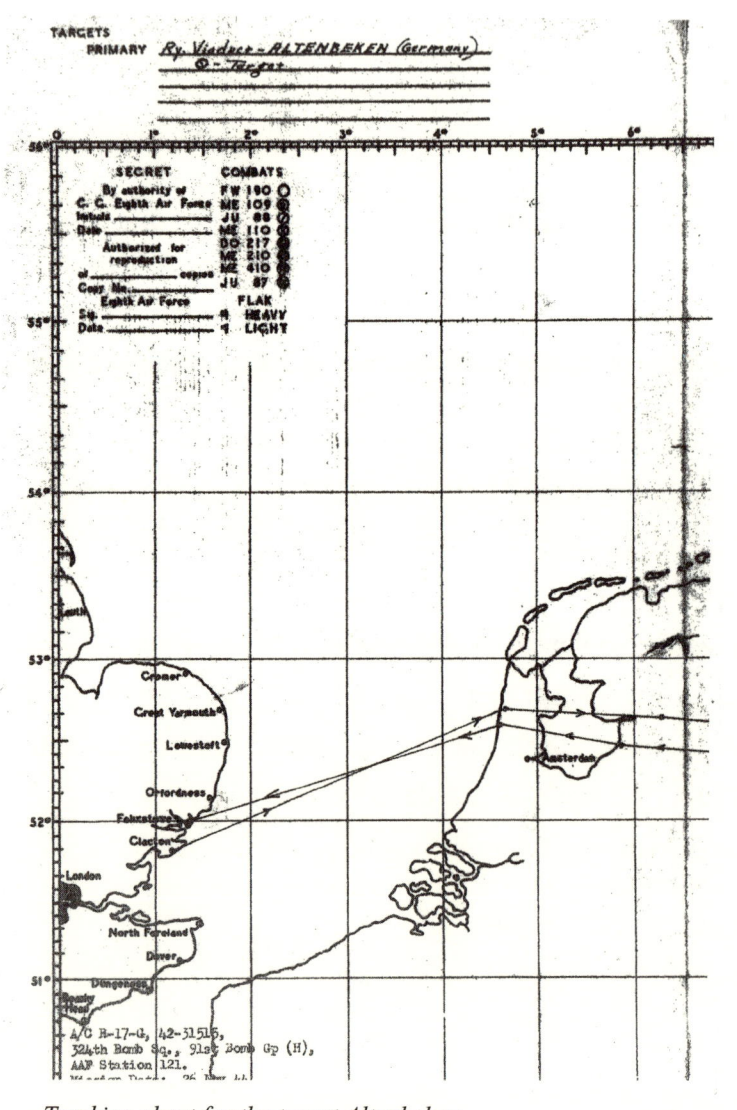

Tracking chart for the target Altenbeken

116

"It crashed at Grossenging, about 10 miles w. of Cloppenburg, Germany. Those who could leave the aircraft landed near Hemmelte and Cloppenburg.

"The Germans identified four casualties and buried them together with one Unknown Airman, who will certainly have been Sgt. Monkman."

In 2001, co-pilot **David Bishop** and waist-gunner **Paul Lynch** wrote their story of their last mission in WW II.

"Both David and I decided that it would be an appropriate time to describe the mission to the Altenbeken rail road viaduct, Germany. Appropriate because, "Father Time" never improved anyone's memory, we have been urged to do so by our families and friends and it was only David's third mission and my first. So what other missions do we have to talk about?

"We participated in this mission on 26, November 1944 at the urgent request of the Eighth Air Force, 91st Bomb Group and the 324th Squadron flying out of Bassingbourn, England. Because to our knowledge, we are the last surviving members of the original crew that flew this mission, it might be of interest to families and friends of those who failed to return to know what happened. As much of this information has become declassified, we are in a better position to piece together events of this day and relate this information to what each of us recalls more than 50+ years ago. Even though we flew together with the same crew and the same plane, our memories may be influenced by what we saw from different positions in that plane. We both agree that we found ourselves in the midst of what turned out to be an intense air battle.

"It was the policy of the Air Force to split new, "green" crews and let them fly with combat veterans for the first few missions. This policy probably had been sound, but it was difficult to adjust to having our original crew, who had trained together, not fly together. We had heard that the substitutes for this mission were very well experienced and these crew members had enough missions on 26, November to be qualified for rotation home in time for Christmas in about a month. Those that comprised the crew that day were:

Pilot Robert Flint: 30 missions
Co-Pilot David I. Bishop: 3
Navigator Robert J. Miller: 3
Radio John S. Kendall: 3
Bombardier Daniel V. Hiner: 26
Top-Turret Charles P. Cumings: 1

NOT HOME FOR CHRISTMAS

Ball-Turret Bartolomeo Zanotto: 34
Tail-Gunner Owen W. Monkman: 1
Waist-Gunner Glenn P. Lynch: 1

"We arose early the morning of the 26, November and filed into the briefing room rather anxious to hear about what was in store for us. After all this was my first mission and the remainder of the day would be all new to me. From now on it was the real thing. David Bishop was a veteran of his third mission so he may not have been as anxious that early in the morning.

"We learned that our target was in the Osnabrück area, south of Bremen and west of Hannover, so we would not have a deep penetration into Germany. The weather was fine with Cumulus and Stratocumulus clouds up to 15.000 ft. And then unlimited visibility. The total mission had five primary targets and more than one thousand bombers taking part. Targets were located at the important Hamm railroad yards, the oil refinery in Misburg and the railroad viaducts at Bielefeld and Altenbeken. Our squadron was part of the group assigned to bomb the viaduct at Altenbeken. Our plane was in the 1st Air Division or the 1st Combat Wing and the code name for the target at Altenbeken was "Gee-H".

"Intelligence information that we were given was that the Luftwaffe had not been operating extensively in this area so we would not encounter much opposition. "We lucked out - a milk run", I thought (and so did David). I was young, green and very optimistic! The briefing was over and we all headed out to get our assigned plane and meet the new crew members.

"The introduction to the new crew members was fast and David's first opinion of our pilot was that he was rather quiet. We later heard that he was one for strict military discipline but there wasn't much that morning. Bart and Dan seemed very friendly and we all seemed to get along.

"Recently, David reminded me of the training mission we flew to Paris and on the way back we lost all radio communication. We had to land on a British airfield and spent the night there. When we got back to our home base the next day some of the pilots told David that we missed a mission that day. The plane we would have flown was shot down. There was a saying that if you were supposed to have been shot down before, you would never be shot down in the future. We wondered if the Germans knew that.

"As we approached our assigned B-17G, I rapidly lost my enthusiasm. Here stood a patched-up, battle weary airplane with bombs painted all

91st Bomb Group, 324th Bomb Squadron

over the nose. It's number was 42-31515 and it's name was "The Wild Hare". Bugs Bunny was carrying a bomb in place of a carrot. It was no comparison to the new one we had to give up after we arrived in the UK. That plane I liked. Well, what did it matter we were on a milk run anyhow. The new guys on the block get the junk - let's go.

"Recently, we have been curious about the history of "The Wild Hare" in order to find what her battle history had been. The plane arrived at Bassingbourn 21, January 1944. The first mission was to Frankfurt on 29, January, twice more by February and on 20, February it received major flak damage on a mission to Leipzig. On 22, March it went on a mission to Berlin and on 10, April it took severe flak damage over Brussels. The following day it made a mission over Stettin and on that mission the entire ship was riddled from end to end by flak. Two days later it was ready for a mission to Schweinfurt. On 29, April it was transferred to the 401st Squadron for its second mission to Berlin. It was loaned to the 322nd Squadron on 15, June and on that mission fighters shot out the hydraulic system. The Pilot, Charley Bell, was faced with the problem of landing the plane without brakes. Earlier, Charley Bell had trained with a pilot who had used parachutes to slow a B-17 on landing, so Charlie Bell tried the same trick on "The Wild Hare". He deployed parachutes to slow the plane on landing. It worked!

"On 21st, June it was back to Berlin for the sixth time with the 322nd Squadron and Pilot David Hanst. During this last Berlin mission the flaps kept creeping down and the radio man had to crank them up by hand every three or four minutes. Approaching Berlin the group was straggling and they were hit by 60-70 ME 410's. The M 410's flew wing to wing right through formation of B-17 bombers with their 20 mm canons blazing. During those four minutes, four B-17 bombers were lost, leaving only two B-17s from the 322nd Squadron. One of these was "The Wild Hare". Upon completion of the bomb run, the antiaircraft gunners began tracking his plane so he opened his throttles, cut over and through the bursts, and in thirty minutes lost No. 1 engine. "The Wild Hare" picked up a P-38 escort along the coast and made it home on three engines. After Berlin, the plane was transferred back to the 324th Squadron and three days later was on it's next mission to Distre. Several crews flew "The Wild Hare" for fifteen more missions but then it was severely damaged in a raid over Cologne. "The Wild Hare" was again repaired in time to bomb the oil refineries at Merseburg on 25, November. Time was running out for the war weary gal as she was assigned to R.J. Flint on 26, November to bomb the railroad viaduct at Altenbeken

NOT HOME FOR CHRISTMAS

"I should have had much more respect for this survivor as she had already paid her way!

"Finally, it was our turn to go. We were airborne and bound for Germany. Just as the weather report said we were through the clouds and we could see for miles. It was so peaceful and beautiful that war seemed far away except for all the planes in the air for that mission. As we got closer to our IP and our target, we all made preparations to get in our respective positions. I helped Owen with his flak jacket and he disappeared into his tail position. Bart got into the ball turret and after the call around, everyone seemed to be ready.

"We had been flying for several minutes when I began to see several bursts of flak but they were not close so I wasn't worried. As I watched the other planes in our formation, I noticed that we were drifting out of formation and away from the protection of the other gunners. I called the pilot to tell him of my concern and he replied, "We're doing the best we can". According to David, it was this time that he became concerned about our problem. He became very disturbed when he saw the No. 3 engine on fire. About the same time I checked the other waist window and saw fire in No. 3 engine. Now I knew - must have been flak. Neither of us realised that we had been attacked by German fighters from the rear.

"Shortly, Flint called, "FW-190 at ten o'clock". I heard popping and hissing inside the plane and Kendall flew out of his chair. I turned to the other window to see the FW-190 making his pass. He was close, so I grabbed the gun and got off a few shots while calling to Bart in the ball turret. "FW-190 coming your way at 10 o'clock". Soon I heard Bart's guns chatter but then he quit. Kendall was gone. How did that guy come up on us so fast? Why didn't we hear gun fire from the top turret? Was he hit by flak? He could have knocked the FW-190 down with the barrels of his gun. Suddenly Flint called, "Abandon ship".

"My chute was in the bottom of my duffel bag. Quick, dig for it. Bart is out of his ball turret and having trouble with his chute harness. I find my chute, get it on and Bart is getting his chute fastened. I step up to the door, kick it open and say a prayer for a quiet reception on the ground. I turn to check Bart and he gives me the OK. I make two quick choices. First, I go out of the door fast and second, I make a delayed chute opening. I wanted to get through this air battle and not be the target of a turkey shoot from some German pilot. In survivors school we were told if you decided to make a delayed chute opening, wait until you see the branches of the trees before you pull the chord. That's what I did, and wasn't in the air very long until I was hung by my chute in a tree. I didn't have enough time in the air to manoeuvre the chute away from that tree. The chute caught the tree and swung me and my leg against a large branch.

"In the forward section of the ship, David was trying to convince Charles Cumings to bail out as he was frightened and almost completely unresponsive. Finally David got his message through and Charles went out. The pilot reported that Cumings was the first to leave the plane at that time. Both pilots followed. We both wondered why Cumings did not survive.

"In the nose, Miller was wounded by shrapnel in his leg and Daniel Hiner was helping him to get out. Robert Miller got out but Hiner did not. We suspect that both Hiner and Bartolomeo Zanotto were caught when the plane exploded, just before they jumped.

"When the order to, "Abandon ship" came, David didn't have any problem with deciding to jump as he believed there was no other choice. We both landed a short distance from each other without serious injury. There were no other crew members in sight. Soon we heard the sound of an aircraft engine and saw a ME-109 heading directly for us on a low buzz job. David took off running towards the woods. I wasn't able to run because of my leg so I rolled over in back of a log and waited for the bullets to hit. None came, but I was soon captured by the local home guard. That was the end of the Altenbeken mission for me. I didn't see David again until the 91st Bomb Group Memorial Assn. Meeting, August 1998 in Savannah, GA.

"After David was captured and on his way to the village, a teen age boy brandished a knife and tried to get David to give him the parachute but the boy did not succeed. Other than that incident, both of us were lucky that we did not encounter any irritated civilians or trigger happy soldiers.

"Robert Miller and David met in the hospital after capture and Robert told David that he pulled his chute cord too soon as a German fighter dogged him most of the way down trying to spill air out of his chute. After he landed he was almost lynched by the local villagers but was saved by a German soldier. Most Germans soldiers understood that both Germany and America were operating under the terms of the Geneva Agreement for the Fair Treatment of Prisoners of War. Then he was pitched into the back of a truck, with the bleeding wound, and bumped along the road to the lockup. A German officer began to describe new types of German weaponry saying, "Soon you will find it not so pleasant to fly over Germany". Robert replied, "How in the hell do you think I found it to-day". This amused the German officer and he replied, "Yank, you told a great joke".

NOT HOME FOR CHRISTMAS

Robert died of lung cancer 1988. He claimed he smoked too many unfiltered Camel cigarettes in prison camp.

"The next stop for David after capture was a train ride to the interrogation centre in Frankfurt. During this time on the train there was only one guard. This made David nervous so he put the guarding business in reverse and made it a point to stay close to that guard for his own protection. There was a time that he rode on a German troop train with German soldiers and had no fear even though they knew he was a POW. One night on the train was frightening when the British conducted an air raid. The train stopped and everyone exited the train. He watched the spot lights trying to locate the British planes, listening to the sirens and hoping they would not be able to spot any of the British planes. I think David was slightly more fortunate than I was as the German guards on our train made us stay on the train during the air raids and they got off - hurriedly.

"It is abundantly clear that I missed seeing the first fighter attack that probably hit Owen and started the fire in the No. 3 engine. I couldn't hear the planes over the roar of our own engines and I was probably looking out of the wrong window at the time of the attack. There were no interphone warnings of the attack. My knowledge of the first fighter attack came from witness statements in the mission report.

"Some new information has surfaced (new to us) that about June 1944, the Luftwaffe planes that carried 20 mm canon were shooting exploding ammunition. The exploding shells were reported to contain two types of fuses. One was a contact fuse that exploded on contact with the target aircraft and a timed fuse that exploded at a preset time and threw shrapnel into any close-by aircraft. When these shells exploded they gave off little white puffs of smoke all in a single line. When the traditional 88 mm or 105 mm antiaircraft guns were used, a group of four large black mushroom shaped bursts would be seen. I read in our Mission Report that antiaircraft fire over Altenbeken was light but David had reported heavy antiaircraft fire. It is possible that David was observing the exploding 20 mm shells from the rear-attacking German fighters. Exploding 20 mm shells may have hit the radio compartment, that may have accounted for my seeing Kendall blown out of his seat.

***

Nose-gunner **Daniel V. Hiner.**

Bishop and Lynch wrote in their above quoted story: "Dan Hiner, in the nose, gave up his precious escape time to help the wounded R.J. Miller get out."

In July 1945, the father of Daniel wrote to the mother of the tail-gunner Owen Monkman:

" . . . We are still trying to check up to find out, if possible, how our son was killed. If we find out for sure that he bailed out we will probably never know how he was killed.

"He was a nose-gunner and when the trouble started, F/O Miller was in the nose with him. (We received a letter from him). There was a flak burst right in the nose and Miller was hit in the leg. He says he doesn't think our son was hurt. The pilot gave orders to bail out and Miller jumped and he thought our boy was right behind him. They were told by the Germans less than two hours after they jumped that our boy was killed. If he bailed out he must have been killed after that because no one we have heard from thinks he was hit before the order came to jump.

"We also heard from Sgt. Lynch and he feels sure he wasn't hit before the order to jump. Lt. Bishop is also home. He says Cumings jumped

NOT HOME FOR CHRISTMAS

from the nose hatch ahead of him. We received a card from Lt. Flint's mother and she has received word that he is in a hospital in England. So he has to be in bad shape."

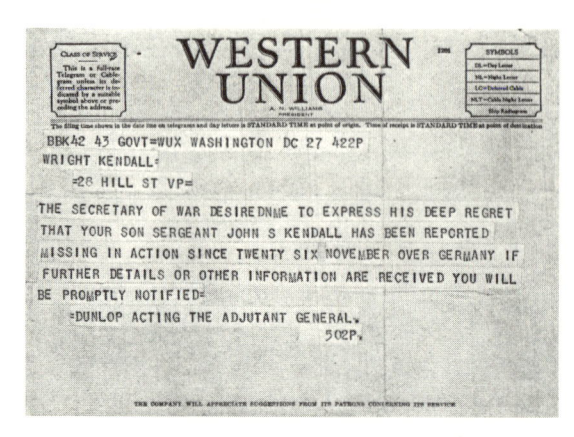

About radio-operator **John S. Kendall,** his niece Jay Kendall wrote:

"I remember my Uncle John. The last time I saw him, I was three or four years old. We lived in the house next to my grandparents,

Western Union telegram:

BBK42 43 GOVT=WUX WASHINGTON DC 27 422P
WRIGHT KENDALL=
=28 HILL ST VP=

THE SECRETARY OF WAR DESIRES ME TO EXPRESS HIS DEEP REGRET THAT YOUR SON SERGEANT JOHN S KENDALL HAS BEEN REPORTED MISSING IN ACTION SINCE TWENTY SIX NOVEMBER OVER GERMANY IF FURTHER DETAILS OR OTHER INFORMATION ARE RECEIVED YOU WILL BE PROMPTLY NOTIFIED=
=DUNLOP ACTING THE ADJUTANT GENERAL.
502P.

Letters to the editor
Dutchman searches for war clues on John Kendall

Editor,

We write Sunday, November 26, 1944. The war is still raging in Europe. The allied armies that had advanced from the beaches of Normandy to the river Rhine in a mere five months have come to a temporary stop. The war in the air, however, continues relentlessly. The Lancasters of the British RAF and the heavy bombers of the American 8th Army Air Force attack German targets without respite.

The "Mighty Eighth" had sent over a thousand bombers, B-24 Liberators and B-17 Flying Fortresses, into the air on that Thanksgiving Day, 1944. In order to deceive the German fighters the main force was to fly — direction Berlin — giving the Germans the impression that the capital was the target of the day. Then the bombers would suddenly turn southwest and bomb Misburg on the way home. This ruse did not completely work out. Due to late arrival over the target two bomber groups were temporarily without fighter escort and came under attack from German fighters who had rushed in from the Berlin area.

Within a quarter of an hour the Germans downed 15 bombers of the 491st and five of the 445th Bomb Group. The sky was suddenly filled with debris of exploded aircraft and airmen descending under the white canopies of their parachutes. Later, the 491st would call that day their "Black Sunday" as they had never lost so many aircraft on a single mission.

But the Luftwaffe also paid a very heavy price. They lost about a hundred fighters out of the five hundred launched.

The 91st Bomb Group lost three bombers that day. One of these, the B-17 called "Wild Hare" was attacked by German fighters, dropped back and exploded in two pieces. Four crew members could save themselves by parachute, the five others were killed during the attack or in the crash. Among those who perished was the Radio-Operator John S. Kendall. His father, Wright Kendall then lived at 28 Hill Street in Newport, Vermont.

John Kendall was initially buried near the crash site in Germany. After the war he was reinterred in the huge American Military Cemetery in the Ardennes in Belgium. At a later stage he found his final place of rest in Vermont, I assume in Newport.

The writer of these lines is a 67-year-old Dutchman now living in Switzerland. When he was a nine-year-old school boy living in Nazi-occupied Holland a B-17 crashed behind his house in the village called Apeldoorn. The date was also November 26, 1944, and this bomber crashed at about the same time as John Kendall died in Germany.

Two of the crew members were killed by German soldiers when they were descending under their white parachutes. The pilot died in the crash. The tail-gunner survived the crash, escaped from a German hospital with the help of the Dutch underground, and was hidden by a family living in the same street as the writer did.

This Dutchman is now researching all 35 heavy bombers of the 8th Air Force lost on Thanksgiving Day, 1944. He will probably write a book dedicated to the brave airmen who lost their lives on that Sunday.

He would very much like to get in contact with family members of John Kendall and or other people who may have known him.

Please write or e-mail to:
John Meurs
Im Gubel 5
CH-8630 Rueti ZH
Switzerland
e-mail: meurs.john@bluewin.ch

Letter to the editor

124

and I remember clearly having breakfast with him there. There was always something wrong with his eyelids. They drooped. His high school classmates called him "Sleepy." My Aunt Medora, his only surviving sister, told me that before he went over to Europe an operation on his eyelids corrected the problem, but those of us who remember him remember him with those sleepy eyes."

For tail-gunner **Owen Wagnild Monkman**, Nancy Granata, daughter of Owen's elder brother wrote the following biography with contributions from Andrew Jenson, a youth time friend.

"Owen was born in Choteau, Montana, on July 31, 1924. He was 20 years old when he died over Germany.

"I know the family lived in Bynum until about 1929 when they moved their house from Bynum to their farm which was about three miles south and west, toward Choteau. That is where the family lived at the time that Owen was killed during the War. He and his brother went to grade school in Bynum. Owen and I started to school together in the fall of 1930. They lived on the farm so someone would take them to school each morning and maybe, if the weather was good they would ride a horse.

"We rode a bus to Bynum to school. The school buses were nothing more than a truck with a big wooden box built on the chassis with one door. It was heated on the cold days by a wood stove, anchored to the floor so it would not fall over. In the winter, at times, the temperature would fall to 40 degrees below zero.

"Bynum and Choteau are both small towns located east of the Continental Divide (Rocky Mountains). Choteau is about 90 miles south of Glacier National Park and Bynum is 14 miles north of Choteau on Highway #89. Sometime around 1900, Choteau and Bynum must have been about the same size as far as population. An election was held to determine which town was to be designated to be the County Seat of government. Choteau won the election by just a few votes and is the Teton County Seat today. The county government is here.

"I can remember when Bynum had a hotel, two lumber yards, two grocery stores, a bank, a school, a post office, a barber shop, several bars, a jail, stock yards, at least two grain elevators, blacksmith shop and three churches. The Great Northern railroad had a depot here which transacted business of hauling freight, passengers, grain {from the elevators} and cattle out of the stockyards. As you can tell this is a big cattle and grain country. They used to ship all the grain, cattle and virtually everything

NOT HOME FOR CHRISTMAS

by rail, but not anymore. The train tracks have been taken out north of Choteau, along with the depots and the elevators. Most everything is hauled by truck now.

"Bynum is not what it used to be; the school is there, a small store, post office, a bar, where the bank was, a dinosaur museum, no churches. I am guessing, the population of Bynum is probably less than 100 people. Choteau population is close to 2000 people. Because of the dry conditions [very little rain or snow for the ranches and farms]; it has been hard on these small towns and cities.

"Owen and I each lived on a ranch, so after school we had chores to do such as milking cows, feeding the animals, haying, harvesting, fencing and lots of other jobs; then when we were old enough, of course, we drove tractors and other heavy equipment. There are lots of things to do on a ranch or farm. Both Owen and I played trumpet in the Choteau high school band. We had a lot of fun. I also played in a dance band too, with four other people. We played almost every week and made a little spending money.

"Owen and I graduated from Teton County High School in the spring of 1942. In the fall of that year Owen started college at Montana State University in Bozeman, Montana. He had a part time job at a radio electronics store with a pay of forty cents an hour. He was able to pay for his board and room out of his own wages.

"He returned to Choteau in the spring of 1943. Believing he would be drafted soon, he did not return to college in the fall. However, the War Department that year, deferred farmers from the draft so he never received the official call-up letter. Anxious to serve his country, Owen did not wait for the deferment to lift. He notified them in the fall that he was ready to serve. Enlisting also had a big plus over waiting for the draft notice, Owen was able to insure that he got his choice of military branches; Navy Air Force or Army Air Force were what he wanted. Owen's hope was to become a pilot.

"In January 1944 Owen was inducted into the Army Air Force at Butte, Montana and was ordered to report to Fort Douglas, Utah on February 14th. At the end of his first day in Fort Douglas, he wrote his parents; "The camp is bigger than all of Choteau! Sure are feeding us good chow and all the guys I've met so far are really swell."

"A week later he was shipped to Amarillo Air field in Texas. He stayed there twenty-eight days and was then washed out of Air Cadets to his great disappointment. About dances he wrote from Amarillo: ". . . . I haven't danced half a dozen times since I left home and three of them were in

Fort Douglas. They dance a different style of jitterbugging altogether. No one from up north can even dance to it. I get along fairly well but I sure miss dances at home. The music here is probably a dozen times as good as I've even danced through. These musicians are out of orchestras such as Tommy Dorsey's, Benny Goodman's, etc. Mighty good!"

"In April 1944, he was sent to the Army Air Force Base in Las Vegas, Nevada to attend gunnery school. There the Commanding Officer found out that Owen could play the trumpet and assigned him the job of bugler, since they didn't have one. Owen wrote; " I sure am having quite a time on the bugle. The darn thing is powerful hard to blow. In the morning I am called half an hour earlier than the rest and get up and blow first call before I even wake up and then fifteen minutes later blow reveille. If I just had my own trumpet here, I'd put a little "swing" in the music."

Owen graduated from gunnery school in June, 1944 at Las Vegas Base Theatre, was promoted PFC. He wrote home: "Finally got my gunner's wings. They are not the same as pilot or navigator wings but the same exact size. Surely do look swell. So you we're getting a lot of moisture up there huh? I hope we get a bumper crop of winter wheat. I'd sure like to be home for shearing but I suppose the rain had delayed it again as it did last year?"

End of July 1944, Owen was shipped out to Gulfport Field, Mississippi where he became part of a permanent crew and had a great deal of flying time in a B-17. During the second week of August he wrote; " We fly everyday down here. Some guys get tired of flying every day but I never do. This is the wettest, swampiest country I have ever seen. . . . .Hearing a lot of rumours about where we might be headed but you can't believe every thing in the army until it happens.

". . . Well, the allies seem to be on the move in pretty good time now. I listened to the news last night on the way back from Birmingham and they reported the allies 120 miles from the German border. It didn't take much to get Paris when they decided to take it. I hope they push the hell out of them right through Berlin. I hardly think Germany will last more than two or three months. Just long enough for me to get over there maybe? If not, I go the other direction.

". . . .You asked where the crew were from, Well: Pilot Bishop, South Carolina, Co-Pilot Bartush from Michigan, Navigator Miller from Missouri, Bombardier Peacock from Utah, Radio-Operator Kendall from Vermont, Engineer Cumimgs from Wisconsin, Right-Waist Gunner Sheen from Utah, Left Waist Gunner Lynch from Connecticut, Ball-Turret Gunner Robertson from New York and Tail-Gunner me from Montana."

NOT HOME FOR CHRISTMAS

Middle September Owen wrote: "Had a little diversion on one of our training missions this week. Took a little out of the way trip and flew over top of Pilot Bishop's parents' farm. Bishop took the plane down real low and really buzzed heck out of the house. It surely was a sight, the chickens went crazy and feathers were flying everywhere and the cows were running all over the place but nobody came out of the house. So he circles and goes back down even lower and buzzes the house so it's nearly shaking the roof off but nobody comes outside. So he finally gets on the radio and calls the county sheriff's office and asks him to please call his mama and tell her it's him who is buzzing the house and for her to come out and wave at him or the next time he's going to set the plane down on the roof. Third time we buzzed over, his mother came running outside in her flowered dress and apron and was waving up at us like crazy. Had to hurry then back on course so we wouldn't get in trouble."

In October, 1944, Owen and his crew flew to Stone, England via Bangor, Maine, Goose Bay, Iceland and Wales. Trip took them ten days. On October 28, 1944, they arrived at Bassingbourn Air Base where they joined the 324th Bomb Squadron of the 91st Bomb Group.

On November 6, Owen wrote home; " . . . .Say, you should be getting some money soon as I took out $ 50 of my pay to be sent home. I don't know how quick you will get it but I would like to have an identification bracelet with my name and serial number on it. They cost about $ 10, I think. Then take the rest and buy X-mass gifts. I can't get a thing here to send at all so you'll have to do it, if you will? I'll send X-mass cards too. Buy for my all the little kids, OK. Then something for my girlfriend, Eileen too. Something kinda nice you know, maybe a pretty piece of jewelry so she will have something to wear to remind her of me until I get home."

Owen was reported Missing In Action on November 26, 1944 but his parents received no further news until the late forties.

Owen's father visited Co-Pilot David Bishop and Navigator Robert Miller immediately after the war, hoping to get more news about the fate of his son. They could only tell him that they were sure he had bailed out safely. This was confirmed by Waist-Gunner Paul Lynch, who visited the Monkman family in 1945.

Some years later the parents were informed that Owen's body had been recovered from a German civilian cemetery and had been re-interred in the American Military Cemetery in Neuville-en-Condroz in the Belgian Ardennes, not far from Liège. In June, 1949,

Owen returned to the States and was buried with military honours in his home town Choteau, Montana.

We know little about engineer **Charles F. Cumings.** "Chuck", as he was called, was born in Neenah, Wisconsin, on November 2, 1924. In 1942 he graduated from Neenah High School and started to work for the Gilbert Paper Company.

On December 29, 1944 his parents were notified that Charles was missing in action and on January 11, 1945 they were informed by the War Department that their son had lost his life. He was twenty when his bomber exploded over Grossenging in Germany. In June 1949, Charles found his final place of rest at the Oakland Cemetery in Neenah, Wisconsin.

Concerning the **target**, Paul Lynch wrote in January 2001:

> "I believe that the railroad viaduct at Altenbeken was so heavily defended by the Germans at that particular time, was that it was a vital supply line for the upcoming Battle of the Bulge. In spite of all the bombs dropped on the structure, I don't think it was ever hit. I checked the home page of Altenbeken and there was the picture of the viaduct still standing. Or course it could have been reconstructed, but it certainly didn't look that way to me."

Contrary to what Paul Lynch thought, the attack on November 26, 1944 was a great success. A young German called Tom Mertens of the "Friends of the Altenbekener Viaduct Association" wrote the author:

The Altenbeken Rail Road Viaduct after the attack of November 26, 1944.

"The viaduct was hit by five bombs of 500 kg. each, destroying pillar 19 and the spans 18 and 19. Due to decreased lateral pressure, span 20 sank several centimetres. The spans between pillar 11 and 14 were more or less seriously damaged. A 500 kg. bomb directly hit pillar 13, cutting the tracks on both sides. Another bomb slightly damaged span 19, increasing seriously the pressure on pillar 20 so that later that pillar had to be blown up.

"After the first attack on November 26, 1944 the Altenbekener viaduct could no longer be used.

"After the bombing, train passengers had to descend a 120 step stairway to reach the Altenbekener station. Their luggage was brought down at a fee by small carts operated by children. Later some farmers discovered this niche in the market and started to bring down handicapped people and luggage by horse drawn wagons.

"Goods traffic over the Altenbeken viaduct was rendered impossible and had to be diverted via Detmold-Herford-Bielefeld."

The Altenbeken Rail Road Viaduct in 2006

***

Acknowledgements:
David Bishop and Paul Lynch for their narrative of their last flight in WW II
Jay Kendall and Faye Kendal Morin for details about Radio-Operator John S. Kendall
Scot Wheeler for his article on John Kendall
Andrew Jenson and Nancy Granata for their contribution about Tail-Gunner Owen Monkman.
Tom Mertens of the "Friends of the Altenbekener Viaduct Association"

CHAPTER 7

91ST BOMB GROUP 323RD BOMB SQUADRON

Aircraft Type: B17G, Serial # 42-37913,
"Seattle Sleeper", MACR: 10837
Airbase: Bassingbourn

"I think they were the most courageous people I have ever known."

—Pilot John Stevens in a post war narrative about the time he spent with the Dutch underground

Pilot: 1Lt John R. Stevens (EVD) Seattle WA
Copilot: 2Lt Stanley F. Johnston (EVD) Hillsboro OR
Navigator: 1Lt John C. Weisgarber (POW) Curwensville PA
Bombardier: T/Sgt Mabry D. Barker (EVD) Long Beach CA
Top-Turret: T/Sgt Quilla D. Reed (EVD) Lansing MI
Radio-Operator: T/Sgt Rene P. Pratt (POW) Fall River MA
Ball-Turret: Sgt Robert T. Anderson (POW) St. Louis MO
R. Waist-Gunner: S/Sgt Richard A. Trombley (EVD) Burlington VT
Tailgunner: S/Sgt Henry M. "Hank" St. George (EVD) Milton NY

Total: 6 EVD, 3 POW
Target: Altenbeken rail-road viaduct

NOT HOME FOR CHRISTMAS

As the fate of six members of this crew is closely connected with what the Dutch call their "underground", I refer to my brief description of the resistance movement in the prologue of this book.

Target for the 91st BG and thus for the Stevens crew aboard "Seattle Sleeper", named after the town of origin of her pilot, was the rail road viaduct near Altenbeken in Germany. According to the evaluation of the American military, this viaduct was one of the two most important in Germany, second only to the Bielefeld-Schildesche viaduct. The railroad through Altenbeken connected the coal consuming, industrial Ruhr area with central Germany and Berlin. The Allies hoped that by destroying these bridges they would accelerate the end of the war in Europe.

Their flight over Holland and into Germany had been uneventful but about five minutes before starting the bomb run on the Altenbeken viaduct, the formation came under attack by German fighters. An official reports says:

> "The 91st BG reported seeing an estimated 75 enemy aircraft, including FW 190s and Me 109s at 11.14 hours. They passed below the 91st BG formation at a distance of about 3000 feet. The German fighters went on to the rear of the formation and seemed to split with approx. 35 to 40 enemy fighters coming in to attack this group from the rear. The main attack lasted about ten minutes with intermittent attacks up to 11.40 hours. The attacks came from level and level low with a few high attacks. Two concentrated passes seem to have been made against the group. Generally the German fighters would break off at points 6'000 – 8'000 yards away from the bombers, although several fighters pressed their attacks to point-blank range. In breaking off the attacks, the fighters would roll over and dive out of range."

Pilot **John Stevens** recalls in the summer of 1945:

> "I will try to recite the events of November 26, 1944 as best as I can remember them.
>
> "This was my 26th mission and it started well before dawn on a foggy day. We were awakened and went to breakfast in the dark fog after which we were briefed on our target for the day; a rail road viaduct north of Osnabrück, Germany. A "milk run" target with little opposition expected.
>
> "It was still dark when we boarded our plane, the "Seattle Sleeper"

91st Bomb Group, 323rd Bomb Squadron

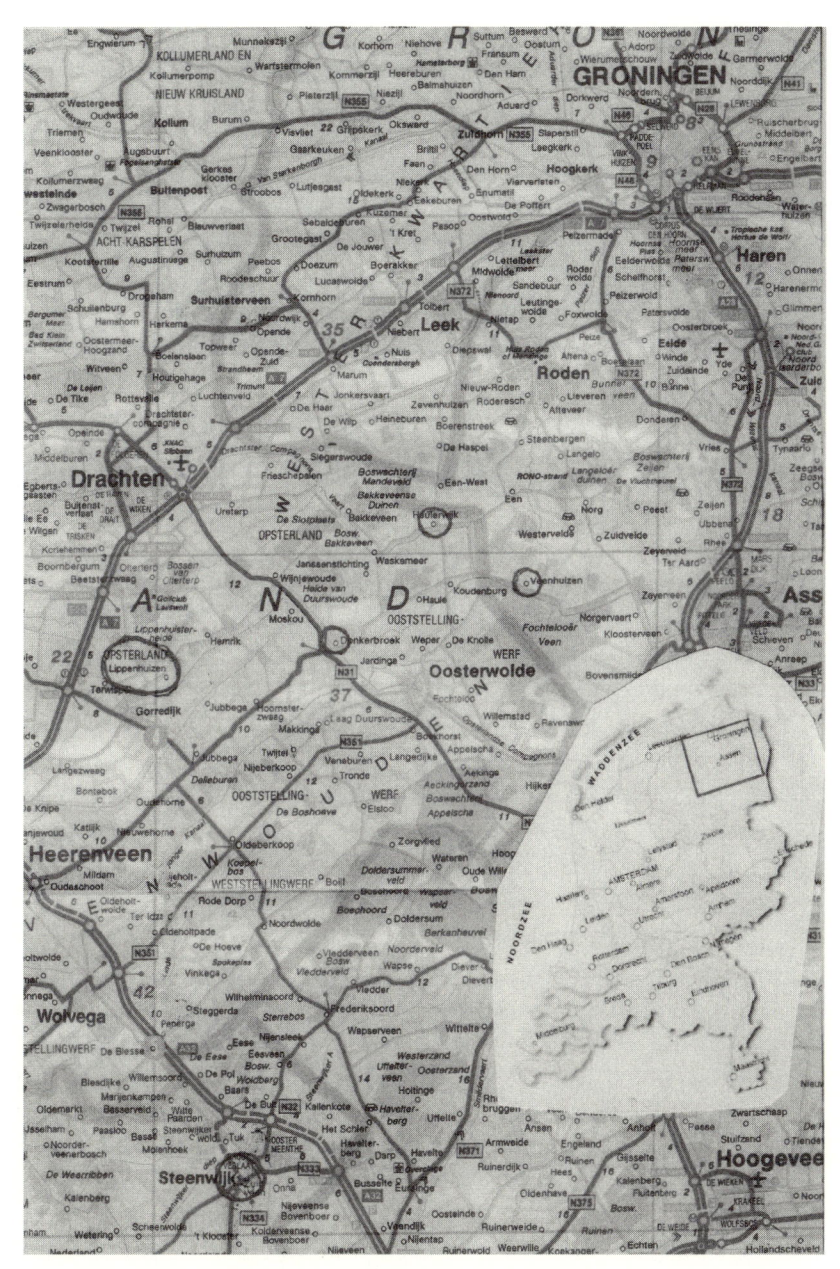

The crash site and other villages. Circled are: Haulerwijk, crash site of "Seattle Sleeper", Veenhuizen, where Don Barker was initially hidden, Donkerbroek & Lippenhuizen, where Don Barker and Quilla Reed were hidden and Steenwijk, where Steven and Johnston were hidden.

and started the engines but it started to get light as we taxied out to the runway for take-off. The fog was still very thick and when I lined up on the runway I could only see two runway lights ahead.

"Take-off was uneventful and we climbed out through the fog heading out at about 12'000 feet. We continued on up to 18'000 feet where we rendezvoused with the squadron and the long stream of bombers headed out over the North Sea, climbing to 27'000 feet. Over the sea, we checked our guns and as we approached the coast, put on our flak suits.

"Things went smoothly until we were approaching the target when we were jumped by approximately fifty German fighters, ME-109's and FW-190's. On their first pass they knocked out our tail guns and wounded the tail-gunner in the leg. Then things got exciting. The electrical and hydraulic systems were shot out, the ball-turret was inoperative and both wings were a mass of holes. Next # 2 and # 3 engines were shot out and one shell grazed my cheek and exploded in the instrument panel. Finally, the ailerons were shot out and the plane started to roll to the left. I clutched in the auto pilot but by the time it took hold we were out of formation and on our own.

"In order to shake the fighters, I drove for the under cast which was at about 20'000 feet. When we reached the clouds we started heading back to England. We tried to jettison our bombs, but since the electrical system was out it had to be done manually. We were able to get rid of all of but two of them before crossing the border into Holland when I ordered a stop as we didn't want to bomb our allies.

"Our situation at that time was 18'000feet in the clouds, 130 miles per hour, # 2 and # 3 engines out, controls out, electrical and hydraulic systems out, and the plane generally full of holes, but we thought we could make it.

"Then it happened: Richard Trombley, the waist-gunner, called that smoke was coming from the right wing tip. I alerted the crew for bail out. In a short time the whole right wing was a mass of flames and I ordered the crew to bail out. When I was sure that everyone was out I went out through the nose escape hatch. As I went out, I looked up and saw the flaming right wing separate from the fuselage.

"I delayed opening my chute so the Germans would not spot me coming down. However, since I was in the clouds, I had no way to judge my height and it was not until I broke out that I realized I was only about 500 feet above the ground. I pulled the rip-cord, the chute opened, and I was on the ground."

"I landed in the back yard of a house. Three or four people where there and they immediately took my chute and hid it in a small barn.

"None of the people spoke English and I wanted to confirm that I was in Holland but when I asked them they kept saying: "Nay, nay, Friesland". Having never heard of Friesland, I was thoroughly confused."

***

Friesland is one of the two northern provinces of the Netherlands. People there speak their own language and although they are Dutch like everybody in the Netherlands, they consider their province as being almost an independent state. It is a standard joke in Holland that as a Dutchman you almost need a valid passport to enter that particular province.

It was about 11:30 and a light rain was falling.

John Stevens landed almost on top of the house of Frits Ludwig in Haulerwijk. His parachute had caught stuck on the roof and his leg had hit the wall of the house. The shopkeeper Uiltje Kampen, who lived next door, approached John and as he did not know if the parachutist was fiend or foe he asked him; "Deutsch", meaning "German". When John had assured Uiltje that he was American, Uiltje told his fifteen years old son Herre to bring John to the farm of Arjen de Boer where John was helped out of his heavy flying gear and got a civilian overcoat.

John and young Herre then went to the farm of Dries Dees and his sister Janna in Bakkeveen, a village not far from Haulerwijk. It was known that Dries and Hanna had hidden quite a few "onderduikers": people in hiding from the Germans. John's leg was bothering him and he spent a few hours with the Dees family laying in bed. After his nap Dries came into the room with civilian clothes. Later that afternoon, Andries van der Wal came to the Drees house and told John that he would come and fetch him later that day. John's leather flying jacket was passed on to Andries who wore it for years after the liberation.

Shortly after dark Andries returned with two bicycles and told John to follow him. They rode for quite a while and finally arrived at a farm where the widow Albert Dijk lived with her crippled son.

NOT HOME FOR CHRISTMAS

John recalls:

"We had some supper and went to bed. Needless to say, I was tired. It had been a long day. I stayed there for three or four days then Andries returned and said it was time to move. This time we rode to Donkerbroek and he took me to a house in the village. I believe the people's name was Van Der Meer. It was there that I was joined by my co-pilot, Stanley Johnson. We stayed there about two weeks and while there I celebrated my 22nd birthday. For a present they gave me a bag of tobacco and some cigarette paper. No small present in these times.

"Our next move was to a dairy farm on the edge of town. The family name was Russchen. There we had milk, butter and cheese to go with the black bread and potatoes.

"We stayed on the farm about six weeks. It was a very cold winter and I spent most of the time around a small stove in the living room playing solitaire.

Mid January John and Stanley went, guided by Jannes Russchen, on bicycles to Steenwijk. They stayed for one night with doctor Bouwer. The next day John was transferred to the family Piet and Annie Logtmeijer on the Gasthuisstraat 35 in Steenwijk and Stanley Johnston was brought to the brothers Verhagen who had an optical shop, also in Steenwijk.

The Logtmeijers had a shop for small electrical appliances. Pieter and Annie Logtmeijer had two sons: Lammert, then seven years old and Wim, nine years old.

The house next door that had belonged to a deported jew, was inhabited by German soldiers.

Upon arrival, John asked Pieter Loghtmeijer if he could send a message to England stating that he was sound and safe. He did not want his wife to live with the idea that he was Missing in Action as she had certainly been informed so by the military authorities in the States.

John's story:

"In order to feed us all Pete would spend all his time scrounging for food. He would take anything he could get and bring it home. One day he got some flour, yeast, and cooking oil, I don't know where. He came home all smiles, ready to make "oily balls"; "oliebollen" in Dutch We ate "oliebollen" for days and days until some of us were tempted to take them out and bury them, but we couldn't waste food.

"Then there came "little fishes". One day Pete came home with a whole bucketful of small fish about two inches long. He proceeded to fry them all. The first day they were good, the second, still tasty, but by the fourth day I couldn't look another "little fish" in the face.

"How was Pete able to spend all his time looking for food when all able-bodied men had to work for the Germans? He had developed a neat trick. He would cut his finger and let it fester until it developed blood poisoning. Then he would go to the doctor and get a six week work deferment. When the time was about up he would repeat the process.

"In the evening, Ko, John, Pete and I would play bridge, or Anna would join us and we would play monopoly. We spent many a fun filled hour in that fashion.

"We had electricity though the Germans had banned its use. Pete had bypassed the meter so when the Germans checked it would show no electricity used.

"The door between the shop and the living quarters was always kept locked, however one morning it was not. We were eating breakfast in the kitchen and didn't hear the outside door to the shop open. The first thing we knew was two German soldiers were walking down the hall toward the kitchen. Pete jumped up and rushed through back into the shop where they bought some small electrical gadget and left. It was about thirty minutes until any of us breathed again.

"I would like at this time to try to express my feelings about these people who helped me and the others like them who helped hundreds of other allied airmen. This was a man and wife with two young, impressionable sons, just to find food for them was a full-time task. They chose to take me, an unknown, in and share their food with me, knowing fully well that if I were caught we would all be shot. I only had myself to worry about myself but Pete and Anna had the boys as well to worry about. This was never mentioned and I doubt that to this day they think of themselves as brave people. I think they were the most courageous I have ever known.

"By the time March rolled around, I was getting very restless and anxious to get out. I asked Pete to see if he could arrange for someone to lead me down to the river Rhine; the frontline of the advancing British troops. My plan was to cross the Rhine somehow and to join the British. Pete was against the idea saying it would be too dangerous and just to be patient. He was undoubtedly right but I persisted. Finally, a few days later he came home and announced that they had found a young man who would take me.

"A couple of days later, in the early morning, Pieter brought me to his brother who had a bicycle repair shop not far from Steenwijk. There I met the young man who was to lead me. He had a bike and they had another one for me. Only mine did not have any tires. After saying goodbye to Pete we started on our way.

"The first morning we rode to Meppel where we stopped to have lunch with a family in their home. After lunch we set off again staying to the back roads. I am not sure of the route but it was evening before stopping in the middle of a wood. I was pooped.

"There was a long ridge where we stopped and in the side of the ridge, behind a bush, was a tunnel. My guide lit a candle and told me to stay there, that he would be back in a little while. My guide let me into the tunnel and in the centre of the ridge was a small room that been dug out and lined with straw. After about an hour he returned with a bottle of milk, some black bread, and cheese. We ate and then hung the bread and cheese from a beam in the centre of the cave so the rats couldn't get it. Even though the rats were walking over me during the night trying to get the bread and the cheese, I was so tired I had a good sleep.

"The next morning we woke up, ate the rest of the food, and went outside into a clear sunny day. My guide said he had to leave for a while and for me to wait for him (I don't know where he thought I was going to go) and that if I heard anybody coming to go back into the cave. I stayed outside for a while, but then decided to go back into the cave and look around. In the cave I discovered another tunnel that led out the other side of the ridge. This was very comfortable because it gave me an escape route in case someone came in the front.

"A short time later my guide (I keep referring to him as my guide because I don't know his name) returned with another man. He introduced me the newcomer and it turned out he was a British security officer. The new man questioned me at considerable length to make sure I was who I said I was.

"After satisfying himself that I was alright, he gave me a revolver in case I should get trapped in the cave. He said there were many Germans in the area and that I should be very careful.

"The next day I was walking down a trail next to the cave to stretch my legs when around a bend came a Dutchman dressed in a German sympathizers' uniform. There was nothing I could do (I had left my gun in the cave) do I just kept walking past him. When I got around the bend I looked and saw my guide, walk up to the man and start talking to him. I didn't know what was going on so I just stayed where I was.

"In a minute my guide came walking down the trail looking for me. When he saw me he told me that the other man was the head of the local underground and that he had come out to meet me. He was sorry that he had forgotten to tell me he was coming. He was sorry. I had almost wet my pants.

"I met the underground chief and we talked for a while. He told me that the British had crossed the Rhine at Weser and were rushing up into north eastern Holland. This was really good news because I still hadn't figured out how I was going to cross the river.

"We stayed in the cave another day (a total of five) and then left on the next leg of the trip. We rode about fifty miles that day and could tell we were getting close to the front lines as we were running into many more German soldiers plus their tanks and guns.

"Since I did not have any papers, it was necessary for us to have a plan in case the Germans were stopping and checking papers at any of the many bridges we had to cross. The plan was this: my guide would ride several hundred feet ahead of me and if he was stopped I would pull of the road into a farm or whatever was available and wait. He would cross the bridge and ride down the road and wait a short while. Then he would come back to me, we would wait for a while and then he would try again. If he got across without having his papers checked then I would go. This system worked out well.

"Later that day, we were riding down the road and went by a farm with three men standing in the barnyard. They were about 150 feet from the road and all were dressed in farmers' clothes but I could tell that two of them were Americans. When I told my guide this he couldn't understand how I could tell, I couldn't understand either, but I could. Later I met one of them in Paris and when I told him about it his reply was: "Were you that Yank riding down the road on that bike?"

"It was obvious that we were getting much closer to the front as there were many Germans and these were not occupation troops but combat soldiers, fully equipped. I was happy to see that that they were moving to the east, in retreat.

"That evening we stopped at a farm house for supper and spent the night in the barn. The next day we left in the morning and continued into the German lines. The further we went, the heavier the concentration of Germans, until by noon we felt if we tried to go further we would surely be picked up.

"My guide left me in a small wood and went to see if he could find

NOT HOME FOR CHRISTMAS

some place for me to stay.

"He returned in about two hours and said that nobody would take me. This is certainly understandable, these people had been at war and under German occupation for four years and their liberation was only a few days away. I could certainly see why they did not want to take a chance now.

"My guide also said that he had to return and that I either could go back with him until he found somebody that would take me or I could stay there by myself. He said that he had found people who were willing to bring me food if I wanted to stay. Having come that far, I couldn't see me back-tracking, besides, it would mean going through all those Germans again. I told him I would stay and wait for the British who were about thirty miles away.

"He had found an abandoned barn or shed where I could hide and we rode over to it. It was in a field behind some houses that had been evacuated, and quite close to the railroad tracks. There was nobody around. One end of the barn had been blown out, it had a dirt floor and there was a loft with some hay in it. My guide helped me get my bike into the loft and hid it under the hay. Then we said goodbye. He told me someone would bring me some food that evening.

"It was late afternoon by then and I was tired from the excitement of the day. I hid myself behind some hay so I would not by visible to anyone looking into the loft, and went to sleep.

"I was awakened about two hours later by someone calling quietly from below. I waited a few seconds and he called again. Hoping it was my provider and not a German I called back. He stuck his head up into the loft and it was a Dutchman with some milk, bread and cheese for me. We talked for a few minutes then he left, promising to return the next day with more food. I never saw him again.

"That night I slept in the loft and the next morning I crawled down to look around. There were several bomb craters in the field around my shed and I saw several Germans going by on the road about a hundred yards away. I could hear the artillery by now and could tell it was getting closer.

"I decided that I had better get some protection in case the shells started to come in around me. I looked around and was lucky to find a broken handled shovel. I started to dig a hole in the floor of the barn but it was slow, hard work. I was starting to get weak from lack of food and had to rest frequently. Finally, after digging off and on all day, I had a hole about six feet long, three feet wide and three feet deep. This I covered with some boards I found. I brought hay down from the loft and lined the hole.

"All day long the artillery, though still a long way off, had been getting closer. During the day I had seen several RAF Hurricanes flying overhead at about a thousand feet looking for ground targets. On time a German 20 mm. battery in a wood across the rail road opened fire at one of the Hurricanes and he in turn came down and blasted them with his rockets. I decided I had better sleep in my hole that night.

"That evening I took my by then empty milk bottle and went out to the nearest bomb crater and filled it with water. When I returned I crawled in the hole and spent the night.

"The next morning the situation was about the same. The artillery was still quite a way off, the Hurricanes were still flying but there were more Germans on the road. That afternoon I crawled into my hole for a nap. When I came out I went to the side of the shed to look out and there were six Germans with a machine gun about five yards away walking towards me.

I was trapped. I couldn't make it back to the hole or up into the loft. The Germans went to the open end of the shed and sat down and lit up cigarettes, I was in plain sight and was afraid to move for fear they would see me. One of them turned around and looked right at me for a few seconds then turned back and apparently didn't say anything because none of the rest of them turned around. I don't know how he could have not seen me but maybe he thought I was just a Dutchman hiding from the Hurricanes.

"Finally they finished their cigarettes, picked up the machine gun and made for some woods across the field. I stood there, shaking all over.

"The next morning the artillery was definitely closer and I could hear small arms fire. The Germans were retreating all around me so I decided to get back in my hole and stay there until I would be overrun by the British. All day long I lay there listening to the sounds of the battle. Finally I went to sleep and when I awoke it was all quiet.

"I lay there and listened for a few moments then crawled out. I went to the end of the shed and looked around. There was not a soul in sight. Then I heard them; the church bells. The church bells were ringing in town. But it was the day before Eastern and I didn't know if they were ringing for that reason or because the town had been liberated. I waited a few minutes then decided to go out to the road and look around. I walked down the short row of trees leading to the road and as I stepped out on to the road a German soldier rode up to me on his bike. He had two rifles, a pistol, two helmets and several hand grenades but he was obviously scared. He asked me if I spoke German and when I said no he gesticulated towards the town and asked: "Tommy? I assured him that they had and directed him down the road. He must have thought the road led away from the British when actually it led right to them.

"After he had left I stood there and thought: "My God, you're this close don't goof it up now". After I pulled myself together I started to walk down the road toward town. After a short distance I met a woman coming toward me carrying a loaf of bread. She stopped and stared at me and then I realized how I must have looked. I had not shaved for several days, I had been in that hole dressed in a tweed suit that was dirty and covered with straw, and I must have looked starved because she didn't say a word, just held the loaf of bread to me.

"I asked her if the Tommies were in town and she nodded her head, again not saying a word, just staring. I returned to my shed, retrieved my ring and watch that I had hidden and again started down the road toward town. I had walked about half a mile when I ran into a group of Dutch people standing on the road. One of them, a young girl, ran up and pinned an orange bow on my lapel. I asked her where the Tommies where and she recognized that I was not Dutch. She asked if I were a Tommy and I told her I was an American pilot. With that she grabbed me by the arm and started to drag me towards the others yelling; "Amerikaanse piloten, Amerikaanse piloten".

"With that they all gathered around me shouting and shaking my hand. I was getting pretty excited and every word of Dutch I had learned left me. Finally one of the men spoke to me in English and I asked him if he would take me to the British. He said he would and led me several blocks to a school. There was a guard at the door but he let me in and told me where I could find the commanding officer.

"I went into the room and there was a very tired British major sitting behind a table. I told him who I was and showed him my dog tags. He was a little apprehensive but I finally convinced him and he agreed to send me back to his headquarters.

"I got on a truck and we went a few miles back to a farm house that was being used by a Lt. Colonel as his command post. I went in and introduced myself to the Colonel and he asked me if I had had breakfast. When I told him I had not eaten for five days he told his sergeant to fix me something to eat. The sergeant took me into the dining room and asked me to sit down and he would fix some ham and eggs. He then went to the cupboard and produced a bottle of scotch and proceeded to pour me half a glass full. He gave it to me and said to drink it while I waited.

"There was a radio in the room and I turned it on, sipped on the scotch and it was then that I realized that I had made it. I started to shake. My hands shook so bad that I couldn't even hold the cigarette they had given me. By the time my breakfast was ready I had calmed down and was able to eat the ham, eggs, potatoes, bread and tea with gusto.

"After breakfast I borrowed a razor and cleaned up as much as I could. Then the Colonel told me that there was an armoured car going back further and that I could go along. I got in the car and we drove quite a while arriving in a small village in the early evening. I didn't realize it but we were in Germany. The south-east corner of Holland juts down into Germany and we had to cross through there to get to the Rhine. That led to an interesting incident.

"The driver let me out in front of one of the houses and told me to go in and that they would take care of me for the night. I went in and told the sergeant who was in charge there who I was. He told me to go to a big white house on the right hand side of the road where they would take care of me. By this time it was getting dusk.

"I went out and started walking and then two American GI's came up to me. They had heard me talking in the house and wanted to know if I was an American. I assured them that I was and while we were talking, two British MP's came up and asked the GI's who I was. When they explained who I was to them, one of the MP's looked at me and said; "You're lucky you were talking to these guys, we shoot civilians around here after dark".

"With that I grabbed one MP with my left hand and the other with my right hand and said, "Boys, you stay right with me until I get in that house," and they did.

"When I got inside and again explained who I was, a sergeant told me I could go into the dining room – that they were just serving dinner. He said that there were several British officers in there eating, but there was a small table off to the side where I could sit.

"I opened the door and walked in the room, all conversation stopped. I went over to the small table and sat down, then looked up. All the officers, who were seated at a long table, were staring at me. I realized that they must be thinking that I was a German civilian, and wondering what I was doing there. Again I explained who I was and was immediately brought over to their table where we all had a good gab.

"The next morning I was up early and in a truck on my way to Eindhoven. We crossed the Rhine on a pontoon bridge near Wesel. On the way we went through the area where the British had crossed the Rhine and saw the hundreds of crashed gliders and aircraft.

"When I reached Eindhoven I had a chance to take a bath and was

NOT HOME FOR CHRISTMAS

given a British field uniform, which, after the experience of the night before, I was glad to get.

"From Eindhoven, I was flown to Brussels where I spent the night. The next day I got a ride on a British C-47 to Paris where I was directed to a hotel that the Americans were using for escaped POW's and evadees.

"I was back."

So far John Stevens story as told in his own words.

After the war, John stayed with the US Air Force and was, as a Lt. Colonel, for some time stationed in Mannheim in Germany The Logtmeijers paid him a visit there and John also came to Steenwijk. He also visited Haulerwijk, accompanied by Piet Logtmeijer and Hans van der Meer of Donkerbroek.

***

Co-pilot Stanley Johnson landed in Holland behind the farm of Harm Cordes. The then nineteen years old Marten Cordes recalls that the heavy boots of the airman were stuck in loose garden earth. Stanley stepped out of his boots, pulled them out of the mud and puts them on again when he had reached the path that led to the Cordes farm.

On that path he was picked up by Sander Bisschop. Sander recalls that Stanley was walking slowly; partly because he was still dizzy after his hard landing and partly because he was wearing his flying boots. The young Dutchman and the American walked arm in arm, like a pair of lovers. Stanley was brought to the personal hiding place of the farmer Graanstra: a pit behind the farm. Sander covered the airman with some branches and went on in the direction of Allardsoog to Mr. Guermonprez, who was a member of the underground. Guermonprez then telephoned another underground member, Douwe Offringa, and explained where Stanley could be found.

Luit Appelhof was hiding for the Germans and stayed with his father-in-law Pieter Offringa in Haulerwijk. His brother-in-law Douwe was also a member of the underground.

Douwe and Luit brought Stanley to Haulerwijk south where he stayed four days with the Douwe Offringa family. Luit Appelhof was conversant in English and could communicate with Stanley. After these four days Douwe and Luit brought Stanley to Van der Meer in Donkerbroek where he met Pilot John Stevens. After the war Luit Appelhof stayed in contact with Stanley Johnston.

They (John Stevens and Stanley Johnston) then stayed with the family Roelof Russchen at 't West in Donkerbroek for six weeks.

Mid January John and Stanley went, guided by Jannes Russchen (Roelof's son), on bicycles to Steenwijk. They stayed for one night with doctor Bouwer in Tuk. The next day, John Stevens went to Piet and Annie Logtmeijer in Steenwijk.

Stanley went to Verhagen brothers, opticians, in the Oosterstreet in Steenwijk. From time to time John Stevens would come and visit his Co-Pilot for a game of cards. Stanley was interested in meeting girls in Steenwijk, but that was too risky in John's eyes.

Stanley remained in Steenwijk until the arrival of Canadian troops in April 1945.

Navigator John Weisgarber was born on February 25, 1922 in Curwensville, PA and graduated in 1940 from high school as number one of his class. He worked in a tannery until he joined the Air Force in March of 1943. He started out as a pilot, but they changed that to navigator.

He volunteered for the November 26, 1944 mission as his regular pilot Bill Eblen was ill and he wanted to finish his tour of thirty-five missions before Christmas. He was on his 33rd mission that day.

In 1996, John recalls:

"I was one of the three flyers of the "Seattle Sleeper" captured on the 26th of November, 1944. I was the Navigator on this mission. We were hit by a ME 109 German fighter plane coming at us from the rear. He shot us very badly, and knocked us out of control at about 27'000 feet. We fell out of control through the cloud cover to about 17'000 feet, at which time the pilot recovered control, and we proceeded towards the English Channel but we were on fire.

"By the way, we did blow up the ME 109 before we lost control.

"The Pilot wanted to ditch in the English Channel, but I got on the intercom and said I was not in favour of this as our bomb doors were down and would not raise back up, and besides we were on fire with largely a full gas load. At this time he changed his mind and told us to abandon ship.

"I pulled the red handle on the escape hatch in the nose of the plane, but it did not open, so I kicked it with my foot at which time it fell away. I then hung down out of the hatch but was afraid to jump as the belly gunner's bottom turret 50 calibre guns were pointed straight down and I was afraid I would hit them. At this time the Bombardier Don Barker wanted out also and told me to let go or he would kick me loose. I cleared the guns by many feet and free fell a long time before opening my chute. It opened but had one panel torn out and I was afraid it would rip completely across, but it did not.

"It seemed to take forever to reach the ground but when I did I found out I was travelling very fast. I tried to turn just before hitting the ground, which was covered by about a foot of water and I threw all the weight on one foot which stoved my ankle so I could not walk. I was wearing only bedroom slippers and felt flying boots which were not well suited for jumping.

"A Dutch family gathered me up and took me into their home just at lunch time about 12.00 and sat me at their table. I remember a very large bowl of boiled potatoes but little else. We could not converse as they knew no English and I no Dutch. I did get the idea that I could escape but could not walk.

"About an hour after I landed I was sitting in a chair when I felt something cold on the back of my neck. It was a Wehrmacht soldier with a pistol and he told me to "Mach-Schnell" or something like that. He took me outside where there were two bicycles and he got me on one and I had to follow him into town pedalling with one foot.

"The Burgomaster was out of town and no one had the jail house key so a German officer nearby who spoke good English said he would take me in for the night if I promised not to escape. This I did as I could not walk away anyhow. He offered me cigarettes and brandy and food and we had quite a conversation. He had been educated in the U.S. and was well spoken. We talked about the war and he agreed with me when I said Germany was already beaten.

"Sometime later we were taken to some old factory where I was put in with some English prisoners.

"I remember the first morning they served us a soup with yellow things floating on top. I asked some of the other prisoners what they were and I was told it was barley soup with weevils floating on top. For several days I did not partake of this until I finally got hungry enough. The coffee I was told was made from parched acorns and it was far from being good but we drank it anyway as it was at least hot.

"Later we were taken by train to someplace called I believe Oberussel where I was interrogated by some German officers who spoke English. Somewhere along the line they had taken my dog tags and other possessions including several hundred dollars of gold Seal dollars which were in my escape kit. They could not understand that I could not speak or understand German as my name was Weisgarber. All I could tell them was my name, rank, and serial number. They later threatened to shoot me as a spy as I had no dog tags. All they did was to put me in solitary confinement for about a week.

"Somewhere along the line we were taken by train and I remember marching across a bombed out city I believe was Cologne. It looked like a crumbled box of wet graham crackers. We were taken that evening into an underground railway station where the German civilians wished to beat us up, but the Wehrmacht guards kept them off. During this time we experienced a Royal Air Force bombing raid.

"Later we were taken by train in 40 x 8 railroad cars and very cramped conditions to Stalag Luft I at Barth, Germany where I stayed about six months until the Russians overran the compound.

"One of the first people I saw when I entered the camp was a Pilot by the name of Jenkins who had always smoked a crooked stem pipe, and I had been flying alongside of him in a previous raid and had seen his plane blow up in the air from a 88 shell. I had no idea he had survived but he must have been blown clear as were so many and he still had his crooked stem pipe in his mouth.

"Colonel Zemke and Colonel Gabreski, both fighter aces, were my next door neighbours.

"I remember one morning directly after roll call muster I rushed through the barracks and wrenched off the brass door pull that was held by four small screws as I needed a hammer to seam the powdered milk cans that we cut open and flattened out to make cooking pans. I fastened it to a stick and made a passable hammer, also I made a metal cutter from a metal table knife to cut the cans open. We put powdered pea powder in the seams that when wet kept the seams in our pans from leaking. We had to do much of our own cooking.

"We spent most of our time planning what we were going to eat when we got released.

"One morning we woke up and there were no Germans in the camp as the Russians had advanced into town. In many respects they were worse than the Germans and the civilians were frightened to death of them. We ran loose for about two weeks until some B-17 bombers arrived at a near-

NOT HOME FOR CHRISTMAS

by airport, and we were flown back to France to Camp Lucky Strike near Le Havre. While there, I took a seven day pass to Paris where we were issued new uniforms and paid a part of our back pay. I also found out that I had been advanced from 2nd Lt. to 1st LT.

"On the way on a Dutch liberty ship I developed a severe infection alongside my left eye as a result of some 20 mm. fragments I had received when we were up by the ME 109.

"I was taken to Camp Miles Standish in Boston and then transferred to Camp Fort Dix where I received much penicillin for several months and they saved my eye.

"After being mustered out in December of 1945 I returned to my home in Curwensville and bought a plumbing, heating and sheet metal business which I managed for fifty years.

"In 1945 I married a girl from New York City and we had three boys, two who are still living. I now live at my present address with my new wife and 3 dogs and 1 cat who are like family.

"I am very active in the Methodist Church, Lions Club and our local Park Commission and do much charity work, as well as much flower and vegetable gardening.

"I am now 82 years old and enjoy very good health and am very active.

Tail-gunner Hank St. George in a taped interview:

"We were flying over Holland at 28000 feet when little black specks came out of the clouds: German fighters. They came four abreast and climbed between two formations of bombers. The broke off at 150 yards and then dived away while turning over as their backs and their bottoms were heavily armoured and therefore difficult to penetrate by the 50. calibre guns of the bombers.

"After the fourth attack the # 3 engine of the "Seattle Sleeper" started to burn followed by the cry from the cockpit "Abandon Ship, abandon ship". A fighter approached the tail and a 20 mm shell cut my pants and whipped this gun out of my hands. I switched my oxygen mask to a portable tank and went to the waist for easier exit.

"Right waist-Gunner Trombley was hit in his leg and lay on the floor. I looked out of the window and saw the # 3 engine still burning. I hoped that Pratt could come out of his Top-Turret. I put my chute on and helped Trombley to put on his after having given him a shot of morphine. He asked the Radio-operator Pratt; "Where are we" and Pratt said: "We're over Holland."

91st Bomb Group, 323rd Bomb Squadron

"We stood by the side door of the B-17, but nobody jumped. I said: "I don't know about you guys, but I go. See you on the ground." I jumped first and after I had pulled the rip cord and had broken through the cloud cover I saw other chutes above me. I was swinging back and forth under my chute like a pendulum under a clock. Before jumping I had forgotten to zip up my flying suit so all my papers, money and my escape kit blew out. I had my flying shoes on. It was recommended to take an extra pair of extra sturdy GI walking shoes into the plane before the mission and attach them to the harness before bail-out. I hadn't.

"I stayed in the air about nine minutes and saw the ground coming up. It was about noon when I landed in a field. I saw a parachute hanging under a tree in a nearby wood. I ran to that chute and saw Dutch civilians taking the chute down and burying it. They said; "Hide, hide!"

Hank started to walk with the intention to ultimately reach the allied lines around 80 miles south from where he had landed. At about 12.30 he approached a house without telephone lines connected to it and as for some time he saw nobody coming to or going from the house he considered it safe to go there for help. He knocked on the back door and a young women with a baby let him in. She didn't speak English and as Hank didn't speak Dutch, communication was on a very low level. She gave him some bread and warm milk and then a man passed by the house on a bicycle and the lady of the house said: "He speaks English". She called the man to come into the house. When he saw Hank he gave him his overcoat to cover up the flying suit Hank was still wearing and said. "I go on my bicycle and you follow me through the woods." They came to his house and the gentleman told Hank to hide outside in a pit used for clamping potatoes.

Hank stayed there until midnight and then the man gave him a local map and showed Hank the way he should take. Hank followed the road for a couple of hours when all of a sudden he was stopped by Mr. Reyss, a uniformed guard of the Veenhuizen civilian prison, who warned him in Dutch that it was after curfew. Hank of course could not answer him in Dutch and as Reijss already knew that several airmen had jumped over Haulerwijk and that most of them had not been captured by the Germans, he assumed Hank was one of them and took him to his nearby prison.

NOT HOME FOR CHRISTMAS

The House of Correction Veenhuizen was started in the early eighteen hundreds as a settlement where poor families from the big cities in the western part of the Netherlands could start a new life as farmers. It came known as "Dutch Siberia". Not all settlers came there on their free will: beggars and homeless persons were forced to settle in Veenhuizen and the institute soon became a kind of low security prison.

In WW II most of the prison guards became active members of the underground. They had two big advantages: they wore uniforms and were allowed to carry weapons.

Hank was put in one of the prison's kitchens. A captain came in, who spoke good English and who told him that Reyss would try to get him to the underground in Apeldoorn: sixty miles south of Haulerwijk and twenty miles north of the river Rhine, then the frontline with the Allies. He also said that Hank would have to ride a bicycle as all motorized vehicles had been confiscated a long time ago by the Germans. Hank was given civilian clothes that he put on but he kept his underwear and also his dog tags.

Reyss and Hank went on the road. Reyss told Hank to follow him at a distance of about 100 yards. When he (the policeman) would step from his bike, Hank had to hide himself until the road would be safe again. The policeman would so to speak "scout ahead".

The two spent the night in a simple hotel and hit the road again the next morning. Before departure Reijs got a letter from a local policeman stating that his companion had committed a theft on the other side of the river and that he was bringing him back to be put in jail.

Between Haulerwijk and Apeldoorn flows the river IJssel, separating the western part of the Netherlands from the east. It's a main river, even by Dutch standards. Reijs wanted to cross the river at Zwolle but as the local policeman had told him that that crossing was heavily guarded he opted for the much smaller crossing (by ferry) in Wijhe a bit more to the south.

The departure of the ferry in Wijhe was guarded by regular German soldiers under command of an officer. Reijs took Hank by the hand and together they went to the officer. Reys clicked his heels, lifted his had and said "Heil Hitler". The officer Heil-Hitlered him back and brought the policeman with his "prisoner" to the top of the line of waiting people and even went so far as to carry Hank's bike on the ferry.

The policeman had an address in Apeldoorn where to go: the Woltman family living on the Jachtlaan not far from the royal palace "Het Loo" the residence of Queen Wilhelmina then in exile in England.

Mid December 1944. Food is scarce. Hank is still with the Woltman family. He had kept his thick flying gloves and as the winter of 1944 was an extremely cold one, he had given these to Tinie, the daughter of the Woltmans. One night Tinie came running to the house and said that a German had stopped her on the road and had confiscated the gloves. As inside the gloves a label was glued reading; "General Electric. Property of the US Army Air Forces" and as Tinie was not quite sure if the German had not seen her disappearing into the house, Hank had to hide for the night in a tree in the garden.

The next morning a member of the underground came and brought Hank to another safe house. The owner of that house was a solid underground member but also a black market racketeer. As there was a lot of coming and going of various people in that house, Hank was moved the next day to the house of a doctor working in the St. Joseph hospital in Apeldoorn, that had been requisitioned by the German army and made into a field hospital.

One day Hank was sitting near the stove in the kitchen when a German doctor of the hospital came to have a Christmas drink with his Dutch colleague. "What's the matter with him", he asked, pointing at Hank "Don't bother", the Dutchman replied, "He's deaf and dumb."

A couple of days later Hank went with the wife of the black marketeer on a bicycle again to the village Barneveld, not far from the river Rhine that separated the Germans from the Allied troops.

After the British First Airborne Division had three months earlier failed to capture the bridge over the river Rhine at Arnhem as part of the Operation "Market Garden", several groups of these paras had been hidden by the underground in the densely wooded area north of the river Rhine.

NOT HOME FOR CHRISTMAS

It was known that British patrols would cross the Rhine to pick up stragglers of the battle of Arnhem. Hank was paired up with a Canadian officer, a doctor of the 1st British Airborne.

They went direction river when Tinie Woltman, who also was in Barneveld, came and told them that the crossing was off due to German patrols. Hank could hear shooting. Back to the farm house they went. The following day Tinie and Hank loaded their bicycles with food and pedalled direction Utrecht. On the way to Utrecht they were stopped by a German patrol. The food they were carrying was confiscated and the Germans let the air out of the tyres. They pumped the tires up again and continued their road.

They went to Best house in Utrecht where Hank spent the rest of the war. Hank had no forged papers, just a card stating that he had lost his papers.

On May 5, Canadian troops entered Utrecht. Hank went to meet them and addresses himself to an officer saying: "I am a American and have been hiding for the last six months".

"Typical American", the officer answered, "They're always ahead of us."

The Canadians sent Hank via Eindhoven and Namur in Belgium to Bruxelles and from there to Camp Lucky Strike near Le Havre in France where American troops awaited transportation back to the States. In Camp Lucky Strike Hank met Rene Pratt again: the Radio-Operator aboard "Seattle Sleeper".

In Le Havre, Hank boarded an Italian ship and came home via New York He had lost fifteen pounds in Holland.

Bombardier Marbry "Don" Barker died in October 1993. His oldest daughter Vicki Robertson and his wife Bobbye rewrote his original story during his last years, and he reviewed the new manuscript as it was reworked. Through the Air Force Escapees and Evaders Society he was reunited with one of the other principals in this story: Top-Turret Gunner Quilla Reed and they kept in touch by phone and by letter, though they never got together in person.

Don wrote about the last minutes of "Seattle Sleeper:

"The Nazi machine guns had knocked out the electrical and hydraulic systems. The ball-turret was inoperable. Both wings were peppered with

91st Bomb Group, 323rd Bomb Squadron

holes. The crew had fared better though than the plane. Waist-Gunner Dick Trombley had been hit in the right leg below the knee. The wound was painful but it did not seem serious at the time. The pilot had a minor cheek wound: just a scratch that had already stopped bleeding. Fortunately no one else had been hit.

John Stevens kept the plane in the clouds for cover.

"Barker to pilot; "Hey, John! You want me to get rid of these bombs?"

"Yeah, let 'em go while we're still over Germany."

"Don reached for the salvo-switch to open the bomb bay doors. But he discovered the switch was gone along with most of the switch panel. He looked around, grabbed a screw driver and slipped it in his pocket. He strapped on his auxiliary oxygen tank and headed toward the bomb bay. Barker gripped the handle and turned the crank to open the bomb bay doors. He carefully worked the crank until it stopped. He recalled how one of his friends, Jerry Romero, broke his right arm when he performed this same task on another airplane and the crank had spun out of control. Don smiled wryly as he remembered teasing Jerry about accepting the Purple Heart for this "accident."

"Don grabbed the bomb rack with his left hand for support. He stepped out onto the narrow catwalk that separated the two bomb compartments then slipped the screw driver from his pocket. For an instant he looked down at the clouds below and wondered what the unintentional target would be. The bombs they carried for this mission were five-hundred pounders, three on each side. He slipped the screw driver into the single shackle that held the first bomb and pried it loose. The heavy bomb fell away into the clouds. Wind resistance would turn the prop on the bomb and unscrew to activate the arming mechanism. He repeated this manoeuvre for the next three bombs.

"Gas fumes penetrated his oxygen mask as he reached for the last two bombs. A tap on his shoulder startled him. He turned and saw the top-turret gunner, Quilla Reed wave him forward. He glanced back at the two remaining bombs, shrugged his shoulders and headed toward the front of the plane.

"The navigator shouted over the roaring wind; "Can't drop 'em now. We're too close to Holland!" The navigator pointed toward the right wing. Don leaned forward and looked out the nose. He expected to see more enemy fighter planes but instead saw flames and black smoke billowing from the wing. Bewildered, he grabbed his headphones and put them on. Just in time to hear John's voice call out; "OK guys! Hit the silk: right now!"

NOT HOME FOR CHRISTMAS

"Son-of-a-bitch," Don said aloud, "On my last mission!" He turned and saw two feet disappear out the escape hatch. Don removed his oxygen mask and saw Engineer Quilla Reed half-way out the hatch, but holding on. Don reached over, released Reed's grip and pushed him forward and out.

"Just as he prepared to jump, Don looked through the hatch and suddenly realized the reason for Reeds hesitation. The bomb-bay doors stood wide open. He shuddered knowing what would happen if a man fell toward the cutting edges. For just an instant, Don Barker's mind raced as he imagined his push sending Reed to his death. His guilt turned to fear as he eased himself down and out of the hatch. He held on and saw the bomb bay doors loom before him. He swung himself back and forth and as he let go, he pushed as hard as he could away from the plane.

"Don tumbled through freezing space. He caught a glimpse of the flaming right wing as it separated from the fuselage then he saw the stream of black smoke as the *Seattle Sleeper* plunged toward the ground. Don did not know what lay below the clouds. Voices of his original crew echoed through his mind; "Delay opening your chute if there is a possibility of enemy planes still in the area. Your open chute will attract their attention." And: "If you're over the North Sea, forget it! A man will last only five or six minutes in that icy water!"

"He fell into the thick layer of clouds. He tried to look down but he wasn't sure which way was down! He had a strange sensation of falling sideways. He could see nothing except the mass of clouds surrounding him. Suddenly a hole opened up. What he saw caused him to react instantly. He tugged at the rip cord. He had seen a house with a fence around it and a young boy standing in front of the house. His mind screamed; "God Damn! You waited to long!"

"The pilot chute dragged the long ribbon of nylon upwards and the harness of the back chute eased up. As the chute filled with air, the loud pop jerked his head forward. The jolt seemed to separate his body from his legs. It was so severe his left boot was pulled from his foot. The roar of the wind that rushed past him as he plummeted through space ceased. He moved his head and looked down. He could clearly see a tree, a canal, and the young boy running into the house. Don guessed the lad was frightened by the noise of the chute as it opened.

"He hit the ground with terrific force. The first thing he thought of was he was sure lucky not to have broken both legs. Recent rains on the ploughed ground had softened the dirt and luckily had cushioned the impact. The chute settled down beside him for just an instant, then suddenly it caught the wind and dragged him face down through the wet earth. He grabbed the shrouds, pulling himself forward enough to spill the chute and get it under control. He was finally able to stand up. He unbuckled the harness and let it fall to the ground. He wiped the dirt from his eyes. He wondered where his helmet was as he gathered up his chute.

"A light rain fell. The house he had seen was at the edge of a small village. People quickly gathered around him. "Where am I?" Don looked at the faces of the strangers as they stared first at him and then at each other. Each time he spoke they mumbled to each other and he realized that they had not understood him. He became more apprehensive. He reached for his shoulder holster and said to himself: "Thank God! My Colt .45 is still here!" It gave him a small bit of self-assurance. Once again he searched the faces of the people around him and decided to try once more. He said; "Where? Belgium? France maybe? How about Holland? For God's sake, where am I?"

"An older woman pressed close to him, her face not more than a couple of inches from his and asked; "Engels?"

"Don nodded enthusiastically and replied; "Yes, English!"

"The woman was joined by others, they crowded around him now and a young man in horn-rimmed glasses touched his shoulder. Don turned slightly to him. The young man asked in perfect English: "You are from England? But this is not the British uniform you are wearing?"

"You speak English? Good! Then tell them I was stationed in England, but I'm American!"

"The young man stretched his arm out and pointed across a field. "You must go that way!" Don stared in the direction the boy pointed, a puzzled look on his face. The young man urged; "Hurry . . . . you must hurry . . . you cannot stay here! Go! Please!"

"Another man stepped out of the crowd and grasped Don's shoulder. Don turned quickly. The older man pointed toward the chute, then to himself, but said nothing. Don thought he understood, nodded and told him; "Yes, take it. You can have it, OK?" The younger man with the glasses translated for him and Barker watched as the man grabbed up the chute, wad it into a small bundle. He pressed the prize against his stomach and ran off toward a building nearby. Don stared as the man disappeared. Strangely enough Don visualized a football player tucking the ball close to his body and running hell-bent for the goal line. Someone in the crowd urged him; "Haast!" The young man with the specs said again: "Hurry!"

"He walked quickly toward the field in the direction they had pointed. Instinct warned him not to run. He decided a man running across an open

NOT HOME FOR CHRISTMAS

field would surely draw attention. As he walked across the ploughed field, he felt the cold mud squish through his sock and between his toes on his left foot.

"He concluded the people he just left had to be friendly. He had seen no soldiers and nobody made no effort to take him prisoner. A few more steps and he turned to look back at the village. It looked deserted. No one lingered where just moments ago a crowd had stood. He thought this strange but decided to keep on walking even though he did not know where he was or where he might be headed.

"He crawled under a barbed-wire fence that seemed to be between him and the direction he had been walking. As he stood up on the other side of the fence he looked around. He noticed a man walking some distance away but seemingly parallel with him. The stranger appeared to pay no attention to him. Nothing was said, but Don decided he'd keep an eye on him anyway. He felt for his shoulder holster again, took a deep breath and continued walking.

"He was guessing of course, but he presumed he had walked about two miles. He looked for the stranger. He was still there. When Don reached a cross-road he heard a low whistle and he stopped. He looked around but there was no one other than himself and the other man in sight. He remembered hearing stories about what happened to Americans shot down over Germany, but then, they were just stories. What he was experiencing now was something totally new to him and he was not the least bit sure of himself. He had no idea what would happen next.

"The other man beckoned to him. Barker shrugged his shoulders and started walking toward the stranger. He could see his face clearly now and it seemed there was something vaguely familiar about him. He surely was one of the men in the crowd back at the village. Don joined him and waved a greeting, not knowing what to say. The man did not speak. Silently the two men walked together down the road.

"Don could see a building that he thought to be a small house, in the distance. The man said something but Don could not understand the words. He noticed the man constantly turned every few steps and looked behind him. This made Don nervous but they walked on. Suddenly he heard a noise in the brush alongside the road. He stopped and instinctively reached for his gun. The stranger pressed Don's arm and smiled, saying; "Neen, ...haas!"

"In all probability the word "neen" was the same as "no" – but in what language? And what was the other word "haas". He had no idea what it meant. The stranger smiled again and pointed. Don saw the rabbit quickly disappear in the tall grass beyond. He relaxed somewhat and returned the smile. They walked on to the small weathered house. Don noticed the cracked paint peeling off the door as he followed the man inside. A woman and two children stood together at one side of the room. The woman appeared frightened when she saw Don. The children too were apparently wary and huddled against the woman. The man spoke to her while Don stood uncomfortably and watched the woman's expression and the children's anxiety. He wished he could understand the foreign words and know what was going on.

"The woman continued to glance at Don but said nothing. Then he thought he saw a tentative smile cross her face. He also thought he heard the word "American" but he couldn't be sure. He looked down at the small boy who seemed to stare at him. Don smiled but the boy turned slyly away. As Don glanced around the room, he saw beds, a table, chairs at the table and others placed around the wall of the room. He saw an old-fashioned cupboard. He noticed no other doors that might lead to an adjoining room. No, it appeared this house only had the one room and the only door through which they had entered. There were heavily draped windows on all four walls of the room.

"He turned toward the woman who had started to speak. He guessed she was probably saying something to him but he could understand none of the words. He smiled at her but shrugged his shoulders and shook his head negatively. She paused a moment then spoke very slowly and he saw her hand move toward her mouth, then she pointed to the table. He only surmised that she was asking him if he was hungry and wanted something to eat. He nodded affirmatively and smiled again. He was hungry. He did not know how long it had been since he had eaten or had even thought about food. He had no watch so he had no concept of time. He looked around the room but did not see a clock anywhere. The woman mentioned for him to sit in one of the chairs. She walked to the cupboard and took out a large loaf of bread.

"The man pressed Don's arm and pointed to a bowl-like pan on a stand against one wall. Don watched as the man got a pitcher and poured water into the pan. Don walked toward the stand presuming he was to wash up. He peered into an old mirror hanging on the wall above the wash stand. The image he saw in the mirror startled him and he stepped back. He had completely forgotten about being dragged through the mud when he first hit the ground. The face he saw was almost completely covered with dried, caked mud. No wonder the woman and her children had been frightened when they first looked at him. He cupped his hands and rinsed his face several times. His hair was stiff with mud also but that would have to wait. He looked at the dirty water in the pan as he stood up and reached for the clean white towel hanging on a hook alongside the mirror. He wanted to apologize to the woman but the words he might say would not mean any more to her than the strange words he heard meant to him. He looked in the direction of the two children and grinned. This time, they smiled back.

"He walked back to the table and sat in one of the chairs. The large wooden table looked heavy and sturdy and was immaculately clean. The chairs all had high backs and matched several others placed against the walls of the room. The man sat down across the table from him. The children sat on one of the beds and watched from across the room. The woman deftly sliced the coarse dark bread and a brick of cheese and placed the slices on a platter. She pushed the plate across the table in Don's direction. He watched as she poured a dark hot liquid into one of the cups that had been placed on the table. Thinking it was coffee, he lifted the cup and sipped. The bitter substance surprised him. It was not coffee as he knew it, but he swallowed and tried not to look as disappointed as he felt. The man and woman did not eat but watched him and smiled. He forced himself to drink the liquid but he did not have to pretend to enjoy the bread and cheese. That really did taste good.

"As he finished eating the man rose and walked across the room toward a huge ornately-carved wardrobe that reached from floor to ceiling. He talked as he moved but Barker did not know if he was speaking to him or to the woman. He watched as the man opened the doors and seemed to be sorting through the clothes hanging inside. He pulled out a coat. He pointed to Don's leather flying jacket and pushed the coat toward him. Reluctantly, Don removed the jacket and handed it to the man. As he did, the woman gasped when she saw the gun in his holster. Don reached for the coat and quickly put it on. It surprised him somewhat that the man did not ask him to give up his gun.

"However the man did insist that Don remove the remaining flying boot. The stranger handed the jacket and the one flying boot to the woman, talking and gesturing to her as he did so. Don could only conclude that he was instructing her how to dispose of the articles. The man made no attempt however to provide him with any shoes.

"Barker was confused because the man kept on talking to him just as if he could understand. He did interpret the motion to follow him though, and the two men left the house. Don followed him out of the road and once again they began to walk. He had no way of knowing where he was being taken and with the overcast sky he really didn't know which direction they travelled. He did sense that they had walked maybe four miles, possibly five. Now both his socks were wet and caked with mud and his feet were icy cold. The coat the man had given him was a good heavy one, but it was not able to keep him warm because his feet were so cold. Don thought of the old saying: "When your feet are cold, you're cold all over!" and he knew that this was true. He was glad there was no snow on the ground and that it was not frozen hard, that would have made it even more miserable. He tried to ask the man about shoes and pointed to his feet but the man merely nodded and continued to walk down the road.

"Don hesitated as they approached another house. This one appeared to be well-kept and was much larger than the previous one. He saw the neat out-buildings that surrounded the house. His companion motioned for Don to come stand beside him as he reached out to knock on the door. As if they had been expected, the door opened and they were ushered into the house immediately. The man who had opened the door talked quietly to the man who had brought Don here. Don shifted from one foot to the other as he was being scrutinized by the new stranger. Don looked down on his muddy feet but the man smiled and motioned him to come into an additional room. After a brief hesitation the man who apparently lived in the house left the room and reappeared moments later with a pair of wooden shoes in his hand.

"Barker thought; "Holland!" I must be in Holland! Dutch people wear wooden shoes!" He looked at the shoes the man pushed toward him. "I hope to hell he doesn't think I can wear those things," Don said to himself. He shook his head but the men gestured first to his muddy socks then to the shoes and intimated that he should put them on. Grudgingly, Don sat down on one of the nearby chairs and put the shoes on over stiff muddy socks. He stood up and took one step. The stiff shoes did not bend and the caked mud made him wince as it pressed into the sides of his feet.

"The man who had brought him there turned toward Don and made it obvious that he should follow him once again. The two men exchanges words and Don obeyed his instincts to do as he was told. It was still raining and the wooden shoes he wore were unyielding and filled with water from the puddles along the way. Don hadn't been this uncomfortable for a long time. Ironically, he changed his thoughts to "when your feet hurt, you hurt all over!" He suddenly stopped walking and said aloud; "Damn . . .these things are killing me!" He pointed to his shoes. The man seemed to understand and stopped but only shrugged. Don took his handkerchief from his pants pocket and tore it I half. He bent over then finally sat down

NOT HOME FOR CHRISTMAS

on the cold ground and moaned as he removed the shoes. He tried to pad his blistered heels but he had his doubts that it would help. He slipped his feet back in the shoes and got up, continuing to follow the stranger. Every step he took sent agonizing pain up his legs. Sometimes it was so severe he feared he might be sick but he didn't dare stop again.

"It was nearly dark when they approached the third house. This time, even in the dusk light, Don could see several other houses nearby and concluded they must have arrived at a small village though every building showed not a trace of light. Without knocking on the door, the man hurried Don inside. As the entered the dimly lit room Don saw several pairs of wooden shoes just outside the door. He hesitated for a brief moment then gladly removed the shoes and placed them with the others. He followed his companion into a large room where other people sat around a huge table. A heavily bearded man approached Don. He reached for the coat and Don took it off and handed it to the man. The big man pointed toward the gun and holster, held out his hand but did not say a word. Don hesitated. He looked around the room at the men who were closely watching him. Slowly, Don pulled the gun out of the holster and placed it in the bearded man's outstretched hand. The man did not budge but kept his hand out. Don unstrapped the holster and handed it to him as well. At this, the man turned, walked toward the table and laid both gun and holster on the table.

"Conversation that had stopped when the bearded one approached Don, now resumed, however a dark uneasy feeling crept over him as he watched the men who occasionally would stop and point in his direction. He shuddered and right at that moment he had doubts about the intentions of his hosts.

"He heard a knock on the door. He was unceremoniously shoved into an adjacent room by the same man who had brought him here. There was no misinterpretation when he warned Don to be quiet as he closed the door. Don looked around. In the obscure light he noticed a window that had been boarded up. He stood motionless just inside the door trying to ascertain what would happen next. He could hear nothing of what was being said in the other room, not that it mattered, he would not be able to understand it anyway. His stay in the room was brief, suddenly the door opened and a stout woman beckoned him to follow her back into the main room with the others. She didn't speak. Don followed her.

"One of the men sitting at the table pointed to a chair that had been moved slightly away from the table and Don sat down. The men spoke, almost in whispers, while Don searched their faces and did his best to try and catch the gist of their conversation. Not making progress at interpreting the words, much less the meaning, he felt somewhat relieved when he noticed his gun and holster still in the middle of the table. He wondered who the visitor had been and what he or she thought if they had seen the weapon on the table.

"Don's attention turned to the heavy set woman who entered the room carrying a large coffee-pot. He watched her fill the cups of the men sitting around the table. She filled another cup and brought it to Barker. Remembering the dark liquid he had tasted before, he hesitated. But when he put the cup to his lips and took a sip, he realized this was real coffee. It was hot and it was good. He emptied the cup and the woman immediately got the pot and refilled it. He moved his chair a little closer to the table and set his cup and saucer down. One of the men was offering him some of the bread and cheese that was on the table. He reached across and took a slice of bread. He took a piece of the cheese and folded the bread around it. He thought to himself; "Now, . . . if I had just some mayonnaise, mustard and maybe a pickle!"

"He heard one of the men snicker as he ate his "sandwich." The woman started around the table refilling cups for the men. Don watched as some of the men turned their cups upside down in their saucers. When they did this, the woman passed them by with the coffee pot. As she reached Don and started to fill his cup again, he smiled but turned his cup upside down as well. She shrugged her shoulders and returned the pot to the trivet on the table. Don smiled as he realized he had finally learned one of their customs. He would try not to forget.

"He reached into his pocket for his cigarettes and matches. He hadn't even considered smoking a cigarette until now. He took a cigarette and placed it between his lips and reached in his pocket for matches. He suddenly realized all eyes were on him and their conversation had ceased. He stood up and reached into the centre of the table, placing his cigarettes and matches in front of them. He noticed the broad smiles as the pack was passed around. He couldn't understand the words but he presumed they were thanking him for his generosity.

"Some time later that day, Don was taken by bicycle to a village called Veenhuizen, about ten miles from where he had come down.

"While on the way there, his mind wandered. He remembered being happy that this Thanksgiving Day in England would be the last holiday he'd have to spend away from home. All the guys flying their "last" mission were thankful all right – the next day after the holiday there had been no flying scheduled so the fortunate one spent the day packing. Don had bought a new AGFA camera and had packed it with his other things. Strangely he could only wonder what would happen to the new camera if he didn't make it back. And what about their car? Four of them had bought a 1945 Ford with right hand steering which they took turns using. There had never been any conflict over "whose" turn it was to take it into London. Don smiled as he thought about their procurement of the 100-octaine airplane gasoline to fuel it!

"There had been lots of talk about what they would all do when they got "home." Don hadn't made up his mind whether he wanted to go home and get one of those soft-jobs or to re-enlist for another tour. All the guys continually talked about their favourite subject, "Women" – ones they had, or ones they whished they had. Don had married when he was just seventeen years old. Things had not gone well for Evie and him. She was three years older and they didn't share many common interests. When he thought about it, he didn't know exactly why they had married in the first place. Well at least she had not sent him a "dear John" letter. Maybe they could work things out when he got home. Home – that word echoed in his mind.

"Don was brought to the grocer of Veenhuizen, Emo Paabst, who had his shop on the main street of the village. Don estimated that Emo and his wife were in their early thirties. Emo handed him a set of civilian clothes and gestured Don to put these on,

"He put on the pants. The course, black material felt scratchy to his legs. The baggy pants fit around the waist but when he looked down he could see they only went half way to the calves of his legs. They were not meant for someone over six feet tall. He picked up the shirt and put it on. He grinned and said under his breath; "a perfect match, the pants legs are too short and so are the sleeves of the shirt!" Don looked for something to put on his feet. He saw no shoes but did find a pair of heavy socks. He sat on the edge of the bed and gingerly pulled the socks up over his blistered heels.

He waited. He guesses several minutes passed. He heard nothing from the other room. He finally got up, opened the door and walked in what he supposed was the main living area. No one was there. He moved to a chair in the room and sat down. He moaned slightly as he stretched out his right leg and reached down to massage the calf of his leg. He applied pressure as he rubbed, trying to soothe the pain that continued to shoot up the thigh. He leaned back and tried to relax. He realized that his whole body ached. His head throbbed. His shoulders and neck were stiff and sore and he suddenly felt weak and somewhat queasy. Don was startled when the door opened and the couple returned. The woman smiled as she passed by his chair and disappeared into another room, but she said nothing.

Don sat there, waiting for something to happen, someone to say something. He saw the man walk towards a table and pick up a very large book. It seemed as if the man was making a motion for him to come and sit on the big sofa at one end of the room. Barker slowly got to his feet and pushed him self to walk across the room. He sat down beside the newcomer who opened the book then pointed to one of the pages. Don looked at what seemed to be columns of words. He found English words and a brief description of their meaning. Another was a foreign word. Don reached for the book, partially closed it enough to look at the cover. It had the words printed on the cover "Engels – Nederlands" and directly under these words he recognized "Dutch – English". It must be a Dutch-English dictionary. The man watched Don's reaction, then nodded and smiled.

The man flipped through the pages. He found the words to ask Don a few questions, such as his name and what the matter was with his leg. Barker continually referred to the book to know what the man was asking. When Don provided an answer the man had to look at the book to find out what had been said. Don was puzzled at times by the man's attempt to pronounce the words that were so familiar to him and he imagined that his words sounded just as strange to his current host. It was a tedious method to use in an attempt to talk with each other, but it worked. Don found that the man's name was Klaas and his wife's name was Berta. When the American said his name as "Don" – Klaas repeated it over and over . . . "Don, Don, Don – goed!" Goed . . . .uh, goed!" Klaas patted Don's shoulder and laughed heartily when one or the other grasped the meaning of another word or phrase.

Barker learned that indeed he was in Holland, but Klaas called it "Nayderrlahnt." During the rather confusing conversation he found out that Klaas and Berta had a " gaynerraal" store on the first floor of the building they were in and that there was a "prisen" behind the store. Berta came back into the room carrying a small tray loaded with pastries. She giggled when her husband spoke several words in broken English. She sat the tray on a table near the sofa and left the room again. In just moments she returned with a steaming pot of coffee. Berta encouraged Don to help himself to the delicious pastries and a cup of coffee.

While Don enjoyed the food and hot liquid, Klaas continued to use the book and asked more questions. He wanted to know about the airplane and he seemed to have a particular interest in what had happened to Don's parachute for some reason. He asked questions about America and what part of that country did Don call home. The process was very slow and required much patience as well as concentration but it was rewarding to both the participants. Barker was surprised when he realized the tray of pastries was empty but he did remember to show Berta that he'd had enough coffee by turning his cup upside down on his saucer.

"This was really the first time Barker had truly relaxed since he had bailed out of the airplane and landed in a strange country. With the realization that he was no longer fearful for his life at the moment, his eyelids became heavy and he rested his head on his hands. Klaas seemed to sense his weariness, promptly closed the book and indicated it was time to sleep. Don had no idea what time it was but presumed it to be late. He had seen no clock in the room. Klaas stood and beckoned Don to follow him. They went up a narrow flight of stairs and Klaas opened the door into an attic room. The room had once been some sort of storage room, trunks and boxes had been pushed against the wall to make room for a narrow bed, a chair, and a washstand. Don glanced at the bed then at Klaas. It was as if his arrival had been anticipated and they had made preparations for a guest accordingly. But he was too tired to ask more questions.

"He smiled as he said good night to Klaas who acknowledged the "good night" with his best English and smiled proudly. Don truly wanted to thank him for his hospitality but he didn't know how and he thought it best if he didn't say anything else at this time. He waved a brief salute to the man and walked into the attic room.

"Don looked at the bed and then glanced around the room. He noticed the washstand had a pitcher, wash pan and a glass. On the wall near the stand hung a gleaming white towel. The bed had been pushed against a boarded-up window. He carefully pulled off the heavy socks and fell back across the bed. The walls of the room seemed to spin around him and he barely remembered pulling up the quilts over his tired body. In moments he was asleep.

"He woke once during the night with a start; he'd been dreaming that he was back at the base with all his buddies but none of them were speaking English! Their words were all a jumble that sounded the same as the strange language he'd heard all day. He tried talking to his friends but they couldn't understand. "My God" he said aloud and tried to shake off the nightmare. But it was several more minutes before he could go back to sleep.

"Wakker, wakker!" Berta shook Don's shoulder vigorously.

"He opened his eyes. He realized that he had not moved since falling to sleep after his unbelievable dream. His legs were stiff and every muscle in his body ached. He rubbed his eyes, ran his fingers through his hair, groaned and stretched. He pulled himself up and sat on the edge of the bed staring at Berta. Suddenly he felt dizzy and grabbed the edge of the bed to brace him self. As he steadied himself the dizziness seemed to leave him. He looked again at the woman and muttered; "Sorry . . . . . for a moment I guess I didn't realize where I was!"

"Of course she didn't understand but she smiled and then asked, "Honger?"

"Don watched as she put her hand up to her mouth and pretend she was chewing on something. He interpreted her actions and nodded. She smiles, pointed toward the door that led down the stairs, and then left the room.

"He once again wondered what time it was. He saw the heavy socks on the floor just in front of him and reached down to pick them up. He felt himself reel forward and once again grasped the side of the bed to keep from falling on his face. The feeling passed and he retrieved the socks, stood up and staggered to the wash basin. He was about to pour some water into the wash pan from the pitcher, then he noticed he still had the socks in his hand. He teetered back to the bed and mumbled; " . . . better try that one more time!" He put the socks on, stretched his legs once more and walked back to the stand. He poured water into the pan, bent down and doused his face again and again. The water was icy cold but it felt good and he felt invigorated as he reached for the towel and dried his face. Barker looked at the open door and started toward it on shaky legs. Going down the stairs posed a challenge. He braced himself against the wall and slowly placed one unsteady foot in front of the other.

"Berta smiled as he entered the room, she pointed to the table and motioned to him to sit in one of the chairs. On the table he saw slices of bread, slices of dark yellow cheese and a cup. She sat a large steaming bowl of thick soup on the table in front of him and filled his coffee cup. He looked for Klaas but is seemed he was not here. He assumed the two had eaten before and Klaas had gone down to the store. He lifted the spoon and was about to taste the soup when he heard a bell jingle downstairs.

"Berta walked to him, put her finger to her lips and whispered, "Stil! Kalm!"

"Don heard Nicolas talking with someone in the store below. He suddenly realized that he could hear their conversation; whatever was said here in this room could also be heard down below. He nodded his head in understanding at he woman. He sipped his coffee, it was very good, but he wished for some sugar to put in it. He always used sugar in his coffee at home but he didn't know how to ask for it. Then he remembered sugar was rationed in the states and it was possible that these people either didn't have any or maybe they didn't use it in coffee.

He drank it black and ate the good soup and some bread and cheese.

"Don finished eating and stood up. He felt better, he decided. He thought walking might loosen up the sore muscles in his leg. He took a few steps over to the window. The black curtains that had covered the window the night before had been pulled back but the outside shutters remained closed. Through the slits in the shutters he could see stone buildings and walls. He guessed this was the prison Nicholas had told him about. He smiled as he thought about the long, drawn-out procedure they had endured to talk with each other the night before. As he turned he saw Berta with the Dutch-English dictionary in her hands. Her warm smile summoned him to sit beside her. "Oh no!" he thought, but he trudged to the sofa, the muscles in his leg complaining with every step. He reached for the book as he sat down. He dreaded the awkward method of trying to talk but then he thought to himself: "What the hell . . . I don't have anywhere to go!"

"He pointed to the window toward the prison, then handed her the book as he asked; "Are there prisoners there?" He watched her turn the pages to the section that had English words first followed by the Dutch interpretation. She explained that the prisoners were "poaeeteek" – political and told how when the Germans occupied the town they had released the criminals and drafted them into their own forces for manual labour.

"She pointed to the socks he wore and then to her own and told him they were made by political prisoners. They also sold them in their store. Time passed and as they talked in this strange way Don felt more and more at ease. She seemed to learn his American words quickly and they had to refer to the book less often. Don wanted to ask more questions about the Germans that occupied the town but Berta suddenly stood up. "Nu . . . bahkern broat!" She let the book fall in Don's lap and disappeared into the kitchen. Don thumbed through the pages of the Dutch section and recognized the words she had spoken – they meant she was baking bread.

"He stared at the words, not seeing them. His thoughts shifted from the realization that he was in this strange country, to the events that brought him here. He did not understand exactly why all these total strangers were helping him and at great risk, he believed. He leaned his head back and closed his eyes. He remembered his grandmother used to bake bread as did most of the women in his family that he had lived with. That was a necessity in "those days" as there was little money to spend on store-bought bread. He was orphaned at age nine. His mother died at age thirty-one when he was not quite six years old. Three years later his father died at age thirty-six. His brother Malcolm, the oldest of the three children in his family had run away when he was sixteen and joined the Civilian Conservation Corps there. He waited until he was old enough to enlist in the Army. Ella, his sister, was fifteen when their parents died and she was taken by one of his mother's relatives to do house work. Don hadn't been old enough to be a "hand" around the farms of his relatives, so he was shifted from one family to the other. He had been made to feel he was a burden in those depression days. When he reached sixteen, he too, ran away to find his brother in Colorado. He had lied about his age and joined the Army but had been given a hasty discharge when his true age was revealed. He finally got a job in a gold mine in Idaho springs.

"Don jerked awake and saw Berta standing in front of him. She was talking to him but it took several minutes for him to embrace reality. Evidently she was trying to tell him that she had to go downstairs to the store. He smiled and nodded as he inhaled the delicious smell of fresh-baked bread. He watched her as she left the room, and he returned his attention to the pages of the dictionary. He looked in the Dutch section and spent some time trying to guess at the pronunciation of the words. He had laughed silently at Nicolas when he attempted to say the American words and he imagined both the man and woman would laugh if he tried to say some of their words. He knew he could not imitate the guttural sounds that seem to come deep in their throats. He heard the bell downstairs again and a conversation between Nicolas and Berta talking to someone. His attention returned to the book and he sat comfortably thumbing through the pages. When he heard footsteps on the stairs he froze. The voices of Berta and another woman became louder. Don closed the book and started to stand. He glanced around, he imagined himself hiding behind a chair, under the table, squeezing behind the sofa. But there was no place here to hide, perhaps up the stairs.

"Before he could move, the door opened and Herta entered followed by a stranger. Don stared at them: his mouth dry and his heart pounding. He felt the colour draining from his face. The woman with Berta merely glanced at him as she appeared to make herself at home, as if his presence was commonplace. Don noticed she was quite tall, taller and much heavier than Herta. She was bundled in a heavy coat and wore a scarf around her head. She carried a large basket. Her apparent calm caused Don to relax a little. The woman placed the basket on the table, removed her coat and scarf and handed them to Berta – a continuous line of chatter that led Don to believe the two women were old friends. He watched her pull some socks, a knitted cap, a dark shirt and a pair of wool pants from the basket and spread them on the table and sat the basket on the floor beside the door. She stopped talking and faced him.

"Berta spoke; he believed she was introducing the woman to him. He understood her to say the name of the newcomer was 'Frauk.' Her attractive smile and pleasant manner surprised him. She turned back to Berta and the chatter between the two began again. Her hands dramatically waved about and she danced around the room as mimicking different characters. Berta covered her mouth as to conceal her laughter. It was contagious and Don found himself laughing also although he did not know why. Berta ushered Frauk into the kitchen and the chatter and laughter followed them as they left the room.

"After a few minutes, Don stood and walked toward the table to inspect the articles of clothing placed there. He presumed they were intended for him. He held his pants up to the waist. The legs of the pants were considerably longer than the one he had on. He folded the pants and placed them back on the table. H reached for the shirt and held it up. It too looked like a better fit than the one he was wearing. The thought occurred to him that his appearance with the too-short pants and the undersized shirt could possibly have been the reason for the giggles from the women. He put the shirt back on the table and turned to see Nicolas entering the room.

"Nicolas called out to the women in the kitchen; then waved for Don to follow him. All four of them sat at the table where food had been placed. The fresh baked bread caught his eye and there was more cheese, fresh coffee and he saw a cake complete with icing sitting on the cupboard. "That looked tempting," he thought, as he sat down. The woman, Frauk, continued talking between bites of food and the conversation incited giggles from Berta and smiles from Nicolas. Don caught himself smiling too though he hadn't the slightest idea what was being said.

"After they had eaten, the women busied themselves clearing the table and putting away the remaining food. Nicolas wanted Don to join him in the other room. Nicolas produced some cigarette papers and a tin of rough-cut tobacco. Together, they rolled several cigarettes and Don watched as Nicolas placed them on a small tray on the table. He motioned for Don to take one of the cigarettes and struck a long match, holding it toward Don. Don lit his smoke and Nicolas did the same. The American leaned back and inhaled deeply thinking how good it was to enjoy a cigarette again.

The women joined them and Frauk went immediately to the piano that stood against the wall at the far end of the room. She sat down at the bench and started to play. Don did not know the song she played but he concluded that she was very talented. He heard Berta sing the words to the strange melody. She too was good; her voice was pleasant to hear. Nicolas seemed to want Don to join in the singing but he tried to explain that he didn't know the song. The man said something to Frauk, she turned and smiled at Don. She reached for some sheet music and leafed through it. She selected one and placed it in front of her and started playing.

"He instantly recognized the familiar song "Star Dust" and although he didn't know the words, he began whistling the tune. Frauk seemed pleased that he knew the song and played it over for him. She played other tunes but only one other time did anything sound familiar. He couldn't be sure because the words Berta sang were not English. Abruptly, Frauk stood up, closed the piano and said something to Berta and Nicolas. She put on her heavy coat and scarf. The two women hugged each other. She smiled and waved to Don. Nicolas followed her down the stairs to let her out through the store below.

"Berta gathered up the pile of clothes Frauk had brought and handed them to Don and she pointed to the stairs to his attic room. He told her 'good night' and climbed the stairs, this time was not quite so difficult. He closed the door to the room and undressed, crawled into bed and pulled the quilts up around him. He had enjoyed the evening and was cheered to have made some new friends. Previously his concept of a good time would have been to spend an evening in a bar, enjoying some beer and the company of his friends. He couldn't help wonder just how long he'd been here, or where he'd be this time next week, or the next month? What else would happen to him? Slowly . . . .he drifted off to sleep.

"In the next few days, Frauk became a regular visitor to the upper rooms of the store after it was closed for business. Don found he looked forward to her visits in the evening; he enjoyed the good company, even the conversation became simpler. Sometimes the book was seldom needed for them to speak to each other. He learned some of their words and phrases and Nicolas, Berta and Frauk quickly picked up the American words, some of them even resembled his way of pronouncing them, including his southern drawl. Most evenings they ate together, the menu simple, but fresh-baked bread with the now familiar cheese, hot soup, occasionally pastries and good coffee filled his stomach and he was grateful to them for it. He noticed the lack of meats and vegetables, all except potatoes which seemed to be plentiful at most of the meals. He truly relished the times when Frauk played the piano and Berta joined her by singing with her pleasant voice. Also, most evenings Nicolas provided the cigarette papers and tobacco for smokes.

"Enjoyable as the days had become, Barker became increasingly restless. In all his life he had never been able to sit and do nothing for any length of time. Nights found him pacing the floor in his room when he was alone, hoping he was not disturbing his hosts sleeping below. He had asked Nicolas about wandering about the house and the man had assured him it was all right. Nicolas had even given him permission to venture into the store if he wished, but never to show any light, and both he and Berta had made it clear that he would never be permitted to leave the building. Never into the small courtyard behind the store either, even though it was fenced off from the prison yard. Don assured them that he would do as he was told; they had nothing to worry about. He had no desire to cause any trouble for the young couple.

"One night he found a supply of something he thought was coal, heaped in one corner of the room. He examined the strange egg-shaped objects, they were different than the coal he was familiar with. When he asked Nicolas about it, he learned that it was compressed coal dust – when burned it threw off a great deal of intense heat.

"He found a Dutch calendar on one wall in the store and he tried to determine what date would be now. He had asked Berta for some writing papers and a pencil earlier which he had tucked into the pocket in his shirt. On the nights he visited the darkened store, he kept track of how many days he had been here and knew approximately what de date was. He calculated it must already be December.

"The second Sunday of his stay, Frauk came up the stairs from the store below followed closely by Nicolas. Don had not known that that the store was open for business on Sunday. He had not heard the jingle of the bell over the door into the store as it had opened. He realized that he was staring at Frauk in surprise as she entered the room. She paid no attention to Don, in fact did not greet him with her usual smile and cheerful words. He watched as she and Nicolas talked their voices know. Frauk approached Berta and they hugged each other, but during the conversation between the two women he thought the animated gestures relayed fear.

"There was no mistaking his interpretation as Frauk turned and quickly left the room, down the stairs, back into the store. This time he listened for the bell that should sound as she exited through the door. He heard nothing. For the days he had been here he had relied on the bell to serve as a warning in case he needed to hurry to his attic room. Now this puzzled him. Perhaps there was another entry but he'd seen nothing during the times he had explored the store below. If they had fixed it so it wouldn't ring, that would explain it, but why?

"He was about to ask Nicolas about the bell when Berta called to him. She motioned to the chair at the kitchen table and asked him if he wanted any more coffee. He saw the anxious look on her face and as Nicolas joined them, he too looked very concerned. Almost apologetically Nicolas told him that he would have to leave as soon as it was dark that very night. Berta scanned his face for signs of understanding as her husband continued to explain. The Germans had narrowed the search for him and the others to this area. Don's immediate thoughts were 'what others'? But he listened as Nicolas spoke; the others had already been moved, but he must pack his things and be ready. He would use the basket that Frauk had brought to put his belongings in. Nicolas pointed to the stairs leading to his room and told him to 'please go now' and smiled tentatively as he told Don 'not to worry'. Don nodded his head, reached across the table and patted Berta's hand and smiled. He wished he could tell Nicolas that he wouldn't worry, but the sense of security he had gained in the past week quickly dissipated.

"He stood, turned and walked towards the stairs and on up to the room he had called 'his' for a short while. He looked around the room. He wondered how quickly the bed, chair and washstand would disappear at his leaving. He also had to smile as he thought of 'his' belongings!' Did they mean the other pair of pants with the too-short legs? The shirt with the too-short sleeves? He did have several pair of heavy socks from the prison, but no shoes. He thought again about walking any distance in his socks, or God forbid, riding another bicycle, just when his leg was beginning to feel normal again. He placed the heavy coat and the knitted cap Frauk had brought on the bed, put the other things in the basket and nervously paced the floor, waiting.

"Berta opened the door, smiled momentarily, and then told him it was time to leave. He picked up the coat and cap and the basket and followed her down the stairs. Nicolas was waiting. He wore a heavy coat and knitted cap also. Don sat the basket on the floor and quickly put on the coat and cap he had carried down with him. He turned toward Berta and held out his right hand. She took it in both her hands and patted them tenderly. She told him goodbye and prayed that good luck would follow him; she

NOT HOME FOR CHRISTMAS

wished him a safe journey. He wanted to hug her and tell her how much he appreciated what they had done. No words fell from his lips however; he could never convey his real thanks no matter how he tried. He bent down and kissed her on the cheek.

"He followed Nicolas down the stairs into the store. From under a counter, Nicolas retrieved a box and opened it. Inside was a pair of leather high-top shoes. Don sat on a bench at the end of the counter and slipped his feet into the shoes. Somewhat tight, but he laced them loosely and said 'Thank you" but he doubted Nicolas heard. He stood up and followed the Dutchman out the door and into the street. It was the first time he had been outside in over a week and the fresh air felt good to him though he realized it was quite cold. He noticed Nicolas glancing around in all direction in a suspicious manner. Don looked too but could see no one. They walked to the edge of town then left the road and headed across the fields now frozen. The remaining grains that hadn't been harvested crunched with each footstep. The coat he wore should have kept out the cold, but Barker felt himself shiver; more in apprehension of what might be ahead for him than the chill of the night. He was also concerned about what would happen to Nicolas and Berta if the Germans found out they had sheltered a 'wanted' American.

"They walked in silence, neither man speaking. Don decided this was not the time or place for any conversation. He looked ahead and saw what appeared to be a farm and other buildings. Nicolas seemed to target it as his destination. As they got nearer, Don saw it to be a rather large house. Nicolas suddenly grabbed Don's arm and motioned for him to crouch down in the tall grass. It was several more minutes before Nicolas spoke. He told Don that the house they could see was where Frauk lived. Being located out in the country, surrounded by a lot of open areas, homes such as this were not searched by patrols as often as homes in villages. He explained that Don should be safe here for a little while. But he didn't explain what had startled him to the extend he felt they should duck down. Don could not guess.

"Barker breathed a sigh of relief at the thought of not having to meet total strangers. Frauk he considered almost a friend by now. Nicolas looked around making sure they had not been followed, then motioned for Don to follow him around the two-story stone house. What happened next surprised Don; he was not prepared for such a hasty exit by Nicolas. Nicolas opened the door to the house and Don stepped inside. Nicolas reached over and closed the door before Don had a chance to say anything to him. Don was even more amazed as Frauk appeared in the small dimly lit entryway and greeted him, this time with her familiar smile. He had no idea how she had known the exact moment he would arrive, there were no telephones at the store or in the upstairs rooms. He concluded this must have been planned earlier, but he thought the timing was uncanny.

"Hello," Don said, "Nothing like bursting in on you in the middle of the night is there? And unannounced at that!" He grinned at her but she didn't answer. She led him into a large room toward the front of the house. She took the basket he carried, told him to take off his coat and hat and she took them as well, and then left him standing alone in the middle of the room. As he looked around the large, elaborately furnished room he could remember Nicolas telling him that in Holland, the home was an expression of the owner's prosperity. And he also remembered Frauk telling him that she lived with her father, mother and sister Dien. Well, Don could only assume that Frauk's father must be a very successful farmer if the furnishings in this room were an indication.

Frauk interrupted his thoughts by returning. She led him into another adjoining where a warm fire glowed in the fireplace. A large chair faced the fireplace and Don sensed someone occupied the chair but he could not see anyone. Just then a large man stood up, walked toward a startled Don, extended his hand and said in perfect English; "How do you do?"

Don shook the hand warmly and replied; "Fine, thanks – and you sir?" His first thought was how wonderful, finding someone he could talk to at last, but his delight was short-lived. The man only looked puzzled. Frauk proceeded to introduce the man as her father. It seemed this was the only English phrase Mr. Meijering knew, one that Frauk had rehearsed him in, in preparation to meeting the American. The older man seemed so pleased with himself afterwards that Don tried very hard not to show his disappointment.

"Mr. Meijering was grey-haired, a giant of a man, taller then Don and much heavier. He walked to the table and produced a large book. It was another Dutch-English dictionary. He laughed a deep hearty laugh as he motioned for Don to join him at the heavy wooden table. Don watched as he placed the book on the table and moves a tall lamp with hanging crystals on the base to the center of the table. There were high-backed stairs, the seats padded with a rich brocade material.

"The chairs were placed on either side of the wide table. Don pulled the chair out slightly and was about to sit down when he looked up to see an older, smiling woman enter the room. He remained standing momentarily when Frauk introduced her mother. Mrs. Meijering wore a clean white apron and a small white cap on her head. She was about the same

NOT HOME FOR CHRISTMAS

height as Frauk, but slight in build. All Don could think of was the lady who worked behind the bakery counter at the grocery store at home in California, the Dutch Girl Bakery!

"Frauk told him she would be delighted to show her home. She led Don through the house and showed him each room. There was electricity in the house. Frauk turned the light on as they entered each room and was careful to turn it off as they exited. Each of the rooms were immaculately clean and all the furnishings in excellent taste. All windows were heavily draped with a dark material. She led him up the stairs. There were three large bedrooms but each of them were furnished in almost exactly the same manner; one bed, one chair, a stand holding a pitcher, wash pan and clean towels on hooks on the wall. She showed him a very large storage room on the second floor. Just then Don heard the strains of a familiar song "Star Dust" coming from the piano he'd seen on the first floor. He looked a Frauk in a puzzled manner. She said; "Dien!"

"She took Don's arm, led him down the stairs to meet her sister. The younger girl stopped playing when Frauk brought the American into the main parlour. Dien stood alongside the piano and much to his surprise; Don saw the girl curtsy politely as Frauk introduced her. He could not help but stare at this young girl; she had the most beautiful complexion he had ever seen, real peaches and cream, as the expression went. Her cheeks were rosy and her blue eyes sparkled. She was just eighteen Frauk told him, and like Frauk and their father, somewhat heavy, but this did not detract from her beauty. Don was somewhat embarrassed by the curtsy, all he could think of to say was; "You play that song very well – like a professional!" Unsure that she understood his words, he clapped his hands several times. She blushed and smiled.

"He was about to urge Dien to play the piano again but Mrs. Meijering pressed his arm and motioned him to follow her into the large kitchen. The family sat around the table in the center of the room. Don had not seen a large old-fashioned wood cook stove like the one here for a very long time. Cupboards lined the walls of the room and pots and pans hung from hooks just over the stove.

"Dien wanted the American to sit beside her. Mr. Meijering took his place at the head of the table, Frauk directly across from Don. There were large bowls of steaming potato soup on the table along with thick slices of freshly baked bread, some cheese and small flat cakes that Don was not familiar with on a small platter. He noticed a miniature crock of honey in the center of the table. Frauk told him that her father had hidden a few hives in the woods a long time ago. He used to have many hives but most of them had been confiscated by the invading Nazis. The concealed hives he had kept produced the delicious honey they served on 'special' occasions; Don's arrival was one of these special times, she explained.

"After they had eaten, Mr. Meijering signalled Don to follow him out of the kitchen. The older man placed another chair before the fire and invited Don to sit down with him. Don stretched his legs out, staring at the flames from the fire, his stomach was filled and he was very comfortable. Minutes passed, neither he nor Mr. Meijering attempted to speak. Don had heard nothing, but suddenly the older man stood up and left the room. Don wondered what had happened. In just moments however, he returned and a younger man was with him. Frauk followed them into the room. An alarmed Don nervously eyed the stranger. Then, Frauk introduced him as 'Paul' her boyfriend. It seemed Paul visited at designated times. Mr. Meijering had anticipated his arrival, thus the reason he had abruptly left the room.

"Don stood to shake the man's hand as he was introduced. Paul was not much more than probably 5'7" or 5'8" and Don judged him to be slightly older than his own age of twenty-four. He was thin and had a slightly receding hairline. Paul could speak a smattering of English although he had difficulty with some words. Paul told Don he was active in the underground. "So, it did exist," Don thought. This man must have felt safe revealing his activities with the American. Don smiled as he imagined Paul and Frauk together; they would make an 'interesting' couple. He looked at Frauk, and as Paul stood there trying to talk with Don, she smiled and looked like she adored the man.

"After the young couple left, Dien and her father and mother tried very hard to hold a conversation with Don. The Dutch-English dictionary lay in the lap of the father and he used it frequently for himself as well as to assist his wife and Dien. All of them showed elation whenever Don understood what they asked and when they understood his answers. He did learn that the farm was located near the town of Veenhuizen and that it was the town where Nicolas and Berta had their store. Dien was extremely quick to catch on to the American words though the two older people had a more difficult time.

"The next day, Frauk and Dien proudly showed Don around the farm. He discovered why the house had looked so large in the dark when he'd first seen it. It was because it was attached to the stable. As the three of them entered the stable, Don saw four large magnificent Belgian horses. The girls explained the well-groomed animals were their father's greatest pride. He wondered why the Nazis had not confiscated these beautiful beasts but he thought better about asking them, knowing it would be difficult to make them understand such a question. They left the stable and walked a short distance to another out-building, smaller than the stable, and it housed a cow, some goats and quite a few chickens. Don could not help but comment on the cleanliness of the buildings. Like the house, everything he saw as neat, clean and well cared for.

The fresh air felt good; once again he was reminded how nice it was to be allowed outside. He was stimulated by the constant chatter of the two girls and the beauty of the countryside. In the sunshine he felt the chill in the air, but there was no wind so he was not cold. He momentarily forgot that he was in a strange land, far from the things he knew best, and he didn't think about the circumstances that had brought him here. He did notice that the two girls glanced frequently in the direction of the canal which they said ran along the edge of the farm. He just assumed they were watching for any stranger who might approach. It didn't comfort him any to recognize that anyone familiar with this family would immediately know that this strange dark-haired men did not belong. He grew apprehensive again. The girls must have sensed his anxiety and led him back into the house. He said to himself: "Tour over, it's just as well.

"Later that same afternoon, Don sat comfortably in the warm kitchen. Mrs. Meijering and Frauk were baking bread. Dien sat in a large chair next to Don, her nimble fingers embroidering colourful flowers on a piece of cloth. Mr. Meijering paused in the kitchen just long enough to invite Don to join him while he tended the livestock, but Don declined.

"The girls coaxed Don to try some of the Dutch words, by repeating what they were saying. Like a game, they said. He did pretty well with words such as 'melk' for 'milk', 'ketel' for 'kettle', 'piloot' for 'pilot'; but when he tried more difficult words that did not sound like the English word, he failed miserably. Each time he tried, both girls would giggle and even Mrs. Meijering laughed at his attempts. He really tried hard to produce the guttural sounds some words required but just couldn't do it. In turn, he grinned at their attempts to imitate some of his English terms. He noticed that anytime he tried to ask a question about other Americans, possibly in this area, they avoided his eyes and pretended not to understand. They would change the subject and talk only about their farm.

"It was after Frauk and her mother had finished mixing dough for the bread and had placed it in pans in the warm oven to rise, did Frauk surprise Don by stating; "The one you call 'engineer' is nearby. I have seen him and he is well. And the other one, the one with the leg shot . . . . he is not so well." The news came as a shock to Don that he nearly felt forward out of his chair. He had to struggle to compose himself.

After several minutes, he asked; "Reed . . . . and Trombley? You've really seen Quilla Reed and Richard Trombley . . . Here? Where? Frauk, where?"

"Reed?" She had a problem pronouncing 'Trombley' but she continued; "Yes. I believe that is as they are called." She smiled and joined him at the table, wiping her hands on her apron.

"You're trying to tell me those guys are near here? What about the others? Do you know if there are others around? Do you think I'll be able to see them, maybe visit them?" Don realized he was asking questions must too fast for her to understand, much less answer him, but he could not contain his eagerness to learn more, to hear about the other members of the crew. He stood up, then promptly sat back again, tried to be patient he waited for an answer. He looked at Mrs. Meijering, she was smiling.

Frauk said; "One time you may see them – I will take you."

"When? Now?"

"No – when it is dark!" She replied.

"The news that Reed was alive cheered him. Unconsciously for days he had been afraid to face the fact that his push through the hatch on the B-17 might have caused Reed to fall into the open bomb bay doors. Now, with the revelation that the other two Americans were nearby meant that at least Reed and Trombley had not been turned over to the Nazis as prisoners of war. This accounted for three of the crew.

"The afternoon passed slowly, Don kept scolding himself silently because he did not seem to be able to sit still or to concentrate on anything. He moved from chair to chair, walked up the stairs and down again. He flipped through the Dutch-English dictionary thinking he might learn more Dutch words, but was unable to focus long enough to do any good. Right now he wished for one of the cigarettes he and Nicolas had rolled, or better still, one of his own that he had passed among the men on the first day. He paced the floor, thinking of all the questions he wanted to ask Reed and Trombley when he saw them; where they had landed, what had happened and how they got to this place. And, was it possible that either of them had any news of the rest of the crew.

"That evening when they had finished the meal and were sitting at the table drinking coffee, Paul entered the room with a 'friend' Frauk introduced as "Bill". Bill was, or looked to be, younger than Paul. Don smiled, debating silently about 'Paul' and 'Bill' – probably not their real names.

"Frauk explained that 'Bill' was Dien's young man. Dien told him that someday they would marry, but that couldn't happen until their country was liberated and they could all live as free people again. Don noticed that Paul now had a side arm with him. The others seemed to be engrossed in preparations for the trip and Don became more anxious to leave though no one else seemed to be in a hurry. Finally, he saw the two girls put on their coats. Frauk picked up the heavy coat Don had previously worn and handed it to him. He reached into the pocket where he had tucked the wool cap and put it on his head. Mr. and Mrs. Meijering talked to the girls, probably instructing them to be careful, if Don interpreted their movements correctly. Both girls hugged their mother, then their father, and it appeared at last as if they were ready to leave.

"Once outside, Don doubted he had ever seen such a black sky. His eyes soon became accustomed to the darkness. As they walked, he decided it was good that there was no moon – the blackness of the night would certainly reduce the possibility of being observed by anyone.

"They entered the woods directly behind the farm until they reached a ditch.

"Paul, Frauk, Dien and Bill all got down on their hands and knees and felt around in the high grass that surrounded the bank. Don watched with interest, not knowing if he should join them on his knees. But he was totally bewildered, he looked at the canal; it looked about six feet across but he had no idea how deep. The darkness of the night did not allow him to estimate the depth. He saw the dark water was moving rapidly through the ditch however. He spied a wide board lying in the grass just ten feet away from where the others were knelt. He guesses it was probably a 2" by 12" board, a little over ten feet long. Finally he walked to Paul and quietly asked; "What did we stop for, did someone lose something?" Paul explained the needed the 'wuden blok' a board that should have been here. Don walked the short distance to where he had seen the board, picked up one end of it and asked; "Is this what you're looking for? This board?"

"He saw the others eyeing him suspiciously. They seemed surprised that he had found it while standing up in the dark, but no one said anything. Paul and Bill lifted the board, placed it across the canal, letting the far end of it fall in place. Paul stepped on the board testing it to make sure it was solid, and then he told them to cross one at a time. Don watched as Paul got down on his hands and knees and carefully crawled along, followed by the rest. When it was his turn, he simply walked across. After Bill had crossed, they carefully retrieved the board and laid it in the brush along a fence that bordered the canal.

"Don gasped realizing these people did not see well in the dark. He presumed instinct and knowledge of the countryside had led them through the woods and over the fields. Until this moment he had not guessed they were virtually blind in the dark. He thought about this as they walked on through yet another field. He remembered that no one he had seen around ate any green vegetables, no meat, and their main diet seemed to be bread, cheese and potatoes. With years of eating primarily these starchy foods he decided that 'night-blindness' could very well occur.

"Shortly after they crossed the canal, Don heard dogs barking ahead. As the sounds grew louder, Bill stepped forward and spoke two quick commands. The barking ceased immediately. Only a familiar voice could possibly have calmed the dogs so quickly; Don could only assume the house they neared was where Bill lived. His suspicions proved to be correct as the group walked up to the door, opened it and entered.

"Don's first glimpse of Quilla Reed sitting with his feet propped up and calmly reading an English newspaper made him smile and shake his head in wonder. He thought the guy looked quite at home: content and very unconcerned, barely aware of the group entering the room. Don looked around; he did not see Trombley anywhere although he had understood Frauk to say he too was here. Don was the first to speak; "Hey, Buddy! The last time I saw you, your butt was in a different position . . . but boy, I'm sure glad that your chute worked ok too!"

Here we have to interrupt Don for a moment.

In his story we see Reed reading an English newspaper and he also mentions drinking real coffee with some of his host: two items that were not to be found in occupied Holland. However, the underground in the part of the Netherlands where the "Seattle" crew had come down, had received massive dropping of weapons and explosives. These were packed in metal containers that were dropped at night from British planes under parachutes. In these containers were always room for small items that had disappeared completely from the Dutch market such as coffee, cigarettes and (it seems) even English newspapers. These exotic products were handed out to underground members of the "reception committee".

On the Sunday that "Seattle Sleeper" came down, Gosse Rodenboog and his wife Joke were paying a visit to Gosse's parents not far from Haulerwijk when they saw parachutists floating down. He immediately went to the spot where he expected the airmen to land.

NOT HOME FOR CHRISTMAS

When he and Joke arrived there they found two airmen surrounded by a group of curious women. These two airmen were top-turret Gunner Quilla D. Reed and waist-gunner Richard A. Trombley.

They wanted to know where the nearest Germans were and Joke wrote "4 km." in the sand, meaning three miles. Gosse decided that the American duo had to be kept out of German hands but there was one problem, Richard Trombley was wounded in his leg during the fighter attack on "Seattle Sleeper". A bicycle was found, Richard was loaded on it and Gosse Rodenboog brought them to the farm of the Assies family, who were known as active members of the underground. They went not directly to the farm but where hidden in some woods nearby, while Gosse went to inform the Assies. After some time, Ap Assies together with Henk Woering came to fetch the two "evadees" and brought them to the Woering farm where they met Don Barker.

Don continues his story:

"Reed stood up, threw down the paper and rubbed his eyes in disbelief. He walked toward Don, a grin on his face and slapped him on the back; "Now, where in hell did you come from? I didn't know you were in this part of the country, but God damn! It's good to see a familiar face." The two Americans looked at each other. Reed continued; "Ya know what? You need a hair cut worse than me! And check the beard! I gotta tell you, you damned sure don't look like a Dutchman with that black hair all over your face!" Quilla Reed grinned broadly.

Paul and the others sat at a nearby table and watched the reunion briefly then engaged in a conversation of their own, glancing only occasionally as the two Americans talked too rapidly for them to interpret the words or meanings. "Have you heard about any of the others? They told me Trombley was with you. Is he ok", Don questioned.

"Yeah . . . he's here . . . don't go away, I'll tell him you're here. These people are trying to get a local doctor to take a look at his leg. Be right back!" Reed left the room, then returned in a few minutes with Dick and helped him to a chair.

"Hey there Dick, how're you doing anyway? Good to see you again." Don didn't think his colour was good, he looked quite pale and he was in pain each time he moved, trying to get comfortable in the chair.

"I've been better!" Trombley once again shifted position in the chair and tried to straighten his leg out in front of him. He moaned almost silently as he asked; "You staying around here somewhere? We sure as hell didn't guess you were anywhere in the territory."

"Reckon you could say we're almost neighbours." Don grinned and pointed, "Those girls over there are the daughters of my 'host' family. I don't know how far we walked to get here, but I'd imagine it was maybe a little over a mile from here . . . real nice farm. But before that, I was staying in the rooms over a grocery store, in the village. You two have been here all the time?"

"Nope, just a little over a week I guess. The first place we were taken didn't have room for both of us, so a man brought us here, " Reed told him. "We've heard that John is around somewhere – they don't know where but they did say the 'piloot' hadn't been caught. Hey, Barker, you having any trouble understanding what these people say?"

"Just some of the words . . . . these two young ladies are trying to teach me, but am afraid I'm a hopeless case." Don grinned.

"Yeah." Dick nodded his head affirmatively, "Bill is trying to help both of us, but this . . . what is it, Dutch? Or German? Or whatever the hell it is, it's like Greek to me!".

Reed told them; "Hey, I even took Latin. It helps some with some of the verbs, but most of it is rough to try and figure out. It's not the words so much as the way they say it . . . it's almost like a growl that comes deep down the throat, you know what I mean? It's easy for them . . .natural . . .But I can't do it! You're getting enough to eat? Ya' look fit enough! Don't get me wrong, I'm not complaining, bread and cheese to fill one up – but I'd sure like to sink my teeth into a good old-fashioned steak . . .or maybe a hamburger!"

"Yep, that sounds good to me too." Don licked his lips at the thought and grinned, "I don't think they eat meat – however where I am staying, they do have some chickens and a cow – but I think she's just for milk! Oh and . . some goats too, yeah, they've got some goats. Reckon that's where some of the cheese comes from – I hadn't thought of that before, sure doesn't taste like goat cheese! But then, I'm not sure what goats cheese tastes like!"

"One thing about it, they seem to have plenty potatoes. I think I've had potatoes fixed every way you can imagine, potato soup and boiled potatoes. I didn't had any French fries, or just plain old fried potatoes, though!" Dick squirmed in his chair again. He looked uncomfortable, then he added, "It could be worse guys . . . guess we should be grateful for anything at all to eat, huh?"

"The girl's father has some beehives stashed out in the woods behind his farm; we had some honey the first night I got there. Now, that was tasty! And while I was in the room over the store, that lady did a lot of baking. She made the best little tiny pastries, and once, a really nice cake, icing and all!"

"Bill's folks have a hog! And I think they intend to butcher it real soon. We haven't tasted any meat since we left England. And ya' know what? Every time I think about bacon, ham . . and all the other good stuff, man, do I drool! Ole Dick here and I have talked about the possibilities ever since they mentioned it. Can you imagine, real, honest-to-goodness pork chops?" Reed leaned back in his chair and smiled as he rubbed his stomach.

"Yeah," Trombley added, " . . . . and if you're really nice, Barker, maybe you'll get an invite to our big barbecue – I mean, we might be willing to share."

"Knock it off you guys! I've had some hunger pangs too . . .well; I mean for other stuff . . . you know what I am talking about." However, Don was glad Dick still seemed to have his old sense of humour and thought that was a good sign. "When is the doctor, they're talking about, supposed to check the leg."

"Maybe tomorrow." Bill talked to him a couple of days ago I guess it was. He has been treating another gunshot wound recently – one of the underground guys from what I've heard."

Reed stood up and touched Don's shoulder. "Hey, want to see what I've been doing the last day or so? I've got a little construction project going . . .come on, take a look at my handy work!"

"What are you building?"

"Come see for yourself . . " Reed led the way through the room into a narrow hallway and proudly opened a double door, . . . whatcha' think?"

Don looked inside. "Pretty neat . . . looks just like a closet to me! Nothing like making yourself useful around the house! Of course, you being an 'old married man' – it's probably easy for you to think of things like this to please the lady of the house!" He grinned.

"Please a woman – my ass!" Reed quipped, "You're missing the point, Barker!" Reed reached for one of the upper shelves. "Follow me, kid!" Don watched as Reed pushed the shelf up and slid it to one side. He pulled himself up and disappeared into the hole above. Don stood there, wondering what the hell Reed was up to. He saw his friend stick his head down through the hole and grin as he invited, "Come on up . . . .take a look for yourself, buddy!"

Don quickly climbed up after Reed. He was surprised to find a space approximately four feet in height and about ten feet long above the false ceiling.

"Welcome to our little retreat! Just in case we happen to have some unwelcome guests you know – like Nazis?" Quilla grinned, and then added, "Of course, getting Trombley up here is not the easiest thing to do, with his bad leg, but we figured, if we could get up there, and then sit on the part that appears to be the top shelf, they'd just think it was nailed down . . .even if they did notice it. Pretty smart, huh?"

"I'll be damned!"

"Let's climb down and join the others where we can be a little more comfortable. Intend to save this for a time when it might be necessary. It isn't meant to be a place to entertain my guests!" They climbed back down into the closet space and Reed replaced the shelf.

"Don stood in the hallway and examined the closet. "Sure looks innocent enough. Boy, I sure hope they don't decide to shoot trough the roof of your closet! I understand bullets in the butt smart like hell!" Don ducked as Reed playfully took a swing at him. "No kidding though, Reed – what made you think you might need a hiding place anyway? Have you heard about any Nazis coming around looking for us?"

"Nope!" Reed acknowledged, "Just wanted to be prepared in case. You know, if they were to find the two of us here in the house, the whole Woering family would be in jeopardy for hiding Americans. It could even get them killed. When I got to thinking about all that, it made me realize I'd best find us a hole to crawl into. It's for their protection as well as for saving our own skins. I'd really hate like hell to get them into any trouble on account of us."

"Point well taken – good God, man! The way you're talking, it sounds as if you think you might be here a while. I hope to hell you're wrong! I was wondering if you'd heard anything about us getting out of here. You don't think we're here for the duration, do you?"

"How the hell should I know?" Reed turned, then added, "Heard of one rather elaborate plan though – some cock-'n-bull story about taking downed airmen to the Zuider Zee and the Brits coming in with a seaplane, landing just long enough to pick them up. You see, the guys are supposed to meet the plane in a rowboat. How's that for a crazy idea? I can't imagine a plan like that working, whatcha' think?"

"Don frowned. "Tell you what! I don't think anything! This whole damned thing is like a dream, no, I should say a nightmare! Who knows what's possible or impossible? Maybe it's been tried already – maybe successfully. I presume they have gotten Americans out of here, you know, the underground, before – uh – someone told me that they had anyway."

"I guess so, and I suppose if and when the time comes, I'll be more

NOT HOME FOR CHRISTMAS

than willing to try any old thing they propose, won't you?" Reed asked.

"Yep."

"Hey Barker – when you jumped did you land near here?" Reed asked.

"Hell, I don't know where I was. I thought it was Germany, but it was before I realized that the Nazi had control of the whole countryside. Wherever it was, it was a long way from here. I gave a bicycle hell one night getting away from wherever it was!

"Throughout the walk back to the Meijering home, Don kept thinking what Reed had done to provide a hiding place for himself and Trombley. Damned good idea, he thought. He decided that tomorrow morning he would see what he could do about making a place for him. He tried to figure the best way that he could convey his thoughts to the Meijering family so they would understand what he wanted to do. He looked forward to having a project that would keep him busy for some awhile.

"Don dressed quickly the following morning and went downstairs. It took some doing, but with Frauk's help in translating and using the big dictionary to find some of the words, he finally saw that Mr. Meijering was beginning to understand. The big man seemed excited about the idea, and let it be known that he was eager to help.

"He led Don to the master bedroom upstairs, but now he realized that the father and mother in this family occupied the bedroom on the first floor. The entry was just off the kitchen, and in this bedroom was a very large closet. Mr. Meijering pointed out that one end of the closet was adjacent to the stairway. The stairs led from the kitchen to the basement, not to the second floor. Just above this portion of the house was the large storeroom he had been shown by Frauk on his first night here. Perfect, he thought.

"Don talked to Mr. Meijering, almost forgetting that the man would not be able to understand what he was saying. He had to be quiet while Frauk spoke to her father about Don's ideas. Mr. Meijering was anxious to begin and quickly brought the tools they would need into the room. Fist they moved all the clothes from the closet and hung them in a large stand-alone wardrobe at one end of the room. Next, they removed the moulding, the knobs and the hinges. Next they sealed the doors shut. Mrs. Meijering and Frauk brought wallpaper and paste, and they covered the entire end of that wall. Once this was finished, they all stood and admired their work. Don decided the wall looked solid, and even on close inspection it was difficult to imagine that it had been anything but an ordinary wall. They looked around for furniture they could move against the wall. Mrs. Meijering decided on a chair, and the washstand would be appropriate, and indicated the towel bar would need to be moved over the washstand, or just above it. Mr. Meijering took delight in discovering that Don, like himself, worked slowly and methodically. The two men got along well together and when the job was finished and everything in place, they walked around and inspected the wall from every angle, and seemed pleased with their work. Don figured that only if someone knew what had been done, would they be able to tell that the room had been altered.

"They went up the stairs to the store room. After measuring, much discussion, and re-measuring again and again, Mr. Meijering pointed to the floor. This would be the exact spot where they could cut the two-foot square hole which would serve as an entry to the closet below. Satisfied with his calculations, the big man produced some cigarette papers and precious tobacco. The two men sat on the floor and proceeded to roll cigarettes. The older man took matches from his pocket, first lit Don's and then his own. Don inhaled deeply, grateful for the pleasurable sensation the smoke provided.

"With gestures and careful words the two discussed how the hiding place would work. If and when the time came, Don would enter the closet through the trap door they were about to build to cover the opening. One of the Meijering family members would then dump a basket of apples over the trap door following them to spread around to conceal the entrance to the hiding place. The carefully calculated the length of time needed for Don to crawl into the hiding place, then it would take to spill the apples, throw the crate into against the far wall, leave the storage room and join the other family members downstairs.

"After they had talked about it in length, they agreed it was a very simple but effective plan. The finished their cigarettes and carefully extinguished them. Mr. Meijering put the butts in his pocket for disposal at a later time. The two men brushed at the ashes, scattering them to hide the fact that they had sat there smoking. They cut the hole and built the trap door, tried it several times to make sure it would open easily and close without making too much noise. When they were satisfied, the two of them filled a large wooden crate with apples that had been spread on the floor to dry and placed the crate near the opening. Pleased with themselves, they went back down stairs into the kitchen. Mrs. Meijering had made a fresh pot of coffee, and she poured them each a cup of the welcome brew.

"That evening, Paul and Bill visited the Meijering home. They were told what had been done in regard to the hiding place. Both the younger men examined the secret room from every direction. They looked first in the bedroom, at what had been the closet doors, and then they went upstairs to the storage room. They climbed down into the hole using the ladder Mr. Meijering had placed there, and both expressed their fervent approval. Don was demonstrating how the trap door would work when Paul mentioned that it could also be an appropriate storage for weapons. He said the underground had a need for someplace to keep some newly acquired arms and ammunition.

"Bill and Paul ate the evening meal with the family, and left soon after. They had been gone about an hour. It was dark when they returned, and were quickly ushered into the house by Frauk and Dien. Don helped carry guns and boxes of ammunition up the stairs to the storage room. They opened the trap door and Don climbed down into the hiding place. Paul handed supplies down to him and watched as Barker neatly stacked them in one corner of the 'closet' room so they could be accessed in a hurry if need be. Paul and Bill left again. They knew Don couldn't go with them to help, but were pleased that he helped them store the weapons they delivered. Don wondered where the two men went, and where they were getting these supplies, but he didn't ask.

"He marvelled at the fact that these people seemed unwearied as they made more trips, brought Sten machine guns, thirty-eight calibre revolvers, hand grenades, and many boxes of ammunition to be concealed in the hiding place. While he waited to help stash the weapons, Don thought how the two younger men would need to carry on with their normal activities the following day, and he wondered when they would find the time to sleep. He admired their strength in leading a double life; typical working citizens during the day, and underground members at night. They made their final trip in the early hours of the morning.

"It had been a long day and night. Don was tired but happy to go up to his room, knowing he had helped them in some way. His inner feelings about Paul continued to plague him as he undressed. He knew Paul had done more than his share that evening helping with the supplies. More than once during the activities that night, Don had the feeling that Paul didn't exactly trust this dark-haired American, that doubts were shared by the two of them about each other. He said, "Oh what the hell! I'm too damned tired to worry about that now." And he crawled into bed.

***

"A few days later, it was barely daylight. Don was awakened by excited voices downstairs. Suddenly the bedroom door was flung open and

Bill rushed in telling them to hurry! Paul and Don scrambled out of bed. They did not take the time to dress, but quickly gathered up their clothes. Before Don closed the door, he rapidly checked to make sure nothing had been left behind. The three of them dashed across the hall and headed for the storeroom.

"Bill told them there were trucks . . . . big ones . . . Germans! Frauk stood in the hall and urged them to hurry. Paul lifted the trap door. Not taking time to use the ladder, Don held tightly to his clothes and jumped down into the hiding place. He winced slightly as his leg felt the impact of seven-foot drop. Ignoring the pain, he moved aside as Bill and then Paul bounded in after him.

"The trap door slammed down on top of them. Don heard the thumping of the apples as they were dumped to cover the trap door. Then he heard the crash of the crate as it was thrown against the wall. All was silent.

"For fear of making noise, Paul and Don did not dress. It was cold in the sealed closet. Barker stood there and shivered. He experienced more fear at that moment than he had ever known in his lifetime. He attributed his uncontrolled trembling to fear instead of the cold.

"Through the walls, they heard pounding on the rear and front doors. There was a lot of commotion. There were loud shouts and Don heard a word that resembled 'open.' The Germans stormed through the rooms, their heavy footsteps resounded from every direction. He heard the sounds of the intruders rushing up the stairs to the upper rooms. The Germans entered the storeroom above their heads. Don shivered even more as he heard the apples being kicked around the floor above them. They seemed to be stomping on the floor. Don realized the sound might differ between the solid places in the floor, and the hollow sounds that might result if they were to stomp on the trap door.

"At that moment, Don did pray, silently, "God! Don't let them find the damned trap door!" His eyes had become accustomed to the darkness in the secret room. He reached in the corner for one of the machine guns he had carefully stacked there the night before. He thought of the night when they had walked to see Reed and Trombley, by the canal, and he knew that neither of the other two men could see in the dark. He touched Paul's shoulder and carefully placed a weapon in his hands. He could see Paul's face; it was chalky white. Bill stood directly behind Paul. Don got another weapon and handed it to him. Then he picked up one for himself. No one moved after they were armed.

"He heard loud orders being shouted by the Nazis. Occasionally he

NOT HOME FOR CHRISTMAS

heard Mr. Meijering's voice deny knowledge of the "Amerikaan pilot!" and Don felt his shoulders sag at the thought of what his presence here had done to this family. Then from one of the bedrooms he heard Frauk scream. A terrible chill enveloped him. Again he heard the word 'Amerikaan' and her reply repeated over and over, 'neen . . neen . . . neen!"

"He thought he heard more than one German voice beside Frauk's and it was obvious they were not merely questioning her. She screamed again and he visualized what must be happening when he heard the dull thud of blows being struck. Don winced as he himself was on the receiving end. It was all he could do to stand still. He seriously thought about climbing up out of this hiding place and put to stop the merciless beating. As if Paul read Don's thoughts, Paul placed his hand firmly on Barker's shoulder bidding him to remain quiet and not move. Don looked into Paul's face: he saw it was contorted with hatred, his teeth tightly clenched, his jaw jutted out in defiance. Don could not imagine how this man could just stand there and listen to what was evidently happening to the girl he loved.

"All three men abruptly turned and pointed their guns toward the wall where the closet doors had originally been. The Germans were banging on the wall with the butt of their rifles. The concealed trio heard sounds of furniture crashing as it was being thrown around. Again overhead, they heard footsteps and someone kicking the apples. Automatically, as if in synchronization the three men aimed their guns toward the trap door. For a brief moment Don almost hoped one of the sons-of-bitches would stick his head through the hole! Don felt the beads of sweat form on his forehead and his temples pounded with each heartbeat. He concentrated on trying to relax, to calm down, knowing that he needed every ounce of strength to stay rational in case he did have to react. There were moments when all shouting and pounding seemed to cease.

"Just when Don figured they had left, the noise would start again. Oh God, he thought if only I could see what was happening. He considered the consequences of making a stand, but he knew he wouldn't have lasted a moment against the Nazis, if there were as many as it sounded out there. And he knew for certain that his appearance now would mean death to all the Meijering family for having him here in the first place. His heart almost stopped as he heard Mrs. Meijering cry out in pain. What in hell are they doing to that gently lady? The image of her in her clean white apron and perky little hat tore through his brain. About then, he also heard Dien scream several times. Then silence. Had they been killed he wondered. Not knowing what was happening was the worst torture of all for him.

"He thought it strange that he had not heard Mr. Meijering's voice again since his denial of knowledge about the American. He had heard several shots being fired and Don feared for the whole family. Then, moments later, the drone of heavy truck motors penetrated through the walls. Don listened as the sounds faded away and he felt he could finally take a deep breath. Relieved as he watched Paul slumped against the wall and drop his arms to his sides, still holding the gun. Bill moved quickly as he relaxed too. Don felt sick, but he quickly dressed and saw that Paul was putting his clothes on as well. He stood there quietly. From the bedroom side of the wall, they heard a gentle tapping and Mrs. Meijering cry out weakly that the Germans had gone.

"Bill was the first to climb the ladder. He cautiously pushed up the trap door and peered through the narrow crack. When he lifted it completely, apples rolled off in every direction, some falling through the hole and dropping down on Don and Paul. Don climbed out next; and then reached down to help Paul, "Come on fella, let me give you a hand." Paul reached up to Don, his hand shaking visibly. Don pulled him up. He heard Bill cry out as he found Dien. He and Paul hurried down the hall. They saw Dien, badly beaten and lying unconscious on the floor of the room she shared with Frauk. They looked around for the older girl, and then Paul quickly headed toward the other rooms searching for her.

"Don rushed down the stairs to look for the older couple. As he searched through the rooms, he shuddered at the sight of broken glass and overturned furniture. He found the lady slumped in a chair in the kitchen. Her right arm was swollen and badly bruised. He knelt beside her and cradled her head in his arms. She sobbed quietly and he realized how difficult it must have been for her to tap on the wall, letting the trio behind the wall know the Germans had gone, and then drag herself into the kitchen. In his search of the rooms, he had not found her husband and had no idea where Mr. Meijering could be.

"In a few moments Paul shouted from upstairs. "Don! Hurry, we must hurry! Come. Help me get the guns out!" Don stood up, once again sensing the urgency of the situation. He patted Mrs. Meijering tenderly on the shoulder, then hurried upstairs to the storeroom. Barker climbed down through the trap door into the secret room. He handed up a machine gun for each of them. He passed up three revolvers which could be concealed under their jackets. He also wanted to assure they would have enough ammunition and extra clips for the machine guns. However he didn't want to slow them down with more than they could carry. He scrambled back up the ladder.

NOT HOME FOR CHRISTMAS

"Don got his first glimpse of Frauk when he walked into the hallway. Paul had told him that he'd found her in the same room he had shared with Don. She had been unconscious with deep wounds on her face and head. After she had regained consciousness he had left her slumped against the open bedroom door. This was when he had called to Don for help with the guns. Though Paul had said she was injured, he wasn't prepared for what he saw. He stared in disbelief at the cuts and bruises and her sweater stained with dried blood.

"God all mighty – I'm so sorry!"

"Through swollen lips she whispered, "They will be back. You have no time to waste on me. Go . . . all of you, hurry . . . You have to hurry! Paul will show you. Go now, and be careful, my friend." Don turned away and looked at Paul. The expression on Paul's face imparted more hatred than Don had ever seen on any man. Paul nodded, then pointed toward the stairs where Bill waited. Don followed him down and glanced once more at Mrs. Meijering as they passed through the kitchen. He stopped for a moment to say something to her, but Bill pulled at him and hurried him out the kitchen door.

"Paul led the way toward the woods. Bill ran off in a different direction. Don remembered them previously deciding on a meeting place if and when it became necessary. He presumed that they thought it would be better to separate temporarily. When he and Paul entered the heavily wooded area all was very still. In just moments, Don heard the roar of the Nazi trucks returning to the Meijering farm. His instincts told him to run. But his better judgment told him to keep low and take advantage of dense undercover. There was also a heavy ground fog, quite normal for this early hour of morning. That too would help prevent detection as they crept deeper into the woods. Paul and Don came to a spot where there was thick underbrush and Paul stopped. Don looked all around, then spread his weapons on the ground. They heard the brush crack and both of them grabbed for their guns and swung around. It was Bill rejoining them. The next few minutes all three of them checked the clips in the machine guns and placed bullets in the revolvers.

"Don wondered what would happen next. He relived the last little while. They had remembered to close the trap door, spread the apples on the floor to conceal the entrance to their hiding place. If the Nazis were to find the trap door, they would find the weapons left behind. That would mean more problems for the Meijering family, He shook his head again not believing what he had seen, Mrs. Meijering with the badly swollen arm, and Frauk's face. Problems? How much more serious could the problems possibly have been, with or without the discovery of the hidden guns, he asked himself.

"The words "Amerikaan pilot" haunted him. He could hear shouts from the direction of the farmhouse. He wanted to know what was happening. He rose up on his knees and watched one of the trucks pull over to the end of the stable. The Germans entered the building, and then returned to the truck. They drove from one building to another as they searched. He watched as the truck approached the woods. Bill grabbed Don's arm and jerked him down. The truck drove past their hiding spot. "God," he murmured, "Why don't we just get the hell out of here?" Then he heard the shooting.

"Paul crawled close to Don and said, "They must be shooting through the walls!" Don grimaced and said, "Guess it's a good thing that we got out of our hole then. I just hope they don't hit any of the ammunition. I don't care if they hit it and blow them all to hell, but not with the Meijering's in there!"

"Paul nodded. The trio simultaneously turned as they heard the trucks start up again. It appeared as they were leaving. Don hunkered down in the brush and the sudden silence bothered him. He couldn't help wonder what was happening in the house. He started to stand up but Paul's hand on his arm cautioned him not to move. Barker had heard no sound but he jumped at Paul's warning touch. Then from nearby, he heard Frauk's voice calling softly, "Paul."

"Don was relieved when he saw Dien with Frauk. Paul and Bill stood up and waved for them to hurry and join them. The girls embraced the two Dutchmen briefly and nodded in Don's direction. Don could see that Dien had suffered the same sort of treatment as Frauk; her face and neck was covered with ugly looking bruises, dried blood covered the cuts about her head. Frauk told them the Nazis had taken away her father. She didn't know where he was and she didn't know whether he was still alive. So far they had not been able to find out any news about him or his whereabouts.

"Dien tearfully described how the Germans had destroyed most of the beautiful furniture in their home, but she seemed mostly distressed about the destruction of her prized piano. Her arms flailed desperately as she repeated how the Nazi had smashed the furniture. All Don could think of was how proudly Frauk had shown him through the house, pointing out the exquisite pieces of furniture. The two girls told of how the Germans had hacked through some of the walls, but the hiding place had not been discovered.

"Paul sighed with relief when he heard the secret closet had not been

NOT HOME FOR CHRISTMAS

found, fearful that if it had the entire family would have been killed. Don couldn't say a word. He stared at the two girls feeling worse than ever; realizing that all of this had happened because of his presence in their home. He thought about Mrs. Meijering; and momentarily he regretted having pulled the rip cord of the parachute that had brought him safely to the ground and to this country. He sat on the ground, leaning against a tree and ran his fingers through his hair, then rested his head in his hands. The others spoke rapidly; though Don could not understand the words they said, their actions and the look on their faces helped him understand what the family had suffered.

"Frauk approached him, gently pulled his hands down away from his head and smiled at him. He looked up at the bruises and swollen face and could feel nothing but despair. She bent over and whispered, "It was not your fault. Do not feel badly. If it were not you, it would have been someone else. " She pointed to her face, and told him, "I know I look bad to you . . . but I heal quickly. Most importantly – you boys are all safe for the moment."

"Paul was there, putting his arms around her and tenderly held her close for several minutes. Bill tried to console Dien who was still crying, about her beloved piano, she did not know if she would ever get another one. Paul stepped back away from Frauk then; the older girl walked over to her sister and hugged her. The two girls said something to the two Dutch men, and started back toward the house. Paul sat down next to Don.

"When it is night out, we will leave. It is not safe for us to return to the house, and it will not be good for the girls to remain there. We will go to the river. We will meet the girls there." Bill joined them and Paul spoke again. "We need to keep watch in every direction until the night comes. I know it is cold, but we cannot build a fire here to warm ourselves. In fact, we need to hide our bodies even more."

"Don looked around; he noticed a large fallen tree near where they were and pointed in that direction. "How about it – don't you think it would make a good shield for us? And we could pile up a little more of the brush around here to hide us from the other direction." He was not sure the two other men understood what all he said, although he saw Paul nod his head, and he stood up. Don began to pile the brush to form a barricade for protection: both Paul and Bill soon were helping, and they moved the guns behind the fallen tree. They worked as quietly as they could; pausing ever so often to make sure no one approached or had heard the cracking of breaking branches.

"Satisfied with their efforts the three smiled. Bill whispered something to Paul, then reached for one of the machine guns and turned to Don. He didn't say anything, merely patted him on the shoulder then disappeared into the woods. Don waited for Paul to explain what that was all about when it was obvious that no explanation was forthcoming, he hunched down against the tree trunk. Finally, he asked, "Where do you suppose they took Mr. Meijering? Do you think he is still alive? What do you think they'll do to him, Paul?"

"Paul did not answer immediately, and then he said softly, "It is hard to say where they have taken him. They will probably try to force him to tell where you are."

"That's what I was afraid of."

"Bill has gone to make sure his family is alright and to see about your two friends – the ones staying at his house."

"Reed and Trombley? My God! Do you think the Germans knew they were there?" For the past several hours he had almost forgotten about them. He had been so engrossed in his own troubles and those of the Meijering family, now; he worried about what might have at the neighbouring home with the other two Americans.

"We don't know, we'll find out in a little while." Paul assured him.

"It was nearly dark: the sound of approaching footsteps startled both men. They reached quickly for their guns. Then Don recognized the figures of the men as they got closer, and stood up pointing toward them. He was alarmed as Paul stood up, raised his machine gun in the direction that Don had pointed, "Wait Paul! It's Bill . . . and the Americans . . . my friends!" He called out softly, "Over here, Bill!"

"Paul and Don both stepped out over the brush pile to help Trombley to the temporary shelter. Reed slung an arm over Don's shoulder and said, "Hey – good to see you all in one piece there buddy! For a little while, we had doubts if we would ever 'see' anyone again!"

"I take it they hit the Woering's place too, then!"

"Hit it! Hell, like a demolition squad! They literally tore the place apart. Never saw anything like that in my life. But my hiding place paid off; even though I had a hell of a time to get Dick up there. They didn't find it – or us – hell, they didn't even com close! And as you can tell, my butt is still intact, not even a scratch." Reed grinned. Then he and Trombley both started talking at once, recounting the furore caused by the Nazis searching through the house.

"Yeah," Dick told him, "Those bastards actually dragged Mrs. Woering through the house by her hair. They tried to make her talk, but she wouldn't! They took Mr. Woering off – we didn't know it at first, but when

NOT HOME FOR CHRISTMAS

we finally got out of the attic, he was gone. Bill thinks they may have taken him to a concentration camp somewhere. God! It was all we could do just to sit there and do – nothing! We could hear everything that was going on – couldn't understand most of the words, but we could hear it!"

"They took Mr. Meijering away too," Don said, "God! I hope they're both OK. When they hit here, I thought al hell had broke loose! You know what guys – there had to be some kind of a tip-off from someone along the line. But who? Finding out where you guys were, and where I was – just too much of a coincidence. Someone *had to tell them* where to look, you know what I mean? It's too weird. The place where I stayed before, at the store . . . well, they knew where I had gone, but they sure as hell wouldn't have known about you, at least I don't think so! Besides, from what I saw, they would never have told!."

"It's spooky all right." Reed's face suddenly lit up, "Wait a minute! Ya' know what? That doctor – the one they brought to look at Trombley's leg. That Dr.Bijl. Damn it Don – Bill told me he was educated in America, and you can bet he understood every word we said. He knew I was there of course, then when he saw Dien with Bill . . . I'm sure he knew who she was, and I'll be he guessed that she and her family had an American at her place too. That's gotta be it!"

"Don nodded his head and said, "Possible . . . they could have made him talk, I guess!"

"Trombley said; "Made him talk – or did he volunteer that information? He could have told them to save his own neck, that's a possibility. I don't imagine we'll ever know for sure."

"Reed asked, "What's the plan? Where do we go from here . . .anyone know?"

"To the river," Don answered, "Paul told me that. We'll meet the girls there. From there, who knows? It's anybody's guess but I suppose we'll find out soon enough." He paused: then quickly said, "What was that?"

"They listened, Paul signalled for all of them to be quiet. Bill pointed to the log. All three Americans ducked down behind it; grabbing for their guns as they tried to conceal themselves. They could hear the angry voices of the Nazi patrol when it returned from the Meijering home to search again for the Americans. Don cautiously raised his head up above the log to look around. Instinctively he formed his lips to whistle, then thought better of it, lowered his head and whispered, "God damn! They're all around us, must be couple dozen of 'em!"

"Bullets whined as the Nazis fired their guns haphazardly into the woods, some of them striking nearby trees with a dull thud. Obviously the Germans didn't know if the men were hiding among the trees, or where they were. They were shooting at random. Then they heard shouts, the orders were in English, "Come out! We know you are there. Come out now! With your hands up!"

"As total darkness fell, the shouts and shooting ceased. Sounds of the moving vehicles faded in the distance as the Germans left. Don eased his hold on the gun for the first time and laid the weapon down beside him; the others were doing the same thing. Don rubbed his right hand briskly to restore feeling. He heard Reed sigh with relief and watched him lean back against the tree trunk and close his eyes. Trombley slumped and for the first time, groaned.

"Bill and Paul talked quietly. Don watched their faces; it looked as if they were formulating some kind of a plan. He watched as Bill turned in their direction, wave his arm and said, "Come on quickly! This way! Let's go!"

"They gathered up the guns and the ammunition. Quilla and Bill helped Dick to his feet and hurried after Paul. Don was directly behind the group.

"At last they reached the river. Dien and Frauk were already there, waiting. The two girls embraced the two Dutchmen, then talked softly to Paul and Bill. Paul turned to the Americans and told them, "Please, it is important we leave here at once!"

"Trombley had sat down at the edge of the river and asked Reed, "What did he say?"

"He said we have to get the hell out of here right now! Sorry, buddy, wish we had time so you could rest a bit, but we don't." Reed looked at the two girls; then asked them, "You two going with us?"

"Frauk quickly explained that her mother had thought it best if they left with the Americans. Mrs. Meijering was concerned about her husband, but she believed her two daughters would be in much danger if they remained behind, and had urged them to leave.

"The group was silent as they walked across fields. They came to a country road, not much more than a rutted path, but they followed it. Don occasionally glanced back at the wounded man who was keeping up but with some difficulty. Dick explained the doctor had not removed the bullet from his leg. He had cleaned and dressed the wound and provided some medication for the pain. They had left in such a hurry he had not been able bring it with him. The wound was healing from the outside, not a good sign. And all this sudden activity, it had opened again, bleeding slightly. Don knew it was causing him pain but they dared not to stop.

"The group continued to walk; they crossed through fields; occasionally they would be on the hard surface of a road. They passed a few buildings, probably farms, Don thought. He was not aware of any group of homes or what might be a village. It was nearly dawn; he heard Trombley groan and saw him sink to the ground. His painfully swollen leg had finally given out. Reed tried pulling him to his feet. The others stopped. Don also tried to help him stand. Reed urged, "Come on, put your arm around my shoulder, Dick. Come on. You can make it!"

"No – sorry guys, but no! I don't think so!" Trombley sank back to the ground. He dropped the gun he had been carrying and rubbed his upper leg. "Hey now, why don't you just leave me here? I'm not kidding, it feels like this damned thing is gonn' fall off! I can't do it!"

"Bill helped Reed get Trombley to his feet once more; all the while the Dutchman was talking softly to him and explaining how necessary it was that they go just a little further. With Reed on one side, Bill on the other, Dick managed to hobble along using only his good leg and swinging the injured one back and forth as they walked. Don picked up the others weapons and carried them as he hurried to join Paul at the front of the group.

"Later that day the group spent the night in the haystack of a farmer who had also supplied them with food. Trombley's leg was getting worse and the following morning the group decided to split up. Frauk, Dien, Bill and Paul were to go directly west. Being Dutch and having papers, they would be able to travel fairly safely, even though the men's underground activities were known by the ones who were looking for them, but the primary targets were the Americans. They were splitting them up. It could be too conspicuous if they all remained together. Trombley was to stay with the farmer while a man they called called Piet de Boer was to take the other two Americans with him. They would travel due north for some distance and then turn west. Pete was a short stocky man and when he spoke to them, Don noticed his exceptionally deep voice. He did however, speak some English words, for which they were thankful. Don and Quilla watched as the two young couples left the house. No one bothered to say goodbye because they all believed they would meet up again at a predestined spot in the next few days.

"This reunion was not going to happen. The seven members of the group would never meet again although they all survived the war.

"After a few days, Richard Trombley went via Auke and Hans van der Meer in Donkerbroek to an address in Lemmer and from there to a safe house in Nieuweschoot/Oudehaske.

"Quilla and Don Barker were first taken to the De Vries family in Oudehorne and came then to the Kroll family in Lippenhuizen.

***

In the late 1930's Johannes Krol came to live in Lippenhuizen in the north-eastern part of the Netherlands as tracker dog policeman. During WW II he used his official function to help allied airmen to avoid capture after they had jumped over his region and used his motor cycle to transport dropped weapons for the underground. Half a century later, his son Dick recalls the war time adventures of his father in an article he wrote in 1995 for a local newspaper:

"Lippenhuizen, winter 1944-1945. It is freezing cold. I am an eighteen years old and doing my homework near the pot-bellied stove.

"It is getting dark when, around five o'clock three men come to a halt in front of our house. Two of them are pulling and the third one is pushing a cart loaded with tree trunks. "Ha", I thought, "Pa has managed to lay his hand on some trees for heating." I put on a coat to help unloading the cart. My father has also arrived on the spot. "Open the doors of the shed", my father says, "and hurry to make some room for the trunks".

"The two men who had been pulling the cart carried the trunks inside without saying a word. They just nodded their heads. They obviously can not spare a hello. After having unloaded the cart, the man who had been pushing, took the empty cart and left. The two others entered the house and there I heard them speaking. They are not Dutchmen, they speak English!

"The two English speaking strangers proved to be Americans, who had been shot down over Haulerwijk on Sunday, November 26, 1944. Their bomber, a Boeing B-17 ("Flying Fortress") had been on the way back from Germany when she had been attacked by fighters. The aircraft exploded in mid-air but the crew could save themselves by parachute. Among them the Bombardier Don Barker who had landed smack in the center of Haulerwijk. Together with the Waist-Gunner Richard Trombley and the Top-Turret Gunner Quilla Reed he had been picked up and hidden by the underground.

"The Germans knew that most of the crew had evaded capture and searched the whole area without finding them. Via various addresses, Don Barker and Quilla Reed arrived at our place in Lippenhuizen. Hiding these airmen was very dangerous but that was never a point of discussion in our family. It went without saying that they could not be handed over

NOT HOME FOR CHRISTMAS

to the Germans.

"Beds were made in the attic where we also had some kind of a place to hide. A part under the slanting roof had been sealed off and offered some room for people. Weapons were also concealed there. It would not pass a thorough search by the Germans who, by knocking on the wooden partition, could easily discover the empty space behind it, but it had to do.

"Between our house and the shed behind it was a small piece of open space hidden from the road. There our two guests could flex their muscles by cutting wood. They had been with us for quite some time when the local baker knocked on the door to deliver the daily bread. He had already noticed that all of a sudden we needed more bread than usual. Our Americans, Don and Quilla, were busy sawing wood. Quilla opened the door, said "Hello" , and went on with his business. After the war the baker said; "I know that you were hiding people, but I thought they were Dutch".

"Every night the two Americans went for a walk through the meadows. My father always took Wodan with him as the dog would warn him when someone suspicious would come near. Whenever that happened, my father would proceed alone with Wodan to investigate while Don and Quilla would remain behind.

"One night, on our way home, we saw the shadow of a man walking in the yard of the Van Weperen farm we had to cross before reaching our house. We hid ourselves behind some bushes and Wodan also was told to lie low. My father went around the farm and grappled the man who was coming around the corner of the house. The man did not start a fight as that was useless when you were in the strong grip of my father. It proved to be the farmer who had been checking his yard for intruders. "Man, you almost gave me a heart attack", he told my father. He went into his farm again and we could cross the yard to go home.

"Those were small adventures for Don and Quilla, who had no inkling about the risks our family was running. Perhaps, because during their bombing missions had been exposed to greater dangers. They noticed however, the permanent fright my mother had when my father was called for underground duties.

"With the advance of the allied troops, the droppings of weapons and ammunition for the underground increased and the activities of the resistance gathered strength. Between September 1944 and April 1945 the RAF executed twenty-one big weapon droppings in Friesland, enough to arm up to three thousand men.

"Pa often had to go with his motor bike and fetch the dropped materiel. The weapons arrived by the side car load at our house and were from there distributed among the underground members. That often happened by bicycles equipped with a baker's basket, big enough to contain the rifles.

"One night, with weapons lying around all over the place, someone rang at the door. Everybody froze. Quilla and Don were in their little room in the attic. Pa opened the door and there were two German officers. "We have to make an urgent phone call", one of them said, "You are a policeman so you certainly have a telephone." My father stepped out of the house, closing the door behind him. "Yes", my father said, "but my phone is out of order. There on the corner is a café where they also have a phone". He accompanied the Germans to the pub, that of course was closed for the day but my father got the owner out of his bed and explained to him that the Germans had to make a call. He stayed with the officers until they had finished their call, wished them a good night and returned home where everybody was waiting anxiously to hear the outcome.

Don Barker describes his first meeting with the Krol family:

"It was almost noon when Don and Quilla arrived in a small village. Don noticed the tree-lined streets and the neatly kept houses, shops and a very old stone church. The two Americans followed their Dutch companion Jan to the far side of the town, and turned off the street into a gravelled driveway. All three of them got off and walked the bicycles up the drive. The house was red brick, had a tall pointed roof and newly painted white trim which accented the bright red bricks. Don saw a brightly polished bell mounted on a post, he assumed it was to announce the arrival of guests, but Jan did not use it. At the rear of the house an extension had been built and he saw a tall chain-link fence which confined a large German shepherd dog who sat there on his haunches watching them approach. The dog barked twice, and then was silent. Don turned to look again at the dog; he was watching every move they made as they followed Jan up to the house. Just as they reached the back door, a man appeared and greeted them.

"Jan smiled and said, "Don Barker, Quilla Reed, this is Johannes Krol."

"The man smiled and extended his hand. Mr. Krol was not as tall as Don, was a bit on the stocky side and Don judged him to be about forty years old. As he shook hands with the Americans, he said in English, "Come in ... come in! And welcome to you both!"

NOT HOME FOR CHRISTMAS

"He led them into a large kitchen. Don immediately noticed the lady, the fresh white apron she wore and that she had a double chin. Jan said, "This is Mrs. Krol." She too shook each of their hands and smiled, then pointed to a door that led to a large, well-furnished living room. She pointed to chairs and indicated they should make themselves comfortable.

"Reed and Barker had just sat down when a young girl came down the stairs and approached them. They immediately stood back up and the girl too offered her hand, "Hello, my name is 'Yah-nny' – in America that would be Jane! Please, sit down."

"Don sat back down but turned to see a handsome young man and a much younger girl than Jane come into the room, so he stood once again.

"Jane quickly introduced the young girl with the blonde curly hair and sparkling blue eyes, "This is my sister Ah-nnie .. and my brother, Dick!"

"Both Don and Reed shook hands with Dick who smiled at them warmly and said, "You are both most welcome in our home! We are happy to have you here. Please sit back down."

"Reed grinned at the young girl, Annie and said "Hello there!" She smiled shyly as she greeted the two in her broken English. Then she sat down and pushed herself back in the big chair. She pulled her dress carefully down over her knees and stared at them as if she was intrigued by their appearance.

"Jan had stood quietly by as everyone had been introduced then finally said; "Mr. Krol will help you now and will take you to the place of the drop when it is time. Then you will learn how you can help our cause. I must leave now, but I truly hope we will meet again, soon."

"Don asked Jane about Mr. Krol. "Our father is the police commissioner here in our village. Actually, he also collaborates with the Germans!" Don looked at Reed and both of the Americans tensed for a moment, then Jane continued, "Or at least that is what the Nazis think. However, it is, how you say, it is his cover. He is also important in the underground and he has many times helped people such as you. We are always happy to have such as you come to us."

"The next morning over breakfast Mrs. Krol said something to Jane and she got up from the table. Soon, she returned with a small wooden box that had a canvas strip fastened to it.

"What is that?" Don asked.

"It is a machine for making cigarettes," she smiled, and handed it to her father. Both of the Americans were fascinated as they watched Mr. Krol roll three cigarettes. He handed one to each of them and put the other one to his lips. Dick was ready with matches and held out a light for each of them. Don took a big drag off his smoke and inhaled. It had been so long since he'd had a cigarette, he felt much like the first time he'd ever smoked, just a little giddy and light headed."

Don and Quilla stayed with the Krol family until the arrival of Canadian troops in April 1945. Meanwhile they instructed the members of the underground in the use of the weapons and demolition material dropped by English bombers in the middle of the late winter nights.

Dick Krol writes after the war:

"In April 1945 the Canadian troops were approaching the north-eastern part of the Netherlands where Quilla and Don were impatiently awaiting their arrival. The underground received instructions that the three bridges in the Lippenhuizen area had to be secured to speed up the advance of the Canadians. My friend Jan van Zinderen and I were assigned to the group that had to keep the bridge between Lippenhuizen and Jubbega open for the Canadians. We also were to function as translators as both Jan and I had learned English in teacher training college. Jan had, together with his father, been listening to "Radio London" a Dutch news program of the B.B.C. They wrote down what they had heard and multiplied and distributed the news among a circle of friends and neighbours.

"One of the last days of the war a motor bike with side car arrived at the bridge we were guarding, manned by two Canadians. We welcomed them with great bursts of cheers and asked them from where they came. They told us they had been dropped near Arnhem and were now preceding the troops as a reconnaissance unit. When I asked them where they lived in America, they said; "Mississippi". I had my rifle ready in my hands, pointed it at the two and said: "Get off your bike. You're not Americans."

"Due to my contact with Don and Quilla I noticed that they spoke differently. Not American slang but English with a Dutch accent. On top of that they wore Canadian uniforms and pretended to come from Mississippi; a State in the U.S.A.

"One of them became furious; "You better take care. My friend has a hand grenade and ready to blow you guys up," he said, pointing to his companion in the side car. Then my commanding officer interfered. He told me to lower my rifle and to get out of the way. He pointed out to me that I was playing a dangerous game and he didn't want to be part of it. A few moments later the two pseudo Canadians crossed the bridge and drove direction Lippenhuizen.

"I was seeing red; my superior did not speak a word of English and should have trusted my instinct. Now perhaps a pair of spies were on their way again. We had a courier in our group with a light motor cycle. I went to him and told him what I had on my mind. I asked him to follow the two guys in Canadian uniforms and to find out where they were going. I took my bike and told my superior that I was going to inform our command post about these two. After having explained there the situation, they contacted my father. He loaded Quilla and Barker, who wanted to come along, on his motor bike and went looking for our courier.

"He was easily found but he explained that the two drove to fast from him and that he had lost them. I went on my bicycle direction Jubbega trying to locate my two "spies" and indeed, after a couple of miles, I saw tracks of a heavy motor bike leading to a farm. The farmer confirmed that the two "Americans" had come to him and had told him that they would come back that night to fetch some cheese.

"I contacted the command post of the underground and they ordered a couple of guys to go with me to that farm and wait for the return of the motor bikers. They also gave me the command of that small group of men although I had no inkling why. We figured out that my command of English was the cause for my quick promotion. We posted ourselves in such a way that we could cover the front side of the farm. Nobody was to do anything before I would give the command. Then our wait began and indeed, after some time, the motor bike arrived and stopped in front of the farm.

"I let them get off and out of their bike and then came forward and shouted that they had to turn against the wall with their hands up. They reacted very quickly, jumped behind a large tree and started to shoot at our people. Without thinking twice I started to shoot, emptying the greater part of the clip of my sten gun. I did not hit them, but came so close that they considered it wise to raise their hands and to surrender. We studied their papers that indeed belonged to two Canadians. I wondered if I perhaps had made a mistake. Our courier was send to our command post for further orders. He returned with the message that we almost certainly had captured two spies who were carrying false papers. We were to keep them in a safe place until the arrival of the Canadian troops who were on their way in our direction.

"They arrived later that night: Canadian scouts. I accosted one of the officers and told him about the men we had captured. Together with him an a few soldiers we went into the barn where we had kept them. The officer talked to them and after a short while they were hauled out of the barn to be executed. They were pro-Nazi Dutchmen working for the Germans and had killed two Canadians and in the uniforms and with the papers of their victims had started to "scout" the area as two Canadians. We did not wait for the final outcome of their actions.

"The Canadian scouts returned to their main force. Later that evening after dinner my father left on his motor bike, taking Quilla and Don with him. Both Americans were armed with sten guns. After a few minutes they met a column of German troops. Three Germans, with their guns ready in their hands, blocked the road and shouted that they had to stop. Pa then yelled to his American brothers-in-arms the "historical" words: "Ready . . . . . shoot!"

"He immediately opened the throttle, slipped in the clutch so that the front wheel came off the ground and ran the German down who was trying to stop him while Don and Quilla emptied their sten guns: first at the two other Germans who were blocking their passage and then, firing backwards, at the rest of the German column. Pa swayed form left to right to avoid the German bullets and at the first opportunity left the road and entered a narrow path into the woods. They got away all right!

"That was the beginning of our liberation from the Germans and the end of our much appreciated contact with "our Americans", because when the following day the Canadians arrived, Don and Quilla joined them without even "going home" and to say "goodbye" to us."

Don recalls these events as follows:

"When the Canadians were ten miles away, Krol said to Don and Quilla; "We have a job to do. We'll take weapons to a village nearby. The Canadians must move heavy trucks over the canals, but the Germans plan to blow these. After they pass ... retreat, you know what I say? We must now go protect bridge. You two help?"

"Both of the Americans agreed eagerly. Reed stood up and shouted, "Whoopee!" He ran around the big table, grabbed Jane and whirled her around. Then he approached Mrs. Krol, took her hand and reached for Annie's too and Reed had the three of them twirling around the room. "Did you hear what he said? The allies are just ten miles away ... what wonderful news. That means some of your Dutch people are already free!"

"Mr. Krol spoke cautiously. "Nazi thinks how to get out, they not looking for evader, but still, must be careful." He headed toward the dining room with Quilla and Don right behind him. Several crates were hidden under a tablecloth.

"Mr. Krol pointed to the crates that were marked 'Grenades' and said, "We will need these."

"Quilla lifted some of the boxes up onto the table and opened them. While they checked the grenades, Mr. Krol unpacked two sten machine guns and several clips of ammunition. He laid the guns on the table and said, "And we may need these." They hauled some of the boxes out through the back door and stacked them on the floor of the sidecar. They put a few on the seat, leaving just enough for one person to sit there, then they went back inside for the guns.

"Mr. Krol pointed to the side car and indicated Reed should ride there. Reed squeezed himself in and placed his feet on the boxes; tucked his legs up under his chin. He placed the gun in his jacket sleeve and crossed his arms. "Anything show?" Reed asked Barker.

"Can't see a thing," Don told him.

"They saw Mrs. Krol standing on the porch with Jane and Annie. Barker heard Jane shout, "God go with you." And the trio waved resolutely.

"The Americans turned and nodded to the group on the porch, and the motorcycle pulled out of the yard and onto the street. They rode past some Germans on foot. Don thought some of the soldiers might get the idea of shooting them for the motorcycle. He placed his hand inside his jacket and gripped the handle of the gun. But the now demoralized Germans plodded complacently along and paid no attention to the trio.

"They pulled into a small village after a short while and Mr. Krol wheeled into the yard of a home almost in the center of the town. He stopped the engine and got off the motorcycle. "We leave grenades here": he told them.

"When the boxes had finally been taken inside the house, the three of them turned the motorcycle around and Reed got back into the now empty sidecar. They both took time to tuck the guns back inside their jacket sleeves. Mr. Krol started the engine once again and Barker got on behind him. Mr. Krol headed down the street; then turned off onto a dirt road. This was a different route than they had taken to get to the village earlier. Don assumed he wanted to avoid the Germans, if possible, believing they would stick to the main roads.

"At last, Mr. Krol turned off the dirt road and onto a paved street again. Don recognized this street as the one they had been on before and he figured they must be about a half-mile from the Krol home. He relaxed his grip on the gun.

"In the twilight, Don saw three horse-drawn farm wagons stopped on the side of the road just ahead. He glanced at Reed, who reached for his gun under his jacket. Mr. Krol did not slow down, speed up, or turn off onto a side road. As they passed, Don saw the Germans had loaded the wagons with furniture, clothing and bedding. Some of the Germans turned to look as they passed by. Some even waved, but no one attempted to stop them. They seemed to be preparing to spend the night at this spot. Some of them were un-harnessing the horses, and some had started a campfire.

"The motorcycle was about to pass by the last wagon when a German soldier stepped out onto the road. He held the reins of a horse and he waved his arms for the motorcycle to stop. Mr. Krol pushed hard on the horn. The blaring horn spooked the horse and caused it to rear up. The distracted Nazi grabbed for the reins as Mr. Krol turned the throttle wide open and whizzed past.

"Barker and Reed looked back over their shoulders. Barker stared hard, half expecting to be fired on. When it seemed nothing would happen, he turned to face forward again. Ahead, he saw the beams of flashlights waving back and forth to signal them to stop. Mr. Krol slowed the motorcycle as three German soldiers came into view. Don figured they might be part of the advanced guard. Unlike the slovenly troops they had been seeing throughout the day, these soldiers marched in full combat uniform and carried side arms and personal gear. Two of the Germans stood on the right side of the road and the other stood directly in front of the approaching motorcycle. They held their rifles erect and yelled, "Stop! Halt!"

"Mr. Krol hit the brakes. The lone Nazi started toward them. Don crooked his finger around the trigger of the gun inside his jacket. His eyes narrowed and his mind raced as he weighed the alternatives. But he saw no way out. He knew instinctively they would not be allowed to pass without papers. It would not do for the Germans to discover they had weapons. He drew the gun from his jacket and fired. The two Germans on the side of the road fell back into a ditch. At the same moment, Reed stood up in the side car and fired his weapon. The body of the German in the middle of the road jack-knifed forward as Reed emptied his clip into the soldier's gut.

"One of the Germans had pulled himself up on the road. Don turned around as far as he could, raised his gun and pulled the trigger. Some of the bullets hit the pavement and sparked in a fiery display. He didn't know if his bullets found their target, but he heard no more shots from behind.

"Barker glanced back at Reed who only gazed straight ahead. Reed's pallor made Barker wonder if he might get sick. Don swallowed hard at the realization that this was the first time he'd ever killed anyone too: at least knowingly. Dropping bombs or firing the guns from a B-17 on distant and anonymous targets was different than actually pulling the trigger of a gun pointed at a human being.

"They rode on without incident. Don presumed it must have been at least a half-hour or forty-five minutes later when Mr. Krol slowed down as they approached another town. He saw dozens of men on the streets, each one wearing an orange arm band. In the middle of the street just ahead, a large machine gun was mounted on a tripod. One man ran toward it and Don instinctively reached for his gun and raised it. Mr. Krol quickly said, "Is all right." The motorcycle went on past the gun, pulled off the street and stopped.

"Men approached the motorcycle and greeted Mr. Krol. It suddenly occurred to Don that these men must also be part of the underground. Mr. Krol explained, "Arm band, our symbol, all men proud to wear it now." Don felt himself relax as he realized they were among friends.

"The group of men ushered the Americans toward a large wooden barn-like structure. The door was opened, but Don and Quilla hesitated as they faced total blackness inside. They stepped inside. When the door closed, darkness enveloped them until someone lit a candle. Although the large interior was still dim, Don could see a number of men standing around them. Three men approached. The large and brawny one spoke to Mr. Krol. Don listened carefully and he heard Mr. Krol say "Amerikaan!" The large man smiled and patted a man standing near him on his back. The second man gave a welcoming gesture and repeated, "American, huh?" Don and Quilla looked at each other then at the men standing in front of them.

"Hey ... you're Americans too?" Don asked.

"One of them let out a cheer, stepped forward and extended his hand, "My God! We sure didn't expect to meet up with any of our guys here! Name's Tyson, Walter J. Tyson, first lieutenant, P-51 pilot from Long Island New York. This character is Robert Harrington, known better to his friends as 'Bobby' – he's from a little place called Newton, Iowa, ever hear of it? Also, first lieutenant, also P-51 pilot!"

"Don Barker; used to live in Long Beach, California. This is Quilla

Reed, he called Michigan home. Our B-17 didn't make it back to the base in England."

"Don said; "So ... how'd you guys end up way out here?"

"Bobby explained, "We just ran out of gas. Set our planes down in a field about four months ago and have been here ever since. We were hidden in some other part of this country, but damned if I know where that was."

"Don asked; "How did you manage to run out of gas anyway?"

"Well, we were chasin' a couple ME-109's that had been giving some Liberators a bad time," Bobby leaned toward Don, "We got so involved we just plain forgot to check the old gage. First thing we knew, we're lookin' for a place to set 'em down. Old Walt here – he was lucky, he found some grass. Me – I got out of the plane knee-deep in yucky mud." He made a face. "We've been foot-boys ever since, well ... except for a couple times when they had bicycles for us to ride."

"Not to be outdone, Reed explained about what happened to the 'Seattle Sleeper' but Don was only half-listening. He studied the other two Americans. They were dressed in clothes similar to what he wore, no doubt borrowed from their Dutch benefactors too. Even in the dim light, Don could make out the freckles on Walt's face and his thoughts were that both these two guys looked incredibly young. He turned when Walt suddenly nudged his arm.

"Heard you guys had some fireworks on the way over here too?"

Surprised, Don looked at him, "How in hell did you hear about that?"

Bobby grinned "Word gets around pal, word gets around!"

"So, what happened?" Walt asked.

"Oh ..." Reed tried to be indifferent, "there really wasn't much trouble," he pointed to the machine gun under his arm, "Sort of hard to argue with these guys." He grinned.

"For hell's sake – here we've been holed up for four months and ain't done nothing, ain't seen any Germans until we were on our way here, and then, the ones we did see were 'parading' down the road on the way out of here!"

"Reed reached over and patted Walt on the shoulder, "Hey buddy! You're just as well off, believe me ... we've seen enough to make up for you guys."

"Damned sure have." Don added. He felt his mouth twitch slightly thinking about the three Germans, but hoped it wasn't noticeable by the others. He decided in this dim light, they wouldn't have seen. He remembered what had happened to Mr. Meijering and decided that tonight's events had evened the score somewhat ... not enough ... but a little bit.

He would have preferred the incident hadn't happened, but he convinced himself that it was a case of kill or be killed.

Krol joined them. Don said: "Tell us how we get to this Heerenveen place? The place where we can find the Canadians!"

"Cross bridge. Stay on road, and then you come to large town. That is Heerenveen. You go through town to second crossroad. Turn to left. Look for big park. Canadians there, in park." Mr. Krol fashioned a smile and added, "Good luck, boys."

"Don turned to the other Americans, "Well ... are you guys with me?" But without waiting for an answer, he headed toward the door, and said over his shoulder, "Let's get going, we've wasted enough time."

"As they reached the door, Quilla turned, waved good-bye to Mr. Krol and said, "We'll be back ... you can depend on it."

"They saw absolutely no one on the road, and none of them said anything to one another. Don was surprised at how quickly they reached the town. And it was much larger than any of the villages they had been in so far. But the biggest surprise was the celebration they seemed to have joined unknowingly. Large banners streamed overhead and pieces of shredded paper littered the streets. Store front windows and fence posts glistened bright with hastily painted signs. Crowds of people waved and shouted as the American's rode past. Of course, no one knew they were Americans, to the ones who saw them, they must have considered them other Dutchmen. The orange arm bands glowed against dark drab clothing and it seemed to bind people together as the people they passed hugged one another.

"Wow, looks like we're just in time for the celebration." Walt shouted as he waved in a friendly manner to a young girl in front of one of the store windows. She smiled and beckoned to him.

"Don shouted, "Not now Tyson! We've got to get to the Canadians first ... you can celebrate later, but right now, we've got to find that park."

"Don remembered Mr. Krol's instructions, this is the first crossroad, he thought. Turn left at the second one ... they turned as directed and found the park about three blocks down this street. Barker pointed to the encampment ahead. Tanks and heavy transport trucks were stationed at the edge of a wooded area. Busy uniformed men worked around the equipment. The Americans pulled up into the park and hurriedly dropped their bicycles. They rushed past a tall Canadian wiping off a tank. The man stopped in front of them and waved his arm, dirty rag in his hand, "Hey, you men! You can't come in here .... This is a restricted area ... Stop! I said!"

The four Americans stopped. Quilla walked up to the Canadian and casually asked, "Have you got a cigarette on you, buddy?"

"Don said, "We're Americans ... Air Force ... but we've all sort of been 'missing the action 'for quite some time!"

"The Canadian turned around and shouted, "Hey everybody! We've got us some Yanks here!"

"Men ran out from behind trucks and gathered around, shaking the American's hands and bombarding them with excited questions such as "How long have you been here" ... "how did you find us" ... and "Where'd you get that artillery?"

"Don, with a sense of urgency, said, "Look guys, it's great to be here, but lives depend on our seeing the commanding officer pronto ... don't you understand?"

"At last two men stepped forward, "Come on ... we'll take you."

"Across the grass and toward a stone building, the Americans followed the two Canadians. "This used to be the caretaker's house," one of the men said as they stepped onto the porch of the building, "now ... it's our headquarters."

"The four pushed their way through the crowd that had gathered and tumbled into the building. Inside a man sat in front of a radio at the far side of the large austere room. He turned as the group was noisily ushered in, a rather bewildered look on his face.

"Another man sat at a roll-top desk but once the Americans were well inside, he stood. "Hey now, what's all this?" he asked.

"It seemed as if everyone spoke all at once. The Canadians tried to introduce the Americans and the Americans tried to explain their predicament. In the middle of the pandemonium the officer shouted, "Quiet! You – Canadians – Wait outside!"

"A startled silence overtook the men. The Canadian soldiers looked at their commanding officer and quickly exited the room.

"Now, what's this all about?" asked the officer.

"All four Americans started to speak at once, each one trying to explain the situation at the bridge. The officer looked from one to the other, then suddenly raised his hands and shook his head ... "Just a moment ... just a moment, please! Now, I understand it's something about a bridge and a German tank ... but let's get the details."

"A large detailed map with miniature bridges, houses, trees, and even fences was mounted on a slanted table. "We are presently here, at this location." The commanding officer used a pointer and indicated the former caretakers' house. "Now, where did you come from?"

"Barker used his finger to trace the route from the park, down the road

NOT HOME FOR CHRISTMAS

and to the village where they had left Mr. Krol and the others. "Here, right here! And this is the bridge. This is the building where we left our Dutch friends. The Germans are about here ..." Barker pointed to another location on the map.

"The officer studied the map impatiently, Don spoke "Please sir ... we need to get started right away. We need to get back to our friends. They have helped us ever since we dropped out of the sky and landed here ... they're underground people and we owe them an awful lot. Now we have a chance to help them."

"Bobby pleaded, "They don't have enough men without us to fight. We promised them we would come back."

The officer looked up at the Americans, "Well ... I'm sorry, but I'm afraid I cannot allow you to return. We must ensure your safety until we can get you back to your own units. Please understand ... I don't make the rules."

"A wave of disappointment swept over Don. They would not be able to go back and help their friends. The last glance of Mr. Krol's confident smile burned in Don's memory. Also, the rest of his family, Mrs. Krol, Jane, Dick and Annie, they were not going to understand why he and Quilla had left without saying goodbye. But at the time, they surely did not know they would not be returning.

"The officer turned to his radio man, "Spears, give a call to Sergeant Mellon."

"A tall lanky soldier appeared in moments. He saluted the officer then turned toward the four Americans. "I heard there were some Yanks here about ... so welcome fellows!"

"The officer said; "See to it that they get something to eat. And Mellon, I believe they could use a shower and some clean clothes. See if you can't come up with something for them to wear."

"They stepped outside, walked across the park and into one of the larger buildings. Once inside, Canadian soldiers flocked to surround the Americans as Mellon ushered them to a long table. Don had to smile as he watched the men scramble for a nearby seat. A large man in a white apron approached the table. With a grin he told the Americans, "I think I can scrounge up some scrambled eggs if that suits you Yanks!"

"Bobby's eyes opened wide, "Real eggs, y'mean?"

"The cook nodded.

"Hey, did you hear that guys," Bobby was elated, "real eggs! I figure I could eat a whole dozen all by myself."

"Where in hell did you find real eggs? Don't tell me the Brits dropped them down in a nearby field!" Walt looked around.

"No, the people in this village presented them to us as a welcoming gift," the cook replied, "they probably came from all around the countryside." He smiled broadly as he added, "And I think we just might have enough for our American friends." He turned and headed toward the makeshift kitchen in one end of the building.

"After their eggs and toast the Americans went to see the commanding officer again who said: "You'll be leaving shortly. I may not be available then, so let me wish you good luck, and a good trip home."

"Have you heard anything about our friends at the bridge?" Reed interrupted.

"Our units have relieved them. Your friends are probably all safe in their homes by this time."

"Barker extended his hand. "Thanks ... I mean, thank you sir ... for helping our friends. It's been a pleasure meeting you and your men. Your hospitality was most welcome, as was the breakfast."

"The officer returned his handshake, and then in turn, shook the hands of the other three Americans. "It has been our pleasure. Right after the mail is delivered here, our mail jeep will take you to our rear headquarters. As the Americans walked out, they heard him say once again, "And, good luck, Yanks."

"The four walked through the park. "Hey, there's the jeep!" Walt pointed. They saw a soldier unloading mail bags from the jeep. He looked up at the Americans. "Hey, are you guys the Yanks I'm supposed to pick up? Well then, let's not waste any more time. Let's get going!" The corporal said as he climbed into the drivers' side and started the motor.

"All four Americans climbed into the jeep. The corporal pulled the jeep onto the street and headed down past the park and out onto a country road.

"Quilla watched the flat countryside pass by and commented, "You know what's really ironic? We can't even say where we've been ... 'because at the moment, we don't know where 'that' was! You know what I'm saying?"

"Yep, sure do," Don replied, "Even if we knew the names of the towns or villages where we've been ... we still wouldn't really know where 'that' was, not knowing anything about this country. It all seems like some kind of a dream to me. Maybe a 'nightmare' would probably describe it better.

"In Nijmegen the little group boarded a C-47 that brought them to Paris. They stayed in the French capital for a couple of days and then boarded a train with destination Camp Chestefield in Le Havre.

NOT HOME FOR CHRISTMAS

"Their stay at Camp Chesterfield was for six long days. On the sixth day, a voice over the loudspeaker announced that each man would be assigned to the ship in accordance to the region in the United States in which he lived. Each specific group was to be designated to an area on the ship. Don learned that he, Walt and Bobby would be in a group of thirty-two men that would dock at New York City.

"From the far end of the camp, they could see the big ship at anchor. Don stared at it as he stood inside the tall fence, and tried to imagine himself sailing across the ocean on it. He had never been on a large ship before and tried to imagine what it would be like. They had flown to England on their own B-17 after training was completed. In his mind he wished there was a plane available for the trip home also but it appeared they were destined to sail instead.

"The following day, it seemed the waiting to get checked out of the camp and onto the ship took forever. They joined the hundreds of men lining the deck railing, shouting and waving to those on the shore. They could see the encampment where they had stayed. They did not know exactly what lay ahead of them but none of the three regretted leaving Camp Chesterfield.

"On the sixth day at sea, the Captain made an announcement that they would be arriving in New York City in two more days. Then to the delight of all the men on board the big ship, the Captain told them they had been able to pick up some radio signals from the States, and would broadcast some 'good old American music' for their enjoyment. He watched some of the men who listened, sway back and forth to the beat and tap their feet. The announcer introduced the Andrews Sisters, singing "Rum and Coke-a-Cola" – Bing Crosby, singing "Don't Fence Me In" – and there was one crazy one about mare's eating oats! He thought the words were dumb, but he couldn't help himself – he enjoyed every bit of it.

"Suddenly in the middle of one song they were playing, the radio announcer broke in with a news update. The man's voice broke as he announced that the war in Europe had ended! Don couldn't believe what he was hearing. He looked around at the others, he didn't know exactly what he expected, something like hats being thrown in the air – dancing in the aisles, so to speak – loud voices cheering, but he heard nothing. No one cheered, throughout the crowd, nothing but dead silence. Don realized everyone else was just like him, too stunned to react in any manner. When he heard the radio voice again giving the date, May the 8th, 1945, he decided it was a day he would never forget. His thoughts were strictly that; he was alive, he was well, and he was almost home.

"As they approached New York harbour two days later, the three friends were standing at the railing of the big ship and watched as another ship pulled alongside. Its deck was crowded with people waving American flags and shouting in their direction. A band played the "Star Spangled Banner" and each and every soldier on deck immediately came to attention. Don felt the huge lump in his throat and figured that everyone else on the ship must be finding it difficult to swallow at this moment. After the salute to their country, the band on the other ship played a lively march while the people lined up at the railing continued shouting welcoming remarks. This must be the first ship to arrive in New York since the war ended, thought Don. As they neared the dock, the horns from several fireboats tooted and coloured water spewed into the air. Other private boats in the surrounding water joined in with toots and whistles and the occupants waving and shouting.

"For the first time, Don saw the Statue of Liberty. He said aloud, "Lady, if you ever want to see me again, you'll have to turn around and look the other way – you know – westward!" He was home.

In February 1946, Dick Trombley's mother wrote to Gosse Roodenboog, who had picked up her son on that fateful Sunday in November, 1944:

"Your letter received and I have sent it on to Richard. He is living about one hundred miles from here in Springfield, Vermont. He worked there a year before he enlisted in the Air Corps. I want to thank you boys for saving my son's life. I'll never forget how you people were so brave and good to our boys.

"There was five months that I didn't know whether he was dead or alive. Well, he arrived home in the U.S.A. on May 13, 1945 and I certainly was one thankful and happy mother. After what he had to tell, about you people in Holland we can never forget you.

"His leg was healed, and it was quite a scar but he was thankful that it was not worse. He is now married to a girl he had before going over to England.

"I hope this letter reaches you all right and I wish all the best of luck and God bless you both for having saved our boys."

In May 1997, a certain Willem van der Ploeg of Donkerbroek in the Netherlands wrote to the Trombley family:

"Saturday, April 22, 1995 I went for practising my favourite hobby. Armed with my metal detector I went over the former skating ring in Haulerwijk, where I earlier had dug up some coins dating from my childhood days. That morning I heard a beautiful sound in my headphone. Tension rose: what would this yield. Soon I recognized in the shiny piece of metal the shape of a bracelet without chain. Wiping it clean on the grass I tried to decipher the applied inscription.

"It was no Dutch marking, but an English name. Yes, I read it well after all: "R.A. Trombley 11056622" with on the backside: "Love Peggie". As a flash of light I remembered a story about a pilot who landed in WW II on this piece of land.

"I had to go home! History had to be researched!

"I contacted the "Resistance Museum" but was directed to the "War Graves Foundation" in The Hague and Belgium. No result. Next I wrote a letter to the British Embassy that was passed on the Air Attaché of the American Embassy. No positive result either.

"Then I read in a newspaper about the visit of Quilla Reed and his

Visit of Quilla Reed to Haulerwijk, May 1997. Shown left to right: Marje Hadderingh, Joke and Gosse Roodenboog, Quilla Reed and Henk "Bill" Woering.

wife to Haulerwijk. I contacted the reception committee and they had the complete list of Quilla's crew as they had bailed out over Haulerwijk on Sunday, November 26, 1944. Richard Trombley was on that list. I have handed the bracelet over to Quilla."

Richard "Dick" Trombley died January 28, 2006 at his residence in Colchester, VT. The Green Mountain College in Poultney, Vermont, writes about Dick in their Athletics Hall of Fame:

"Dick is the personification of Green Mountain's sportsmanship code, a fine athlete and a gentleman on and off the field. He was an outstanding three-sport athlete, member of the basketball and track teams and co-captain and member of the football team. In football, Dick was a triple-threat on offence and a deadly tackler on defence. He was a solid basketball player and performed well in track and field.

***

Acknowledgements:
U.S.A.
Pilot   John Stevens
Dorothy Johnson for co-pilot Stanley Johnson
Navigator   John C. Weisgarber Sr.
Bobye Barker   for bombardier Marbry "Don" Barker
Top-Turret Gunner   Quilla Reed
Martha Reid   for waist-gunner Richard "Dick" Trombley
Tail-Gunner   Henry "Hank" St. George
Denise Labs   for tail-gunner Henry St. George
Robert St. George   for tail-gunner Henry St. George
Netherlands.
Jan Hey   for summary of MACR
Sander Reinders   Haulerwijk
Melle Postma   Haulerwijk
Dick Krol   Haulerwijk
Col. Arie de Jong for tail-gunner Henry St. George
Job Woltman   for tail-gunner Henry St. George
Ab Jansen   author of "Sporen aan de Hemel
Willem van der Ploeg   for waist-gunner Richard "Dick" Trombley

CHAPTER 8

91ˢᵗ BOMB GROUP
324ᵀᴴ BOMB SQUADRON

Aircraft Type: B17G, Serial # 42-38128
"Dear Becky", MACR: 10838
Airbase: Bassingbourn

"I felt like I died and went to heaven when I finally got to my parents front door, and after that we stayed up and talked the rest of the night and gave thanks that I made it back home."

—Pilot Adolph Miller when he returned home on June 19, 1945

Pilot: 2Lt Adolph P. Miller Jr. (POW) Texarkana TX
Co-Pilot: 2Lt Richard E. Prunty (KIA) Charleston NV
Navigator: 2Lt Thomas A. Bottomley Jr. (POW) Dillsburg PA
Bombardier: S/Sgt Alton Lowe (POW) Cairo IL
Top-Turret: S/Sgt Thomas E. Kincade (POW) Ardmore PA
Radio-Operator: S/Sgt Daniel D. Moynihan Jr. (POW) Flushing NY
Ball Turret: Sgt Lester R. Pearson (POW) Sumner WA
Waist-Gunner R.: Sgt William S. Hurtley (POW) Mondovi WI
Tail-Gunner: Sgt Glenn C. Knudson (POW) Larimore ND

Total: 1 KIA, 8 POW
Target: Altenbeken rail-road viaduct
Place of Crash: Elstener Swamps, Germany. SE of Cloppenburg
Time of Crash: 11.00

NOT HOME FOR CHRISTMAS

S/Sgt. John R. Rosenthal during debriefing after the mission.

> "About ten minutes prior to the Initial Point, altitude about 21.000 feet, we were attacked by about seventy-five enemy fighters. At this time I observed aircraft B-17G, serial # 42-38128, to be hit by enemy aircraft fire and the No. 2 engine caught fire. The aircraft flew along with the formation for approximately two minutes during which time I saw two men leave the ship. I did not see their parachutes open and believe that they made delayed jumps. Immediately afterwards, the aircraft slid to the left of the formation and exploded, disintegrating completely."

Pilot **Adolph P. Miller, Jr.** and his twin brother John Frank were born in 1922 in Fort Worth, where their father worked as a railway mail clerk. The family moved to Texarkana in 1924.

Adolph graduation from High School in January 1940, he went to work for the Hotel Grim Drug Store, where he operated the soda fountain for a wage of ten cents an hour.

"We sold hamburgers for five cents a piece, but working fifty-nine hours a week for $5.90 a week made me realize I needed to further my education," Adolph said in summer 2006 in an interview with the *Texarkana Gazette.*

Adolph started attending Bethany Nazarene College in Bethany, Oklahoma in the fall of 1940. "We went to the Nazarene Church when we were kids," Adolph said in the same interview, "The pastor took us up to that college to visit one day and that's how we eventually enrolled. He was instrumental in getting us there."

In September 26, 1944, the then 20 years old Adolph was inducted into the U.S. Army Air Corps. On February 7, 1944, he received his wings at Stockton.

He flew his first mission on November 2, to the fuel plant at Merseburg, Germany .

Miller and his crew were told that the November 26, 1944, mission would be a milk run, lasting only six hours ten minutes. Having flown to Merseburg on three of their first five missions, the crew felt confident.

After the usual early morning briefing and formation over England, the "Dear Becky" crew was on their way to the railroad viaduct at Altenbeken, Germany.

"After leaving the initial point, we were struck by a wave of ME-109s coming in a line abreast, approaching from our right," Adolph recalls.

One of the bomber's four engines burst into flames immediately and soon the whole plane was on fire and full of smoke on the inside.

"My co-pilot Richard Prunty was killed on the first pass the fighters made," Miller said. "I put the plane on autopilot as the aircraft took a steady downwards descent. The bomb bay doors wouldn't open, the communication system was out, and fire was raging everywhere."

Miller said he hoped the crew members in the rear of the aircraft realized that parachuting out was the only option.

"I got out through the forward hatch along with Tom Bottomly, the navigator, and I pulled my ripcord immediately after exiting the aircraft. I estimated I was between 15.000 and 20.000 feet.

"It was a beautiful descent, although scary with the battle continuing all around," he recalls. "I could tell there were other planes hit because I counted nineteen parachutes during the trip down."

Miller did not make it to the ground because he got dragged through tree tops and stuck in one of them.

"Immediately, I realized that quite a crowd had gathered below me," Miller remembers. Some had guns and other had clubs, hoes, rakes; but my real concern was to get down before someone used me for target practice."

Fortunately for Miller, some German soldiers at the scene took charge.

"They asked for my pistol – I had none because our commanding officer wouldn't let us fly with side arms, "Miller said to the Texarkana Gazette reporter. "He told us no one could fight their way out of Germany with just a pistol."

After taking Miller's fleece-lined flying jacket, his watch, and rings, the soldiers dismissed the crowd and started walking him to the woods.

"Not speaking German, I had no idea what their game plan was," Miller said. "I thought at first they might be taken me into the woods to shoot me. However, such was not the case because we soon came upon a farmhouse used by their military."

NOT HOME FOR CHRISTMAS

Ulrich Haussmann
Innsbruck /AUSTRIA
Sonnenstr. 30 (French Zone)

Mr. Adolf Paul Miller Jr.
1619 , 9th street
Bowie, Tex.

Dear Mr Miller,

Or should I just say dear Tex? I bet I've got you guessing who the writer of this letter may be. The solution would be really too hard if I would not help you along. First turn the hands of the clock back two years. You then were shot from the sky, and were brought to an interrogation camp for grilling . First they frisked and mugged you , to use the nearly appropriate slang and then they stuck you into a cell all by yourself, in other words buried you alive. That is how about one feel going through the whole ordeal. (I know as well as you do , because I had to go through the same thing a few month afterwords.) You were then brought into an office to a man with a goatee. This officer whom you distrusted at first very much, turned out a pretty decent sort of fellow, according to your own judgement. Funny how little things , normally selfunderstood things become so important. I just think how much you appreciated that shave. Same here. They gave us one razor blade in four month so I just let the old whiskers grow into hillbilly style. But now they are all gone. , goatee and everything and the ragman who returned from the PW camp has transformed himself into a respectable looking civilian.

And yet there is a vast diffenrence between us. You returned to the land of plenty, whereas I came home into a devastated land of need. I found my home standing but my wife and kids together with a sick sister badly undernurfished and star/ved. . They sure would make swell extras for a concentration camp film. To have to stand by without being able to help, is enough to xxx drive a man crazy. Because, no doubt, if things keep up as they are now for any length of time will result in a serious harming of the childrens health and growth.

For this reason I am sending out a SOS call. Should you or any of your friends feel inclined go lend a helping hand to the starving children in Europe I would be thankful from my deepest if you would think of my kids, because they a p e in dire need. I have a job and I have money and yet the rations are far too short. There is a drive on in the States for 'Care packages' to be distributed

91st Bomb Group, 324th Bomb Squadron

in Europe. I bet they've got an agency in your town. Or what if you would make up a package yourself containing some lard, sugar, cocoa, and powdered milk. That would hit the spot better still, because those are the things children need most and are not contained in the care packages. The only danger of such individual parcels is that they arrive here half or threequarter empty whereas 'care packages' have to be picked up by the adressee personally at the US distributing agency and furthermore it goes much quicker because the CP are here already and are handed out upon notice.

Please understand my motives right. I hate to be thought of as a scrounger, but a man will go a long stretch when his little one are starving. And I am sure you are coming to Europe later on on a visit, when times are normal and then I shall gladly more than reciprocate. I live in about the most beautiful town in Europe, cupped in by high mountains and you would sure enjoy it here. But such things are probably a few years off yet.

For the holidays I am wishing you lots of fun and the very best for the year 1947. I would love t receive from you a nice long letter telling me, how you fared after you left me, where you were at camp, how you went home and what you are doing now. By the way I am writing a book about the old Dulag titled: Name, Rank, and Number revealing all the inside dope on Dulag-Luft. I shall let you know when it comes out.

With best regards sincerely yours

PS: Should you really be able to send something pleas adress it to my wife, because I am on the road a lot and may not be able to pick it up personally. for a long time and hurry is needed.

    Frau
      Cornelia Haussmann
      ~~xxxxxxxx~~ /AUSTRIA
      Innsbruck / AUSTRIA
      Sonnenstr. 30 (French Zone)

This letter which I had addressed to you and had left off a Texasarma returned yesterday. So I am trying again. 4 Febr. 47

Two-page letter from German interrogator Ulrich Haussman to Pilot Adolph P. Miller

From there Miller was taken to a nearby airfield.

"I stayed there two days and nights before being taken to the interrogation centre at Oberurssel. It was night and two other POW's and I where being walked through Frankfort when the air raid warning sirens sounded. We were ushered into the air raid shelter along with the local residents, but, lucky for us, Frankfurt was not the target that night."

Upon arrival in Oberurssel, Miller's captors took his shoes from him and placed him in a small cell with only a straw mattress in it.

"The window in it was small with shimmering glass, which only let you know whether it was day or night," he said. "For rations, I was given a jug of water and two slices of black bread a day. After six days, I was taken for interrogation and asked multiple questions, to which I gave only my name, rank and serial number."

About co-pilot **Richard E. Prunty,** Shirley Murdoch, whose mother was Richard Prunty's sister, wrote in 2005:

"The Prunty family came to America from Ireland in 1749. They married into the Finney family, who had arrived in America from Ireland in the late 1500's. Since that time, our line of the family has remained in agriculture. My great grandparents came to Nevada in 1889. At that time they homesteaded the ranch that the family still lives on. Richard was the oldest son and, therefore, the first heir to the ranch. After he died it went to his two brothers Harold (Corky) and Franklin (Shorty). Both brothers have since passed away. The ranch is now run by my aunt and cousins. If you would like more information about the Prunty ranch you can find it on www.pruntyhorses.com. This site will show you where Richard was born and raised. The ranch has really not changed at all since his death. They now use vehicles in addition to horses, but most of the work is exactly the same as when Richard did it. He went on the same round-ups and branded in the same corrals. The houses, barns, and corrals are all the same as when he was there."

91st Bomb Group, 324th Bomb Squadron

German report KU 3374 pertaining to the death of co-pilot Richard E. Prunty. Stating that he died on November 26, 1944 at Hemmelte, Germany and was buried in the POW cemetery in Vechta, Germany. Remarks in English were added after the war by US officials.

```
                                    Charleston, Nevada
                                       July 6, 1945
J. A. Ulio
Washingtion 25, D. C.

Dear Sir
       We have received a letter from the pilot of the B17 my son was on
He writes that my son Richard was not hurt when he bailed our of the plane,
but that when the rest of the crew were taken to a station by the German
that Richard was not there.
Have you ever received his tag or any information concerning Richard E.
Prunty. Was he injured when he hit the groud or was he killed by the
Germans? I wish I knew the case of his death. If he is dead. Also the
burial place. Please help me to get more information if possible.
                                   Sincerely

                                   Mrs. Earl Prunty

P.S. We have never received any of Richards belongings from England.


                        C
                         O
                          P
                           Y
                           of handwritten letter
```

Transcription of a letter from the mother of Co-Pilot Richard E. Prunty.

NOT HOME FOR CHRISTMAS

Waist-gunner **William S. Hurtley** was born Aug 10, 1925 in Movdovi, Wisconsin to Archie and Rose Hurtley. He attended school Mondovi and graduated from Mondovi High School in May of 1943.

After graduation, his family moved to California where William worked at Solar Aircraft Factory until he was inducted into the U.S. Army Air Corps in January of 1944. He was shipped overseas to England in October 1944 and joined the 91st Bomb Group based at Bassingbourn in Cambridgeshire.

After the war he wrote about his last flight in WW II:

"We were on a mission to Altenbeken Germany on Sunday, November 26, 1944 when the bomber I served on was hit by fighter planes. The plane burst into flames and the crew had to jump for their lives. I landed outside Altenbeken, and was captured by German civilians. I was searched and taken into a house near by. They bandaged my wounds, while I waited for the German military to come and get me.

"When the German military came, I was loaded into a truck along with other prisoners and taken to a hospital. There my wounds were treated and bandaged again. Then we were taken to a little town near Altenbeken and confined in a place that looked like a jail. We were confined there one day. For food they gave us some kind of thin soup and nothing else.

"On 28 November we were placed on a train and taken to Frankfort. They questioned us about all phases of air warfare. We stayed in that place about a day and a half. For food, they gave us some thin soup and some vile tasting dark bread that was hard as stone.

"From Frankfort we were taken to Wetzlar. This seemed to be an assignment and distribution camp. Until arrival in this place, we barely had enough food to keep us going. Here we got some Red Cross food parcels. They were sent to the mess halls and divided. For food they gave us potatoes mixed with meat and things from our parcels.

"Next transfer was to Grosstychow, Germany. I was confined there until 6 February 1945. We were crowded into small rooms. There were about 25 men in a room, 10 by 30. Bunks were three tiers high. The first three weeks after arriving, I had to sleep on two tables placed together.

"I had no work assignments at this place. We received one Red Cross food parcel about once a week. The Red Cross parcels were always damaged and taken apart. We were allowed one item a day from these parcels. For breakfast we would get a cup to thin coffee and at noon a cup of some kind of thin soup. At night we would get some potatoes mixed with corned beef or meats taken from our parcels. We were allowed one eighth of a loaf of bread per day per man. One day when a German guard lost his pass, we were accused of stealing it and our food ration was reduced for a week.

"On February 6th, we had to leave Grosstychow. The Russians had advanced close to this place, so the Germans had to move us. We were forced to march twenty or more kilometres a day until we reached Stalag 357 south of Hanover. When we left Grosstychow, we were allowed to take one Red Cross parcel with us. At night they would confine us in barns. For food they dumped in a few bushels of potatoes, we had to scramble for them. We never had enough to eat.

"One time we marched all day and then at midnight we got some thin soup from a wagon that went by. The evening we slept in the rain.

"When the British came close to Stalag 357, we started marching again, and re-crossed the river Elbe. Then the Russians approached and we turned about again. We marched rather aimlessly. They confined us to barns at night and the food always consisted of potatoes, but not enough of them. While marching, we went into potato fields and carried all the potatoes we could stuff into our shirts. We took turnip tops and made soup from them. We traded cigarettes and soap for onions, salt and extra potatoes.

They finally marched us to the British lines and we were liberated.

William was liberated May 2, 1945. He was awarded the Purple Heart because he was wounded in the shoulder and arm from cannon fire.

He returned to Mondovi, WI, and worked as an electrician constructing electric high lines in Wisconsin and other states. Bill never married. He passed away in April 1979 of heart attack, survived by two sisters and a brother.

William was buried in Mondovi with full military honours conducted by the Mondovi American Legion Post.

About tail-gunner **Glenn C. Knudson,** Edith Lee wrote the following:

"In December, 1943, a North Dakota farm boy who was "crazy about airplanes" enlisted in the U.S. Air Corps, hoping to become a pilot. The Air

NOT HOME FOR CHRISTMAS

Force had enough pilots but they needed gunners; so angrily protesting, Sgt. Glenn Knudson became an aerial gunner.

"In the crew of nine, Knudson and co-pilot Richard Prunty became especially close friends. When Prunty was piloting the B-17, he often invited Knudson join him in the cockpit. Sometimes Prunty let him fly the plane although that was against regulations.

"The crew made three bombing missions over Germany. The first plane they flew back to England in good condition. The second was flown home shot to pieces by anti-aircraft fire but remained in the air. Their third plane was riddled with bullet holes and caught fire. That was on Sunday, November 26, 1944.

"The crew was ordered to bail out and by the time Sgt. Knudson squirmed forward out of his cramped tail gunner's position and over the bomb load, the pilot and crew members had jumped. Co-pilot Prunty

Front Row from l. to r.: Pilot 2Lt. Adolph P. Miller Jr., Co-Pilot 2Lt. Richard E. Prunty, Navigator 2Lt. Bottomley, *Bombardier Joe Nieaecks
Bottom Row: *Engineer Andrew G. Lucas, Radio-operator S/Sgt. Daniel D. Moynihan, *Gunner John Nelson, Ball Turret Sgt. Lester R. Pearson, Waist-Gunner Sgt. William S. Hurtley, Tail-Gunner Sgt. Glenn C. Knudson
* did not participate in this mission.

226

was holding the plane on course, allowing the men to jump, and tried to remain high to avoid enemy fire. Knudson bailed out and remembered waiting what seemed a long time before he pulled the rip cord and floated down. A hero who saved his crew, Prunty never got out of the plane. When he returned to the United States a year later Knudson contacted and talked to Prunty's mother. She had lost her only son.

"Glenn was taken prisoner. In January 1945, two months after he had bailed out, he started the 600-mile trek across northern Germany from the Baltic Sea until his liberation during the following April. The terrible walk started when Soviet troops were moving west. During one of the severest winters northern Germany had experienced, 8000 U.S. and British prisoners (nearly all of them airmen) began a forced march that was completed 86 days later, east of Hamburg, by 5.500 starving, crippled men on April, 1945.

"Their path was littered with by the bodies of men who had died on the march – from diphtheria, pneumonia, dysentery, pellagra, exposure. They endured frostbite and slept on the frozen ground. They got wagons to transport the ill but no horses; the men had to pull the wagons. Knudson told his wife years later that he repeated his catechism lessons as he walked and it helped. He remembered all he had learned for confirmation.

"When the prisoners were handed over to allied forces they were taken to hospitals in England. Ole and Emma Knudson in Hegton Township learned that their son was no longer "lost in action" but was coming home when well enough.

"When they had been fed regularly in the hospitals somewhat, they were shipped across the Atlantic, then put on trains to go west across America to a rest camp in Washington.

"Airman Glenn Knudson stepped off the train in Larrimore and went home. He spent two weeks with his parents then resumed his train ride to Washington. When he entered the rest camp, the Air Corps busted him a rank for going home AWOL.

"When he left the service Knudson wanted to be an engineer. He enrolled at the University of North Dakota in Grand Forks but he found that he couldn't stand being in crowds and around people all the time.

"He went back to his father's farm. The first thing he did was get his pilot's license, taking flying lessons from Vince Buraas in Northwood.

"One day the Knudsons were moving grain bins when a young girl rode by "on a crazy horse". Glen asked his brother Ivan who "that wild rider" was. It was Joyce Gullikson, daughter of a neighbour.

"Orin Knudson set up a blind date for his brother Glenn and Joyce. In

NOT HOME FOR CHRISTMAS

March, 1947, the couple went to the parsonage in Mekinock to exchange their vows, "Neither of us had any money". Joyce's aunt made the wedding cake and her little brother Jerry managed to get his share before the cake was cut.

"They farmed, living in the house where Glenn was born. They bought one more quarter of land and farmed in Hegton Township where many of their neighbours were Glenn's brothers and, later, his nephews. His wife said; "I was the hired man".

"Early years he was ill some. Sometimes he jumped from their bed, ready to bail out of the plane. Gradually the marks from his war years faded.

"Then there were good years: Joyce took flying lessons from Vince Buraas too, so she could solo. Then she did Glenn do the flying and they did a good deal of it.

"They had three daughters – Cathy, Merle and Wanda – who were pride and joy to the Knudsons. They bought horses so Joyce and the girls could ride while Glenn flew. Glenn did some inventing and engineering, getting several patents and even earning some money from that sideline.

"The girls grew up ambitious and achieving. They all married and each family had two sons and Wanda had a girl too. Glenn and Joyce were happy farmers and happy grandparents.

"In 1997 Glenn contracted cancer. They drove to Grand Forks for chemo treatment. There were heavy snows that cold winter and deer starved and froze. One day as he and Joyce drove by one dead deer after another on their way to Grand Forks Glenn broke down and cried; "That's like we died," he said, "and that's how we left the dead in the snow."

"Mostly, his life was far away from the cold and the snow. He got to fly. He married the girl he chose. He farmed his home farm with family all around him. He made his parents proud, his children made him proud, and he watched his grandchildren grow and bloom. He served his country and his God.

"Well done, Glenn Knudson.

Report filled out after the war by bombardier Alton Lowe (page from MACR 10838)

***

Acknowledgements:
For pilot Miller: Interview with the *Texarkana Gazette,* Summer 2006.
For waist-gunner Hurtley: Malvin Koehn, brother-in-law
For tail-gunner Glenn Knudson: Edith Lee.
For co-pilot Prunty: Shirley Murdoch

CHAPTER 9

305TH BOMB GROUP
365TH BOMB SQUADRON

Aircraft Type: B-17G, Serial # 43-37955,
MACR 11202
Airbase: Chelveston

> *"Hide. Some one will come for you tonight."*
> —A Dutch woman said to waist-gunner Lattimore after he had landed on Dutch soil

Pilot: 2Lt Henry D. Schmid (POW) Coachella CA
Co-Pilot: 2Lt Owen L. Mayberry (EVD) Fair Oaks CA
Navigator: 2Lt Terrence F. Messing (POW) Caceola NE
Bombardier: Sgt Theodore "Ted" E. Roblee (EVD) Milwaukee WI
Top-Turret: S/Sgt Thomas "Ton" G. Horger (POW) Dearborn MI
Radio-Operator: S/Sgt Robert E. Willson (POW) Magnolia MS
Ball Turret: Sgt Leo C. Wloczewski (POW) West Natrona PA
Waist-Gunner: Sgt Thomas W. Lattimore Jr. (POW) Sullivan MO
Tail-Gunner: Sgt Keith D. Hereford (POW) Fort Scott KS

Total: 7 POW, 2 EVD
Target: Synthetic fuel plant at Misburg, Germany

NOT HOME FOR CHRISTMAS

Summary of Missing air Crew Report 11202, made by Jan Hey of the Netherlands:

"Bomber was hit by flak over the target area. One prop had to be feathered. When, on return, a fire developed all bailed out north of Deventer, Netherlands.

"When all had jumped, the B-17 exploded in mid-air and crashed near the farm of Mr. G.J. Rechterschot in the hamlet called Tjoene, Community of Diepenveen near Deventer. A barn was destroyed by fire and the brother of the farmer was killed under one of the wings. The location is near the Monastery "Sion", at the left side of the road from Deventer to Raalte, Community of Olst.

" Co-pilot Owen Mayberry and bombardier Theodore Roblee evaded at Olst."

Top-turret gunner **Thomas "Ton" G. Horger** wrote the author in 2004:

"I was a nineteen year old from Dearborn, Michigan when I entered the Army Air Corps in February, 1943.

"It was a cold, clear morning in England on Sunday, November 26, 1944. There were three squadrons, 12 planes to a squadron, and 36 in a group. They were positioned high, low and lead squadron. Plane 43-37955 was in the lead squadron, flying at 25,000 feet.

"Ted Roblee, the bombardier, opened the bomb doors at the initial point which was about 25 miles from the target, Misburg in Germany. The lead bomber salvoed his bombs, led by two bombs trailing smoke. All the other planes in the group dropped their bomb load at the same time, following the trail of smoke. The bomb doors were closed right after the release of the bombs to decrease resistance.

"The plane was hit within seconds of hearing "bomb door fully closed" from Willson, the radio-operator. It sounded like a huge firecracker going off in a box, a very hollow sound. The plane left the formation, dropping immediately. I got out of the top-turret and looked at the engine instruments. All the needles on the gauges were jumping, except for #2 engine. Every instrument for that engine read zero. Co-pilot Mayberry hit the feathering switch on #2 engine but it would not feather. It windmilled the rest of the time. They feathered #1 engine. The plane went into a long glide from there, with a little power, but not enough to maintain altitude.

"Three fighter escorts flew along side and waved, staying with our plane. We threw everything not needed, out of the plane to lighten the load – guns, ammo, anything loose. At 12,000 feet, the plane was hit again by flak. There was no visible damage, and that hit did not hamper the flight any further.

"At 1200 feet, Schmid, the pilot, said, "We're going to jump." I said that I was going to jump from the waist. I grabbed my shoes so I would be able to walk when we hit the ground (to replace the soft heated boots that we wore on the plane), and my parachute. I went through the bomb bay, into the radio room, and told Wilson that we were going to jump. Wilson and I went back into the waist, where someone had already kicked out the waist door. Our tail-gunner Keith Hereford was standing at the waist door when we arrived, along with waist-gunner Lattimore and Wloczewski, our ball-turret gunner. We all looked forward to the front of the plane, where Schmid waved us out. Hereford bent over, grabbed his knees, and rolled out. We all followed right after him.

"It was a sunny, chilly mid afternoon. We all landed within 700-800 feet of each other because we jumped at such a low altitude. We hid our parachutes and Mae Wests where they would not be noticed, and hid ourselves in a small wooded area. There were people wandering around in the area. They told us to stay until dark and they would come and get us. Before dark, armed German soldiers arrived and captured our group.

"The German soldiers marched us into a village approximately two miles from where we came down. They took us one at a time into a house where we were strip searched. After that, they loaded us into a half-track truck and drove us to a schoolhouse, where we stayed that night and the next day, until about 11 pm. The night of Nov. 27, 1944 the Germans put all of us on a small bus. There were five men already on the right side of the bus and two men on the left, where we also sat. Everything was blacked out. We recognized the voices of navigator Terrence Messing and Schmid on the bus.

"Every time we hit a pothole in the road, which was frequent due to the blackout conditions, the men on the right side of the bus would cuss out the driver loud and clear.

"We arrived at a factory or warehouse as daylight broke. The Germans asked us to help the men on the right to get out of the bus. They were all bandaged up and in bad shape. We helped them into the factory and never knew what happened to them from there. We assumed they were from the air corps. At the factory, we were interrogated. The Germans were interested in the names of the co-pilot and bombardier. They were still on the loose.

NOT HOME FOR CHRISTMAS

"From there eight of us were taken to the main interrogation center in Frankfort by passenger train with two guards. I remember arriving at Frankfort, but have no recollection of being there or how I was taken to Wetzlar, my next stop. From Wetzlar, we were put on boxcars and taken to Stalag Luft IV. The trip took three days, without food and with very little water. It was so crowded in the boxcars that we were unable to lay down so we sat or stood the entire trip. The first part of February, we were marched out and remained on the road until we were liberated by the English on May 2, 1945

Bombardier **Theodore "Ted" Roblee**:

TOP SECRET.
I.S.9 (WEA)

APPENDIX "C" TO E. & E. REPORT No. IS9WEA/1/324.

If further circulation of this information is made, it is important that its source should not be divulged.

No. 36827301   Rank Sjt   Name ROBLEE Theodore Edward.

Date of Interview 31 Mar 45.

GSGS 4416, 1:100,000 Sheet N.1.

a. Miss BAKE, OLST (8916)
   6 days (27 Nov - 3 Dec 44) Board and lodging.

b. On an estate belonging to an Englishman and his sister situated, I was told, one km NE of OLST (8916) I lived in the house of his chauffeur.
   8 days (6 DEC - 14 DEC 44) Board and lodging.

c. BERNARD PRINZEN, 74, IJZERLO.
   3½ months (14 DEC 44 - 30 MAR 45)
   Board and loding. Clothes.

Evasion Report Bombardier Ted Roblee.

305th Bomb Group, 365th Bomb Squadron

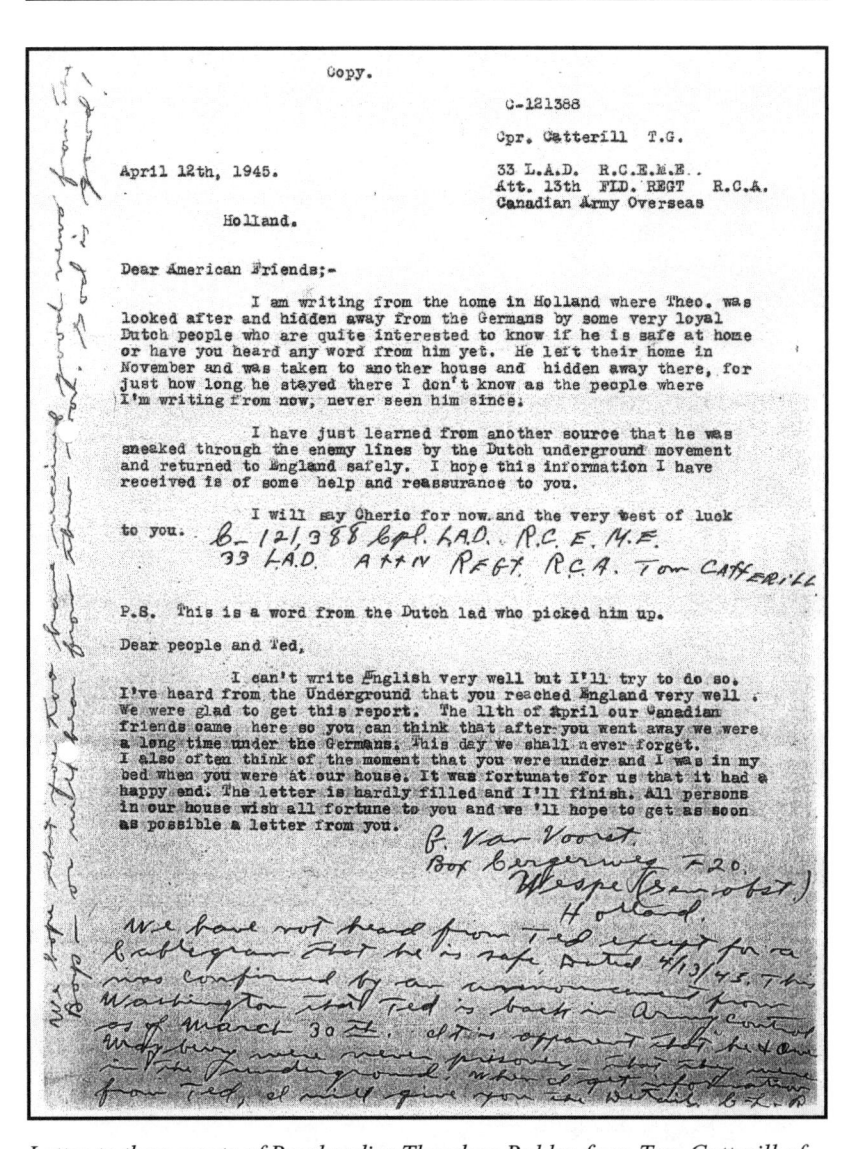

Copy.

C-121388
Cpr. Catterill T.G.
33 L.A.D. R.C.E.M.E..
Att. 13th FLD. REGT R.C.A.
Canadian Army Overseas

April 12th, 1945.

Holland.

Dear American Friends;-

I am writing from the home in Holland where Theo. was looked after and hidden away from the Germans by some very loyal Dutch people who are quite interested to know if he is safe at home or have you heard any word from him yet. He left their home in November and was taken to another house and hidden away there, for just how long he stayed there I don't know as the people where I'm writing from now, never seen him since.

I have just learned from another source that he was sneaked through the enemy lines by the Dutch underground movement and returned to England safely. I hope this information I have received is of some help and reassurance to you.

I will say Cherio for now and the very best of luck to you. C-121,388 Cpl. L.A.D. R.C.E.M.F. 33 L.A.D. ATTN REGT. R.C.A. Tom CATTERILL

P.S. This is a word from the Dutch lad who picked him up.

Dear people and Ted,

I can't write English very well but I'll try to do so. I've heard from the Underground that you reached England very well. We were glad to get this report. The 11th of April our Canadian friends came here so you can think that after-you went away we were a long time under the Germans. This day we shall never forget. I also often think of the moment that you were under and I was in my bed when you were at our house. It was fortunate for us that it had a happy end. The letter is hardly filled and I'll finish. All persons in our house wish all fortune to you and we'll hope to get as soon as possible a letter from you.

G. Van Voorst
Box Cooperweg F.20.
Weespe (Bambost)
Holland

Letter to the parents of Bombardier Theodore Roblee from Tom Catterill of the Royal Canadian Artillery. He wrote on behalf of G. Van Voorst who for some time had hidden Theodore after he had bailed out over Holland. (As immediately after the liberation of the Netherlands in April/May 1945 by Canadian Troops, there were no postal connections between Holland and the USA, Canadian soldiers often acted as in-betweens)

NOT HOME FOR CHRISTMAS

Waist-gunner **Thomas W. Lattimore Jr.** in a January 2004 letter to the author

"Our mission that day, Nov 26, 1944, was to fly to and bomb the oil refinery at Hannover, Germany. We were briefed early that morning, took off sometime around 7 o'clock, flew to the target, and dropped our bombs and headed home near 12 o'clock.

"The sky was full of flak - we were hit several times as we flew over the target. Some small pieces came into the plane. One motor was badly damaged and had to be cut. We may have been hit again as we left the target because another motor caught on fire and had to be cut and prop feathered.

"We still had two engines (supposedly operating) and thought we should be able to get back to base or at least west far enough to be in Allied territory. We were flying at 20,000' feet when we went over the target.

"After the engines shut down we started losing altitude.

"The pilot, Hank Schmidt, ordered us to throw everything out of the plane that we could - we threw flack jackets, ammunition everything that was loose out. Our plane kept losing altitude, finally at about 1200'-1500' off the ground, the pilot ordered all to bail out. This was near 2:30 or 3:00 p.m.

"Tail-gunner, ball-turret gunner, radio man and myself the waist gunner went out the waist door. We four hit the ground near each other. Rolled up our chutes and hid them. We had landed in a small wooded area and hedgerow. The four of us hid the best we could.

"About twenty minutes after we landed, a woman riding a bicycle rode down a path or trail and said in English; "Hide. Some one will come for you tonight."

"About thirty minutes later a squad of German solders came looking for us - as they came near our hiding place we stood up threw up our hands and surrendered. This was near 4:30 p.m.

"We were walked to a small town near by and locked up in a school house for the night.

"The next day or soon after, we were taken by truck to an interrogation center at Frankfort Germany. I was there for several days in solitary confinement. We were questioned about our crew, mission and so on. The German officer knew more about our plane and mission then I did. He spoke English very well.

"From there, I was moved to a staging center for POW's. We stayed several days - received items from the Red Cross including personal items and articles of clothing. Seems like I was there four to five days.

"From there I was taken along with other POW's by train (box car) to Stalag Luft IV in Northern Germany and arrived there on December 16th 1944. I was assigned to Lager C Barracks #10 Room 9. There were 20 in this room.

"The Russian Army was coming toward our camp from the east. We left camp on Feb 5th (on foot) and marched for the remainder of the war until finally being liberated on May 2, 1945 at Halle, Germany on the river Elbe, by the American Soldiers of the Timber Wolf Division.

Ball-turret gunner **Leo C. Wloczewski**

"We were debriefed and deloused by the Infantry Division, staying there in Halle for several days. We were taken by C-47's to camp Lucky Strike at La Havre, France, where we were prepared to be sent back to the U. S.

"We (several hundred) boarded a victory or Liberty ship about June 1st 1945 and landed in New York Harbour and transported to Fort Dix New Jersey about June 15th 1945

Tail-gunner **Keith D. Hereford** wrote in 2001:

"We were hit with flak as soon as our bombs were dropped, we lost # 3 + # 4 engines at that time. On the way back west we threw everything out of plane that we could. The pilot (Hank Schmidt) tried to get us back to Channel but at about 12'000 feet flak hit us again from a small town knocked out # 2 engine that could not be feathered. Later we were informed to bail out. I think I bailed out at about 1200 feet. Several of us got into a tree area and a Holland man drove by on a bicycle and told us to wait till dark and they would come get us.

"Real soon a truck came by with troops and captured us. I think our first night was spent in a school house. I was taken to Hannover for about two weeks then transported with a lot of prisoners by cattle car to Stalag-4.

"Some time early Feb. we were marched out in groups of 3 to 6 hundred people. We spent nights in open fields and barns. The English finally liberated us on May - 2. It was figured that we marched about 500 miles on the trip. The English treated us for lice for a few days and then flew us to Brussels, where the American army took over.

"We were transported to La Havre France where we stayed for about two weeks. The camp there was called camp Lucky Strike. From camp to La Havre to a ship and thank God back to U.S.

***

Acknowledgements:
Thomas G. Horger
Thomas W. Lattimore
Keith Hereford
Jan Hey
Kenneth Wloczewski

CHAPTER 10

303RD BOMB GROUP 358TH BOMB SQUADRON

Aircraft Type B-17G, Serial # 42-97972,
MACR 11200
Airbase: Molesworth

"No matter what you hear, I am coming home!"
—Pilot Chet Jameson to his wife the day before he went overseas

Pilot: 1Lt. Chet H. Jameson (POW) Anadarko OK
Co-Pilot: 2Lt. Robert N. Blazey (POW) *
Navigator: 2Lt. Maurie S. McDade Jr. (POW) Atlantic City NJ
Bombardier: T/Sgt. Ferdinand P. Haevers (POW) Greenbay WI
Top-Turret: T/Sgt Glenn W. Hall (POW) San Rafael CA
Radio-Operator: S/Sgt Howard D. Hole (POW) Honolulu HI
Ball-Turret: Sgt Roland J. Bender (POW)*
Waist-Gunner: S/Sgt Gasper Pizzolato Jr. (POW)*
Tailgunner: S/Sgt William L. Hoots (POW)*

Hometown not available

Total: 9 POW
Target: Altenbeken rail road viaduct.

NOT HOME FOR CHRISTMAS

HEADQUARTERS
AAF STATION 107
APO 557 - US ARMY

D-A-2

26 November 1944.

SUBJECT: Narrative Report of Mission - 26 November 1944.

TO : Commanding Officer, AAF Station 107, APO 557, U.S. Army.

1. Fifty-eight A/C from this Group were dispatched this date to attack a railway viaduct at Altenbeken, Germany (Visual or G-H). The last resort target was the M/Y at Osnabruck, Germany (PFF). Thirty-six A/C flew as the "A" Group of the 41st Combat Wing which was led by Lt. Col. Walter K. Shayler, of 360th Squadron. The remaining A/C flew as the lead and low squadrons in the "B" Group which was led by Major Charles E. Kerwin, 359th Squadron.

2. The A/C of the Group took off between 0740 and 0823 hours, and returned to base between 1351 and 1451 hours.

3. A/C 43-37590, Lt. McGilvray, 358th Squadron, turned back at 1025 hours at 52°22'N-04°00'E when the bombs came loose in the bombay.

4. Two A/C are missing: A/C 42-97972, Lt. Jameson, 358th Squadron, was hit by E/A between the IP and the target, and was seen to go down in flames. Four parachutes were observed. A/C 42-97691, Capt. Healy, 427th Squadron, was hit by A/A gunfire over the last resort target. The A/C was forced out of formation but when last seen, it was still flying. Nineteen men are missing. In addition six men were wounded.

5. The lead and low squadrons, "A" Group, and the lead squadron, "B" Group, bombed the primary target G-H with unobserved results. The first pictures show no bomb bursts. The other squadrons bombed the last resort target visually because their G-H was out. The first pictures indicate good results. 209 x 1000 GP bombs were dropped on the primary; 104 x 1000 GP bombs and ten units of T-223 leaflets were dropped on the last resort.

6. About 25 E/A were reported. Only a few were able to penetrate the excellent fighter support and make attacks which were sporadic and not concentrated. One A/C was lost to E/A. One claim has been filed, and it has been tentatively assessed as probably destroyed. The E/A were seen from 1100 hours to 1200 hours in the area from Dummer Lake to the primary target.

7. The A/C attacking the primary encountered meager and inaccurate A/A gunfire at Zwolle only. The other A/C also encountered intense and accurate A/A gunfire at the last resort.

8. Ten A/C sustained major battle damage and nine minor, all from A/A gunfire. They were all in the squadrons which attacked the last resort.

9. Going into the primary target there was 4-6/10ths patchy cloud, tops 14,000, becoming 10/10ths over the primary. This cloud layer broke north of 52 degrees so it was clear over the last resort.

10. Friendly fighter support was excellent. It cannot be determined whether chaff had any effect at the primary. It was ineffective at the secondary.

W. Robert Thompson
W. ROBERT THOMPSON,
Major, AC,
Group S-2.

Group Report

From Harry Gobrecht's book *Might in Flight,* the story of the 303rd Bomb Group.

"The 303rd dispatched 58 B-17s. It was later verified that this mission comprised the largest number of bombers airborne on any of the eventual 364 combat missions flown by this Group.

"Primary target was the rail road viaduct at Altenbeken and the last resort target the marshalling yard at Osnabrück.

"The aircraft attacking the primary target found meagre and inaccurate flak. Intense and accurate antiaircraft fire was encountered at the last resort target that resulted in ten major and nine minor instances of battle-damage, six wounded crewmen, and the loss of two B-17s.

"Returning crews reported that the aircraft # 42-97992 had been hit by two enemy aircraft at 11.25 hours, caught fire between the Nos. 3 and 4 engines, peeled off to the left, went down in a tight spin, and blew up at 5.000 to 6.000 feet.

"The Pilot, Lt. Jameson, and togglier, T/Sgt. Haevers, were contacted by tail-gunner, S/Sgt. William L. Hoots, in September 1992. They related an entirely different story. They stated that no crewmen had seen any fighters or flak. They believed that only minutes after they had started fuel transfer from the Tokyo tanks, the No. 4 engine had white vapour trails. The tail gunner reported this to the co-pilot, who noted that all engine instruments were normal. About two minutes later, a fire blazed around the No. 4 engine super charger. The aircraft had flown a mission the previous day and sustained extensive damage to the right wing just beyond the No. 4 engine."

Pilot **Chet Jameson**' wife Betsy wrote about her husband:

"Chet was born Oct 5th 1918 in Anadarko, OK. He and his parents came to Tulsa in 1921. Soon after they came, they moved next door to us. My brother was his age and they became life long friends. Chet considered me my brother's pesky little sister until we started dating in 1940! Chet spent one semester at the University of Oklahoma in Norman after having graduated from public school. He left college and worked cattle on some property his Dad owned just outside of Tulsa.

"The war started and he enlisted in the Army in March of 1941. He wanted to go into the Air Corps but at that time they were waiting to have enough men for a class before calling them up. He was stationed at Ft. Sill, OK and in very short time entered Officer Candidate School. He

NOT HOME FOR CHRISTMAS

"Just Married" Chet and Betsy Jameson

became a 2nd Lt. just before Pearl Harbour and was assigned to duty at Ft Meade in Maryland. Shortly he returned to Ft Sill as an instructor for the Field Artillery. We married on April 25th 1942. In September he was transferred to the Air Corps and started flight training.

"He started his Air Corps training in Santa Anna, CA. From there we went to Tucson, AZ, then Roswell, NM. When he finished 4 Engine School, he was sent to Walla Walla, WA. Well, once again he was made an instructor. He, like all other volunteers, wanted to "go where the action was", so he was disappointed. However, the weather was so bad they couldn't get enough flying time in so they moved to Avon Park, Florida. I joined him there and stayed until he went overseas.

"The day he left, we said our good-byes. We were standing in the hall at the hotel where we lived in front of the elevator. He said, "No matter what you hear, I am coming home!" Of course we were young and I was naive, so it didn't seem so bad. Fortunately it turned out OK. His whole crew made it back, so that was even better.

"I can fill you in on some of the highlights of his last flight and the ultimate consequences.

"He stayed with the plane as long as he could, trying to keep it level so all could get out. When he finally jumped, he landed away from the other crew members close to a very small town on Sunday November 26th. A girl rushed up and he had visions of being "saved" by a member of the underground but all she wanted was his parachute which she took and disappeared with. Unfortunately his boots were tied to it. Walking around with flying boots with heating wires across the soles wasn't good. At the time he came down, people were coming out of church so he drew a crowd quickly. Apparently he was the first Allied airman they had ever seen and they didn't know what to do with him.

"The local Bürgermeister had to go to his office - put on his official uniform - and get out his manual to find the proper procedure. Meanwhile the crowd became intrigued with the receptacle in the left shoulder of Chet's flight suit. It was the opening for the plug that operated the heating system - a real necessity since the temperature inside the plane often got to 50 degrees below zero. A bystander took out a knife and cut the top off and started pulling on the wire. Not knowing what it could be, he cut it off at the opening. Actually, it was a good thing. Chet hid his lighter and a Catholic medallion in the hole.

"The medallion depicted the Patron Saint of Travellers. A friend of my Mom's had it blessed by the Pope when she was in Rome. She gave it to Chet when he joined the army.

"While waiting for an official person to arrive, Chet, with the help of a young man about twelve or fourteen years old acting as an interpreter got his boots and parachute back. He was then taken to an Army Base guard house in Detmold overnight. The next stop was an unknown base which they reached by travel in a charcoal driven bus. They had to stop often, particularly at the bottom of hills, to refuel so they could make it up hills and continue to run.

"At this base, he was escorted to a tremendous underground hangar where he was told to leave his parachute on a large pile of others. He'd had to carry it with him the whole time as he was moved from place to place. Also in the hanger were hundreds of Stukas lined up with their propellers down and under the tail with the one in front of it. Obviously, Germany's production of planes exceeded their ability to produce fuel.

"He was then taken by train to the interrogation centre in Oberussel, a suburb of Frankfurt. They held him there in solitary confinement for about a week. At that time, he met

Betsy and Chet Jameson at their daughter's wedding in Colorado, 1992

with the rest of his crew for about thirty minutes. The officers were put on one train and the enlisted men on another. He never saw any of them again until he was back in the States.

"He was sent to Dulag-Luft West. There he was issued his first Red Cross supplies of clothes, and transferred to another train that took him to Stalag Luft #1 in Barth. It was the first camp established by the Luftwaffe. He stayed there for the rest of his incarceration. Toward the end of the war, as the Russians approached, the Germans left the camp. In a few days, they were all flown out and he went to Camp Lucky Strike in Le Havre, France to wait for transportation home.

"After he got home in the summer of '45, we enjoyed his accrued leave. January '46 he went to work for an exploration company - looking for likely drilling sites for oil wells. Shortly afterwards the company stopped hiring anyone who didn't have a degree - so we moved from Kansas back to Tulsa for him to attend the University of Tulsa. After 4 years he got his degree in Geological Engineering.

Bombardier **Ferdinand Heavers** wrote after the war:

"On November 26, 1944, as we were flying our seventh mission over Germany, our plane was hit by flak and started to burn. The right wing of our B-17 began to buckle so we bailed out. I landed in the Weser River about five miles from Minden. I hit the river with the small of my back.

"As soon as I reached shore, I was taken prisoner and taken by the guards to a farm house where two members of my crew had already been escorted. From there we were marched to Minden where we were placed in solitary confinement in the city jail. Here we remained for four days without heat or blankets. Shortly after this my back began to cause me great pain. When I reached prison camp the English doctor gave me pills to relieve or deaden the pain so I could sleep.

"From Minden (all of my crew but the pilot were together) we were taken by train to a camp where I received American Army clothes brought in by the Red Cross. About a week later the officers were sent to one camp and we enlisted men to Stalag Luft # 4 near Kolberg by the Baltic Sea. We arrived there about December 17, 1944 and were placed in a barrack which had about ten rooms – each room housing about 25 to 28 men.

"February 6, 1945 we were placed on a forced march as the Germans were afraid of the Russians who were approaching through the Polish corridor. We were marched west through Schweinemunde and Anklam through to Hamburg. From there we were marched south to an English prison camp. About a month later we were released by a British patrol on May, 1945. This march was figured to be 900 kilometres.

"On this forced march we were bedded in barns and also open fields. The food consisted of very few potatoes a day augmented by a few slices of German bread a week. Because of this poor diet, many of us suffered from dysentery. We received about a quart of drinking water a day as most of the well water had to be boiled before it could be drunk.

"Weather conditions were about the same as winters in central Wisconsin. On this trip I lost about 45 pounds.

In 2004 Ferdinand Heavers' eldest daughter wrote about her father:

"Dad's answer to how he got in the Air Corp: he apparently did not need to worry about the draft as he was a government employee doing an essential task, delivering the mail. It seems though he and some friends decided over a couple of drinks that the war would end quicker if they were involved. They enlisted the next day. They did basic training and then specialty training. And Dad ended up in Walla Walla, Washington teaching others to drop bombs and the like. He told me that after a couple of months of that chicken shit, he and some friends decided that if they could get a complete B-17 crew together, then maybe they would see some action overseas. They did and they went. Dad said that they only flew about 6 or 7 missions before they got shot down. So much for ending the war sooner!

"Before he joined the Air Corps, Dad had his eye on a yellow Chrysler coupe. He really wanted that car. Eventually he saved enough to buy it. All went well for about two months: then bills, gas, and car insurance started to mount up. Dad finally had to take the wheels off and put the car upon blocks until he got more cash. About six months later, he took the car down and drove it awhile. He sold it about two months later. He always talked about how great that car was and the lessons that he learned about finances. Later, after all of us girls were out of college, he and Mom bought a beige Chrysler. He drove it for about four years and then traded it in for another Chevrolet. Kind of his way of saying that he finally had everything and that he really did not need it after al.

"About his long march through Germany, he said they would eat grass and roots because there wasn't a lot of food. They also would sleep on manure piles to keep warm and eat charcoal. The other POWs would also try to sleep next to Dad because he gave off so much body heat. I know that on the march to Germany, one of the POWs fell down and they were going to kill him. Then Dad picked him up and carried him. I think the guy survived. Dad told me that the last night of the march everyone went to sleep on a farm. The guards were there. In the morning when the prisoners woke up it was very quiet and the guards were gone. They then realized that they were free.

"After he arrived back home, Ferd returned to his pre-war job at the U.S. Postal Service. He remained in an Air Corps Reserve unit based in Milwaukee, Wisconsin. In 1947, he married Arlene Clemens, a teacher who was his pre-war sweetheart. They had five daughters, Phyllis, Patricia, Betty, Ruth and Mary, who died in infancy.

"He was called back to active duty for the Korean War, but was discharged due to the nature of injuries received when he bailed out of his B-17. While his children were small, Ferd got a second job working for his brother-in-law as a gas station mechanic. Once his youngest daughter was in school, Arlene returned to work, and Ferd quit his second job to spend more time with his family. Ferd spent most of his free time with his family. The one exception to this was his two week trip "up north to the shack" with his father and hunting buddies. Once there, they played cards, walked in the woods and of course, hunted deer. His high point of hunting season was getting three deer in one season.

"He also enjoyed fishing - building a 16 foot boat that he enjoyed taking out in the water of Green Bay. Ferd and his friend, Dick, constructed a red brick house on the shore of Green Bay. His knowledge of "fixing things" was vast: electrical, plumbing, carpentry, and mechanical. He would sometimes sit and hum for long periods, gazing at some project. Then suddenly, having thought it all out, he'd get up and do whatever needed to be done, rarely with bad result.

"He also played community volleyball with his friends once a week. Having lived in Green Bay and delivered mail to many of its citizens, it was only natural that he enjoyed Packer football games and knew many of the coaches and players. He taught all his girls the meaning of loyalty through good seasons and bad: "your team is your team, no matter what happens." And they all learned to "punt when you're out of downs". They also learned the security of sitting in his lap in his rocking chair: the world wasn't such a scary place after all. He always made the time to kiss away boo-boos and give extra special hugs. Ferd was also an excellent whistler. He could whistle opera, swing or nursery songs. He whistled when working, reading the paper, dancing with his children, or doing household chores.

"When Ferd retired from the Post Office, he and Arlene travelled to

Europe to see Germany, France, Austria, and Switzerland. They also took a cruise to Alaska. They always kept a bag packed for travelling, because they never knew when Ferd would wake up and decide he wanted to go to Mount Rushmore or to the Grand Canyon or the California redwoods. It was his great joy to get into his car and go wherever he might want to go, perhaps an unconscious response to have been imprisoned and confined. When at home, he read western novels, watched John Wayne movies, and played volleyball five times a week.

"In 1980, Ferd was diagnosed with lymphoma cancer and went through chemotherapy. His strong belief in God and Arlene kept him going through this trying time. Thankfully, his cancer went into remission. During this time he became grandfather to three delightful little girls, Angela, Megan and Nicole. He and Arlene spent a lot of time playing with them and loving them. He developed cataracts as a result of the chemotherapy which interfered with his volleyball playing. After his cataract surgery, he returned to playing volleyball for many years. He even played with the community college players, only giving it up many years later when a ball was "spiked" on his head, dislodging the implanted lens.

"Ferd also grew impatient with the politicians of the time. He was invited to the inauguration of Ronald Reagan in 1980 and 1984, but did not attend. He felt great relief when the wall in Berlin was torn down – finishing the war forty years later.

"Then in 1987, the cancer returned, followed by chemotherapy and another remission. The next few years brought another granddaughter, Katie, and his only grandson, Tommy. His eyes twinkled when with the children, whether reading, rocking, or playing. In the fall of 1994 the cancer returned. This time chemotherapy had no effect. Ferd died at age 79 in June of 1995. He and Arlene had been married for 48 years. He left behind a legacy of undying love and strength of spirit to those who survived him. After his death and through the efforts of his daughter Betty, The United States awarded Ferd the Purple Heart.

In May 1945, top-turret gunner **Glenn W. Hall** wrote to his parents:

"We were evacuated from Stalag IV by the Jerries on February 6, 1945, and marched for 43 days. We finally arrived here at "357" on April 6th. They tried to move us again but the British forces moved too fast for them and they abandoned us and retreated before the enemy.

NOT HOME FOR CHRISTMAS

"The British armoured division drove in and liberated us on the morning of April 16th. There were several thousand prisoners here of all nations and we are repatriated according to length of time spent as a POW. My name will come up soon.

"In the interim we are free to do as we please. Food and "cigs" are coming in regular now, and everybody is happy and anxious to get going for home. I believe I will be in the States within a month from to-day. Will probably get a furlough as soon as I get back – sure hope so – I weigh 160 now and have a tremendous appetite for some of Lora's real home cooking.

"Hope you are both well and have not worried too much. See if you can get me a Parker "51" pen. The Jerries got mine."

In 2001, Glenn's grandson Steve Polaski wrote me :

"Your information that the aircraft crashed in Kalldorf agrees with mine that Glenn was captured "near Minden on 11/26/1944", as Minden is about 12 kilometres north of Kalldorf. He remained in Minden for four days, then was transferred to Stalag Luft I in Barth. He remained there for only 9 days then was transferred to Stalag Luft IV in Gross Tychow (now in Poland) which was a camp for enlisted aviators (NCO's). Later he was transferred to Stalag 357 in Orbke (also spelled Oerbke) located near Fallingbostel.

"He was liberated by the British 2nd Armoured Division on 16.04.1945 and flown to Oxford England hospital to recuperate. He returned back to America on 03.06.1945 aboard a liberty ship arriving in Newport on June 15th.

"Due to the marches from camp to camp during the winter, he developed trench foot and had difficulties with his feet for the rest of his life.

About radio-operator **Howard D. Hole** his widow wrote:

"Howard Douglas Hole – consulting engineer and mechanical engineer – was born in Honolulu December 29, 1920 to William Warren Hole and Julia Sylva Hole. He married Dorothy Burnham Rowe on August 31, 1946. They had two children.

"Howard dropped out of Roosevelt High School to help earn money to send his older brother Bill to Georgia Tech. Howard was an apprentice at the Navy Yard at Pearl Harbour and became a graduated machinist in 1941. In 1938 Howard joined the Inter-Island Steam Navigation Co. as a machinist and left in 1941 to join the U.S. Air Force (which was called the U.S. Army Air Corps then).

"He flew 98 missions in the Pacific and was then sent to England. He and the entire crew were shot down over Germany. He was in a prison camp for 6 months. Your father and another soldier escaped to the British lines after crossing through enemy territory. When they arrived at a British outpost, they had to prove they were Americans. Your father told me they were asked to name baseball players that only American soldiers would know about. They had only found potatoes on their way, and were thin and in need of a good shower and food to eat. Dad told me those first few days they were only allowed small portions of food and drink so that their bodies would tolerate it.

"He never told me very much about the prison camp. However, he did say that when they were shot down, the German civilians hit them all over the head with baseball bats, and the German guards came and took them away. I used to wonder if that may have been the reason he had so many headaches over the years?

"In 1946 Dad returned home on a troop ship that docked in New York. Because he had been a prisoner of war, he was allowed to do whatever he wanted to aboard the ship.

"When he returned to Honolulu in 1946 he went to work for the Hawaiian Ordinance Depot for the U.S. Army. After a short time with them, he left to teach automotive maintenance at Kamehameha School. He was there over one year. Then he went to the work in the engineering department of the Hawaiian Sugar Plantation Association from 1947 – 49.

Tail-gunner **William L. Hoots** recalls:

"This is my memory of the 144 days that took place after I bailed out on November 26, 1944. We took off that morning from Molesworth, England heading toward our target, the rail road viaduct at Altenbeken, Germany.

"After we got to rendezvous altitude (18 – 20.000 feet), the pilot called and told us to put on our extra clothes because the weather was going to be a lot colder than they briefed us. Since I was flying in the tail, I didn't have much room to put on my old fleece-lined britches. When I did, my parachute straps wouldn't buckle back up, so I stretched them out to lengthen them and made the mistake of not adjusting them. That was a mistake I paid for later.

We had a 20-minute IP point (the time the aircraft is lined up to target and bombs are dropped). This was a much longer IP point than normal.

NOT HOME FOR CHRISTMAS

Right after we got lined up I called the co-pilot to check the instruments on engine # 4 because it was smoking, and he said everything was running well. We hadn't seen any fighters: the flak was way off and not close.

"In just a little while, I looked out on the right wing and # 4 was now on fire. I called the pilot and they feathered the # 4 and we went into a dive to try and put the fire out. We were at 24000 feet. We were probably in the dive for 4.000 feet and when we levelled out the fire was really out of control, so he gave the order to bail out.

"I snapped my chest parachute on, which was in the tail with me. I turned around and tried to get the door off in the tail so I could bail out but for some reason it wouldn't come loose from the airplane. I was going to have to go to the waist by the tail wheel to bail out. Each time I started crawling through our crawl space, I would get just a little way before the airplane would bank up real hard. I would be thrown against the side of the airplane by centrifugal force and I couldn't figure out why. When I finally got to the door of the waist to bail out, I would say we were probably still 18-20.000 feet high with just a few clouds floating between us and the ground. The right wing had burned so much that the skin on the top of the wing had burned off and I could see the fire in the fuel tanks.

"I bailed out, trying to remember all we had been trained to do for survival. When I went out I was lying on my back and spinning. I fell for some time and opened my arms and legs to stop my spin. The aircraft had blown up in front of me and there were pieces flying everywhere. So, I pulled my arms and legs back in and the debris from the airplane was falling down. Up above me was one open parachute and there was a guy floating down. I could see no parachutes below me so I pulled in my arms and legs and fell for some distance again. I then pulled my ripcord and when my parachute blossomed I was lying flat which gave me quite a jolt. The parachute I used had a 28-foot canopy and was for a paratrooper of 190 pounds with full pack. I probably weighed 135 pounds.

"When the parachute opened, the harness was not properly secured around my legs since I hadn't fully adjusted the straps. I took another major jolt. My oxygen mask was originally on my face since they told us to leave it on in case there was an explosion so the fire wouldn't get into my lungs. But after the force from the parachute opening, the mask was now up on my forehead. They had trained us not to pull the ripcord when we jumped from a burning aircraft because the flame was trailing behind the wing. When the parachute opened, the flame would hit the silk and in one flash it was gone. You would then have just a short time to think about your life before you hit the ground.

"After my parachute opened, the wind was really blowing so instead of going down, I was doing more drifting and going sideways. I attempted to spill my parachute by holding the shroud lines on one side and pulling it down. That lets the air go by the parachute and allows for a faster fall. I did that twice after resting for a minute and the second time I let go. For some reason I was oscillating in the air. Instead of being underneath my parachute where I was supposed to be, I was swinging out so high to the side that I was about to collapse my parachute.

"I had looked at my watch after my parachute opened to see about where I might be, but of course it was well into enemy territory and it was in the Ruhr Valley. That is where we were going to bomb a railroad marshalling yard where they were bringing army supplies into to start the Belgium Bulge. That would be the last big offensive the Germans put out in 1944.

"As I kept drifting, I wasn't going down, just floating further into German territory with the wind. It was Sunday morning and when I looked down, people were coming out of church but they hadn't looked up to see me. I was over a small village of about one hundred people. The wind stopped blowing and making me float and I started going down, falling, and I thought I was going the fall into some power lines. I crossed my legs to keep from straddling anything as I went down and went right down beside some trees by a house.

"I landed in sandy soil with my legs still crossed and why they didn't break I'll never know. When I got up to try to get out of my parachute, the wind was still blowing and it would jerk me down so I had to drag my parachute in and stand on it while I undid my harness. While I was attending my harness, a German showed up who was the burgomaster of the town. He had a pistol and made me put my hands up and kept telling me the "wars kaput". I was thinking, now isn't this lucky, the day I bail out the war is over. What I did not understand was that he was telling me the war was kaput for me since I was on the way to jail. As we went I had my hands in the air so I couldn't pull a weapon on him. He would not know that I didn't even carry a gun with me.

"The fleece-lined pants I had put on for the cold weather didn't have suspenders or a belt. They had been held up with the parachute harness that was now lying in the garden by the house where I landed. I had to reach down to get hold of my pants which were hanging way down on my hips and when I would do so the German would hit me in the head with his pistol. I, of course, put my hands back up in the air and my pants kept falling further down. I finally stopped and we came to an

NOT HOME FOR CHRISTMAS

agreement that I could hold them with one hand and hold the other hand up in the air.

"He took me to what I presumed was the city hall that was staffed with two women. I would say one was young, maybe in her late teens and one probably 40 or 50 years old. I was hurting so badly from where the parachute straps had come up on my legs that I could hardly sit up.

"One of the ladies asked me if I wanted to pray and I declined. She was telling the young lady in English that all Americans were Christians.

"I don't know how long I was there, but German soldiers eventually came to pick me up and took me to another house. They said they had my comrade there and I told them I didn't have a comrade. They opened a door a little so I could look through a crack and there was my togglier on the crew, sergeant Haevers. He was sitting in a chair in wet clothes and was not looking towards me so they said; "Your comrade"? I said; "No, I never saw him before". In the meantime, unbeknownst to me, they had let him look through the door at me. He had said, "That's not my comrade, I've never seen him before." We were in luck that we both denied knowing each other. They left the house and starting looking for other crew members.

"Later on, Sergeant Haevers and I left the house and they brought Sergeant Hall, the engineer. Now there were three of us and they took us to a larger place in town to catch a bus or train, I don't remember which. The town had been bombed and it wasn't long before the civilians gathered around us and were spitting and hollering and telling us we were bombing churches and school houses; killing women and children.

"There were three or four men that got very close. One of hem hit me on the left ear or the left side of my head with his fist. When he hit, it was so hard that it knocked me down. While I was on the ground several of them were kicking me and I knew if I was going to survive, I had to get up. As luck would have it, when I did manage to get up, they were working on the other two crew men. The Germans held their guns on us so that we couldn't fight and the three of us took a pretty good beating from those civilians. I can't really remember anything else that took place there. I know we left and the next thing I remember I was being put in a city jail.

"I can't say that it was complete solitary confinement, but it was next thing to it. I was put in a room probably 10 or 12 feet long and 6 or 8 feet wide. The only piece of furniture was a thing like a small table, which was to be my bed. One end was a little bit higher than the other was. I was about 6 feet long and 4 feet wide. No blankets, no pillow, no nothing. There was a hole in the floor where I could relieve my kidneys and that was it. I wasn't long till it was beginning to get dark and I had only had breakfast that day before daylight. I was hungry and thirsty, so finally they said that I could eat and they brought in this horrible tasting, tacky cheese. My first thought was that they were trying to starve me, so I was going to have a drink of whatever they brought me, not knowing it was their German coffee. I had a taste of that and spit it out. That and the cheese were my supper. I was afraid to eat, but later on this stuff tasted good.

"The lick I had taken on my head had ruptured my eardrum and I was bleeding out of the left ear, so I didn't rest much that night. The next morning it had run down on my face and dried a mixture of blood and fluid coming from my ear.

"I knew that one way to save my sanity, being in there by myself, would be to try and keep track of time. I took my dog tag and made a calendar on the wall. I scratched a place into the wall and since I knew the 26th of December was Sunday, I started there and made it go into December. The room wasn't really solitary confinement. I could stand real close to the wall and there was a window that went outside where I could see daylight, but nothing else. The door, up above my head where I couldn't see out, had a hole probably of a foot square with iron bars across it. I could hear voices in the hallway – some English, some German. I could recognize the voice of the engineer.

"They finally came to take me to the bathroom on Monday morning. It was down a hall. The co-pilot was already in there using a safety razor they had given him so he could shave. There was also a German standing there shaving. The co-pilot and I talked a little bit about what happened, whether everyone made it out of the airplane or not, and our condition. He didn't seem to be hurt at all. They brought a doctor in sometime that day and he just looked in my ear. To the best of my recollection, he put some glycerine in my ear and that was it.

"Since I still hadn't slept much since bailing out of the airplane, I dozed off to sleep several times during the day on Monday. Each time I woke up, I would be very disoriented and would mark a day off the calendar as if I had been asleep the entire night. After the fourth or fifth time, I looked at my calendar wall and there it was approaching December. I knew full well it wasn't December and I had to get things straightened out.

NOT HOME FOR CHRISTMAS

```
FORM #1                              Pge 1                          KU 3376
                           REPORT ON CAPTURED AIRCRAFT

  POST:                   Air Bs. H.Q. DETMOLD, Air Bs Command 8/III
  LOCATION:
                          3 Dec 44
  DATE:

  DATE AND TIME:          26 Nov 44, Time 11.15
  AIRCRAFT WAS SHOT DOWN

  PLACE OF CRASH:         Kalldorf, about 7 km east of Vlotho/Weser
  (NEAREST TOWN)

  KIND OF CAPTURE:        Unknown
  (FLAK, HUNTER, NIGHT HUNTER,
  EMERGENCY LANDING)

  TYPE OF AIRCRAFT:       B 17 G 40 VE, Flight to target

  MARKINGS OF CRAFT:      On Tailassembly Red Triangle with Nr. 2979, in red Triangle
  (LETTERS, FRONT OR REAR OF INSIGNIA)  a white triangle with letter "C" in black.
                          V K Star N above O

  ADMITTANCE NO:          297942

  EQUIPMENT:              N
  F.T. FREQUENCIES:
  CONDITION OF AIRCRAFT:  98 % Loss, Crashfire

  DELIVERED TO DISTRIBUTOR:  Guarded by Auxiliary Police Kalldorf
  (DULOG -LUFT, ETC.)

                          1 Man captured:
                          Jameson, Chest. H. O-451979

                          9 Men probably at large. Names unknown, crew bailed out
                          and were drifting off to the East, whereabouts unknown.

                          Investigation made by: Becker, S/Sgt.
```

Translated German document KU 3376, captured after the war, pertaining to the crash of this bomber.

***

Acknowledgments:
Betsy and Chet Jameson
William Hoots
Dorothy Hole, widow of radio-operator Howard Hole
Trish Burton, daughter of bombardier Ferdinand Heavers
Steve Polaski, grandson of top-turret gunner Glenn Hall

CHAPTER 11

381ST BOMB GROUP 532ND BOMB SQUADRON

Aircraft Type: B-17G, Serial # 42-106994,
"Little Guy", MACR 11205
Airbase: Ridgewell

"Jump, I'll be right behind you".
—Last words spoken by Pilot Kyle Smith to his co-pilot Don McGurk

---

Pilot: 2Lt Kyle S. "Scott" Smith (KIA) Albany OH
Co-Pilot: 2Lt Donald F. McGurk (POW) Springfield MA
Navigator: F/O Melvin A. LaLuzerne (POW) Green Bay WI
Bombardier: S/Sgt Byron F. Wear (POW) Princeville IL
Radio-Operator: Sgt Lester F. Colson (POW) Brooklyn NY
Engineer: Sgt. Robert K. Porter (POW) Danville VA
Ball-Turret: Sgt Gustavo "Gus" E. Contreras (KIA) Tucson AZ
Waist-Gunner: Sgt Thomas Arnold (POW) Milwaukee WI
Tailgunner: Sgt Francis R. DeLange (POW) Minneapolis MN

Total: 2 KIA, 7 POW
Target: Osnabrück Marshalling Yard

NOT HOME FOR CHRISTMAS

Already over the North Sea, en route to the target Altenbeken, "Little Guy" lost one engine. Pilot Scott Smith could have aborted the mission and could have returned to the base Ridgewell but he decided to continue his flight to the target.

Navigator **Melvin LaLuzerne** in a letter to the author dated August 2001:

> "Reading the information you sent me sparked a bit of memory regarding engine failure. We lost the first engine before or while crossing the Channel from England. With only three engines it was not possible to keep up with our group and we became a "straggler". We did manage to go over an alternative target with another group which I cannot identify.
>
> "The second engine failed shortly after bomb release and that failure was believed to have resulted from flak damage. There is no way to determine the accuracy of this assumption. It is possible that mechanical failure occurred since full power was probably used during the bomb run to maintain formation and altitude position within the attack group of the four engined bombers. Engine failure was not uncommon even without the additional demands that had been required.
>
> "With only two engines and the weight of the two bombs that failed to release, there was no possibility of maintaining altitude. We again became a "straggler", this time west. It should be obvious at this point that there was no way of landing this plane. Bailing out near the coast and letting the plane crash in the Channel or bailing out into the Channel and hoping for a quick rescue were our alternate choices if the plane could be kept air-born long enough.
>
> "The Missing Air Crew Report mentioned in your letter of August 5, states that only one engine - # 4 - was running when the plane crashed. My memory is very fuzzy about failure of the third engine but I believe the report is correct as we were losing altitude at an accelerated rate just before the crash. Failure of the third engine would definitely be due to mechanical problems.
>
> "Details beyond what I've already stated are not possible. They've been

F/O Melvin A. LaLuzerne

kindly erased by whatever nature provides for blotting out those events which otherwise might trouble us forever."

In March 2009, Melvin provided the following biographical information:

"I was born in October 1923 on a farm near Dyckesville, Wisconsin, an area settled by Walloon speaking Belgian emigrants. Walloon was my first language. I was the oldest of four sons born to Mayme and Alvin LaLuzerne.

"I was educated through high school in Green Bay, Wisconsin and completed one year at St. Norbert's College where I enlisted and was accepted as an Air Force Cadet. I graduated from the Pan American School of Navigation in the summer of 1944 and was assigned to the 8th Air Force stationed in England.

"After my return to the States I earned a Mechanical Engineering Degree from Michigan College of Mining & Technology in 1949. While in college I met my wife of 59 years. (Still counting).

"I joined Factory Insurance Association after graduation and stayed with them 36 years, retiring in 1985 as District Manager of an area encompassing the states of Minnesota, Iowa, North Dakota and South Dakota.

"My wife and I have lived in Minnesota since 1962. We have two sons, two daughters, five grandchildren and two great-grandchildren.

***

Over Apeldoorn, in the central part of Nazi-occupied Holland, Smith ordered his crew to bail out. When the crew with the exception of the two pilots had evacuated the bomber, Kyle said to his Co-Pilot Don McGurk: "Jump, I'll be right behind you". Kyle however remained behind the controls to prevent that "Little Guy" from crashing on the village. He crashed his bomber in the municipal open air swimming complex just outside the village, deserted at that time of the year.

Tail-gunner **Francis "Bob" DeLange** in a post war letter to the sister of Pilot Kyle "Scott" Smith:

"Words cannot express my sympathy or explain my admiration for your brother. He was one of the best pilots I've ever known and each and every one of his crew was proud to have him as their pilot.

NOT HOME FOR CHRISTMAS

"We took off the morning of November 26th on the mission to Osnabrück, Germany. We were only an hour from our base when number two engine began to leak oil. Co-pilot Don McGurk and the engineer Bob Porter, did all they could to save the engine but finally it had to be feathered. Scott could have then turned back but being the man he was he decided to go on to the target with three engines. In order to do this we had to drop behind our own formation and that was when things began to happen.

"We had fighters but I don't believe they damaged the plane. We finally got rid of the fighters and got to the target. We had to make two passes over the target because the bombs stuck in the bomb bay. Finally we got rid of six of the one thousand pounders but could not get rid of the other two. We were going to take them back with us.

"We then lost number three engine. Lester Colson and I believe it was due to the fact of having so much weight with only three engines. Finally Scott rang the bail out signal as number four engine was acting up, he stayed with the ship so that we could have time to bail out. He then only had one engine and still had the live bombs. He was killed, so I was told, from the concussion when the plane crashed.

"You can be proud of your brother. He was the type of man that was necessary for the defeat of Germany.

"Scott was buried in Apeldoorn, Holland and a British chaplain (Padre Buchanan) who was captured at Arnhem and was in the prison hospital where I was, laid Kyle to rest. Gus Contreras was also buried there."

Francis "Bob" DeLange was wounded by German soldiers when he floated down over the village center and was brought to the civilian St. Joseph Hospital in Apeldoorn. There he met Major Gordon Sheriff of the British First Airborne Division, who was captured during the Battle of Arnhem in September 1944, and David Ward, a British navigator with the RAF.

This trio escaped from the hospital in January 1945 with the help of a Dutch nurse and were hidden by the Dutch underground. Bob spent some time with the Woltman family in Apeldoorn. He was liberated by Canadian troops in April 1945.

After the war, pilot **Kyle Scott Smith** was re-interred in the Netherlands American Cemetery near Margraten. On December 29, 1948, his remains arrived by train in Athens, Ohio.

At the request of the author, Fred Williams visited Kyle's grave. He reported:

"Well, I finally headed to Albany, Ohio to see if I could find Kyle Smith's grave. I knew that his father had resided there from the MACR. I could not find Kyle's listing at any military cemetery so I assumed that he was buried in Albany, a very small town (or village) near the university town of Athens, Ohio.

Pilot Kyle "Scott" Smith

"It is in south eastern Ohio, about 140 miles from Cincinnati. Upon arriving, I could not locate any cemetery in town. I stopped in at the local library and was told that there was no cemetery in town but one was located between Albany and Athens. I headed there. I found a large cemetery adjacent to a small country church. After much searching, I found Kyle Smith's final resting place. It was marked with a flag as with all the other veteran's there. He is in good company. I found graves of veterans from the revolutionary war and the Civil War nearby. Kyle is buried next to his father and they share the same tombstone. The dates for Kyle are 1920-1944. The dates for his father are 1877-1965."

John Meurs, who had witnessed the crash of "Little Guy", wrote almost fifty years later in his memoirs:

"That Thanksgiving Sunday 1944 was a clear and sunny day. I then was a nine year old schoolboy living in a village called Apeldoorn in Nazi-occupied Holland. We were having our meagre war-time lunch, when a B-17 "Flying Fortress" bomber came rumbling low over our house. So low that we had the impression that it would take our roof away. The sound was overwhelming; it made the cups on the table dance on their saucers: then followed the deafening sound of the final crash.

"We ran to the rear window and saw, half a mile behind their house, a large ink black cloud billow to the sky, followed by the noise of gun shells exploding in the fire. Our family of five and our neighbours ran in the direction of the crashed bomber but were stopped by nervous German soldiers, who had come speeding out of the nearby schoolhouse where they were billeted.

NOT HOME FOR CHRISTMAS

It soon became known that the bomber with three engines dead had approached Apeldoorn at a very low altitude. The crew had bailed out over the centre of the village, but the pilot had stayed behind the controls and had kept the plane in the air, long enough to avoid the built-up area of our village. He had managed to ditch his B-17 in the circular canoe pond of the open air public swimming complex, killing himself in the crash. Some of his crew did not fare better. They were shot at by the Germans while dangling helplessly under the white canopies of their parachutes. The ball-turret Gunner Gustavo Contreras was killed and came down on the market square. The tail-gunner Bob DeLange and the radio-operator Lester Colson were wounded and were taken to a German hospital just outside the village, from where Bob two months later escaped with the help of the Dutch underground. He spent some time with a family living on the same street as we did and was liberated by Canadian troops in April 1945.

> "I visited the crash site as soon as the Germans had cleared out. It lay in a vast swimming pool area the municipality had built in the long period of recession before the second world war as a program of unemployment relief work.
>
> "What was left of the bomber lay straddling the canoe pond. The almost intact tail-piece stuck out high on the island in the middle of the circular ditch: the fuselage was lying in the water. Debris of the cockpit, engines and wings were spread out on the bank. The typical stench of a burned-out airplane lingered in the air. A few machine guns, their perforated barrels twisted by the impact were lying there next to yellow painted, portable oxygen tanks. A strange, quiet atmosphere reigned over the wreck as if the brutal impact had chased all the noise away."

Three young girls from Apeldoorn visited the site on the evening of the crash. One of them, Titia Speldekamp, wrote the author:

> "It wasn't new: it happened quite frequently during the last years of World War II; bombers tumbling from the sky in flames, after having been hit by German anti-aircraft guns. Sometimes the crew members managed to leave the aircraft in time, hanging in the air under their parachutes as helpless targets.
>
> "That's what happened that glorious Sunday afternoon when an Ameri-

can bomber on its way back from Germany eventually crashed on the Apeldoorn swimming pool site. I don't remember how many men came gliding down: one of them on the market square and about three others in neighbouring streets. The man who came down on the market square was probably dead before landing – he was fired at by the Germans while dangling in the air, quite in defiance of the rules of the Geneva Convention.

"It was extremely spectacular: before our eyes the aircraft seemed to crash exactly on the spot where there was an island in the narrow winding lake, on which we used to canoe in normal times, as if it was the result of careful and deliberate planning.

"One of my friends lived at a distance of a quarter of a mile from the Bos Bad, "our" swimming pool. Our plan de campaign was quickly made: as soon as it was dark that evening, we (three 14-year old girls) left our houses – unseen and unheard. We went through the woods, where we knew every curve and bend in the road. We climbed the fence of the Bos Bad and in spite of the dark we easily found our way to the lake. Our guess had been right: there, on the island, lay the wreckage of the aircraft, like a lame and wounded bird.

"We watched it from a distance for some time, excited and perhaps a little frightened too, although children at that age are convinced they possess nine lives.

"We must have had a guardian angel, no doubt about that. We saw armed German guards around the lake, not many, two or three perhaps. We approached carefully, creeping rather than walking. One of us saw it first; a strange, large object on the bank of the lake, half lying or hanging in the water. It looked like a parachute and on closer inspection we found out that it was. The material of which parachutes are made was very popular among young girls these days: we used it for hankies, blouses and many other things. So we felt as if we had discovered a gold mine. And such a lot there was. We started pulling gently at the parachute so as not to draw the attention of the guards and then – suddenly all three of us at the same time seemed to go entirely numb. Attached to the parachute there was, half lying in the water, perhaps 25-30 meters from the perished aircraft on the island, a body in uniform. We gazed at it in terror for a couple of seconds, the body seemed so small. Our eyes had become adjusted to the dark by now and in utter amazement and horror, we saw that from the body the head was missing.

"It made our blood run cold and, looking back, I still find it difficult to believe that we indulged in such an adventure – and survived. The parachute silk had lost it's attraction and at some distance we saw one of the

German guards slowly walking into our direction. I remember we could distinguish the glow of his cigarette. We hid in an artificial grove and sat there, arms around each other shoulders. The guard approached, stopping very close to us, by the edge of the grove, to light another cigarette. As if he instinctively felt that something was wrong, he walked around the grove, pausing now and then as if he was listening. One of us could hardly suppress a sneezing fit and we almost suffocated her in our attempt to stop her. How, I don't remember, but we must have got home safely after our nightly adventure.

"I often wondered in the more than 55 years that have passed since then about the person behind the headless corpse – who was he, what were his thoughts at the moment of his untimely death, did he have parents, or perhaps a family?"

Later that Sunday, on the Ridgewell base in England, Chaplain **James Brown** of the 381st Bomb Group, wrote:

"A large crowd assembled at the control tower on this day, November 26th, to await the return of our planes from combat over Germany. It is the Thanksgiving season and the base is endeavouring to celebrate Thanksgiving in typical fashion -- a big turkey dinner with all the trimmings and a happy family atmosphere. Even the English people are helping us to observe the American holiday.

"I was invited to give the address at a large assembly in the cathedral in Bedford, England. The community of Bedford observed our American Thanksgiving by holding a special service in the cathedral for the benefit of all Americans in the area.

"An American airfield is located in Bedford. The cathedral was filled with both English people and Americans. It was an inspiration to speak before the large assembly. A colourful procession of English dignitaries marched into the church, led by the Lord Mayor of the city and the English clergy dressed in their churchly robes. How thoughtful of the English people to hold this Thanksgiving service for the benefit of the Americans stationed in England.

"Likewise, on Ridgewell air base we were endeavouring to create a joyous spirit befitting the occasion. In this atmosphere, we gathered at the control tower to welcome our fliers back home from combat. The crowd soon learned how many planes went out this morning. Now, as the planes began to appear on the horizon, and as they came nearer to the base, we began to count them.

"Spirits were high -- until the count showed one missing. No one anticipated that on this Thanksgiving Day, the 381st would lose a ship. What was supposed to be a day of rejoicing and gaiety turned suddenly quiet and sombre. No one felt like cheering.

"My unpleasant task continues when I return to my room to write letters of condolence to the families. What can one say to them at this Thanksgiving season of the year?"

Co-pilot **Don McGurk** served as a lieutenant in the Army Air Corps in World War II and was a B-17 pilot in the 532 squadron of the 381st heavy bomb group in the 8th Air Force at Ridgewell, England. He flew 18 combat missions over Europe before his aircraft "Little Guy" came down on November 26, 1944.

Captured by the Germans, he spent the duration of the war as a POW at Stalag Luft I in Barth, Germany until liberation by Russian troops in May 1945. He was awarded the Purple Heart, Air Medal and the POW medal.

Co-Pilot Don McGurk

After the war he worked in various capacities in material at Hamilton Standard, General Instrument and Digital Equipment Corp. in Westfield, MA before retiring in 1986. After retirement he served as a Director with the File of Life Inc., a non-profitable organization.

About bombardier **Byron F. Wear** his sons Ross and Boyd wrote in 2008:

"Our Dad, Byron F. Wear, grew up on the family farm in Princeville, Illinois. He was raised with his brother Harold and sister Phyllis on their grain and livestock farm in a house built by his Great Grandfather in 1865: the same house where my brother Boyd and I spent our childhood.

"He actually lied about his age to enlist at 17 in the Army Air Corps.

"He successfully completed his first tour as a toggler aboard "French Dressing" flown by Bruce Rivett, and was scheduled to go home when

NOT HOME FOR CHRISTMAS

the 8th Army Air Force was in desperate need of crews, so with a sense of responsibility he signed up for his second tour in "Little Guy". On that fateful day November 26, 1944 he was acting as bombardier due to his experience. When it came time to drop "Little Guy's" bombs, they jammed. Dad explained how he stood over the open bomb bay in an attempt to dislodge bombs in the racks with a pry bar, but without success.

"Little Guy" had already lost an engine over the North Sea on the way to Germany and over the target a second engine stopped functioning. Pushing the remaining engines to the limit in an attempt to stay in the air resulted in the loss of the third engine. Over Apeldoorn in the Netherlands they lost their battle and my Dad left the plane with the rest of the crew except for pilot Kyle Smith. Before Dad jumped he asked Kyle "are you coming", to which he responded "I'm right behind you". Our Dad told of the the horror of parachuting from his ailing B-17 with the SS troops on the ground shooting at him.

"When he hit the ground, or possibly a stone wall, his ankle broke. An 18 foot diameter parachute didn't slow descent that much he would say. A German soldier immediately hit him in the head with the butt of his rifle and knocked our Dad out for a period of time. Prisoners were moved by night to Stalag Luftwaft 1 in a coal fired bus to avoid the accuracy of allied bombing during the day.

"He said the Germans took good care of the prisoners in Stalag Luftwaft 1 until their supply lines were cut off, then he only got rutabagas and water...to the day he died, he could never eat another rutabaga or turnip! He lost 60 pounds in 6 months, but felt sorry for the German's who were also starving. As Germany was losing the war, Hitler ordered the Stalag commandants to kill all the prisoners, but they had too much integrity according to our Dad. As the Russian's rolled in to liberate the camp, the German commandant ordered his soldiers to open the gates, throw down their weapons, and surrender. To our Dad's horror, the Russians killed all German soldiers and took no prisoners because of what Germany had done to Russia. He trusted the Germans more than the Russians, who liberated him at the end of the war, because of what the Russians did to the townspeople as they advanced.

Back in England, he discovered all his possessions and souvenirs from the war were gone. To add insult, he described how most POWs went home on landing ships that were not really worthy of the open seas, while the more able bodied soldiers went home on cruise ships and destroyers..

Back home, he found his girlfriend had dumped him, but then he would have never met our Mom Marta who was always so proud of what he had done in the war and enjoyed the ex-POW reunions they attended. He said he was treated as a hero and couldn't remember buying a drink or dinner for a year. However, Dad was always saddened and humbled by the fact that he survived while so many others paid the ultimate sacrifice. Boyd and I have always had a special admiration for B-17's, the role they played in winning the war, and the extreme adversity these young men endured for our freedom.

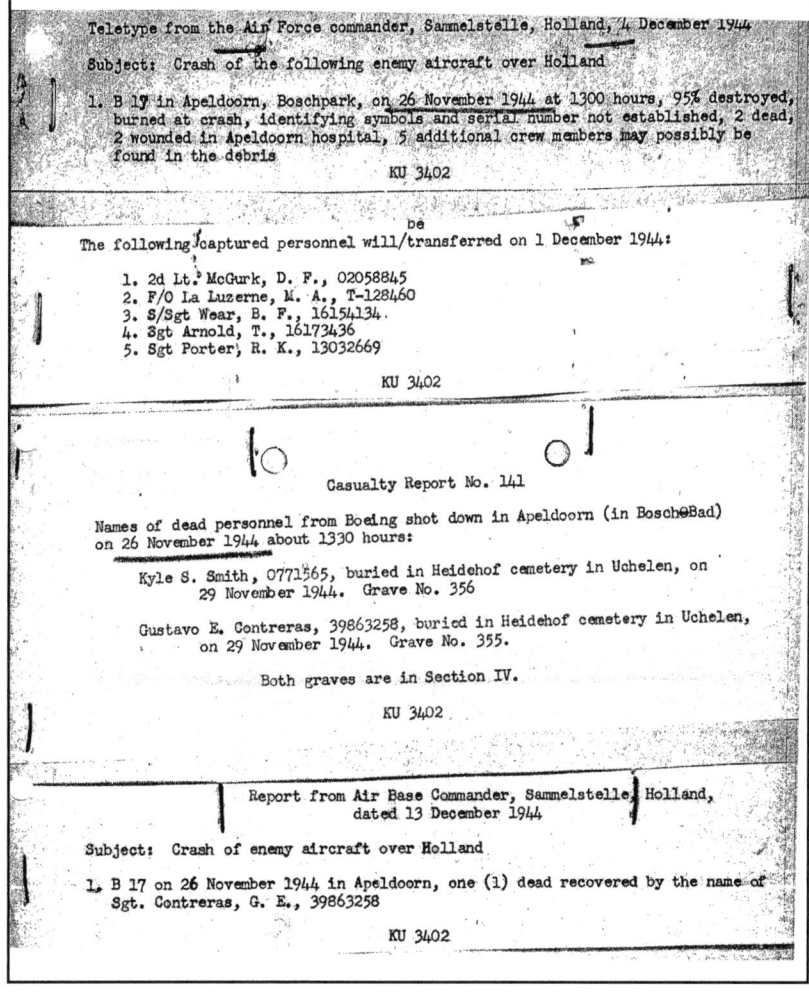

```
Teletype from the Air Force commander, Sammelstelle, Holland, 4 December 1944
Subject: Crash of the following enemy aircraft over Holland

1. B 17 in Apeldoorn, Boschpark, on 26 November 1944 at 1300 hours, 95% destroyed,
   burned at crash, identifying symbols and serial number not established, 2 dead;
   2 wounded in Apeldoorn hospital, 5 additional crew members may possibly be
   found in the debris
                               KU 3402

The following captured personnel will/be transferred on 1 December 1944:

   1. 2d Lt. McGurk, D. F., 02058845
   2. F/O La Luzerne, M. A., T-128460
   3. S/Sgt Wear, B. F., 16154134
   4. Sgt Arnold, T., 16173436
   5. Sgt Porter, R. K., 13032669
                               KU 3402


                     Casualty Report No. 141

Names of dead personnel from Boeing shot down in Apeldoorn (in Bosch@Bad)
on 26 November 1944 about 1330 hours:

       Kyle S. Smith, 0771565, buried in Heidehof cemetery in Uchelen, on
           29 November 1944. Grave No. 356

       Gustavo E. Contreras, 39863258, buried in Heidehof cemetery in Uchelen,
           on 29 November 1944. Grave No. 355.

                  Both graves are in Section IV.
                               KU 3402


              Report from Air Base Commander, Sammelstelle, Holland,
                         dated 13 December 1944

Subject: Crash of enemy aircraft over Holland

1. B 17 on 26 November 1944 in Apeldoorn, one (1) dead recovered by the name of
   Sgt. Contreras, G. E., 39863258
                               KU 3402
```

Translated German Report

NOT HOME FOR CHRISTMAS

AFPPA-12

CASUALTY QUESTIONNAIRE

1. Your name BYRON F. WEAR   Rank S/Sgt   Serial No. 16/54134
2. Organization 381 Gp Commander _____ Rank Col. Sqn CO Fitzgerald Rank Lt. Col.
   (full name)   (full name)
3. What year 1944 month Nov. day 26 did you go down?
4. What was the mission, No. 29. Missery, target, INDUSTRIAL, target time, 12:04, altitude, 24,500 route scheduled, _____, route flown _____
5. Where were you when you left formation? OVER The NORTH SEA.
6. Did you bail out? YES
7. Did other members of crew bail out? YES — ALL
8. Tell all you know about when, where, how each person in your aircraft for whom no individual questionnaire is attached bailed out. A crew list is attached. Please give facts. If you don't know, say: "No Knowledge". ENTIRE CREW BAILED OUT IMMEDIATELY.
9. Where did your aircraft strike the ground? 8 MILES W. of APLEQOUN
10. What members of your crew were in the aircraft when it struck the ground? (Should cross check with 8 above and individual questionnaires) NONE
11. Where were they in aircraft? —
12. What was their condition? —
13. When, where, and in what condition did you last see any members not already described above? I SAW The ENTIRE CREW WITH EXCEPTION of (PILOT SMITH) (BALL TURRET GUNNER GUSTAVIOUS) IN CAMP LUCKY STRIKE, FRANCE.
14. Please give any similar information on personnel of any other crew of which you have knowledge. Indicate source of information. _____

(Any additional information may be written on the back)

Pages from Missing Air Crew Report 11205. Questionnaire filled in after the war by Togglier S/Sgt. Byron F. Wear.

381st Bomb Group, 532nd Bomb Squadron

```
                                         ..JLLLAND
                                         # 2374
                REPORT

Copied from our Report Book:

     On the 26th of November 1944 at 1304 hours an American bomber
crashed down in the "Bosbad" in Apeldoorn. One of the men, Lt. Smith,
died in the plane. His body did not burn. The remainder of the crew
had jumped out. One member of the crew was shot by the Germans while
descending. This man was Gustav Contreras. Two other men were wounded
and hospitalized in the German hospital "St. Joseph". Three other men
were made prisoners by the Germans.


                         Apeldoorn, 11 Jan. 1946


                              s/ Tiemens.
                                 Fire station Commander


A TRUE TRANSLATION:     ...1st Platoon, 3059th QM GR CO.

A CERTIFIED TRUE COPY:

CHESTER S. MILISZKIEWICZ,
2nd Lt. Inf.
```

From the Report Book of the fire Brigade of the village of Apeldoorn.
Page from the Individual Deceased Personnel File (IDPF) pertaining to Ball Turret Gunner Gustavo Contreras.

***

Acknowledgements:
Navigator Melvin A. LaLuzerne
Co-pilot Donald F. McGurk and his son Peter
Ross Wear, for his father bombardier Byron F. Wear
Chaplain James Brown in his book: "The Mighty Men of the 381st: Heroes All"
Fred Williams.

CHAPTER 12

390TH BOMB GROUP 568TH BOMB SQUADRON

Aircraft Type: B-17G, Serial # 44-6491,
"I'll Be Around", MACR 11209
Airbase: Framlingham, Suffolk

"I'll tell you something about November 26, 1944, a very sad day in my life."

—Top-turret gunner John Bartram in a letter to his mother, dated April 1945

Pilot: 2Lt Gilbert A. Meyer (POW) Oakland CA

Co-Pilot: 2Lt Alfred W. Burkhart (POW) Athens PA

Navigator: F/O Irving Aschendorf (POW) Portsmouth OH

Bombardier: 2Lt Dan W. Finlayson (POW) San Antonio TX

Top Turret: S/Sgt John L. Bartram (POW) Arkadelphia AR

Radio: S/Sgt Dale T. Westell (POW) Pocahontas IA

Ball Turret: Sgt Raymond W. Maul (POW) Lyman NC

Waist Gunner: Sgt Aaron E. Mickelson (POW) Au Claire WI

Tail Gunner: Sgt Richard W. Kuerten (POW) Omaha NE

Total: 9 POW

Target: Hamm Marshalling Yard

Crash Site: Bad Dissen-Rothenfelde on railway track at exit of village

NOT HOME FOR CHRISTMAS

About bombardier **Dan W. Finlayson** his son Richard wrote in 2001:

"Regarding his crew members, the only one he ever talked about was the radio operator/navigator, I don't know his name, but he was Jewish. Therefore, it was doubly dangerous for him to fly missions if he was ever captured.

"During this raid, the weather was OK, but the primary target was heavily overcast with clouds. They were well back in the original formation and they were directed to their secondary target -Hamm railway yards. There was scattered light flack and I think the fighter attacks were no too bad.

"During the flight they did see one of the Luftwaffe "new" jets go streaking past - really surprised and scared them as it was so fast. As they approached the target, they opened the bomb bay doors to drop the bombs and were hit by a burst of flack in the bomb bay. It started a fire and had knocked out one or two of their engines. They began to lose altitude and control and a fire was burning within the bomb bay among the live bombs.

"The pilot gave the OK to bail out. Everyone evacuated the plane as quickly as possible but the radio operator/navigator was unconscious. My Dad crawled into the compartment above and lowered him down into the nose and pushed him out the escape hatch for the bombardier. He was partially conscious and managed to open his chute. My Dad received the Air Medal for this heroic action in saving his comrade. My Dad then bailed out hitting his head and receiving a serious laceration getting out of the plane. He thinks he hit the rear radio antennae as he sailed through the slip stream of the airplane. Shortly thereafter, the plane exploded. He thought he was the last one out.

"He came down in a field covered with pig shit. The navigator/radio-operator had already been captured by a farmer, an old man, carrying a single shot shotgun. He herded my Dad and the radioman ahead of him. They were brought into a village and were beaten, spit upon and put up in a farm house.

"The next day, as they were being transported in a train, a crowd stopped them and wanted to put them, I think there were three of them, under the train wheels to cut off their legs. The only thing that saved them was their German guard who prevented this atrocity from happening. My Dad greatly admired the man for standing up to the crowd to save them.

They continued on to the camp where he stayed for about 6 months, liberated eventually by the Russians. He developed a great aversion to eating turnips from this experience as that was all they had to eat. He also saw terrible abuses of Russian POW's in the camp next to theirs, and told how they would toss their Red Cross bundles to the Russians because they felt sorry for them. He also never drove a German or Japanese car in his lifetime, but he really loved German food as that is very common in this part of Texas as many of the early settlers were German.

Top-turret gunner **John Bartram** wrote to his mother in April 1945 immediately after his liberation by the British:

"I'll tell you something about November 26, 1944, a very sad day in my life.

"We were to bomb a bridge at the city of Hamm. We arrived there alright. We were the #2 plane in the formation, right up front. There was a lot of flak and we were over the target ready to drop our bombs (we had six 1000 lb. bombs) when we were hit by a heavy 88 mm flak shell right in the bomb bay. It almost tore our left wing off. It burst the #2 gas tank and the plane caught on fire. It was a very big fire too. You can imagine how 400 gallons of gasoline will burn.

"I used all the extinguishers and then told everyone to bail out. All of the crew in the rear of the plane jumped at once – that was Kuertin, Westell and Mickelson. By this time, the ship was one mass of flames. I told Lt. Finlayson and Aschendorf to jump (they were in the nose), but they refused to go unless I would jump first. I expected the ship to blow up any minute, so out I went.

"We were in a dive by this time and doing 200 miles per hour. I did not open my parachute at once but waited until I got down to where the air was warm so that I would not freeze. I fell about two miles before I opened my parachute. It did not take long to make those two miles either – only about thirty seconds. After my parachute opened I noticed that there were two more chutes in the air about a mile above me (they were Lt. Finlayson and Aschendorf) and also I saw that the airplane had already blown up and was coming down in about 4 pieces all in flames. You see I just got out in time. The pilot and co-pilot did not get out I am sure, as I did not see any more parachutes. They did not have time as they were still flying the plane when I left and had not put on their parachutes. The pilot was Lt. Meyer and co-pilot was Lt. Burkhart.

"I landed in a tree in the back yard of a farmhouse. There were two men with shotguns waiting for me. They turned me over to the police and

NOT HOME FOR CHRISTMAS

I was taken to town and put in jail. Lt. Finlayson and Aschendorf were already there. None of us was hurt. We were taken to an Army guardhouse that night where we were put with Maul, Mickelson, Westell and Kuertin. All of these boys were OK too.

"We never did hear anything about Lt. Meyers or Burkhart so I feel sure they burned up in the ship.

"The next day we were put on the passenger train and taken to Frankfurt. It took three days and two nights to make this trip. Here they gave us the third degree and tried to make us talk, but of course, we would not. I will tell you about all the methods they used in trying to make us talk when I get home. We left Frankfurt the next day and went to Wezlar where we were issued new clothing and cigarettes. This was done by the Red Cross. The only thing I had to eat the first four days in Germany was one bowl of soup. They would not even give me any water to drink.

"I do not believe I ever told you about us cracking up our airplane "Little Butch" on the night of November 25. This crash was the indirect cause of us being shot down on November 26. On November 25, we went to France on a practice mission. We did not get back to our base until after dark and it was snowing so hard we could not see the runway. We came in for a landing anyway but we were way too high. The control tower told us to go around that we were too high but Lt. Meyer was afraid he would loose the field completely if he went around again so he landed anyway. We missed the runway completely and landed in a muddy field. "Little Butch" sunk down in the mud and could not be gotten out that night.

"We were scheduled to go on a mission the next morning at 3 a.m.; so therefore, we had to take a different airplane. We took a new one. The regular crew for this new one was in London on a 3-day pass. As we were flying this new airplane which belonged to another crew, we flew in a different place in the formation (up in front). Our regular place with "Little Butch" was back in the rear on the outside. So you see if we had been in "Little Butch" on Nov. 26, we would have been in a different spot in the formation and would have been safe, but as it was, we were knocked down. Oh well, we probably would have been shot down anyway later on even in "Little Butch".

"There were four crews at the 390th that came over with us from Alex. All four were shot down, one on their first mission, one on their third mission, us on our 12th mission and the last crew went down about Jan. 1 (we saw some of the men of this crew at Stalag 4). Of these four crews I am the only engineer that got out alive."

In 2002 daughter Sarah James wrote the author about her father, top-turret gunner **John Bartram:**

"After the war, he worked for the Army Corps of Engineers as an inspector. One of his job sites was NASA (National Aeronautics & Space Administration). He helped build the vacuum chambers and centrifuges NASA used to train astronauts.

"He worked for the Corps until a heart attack forced him to retire two years early. He married my mother in 1935, and they had been married 62 years when he died at the age of 87. He had two kids - my sister and me. I was a total shock and surprise. When my mother was 38 years old, her doctor told her that she would no longer be able to bear children. At age 42 for her and 44 for him, surprise - they have a baby girl (me). There's 14 years difference between my sister and me, so I basically grew up as an only child. As a child, he grew up in Warren, Arkansas (the same state that former President of the US, Bill Clinton, was from).

"Arkansas is an extremely beautiful place with large green rolling hills and mountains with beautiful lakes. He liked to hunt and fish when he was young, and as he grew older, he mainly enjoyed fishing and baseball. His true love was automobiles. He loved to work on them as a hobby. I remember he custom ordered a 1965 Ford Mustang. It was the first year this really hot looking sports car was introduced to the public, and he just had to have one. A lot of teenagers drove them, and there he was - an old man with grey hair - driving this hot rod. He was getting gasoline for his Mustang one time, and the attendant (a young kid, of course), said "What's an old man like you doing driving a car like this?" I think that question bothered him until the day he died, although it didn't keep him from driving Mustangs the rest of his life. He even drove one before he died. Now my husband drives it.

Pilot **Gilbert A. Meyer** died on 8 February, 1999 in San Leandro, CA, just south of Oakland. He was survived by his wife of 55 years, Helen L. Meyer of San Leandro. He left a son, Gilbert Michael Meyer and a daughter Diane Doohan.

He was a plant manager for Bethlehem Steel for 37 years.

Concerning Co-Pilot 2Lt **Alfred W. Burkhart** I got in contact with Jean Bosworth, a former girl friend and with Edward Peterson, who graduated with Alfred at Athens High School. Both sent me Alfred's obituary. Summary from their letters and the obit:

"Ed Pattersen, now living in Homosassa, FL, graduated with Al at the Athens High School. Ed also joined the USAAF and became Co-Pilot on a B-17 bomber of the 447th Bomb Group. Like Alfred, he was shot down over Germany and spent the rest of the war in a German POW camp.

"Alfred William Burkhart died at the age of 77 in May 2001 in New Canaan, where he had lived for many years. He had gone out to do some garden work while his wife was doing some shopping. When she came home she found him lying in the yard. Alfred, who was born in Athens in 1923, had a peaceful death.

"After the war he studied at the Cornell University in Ithaca, New York. After graduation from the Cornell Law School in 195, he began his career as attorney with the firm of Mendes & Mount in Manhattan. Meanwhile he had married a girl from New York City.

"Later he moved to Norwalk and joined John Keogh Sr. in practice. For more than fifty years he worked for the firm now known as Keogh, Burkhart and Vetter.

"Alfred was very active in the community: past-president of the Rotary Club, past president of the Norwalk-Wilton Bar Association, honorary member of the Knights of Columbus and member of the Shore Haven Golf Club. Tennis was a hobby and he also played the trumpet in the Cornell Band."

Crash Site.

The Neue Osnabrücker Zeitung published the following story in their March 16. 2002 issue:

"Who knows the background of the American bomber crash on the railroad Haller Willem in Dissen on November 26, 1944?" This question was asked by John Meurs, a Dutchman living in Switzerland, who in his search for eyewitnesses had addressed himself to the municipality of Bad Rothenfelde. Meurs would like to write a book about this subject. His question did not remain unanswered.

"The first reaction came from aviation expert Martin Frauenheim in Hagen. His files confirmed the crash and the bail-out of the crew. He wrote though: "the aircraft was not a B-24 'Liberator' but a Boeing B-17G 'Fortress' piloted by Gilbert A. Meyer." The Bombardier Dan W. Finlayson who appeared in the article belonged according to Frauenheim also to this crew.

"A further "ear witness" was Wilfried Zöllner of Dissen who, at the age of thirteen at that time, only heard the explosion. He could however not give further details about the crash, the bail-out of the crew from the burning machine and the capture of a crew member in a pig field by "an old man with a shot gun."

"The now seventy years old pensioner Helmut Gartschmidt, who witnessed the crash from the farm of his parents, still remembers quite well what happened. "It was a Sunday, November 26, 1944, " he says, "and we had heard already the whole morning the drone of allied bombers, who flew accompanied by their fighters at a high altitude over our area direction Ruhrgebiet. There was only a light overcast, so we could see from time to time some of the many bombers.

"Our complete family and also the other habitants of our house, people from Osnabrück who had lost their house through allied bombing, were standing outside looking at the sky. Later we heard bombs exploding from the direction of Munster after, as we learned afterwards, an attack on Hamm.

"Between ten and eleven it became quieter in the sky. I stood looking through a pair of binoculars and saw an aircraft with an altitude of 600 to 700 meters fly approaching directly our house. She was trailing smoke and burning between one of the engines and the fuselage. She came closer and closer and I noticed that the prop was feathered. Our Dad stood behind me and said, "if she can stay in the air for a couple of minutes, we will be lucky and she'll come down in the Teutenburger Forest."

"Gartschmit continues; "I saw the crew bail out and five parachutes opened. The crew had hardly left the plane when a huge fire started all along the fuselage. The plane made a 180° turn and exploded with a loud bang. Then the various parts came down. One of the engines landed near our farm house. The propeller made a ditch about two meters long. The cockpit came down before the front door of the postman Johannes Appelbaum, a wing and an engine near the Pöttings and the other wing on an adjacent field.

"When all had become quiet our mother counted the heads of her dear ones. There was no harm done to anyone of us.

"We went to see the various parts. I was interested in a blue dinghy with a survivors' kit but before I arrived there I had already collected a leather flying helmet with earphones and goggles. In the dinghy I found a pair of huge gloves, a flare pistol with ammunition. My father took the pistol away but I could keep the rest of what I had found.

In 2002 Richard Finlayson wrote the following letter to eye witness Helmut Gartschmidt in Dissen, Germany:

NOT HOME FOR CHRISTMAS

"I apologize for this letter not being in German but I hope that someone may be able to translate it for you. I have written a similar letter to Herr Wilfred Zollner regarding a letter I received from my friend, Mr. John Meurs, now living in Rüti, Switzerland. He had sent a request to the Neue Osnabruker Zeitung previously asking for witnesses of the crash of a B-17 on 26 Nov 1944. You had responded to the newsletter saying that you had witnessed the crash and had some pieces of the airplane.

"Mr. Meurs is currently writing a book concerning a day in the air war, that being Nov 26th 1944. He is originally from Holland and had witnessed the crash of a B-17, Little Guy, in his village hence his interest on the subject. As for myself, I am the son of the Bombardier mentioned in the article. Although I spent 24 years in the U S Air Force, (of which 5 were in beautiful Wiesbaden Germany), I was not a pilot or aircrew member but a dentist, a specialist in Periodontics. I along with Mr. Meurs am interested in the historical aspects of the war, but also for me, a personal one as well. If it had not been for a German soldier protecting my father and two other aircrew members from an angry crowd in Hamm, I would not be here today!

"I would ask you to consider a request from me to possibly donate any pieces of the aircraft you might want to get rid of to the 390th Air Museum in Tucson, Arizona. It is interesting that the only B-17 aircraft restored by the museum is named for the one that you have pieces from. I am enclosing a picture of the aircraft, named *I'll Be Around* for your inspection. I am sure the museum would find a significant place for any artifacts you might want to donate. Of course I understand that you may want to keep these items and certainly respect your wishes but if you are considering discarding them, please consider a donation to the museum. I will be happy to arrange this. Also, if you know any other facts regarding the capture of the crew I would be very interested to know. My father talked very little about this aspect of his life, only at the very end, so I know only a small part. Thanks to the historical research of Mr. Meurs I am learning more. Again, I appreciate your time and effort in reading this letter and look forward to hearing from you."

***

Acknowledgements:
Bill Burkhart for co-pilot Alfred Burkhart
Richard Finlayson for bombardier Dan Finlayson
Sarah Bertram for top-turret gunner John L. Bartram
Crash Site: Wilfried Zöllner

CHAPTER 13

487TH BOMB GROUP 839TH BOMB SQUADRON

Aircraft Type: B-17G, Serial # 43-38141,
MACR 10758
Airbase: Lavenham

"Even today when I think of my first parachute jump into unknown territory I get the sweats."

—Waist-gunner Milton O. Price in a letter to the author

Pilot: 2Lt Burr E. Davidson (POW) Graniteville SC

Co-Pilot: 2Lt Douglas C. Brink (POW) Minneapolis MN

Navigator: 2Lt Willard J. Blanchard (POW) Whaleyville VA

Bombardier: 2Lt Roy R. DeNure (POW) Fort Jones CA

Top Turret: Sgt Clarence R. Becker (POW) Fresno CA

Radio: Sgt William Millard (POW) Los Angeles CA

Ball Turret: Sgt Charles A. McBride (POW) Muscatime IA

Waist Gunner: Sgt Milton O. Price (POW) Brookline MA

Tail Gunner: Sgt Joseph W. Dory (POW) Austin NV

Total: 9 POW

Target: Hamm

Crash Site: Estate Lage, 11 km NE of Bramsche, 21 km NNE of Osnabrück

Time of Crash: 13.15

NOT HOME FOR CHRISTMAS

Back row from left to right: William Millard, * Bill Cowan, Milton Price, Joe Dory, Charles McBride, Clarence Becker
Front row from left to right: Roy Denure, Willard Blanchard, Burr Davidson, Douglas Brink
* not on the November 26, 1944 mission

Bombardier **Roy "Robert" Denure** made handwritten notes about his last flight in WW II and the following months as a POW in Germany. The notes were transcribed and sent to me by his daughter Beth DeNure Tillman. Robert called it "My Horror Story".

"On November 26, 1944 we were briefed at 0500 for a mission to the marshalling yards in Hamm, Germany. Bomb load; 6 - 1000 pounds GP.'s.

"We took off climbed up through the usual soup, came out on top at about 1600 feet, and joined our Squadron. Then we formed with our group and headed for Germany, climbing on course.

"Everything went as usual. We crossed the lines at about 26000 ft. at 1045. We had a little trouble with oxygen in the ball turret. Charles McBride, the top-turret gunner, passed out and then our waist-gunner Milton Price also passed out while helping him out of the turret, but it came out OK.

"We picked up a little flak here and there but it was meagre and inaccurate. Not worth worrying about. The condensation trails made by the High Squadron were very pretty that morning and Smiley (navigator

487th Bomb Group, 839th Bomb Squadron

Willard J. Blanchard) was getting some good pictures with Burr Davidson's camera.

"We hit the Initial Point right on the nose and were about two minutes from the target when it happened. Number two engine must have gotten a direct hit somewhere in the prop pitch control because it immediately ran away. Dave said afterwards that it must have wound up to around 4000 RPM's because the needle ran clear past the end of the dial. The engine also must have had one or two cylinders blown out because it started vibrating so badly we thought it would tear itself loose from the wing. Even after Dave got it turned off it continued wind-milling and vibrating so the whole ship was shaking like a leaf. To add to the confusion a small fire started right back of the prop hub.

"We drifted back out of formation and couldn't keep up so Dave called me on inter-phone and said "Bob, get rid of your bombs, we're going home." So I dropped that load of destruction right into somebody's calf pasture. I hope!

"The fire went out for a while but the vibration was really terrific; shaking down the landing gear and everything else that was loose. The bomb bay doors wouldn't close either, but the fire was out, we were heading back for our lines and still had 20,000 ft of altitude. Everything looked OK but in just a few minutes the fire in #2 was burning again and that time someone reported fire coming out from under the wing so Dave said: "Bail Out!" I didn't waste much time getting ready to part company with the old "Bama Blitz Buggy".

"My last look at the inside of the ship showed me Smiley sitting there in the nose getting ready to follow me I supposed and Dave still in his seat holding the ship level and making some last minute adjustments on the C-1. The co-pilot jumped out through the bomb bays just ahead of me. A glance back through the waist showed me a deserted ship except for Price, who was just then disappearing through the waist door.

"I stepped down into the bomb bay, took a last check on my chute, got the D-Ring in my hand and jumped!

"The slip stream started me tumbling and spinning so that I could not see the ship, ground, sun or anything else for the first few seconds. My first thought was how suddenly quiet it was and how very much all alone I felt! I didn't pull the rip cord for sometime because of being briefed that a delayed jump was very desirable and also I knew that there was plenty of time. However I was still spinning and couldn't seem to stop so I pulled the D-Ring and was snapped out of my spin like a wet dish rag.

"It seemed like about ten minutes before I started getting close to the ground so I had lots of time to think over the situation and make some plans for when I reached the ground, but coming in sight of the place where I was going to land, any hopes or plans I may have had for evading capture were very much subdued to say the least, for it was a country of farmers and there were dozens of them in every field for miles around.

"I made a nice "5 point" landing and was surrounded within a few minutes.

"The peasants either had no evil intentions or else were afraid that I had a gun because they didn't act hostile at all, much to my relief. Presently two soldiers arrived and by signs, made it known to me that I was their prisoner. We walked about a mile to where they got a car then drove about four miles to an air base, where I was put in the guard house, after searched and relieved of all my personal articles. They even stole my cigarettes! However my crew were all there except Joe, the tail gunner, who had sprained his ankle on the landing. That night we were given a chunk of black bread, a slice of blood sausage, a little square of margarine and a drink of erzats. (coffee). Then with one blanket, we slept on the floor."

So ends the first day in German captivity of Robert Denure. Daughter Beth Tillman further wrote me:

"My father died September 13, 1996 after a reoccurring illness of lung cancer. He was 69 years old and was able to live a very active and full life until the immediate months before his passing.

"My father was captured and was finally held at Stalag Luft 1, near Barth, Germany from December 8, 1944 to May 1, 1945. When my father returned from the war, he was malnourished, extremely broken in spirit but most grateful to be alive, I was told. He announced to parents and six sisters and their husbands and children that he would tell the story once. So it was done. Some of my older cousins who were very young then tell me they remember that day with awe. My dad wasn't a large man, however, I am told he returned weighing 97 pounds, some 50 pounds less than when he first entered the Army Air Force.

"After Dad returned to Scott Valley and gradually regained his strength, he worked for a brother-in-law, as a mechanic, then for another brother-in-law as a cabinet maker, then he was hired by our local electric utility company, Pacific Power. This is where he worked for 33 years until retirement. He was an estimator-engineer for the power company, providing the field work for many of the homes and power lines located in Scott Valley today."

487th Bomb Group, 839th Bomb Squadron

Ball-turret gunner **Charles A. McBride** wrote in May 2001:

"We were awakened at about 0330 hours and told we were alerted for a mission that day. I felt our crew was the best in the 8th Air Force. The weather on the ground was cold and misty. Above the clouds it was a sunny day.

"Our target that day was the marshalling yard at Hamm, Germany. While on the bomb run our aircraft was hit by ground flak. We had not dropped our bombs at that time but our airplane was on fire. The pilot gave the order to abandon aircraft so we all jumped at approx. 25000 feet. The temperature was about 57 degrees below zero (Fahrenheit). The last thing I did before we bailed out was to look at my watch. It was 11.40 hours.

"I landed in trees and was captured by members of the Hitler Youth. We were then taken to an interrogation center and held for a few days. We were then sent to Stalag Luft 4 to be incarcerated. While at Stalag Luft 4, I contracted pneumonia and was confined to the camp hospital. The Russians were advancing on Germany from the east and it was decided to evacuate the camp. We were loaded into box cars and sent to Barth, Germany. That is where we were liberated.

Ball-turret gunner Charles McBride

"I was supposed to meet my sister who was an army nurse on the 27th of November. She called the air base the 26th to finalize our plans to meet the next day and was told that our plane had gone down but there were no parachutes sighted. We did however all get out of the plane and were incarcerated until the end of hostilities.

Waist-gunner **Milton O. Price** dictated in May 2001 his following story to his granddaughter Sandy:

"At approximately 4:00 AM on November 26, 1944 we were awakened to receive a briefing for our 7th mission. We were told the target, Hamm, Germany would be a milk run (an easy one) with little flak and no fighters.

NOT HOME FOR CHRISTMAS

"After breakfast and loading the guns on our B-17 we were ready to take off. To this day I cannot understand how an island as small as England was able to have so many airfields for RAF (Royal Air Force), USAC (US Air Corp), Polish, Dutch, and so many other Bombers, fighters plus other ships of other countries. Of course the crowded conditions, I am sure, had a lot to do with our losses before we crossed the channel.

"Now back to the mission. After we were underway and had crossed the channel, I removed the safety pins from the bombs. That was my duty on all missions after we were in flight. I would replace the pins if the mission was aborted.

"It was a beautiful day and our bombs had been dropped on the marshalling yards when our #1 engine was hit by flak. Our pilot told the co-pilot to feather #1 and he mistakenly feathered # 2. Upon trying to correct the error neither prop would respond so our ship was shaking itself to pieces and our pilot could not correct the mistake. He gave the order to bail out and I believe I was the last of our crew to jump. We had removed the waist door and that was our exit.

"Even today when I think of my first parachute jump into unknown territory I get the sweats. I was scared to death and did my full share of prayers to the Lord above. As I jumped into the unknown the slipstream tossed me around like a rubber ball. When I finally thought I was in the right position I pulled the ring on my chest chute. As the chute came out it hit me on the chin and turned my neck around, I looked up and noticed a lot of small holes in the chute. To this day I wonder if those holes were supposed to be there.

"As I floated down, I thought it was slow until I got within 200 yards of the ground and then realized I was falling pretty fast. Luckily I landed in a farmer's field and recent rains made the ground soft. So even though my tail was wet I was not hurt and could pick up my chute and head for a wooded area. My bombardier landed within 100 yards of me, so the two stunned Americans were in hostile territory. After spending about ten minutes in the woods we were picked up by two German Luftwaffe soldiers. They marched us back to a farmhouse where a car was waiting to take us to a prison camp.

"My six months spent as a prisoner of war were the worst times of my life. It's an experience that some of us will never forget and the hardships and cruelty of men towards men will never be forgotten. Our message to all we come in contact with is appreciate your freedom it is your most precious possession.

"I am 82 years old, my wife Vera is 80. We have a son and two daughters, a grandson and two granddaughters. The Lord has blessed us, if we get to December 27, 2001 this year we will celebrate 60 years of marital bliss. Our family is the most important possession of our life."

The following details about tail-gunner **Joseph "Joe" Dory** were provided by Justin Merriman:

"While over the target area Joe said the flak started hitting his aircraft sounding like small rocks thrown by some one at the side of a metal building. He heard a loud bang and looked back at the engines and saw the #1 was hit and smoking. He instinctively knew the aircraft was doomed after it started shaking and that bail out orders would soon be given to the crew over the intercom. He prepared for this by tying his boots together by their shoe laces and placed them around his neck. He was wearing leather sheepskin heated flight boots at the time and knew he would need shoes on the ground. He also partially released most of the escape panel attachments that held the panel in place.

"A tail-gunner on a B17 had a small tight space in the very rear of the bomber. One entered it by crawling on hands and knees. After take offs and before landings the gunner would be confined in this limited space. In the event of an emergency such as this, one could escape by pushing or kicking out the escape panel and rolling out. It was about the size of an average person's body parallel to the gunner.

"When word was given over the intercom to "bail out", Joe was well prepared to exit the aircraft, more so than other crew members. He immediately kicked out the escape panel, took a big gulp of oxygen and rolled out. He knew they were between 20,000 and 25,000 feet elevation and couldn't breathe until he was down to around 15,000 feet. He immediately started tumbling over and over. He said he had heard in training to stop the tumbling, extend arms and legs and open them wide. When reaching the altitude he felt it would be okay to breathe he did so, and still tumbling, pulled the parachute rip cord.

"The parachute failed to open to his dismay. A small pilot chute contained in a chest pack attached to the main parachute was located on his chest. He ripped open the small cover held by small metal snaps. With his hands and with help from the wind he deployed it. It unfurled above his tumbling body and in turn pulled out the big main chute. The big chute then opened, he felt a tremendous shock, oscillated once and hit the ground hard. Joe had been very close to hitting the ground with no open parachute. Being somewhat stunned he lay in a heap looking skyward and

NOT HOME FOR CHRISTMAS

was unable to see any other chutes above. His shoes that had been secured around his neck were long gone. They had probably been torn loose during the chute's opening shock. Being the first out of the aircraft, and with his fast descent, the other crew members were miles down the air space. They in turn never saw his chute so reported him missing. They were all surprised after the war to hear he was alive and well.

"In a few minutes he was frantically getting out of his chute harness after spotting some trees not too far away. His idea was to evade capture somewhere in the trees. A German sergeant driving a motorcycle with an officer in the sidecar drove up the hillside and captured him. The officer stuck a pistol in his face and they searched him, took his pistol, billfold, rings, wrist watch and leather helmet. He was then transported to a POW transient camp near Limeburg, Germany."

"Joseph William Dory died in Jarbidge, Nevada on July 1, 1968, in a tragic airplane crash with his wife Ruth. They were the only occupants and Joe was the pilot of their airplane.

"Joe lived all his life in Austin, Nevada. He was a good handyman/carpenter and worked on small jobs for neighbours and other townspeople. He worked on these jobs through his school years on weekends and summers.

"Upon returning home after his liberation on May 2, 1945 he worked at a large open pit copper mine in Ely, Nevada and later for the Nevada State Highway Department located in Austin, Nevada.

"Joe and his wife Ruth purchased the Pony Canyon Motel and the Chevron gasoline service station in Austin, Nevada and successfully managed them together until their untimely deaths in Jarbidge, Nevada on July 01, 1968.

"Joe loved to fish and hunt, he was a crack shot and an expert at stream trout fishing. I personally spent many hours fishing with him and flying in his several airplanes. He was a licensed pilot and bought and sold several aircraft. He loved to fly and was always flying some local resident to various places. Joe was a very good business person and had a real friendly, hearty loud laugh.

"After his parachute jump into Germany Joe developed a stutter that he never had prior to the jump. This stutter continued for years; however, before his death it had almost disappeared. .

487th Bomb Group, 839th Bomb Squadron

> MuscatineJournal.com
>
> **Obituaries**
> **Charles Arthur McBride**
>
> MUSCATINE, Iowa n Charles Arthur McBride, 80, of Muscatine, died Friday, Nov. 18, 2005, at his home surrounded by his family.
>
> The Rev. Dan Schoepf of the Calvary Church will officiate the service. Honorary casket bearers will be Jim Diveney, Keith Brookhart, George Blackwood, James McAtee, Eric Torgerson, Tom Guck and Milt Price (Former B-17 Crew Member). A time of food and fellowship will follow the service at Calvary Church. Burial will be in Arlington National Cemetery at a later date.
>
> Memorials may be made to Genesis Hospice Program. Online condolences for the McBride family may be left at www.wittichfuneralhome.com.
>
> Mr. McBride was born March 22, 1925, in Muscatine, the son of Ralph A. and Mabel Trader McBride. He married Phyllis Drumm on Jan. 12, 1951, in Muscatine.
>
> He graduated from Musca-tine High School in 1943 and attended college in Missoula, Mont.
>
> He owned and operated Carriage Corner Body Shop, retiring in 1998.
>
> He was a U.S. Army veteran serving during World War II in the Eighth Air Force as a Ball Turret Gunner on a B-17. He was a Prisoner of War from Nov. 26, 1944 until June 6, 1945, when he was liberated. He was a Purple Heart Recipient and also the Air Medal Recipient. He retired with the rank of major from the U.S. Army Reserves.
>
> He was a member of the First Baptist Church, Moose Lodge #388, a lifetime member of the National Disabled American Veterans (DAV), a lifetime member of the American Ex-Prisoners of War. He was a member of the Caterpillar Club when his life was spared because of an emergency parachute jump from a B-17 on Nov. 26, 1944. He was also a charter member of the World War II Memorial.
>
> He and his wife very much enjoyed their trip back to his POW camp in 1995 with other former POWs.
>
> He loved his grandchildren and shared his favorite pastimes and most memorable experiences with them. He enjoyed woodworking and loved to golf.
>
> His is survived by his wife, Phyllis McBride of Muscatine; two daughters, Pamela Leaman and husband, Don, of Raleigh, N.C. and Susan Workman and husband, Mark, of Macungie, Pa.; four grandchildren, Allison and Cate Richardson of Raleigh, N.C., and Seth and Sam Work-man of Macungie, Pa. and one sister, Virginia Guck of Muscatine.
>
> He was preceded in death by his parents and one half-brother, Donald Stephens.

Obituary Charles A. McBride

***

Acknowldgements:
Beth Tillman for Bombardier Roy R. DeNure
Sandy Shefcheck for Waist-Gunner Milton O. Price
Justin Merriman for Tail-Gunner Joseph W. Dory

RINGMASTERS

A History of the 491st Bombardment Group (H)

by Allan G. Blue *(Summer, 1964)*

(Editor's Note: The 491st Bomb Group, also known as "The Ringmasters," played an integral role in the mission of Sunday, November 26, 1944. Of the 34 planes lost that day, the 491st lost 15 of them—more than half of the B-24s they sent on the mission. This chapter serves as an introduction to the 15 chapters that follow and gives a bit of insight into the 491st and the Misburg mission.)

***

MISBURG

On the 25th of October 1944, a sleek P-51 Mustang from Steeple Morton dropped its gear at North Pickenham, home of the 491st Bomb Group. Pilot Getz, former Liberator driver, had stopped by to give the old crowd an envious peek at his new mount. Getz, one of several 491st pilots who did fighter tours after completing their missions with the 491st, was assigned to the Second Air Division Weather Scouts, an outfit composed entirely of former B-24 pilots, and whose job it was to precede the 2ADs Liberators on each mission to report on weather conditions at the target. In the good-natured banter that afternoon Getz' former associates would not concede that Weather Scouts were really *fighters*, even though they flew Mustangs. A month later, however, there wasn't a man in the 491st who wasn't convinced in all seriousness that the Weather Scouts were among the "best damn fighters in the world."

The events leading to this change of heart began in the late

NOT HOME FOR CHRISTMAS

hours of 25 November as the teletype in Group Ops began ticking off the field order for the following day's mission. The Eighth would be after four major targets in Northern Germany. Objective for the 491st: The one remaining oil refinery still in production at Misburg. The target was no stranger to the Group -- it was over Misburg on 12 September that the 491st had lost Sparrow and Eckard. But that was over two months ago and the Group just wasn't losing airplanes these days. Still, there were some who noted that the strike at Misburg would require deeper penetration into Germany than any of the other targets for the following day.

Briefing was at 0530 and by 0904 thirty-one aircraft were up and forming. At 1012, # 44-40162 aborted with a gas leak and, shortly after the formation left the English coast at 1030, another aircraft, # 42-95341-W, turned back with no radio. After a few minor adjustments to cover the holes thus opened, the 491st formation was as shown.

LEAD SQ (855th)

Metcalf-Parmele
622 L

Elliott   Bridges
482 M+   746 V

Martin   Murf   Hunter
296 H+   680 V+   156 F

Campbell   Greer   Fandell
114 F+   462 L+   164 J+

LOW SQ (854th)

		Haney		
		735 Z-		
	Weitz		Wentzel	
	117 J		294 G-	
Warczak		Rath		Lenning
253 R-		459 F-		610 I-
Vukovich	Simons		Wynn	Meuse
108 A-	172 H-		007 S+	271 K-

HIGH SQ (853rd)

		Stewart		
		530 -F		
	Ecklund		Moore	
	534 B		205 -G	
Butler		Bennett		Budd
485 K		073 -B		167 -O
Hite		Cloughley		Stevens
884 -X		212 -I		464 -Y

At 1111 hours this formation crossed the enemy coast as a part of the bomber stream. At almost the same time, some 150 enemy fighters attempted an attack on the B-17 groups at the head of the column. The Fortresses at this time were just approaching Dummer Lake, the point where the stream would split into segments to attack the four different assigned primaries. The German fighters were successfully driven off by the B-17s' fighter escort, assisted by additional area coverage fighters called in to help. The action, however, drifted southward with the Fortresses as they headed for their targets at Altenbeken and Bielefield.

NOT HOME FOR CHRISTMAS

For the 491st the mission was uneventful until some 45 minutes later when it passed the Dummer Lake area. At 1155 three enemy jets were observed flying parallel to the formation about 2000 yards to the left. They made no move to attack but stayed with the Group long enough (it was reasoned later) to chart its strength, course and speed.

The IP, which the 491st reached at 1226, was the town of Wittingen. Located some 16 miles east and north of the target, it thus marked the deepest point of penetration and, in effect, the Group would bomb on the way out. Just prior to the IP-turn a large number of enemy fighters appeared in the distance, southeast of the bombers. They made no move toward the Liberators but were "just playing around in the clouds" as if daring the Mustangs and Thunderbolts to come over and mix it up. The chance seemed too good to miss and the entire close fighter escort, consisting of 197 P-51s and 48 P-47s, went storming after the Germans, estimated at from 150 to 200 strong. In a matter of minutes they were fully engaged, leaving the B-24s on their own. Area coverage fighters, as noted above, had already been diverted to meet an earlier appearance of the enemy.

The Air Commander, 854th CO, Lt. Col. Parmele, now faced a decision only he could make: "...whether to uncover his three squadrons in the face of imminent enemy attack or to preserve the Group formation and meet the enemy with a united front. Realizing that superior bombing results could only be achieved by uncovering, he unhesitatingly ordered this maneuver." The 491st wheeled into the Big Turn and came out on the bomb run. Almost immediately a chance mishap occurred in the lead aircraft of the low squadron -- the nose gunner brushed against the bomb toggle switch with his shoulder. (At this stage of the war most Lead and Deputy Lead aircraft carried an extra, or pilotage, navigator who normally occupied the nose turret. This put four people in the nose compartment of a B-24 which was considered overcrowded with three.) The entire squadron, as briefed, dropped on their leader and 30 tons went down into open fields 15 miles short of the target. In order to avoid further exposure to flak, which had become heavy since the IP, the low squadron veered away from the formation and angled for the rally point south of Hanover, bypassing the target.

This opened a gap between the lead and high squadrons and the low squadron was now off to the left by itself. With all fighter escort lured away, the stage was set for disaster. It came swiftly.

As if by prearranged signal, which it undoubtedly was, the flak suddenly ceased and another, previously unseen hoard of 100 plus German fighters (nearly all FW 190s) struck the high squadron like a scythe. They came in line abreast from six o'clock high, 10 to 15 at a time. The second pass took out the two B-24s of the high right element, Stevens and Budd. Moments later, just as the squadron was approaching the release point, Moore and Stewart were hit badly but managed to make it over the target before going down. Hite, Cloughley and Ecklund followed soon after. The two remaining aircraft, Butler and Bennett, tried to join up with the lead squadron but only Bennett made it.

The fighters now swung southwest and turned their attention to the separated low squadron, pressing their attacks home with almost reckless determination. They obviously wanted to finish their slaughter before the decoyed fighter escort could disengage and return. The pattern was the same, wave after wave in line abreast, followed by individual attacks from almost any angle to finish off the cripples. One FW 190 came screaming down from 6 o'clock very high and sliced through a few feet of space between the Lead and Deputy Lead Liberators. The crew of the latter, AIRBORNE ANGEL, estimated the German missed their plane by less than ten feet. Warczak's unnamed B-24 blew up (Warczak did not survive this one, his second B-24 explosion in two months) and a few moments later Wynn's SCARFACE also exploded. Vukovich's B-24 fell off in a vicious spin that trapped everyone inside.

However, the Liberator gunners were scoring too. T/Sgt. Gerald Burbank, top turret with Lanning, tracked an FW 190 as it came in from 4 o'clock. He opened fire at 700 yards. At 500 yards he began getting hits in the cockpit area and the 190 stopped firing, the pilot undoubtedly dead. The e/a continued to bore in, the nose going down just before a collision seemed inevitable.

Burbank's own plane had problems. Its bomb bay doors had not been open during the low squadron's premature release and as a result two of the doors were left dangling below the aircraft.

NOT HOME FOR CHRISTMAS

The sight of the mangled metal of a cripple brought the fighters like flies.

In the lead bomber 1st Lt. Lester Faggiani blew up a 190 from the nose turret. Faggiani was the pilotage navigator but hadn't taken time to swap places with the regular nose gunner. At the other end of the plane, tail gunner S/Sgt. Donald Newsholme flamed another 190 while S/Sgt. Walter Jarzynka in the right waist took care of a third, sending it down in an uncontrolled spin.

The fighters accounted for three more B-24s before leaving the low squadron for more unfinished business. HARE POWER (Weitz) went down with its bomb bay on fire. First Lt. Robert W. Simons' GREASE BALL caught a fusillade of 20 mm explosive shells that killed two gunners, knocked out all communications and most of the controls, and set fire to the bomb bay. The plane dropped like a rock with only three of the crew able to get out. HOUSE OF RUMOR (Meuse) was also burning. As the pilot rang the bailout bell, bombardier 1st Lt. Harry W. Sonntag went through the plane making sure that everyone had the word. "I found Yuzwa (NG), Caruso (LW) and Byrnes (TG) completely ignoring the order to bail out. Yuzwa (S/Sgt. Samuel Yuzwa) absolutely refused to stop firing and put on his parachute." Sonntag was blown out while checking the rear escape hatch and the three gunners went down with the plane.

Meanwhile the lead squadron, having reached the target unmolested, bombed with good results. With at least some warning as to what was coming, they had tucked it in as tight as possible and the gunners were ready when the first wave of fighters hit. Again they came in from 6 o'clock. S/Sgt. Michael F. McNamara, right waist gunner in Martin's aircraft, flamed an FW 190 on the second pass and S/Sgt. William E. Marsden, left waist in the same plane, exploded another soon afterward.

First Lt. Thomas J. Talbot, a bombardier manning the nose turret in Murff's plane, BIG'UN, also got a destroyed on one of the early passes as a 190 came in high, over flew his target and began his breakaway too late. Talbot picked him off going away and the pilot bailed out. The gunners in PADDY'S WAGON, flown by Lt. Campbell, were busy and accurate, with top turret, right waist and left waist each claiming a kill. Top turret and right waist in Greer's

#462 shared a 190 and waist gunners in both #482 and #164 got probables.

Understandably, the radio had been filled with suggestions that the fighters return and do their fighting where it would do the most good. However, the first to respond to the urgent call were eight P-51s of the Second Air Division's Weather Scouts. Led by Bob Whitlow, who was to become the first Athletic Director of the Air Force Academy, the eight Mustangs waded into the 100 plus enemy fighters, broke up the coordinated attack and kept the 190s busy until reinforcements arrived. When they did, it was a fairly good turkey shoot, resulting in claims of 47-1-20.

With the pressure off, the remaining 12 B-24s of the 491st reassembled into a single formation and headed for home. The concentrated attack on the bombers had lasted only 15 minutes, with some sporadic passes for an additional ten. The high squadron had been completely wiped out and the low squadron had lost seven out of ten. (Lanning managed to make it over Belgium where the crew bailed out.) Due in large part to the timely appearance of Whitlow and company, however, all nine Liberators of the lead squadron were, if not wholly intact, at least still airborne.

The first returning aircraft to land was Greer. His plane had two flat tires and came to a stop at the intersection of two runways, blocking both. One by one the others came in, nearly half of them with wounded or dead aboard. The reaction of the ground crews at the hardstands of the 853rd Squadron are described below -- hardly award-winning prose but nonetheless authentic.

"Today nine crews departed on ops. The ETR was 1600 hours. A few minutes after the ETR a squadron and a half of the 491st planes appeared over the field but, as none of our ships were among them, we waited for the second formation to appear. But the clock moved around from five, to ten, to fifteen minutes and then to half an hour... At first it never occurred to us that maybe our ships had gone down. But gradually, after we had checked and rechecked with the tower, gradually we began to realize that such a thing could happen -- that maybe it had happened. We fought the thought for a long time, tried to make ourselves believe that the ships had come down in France or Belgium, or at least some of them would come back...

But after interrogation, there was no hope left at all. Reports vary as to the number of chutes seen. One gunner estimates 95% of the men got out. Others are not optimistic. A reasonable estimate would seem to be between 50-75% of our 84 men got out safely..."

Hope ran higher than reality. Of the 84 men of the 853rd, 50 were already dead and many of the rest badly injured.

Stevens had been flying his first mission since 20 June, when he crashed at Dover as previously described. Just after the first fighters hit, his engineer, F/Sgt. Joseph L. Boyer, yelled, "They're coming in again!" An instant later he was killed by a 20 mm shell, his body falling out of the open bomb bay doors. Moments later the plane exploded. Stevens, blown clear, again survived.

THE MOOSE (1st Lt. Warren Moore) was hard hit on the first pass, which left #2 burning, the bomb bay on fire and the intercom and hydraulics out. "Our engineer (T/Sgt Francis S. Hawkins) went into the blazing bomb bay and opened the doors manually. He must have been burned badly." (Moore) Bombardier George K. Patten had been manning the nose turret and had tracked an enemy fighter too far, jamming the turret. Navigator Ross S. Houston worked frantically to try to crank the turret back so that Patten could get out but it was no use. Two explosions in the aft section sent the plane down out of control and Houston was forced to leave Patten trapped. Five survived.

Stewart's crew were on their 30th mission. Five managed to bail out before IDIOT'S DELIGHT blew up.

Butler's DORTY TREEK was shot to a shambles in the air. "There were two more fighter attacks between the time I ordered bailout and the time I left the aircraft. Yergey (B) and Fuller (RW) were dead, Callicrate (LW) had a bullet through his arm, Jones (E) and Ostrander (CP) were badly burned, and Trombly (TG) had been shot through the hand. The aircraft was covered by fire and all the engines shot out when I left the plane." Kamarainen (Radio) was beaten by civilians when he landed, but survived.

Bennett, in ARK ANGEL, succeeded in joining up with the Lead Squadron. "He slid underneath us. His whole Martin (upper) turret was missing and there was a large hole in the right wing. He couldn't keep up and was last seen at 1258 hours still losing altitude." (Fandell) Nobody knows what happened after that; nobody in ARK ANGEL lived.

Little is known also of the events aboard PROBLEM CHILD (Hite), FIREBIRD (Budd) or Cloughley's unnamed B-24. Of the 28 men manning these planes, 24 were KIA. German records do state that the wreckage of these aircraft, together with Warczak's from the low squadron, were so close together that it was impossible to determine what bodies belonged to what B-24. The remaining 853rd aircraft, Ecklund's, faired better; the entire crew bailed out and were taken prisoner.

Casualties in the other squadrons brought the total 491st bill for Misburg to 90 KIA and 52 POW. Verified claims were 7-11-3, which of course did not include any enemy fighters downed or damaged by aircraft which were shot down.

A Sidelight on Misburg is given in a letter from Col. William M. Shy: "The night prior to Misburg we were working up the mission in Group Ops. After the field order came off the teletype, Jack Merrell came down to go over the mission. Meantime, Capt. Verle Pope, our Intelligence Officer, had looked into his crystal ball and established that there was a large number of German fighters in the area adjacent to our target, and that they had been acknowledged through intelligence channels as having quite a potential left. These boys had been rather inactive for a while, and 8th AF believed that they were being held in readiness for one big effort. At this stage of the game our Group had never sustained a concentrated fighter attack, and Jack said he thought we had better shakedown our gunnery equipment and include a strong specialized briefing for the gunners going on this mission. This was exactly what was done, and Jack personally gave the gunners hell the next morning, since the night's efforts had turned up some careless housekeeping in regard to turrets and cleaning of gun barrels. I am sure that some of our crews returned home from this mission as a result of Jack's efforts with the gunners that night. This was typical of his leadership and foresight. I saw a few gunners go up and shake hands with him after landing back home the next day."

A final Sidelight on Misburg comes from the Control Tower Log entries for Monday, 27 November:

NOT HOME FOR CHRISTMAS

0050 Alerted.
0530 Briefing.
0849 17 A/C off on ops...
17.25 hours. Sixteen replacement B-24's arrived from Stanstead. Shades of Dawn Patrol.

***

Reprinted by permission.
Ringmasters article "491st History: Part IV, Misburg": Allan G. Blue

"The Ringmasters" is published quarterly by the 491st Bombardment Group (H), Inc. and printed at Rocky Mount, North Carolina. A Tax Exempt Non-Profit Veterans Organization.
www.491st.com

CHAPTER 14

491ST BOMB GROUP 853RD BOMB SQUADRON

Aircraft Type: B-24H, serial # 41-28884,
"Problem Child", MACR 10762
Airbase: North Pickenham

"War is hell and there is no doubt about it in my mind now."

—Bombardier Vince Cahill whose plane was aborted this mission due to engine failure over the North Sea

---

Pilot: 2Lt John P. Hite (KIA) Christiansburg VA
Co-Pilot: 2Lt Morris J. Volden (KIA) Cottonwood ME
Navigator: 2Lt Thomas R. O'Brien (KIA) Waspeth NY
Bombardier: 2Lt Bill H. Sutton (KIA) Little Rock AR
Top-Turret: Sgt Edward B. Tykarsky (KIA) West Aliquippa PA
Radio: Sgt Kenneth F. Weible (KIA) Chappell ME
Left Waist: Sgt Andrew Marko (KIA) Bridgeport CT
Right Waist: Sgt Carl Negrin (KIA) Brooklyn NY
Tail Gunner: Sgt Harold R. Wagers (KIA) College Corner OH

Total: 9 KIA
Target: Misburg (Hannover)
Crash Site: 800 m. NW of Hiddesdorf, 10 km. SSW of Hannover
Time of Crash: 12.45

NOT HOME FOR CHRISTMAS

Exerpts of the MACR made by Jan Hey, Hengelo (Netherlands)

"Lost to fighters in the target area between 1240 and 1300 h. No further details in MACR. However, in MACR 10763 is a German report that a B-24 (‹green cross bar') crashed at 12:45 h. about 800 km NW of Hiddesdorf, 10 km. SSW of Hannover, all of crew (9 men) killed. After elimination of other B-24s lost, this one must be the B-24, serial # 41-28884."

This whole crew was killed in action. I have tried to get in contact with family members but did not succeed. In honor of this crew I quote some survivors of the 491st who flew this mission. Bombardier Vince Cahill's crew of the 853rd Bomb Squadron had to abort this mission because of engine failure over the North Sea and returned safely to North Pickenham. His impression:

"There were only nine aircraft in the 853rd Squadron over Misburg. Our crew was to be the 10th aircraft but shortly after crossing the enemy coast we had to feather #1 engine and were having trouble with #2. We salvoed our bombs into the Zuider Zee, returned to the base and had lunch. After lunch I went to the gun shack to clean my guns that had been test fired over the channel. It was getting close to the time for return of the group.

"We heard the incoming aircraft, expecting twenty-nine to return. As they approached the field, red-red flares filled the sky. This meant wounded aboard, they had priority to land. I counted the ships, only fourteen of the twenty-nine we had sent into the air that day.

"The ships landed and I ran over to the one nearest to me. The bombardier, who was in my class at Childless (Sammy Heinfling) looked at me as if he'd seen a ghost. "What are you doing here? Your squadron was knocked out of the air by fighters. I thought you went down." Had we not aborted our mission, we would have been shot down as they did not leave the 853rd Squadron until all aircraft were destroyed.

"This was the greatest loss our group had experienced. Over 90 men were lost from our squadron alone. Over 140 men of the group were lost. It was a quiet hut that night. Pilots Budd and Orley, Navigator Hirsh and Bombardier "Shorty" were gone. I wondered if we would ever be lucky enough to complete our 35 missions. This was Budd's crew's 26th mission, four more to go for 30 and a complete tour.

"November 26 was a Sunday. The small chapel which was never crowded for evening Mass could not hold the many who were there tonight. As I wrote my mother, I want to thank you for the mission you made at church. I wish to assure you that your prayers were answered. (The first of three times.) War is hell and there is no doubt about it in my mind now."

Lead crew on the November 26, 1944 mission to Misburg was Pilot Joe Metcalf with Col. Parmale as Command Pilot. Plane was "Ragged but Right". Joe reports:

"To the best of my recollection, the 491st Bomb Group was flying ‹tail end Charlie' for the Air Force on this date and as such would be a prime target for fighters. As you may recall, we didn't have fighter support the last 30 minutes of our flight to Misburg. Enemy fighters attacked as we turned on our Initial Point toward the target.

"On the initial , we lost some four to six planes. The enemy fighters continued the attack as we flew the last ten minutes from the IP to the target. There were fighters flying thru our formation. We were determined to drop our bombs which we did and immediately turned away from the target because of heavy flak. After leaving the target area, we were under constant attack for the next 20 minutes (maybe it was only 20 minutes, but it seemed like an hour) or so until we got over the Minden Canal and Drummer Lake area where we received fighter support from P-51's.

"To the best of my knowledge, we started out with a flight of 36 planes and arrived back at our base with 16 to 18 planes. We were very fortunate in our plane since we did not sustain any injuries nor was our plane damaged to the point that we could not get home. We did have several bullet and flak holes in the plane.

"I recall the plane flying on our right wing, flipping over their right side. Our crew members reported seeing parachutes opening. As you can imagine the flight from target back to where our fighters were was a hairy one. Our gunners claimed 1 fighter shot down and another probable."

Hell at Misburg, by Al Oliviera, armorer/gunner on Fandell's crew:

Our second mission was to Misburg where we went after the oil refineries carrying twelve 500 # GP bombs. We encountered heavy flak from the IP to bombs away, then the flak subsided and all hell broke loose with enemy fighters coming at us from all directions. Our tail turret received a direct hit on the armor plate.

Shorty Richardson was not injured but sat in the turret helpless as his guns froze from the extreme cold. Apparently the same FW 190 that disabled the tail turret perched on the right wing where I was manning the right waist gun. I could clearly see the pilot with his oxygen mask in place and I could also see the four American flags painted below his canopy. Twenty milimeter shells were bursting in bright flashes as he attempted to down the aircraft. Out of the corner of my eye I saw one of those flashes at the left waist position and Bill Meerdo who had been firing from his position fell against my gun jarring it loose from the mount. I repositioned the gun and continued firing at the FW 190 on the right wing. The FW 190 began to smoke from the cowling and lose air speed, descending out of sight. I was credited with a "probable". I tended to Bill Meerdo with morphine and sulpha but he had a neck wound and apparently died instantly.

Off to the right, the devastation was bad. B-24s on fire, some exploding in the air falling in flames. Other B-24's completely engulfed in flames and some completely out of control spiraling down. I saw only five chutes.

With aircraft damaged and control cables severed Fandell did a great job returning to North Pickenham.

Misburg, a tail-gunner's view, By Warren Doremus, tail-gunner with Bill Martin's crew.

"The evening before I had an uneasy feeling that promted me to write my mother and girl friend (later my wife). At briefing possibility of fighters was stressed and for the first time on any mission, I test fired my guns. About fifteen minutes before the target, I saw aircraft in the distance and notified our pilot. When we were attacked by enemy fighters, I fired my guns and it spit out a couple shells and then jammed. The next thing I knew I was lying on my back looking at the plane's ceiling with one eye and gasping for breath. My oxygen line was damaged and had collapsed. I disconnected my oxygen mask and tried to fix my guns. I couldn't fix them and was losing coordination due to lack of oxygen. In a few minutes the fighter attack was over and the flak came. The waist gunners looked at me and asked if my head hurt. I said no and was puzzled why they asked.

"The base sure looked good that day. After landing, we examined the tail section and realised how lucky we had been. Part of the left fin, rudder and elevator were missing and the side of the plane next to the tail turret was full of holes. Also, our top turret gunner had been injured in the face. A 20 mm shell from from one of the enemy fighters had hit one of his 50 cal shells sending fragments of it into his face. I ended up in the area hospital with 20 mm fragments in my right shoulder and a couple of lacerations on my face. Thank God for our flak suits that in this case had taken most of the punishment. After release from the hospital, I was chosen to go to London to the "Armed Forces Radio Center." There I was interrogated as to the happenings of the group and my crew. From this a speech was written and I made a recording to be broadcasted into enemy held territories.

"I flew my last three missions as a fill in gunner, and I sure missed my original crew. Today there are six of us left of the original ten and we are in contact with each other on a regular basis."

***

Acknowledgements:
"As I saw it": from Vince Cahill (B) Greaser's crew.
Pilot Joe Metcalf
"Hell at Misburg", by Al Oliviera
"Misburg, a tail-gunner's view," By Warren Doremus
Jan Hey fror summary of MACR

CHAPTER 15

491ST BOMB GROUP 853RD BOMB SQUADRON

Aircraft Type: B-24H, serial # 41-29464,
"The Unlimited", MACR 10763
Airbase: North Pickenham

"I glanced out of my side window and saw the right wing with #3 and #4 engines still attached...break off completely. The aircraft went into a wild gyration and there was a loud explosion. I was blown clear of the aircraft."

—Co-Pilot Brice Thornburg in a letter to the author

Pilot: 1Lt Charles W. Stevens Jr. (POW) Charlotte NC
Co-Pilot: 1Lt Brice E. Thornburg (POW) Davidson NC
Navigator: 1Lt David W. McCarty (POW) New York NY
Nose Turret: S/Sgt Troy L. Ryan (KIA) Baldwyn MS
Top Turret: T/Sgt Joseph L. Boyer (KIA) Mullen NC
Radio: T/Sgt Joseph P. Dechaine (POW) Waterville ME
Left Waist: S/Sgt John D. McJimsey Jr. (POW) Bethany LA
Right Waist: S/Sgt Elmore W. Shepherd (KIA) Virgilina VA
Tail Gunner: S/Sgt Elmer Steinman (KIA) Bayonne NJ

Total: 4 KIA, 5 POW
Target: Misburg
Crash Site: Hüspede, 18 km NW of Hildesheim
Time of Crash: 13.10

NOT HOME FOR CHRISTMAS

Jan Hey of the Netherlands who has summarized all Missing Air Crew Reports pertaining to the 8th USAAF, say about this crew:

> "The Unlimited" exploded in mid-air and crashed in Hüpede, Germany, 12 miles NW of Hildesheim killing a mother with her daughter. Another daughter lost one of her legs.
>
> "Engineer Joseph L. Boyer was killed in the aircraft and fell through the bomb bay doors. Nose-gunner Troy Ryan, waist-gunner Elmore W. Shepherd and tail-gunner Elmer Steinman were found in the wreckage of their bomber. All four were initially buried in the civil cemetery of Pattensen-Hüspede in Germany. After the war they were re-interred in the American Military Cemetery in Neuville-en-Condroz in Belgium.
>
> "Navigator David McCarty and waist-gunner McJimsey could bail out just before the explosion of "The Unlimited". Pilot Charles Stevens, co-pilot Brice Thornburg and radio-operator Joseph Dechaine were blown out during the explosion. All five were captured and survived the war.

Back row, left to right: Elmer Steinman, David McCarty, Brice Thornburg, John McJimsey
Front row, left to right: Joseph Dechaine, Elmore Shepherd, Joseph Boyer

We know very little about the pilot **Charles Stevens**. From the database of the 491st Web Site I learned:

> "During the mission of June 20, 1944 to France the flak "was the heaviest the guys have seen yet." One burst of flak took away the entire nose section of Charles Stevens' B-24, # 42-95171, instantly killing the Navigator Lt. Harold R. Meng, and the Bombardier William F. Weck.

> "The plane left the target area with two engines gone, a third one was lost over the Channel and the remaining engine was losing power as Stevens brought the wreck in. He made a magnificent one-engine crash landing on a beach near Greatstone in England, but two crew members; Thomas E. Fullbright and Bernard E. Peak, had jumped before the landing and delayed their chutes too long. Both were instantly killed. Stevens came back yesterday, is taking it hard."

NOT HOME FOR CHRISTMAS

Co-pilot **Brice E. Thornburg** wrote the author in 2002:

"I am Brice E. Thornburg and was the co-pilot on the mission you described. Prior to that mission we were briefed that its purpose was to get the German fighters of 400+ to come up in force after us. We were told that the 8th Air Force would be sending 400+ fighters with us. There were 3 groups of B-24s with 30 aircraft per group. The 491st Bomb Group was one of these groups.

"Everything was normal until we were in the target area. Over the target, flak was heavy. I saw 200 or 300+ fighters milling around outside of the target area. To avoid the flak after bombs away over the target, we turned to get out of the flak. Immediately the Me-109's attacked the formation. The aircraft was a blazing inferno within three or four seconds. I looked back into the bomb bay area and saw a crewman in a complete fireball. I got up from the seat to try to extinguish him. As I got up I glanced out of my side window and saw the right wing with #3 and #4 engines still attached...break off completely, The aircraft went into a wild gyration and there was a loud explosion. I was blown clear of the aircraft.

"I delayed pulling the ripcord because I was fastening the parachute leg straps. (It was uncomfortable to sit in the seat for eight hours with the straps fastened.) While coming down, I fell through a group of fighters firing at each other. Then I saw people on the ground and I pulled the ripcord. I landed in a freshly ploughed, soft field. I rolled in the mud to try to extinguish the fire on myself. My clothes were on fire and my oxygen mask had melted onto my face. I was the first on the ground from the battle. I saw many men in parachutes descending from the air battle. Many aircraft were on fire and pieces were falling all around me.

"Within a few minutes, there were several German soldiers with rifles and bayonets against my stomach. They were hollering "Pistol." An eight to ten years old kid appeared and acted as interpreter. The boy spoke good English. I was ordered to get my parachute and go with them. About this time, someone hanging from a parachute above me started yelling at these German soldiers. He was a German fighter pilot who was shot down in the battle. He also spoke good English and asked me for a cigarette. I gave him the cigarettes I had and we walked side-by-side discussing the battle that was still going on about us. He put me in a room of a small building, shook my hand and disappeared. I never saw him again.

"A man came into the room and said he was a doctor. He saw that I was pretty well burned and he put some kind of grease all over my face

NOT HOME FOR CHRISTMAS

"We rode the train for a day or two to a railroad station where we waited. While at this railroad station, the Brits started bombing it. We were rushed out of the station and got on a trolley car. We rode this trolley for a mile or two. We were then taken off of the trolley and taken to an interrogation centre. The German officer interrogating me kept asking me if my name was THORNBURG. After about 30 minutes of this, I told him that I had always thought of the German people as being humane and I needed to see a doctor for my face where I had been burned. He said, "I'll show you how humane the Germans are." He called someone on the phone and told me a staff car would pick me up and take me to a hospital.

"Immediately two people came in and escorted me to a waiting staff car. The car took me to a two-story building. I was then taken up to the second floor where they gave me a nice, comfortable, double bed and nice room all to myself. A German woman came in and gave me a bowl of mashed potatoes and a bowl of apple sauce. It was good food. I stayed there for several days in that nice room and the same good food.

"After staying there, living good and being interrogated by a German officer several times, I was taken along with about twenty Americans to a German hospital, where medical personnel of the 1st British Airborne Division, who had been captured during the battle for the bridge of Arnhem in the Netherlands, was taking care of the medical needs for the Allied POWs. After four to five weeks treatment at this hospital, I was transferred to a regular POW camp and was moved around three or four times until the war was over.

"I was never mistreated by the Germans.

Brice Thornburg's wife Betty sent me the following post war details:

"About six months after he came back to the States and had his Rest and Recreation in Miami, we got married and were sent to Turner Field, Georgia--then to Langly Field in Virginia--then to Ft. Bragg. Then to Shaw Air Force Base in Sumter, SC and then to Scott AFB in Illinois--all in a year's time!! Our first son was born at Scott AFB. He was three months old when Brice got orders to go to Japan. After being over there a year or so he decided to get out and joined the National Guard. Our second son was born just before Brice was recalled during the Korean War and we were sent to Scott AFB again. Brice had orders to go to Korea after about a year but then his orders were cancelled.

"We were sent to Symerna, Tenn. near Nashville--then to Pope Field in

NOT HOME FOR CHRISTMAS

"We rode the train for a day or two to a railroad station where we waited. While at this railroad station, the Brits started bombing it. We were rushed out of the station and got on a trolley car. We rode this trolley for a mile or two. We were then taken off of the trolley and taken to an interrogation centre. The German officer interrogating me kept asking me if my name was THORNBURG. After about 30 minutes of this, I told him that I had always thought of the German people as being humane and I needed to see a doctor for my face where I had been burned. He said, "I'll show you how humane the Germans are." He called someone on the phone and told me a staff car would pick me up and take me to a hospital.

"Immediately two people came in and escorted me to a waiting staff car. The car took me to a two-story building. I was then taken up to the second floor where they gave me a nice, comfortable, double bed and nice room all to myself. A German woman came in and gave me a bowl of mashed potatoes and a bowl of apple sauce. It was good food. I stayed there for several days in that nice room and the same good food.

"After staying there, living good and being interrogated by a German officer several times, I was taken along with about twenty Americans to a German hospital, where medical personnel of the 1st British Airborne Division, who had been captured during the battle for the bridge of Arnhem in the Netherlands, was taking care of the medical needs for the Allied POWs. After four to five weeks treatment at this hospital, I was transferred to a regular POW camp and was moved around three or four times until the war was over.

"I was never mistreated by the Germans.

Brice Thornburg's wife Betty sent me the following post war details:

"About six months after he came back to the States and had his Rest and Recreation in Miami, we got married and were sent to Turner Field, Georgia--then to Langly Field in Virginia--then to Ft. Bragg. Then to Shaw Air Force Base in Sumter, SC and then to Scott AFB in Illinois--all in a year's time!! Our first son was born at Scott AFB. He was three months old when Brice got orders to go to Japan. After being over there a year or so he decided to get out and joined the National Guard. Our second son was born just before Brice was recalled during the Korean War and we were sent to Scott AFB again. Brice had orders to go to Korea after about a year but then his orders were cancelled.

"We were sent to Symerna, Tenn. near Nashville--then to Pope Field in

491st Bomb Group, 853rd Bomb Squadron

N.C.--then to Keesler in Mississippi--then Brice was sent to Saudi Arabia for a year and the kids and I were sent back home. After that tour Brice came to Charleston AFB--then while Charleston was still his home base, we all went to the Canal Zone where he was a Liaison Officer for three years. After being back for about three years, he retired with 30 years service as a Bird Colonel.

"We moved 10 miles up here to Summerville and have been here ever since. We really like it here. Brice said he's been everywhere except Australia and New Zealand. While at Charleston, he flew all over the world just about. After he retired, he went to work as an Aircraft Control Officer and worked there for 15 years.

About left-waist gunner **John D. McJimsey Jr.** his daughter DeeLee McJimsey wrote:

"John DeWitt McJimsey, Jr. whose friends and family called him Jack, was born December 25, 1922 in Elysian Fields, Texas He always said this was not a good day for a birthday because you would get only one present and it would say "Happy Birthday AND Merry Christmas.

"His father was John DeWitt McJimsey Sr. and his mother was Hattie Maude Jernigan. He had one sister Mae Margaret, two years older, and one brother, Bert, fourteen years younger. He and Bert were best friends: they loved to hunt and fish together.

"He attended Elysian Fields ISD, Elysian Fields, TX and graduated from Greenwood High School, Greenwood, LA. He entered the Army Air Corps in January, 1943 at Camp Beauregard, LA. He departed for overseas duty (European Theater) on April 18, 1944 and arrived at North Pickingham Air Base in England on April 30, 1944. He participated in the Misburg Oil Refinery Misson on November 26, 1944, when his entire "High Squadron" was shot down approximately 15 miles from Hanover, Ger-

Left-waist gunner **John D. McJimsey Jr.**

309

many. This was his 32nd mission. He was honorably discharged Sept,. 24, 1945 at Barksdale Seperation Center, Barksdale Field, LA.

"In August he married Abbie Ruth Graves. One daughter, DeeLee, was born November 30, 1951.

"After the war, he taught at a mechanical trade school in Marshall, Tx. He worked on several oil well drilling rigs as a "rough neck", and at Arkla Gas (now Center Point Energy) putting in pipe lines in Arkansas, Oklahoma, Texas. This was his last job, from which he retired. He served his community as a member of Mt. Zion Methodist Church, Waskom Masonic Lodge, Sottish Rite, Community #4 Volunteer Fire Department, helped establish the Panola Bethany Water System, and served on the Elysian Fields School Board from 1960-65.

"He also did farming, raising corn and cotton, and had some cattle. He loved this, but said he could not make a living from this. That's when he started working in the oil field.

"Jack died August 16, 2005 at his home in Panola, TX. He suffered from Alzheimers and lung cancer. He is buried in the Woodley Cemetery in Elysian Fields, TX.

***

Acknowledgments:
Lia Thornburg for Co-Pilot Brice E. Thornburg
Jan Hey for the summary of the MACR
DeeLee McJimsey and Robbie Sutlive for waist-gunner John D. McJimsey
    Jr.

CHAPTER 16

491ST BOMB GROUP 853RD BOMB SQUADRON

Aircraft Type: B-24J, serial # 44-40212,
MACR 11158
Airbase: North Pickenham

"The body was properly identified before re-interment, and at the time of re-interment his identification tag was buried with his body for future identification."

—From a letter from the War Department
to the widow of Bombardier John H. Singley

Pilot: 1Lt Robert E. Cloughly (POW) Kansas City KS

Co-Pilot: 2Lt Gerald M. Greer (POW) Bakersfield CA

Bombardier: 2Lt John H. Singley (KIA) Columbia SC

Nose Turret: S/Sgt Leo R. Lehr (KIA) Springfield MA

Top Turret: T/Sgt Paul W. Manter (KIA) Freeport ME

Radio: T/Sgt William L. Carlisle (KIA) Minneapolis MN

Left Waist Gunner: S/Sgt Jesse W. Cole (KIA) Sanford NC

Right Waist Gunner: S/Sgt William E. Reutener (KIA) North Olmstead OH

Tail Gunner: S/Sgt Russell C. Stewart (KIA) Indianapolis IN

Total: 7 KIA, 2 POW
Target: Misburg
Crash Site: Müllingen near Hildesheim

NOT HOME FOR CHRISTMAS

Back row, left to right: Paul Manter, unknown*, William Carlisle, unknown*, Russell Stewart
Front row, left to right: John Singley, Robert Cloughly, Gerald Greer, unknown*
*not on this mission

Only the two pilots could save themselves by parachute and were taken prisoner.

Jan Hey, of Hengelo, Netherlands, writes about this crew:

> "The bomber formation was heavily attacked by many German fighters when on the bomb run and getting off the target. Many bombers crashed in that area. Police and recovery teams from various airfields in the vicinity of Hannover were involved in recording the crash sites and the identification of dead and POWs but their reports are not always clear. The available documents do not shed light on the crash-site of this aircraft.
>
> "Dead List A/Z" revealed that Sgt. William Reutener was buried at the time in Hildesheim; a series of micro-fiches with "Crashes arranged by Date" includes a B-24 at Müllingen near Hildesheim so it is believed that this one may have been the 44-40212."

In April, 1946, almost a year after the end of the war in Europe, **Ray McDonough**, an investigator of the 46th Grave Registration Company visited the crash site and wrote:

"On the 26th November 1944 a four motored bomber crashed in the vicinity of the town of Harkenbleck, about 10 miles south of Hannover. The plane was brought down by flak and the main fuselage fell in a small lake near Harkenbeck, the parts protruding above the water burned for two or three hours.

"Two fliers were found in the surrounding area, one found alive and one found dead.

"Waist-Gunner Sgt. William Reutener, service number 15140449, was found wounded, was given first aid by a nurse and then taken to a hospital in Hildesheim by streetcar. The second flier, Tail-Gunner Russel C. Stewart was found dead in a field next to the pond. His body was removed to Grasdorf.

"When investigating the scene of the crash it was found that the plane wreckage laid in about 20 to 25 feet of water. Some of the wreckage laid near the shore of the pond, but no markings or numbers were available.

"When questioning persons in Harkenbleck they assumed that there may be more bodies in the plane, but the number was not known.

In April 1946, about a year after Germany had surrendered, the Mayor of Grasdorf, Germany, stated:

"In October 1944, Sunday-noon, there was an air attack on Misburg. The last squadron was attacked by German planes and released one part of the bombs near Grasdorf. After the bombardment I saw some wreckages of a plane falling down.

"If I remember right, the part which crashed on the right side of the river Leine in the vicinity of Grasdorf was burning. On the other side, on the east bank, another part was laying.

"One wounded soldier was reported to me. I informed the nurse of the vicinity to bandage him and he was found 300 metres north of the river. Near him the tail of the plane was laying. The pilot had a small wound and I helped him to put some compress on it.

"Another soldier was found near the ice-cover on the water on December 26, 1944. He was buried in the cemetery in the cemetery of Grasdorf.

Co-Pilot Gerald M. Greer's story as dictated to Peggy Greer, his daughter-in-law:

"On November 26, 1944, Second Lieutenant Gerald M. Greer began his 16th mission. Their target was the synthetic fuel plant in Misburg, Germany. They were flying a B-24 that was loaded with twelve 500 pound bombs.

"The plane flew at about 24000 feet along with twenty-nine other planes of the 491st Bomb Group on the same mission. Their target area was thought to have a lot of flak but little was incurred. As they started the bomb run ME109 fighter planes attacked them. Gerald didn't see the fighters but knew they had been hit. The pilot, Robert Cloughly, said to turn on the bailout switch to notify the crew to get out. Gerald and Robert began to make their way out of the pilot's compartment. The plane was in a shallow dive as Gerald crossed the flight deck but Robert wasn't with him. He noticed that the engineer and the radio operator were already gone. As Gerald worked his way to the bomb bay doors he discovered that the area was on fire which he thought was a fuel fire. The bombs were all gone and the bomb bay doors were still open which gave him a good escape if he could get through the fire.

"He covered his face trying to get some protection as he moved through the flames and out the bomb bay doors. As he fell through the sky, he noticed that he was smouldering from the fire. He waited a long time before pulling the ripcord to make sure he was not longer on fire. Gerald looked around trying to spot other parachutes in the air but saw none. He did see a FW190 fighter plane coming towards him but an American P51 fighter plane shot him down and the pilot didn't bail out.

"As soon as he landed German soldiers were there to take him prisoner. They couldn't understand each other but from a few gestures and hand signals Gerald knew they wanted to know if he had any weapons but he didn't. He was then taken prisoner and transported to a German Command Post where a German Medic gave him first aid. The Medic applied bandages to Gerald's burnt face.

"A little later the German's took Gerald outside to see William Reutener who was badly hurt on a stretcher. Gerald asked him if anyone in the back of the plane got out and he said that they were all dead. William died a short time later.

"Gerald thought that the engineer and the radioman had gotten out before him but he never saw them again. The pilot was leaving at the same time but Gerald never saw him again either.

"Gerald was taken to a holding centre and interrogated for several days. He was then sent to a hospital where an American Doctor, who was a fellow prisoner, performed a skin graft operation under both of his eyes. This surgery was performed using drugs to keep Gerald from feeling the pain.

"Later he was sent to a burn hospital where he received another skin graft operation. This time he would have to be awake for the operation because they didn't have any drugs except morphine. An English Doctor, who was also a prisoner, would be performing the surgery. They gave him two shots of morphine and a short time later two helpers, one on each arm led him up a flight of stairs to the operating room and laid him on a gurney.

"The English doctor told him to grab hold of the gurney rail, hold on tight and don't move his head. The doctor's assistant Jock, a big Scottish man held Gerald's head down so he couldn't move it. The doctor picked up the scalp and cut a slit just under one eyelid, which felt like a hot wire scraping under his eye. The doctor pushed his lower eyelid up to meet the upper and took a look to see what size and shape was needed to patch the hole. He then cut a piece of soft skin from behind his ear and stitched it under his eye. He repeated the procedure for the other eye and the operation was over.

"His eyes were kept bandaged over night, and a few days later his stitches were removed.

"After he recovered he was transferred along with two other prisoners to a regular POW camp. Two German soldiers were assigned to escort them to the camp. Part of the trip was by train, part was by truck and part was on foot. They spent one night at a farmhouse owned by a friend of one of the guards. A member of the SS who was the grandson of the woman who owned the farmhouse came to visit and the prisoners were locked in a near by barn until he left. Later the prisoners were brought inside and given a feather bed to sleep on. The guards knew that the prisoners had Spam that was given to them by the Red Cross so they asked them to give the Spam to the woman at the farm and she would make breakfast in the morning. They gave her the Spam and in the morning she cooked fresh eggs and Spam. Gerald had not had fresh eggs since he left home to join the war.

They finally arrived at the Moosburg prison camp and settled in with the other prisoners. Gerald was liberated on April 29th 1945.

As I knew that nose-turret Gunner **Leo R. Lehr** originated from Springfield, MA I sent a letter to the Editor of *The Republican* for more information about him. The Managing Editor, Special Projects, Cynthia Simison not only published my letter but also gave it full follow-up. She wrote in the November 10, 2004 edition of her newspaper:

NOT HOME FOR CHRISTMAS

"Casey Renkowicz never knew Staff Sergeant Leo R. Lehr but she knows the pain his family must have that day in October 1945 when news of his death finally arrived at a house on Hungry Hill in Springfield. Six months earlier, in another neighbourhood of Western Massachusetts, the same kind of telegram had arrived at her family's home.

"And she also knows the beauty, if you will, of the American military cemetery in the Netherlands where Leo Lehr is buried. It is also where her brother, Casimir Witalisz, an infantryman killed in Germany just days before victory was declared in Europe that spring, is buried.

"I want the family to know it is such a beautiful cemetery," Renkowicz told me as she described a visit to her brother's grave. It was a visit, she said, that she had promised her ailing mother before she died.

"Renkowicz, who now lives in Westfield, was among those who called in response to a column published on these pages about Leo Lehr I wrote in search of relatives and friends of the airman who, along with his crew aboard a B-24 Liberator heavy bomber, was shot down over Germany on the Sunday after Thanksgiving 1944.

"I didn't have to wait long for response when my column was first published. I had barely been at my desk for a half-hour that morning when a niece – though not of an age old enough to remember Leo Lehr – e-mailed from Westfield the sad news that most of that generation of her family were dead. But her aunt, Geraldine Lehr, who now lives in Norton, might provide some assistance to researcher John Meurs in Switzerland, said Linda Lehr.

"A cousin, Bill Duffy of Southwick, responded the same within hours. "We all know of Leo is what we have heard in family stories," said his wife, Nancy Duffy. They are the son and daughter-in-law of Leo Lehr's sister.

"Then a telephone call to my desk caught me most by surprise. A soft-voiced gentleman inquired if I was the person who had authored a piece about Leo Lehr. "I sat behind Leo during our senior year at Cathedral high School," the man told me..

"Bob Campbell now lives in Avon, Conn., and turned 80 recently. His personal story is probably very much a mirror of what Leo Lehr's would have been, save for one twist of fate. Had Campbell been with the crew of his B-17 Flying Fortress heavy bomber on September, 13, 1944, he, too, might not have returned home.

"I was grounded that morning. They went down over an oil refinery in Blechhammer, Germany," Campbell recalled of the city which was the target of a major Allied offensive that fall.

491st Bomb Group, 853rd Bomb Squadron

```
C A S U A L T Y    R E P O R T        U.S. AIR FORCES.

Date              :   20 November 1944        Time  :  ± 1300 h
Aircraft          :   B-24J   44 - 40212               8th AF.
Codes             :   T8 : I
Group/Squadron    :   491 BG -H- 853 BS        Base : Metfield, Suffolk
Details of loss   :   The bomber formations were agressively attacked by
many German fighters when on the bomb run and coming off the target. Many bombers
crashed in that area. Police and recovery teams from various airfields in the
vicinity of Hannover were involved in recording the crash-sites and the ........
Target            :   Hannover-Misburg Oil Refinery, Germany.
```

..... identification of dead and POWs but their reports are not always clear. The available documents do not shed light on the crash-site of this aircraft. 'Dead List A/Z' revealed that Sgt. Reutener was buried at the time in Hildesheim; a series of micro-fiches with 'Crashes arranged by date' includes a B-24 at Müllingen near Hildesheim so it is believed that this one may have been the 44-40212.

Killed : reinterred in Netherlands on about 10.08.45, initial plot numbers between brackets.

E	:	MANTER Paul W., T/Sgt.	31321694	
		(PP-1-22)		U.S.A., MAINE.
NG	:	LEHR Leo R., S/Sgt.	11034382	MASS
		(PP-10-247)		Netherlands A-11-20

reinterred in Ardennes, initial plot numbers between brackets. A German report states that the Sgts. Carlisle and Cole were recovered and identified, but no name of cemetery is recorded.

B	:	SINGLEY John H., 2/Lt.	0-707445	S C
				Ardennes D-16-7
RO	:	CARLISLE William L., T/Sgt.	17115091	MINN
				Ardennes B-37-16
RWG	:	REUTENER William E., S/Sgt.	15140449	OHIO
		Buried in Central Cemetery of		Ardennes D-4-8
		Hildesheim, VIb left, Row II		
		Grave 19.		
LWG	:	COLE Jesse W., S/Sgt.	34854210	N C
				Ardennes C-19-20
TG	:	STEWART Russell C., S/Sgt.	35892782	
				U.S.A., IND.

P.O.W. :

P	:	CLOUGHLEY Robert E., 1/Lt.	0-700599
CP	:	GREER Gerald N., 2/Lt.	0-768523

Sources : MACR. 1 1 1 5 8   'Dead List A/Z'

Details collected by : J.A. H e y - A.v.d.Leeuwstraat 12 - 7552 HS Hengelo, Holland.

"He received the column thanks to a sister who still lives in Western Massachusetts.

"I read it with wistful memory," he said. "Leo Lehr sat directly in front of me in Sister Rose Williams' home room in the Beaven Building on Elliot Street. Leo was a pleasant low-key type with a quiet sense of humour. He was very unassuming and a very nice appearing guy."

"Campbell says that he and Leo graduated from Cathedral in June 1941. He went off to college before entering the service, while Leo went to work at American Bosch Corporation, and did not enlist until December, 1942.

"I know I heard about Leo being lost, but that was about it," said Campbell, who would later complete his schooling at the University of Notre Dame. Several of his other buddies from Springfield – Bill Brick, Don McGurk and Bob Nothacker – wound up in basic training with him, Campbell recalled. And some of them were shot down over Germany, but survived to return home.

***

Acknowledgments:
Jan Hey of Hengelo in the Netherlands for the summary of the Missing Air Crew Report
Peggy Greer for the story of co-pilot Gerald Greer.
Cynthia Simison, Managing Editor, Special Projects, "The Republican" for nose-gunner Leo R. Lehr

CHAPTER 17

491ST BOMB GROUP
853RD BOMB SQUADRON

Aircraft Type: B-24J, serial # 44-40073,
"Ark Angel", MACR 10764
Airbase: North Pickenham

---

*"I pray that I can have the courage
to face the future."*

—Raymond McKee in his diary dated July 15, 1944

Pilot: 1Lt David N. Bennett Jr. (KIA) Norwood NC
Co-Pilot: 2Lt Jessie F. Blount (KIA) Hood TX
Navigator: 2Lt George H. Engel (KIA) Pittsburgh PA
Nose-Turret: S/Sgt Irving B. Starr (KIA) Brooklyn NY
Top-Turret: T/Sgt Norman G. Warford (KIA) Frankfurt KY
Radio: T/Sgt Pete Patrick Jr. (KIA) East Point KY
Left-Waist: S/Sgt Raymond O. McKee (KIA) Baton Rouge LA
Right-Waist: S/Sgt Charles E. Hixson (KIA) Cleveland TN
Tail Gunner: S/Sgt Henry P. Stovall (KIA) Beckly WV

Total: 9 KIA
Target: Misburg
Crash Site: 3 km S of Oerie, 15 km NW of Hildesheim

NOT HOME FOR CHRISTMAS

A pilot in the bomber stream who had witnessed that "Ark Angel" was losing height and was leaving the formation, later reported:

> "Bennett (the pilot) managed to link up with us but drifted down under our aircraft. The top-turret was completely gone and the right wing showed an enormous hole. She could not keep up with us and was last seen at 12.58 hours. She was continuously losing altitude. Nobody saw what happened to Ark Angel afterwards.

Exerpts from the Missing Air Crew Report made by Jan Hey, Hengelo (Netherlands):

> "It was observed that this aircraft was shot down by German fighters over the target area. The ball turret had been shot away and there was a large hole in the right wing. The plane lost altitude. German reports confirm that this serial crashed three kilometres south of Oerie. The B-24 may have exploded in mid-air killing the entire crew.
> "Six men were identified by name but Bennett, Hixson and Stovall were buried as Unknowns. All buried in the cemetery of Oerie and re-interred after the war in the American Military Cemetery in Neuville-en-Condroz in the Ardennes.

In 1999, forty-five years after the crash of "Ark Angel", a relative of John T. Keene who had been the crew chief (head mechanic) looking after Ark Angel, visited the cemetery where the crew had been initially buried:

> "When Fred Thaxton asked that I help find the graves of the crew of "Ark Angel" that had been shot down over Germany on the last Sunday in November, 1944, I knew only that they were supposed to have been buried in the village of Oerie somewhere north and west of Hildesheim. When I checked the map, I realised that my Danish family and I would be driving through Hildesheim.
> "As we could not find Oerie on any of our maps of Germany, I asked some German friends if they could tell us where it was. We were told to look in the area of Pattensen, which is a small town north of Hildesheim and south of Hannover.
> "The next day as we drove out in the country we thought we'd never

491st Bomb Group, 853rd Bomb Squadron

find it. At last we came to a sign with Oerie pointing down a narrow side road and after a few kilometres we were there. As we drove towards the village, we stopped at a cemetery. Like everything in Germany it was neat, clean and attractive. As soon as we got out of the car, a woman riding a bicycle stopped to ask if she could help us, and minutes later, a man driving a car also stopped. I'm sure on a dead end road to a tiny village, it was unusual meeting a car with three Danes and one American.

"Imagine our surprise when two people came along, both of them knew about the plane. The man said that farmers were still finding parts of the plane in their fields. The woman, Hannelore Pohl, told us, that the graves had been moved by the Allied military authorities about three years after the war.

"Hannelore told us that, although the plane crashed before she was born, she had heard about it all her life. As it was the only plane to crash near Oerie, it was part of the village folklore. She also told us that it crashed on property owned by her father, who is dead and who at that time was mayor of the town. She invited us to her house for something cold to drink.

"Driving to her house we realised that Oerie is a typical German village consisting of fifteen to twenty houses altogether. While we were at Hannelore's house, we talked about the crash. She told us that the villagers had never known whether the crew was English or American.

"By this time the whole village knew about us, and everyone was excited that finally they knew which country the bomber was from.

"Hannelore brought out a large framed aerial photo of Oeri and the fields surrounding it. I took a picture of it as it showed the crash site. She and I exchanged addresses and she promised, if any other parts of the plane turned up, to send a piece. For example, just a few weeks before we were there, a farmer had found a piece of a propeller.

"We then walked the field where the plane had crashed. As we were walking, her mother came to meet us and to tell us her memories of the crash. She said that everyone in the village had been very frightened because it was the first crash any of them had seen. They all ran across the fields to the plane and discovered that all crew members had burned to death.

"Hannelore's mother was anxious that we would know what they did with the bodies and told us that they gave each a proper Christian burial. We thought this was remarkable for a poor village in the middle of a war zone to treat their enemy in such a humane way. I wished the families of the crew members could have been there to see the peaceful scene. It

NOT HOME FOR CHRISTMAS

would have been a comfort to know that the remains had been well cared for by the villagers.

Hannelore Pohl's mother, Else Mensing, then 24 years old, had been on her bicycle on the way from Bennigsen to Oerie. When going through the neighbouring village called Hüspede she saw several allied airmen standing in a ditch under guard of a couple of men. She wanted to bring flowers to the cemetery of Oerie on this "Remember the Dead" Sunday.

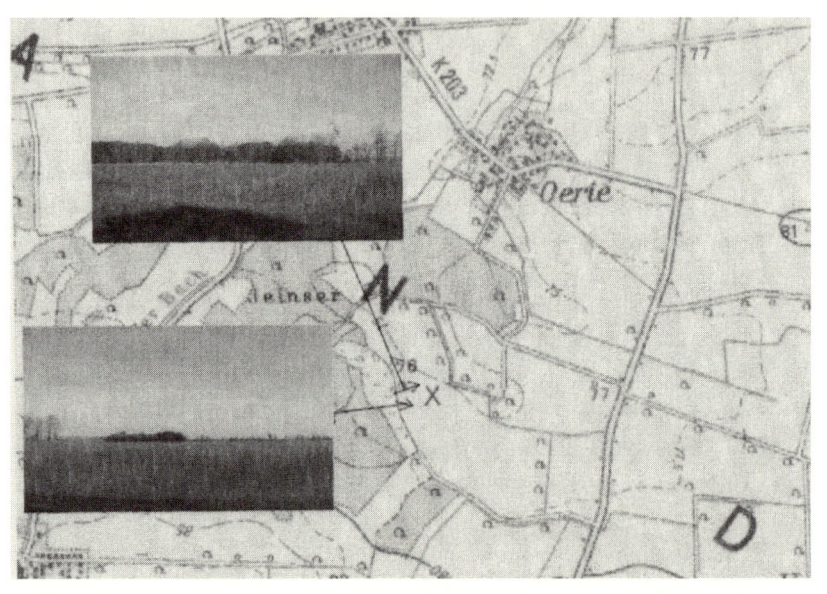

Crash Site

On the road leading to the farm of her future husband Heinrich Mensing, she learned that an aircraft had probably crashed behind the woods of Oerie. Driven by curiosity she went with her sister-in-law Hilde, then 25, into this forest.

Having arrived there, they discovered that they were the first to visit the crash site. The nose of the aircraft had ploughed into the field and the wings had broken off. When approaching the wreck they saw the burned and still buckled up corpses of the crew. The pilots were in their seats. Totally upset they cycled home and told the people in the village what they had seen.

322

Already some years ago the author came in contact with **Thomas Pohl**, a young German engineer and son of Hannelore Pohl. He created a web site concerning the village Oerie and devoted a very great part to the crash of Ark Angel. This part is also in English. Website is www.oerie.de . Click on the yellow sign "Oerie", then comes "information for English speaking visitors", click on "the crash of the B-24 "Ark Angel" then on "link to the B-24 story" and you'll find a wealth of information including pictures of the crash site.

About Pilot **David N. Bennett Jr.** of Norwood, North Carolina, his sister's daughter Bennett wrote the following:

"David Neville Bennett, Jr. was born on September 24, 1919 to Lillian Menefee and David Neville Bennett of Norwood, North Carolina, USA. He was the oldest of three children, with a sister, Menefee Bennett (Little), and a brother, Thomas Benton Bennett (now deceased).

"Norwood is a very small rural town on the Pee Dee River in North Carolina, and the Bennett family had several enterprises: farmland, a livery stable, and a ferry to cross the river. Neville's grandfather had been a legislator in the North Carolina General Assembly and was appointed by the NC Governor as the 1st Mayor of Norwood when the town was incorporated in 1881. His father managed the farm and businesses. His mother, Lillian, had come to Norwood to open a hat shop, making hats for ladies and traveling to New York every year to discover the latest fashions. When she married Mr. Bennett she turned from making hats to family life.

"In boyhood Neville was handsome, smart, and a natural leader. He was a good athlete and played on football, basketball, and other teams at his school. Never without a girlfriend he made friends wherever he went. When the US entered WWII, he was very eager to join the military and fight. But his parents insisted that he temper his eagerness and go to college instead. He enrolled at North Carolina State University in Raleigh, NC. After a year in college he either persuaded his parents to change their minds, or his eagerness to enlist overwhelmed his obedience to them. He enlisted and left for the military

"Neville served in the Air Force ground forces and got his flight wings two years into his service. In December 1944 he was awarded the Oak Leaf Cluster for meritorious achievement in accomplishing air missions over Germany. He flew 14 combat missions. During his service Neville wrote home frequently. In late December 1944, the Bennett family received a telegram notifying them that Neville was Missing in Action.

About co-pilot **Jessie "Jake" F. Blount** of Hood, Texas, Jennifer Sicking, a reporter for the *Gainesville Daily Register* (Texas), published on March 7, 2004 an excellent article about Jake. A few excerpts:

"For about 14 miles, the taxi driver drove the Texas roads, bearing the news no one wanted to hear and the piece of paper no one wanted to see. At the farmhouse in Hood, he handed the telegram to the father and left.

"At the farm on that winter afternoon, the Blount family's fears were confirmed: the son, brother and husband, Jesse "Jake" Blount, a co-pilot of a B-24 based in England, had been killed in action in the European theatre of war.

"When Mom and Dad received the telegram, they went all to pieces," Jim Blount remembered about the news of his brother's death arriving that December day in 1944 at the farm house. "Jake was good to write, but we hadn't received a letter from him in over a month so we were expecting the worst."

"Military officials had sent the letter to Gainesville, but without telephones in the Hood area, a taxi brought the message to the house.

"For many days and years after that winter day, the family knew little of what had happened to Jake. Later, Blount's mother received a Purple Heart and a letter of the government of England honouring Jake Blount, but the circumstances surrounding his death remained a mystery.

"Even in the 1950s when Blount's body was found and he was re-interred in Fairview Cemetery in Gainesville, the family learned little other than that he had been buried with his fellow crew members in a single grave.

"Jake, the middle brother of seven, joined the Air Corps in January 1942. He first went to Wichita Falls where he trained as an airplane mechanic. At Barksdale Field (now Barksdale Air Force Base), Jake passed the test to become a flying cadet and was accepted as a pilot. He trained in Bonham, Sherman, Fort Worth and Montana before going overseas in June 1944 as a co-pilot of the B-24 named "Ark Angel" He was 26 years old when he died.

"In 1943, Jake had married Mary Ruth Patton, who lived between Hood and Era. "He was the one that was liked real well," Jim said remembering his older brother. "Everyone thought real well of him. I don't know if you'd call him a clown or not, but he's always one to be upbeat.

Jim, too, wanted to join the Air Corps following in his brother's steps. However, family obligations kept him on the farm until his younger brother finished school.

"Dad was an older person. He couldn't really run the farm. When Jake left, I was running the farm", Jim said.

"Six of the Blount boys served in World War II, the seventh and youngest served in Korea.

"Recently John Meurs contacted the Register looking for members of the Blount family as part of his research.

"I want to give them whatever information I have gathered about Jessie's last flight," Meurs said. "My present research is very rewarding, especially when it concerns airmen who were killed in action.

Such information is welcomed by the Blount family. They were also contacted by a man in Germany in 2003 with information about the "Ark Angel".

"I was real glad to get it," Blount said. "After fifty something years, it's more or less out of your mind. After this guy contacted us and told us the information, it sure did answer some questions."

On January 4, 1945 the *Paintsville Herald* published a letter radio-operator **Pete Patrick Jr**. of East Point KY, had written to a friend:

"This leaves me feeling fine and hope you are the same. I haven't done much since I have been in service but to think of it, I have done and seen quite a bit.

"I enlisted in the Army May 17, 1943, and was inducted at Fort Myers, VA. From there I was sent to Camp Lee, VA. I stayed there for two weeks and from there I was sent to Keesler Field, Miss. I took my basic training at this field, then was sent to Sioux Falls, SD and was made private first class and started to radio technical school. In six months I graduated from radio school and went to Yuma, Arizona, for gunnery school. After seven weeks I was promoted to the rank of corporal. I was given ten days leave which I spent with my parents at Hager Hill. It was a great pleasure seeing my folks again: I had a wonderful time when I was on leave at home.

"When I came back to camp I was sent to Lincoln, Nebraska and assigned to a bomber crew. I made many friends while I was there. I was sent to Carper, Wyo for three months for further flying training. This was for combat flying and the going was pretty tough. I was then shipped to

NOT HOME FOR CHRISTMAS

Topeka, Kann., and assigned to a plane and was flown here to England. We were here for two days and I was promoted to sergeant. After a few missions I was awarded the Air Medal. After this great experience I was promoted to the rank of staff sergeant and a few days ago I was promoted to technical sergeant.

"I have made several trips to London and had some swell times. There isn't much difference in the way of living here and at home. The streets are a great deal smaller and the steering wheels of the cars are on the other side. I have enjoyed every day of my life in service and I am proud that I have been chosen to serve my country.

"Glad to hear that you bought that $ 250 War Bond. Sure am glad to hear that the folk on the home front are doing their part in helping win the war.

About Left-Waist Gunner S/Sgt **Raymond O. McKee** of Baton Rouge, LA, his son Raymond wrote the following:

"He was born Oct. 14, 1919 in Folsom, La., which is about 70 miles north-east from New Orleans. Folsom is a rural town similar in size to Oerie in Germany, where he was originally buried. My dad attended Covington High School and got his GED in Baton Rouge. I'm told my dad was quite smart but never applied himself to school and his studies, smoked too much, slept too late which resulted in a lot of kitchen patrol when he entered the service. It seems the military brought out the best in him, taking a boy and making a man. Before entering the service, he worked for a construction company.

"While working a job in Woodville, Miss. (where I was born), he met my mother. Woodville is also a small rural town similar to Folsom and Oerie. It's 50 miles north of Baton Rouge. My parents were married September 15, 1942. They kept it a secret for six months, she living in Woodville.

Waist-Gunner Raymond O. McKee

Despite the short average life of a combat aircraft, many hours were spent in embellishment with a paintbrush. In addition to the main painting for Ark Angel, small green and yellow representations of this were placed close to the position of each of the aircraft's crew members. B-24J 44-40073 Tec B of the 853rd Bomb Squadron has the outer propeller bosses painted light blue and a yellow bomb-by door stripe. (USAAF)

"My Dad entered the Army at Camp Beauregard, La. in September 1942. Then went to Keesler Field, Gulfport, Miss. He received his wings at Harlingen, Texas and completed his combat training at Casper, Wyoming. He left to go overseas from Topeka, Kansas, on July 15, 1944.

"My Dad wrote in his dairy on July 15, 1944:

"We took off at Topeka at 300 a.m. EST on the first leg of our journey to Bangor, Maine. We landed in Bangor nine hours later, after having almost run out of gas. This was our port of embarkation and we were restricted from sending telegrams or making phone calls. I miss my wife a lot today. Just twenty hours previously I told her goodbye in Kansas: the distance between us is growing fast now.

"July 16, 1944. Today was lonesome. It was Sunday and we were not cleared to take off so I spent my last day in the United States doing nothing. We received the news that one of our crews didn't make the first leg of the journey. They crashed in New York State.

"Maybe they are fortunate maybe not. I suppose my dear wife is in Memphis. Maybe she is happy. I'm not.

"July 17, 1944: This morning I woke up early and we took off. A couple of hours later we crossed the U.S. border, we were out of the States. I pray that I can have the courage to face the future. At 11 AM we landed in Labrador and there wasn't anything but a field.

"July 18, 1944. This morning I awoke and went out to the plane. The plane is beginning to feel like it is alive and is a friend. I am beginning to love her and I trust her. She is so beautiful when her four big motors pull her into the sky." "

***

Acknowledgments:
For all crew, Sue Thorton, visit to Oerie, Germany
For all crew, Jan Hey for the summary of the MACR
Thomas Pohl, Oerie.
For pilot David Bennett, Bennett Cotton
For co-pilot Jessie "Jake" F. Blount, Jennifer Sicking, *Gainesville Daily Register*
Raymond McKee son of left-waist gunner S/Sgt Raymond O. McKee
Ark Angel photos provided by Gordon Carline

CHAPTER 18

491ST BOMB GROUP
853RD BOMB SQUADRON

Aircraft Type: B-24J, serial # 44-40205,
"The Mooose", MACR 10765
Airbase: North Pickenham

"The fire was still not up to the wing tanks yet so we made it to the target and dropped our bombs. Then I gave the bail out signal. I hadn't had time to set the auto-pilot so I held the ship level while all the crew bailed out and then I bailed out."

—Pilot Warren Moore

Pilot: 1Lt. Warren C. Moore (POW) Seattle WA
Co-Pilot: 1Lt. Robert D. McIntyre (POW) Clearwater, KS
Navigator: 1Lt. Ross S. Houston (POW) St. Louis MO
Bombardier: 1Lt. George K. Patten (KIA) Milton MA
Nose-Turret: 1Lt. Richard K. McDonnell (POW) Maspeth NY
Top-Turret: T/Sgt Francis S. Hawkins (KIA) Setauket NY
Radio-Operator: T/Sgt Joseph F. Rimassa (POW) Newark NJ
Left-Waist: S/Sgt Frederick F. Borger Jr. (KIA) Nazareth PA
Right-Waist: S/Sgt John P. Murray (KIA) New York NY
Tail-Gunner: S/Sgt Marshall E. Williams (KIA) Little Rock AR

Total: 5 KIA, 5 POW
Target: Misburg
Crash Site: 1 km S of Gehrden, 15 km SW of Hannover
Time of Crash: 13.30

NOT HOME FOR CHRISTMAS

Taken April, 1944 in Pueblo, Colorado in front of "Delirious Dolores"
Back row, left to right:Engineer Francis Hawkins, Co-Pilot Bob McIntyre
Front row, left to right:Navigator Ross Houston, Bombardier George Patten,
Tail-Gunner Marshall Williams

The Missing Air Crew Report, pertaining to this crew, mentions that his bomber was shot down by a large group of German fighters. One engine caught fire and canon shells riddled the rear part of the bomber. The plane exploded in mid-air.

George Patten, Francis Hawkins, John Murray, Frederick Borger and Marshal Williams were either killed by fighter shells or in the crash of the aircraft. They were, after the war, re-interred in the American Military Cemetery in Neuville-en-Condroz in Belgium, nine miles south-west of Liège. In this cemetery many soldiers rest who lost their lives during the Battle of the Bulge in late 1944.

According to his Individual Deceased Personnel File (IDPF), the bombardier George Patten was initially buried in a group of 19 unknowns in the Seelhorst cemetery in Hannover on December 4,

1944. In April of 1946 he was exhumed by the Quatermaster Corps and re-interred in the American Military near Neuville-en-Condroz.. George found his permanent place of rest in the American Military Cemetery in Epinal, France. He rests there next to his brother Irving Patten. Irving was also a Bombardier, belonging to the 15th USAAF operating then out of Tunis in north Africa. He lost his life over Switzerland on October 1, 1943 on a mission to Augsburg in southern Germany.

The other four crew members who were killed were repatriated to the States and buried in their towns of origin.

Five crew members: Warren Moore, Bob McIntyre, Ross Houston, Richard Mc Donnell and Joe Rimassa, could save themselves by parachute and were taken prisoner.

As twenty bombers came down almost at the same time and in most cases in the same region, the Germans had trouble finding out which prisoners and/or killed airmen belonged to which aircraft.

Pilot **Warren C. Moore** wrote in June, 2002:

"Our target on November 26th was a refinery at Misburg. Everything was uneventful until we reached "initial point" to start our bomb run to the target. We had picked up P-51 fighter cover just before we got to initial point however that is where we lost our fighter cover. Some German fighters were heading towards us and while they were chasing us another large group of fighters attacked our bomb group.

"Our ship was set on fire and the rear section was riddled with 20 mm shells. All the crew members in the rear section were killed. The fire was still not up to the wing tanks yet so we made it to the target and dropped our bombs. Then I gave the bail out signal. I hadn't had time to set the auto-pilot so I held the ship level while all the crew bailed out and then I bailed out.

"As I was nearing the ground with my parachute, I saw a group of people following my descent path. When I landed I was circled by about fifteen people. I think the reason they didn't rush me was because they may have thought I had a gun. Fortunately two soldiers drove up and took me in their truck into the city and placed me into a jail cell. When it got dark and during the blackout they took me by street car to a building on the outskirts of the city where all the other captured crew members were. From there we were all shipped to Oberursel; the interrogation center.

NOT HOME FOR CHRISTMAS

"We were placed into individual cells with no windows with a slot in the door to push the food through. Our toilet was a bucket. On the second day it was my turn to be interrogated by a German officer.

When I entered his room the first thing he said was "you can't tell me anything". He replied; "I know the bomb group you were with, I know the target, I know your altitude and I know the type of bombs you used". He was very proud of that and liked to brag about it but he sent me back to my cell. After a day or two we were put on the train and sent on our way to the Stalog Luft #1 a camp across the East Sea from Sweden.

"While in prison camp our barracks had bunk beds eight across and three high with a straw mattress. Once a week we were sent to the showers and we treated each other for lice. Prison camp was boring but we were not mistreated if we behaved. If we were to open a window during a blackout they would shoot at us. The camp consisted of both English and American officers.

"There were Russian prisoners there also but they were not allowed in our compound. "They were given the less desirable chores like empting the toilet buckets and they did not mix with us. Once in a while we would receive a Red Cross food parcel and those of us who did not smoke would give the cigarettes to the Russian prisoners.

"There was a library with books written in English which helped us spend our time. The food was eatable and consisted of potatoes, cabbage, and a dark bread (some said it had sawdust in it). Once in awhile we were fed horse meat which we looked forward to. Near the end of our prison term the food was very bad, but of course the German people were not eating well at that time either.

"Some time about May we knew the Russians were on their way to Barth because we could hear the cannon sounds and the fighting. I think about May 15 we all woke up and noticed that all the guard towers were empty. The first thing all the POW's did was to knock down the guard towers and tear up the barb wire fence. I think after the Russians arrived we remained there for a couple of days until the US air force flew in B-17's to an airfield next to our prison. We were all then flown to a rehabilitation camp on the coast of France where we stayed for about a week for debriefing before we were sent home to the States by boat.

"When we arrived in the States we were given a fortnight off at an ocean tourist resort in Malibu, California. We were then sent to a refresher school of ground and flight instruction. We were being retrained to be sent to the war in the Pacific. Thankfully the war ended and we didn't have to go.

Earlier that year, in June, 1944, on a mission to the Creil air base in Nazi-occupied France, Warren Moore lost two engines over the target due to flak and had to ditch in the Channel. Warren recalls:

"Our mission that day was an airport on the outskirts of Paris. As we approached the target we could see the anti-aircraft shells bursting in the air in front of us. It was our hope that the gunners did not have our exact altitude but that hope was short lived.

"The shell exploded in front of us and knocked out engines number one and two. That left two engines operating at full throttle on the right side of the plane and in order not to be pulled into a flat spin (which is extremely difficult to recover from) it was necessary for us to bank into the good engines in order to go straight ahead. With two engines we also had to go into a slight descent in order to keep up air speed. I had the bombardier immediately jettison our bomb load. Fortunately they had not yet been armed. I should have been extremely frightened by what was occurring but there was no time. All my time was taken up in flying a crippled ship hopefully back home.

"We started a long slow descent towards England. We contacted British air-sea rescue and they were directing us to a landing field on the coast. We were finally able to level off our descent at about 3000 feet but when we were approximately two miles from the English coast we lost engine number three. I notified air-sea rescue that we lost number three and we were ditching.

"I remembered that in flight training we had been told that if it was necessary to ditch a B-24 you should approach the water in a low tail approach. Presumably the theory was that hitting the tail first would allow the plane to slow down long enough before the nose section hit the water. If you went in on level approach at approximately 85 miles per hour (that is the stalling speed of the B-24 without using flaps), the nose section would build up a wall of water in front and be pulled straight down.

"The flimsy bomb bay doors were ripped off, the tail section filled with water immediately, it broke the airplane in half just behind the wings and the tail section went straight down with four crew members. The nose section with partially empty wing tanks floated long enough for the rest of the crew to get into the water and to inflate their life vests.

"I do not remember how long we were in the water before we were rescued. The air-sea rescue unit had a "fix" on us and all of the crew except myself got into a long boat that they brought out. I don't know how I became separated from them, but I was a short distance away and was picked up by a float plane. I was taken to one hospital and the crew was taken to another. We all suffered from mild hypothermia but were able to be treated and in a few days we were able to return to our base.

"I was awarded the Distinguished Flying Cross and it was presented to my mother in a ceremony while I was in the prison camp.

After discharge from the service, Warren returned to school to earn his degree in finance and economics. Then he spent one year in Paris for more study. Warren wrote:

"However there was very little studying. I wasn't that dedicated .I returned to the States and spent 30 years working for Bank of America. During that period I married and we raised two children. After I retired my wife and I spent two years in the Philippine Islands as Peace Corps Volunteers. A few years later we spent a year in China teaching English as a second language at a college in south central China.

About co-pilot **Robert D. McIntyre** his daughter Karen Crane wrote:

"He said when he jumped out of the plane, all four engines had shut down and were on fire and he jumped out from the bomb bay. His flight suit had caught fire as well, and his oxygen mask was hitting him in the face. When he went out of the plane, he fell until approximately 3,000 feet before he opened his parachute. When he landed, there was a German there waiting with a rifle. He knew enough English to ask him for his .45 gun.

"He and about four or five members of the crew were taken into town. Frederick Borger, a gunner from his plane spoke German. He complained about the building they were taken to as it was very cold. All of the windows were broken. They were told if they hadn't bombed so hard they would have had windows. A few days later they were taken to another town near Frankfurt in the back of a truck.

"At this point they were "interviewed". His captors already had all of the information about him… serial number, when he graduated from flight school… basically everything. From there he went to the German prison camp. He wore the same flight suit from when he went down until the day he was released. My mother said she remembers when he got home that he was so thin and so hungry.

Bob McIntyre had another near escape. On June 15, 1944, on a mission to the Saint Cyr airbase in France, his B-24 was seriously damaged by flak. His Pilot, James C. McKeown was hit in both ankles and was bleeding profusely. He was laid out on the flight deck and given aid what the crew could accomplish, including several shots of morphine. Bob took over and brought the bomber home on three engines.

Arriving over base, McIntyre found he would have to land the crippled aircraft in a strong cross wind – something he had never done before. The first pass was unsuccessful – at which point McKeown got up off the floor and, in spite of a serious loss of blood and the intense pain in his ankles brought about by the strong rudder pedal pressures required, landed the plane safely.

Bob McIntyre claimed later that his pilot could not wait to get down to collect his Purple Heart while McKeown (who was actually awarded the Silver Star) claimed he was afraid if the stayed airborne any longer the crew would give him more morphine – and, according to Mac, a needle in the hands of a nervous gunner was as bad as the flak.

After the war Bob told his wife that afterwards they had counted 140 holes in the B-24.

Bob McIntyre passed away in June 2005.

Navigator **Ross S. Houston** was, in his own words,

"I was born in St. Louis, Missouri on January 2, 1921, the home of Anheuser Busch beer, St. Louis Cardinal baseball team, Rams football team, also the Gateway Arch. After completing my primary and secondary education in St. Louis, I took business training at a local college along with some piano and violin education.

"This was interrupted by our entrance into World War II, at which time I enlisted in the Army Air Force. After a year of navigational training, I was assigned to a crew of a B-24 in the 491st Bomb Group. This was a big task for someone who was 22 years old but some were younger.

"On Sunday, November 26, 1944, I bailed out of our B-24, "The Moose" through the nose wheel door after feeling the downward motion of the plane and the sound of the warning bell. After delaying the opening of the chute, the noise of the fighter combat and the B-24's engines ceased. I pulled the ripcord and with the jerk of the chute opening, I remembered the lectures about always having our harness adjusted tight. It must have been the looseness and the amount of clothing that caused the harness to pull tight, too high on my body. Enough said about that.

"The quietness of my descent sobered me to the point, that with three missions to go, I wouldn't be home for Christmas. The next thought was "Where am I in Germany and what kind of reception would I get on the ground". It was a clear day and I saw the ground getting closer. It was good that I didn't know how fast, as I would have braced myself, causing myself possible injury on landing. In contrast, I hit the ground before I knew it and doubled up like an accordion. The wind was blowing so hard, it took my chute and dragged me across the frozen ploughed field ripping my flight parka on the left sleeve to shreds. The dragging motion stopped and allowed me to stand up and unfasten my harness which was still unbearably tight.

I then realised that some German civilians had collapsed my chute and were running off with it, leaving me standing in an open field trying to orient myself.

I wasn't alone very long, as a German soldier was running across the open field towards me. With caution he approached, not knowing whether I was armed or not. While searching me he relieved me of my watch and escape kit and directed me to go toward a dirt road a short distance away. We walked down this road with the soldier behind me with my hands raised. An elderly man with a cane walked toward us and asked whether I was Yank or British. With the answer of Yank, he swung his cane and hit me in the head, causing an open cut above my left eye. The scar is a reminder of that incident.

The guard and I entered a small town, where I met my co-pilot, Bob McIntyre, still carrying his chute, and being escorted by another German guard. My guard stopped at a first-aid station, where they put some white powder on the cut and stopped the bleeding with a piece of adhesive tape. While we were going through town, the villagers took pictures, shouted and spit on us. We were taken to a shower room at a garrison outside the town, where we saw our radio-operator, Joe Rimassa, and other downed fliers. We were searched again and our shoes were taken from us.

That night, we were taken to town by truck to another military facility in Hannover, where we saw the devastation of that city. Upon arriving there, I saw my pilot, Warren Moore, who was burned about the face. We were given some hard sausage and bread to eat, which was the first food we had since breakfast. After giving the German officer my name, rank and serial number, my interrogation included being informed by him the names of the crew that did not survive the ordeal. We complained about being kept in a room with the windows broken out and the Germans reminded us that we did that.

Ross Houston arrived in the POW camp in Barth, Germany, where he stayed for about five months.

The German, who had assaulted Ross immediately after landing on German soil, was arrested in April 1945 and sentenced a year later to imprisonment for five years beginning May 1, 1945.

The evidence for the Prosecution reads:

"On or about 1200 hours, 26 November 1944, a plane crashed in the vicinity of Roloven, Germany, and the pilot (sic), Ross Houston, an American, parachuted down near the village. Several local people from the town gathered around the pilot. Among the first to approach the victim was the accused, who had picked up a stick and struck the victim from three to several times about the head, until he began to bleed and was caused to fall down. The accused in his confession states that he struck the victim only on the back. A member of the crowd told the accused "not to beat him anymore" and shortly thereafter a lieutenant from the Luftwaffe and two soldiers from the anti-aircraft division, took the pilot to the office of the commandant of the Luftwaffe.

For the Defense, the accused testified as follows:

"On the morning of 26 November 1944, I saw four aviators bail out of a plane in the vicinity of Roloven and one of them landed near our village. I jumped on my bicycle and pedalled to where he had landed, for the purpose of seeing what he looked like. As I approached him about twenty persons, mostly women, had already gathered around the pilot. I noticed no gun on the pilot. He was neither wounded nor bleeding. I found a stick about 3/4 of a meter long and as thick as my finger and hit him over the back twice. He offered no resistance but as "he back-stepped he stumbled." Then a German soldier appeared and took the pilot away and I don't know what next happened. I have a goitre, which is my explanation for becoming excited and hitting the pilot."

The prosecution did not have a strong case. They argued that Ross "was an unarmed prisoner of war in custody of the German army" when he was hit by the accused. This was besides the truth:

NOT HOME FOR CHRISTMAS

Ross was surrounded by civilians when the accused hit him and the accused could not have known if Ross was armed or not.

Ross continues;

"After liberation from Stalagluft I, I was sent back to the States. When on a sixty days' leave, Japan gave up. The government sent me to business and law college for 3 ½ years which terminated with my marriage to a girl named Jean, who had a little boy from a previous marriage. Our first son became a mathematics teacher for a few years and eventually was in management of Southwestern Bell System. Our second son lives nearby. Our first and only daughter is a Project Engineer with the Union Pacific Railroad.

"After almost thirty years of marriage, my wife Jean became ill with cancer, from which she did not survive.

"I am not one to being along and still wanted to share my life with someone. In answer to my prayers, I met a widow, Vell, from my church, who had two grown daughters. I now have four children, two step children, fourteen grandchildren, three step grand children, one great grandchild, four, soon five, step grandchildren. I have retired since 1985 doing volunteer work for the senior people and keeping fit.

Of all members of the 491st Bomb Group, who had lost their lives on this mission only bombardier **George K. Patten** found his final place of rest in the Epinal American Cemetery in Epinal, France. He is buried there next to his brother Irving who also was a bombardier in the Army Air Force but was operating out of North Africa with the 99th Bomb Group of the 15th USAAF.

On October 1, 1943, on the way home after a mission to Augsburg in Germany, his B-17, serial # 42-30126, "Sugar Foot", violated the air space of neutral Switzerland and was downed by Swiss anti aircraft batteries located near Bad Ragaz, in the eastern part of Switzerland. Seven crew members, among them Irving Patten, lost their lives in the crash of their bomber and were buried in Bad Ragaz with full military honours and in the presence of most American airmen then interned in Switzerland. After the war he was re-interred in Epinal, France where he was later joined by his brother George.

When he was reported missing in action, George Patten was 28 years old. He was a graduate of North Quincy High School in Massachusetts, where he was on the wrestling and football teams. He was also a member of the Squantum Yaught Club, sailing his boat "Manitou" in the Indian class.

He later graduated from the Wentworth Institute in Boston and was a designing draftsman for General Electric when he joined the U.S. Air Forces.

George had three brothers in the services; Irving with the 15th USAAF, Ainsly serving with the U.S. Army in France and Elliot serving with the U.S. Navy in the Pacific.

In September 2003, George's son Bruce and his wife Cheryl,

QUINCY PATRIOT LEDGE

Second Son In North Quincy Family Is Reported Killed

News that the second of their four sons, who served their country in the time of war, had been killed in action was received recently by Mr. and Mrs. A. Harold Patten of 105 South Bayfield road, North Quincy.

Lost Nov. 26, 1944

The War department notified the Pattens that First Lt. George K. Patten, bombardier on a B-24 Liberator, who was reported missing in action over Germany on Nov 26, 1944, is now presumed to have been killed in action on that date.

Lieutenant Patten's brother, 2nd Lt. Irving B. Patten, AAF bombardier, was killed in action Oct. 1, 1943. Two other sons of the Pattens recently were discharged from the service. They are Ainsley T. Patten, who served in Europe with the U. S. Army, and Elliot C. Patten, who served in the Pacific with the Navy.

The son just reported as killed in action had been awarded the Air Medal with four Oak Leaf clusters. He was the husband of Mrs. Marjorie (Crosby) Patten, of 181 High street, Hingham. He is survived by a son, Bruce Kenneth, whom the father never saw.

Lieutenant Patten, who was 28, was a graduate of North Quincy High school, class of 1934, where he was a member of the wrestling and football teams. He was also a member of the Squantum Yacht club and sailed his yacht "Manitou" in the Indian class.

After graduating from the Wentworth Institute in Boston he worked as a designing draftsman for the General Electric company in Lynn.

Mr. and Mrs. Patten have another son, Ralph W. Patten, of the home address.

LT. GEORGE K. PATTEN

Hospital Group Has Silver Tea And Yule Party

The South Shore auxiliary of the Massachusetts Osteopathic hospital, Boston, enjoyed a silver tea and Christmas party Thursday afternoon at the home of Mrs. Harvey Copp, 20 Hawthorn road, Braintree. Mrs. Abbie Barrett of Hingham was co-hostess, with Mrs. Abbie Wyman, president, and Mrs

1Lt. George K. Patten

339

NOT HOME FOR CHRISTMAS

Funeral with full military honours of members of the "Sugar Foot" crew in Bad Ragaz, Switzerland. Present were all American airmen interned in neutral Switzerland

visited the Epinal Cemetery where they were received by Roland Prieur, the superintendent. Bruce wrote:

> "Mr. Roland Prieur greeted us immediately as we entered the parlor of the administration building. After explaining who we were and signing the guest book, he led us out to the graves. Along the way he cut a pair of red roses from a garden and got a small pail of earth. At the graves of Irving B. Patten, my uncle, and George K. Patten, my father, he stuck a rose into the ground in front of the marble stone and rubbed earth into the inscription to make engraving stand out. Then he took a Polaroid picture of each grave and left us to continue our visit.
>
> "It was a bright sunny day and a beautiful setting. We must have spent a couple of hours taking it all in, wandering around and taking pictures. It's good that we took the bus out and not a taxi, as we felt completely unhurried. Upon returning to the administration building, Mr. Prieur presented us with a thick folio of information. He had looked up the addresses of the veteran associations for the 99th and 491st bomb groups on the Internet, and that was included, along with the mounted Polaroid pictures. He had looked in his data base and found that a woman had come for many years and placed flowers on both graves. It was Katherine

Hack, an ex Army nurse who had been a close friend of Uncle Irving during the war.

"It just so happened that we had come out to the cemetery on the anniversary of the allied liberation of Epinal. Mr. Prieur explained that the local people took this very seriously, and had wreath laying ceremonies in the evening at all the war memorials in town, starting with the American cemetery. He invited us to come out that evening to participate, and we gladly accepted.

"After having had a rest in our hotel, we took the bus back out to the cemetery. I was expecting to stand off to one side and watch the ceremony, but Mr. Prieur had us stand in the front row on the bottom step in front of the memorial. There were speeches and each veteran's group placed a wreath on one of the five stands out in front. At the conclusion Mr. Prieur led me out in front of the throng and introduced me. All I could think of to say was, "I'm very pleased to be here." After most of the people had departed for the next ceremony, Mr. Prieur beckoned us to his car, and we proceeded down to the suburbs of Epinal where there was a monument at the firing wall where the Germans had executed 336 resistance fighters. As one man read the name of 48 of the resistance fighters, another answered, "Mort pour la France." Then three groups of three people placed a wreath on the monument, followed by a line of school children with bouquets. Afterward the mayor invited us to the wine reception at the conclusion of all the ceremonies.

"But we weren't done, yet. We got back into Mr. Prieur's car and went to the monument to the fallen French soldiers of World Wars I & II near the center of town. We were introduced to the Bishop, to the Chief Rabbi and to a professor of Greek and Latin. A band played the Star Spangled Banner and Le Marseillaise, followed by the placing of wreathes on the monument. Mr. Prieur had Cheryl and me join him in placing the wreath on behalf of the Americans. Another long line of school children filed past and placed bouquets. At the conclusion there was a receiving line, of which we were a part, then we all walked through the adjoining park to a huge indoor pavilion for the wine reception. Mr. Prieur had me stand next to the deputy mayor while he read his speech. When he finished, the deputy mayor signed his notes and gave them to me. The wine that followed was very good. There was much toasting and shaking hands with individuals. I toasted all my wine away, and a woman brought me seconds. Eventually people started drifting away, and we did too, by foot back to the hotel. It had been an emotionally exhausting day.

NOT HOME FOR CHRISTMAS

Radio-operator **Joseph "Joe" Rimassa** wrote in February 2004:

"I was the radio-operator and my position on the plane was on the flight deck behind the pilot (Moore) and the co-pilot (McIntyre). The engineer (Sgt. Hawkins) was also on the flight deck.

"As I recall we were attacked after leaving the target by many Focke Wulf's 190. I remember them coming at us in a group of 8 or 9 abreast and raking our formation with machine guns and 22 mm. canon fire. After they made their second pass at our formation I remember our wings and the area under the flight deck was on fire. The pilot pushed the "Bail Out" alarm and I remember bailing out through the top hatch.

"I delayed opening my parachute so I could get clear of the combat area. I believe "The Moose" blew up shortly after we exited the plane. As I slowly descended under my parachute, a German pilot of one of the Focke Wulf's that had shot us down flew past me and gave me a soldier's salute. I'll never forget this gallant act. He could easily have shot me.

"Once on the ground, a farmer and a young lad about twelve years old came after me with a rifle and held me until the SS troopers and the Wehrmacht soldiers came for me. After they had argued a while as who should take me into custody, the Wehrmacht won out. Needless to say that I was happy about that,

When I bailed out of "The Moose" and finally opened my parachute, I lost my flight boots. They flew off my feet when I was suddenly slowed down by the opening of the chute. When I hit the ground I only had my felt heated suit slippers on my feet. It was November with a couple of inches of snow on the ground. Needless to say they were worn through in a couple of days of walking.

"When we arrived at Dulag-Luft at a town called Wetzlar for our interrogation a German sergeant got me a pair of shoes from the Swiss Red Cross.

"After interrogation, I and the rest of the captured non commissioned officers were sent to a prison camp in Upper Silicia (now Poland) called Stalag Luft 4. I remained there until the end of January 1945. When The Russian army was moving towards us the Germans placed a couple of thousand of us in small box cars (52 men crowded in each car with one bucket for a toilet). After nine days we arrived at Stalag-Luft 1, near a town called Barth on the Baltic Sea. It was at that camp where I saw Lt. Moore, Lt. McIntyre and Lt. Houston again. It was a cool winter and I lost a lot of weight.

"I had lived in the same clothing from the day I left England on our last mission until we were liberated by the Russians. Several days later we were flown to Lyon, France, where we were deloused, given several showers and new U.S. Army uniforms. From there we were taken to Camp Lucky Strike on the French coast near Cherbourg. We stayed at the camp for about a month. I remember they fed us several times a day and also gave us complete physical examinations. By the time I sailed to the U.S.A. in mid June I had regained some of the weight I had lost.

"When I arrived home on leave my mother completed the job by feeding eggnogs, milk shakes and her good home cooking.

A German gentleman, Georg Weber, witnessed the crash of "The Moose" near Gehrden. He wrote in 2002:

"My neighbour Friedrich Kirchhoff, then a 22 years old soldier on home leave, and myself watched on that particular Sunday the heavy air battle over Gehrden. He also saw the "Liberator" bomber being hit and explode. He saw some bodies falling through the sky when the bomber exploded. Their parachutes remained unopened so we can assume that they were already dead. About 1000 feet from where he stood part of an engine came down in a garden with the propeller still whirling. As a soldier he reported to the Gehrder police and went with them to the crash site.

Georg's own story reads as follows:

"As a 14 years old apprentice working for the town of Gehrden I had to go, as auxiliary policeman, with my boss Von Reden to the crash site. For the first time in my life I saw the bodies of dead people. They were scattered on a field, most of them buried a foot deep in the soil. Thanks to their heavy overalls their bodies were intact. I can vaguely remember that we collected the dog tags from their wrists. I especially remember that one of the airmen carried a coloured map in a leather holster on his breast. I also remember an iron ration of chocolate and glucose.

Another German gentleman, Friedrich Hunte, told Georg Weber:

"I was at that time seven years old and went on Sunday together with my father (who as a design engineer was exempted from military service) over the Gehrdener hill. About a kilometre west of the hill we saw a man came down on the field under a burning parachute. During the fall he moved his arms violently. In my opinion he was not dead yet at that time.

NOT HOME FOR CHRISTMAS

"My father told me to stay put at the ditch and went alone to the man. Father did not want me to see him. He was, according to the watch we found, probably Francis Hawkins. A wrist watch laid about twenty meters from him on the field near the ditch. The strap had probably snapped during the fall. My father took the watch and kept it almost sixty years in our cub board. The watch had stopped at 12.19 hours.

```
CASUALTY        REPORT              U.S. AIR FORCES.

Date            :   26 November 1944        Time :   1330 h
Aircraft        :   B-24J  44 - 40205                8th AF.
Codes           :   T8 : -G             ' THE MOOSE '
Group/Squadron  :   491 BG -H- 853 BS   Base : Metfield, Buffolk.
Details of loss :   Shot down by a mass of fighters. No. 2 engine was on fire
and the rear section was riddled by 20 mm shells from bomb bay back to the tail.
The Engineer attempted to crank the bomb bay doors open that were stuck after
exploding 20 mm shells. When a fire in the bomb bay started the crew bailed out.
        Target  :   Hannover-Misburg, Germany.

Then the ship exploded two times and desintegrated.
Crashed 1 km S of Gehrden, 15 km SW of Hannover.

Killed : no info on place of burial. Reinterred in Ardennes; initial plot
         numbers between brackets.
    B   :   PATTEN George K., 1/Lt.         0-754761    MASS
                                                        Epinal B-42-12
    E   :   HAWKINS Francis S., T/Sgt.      12122898
                                                        U.S.A., N Y.
    RWG :   MURRAY John P., S/Sgt.          12193506    N Y
                                                        Ardennes A-37-16
    LWG :   BORGER Frederick F. Jr., S/Sgt. 33623530
                                                        U.S.A., PA.
    TG  :   WILLIAMS Marshall E., S/Sgt.    18219340    ARK
                                                        Ardennes B-11-5

        Note : The reason for the permanent burial of Lt. Patten in Epinal (and not
               in Ardennes) may be, that in Epinal Plot B-45-21 is buried
               2/Lt. Irving B. PATTEN 0-735143, also from Massachusetts, who was
               killed on 1st October 1943 and served in 99 BG (H) 416 BS. The B-17
               in which he was flying as Bombardier was shot down by Swiss flak.
               He was initially buried in Ragaz, Switzerland.
               Maybe they were relatives ?

P.O.W. :
    P   :   MOORE Warren C., 1/Lt.          0-547092
    CP  :   MC INTYRE Robert D., 1/Lt.      0-699618
    N   :   HOUSTON Ross S., 1/Lt.          0-886646
    NG  :   MC DONNELL Richard K., 1/Lt.    0-754752
    RO  :   RIMASSA Joseph F., T/Sgt.       32159109

        Note: in 5 films M1217 (Nat.Archives) with 'War Crimes Trials in Dachau' is
              the Case 12-1894. Lt. Houston was captured and assaulted. One German got
              5 years imprisonment. The assault took place at Roloven, 6 km E of Gehrden.

Sources : MACR. 1 0 7 6 5

--------------------------------------------------------------------
Details collected by : J.A. H e y - A.v.d.Leeuwstraat 12 - 7552 HS Hengelo, Holland.
```

491st Bomb Group, 853rd Bomb Squadron

***

Acknowledgements;
Pilot Warren C. Moore
Karen Crane for co-pilot Robert McIntyre
Navigator Ross Houston
Bruce Patten for bombardier George K. Patton
Radio-operator Joseph S. Rimassa
Georg Weber

CHAPTER 19

491ST BOMB GROUP 853RD BOMB SQUADRON

Aircraft Type: B-24J, Serial # 42-51530,
"Idiot's Delight", MACR 10767
Airbase: North Pickenham

"We knew that the German anti-aircraft gunners would pick us up at about IP and follow us all of the way into the target with the barrage, and for a goodly distance beyond the target"

—From Co-Pilot Frank Spady's autobiography

Pilot: Capt. Wayne E. Stewart (KIA) Meadow UT
Co-Pilot: 1Lt. Frank A. Spady Jr. (POW) Chuckatuck VA
Navigator: 1Lt. Woodrow G. Johnson (KIA) Iron River MI
Bombardier: 1Lt. George A. Valashovic (POW) Johnstown NY
Pil. Navigator: 1Lt. William L. Reese (KIA) Garfield Heights OH
Top-Turret: T/Sgt. Laverne G. Anderson (KIA), Litchfield WI
Radio: T/Sgt. Harry H. Pollak (POW) Clifton NJ
Left-Waist: S/Sgt. Henry K. Mosley Jr. (POW) Arwado NY
Right-Waist: S/Sgt. George H. Corona (KIA) San Francisco CA
Tail-Gunner: S/Sgt. Walter W. Reichenau (POW) Fredericksburg TX

Total: 5 KIA, 5 POW
Target: Misburg
Crash Site: Annaturm on the Deister, 5 Km N of Springe, Germany
Time of Crash: 12.40

NOT HOME FOR CHRISTMAS

Calvin Stewart about his brother pilot **Wayne E. Stewart**:

"You can imagine my surprise and how thrilled I am to hear from you with details concerning my brother Wayne when he was killed along with his crew November 26, 1944. The rest of the family have wondered all this time what exactly happened to Wayne. I knew it was his return flight after dropping his bombs over Germany, and it was to be his last flight over there. How ironic and sad that he never made it into safe countries. The information from you is the only thing we have ever received about his death.

"My mother Sarah E. Stewart did receive some sort of communication stating that he (Wayne) was supposed

Captain Wayne E. Stewart

Nov. 20, 1946

OMGMr 293
Stewart, Wayne E.
SN O 811 152

Dear sirs
Is their any way to find out where and how, my dear son Wayne met his death,
I have heard so many reports I donot know which one is right

Mrs Sarah E. Stewart
Meadow, Utah

to have been seen at a railroad station in Germany on or about 11-27-44. (I also noted that in the USAir Force paper). You can imagine how much we have wondered if that was so, or if he went down with his plane. She was also informed he was presumed to have been shot down over Belgium. How records do leave one in doubt.

"Out of five brothers, I am the only one living. Four of the five brothers served in WWII in various branches of the service:

Verl E. Stewart	US Army
Arlo Stewart	Capt. Army Air Force (pilot)
Wayne E. Stewart	**Capt. Army Air force (pilot)**
Calvin P. Stewart	U.S. Navy (myself) Also served in US Army in Korea.
Charlie Stewart	U.S. Army

Wayne was the only one killed in the war. Youngest brother Charlie served in Korea in the Army later on.

Co-pilot **Frank A. Spady Jr.** wrote in the foreword of his autobiography:

"For a number of years my children have asked me to place in writing some of the things I remember and expound on to them from time to time. They refer to my ramblings as talking about "olden times" meaning anything that may have happened fifteen or twenty years previously.

He describes his last flight in WW II;

"The 491st Bomb Group, our Group, flew by itself that day, since no other Group in our Wing flew with us. We flew the lead plane in the high squadron (No. 2 Squadron) and we had the regular nine planes in our squadron that day. The Group Lead Squadron had two extra planes for a total of eleven planes. The Low Squadron also had three extra planes. The Group as a whole had a total of thirty-one planes.

"Our target was a diversion target that day, and the primary target was a railroad viaduct in another area not too far away. I believe it was between Hamm and Hannover.

"There was light flak from several places along our route to the IP. Many miles before we reached the IP, we could see the flak barrage over Misburg, and it was as severe as any. The barrage covered an area at least twenty-five miles square and was exactly at our altitude. We knew that the German anti-aircraft gunners would pick us up at about IP and follow us all of the way into the target with the barrage, and for a goodly distance beyond the target.

"A description of our Bombing Plan is as follows. We were flying east to the IP. The IP was about fifty miles north of the target Misburg. Hannover was about five miles west of Misburg. Therefore we were to turn ninety degrees to the right at the IP, open the bomb bay doors, and start the Bomb Run South to Misburg. Hannover was only five miles west of Misburg and we did not want to make a direct turn West after bombs were released, since we would run into the most severe flak that one can imagine. Therefore, our course immediately after bomb release was to begin a shallow dive while turning another ninety degrees to the right and heading west toward home.

"Bomb bay doors were opened at the IP and all planes had to fly straight and level from the IP until bombs were released over target. The most vulnerable part of a mission over enemy territory was from IP to the point of bombs release: the bomb run. We were flying at an altitude of about twenty-seven thousand feet.

"In addition to the flak barrage, we could see hundreds of contrails on the other side of the IP and the target, which indicated single engine fighters. Those contrails were about two to three thousand feet above our altitude. I knew that a concentration that large of fighters had to be German fighters because our close fighter support was not that large. Also, some of our close support fighters seemed to disappear.

"Due to the intense flak and the presence of German fighters, we were sure that we would bomb in Group Formation, but as we approached the IP, Colonel Parmele came on the radio and ordered us to uncover the formation and go over the target in Squadron Formation.

"When the Lead Squadron reached the IP, they made their turn and headed for the target. We, the High Squadron, reached the IP and started our turn at about the time the Lead Squadron had completed three-fourth of their turn. We opened the bomb bay doors and the bombardier started aligning the bomb site. By this time, the Low Squadron had almost completed its turn onto the bombing run.

"Some of our close fighter support had closed with some of the German fighters on the other side of the IP, but some of the German fighters were getting through to our bombers. About half way from the IP to the target, flak started coming up at the Lead Squadron and our squadron. This flak was at our altitude and was very close. There were many near-misses around us and the other planes. We were buffeted several times by the force from near misses.

491st Bomb Group, 853rd Bomb Squadron

"About the time the Lead Squadron's bombs were released, German fighters were all over our squadron. Since we were on the bombing run, we could not take any evasive action. We had to fly straight and level until the bombs were released, regardless of enemy action.

"ME-109s and FW-190s were coming at us from all directions. I could feel the plane shutter from reactions of our machine guns firing. There was no reason to call on the intercom radio to tell the gunners that an enemy fighter was coming from a specific direction, since all of the gunners were busy firing at enemy fighters that were coming from all directions. I could hear the shatter of glass breaking and falling as enemy bullets came through the nose section and the cockpit.

"Some of the enemy fighters were firing 20 mm guns from their planes. I could see the shells exploding about twenty feet in front of our plane and they looked like someone had thrown a package of small fire crackers in front of the plane. These shells were timed to explode at a pre-determined distance in front of the guns. The German pilot had to make his run on his target, estimate his distance from his target, and fire his guns when he thought the range was right. I thank the Lord that most of their shells exploded in front of, to the side of and in the rear of our plane.

"A bullet came through the left side of our plane on an angle that made it pass between my left arm and my chest. I felt a jolt, my arm jerked forward, I heard glass break and fall, and there was a hole in the instrument panel in front of me where the bullet had gone through it and out of the nose section of the plane. I put my hand under my arm where the bullet had gone through, removed my hand very quickly, looked at it and saw no blood, then promptly forgot about it.

"I heard Reese, our pilotage navigator in the nose turret say over the intercom that he could not get the turret to operate. I knew immediately that the wiring to the operator had been cut or damaged, so I told to him that he would have to turn the turret manually.

"Finally, I heard the bombardier say over the intercom, "Bombs away". We immediately started a slow descent. By that time, we were over the target and we had been getting the most severe flak that I had ever seen. Then almost instantly, the flak stopped coming up and the enemy fighters really did come in. One came so close to my right side that I could see the pilot's face. Another one came into my right side within pistol range and banked away after his firing run. Several were so anxious to get to us that they came in a few seconds before the anti-aircraft gunners stopped firing, and these got some of their own flak.

"I am not sure how many passes the German fighters made on our squadron, but I do know that all of our planes dropped their bombs on the target. Several minutes (may be three or four) after passing the target, I looked around and saw that all of our squadron was missing except the leader of our high element of three planes, one plane in the low element, and our plane. The German fighters came in again and shot down the leader of our high element and the remaining plane in our low element. Then we were the only plane left out of our squadron of nine planes.

"Almost immediately, a swarm of German fighters came in on us, and after they passed by, Harry Pollak the radio-operator yelled, "The plane is on fire". I looked back in time to see him go out of the bomb bay, and at the same time, I saw fire on the flight deck where the oxygen tanks were stored. Realizing that oxygen would support combustion, and that the fuel tanks were just above the oxygen tanks, I knew that we had no choice but to bail out.

"We had practiced the emergency bail out procedure many times and everyone knew exactly what to do and when to do it. In the nose section, the bombardier and the navigator were to get the person in the nose turret out, then all were to open the nose wheel door and bail out. In the tail section, the two waist-gunners were to get the tail turret gunner out of the turret and then all were to bail out through the bomb bay. The pilot in the right seat was to get out first through the bomb bay, and then the pilot in the left seat was to go out through the bomb bay. Every crew member knew and understood that when the bail out order was given, everyone would go immediately with no playing around.

"I looked back again at the flight deck where the fire was, the fire was getting larger, so I immediately told Stewart that we had to bail out. He looked back and ran the emergency bail-out bell at the same time. I gave the order three times over the intercom to bail out and explained that the plane was on fire on the flight deck. Then I disconnected my oxygen mask, the radio cable to me headphone set, the cable to my electric heat suit, removed my flak jacket, unbuckled my safety belts, grabbed my shoes (the strings had been tied together previously for just such an emergency) and headed for the bomb bay.

"When I started by the top turret, I noticed that the door at the bottom of the turret was open and saw two feet coming out. Since Mosley was almost out of the turret, I went by him to the bomb bay and bailed out. From that point, I learned nothing else about the crew until I had reached the ground. When I bailed out, I stepped on the cat walk in the bomb bay, then stepped left and went out through the right front bay.

"When I jumped, I was facing the rear of the plane with my shoes in my left hand and my right hand was on the rip cord ring of my parachute. As soon as my feet hit the air stream, I was thrown into a horizontal position with my head lower than my feet. I was falling in the direction that the plane was headed, on my back with my feet elevated. My shoes did not fall as fast as I was falling, so I had to keep a firm grip on the strings that were tied together, and pull the shoes down with the air current trying to pull them out of my hand.

"I knew that the terminal velocity of a human body falling in space was about 110 miles per hour and that I was about 27'000 feet up when I bailed out. Several years before that date, I had calculated that in a free fall in space, a body would fall about two miles per minute. Knowing the altitude when I bailed out (27'000 feet), I did a fast calculation and determined that I would hit the ground about two and a half-one minutes after bailing out, if I did not open my parachute.

"My immediate goal was to fall through the air battle that was going on around me before opening my parachute. Also, I wanted to be as close to the ground as possible when the parachute opened, hoping that I would have a chance to hide in a wood, or anywhere else that might me available.

"I calculated that I should not open my parachute until I had fallen at least 21'000 feet, or about 5'000 feet up, in order to be sure that I would be well below the air battle. The ideal situation would have been to pull the rip cord when only about 2'000 or 1'000 feet above the ground, but I needed a safety factor of several thousand feet. Therefore I began counting slowly and hoping that I would have the nerve to reach 120, or two minutes, before opening my parachute., which would place me about 5'000 feet or 6'000 feet above the ground. At the count of 120, I pulled the rip cord and the parachute opened.

"Immediately after the parachute opened, I began trying to untie the knot in my shoe strings and put my shoes on so that I could hit the ground, slip the parachute harness instantly and start running. The temperature at 27'000 feet altitude was about forty degrees below zero centigrade. I do not know what the temperature was at my altitude when my parachute opened, but my fingers felt like they were freezing. Therefore, I gave up trying to untie my shoe strings and started looking down to see what was below.

"Directly under me was a large forest and I thought how lucky I would be to land in that. About that time, I heard several fighter planes and machine guns firing nearby, and at least one plane came by me close enough to disturb my parachute. I looked down again and saw that the forest that

NOT HOME FOR CHRISTMAS

was under me was not there, so I knew that I was drifting with the air current. I tried to slip my parachute back to the forest by pulling on the parachute's lines. That was a failure, so I gave up and waited.

"When I got to within about four or five hundred feet above the ground, I saw a settlement of about six or eight houses and about eight or ten people there looking up at me. I was drifting toward that settlement fast, and there was nothing I could do but hope for the best. I came in just over the electric power lines at a road by the settlement and landed in a vegetable garden between two of those houses. Immediately, two men and two women who appeared to be in their seventies, one boy who appeared to be about eighteen years old, and two or three children surrounded me.

"The boy had an old rifle that looked to be World War I vintage and from his actions I understood that he was telling the people around me to get out of the way so he could shoot me. One of the older men got behind me, wrapped his arms around me and asked me if I had a pistol. When I responded that I had no weapon, he told the boy in English to get away from us. The man who had wrapped his arms around me saved my life.

"While that was going on, the other older man and one of the older women had pulled my parachute in and folded it while I got out of the harness. About that time, two German soldiers arrived and marched me down the road about one-quarter mile where several other German soldiers had Reichenau our tail-gunner, Mosley our top-turret gunner, and Valashovic our bombardier.

"During the air battle, a 20 mm shell from a German fighter plane exploded in the tail turret and several fragments hit Reichenau in both legs and his face. Though he was bleeding some, the wounds were not serious. He had a towel that he had been using as a scarf around his neck, and he was using that to clean some of the blood off of his face and legs. I asked one of the guards about medical attention for Reichenau and he said we would receive some at the Army Station that we were headed toward. Valashovic and Mosley did not have a wound.

"The soldiers marched us several miles further along that road to a small German Army Station of about three or four buildings. At that Station, the Germans had Pollak, our radio operator. Fortunately, Pollak had not received a wound.

"On the way from where we were captured to the Army Station, we passed through three more built up areas with a store or two. In several instances, a woman leaned out of a second floor window and yelled something at the German soldiers who were guarding us. Reichenau was from Fredericksburg, Texas, a German settlement, and he and his family could speak German. I asked Reichenau what those people were saying. He smiled and said they wanted the German soldiers to kill us.

"At the Army Station, we were strip searched, and the Germans tried to get some information from us, but no one told anything. The Germans did clean Rechenau's wounds and put some medication and bandages on them. I looked at my arm and chest when I had my clothes off. A place about six inches in diameter on my left chest under my left arm was almost black. Also, a place on my left arm, about the size of a half dollar, was cut out about one-sixteenth of an inch deep. That spot was very close to me smallpox vaccination scar. Since it was not serious, I decided to wait until later to say anything about it.

"In addition to our crew members, the Germans had two or three other Americans at that Station, and they had been captured that day. There were no facilities at that Station to hold prisoners, so the Germans locked us up in their bath facility, which was a building about twelve feet square. They kept two soldiers around the building as guards for the night.

"The next day, we were marched about six or eight miles to a small city and placed on a train. I have no idea where we were captured or what towns or cities we passed through. As well as I can remember, we traveled one day and one night after boarding that train before reaching the first prisoner of war camp the next morning, November 28, 1944.

"The first prisoner of war camp we were taken to was Oberursel, which was about eight miles Northwest of Frankfurt am Main. Oberursel is about 170 miles Southwest of Misburg. We rode trains and walked from where we were captured to Oberursel. I do remember that we rode on one train that was a local train. That train carried children to and from school. While we were on that train, it made several stops for school children to get on and off.

"These children were in elementary school and appeared to be from about six years old to about twelve years old. The children were not afraid of us and we carried on conversations with them, since the guards did not care. They could speak English as well as we could, but they did have an accent.

"During one change of trains, we had to walk through the train station. Just as we were getting ready to go down some stairs to get to the other train, I saw a man picking his way through the crowd and heading straight toward me. He did not take his eyes off me the whole time he was walking toward me, and he reminded me of a snake trying to charm a bird. When he got to within about ten feet from me, he started talking and continued to talk until he was almost in my face. Since I did not understand

NOT HOME FOR CHRISTMAS

German, I could not understand what he was saying to me, but the look on his face told me that it was not complimentary.

"Walter Reichenau was next to me, and when the man moved on I asked Reichenau what the man had said. He smiled and told me that I had just gotten the worst cussing out that I ever had. I asked Reichenau why the man had singled me out from across the room rather than one of the other Americans. Reichenau responded that the man had a son who was a pilot in the Luftwaffe, and his son had been killed. The man spotted me as an officer and a pilot and had vented his wrath on me.

"About two days after we were shot down and captured, we reached Oberursel. We got off the train and boarded a street car to the end of the line. We walked the rest of the way to the prisoner of war camp.

"From the time we were captured to the time we reached Oberursel, our crew talked among ourselves when none of the guards were close enough to hear what we said. Though all of the guards could speak English, they did not appear to care that we talked among ourselves, as long as the conversations were short. All of us wanted to know what the others had experienced during the run over the target and during the air battle.

"I asked George Valashovic, the bombardier, what happened in the nose section of the plane. He said that before and after "bombs away, he heard glass shatter and thumps when bullets or flak fragments went through the nose section. He said that William Reese, the pilotage navigator, got out of the nose-turret, then he (George) opened the nose wheel door and bailed out. He said that Reese and Woodrow Johnson, the regular navigator, were standing there waiting to bail out after he did. I never heard from them again until I reached home after the war and learned that Reese and Johnson were both killed.

"I asked Walter Reichenau, the tail-gunner, what happened in the tail section of the plane. He said that he shot down one German fighter and damaged another one. He also said he was sure that George Henry Corona, the waist-gunner, shot down one German fighter, but he did not know whether Anderson shot down any German fighters or not.

"Reichenau said that a minute or so after the 20mm shell exploded in his tail turret, he heard the bail-out bell and the call from me over the intercom to bail out. He then started getting out of the turret and he said that Corona and Laverne Anderson, the flight engineer who was on the other waist gun, helped him getting out of the tail turret. After he had gotten out, he bailed out of one of the rear bomb bays and that Corona and Anderson were standing there waiting their turn to bail out. I never

491st Bomb Group, 853rd Bomb Squadron

heard from them again until I reached home after the war and learned that Corona and Anderson were both killed.

"Harry Pollak, the radio-operator, saw the fire and bailed immediately after yelling that the plane was on fire. He was the first one out of the plane and did not know anything about what had happened in the plane after he bailed out. It was the radio-operator's duty to close the bomb bay doors after the bombs had been released. He was in the act of closing these doors when he saw the fire on the flight deck. Instead of closing the doors, when he saw the fire, he yelled and bailed out all at the same time. Therefore, when the other men on the flight deck got ready to bail out, the bomb bay doors were already open.

"I asked Henry Mosley, the top-turret gunner, what he knew. Mosley said that he unlatched the bottom door to the top-turret, which was also the gunner's seat, started to drop out and then his parachute harness got caught on something. He climbed back up, freed his harness, and was coming back down when he saw me come by. He said that as soon as I went by, Wayne Stewart, the left seat pilot, pulled him all the way down and handed him his parachute chest pack. Mosley then snapped his chest pack on and bailed out of the front bomb bay. He said that Stewart was standing on the cat walk at the bomb bay waiting to bail out, just as he (Mosley) bailed out. I never heard from Stewart, directly, again until I heard after the war he was killed.

"About five months after the war, I was stationed again at Turner Field near Albany, Georgia. Stationed there also, was Brice E. "Chuck" Thornburg, another pilot who was on Charles Stevens crew and was in the barracks with us at Metfield, England. Stevens had three engines shot out and got a direct hit in the nose section of his plane on June 20, 1944, but made it back to the English shore line.

"Based on information I received from Valashovic, Reichenau and Mosley, all members on our crew who were killed were standing at their escape opening waiting to bail out. They could have been killed from bullets or 20mm canon fire from German fighters after we left the plane and before they could bail out. They could have been killed after bail out by failure of their parachutes to open, or by fighter planes before they landed, or they could have gone down with the plane for some unknown reason. Also, they could have been killed on the ground by civilians or by German soldiers, and this did happen to many of our airmen.

"The German camp at Oberursel was a transition center for captured American and British airmen. When captured after being shot down over

NOT HOME FOR CHRISTMAS

Germany or German controlled territory, the prisoners were sent to the camp at Oberursel for processing and interrogation.

"When we arrived at Oberursel, we were separated and I was interviewed in a small room by a German non-commissioned officer, probably a corporal or sergeant. I gave my name, rank and serial number in accordance with the Rules of the Geneva Convention. He insisted that the Geneva Convention Rules allowed a prisoner of war to give his organization number. I agreed and told him that my organization number was the same as my serial number, which was the Geneva Convention interpretation of organization number.

"He asked my father's name. Since I was a Jr. I assumed that he knew that my father's name was the same as mine and I informed of that. He asked my birth date and my religion, so I told him, since I saw no harm in that. Then he asked me my mother's name and I told him she was Mrs. Spady, with no further elaboration. He had my dog tags, so he knew my name, my serial number, my blood type, and my religion was as P for protestant on the dog tags. After that, I answered no more questions.

"The German continued to ask questions, especially about my Group, Squadron, where I was stationed, our target the day I was shot down, and other questions related to the military. I sat silent, except that once or twice I said that under the Rules of the Geneva Convention, I was only required to give my name, rank and serial number.

"He continued to ask questions and I remained silent. Several times the silence continued for two or three minutes at a time while he waited for me to answer his question. Then he would ask another question and there were several more minutes of silence. This continued about twenty minutes. I felt silly sitting there at the table with the German, who had a writing pad and pencil, while dead silence prevailed most of the time.

"Finally, the German asked another question, and told me to answer his question since he did not have any more time to spend with me. I replied that I was not holding him from doing something else and that he should go ahead with his other duties. He said that he had no more time to waste, got up out of his chair and told me to follow him.

"I followed him down several long corridors until he stopped at a door. He told me to take my shoes off and place them in the hall by the door. He opened the door and told me to go in. As I went into the room, he told me to think about the questions he had asked, and if I decided to answer them, call the guard and tell him I was ready to talk. I realized that I was being placed in solitary confinement.

"I found myself in a cell about five feet wide by about nine feet deep. The room had a small window with obscure glass, a small hot water heater that never was warm, and a bunk. The bunk was about thirty inches wide by about six feet long by about eighteen inches high. The thing resembled a tray more than a bunk.

"The bunk was the only thing in the room, except me. There was no mattress or pillow or blanket or any other covering, and it was cold. The clothes I had on were the same clothes I dressed in the morning of November, 26, 1944, the day I was shot down. I had on long winter underwear, heavy socks, regular officers winter shirt, trousers, necktie, regular army brogan shoes, and a jacket. The jacket was Air Force issue green heavy cloth with heavy alpaca lining and collar. I did not have a cap or hat and I did not have any gloves.

"Before I bailed out of the plane, I removed my sheepskin lined helmet with the headphone set, and my sheepskin lined gloves, so that my hands would be free. When my parachute opened, my sheepskin lined flying boots flew off and left me barefoot, except for the heavy shoes I had in my hand. Therefore, when I landed, I did not have a cap or hat or gloves, but I did have good, heavy shoes and put them on.

"After I had been in the solitary confinement cell a short time, a guard opened the door and placed a quart bottle on the floor next to the door. The bottle was filled with cold, ersatz coffee. On the wall next to the door was a gadget that stuck through the wall. The guard told me to push the lever on the gadget when I needed to go to the toilet, and a guard would come, unlock the door and go with me to the toilet. I asked him about getting a bandage for my arm, where I was hit with a bullet during the air battle. The guard took me down the corridor, turned and went into a large room at the end of the corridor.

"This room served as headquarters for the guards. There were a few shelves with books, and one corner served as an infirmary. An American airman was in the corner where the infirmary was located, and he was acting as a medic for the American prisoners. I removed my jacket, shirt and underwear top. This was the first time I had seen the wound since I was strip searched the day after I was captured. The large black bruise on the left side of my chest under my left arm was still there and was a little darker then it was the last time I saw it. The gouged out place on the back of my left arm was raw and wet.

"The American airman had a little cabinet that contained a few medical items. He rubbed some salve on the large black bruise on my chest, a kind of medication on the arm wound, and put a bandage on the wound.

NOT HOME FOR CHRISTMAS

Then he asked me if I would like to take book to read. I said I would, and we walked over to the book shelves.

"The books were given by the International Red Cross for prisoners of war to read, and I began looking at the titles, which were all in English. The senior German guard walked over, took a book off the shelf, handed it to me and said that would be a good one for me to read. At the same time, he told the guard who had brought me to the room, to take me back to my cell.

"That night, the guard opened the door and handed me a slice of dark brown bread that was smeared with about one half teaspoon of margarine and poured some ersatz coffee in my bottle. The next morning, I was given another slice of bread and ersatz coffee. At noon, I was given a bowl of thin grass soup and more ersatz coffee. That night, I was given another slice of bread with the same one half teaspoon of margarine smeared on the bread. The same food routine was followed for the next seven days.

"During the solitary confinement, there was nothing to do but lay on the tray (or bunk) and try to sleep. I was too hungry to do any type of exercise. Furthermore, exercise would have made me hungrier, if that were possible. Two or three times a day, I would give the signal that I wanted to go to the toilet. That gave me about three minutes out of the cell each trip to the toilet, and helped break the monotony. After a few days in the cell, I got scabies and scratching occupied most of my time after that.

"I found solitary confinement troubling, including the hunger, the cold, and the scabies. There was no one to talk to, I had no idea where I was in Germany, and I had just about lost track of time and date. I had time to think about the air battle that resulted in my whole squadron being shot down, and I wondered where the other men of my crew were and if they were safe, or not. In times such as that, one communicates with his maker, and it can be safely said that there were no atheists in a solitary confinement cell for prisoners of war. While I wondered what to expect next, I refused to allow my mind to wander into the unknown, and forced myself to consider future adverse possibilities and devise ways in my mind to counter these possibilities.

"A day or two after I was placed in solitary confinement, a man in the next cell knocked on the wall and called to me. I answered, and he said that solitary confinement was getting to him. I agreed that it was rough. Then he began to ask questions, such as what outfit I was with, etc. Immediately, I recognized that he was a German trying to get information, so I told him that I was not interested in talking.

"Some of the Germans could speak English without an accent, some had been in America and went back to follow Hitler, and some from

America were back in Germany visiting when the war started and could not get out of Germany. These Germans were used to interrogate Americans, guard Americans, and similar duties. Also, some of the American airmen, who were prisoners of war, gave the Germans information and assisted the enemy in other ways.

"During my training in America before going to Europe, an Air Force Sergeant who had escaped from the Germans through France and Spain, and back to England, gave a talk to all of the men on the field and described his experiences. He said that American airmen who gave information to the Germans at the interrogation center, were kept at the center as long as they continued to give information to the Germans. If you did not give any information, you would be sent to a permanent POW camp and held there without further interrogation.

After about a week in solitary confinement Frank Spady together with George Valachavic were transported to Stalag Luft I camp in Barth where they stayed until their liberation by the Russians. Frank recalls:

"At 01.00 A.M. April 30, 1945, Major Steinhauer of the German Command, notified the Senior Allied Officer of the Barth camp, Colonel Zempke that all German guards had evacuated the camp, leaving it in command of the Americans and the British. When we woke up that morning we found that we were no longer under armed guard. The first thing we did was to raid the warehouse holding Red Cross food packages and eat a decent meal for the first time since I was shot down on November 26, 1944.

"The next problem was to establish contact with the Russians. Early morning the following day, two or three men were sent south to look for our liberators. Eventually, contact was made and the Russians came to our camp. The Russian Army that came through Barth was what we called a "Rabble" Army, not the first quality army. They were walking or riding in horse drawn carts, and some of these carts had wheels that were about a four-inch slice from a tremendously large tree trunk.

"A Russian Colonel rode up in a very high two seated buggy drawn by two of the most beautiful bay horses I had ever seen. In addition to the two seats, there was a driver's seat higher than the coach seats, and the driver was a really dressed up Russian soldier. The whole contraption, with Coat-of-Arms on each buggy door, had been "liberated" from some German estate.

"After the German guards had left the camp and went west to sur-

NOT HOME FOR CHRISTMAS

render to the Americans, we walked around the area outside of the camp. Colonel Zempke ordered all POW's to remain in the camp or its immediate area until he made arrangements to have us flown out in American planes. A few venturesome souls took off and headed west to see some of Germany and eventually made contact with the American Army. I followed Colonel Zempke's orders and remained in the camp. There were too many disgruntled German civilians and too many Russian and German soldiers running around.

"There were several other prison camps around Barth, some of which held political prisoners of different nationalities. One prison camp was on the airfield of Barth and those prisoners were primarily Poles, including some Polish Jews. When the German soldiers left Barth and headed west, they left the doors to the prisoners' barracks on the airfield locked with the prisoners inside.

"When American and British POW's from Stalag Luft No. 1 opened the doors to the Polish prisoners barracks on the air field, they were met by conditions so horrible they were almost beyond description. All of the people there were skin and bones from hunger. Only a few were on their feet, the rest being confined to their bunks with dysentery, weakness from hunger and only God knew what else. They had been on a starvation diet for months, and the Germans had not given them any food for the past two or three days. Most had been in their bunks since before the Germans left. They did not have enough energy to get up to get to the toilet, and their condition was such that I shall not describe it further.

"Several days after the German capitulation, American planes landed at Barth airfield to fly the POW's out. They were troop transports and four engine bombers. I flew out in a B-17 bomber that had wood platforms built in the bomb bays. These converted bombers carried about twenty or thirty men on each trip.

"We were flown to an air field in France, then taken by truck to a very large tent city named Camp Lucky Strike. There were two things that all of us were looking forward to with great anticipation. The first thing was being able to take a good shower, with soap, and staying in the shower long enough to get clean, and a little longer for good measure. The second thing was being able to eat our fill. Both of these things were fulfilled as soon as we arrived in Camp Lucky Strike.

"June 13, 1945, we boarded a troop transport named "General Butner" in the port of Le Havre and a day or two later we set sail for home. Four or five days later we docked in Newport News after a very fast and uneventful crossing.

"The ship entered the James River early in the morning of June 20. It was met by several tug boats and all of the ships anchored in the area blew their horns or whistles as we went by. As we were preparing to dock, an Army band was there playing welcome songs. There were also a lot of people on the dock to welcome us home.

"We went down the gang plank of the ship, boarded a train that was waiting for us, and were taken to Camp Patrick Henry. The Camp was located in the area of the present Patrick Henry airport.

"My sixty day leave started June 25, 1945 and for the next two months, I reveled in being able to do just what I wanted to do and when I wanted to do it. I slept mornings until I wanted to get up, visited old friends, sat around the stores in Chuckatuck and talked to the village people when they came in, just as I had done all my life.

"Morning in Moore's store, where the post office was located, was where I saw the people who lived outside of the village when they came to collect their mail. All of the "home folks," people in the village and those on farms outside the village, were glad to see me home in one whole piece.

"One thing in particular I remember when I got home. I went to Suffolk to visit my friends and take care of business at the bank. When I went in January's Men Clothing Store to see the people there, Mr. and Mrs. January gave me a big hug. Then Hillary January, who owned the store, said that he had something for me. He went to his office, got a package, brought it to me and said, "I knew you would come back here and I kept it for you. " It was a package with a necktie that he had sent to me for a Christmas present the previous Christmas. The package had been returned to him marked "Missing in Action." Mrs. January said that when the postman returned the package to the store, Hillary went to his office, put his head on his desk and cried. Then he said that he would keep it and give it to me when I came home.

"One of the great joys during my leave was eating all of the good food I could hold. At home, Mamma cooked everything I mentioned that I would like to have. After a while, I began to regain some of the weight I had lost in Stalag Luft No. 1.

Navigator **Woodrow G. Johnson** was born in June 1918 in Iron River, Michigan. His mother Agnes was widowed very young and had to raise her two sons, Woody and Lloyd, alone. Her husband Alex had died of the great flu epidemic in the 1920's, Agnes also had the flu and was quarantined to her house. Before Alex was buried, the hearse went by the house so Agnes could at least see it. That must have been heart wrenching for her.

Mother Agnes ran a rooming and boarding house and the two brothers learned to split wood at a very young age. Their house had to be heated, and wood was also needed for the cooking stove. She not only cooked, but baked her own bread.

After graduation from Iron River High he served as deputy city clerk and for two years was employed by the M.A. Hanna Company prior to enlisting in the Air Corps.

After his advanced training at Pueblo, Colorado, he was sent to England in March 1944. He had won the Air Medal with six clusters, DFC and the Purple Heart. The November 26, 1944, mission was to be his last before qualifying for home leave. In his last letter home, dated the day before he died, he mentioned: "It seems strange but I don't feel the elation one should when they are practically thru their tour"

Woodrow was initially buried near the crash site in the cemetery of Eimbeckhausen in Germany. After the war he was reinterred in the American Military Cemetery in the Belgian Ardennes. His body was returned home in May, 1949 and his funeral was held on Saturday, May 21, 1949. His mother never recovered after that; she mourned his death the rest of her life.

1Lt. Woodrow G. Johnson

Woodrow was awarded 2 Air Medals, 6 Oak Leaf Clusters, the Distinguished Flying Cross and the Purple Heart. Woodrow was admired for his bravery, his devotion and his superior navigation ability by all who knew him. He was devoted to his mother and extended family and enjoyed boating, hunting and skiing in his spare time.

About bombardier **George A. Valashovic** his son Thomas wrote in 2006:

"He was born in Johnstown, graduated from Johnstown High School 1937. He was a good athlete playing football and baseball. He married Geraldine Kelly October 14, 1943.

"After the war, he went to work for Independent Leather Corp., a large tannery in Gloversville, NY.Johnstown and Gloversville, NY were home to over 20 tanneries and over 100 Glove companies. George worked his way up and eventually owned 35% of the mill. He sold out in 1990 and basically only had "one" job for 45 years. I also worked at the tannery for 25 years, 1964-1989.

"Besides work, George enjoyed golf and gambling. And boy did he enjoy gambling! He played poker twice a week, bet the horses every day and most of all loved to bet on sports - mainly football. I often tell people that I think my father bet on every professional football game ever televised, starting in the 1950's until his death. He loved living on the edge.

"I will say though that despite his losing a lot of money through the years, he worked hard and made a good living. My brother and I lived in nice homes and he was generous with his money. Probably his favorite saying was "It's only money".

"I think my dad was typical of the men Tom Brokaw describes in the Greatest Generation.

"He died in October 1995, a week before his 74th birthday.

About pilotage navigator **William Reese**, his nephew Al Butterfield wrote:

"William Reese was born December 11, 1920 at Cleveland, Ohio. His father was of Welsh descent and his mother came from an Irish family. When he died on November 26, 1944 he was just short of his 24th birthday.

"He attended Miles School where he played the trombone and bass drum in the band and orchestra. He also became the drum major. On December 4, 1938 he performed on Bert's Big Broadcast which aired on WCLE Radio.

"While at John Adams High School Bill played in the Brass Sextet, The Trombone Quartet and the Dance Band. He was the Drum Major with the marching band. He was the Class Treasurer, Central Committee Vice President, was on the Prom Committee and a member of the National Honor Society.

NOT HOME FOR CHRISTMAS

"After High School he worked in Cincinnati, Ohio. He hitchhiked home to Cleveland for Christmas, 1940. The family moved to 4523 E. 126th Street in Garfield Heights. It is a stucco house on the corner of Rexwood.

"In September 1941 His sister and her husband Bill Butterfield drove Bill to Blackburn, VA where he started College at Virginia Polytechnic Institute. His mother accompanied him on this trip. Bill made the wrestling team for VPI and wrestled at North Carolina State in Raleigh, NC.

1Lt. William L. Reese

"After his mother had given him the permission he joined the Army Air Corps in May, 1942 in Richmond Virginia. He graduated from the Army Air Force Navigation School December 1943 at Hondo, Texas. Next stop: Pueblo, Colorado. He was assigned to the 8th USAAF, 491st Bomb Group, 853rd Bomb Squadron. Bill came home on leave in March 1944, it was the last time his family saw him.

"Early May 1944 the 491st left Pueblo for Harrington, Texas where modifications were made to the aircraft. Then to Palm Beach, Florida for further modifications. Upon departure from Florida they opened their sealed orders. The final destination was Metfield in England by way of Trinidad, Belem, Brazil, Fort Alaza, Brazil and the across the Atlantic ocean to Dakar in Senegal, Marrakesh in Marocco.

"On June 8th 1944, in support of the Allied invasion in France, the target of the 491st for that day was the rail road bridge spanning the River Rance. Bill was taken off their bomber "Lucky Penny" and assigned to one of the lead planes as he was such a good Navigator.

"Lucky Penny" lost an engine before reaching France and was forced to abort the mission and to return back to Metfield. The aircraft, with a full load of bombs and kerosene, crashed while trying to land. She exploded and killed the entire crew. Bill was on the runway and witnessed the accident. Some time later he wrote the following letter to the mother of Warren Rudolph:

"Your letter arrived just as I was writing to you for the second time. My first letter was sent back to me by the censor department. They felt that not enough time had elapsed since the accident, and in accordance with their strict policy as to what can and cannot be said about accidents, they wouldn't let it go thru. I feel now though, that enough time has elapsed so that this letter, telling you what you wish to know, will be allowed.

"As my father wrote you, I was taken off the crew and that proved to be most fortunate for me. I was supposed to fly with one of the lead crews for that mission, but we were taken off the list at the last moment and it was too late for me to go and fly with Warren and the rest of the boys.

"I was here when the accident happened. They were coming back from the mission and had one engine gone. It was just one of those accidents that will happen when men fly. They crashed trying to land here at the base, and the ensuing explosion killed everyone aboard. That it was quick and decisive, that no one suffered any pain was merciful.

"After living and flying with the fellows as long as I had, it was just too hard to believe that anything could happen. I liked Warren so much. He knew everyone's job on the ship, and lots of time he used to come up in the nose with me and I would show him all about navigation. Our crew was one of the best in the groups. On June 13 Chaplain Spense and I buried them all together in the American Military Cemetery at Cambridge. It's very beautiful there, and the services were conducted with all the military honors due them. They are due so much too. Every boy who places himself in a plane and goes deep into enemy territory day after day is a brave man in every sense of the word.

"No matter how much I write or say can dim the sorrow you must have Mrs. Rudolph. I just hope you will get some satisfaction out of the knowledge that he was doing much more than his share of the work on the crew; that he was doing a swell job; and that he was called while he was doing his part to end this war so all of you, the ones he loved, could live happily.

"Bill was then assigned to the "Flying Jackass" piloted by Wayne Stewart. On 15 August 1944 the 491st moved to North Pickenham, England.

"Sunday, November 26, 1944 found the Stewart crew flying "Idiot's Delight" named after the 1939 movie starring Norma Shearer, Clark Gable, Ed Arnold, Burgess Meredith and Charles Coburn. Target was the synthetic fuel plant in Misburg near Hannover. The Germans sent 500+ fighters into the air that day and annihilated the complete 853rd Bomb Squadron including "Idiot's Delight". Five crew members could save themselves by parachute and five members, among them Bill Reese, were either killed during the attack or in the crash of their bomber.

"Bill Reese was initially buried in the cemetery of Eimbeckhausen together with Woodrow Johnson and an unidentified airman who was totally burned and could have been either Captain Stewart or the Waist-Gunner George Corona. After the war Bill was exhumed and re-interred in the U.S. Military Cemetery in Neuville-en-Condroz in the Belgian Ardennes.

"My grandfather had my uncle's remains returned to the United States and in 1949 Bill found his final place of rest in Crown Hill Cemetery in Twinsburg, Ohio.

"In September 1993 someone decorated Bill's grave with bouquets of homegrown roses. Every year for two years on every holiday his grave was decorated. All the decorations were from someone's garden or were home made. It stopped in 1995. I always thought it was an old girl friend but we never found who it was.

About radio-operator **Harry H. Pollak** his obituary in the New York Times of October 1980 says:

"Born in Passaic, NJ. He held degrees from Rutgers University and the University of Chicago. Died at the age of 59 at the George Washington University Hospital.

"Had been associated with the State Department since 1962, when he was appointed labour adviser at the United State embassy in Tokyo.

"He had been an official of the Congress of Industrial Organisations before its merger with American Federation of Labour in the mid-1950's. He became the Asian representative of the AFL-CIO, and in 1961 President Kennedy named him to handle liaison between the labour movement and the Peace Corps.

"From 1967 to 1973, Harry Pollak was the labour attaché and political officer of the United States Mission to the European Economic Community in Brussels. He was the labor attaché and First Secretary of the United States embassy in London from 1973 to 1977, when he returned to Washington to work at the State Department.

***

Acknowledgements:
Frank Spady Jr.
Ralph & Bruce Valine for navigator Woodrow Johnson
George Painter for nose-turret gunner William L.Reese
New York Times for radio-operator Harry H. Pollak

CHAPTER 20

491ST BOMB GROUP 853RD BOMB SQUADRON

Aircraft Type: B-24J, Serial # 44-10485,
"Dorty Treek", MACR 10760
Airbase: North Pickenham

"A flight of transports came in to evacuate the sick. There were six nurses on board, and man, were they easy on the eyes!"

—Co-Pilot Robert Ostrander, awaiting transport to England after his liberation

---

Pilot: 1/Lt Ralph J. Butler (POW) Broadlands IL
Copilot: 1/Lt Robert G. Ostrander (POW) River Forest IL
Navigator: 1/Lt Herman C. Bauer (KIA) West Lafayette IN
Bombardier: 1/Lt Stanley A. Yergey (KIA) Omaha NE
Engineer: T/Sgt Elmer R. Jones (POW) White Creek KS
Tailgunner: S/Sgt Robert V. Trombly (POW) Riverton VT
Waistgunner R.: S/Sgt Gordon B. Fuller (KIA) Oakland CA
Waistgunner L: S/Sgt Victor E. Callicrate (POW) Fort Collins CO
Radio Operator: T/Sgt Edwin E. Kamarainen (POW) Iron River WI

Total: 3 KIA, 6 POW
Target: Misburg
Crash Site: On railroad between Sarstedt and Heiside, Germany
Time of Crash: 12.30

NOT HOME FOR CHRISTMAS

Co-pilot **Robert G. Ostrander** wrote an excellent account about his last flight in WW II:

"On November 26, 1944, I was awakened at 3:00 a.m. by an orderly who had the job of arousing the squadron. His greeting, "breakfast at three, briefing at four, sir," was given in the same dull, flat tone of voice with which he had aroused me from my slumbers on nineteen previous occasions. I poked my head out from under the covers, and the cold air that whistled through the numerous cracks of our barracks was enough to freeze one's nose. I gradually became aware of the fact that I was going out on my twentieth combat mission, and the thoughts of it were not pleasing.

"My first move was to slip on my "long handles" (long underwear) which I kept under one of the layers of the blankets. Then my olive drab pants, shirt, and flying suit were the next of my attire. When I put on my shoes, I felt as though I was putting my feet into an icebox. My parka hood was the last item I donned. Picking up a flashlight, I was ready to leave my quarters and go out into the black night. As I stepped out the door, the wind from the North Sea bit into my face. I could tell that it was really going to be cold upstairs that day.

From left to right: Herman Bauer, Stanley A. Yergey, Ralph J. Butler, Robert G. Ostrander

"It was about a mile to the mess hall, and I often wondered why I even bothered to go in. The food that was served was nothing at all like the Palmer House cuisine. In fact, many times, quite a few of the fellows were sickened by the fare, but it is better to eat something than to fly with an empty stomach. Day after day the menu was invariable powdered eggs and coffee with burnt toast. After a certain length of time, one took it as a matter of course.

"Another mile hike brought me to the briefing room. Here is where all the pertinent "poop" for the mission is handed out. First the chaplain gave us his blessing for a safe return. Then the C.O. stood up, and there was a silence in which you could hear a proverbial pin drop. When he raised the curtain, there was a chorus of "Oh's" and "Ah's" as everyone followed the red line in to the heart of No Man's land. We were told that our primary target was the oil refineries at Misburg, a suburb of Hannover. The latter was the largest defended city in Germany. I knew what it was like because I had been over the flak-infested area twice before.

"The intelligence officer was the next speaker, and he told us everything that was to be known about a mission. The only thing I liked about it was the slight chance of hitting a secondary target if the weather conditions were bad at the primary. The weatherman got up and tried to make things look pleasant for us by saying that a lot of activity would take place over the target when we were due there. But a weatherman's predictions come true in about one of one hundred times, so I just overlooked his statement.

"The briefing was broken up into sections: the pilots copying down their information on the flight; the bombardiers finding out the types of bombs and how to drop them; the navigators getting all their data to take us to the target and back home again; and the gunners being told about the possibility of enemy fighters attacking the formation, as to-day was a good day for Jerry to make a call on the bombers for such deep penetration.

"After briefing was over, the next step was the dressing room where everyone was issued a flying suit and a parachute. I picked up the escape kits and moved out where the trucks were awaiting the crews. When my truck was filled, it shoved off. There was no idle conversation. Each man was busy with his own thoughts. The expectant hush of dawn was broken only by the rumble of the trucks and the tense voice of each man as he called out his hardstand, (area in which a plane is stationed) number. In the fading darkness, we were shadows to each other, with individual faces suddenly silhouetted, for a moment, in the eerie glow from a cigarette.

NOT HOME FOR CHRISTMAS

"Arriving at the hardstand, I found my gunners assembling their guns and the crew chief checking the engines. Each man had to fulfil his assignment, and not much was said during the procedure. One could see that everyone's nerves were on edge, and I think we were all hoping for the mission to be scrubbed or cancelled. Time dragged on until a red flare was shot up which meant that it was time to start the engines. I climbed up into my seat and commenced going over the checklist. The other pilot checked each instrument as I added them up, and we found everything in order. We started each engine, and they all showed signs of the cold . . .. coughing and sputtering. However, in a few minutes, they were purring like kittens. It came our turn to taxi out, and our hopes of the mission being scrubbed dwindled away.

"It was a typical "limey" day, with the ceiling tight down on the ground and the visibility practically nil. Nevertheless, there we were, out to bomb the Hun. When it became our turn for take-off, we poured the coal to it, and away we went. As soon as we left the ground, we had to go on instruments and intermittently we would catch the prop wash from the plane ahead of us. As we kept climbing, it got colder and colder. We finally broke out on top at 18.000 feet and found the temperature reading -22. There was slight condensation trails at this altitude which meant that they would be thicker as we ascended. The planes were already forming, and by the time we got into formation, the group was almost intact. In time we had formed with the other two groups of our wings, and in turn, we assembled ourselves in the assigned place in the Division Assembly Line.

"The Division climbed out on course, and we noticed that the temperature was decreasing and the con-trails were increasing. There was no talking over the radio, and I was listening intently on hearing the C.O. say that we would hit the secondary target, but to no avail. When I saw our half of the Division make a turn eastward, I knew we were on our way to the oil refineries. I knew we were approaching the target, and pretty soon I heard "Snow White, Snow White" which meant that it was time for us to start throwing out chaff (bits of paper thrown out of planes to foul up the enemy's radar). In a matter of minutes, I heard "Easy Dog, Easy Dog", and we had started our bomb run. With the bomb bay doors open, I had to increase settings on the engines. I was amazed at the scarcity of flak that was coming up and its ineffectiveness. The suspense of riding down that bomb run without the flak around us was enough to drive anyone insane. My eyes were set on the leader, waiting to see his bombs go away, and it seemed as though time would never come. Finally, I saw them go, and I knew that ours had gone too because the plane lurched forward as if giving a sigh of relief to be rid of its heavy burden.

"As we left the immediate target area, I cut everything back to normal cruising speed. I was still stunned by the fact that we were apparently getting by so easily, but I came to the conclusion that we had pulled a "quickie" on the Hun, and that it was another milk run (easy mission). Everything seemed to be in our favour. The sky overhead was filled with friendly fighters, and we were homeward bound. Then I saw the three planes that were twelve to fifteen thousand feet above us. I saw thick condensation trails pouring from the rear of the planes, and I knew that they were enemy jet planes. Our fighter coverage left us in hot pursuit. I felt as though we were all alone.

"Suddenly, I realized that we were left as bait for the enemy. For within five minutes, flight upon flight of Me 109's and FW 109's swept through our formation and raked us with their machine guns. My plane was a mass of flames, and my engines sounded as if they were falling apart. The pilot gave the bail out signal, and I left as soon as the radio-operator and engineer had gone. It took about one and a half step to clear the plane. I have never experienced the sensation that I experienced in those few minutes of my fall through space.

"During my course of training, I had been told to delay the jump as long as possible. I estimated my free fall to about fifteen thousand feet before I pulled the rip cord. I went through quite a few acrobatics as I was falling. With each different position of my legs and arms, I found myself spinning or spiralling downward. The prescribed way to fall is with one's arms and legs straight down.

"After passing through cumulus clouds, I thought it was about time to see if my chute would open. Pulling the cord out to approximately an arm's length, I waited anxiously but nothing happened. I became frantic. I threw my arm out to its limit and waited again. All I could hear was a flapping noise in the breeze. Suddenly, I received a terrific jerk, and I was floating earthward. I couldn't see my chute because my hood had flown up and limited my view.

"Observing the surrounding area, I noticed I was just south of a village. A fighter plane was quite some distance away, and my first thought was that it might be a Jerry looking for parachutists. I slipped my chute and within a matter of minutes, I had hit the ground. I landed rather easily and went to my knees. Quickly I got up, dumped my chute and climbed out of the harness. I also got rid of my Mae West life preserver. I thanked the Lord for being alive and for feeling terra firma under my feet again.

NOT HOME FOR CHRISTMAS

"During my fall through the atmosphere, I had lost one of my flying boots, and all I had was a heated slipper. I went for my escape kit, and I discovered my pockets were empty. I remembered that only eight bags were in the bag that I received and that I had given them all to the other members of the crew. Wiping the sweat from my brow, I felt a stinging sensation and looked at my hand. I then realized that I had a handful of loose skin, and then, for the first time, I realized that my face had been burned from the flames in the plane.

"I thought it was about time to get out of the vicinity so I headed for some trees that seemed to be about ten miles away. Suddenly, I noticed a soldier about a thousand yards to the left. He was screaming at me and was brandishing a gun. I didn't know whether to run or to go over to him. After hesitating a moment, I decided to go over to him as I was not anxious to learn how accurate an eye he had.

"My captor was an elderly man who was old enough to be my grandfather. I could not understand a word he said, and since it was vice-versa with him, we carried our discussion in sign language. He asked for a gun, but I didn't carry one. While he was searching me, I saw that people were coming out to see who or what had landed in their great land. A squatty fellow, garbed in Alcatraz type uniform, was leading them all. Approaching me, he muttered something in his guttural tongue, and, since I couldn't understand him, I shrugged my shoulders. With no warning whatsoever, he hit me full in the mouth. It just knocked me flat on my back. Immediately, my lips swelled up like I had been stung by a bee.

"By this time, a congregation of men had surrounded me and were taken their turns hitting me. I was very weak and did not think I could stand anymore. After they had had their fun, my guard started mentioning for me to walk, and we headed back to the village. Walking with one shoe on and one shoe off didn't help things, and one of the men was poking me in the back with a pitchfork handle. As we neared the village, another allied airman was pushed out into the road to join our little parade. I did not recognize him at all until we looked into each other's eyes, and I realized with a shock that he was my engineer Elmer R. Jones of White Creek in Kansas. It was wonderful to see someone I knew. We were marched into a backyard and searched again. Up to this day, I still think they planned to line us up and shoot us. Just then, a well-dressed man came up to our assailants and said something loud enough for everyone to hear. The crowd disappeared as into thin air.

"We were taken to a cell in the basement and given time to collect our wits. Presently, the door was opened, and our left waist-gunner Victor

A. Calligrate of Fort Collins in Coronado was pushed into the cell. This made three of us, and we wondered how much of the rest of the crew we would see. My gunner told us that a bullet had grazed his arm, but other than that, he was in good shape.

"Within an hour time, we were on a trolley – destination unknown. I happened to look back into the cab of the trolley. Three little girls were looking at us fearfully, and when they saw me, they started to cry. I asked my engineer if I looked that bad. He said I should see myself.

"We arrived at an airbase, and the pilots mocked us as we went by. A huge truck pulled up, and a group of American fliers piled out. Among them I recognized my pilot Ralph J. Butler, of Broadlands in IL. That made four, and our happy family getting back together again. We were treated for our wounds and put in a cell that had cardboard mats for bunks.

"By this time, night had fallen, and we couldn't see a thing in this dismal room. Of the eight men in my cell, I knew only two. I surmised that the famous Luftwaffe had had a field day on the heavy bombers. It had been fifteen hours since I had anything to eat, and my stomach felt like an empty barrel. We asked for food but received a sneering "Nix" from the guard. Overcome with fatigue, I soon fell asleep.

"The next morning brought no sign of relief. About nine o'clock, we were given some cold ersatz coffee which I could hardly down. Our next feeding came about four o'clock in the afternoon. This consisted of a bowl of cold stew which made me sick to see. I sampled a few mouthfuls but turned the rest away in disgust. The next course was black bread made out of sawdust and served with a tiny speck of margarine. This was the first morsel of food that I had been able to down with any satisfaction. Another day was done, and being a prisoner of war was not exactly what I call living like a human being.

"The following morning we were awakened by the guards and summoned to move out. We were shipped by bus to a railroad terminal, and there we met the last two members of our crew who had survived. They were the tail-gunner Robert V. Trombly of Riverton in Vermont and the radio-operator Ed Kamarainen of Iron River in Wisconsin. I was told that our other waist-gunner. Gordon B. Fuller, had died at his position, but nobody ever heard of the navigator Herman C. Bauer and the bombardier Stanley A. Yergey. It was hard to believe that we had lost so good buddies. The crowd in the terminal gathered around us, and the guards had to use their authority to keep them off. The people reminded me of a bunch of snarling dogs. As we were about to board the train, a high ranking German officer came up to the officer in charge of us. He said he would not ride on the same train as American swines so we all had to wait for another train. No "brass" was on this train, and we headed for south western Germany to a town called Oberursel, which was well known for its solitary confinement quarters.

"The journey took us all day and night, arriving at six the following morning. There was snow on the ground, and it was very cold. We were herded into a cell, one by one, and when they had finished, there were eight men in mine. I recognized two gunners from another crew, and we got a few cheers out of one another.

"Then, one by one, we were taken out of the cell. I was the last to go and found that it was the same routine that they had showed us at the air base. The interpreter had a pleasing manner in his cunning way, but all I gave him was my name, rank, and serial number. After I convinced him that I wasn't giving him any information, I was taken to a cell that was six feet by thirty feet. There was a cot with a sawdust mattress, two blankets, a jug of water, and a radiator, not on. On the walls were several calendars made by previous Allied tenants. On ten roughly drawn calendars were marked ten days that each man had spent in the cell, and some did not look too encouraging. No sooner than I had sat down, I was taken through the processing line. I was fingerprinted, examined, searched, and my flying equipment was taken away from me. Next, a doctor looked at my face and gave me some salve.

"For the first time, I got a look at my face. I was quite surprised that I didn't recognize myself. My stubble was four days old, and the burns had left a number of unpleasant sights. My forehead and the outer parts of my face had received the most severe burns. I administered the salve, and the doctor wrapped my head in what appeared to be toilet paper. When he had finished, only my left eye had been uncovered. I was then taken back to my cell. The time had gone so fast that feeding time was again on hand. When they opened my door, I was dreaming of a steak dinner, but settled for two slices of bread with margarine and some of that ersatz coffee. I asked what time it was, and one of the guards showed me his watch – a GI issue – reading 7 p.m. I was beginning to "sweat out" the time. Presently, a guard opened my door and commanded me to take off my boots and set them outside my door, a precaution so we wouldn't try to escape. My lights went out, and I was left no alternative but the hit "Ye Olde Sack".

"The next morning I was aroused at six and given a hearty breakfast of two slices of bread and jam and the usual coffee. At ten the doctor came, looked at the bandage, and told me to see him to-morrow. Noon time brought the feeders, and the menu was meant to be vegetable soup. It had a few leaves and a couple of carrots mixed with water. By this time, I took it as a matter of course. For eight days this same procedure was repeated. Day in day out I lived my life over a thousand times. I was beginning to wonder if I was ever going to get a bath or a shower or a shave. I could have joined the House of David with the beard I had grown. I marked each day upon the wall, and eight days had gone before I received any attention. An inspector came around to see if I had done any damage to the room, and I asked him if I was going to get a shower. He told me that I would have to see the interrogator. I inquired how to do that, and he said he would arrange for it.

"That afternoon I was marched to another section of the camp and had my first sniff of fresh air. I was taken to a building that had a number of different offices in it. Here I met my interrogator. He was a refined man who appeared very learned and could speak English as well as I. Instead of asking me questions, he told me everything about my experiences of the past two weeks. The only mistake he made was in saying I was from the 852nd Bomb Squadron, but I was from the 853rd. He told me more about the USAAF than I knew.

"I was stunned at the amount of information he presented to me. All he wanted from me was the verification of a few instruments that were being used, but I told him that he probably knew more about them than I did. After a forty-five minute grilling, he called the guard, and I was taken away. While crossing the compound, a Russian prisoner pointed upward, and I saw a group of Fortresses on their way home. He gave me a smile and said, "Kamarad." The guard pushed with his gun muttering a lusty "los" (move on). I was lead back to my cell, and I wondered how long it would be before I got out again.

"Within two hours, I was released from that cell-hole, and I picked up my belongings: a comb, wallet, knife, dog-tag, and receipt for my watch. I was then marched to another compound where I met quite a few fellows who had gone down the same day that I did. Each took his turn telling his horror story, and the laughs were numerous when the interrogation stories were told. After being fed, we were assigned to bunks of the same calibre as before, and we had to hit the sack. We were aroused at dawn and marched to a rail road station where we boarded a train. It was a full day's journey to our new camp which was Dulag-Luft (a transient camp for prisoners) at Wertzlar.

"The camp was about five miles out of town. As we were marched through the town, we had a chance to see what destruction the air force had wrought on this small place. I was gutted with bomb craters, and

NOT HOME FOR CHRISTMAS

fallen debris was strewn all over the area. Some of the people looked at us as if we were friends, and others were just standing there dazed. I was almost exhausted by the time we arrived at the camp. Some instructions were given, and then we were issued clothing, and I had my first bath in over two weeks. I thought I would never get all the dirt off myself. Next some chow, and I had my first full meal in that period of time. Finding a bunk was next, and after securing a place to rest, I examined the contents of my "joy box": a clothing box presented by the Red Cross. It contained all the necessities, from shaving equipment to a shoe brush. In the course of the evening, I met more fellows from my group and learned more of what had happened. Our group alone, lost sixteen out of thirty planes and quite a few men failed to show up. The 491st really took a beating.

"The chaplain came around and told us he would hear confessions that night and would say Mass and serve Communion the next morning. I attended both services and was surprised at the number of Catholics who were there. I made this a daily habit during the five days that I was there. During this time, I had access to a library and spent most of my time reading. If I was not buried in some mystery novel, I was playing cards. The latter became an everyday pastime. The reason for the long stay here was because there was no transportation available to ship us out. A play was put on by a group of old "Kriegies": the German word for prisoner, short for Kriegsgefangenen, and it turned out to be quite a morale booster. It was interrupted by our friends, the RAF. We had to lie down on the floor, and all that could be heard was the eerie wailing of the alarms, and then the bomb came whamming down. I was praying that those boys knew where to lay their eggs. They did a good job on their target, which was a nearby factory works, left in ruins.

"The next day, a train came in, and we were shipped out. It was a coach, and they squeezed twelve of us in a compartment. There were five men on each side and two men in the baggage racks. Each man received half of a Red Cross parcel, containing food: Spam, beans, sardines, meat, candy, etc. We sat in the station until dark before pulling out for fear of being strafed by the Allies. My companions were a comical bunch, and I could see we were going to have some fun, no matter how bad it was.

"The first day was spent in getting to know one another. We had fellows from the "Land of the Free." One of the boys and I discovered that we had spent the summer at the same lake in Michigan, and we did some very enthusiastic reminiscing about Corey Lake. Due to the close quarters, each pair would take turns eating. My buddy was a quiet sort of fellow, quite agreeable in everything, so we got along fine. Our journey northward was halted several times because the railroad lines were blown up. This seemed to be the main objective to our air force: to bottle up communications. Apparently, they were doing a good job of it.

"Our rate of progress became so slow that I thought it would take the rest of the war to get up to our permanent camp. As we wound northward, I noticed that the snow was getting deeper and deeper. One of the guards told us that we were in Goering's hunting estate. We saw several deer, rabbits, and flocks of geese and ducks. We arrived at our destination on the fifth day, and it was a relief to get off that dirty, beat-up coach. We were really welcomed by a committee of two: a German soldier with a police dog that looked as though he could eat the whole detachment.

"We had reached our destination for the duration and were informed that the camp was three miles out of the town of Barth, which is located at the base of the peninsula on the Baltic Sea, due north of Berlin. Marching through the town, we were snarled at, cursed, and even run down. As we left the town, I wondered if I would ever see it again. From the outskirts of the town we could see our new home, Stalag Luft I.

"As we approached the camp, the first thing we noticed was its enormous size. Once inside the gate, we were herded into an enclosure, and here we met "Herr Kommandant" of the camp. He told us all the rules and regulations by which we must abide. They interrogated us again, and it was the same old story; tell us this, and you can go. After being interrogated, we were permitted to send a radiogram which I never thought would go through. To my surprise, it did.

"Next, we were given our second bath, and our clothes were deloused. When I redressed, I discovered that all my clothes had shrunk. My parka hood was ruined. In fact, I couldn't even button it. We were led through the camp to our quarters. En route I saw men who had been shot down back in September and October, and many more who had gone down the same day that I had.

"The compound in which I was placed was a new one. Our forlorn little community was comprised of just a handful of men. I first located my room and grabbed a bunk for myself. Bed clothing and eating utensils were issued. I received a mattress cover, two blankets, a bowl, a cup, and a knife, fork and spoon. The room to which I was assigned was one of fourteen, which composed the barracks. It was twenty-four by thirty feet, and had a stove, a table, and two benches. The bunks numbered twenty-four and were made of wood slats. On one side of the room there were six across and three deep, and on the other side there were four across and three deep. Twenty-four men were put in here, and we went about our

NOT HOME FOR CHRISTMAS

business. We received a Jerry ration of potatoes and bread which was made into the best meal possible. Some of the boys had leftovers from their parcels, and their contributions were most welcome. I climbed up to the third tier to my bed and commenced making it up. Gathering all the wood shavings around me, I stuck them in my mattress. Over this downy bed, I arranged my blankets. I found a board and nailed it up for a shelf. The evening passed so quickly that I didn't realize it was time for lights out.

"My second day in Stalag was a busy one. I was told to pick up every little odd and end on which I could lay my hands. Nails were a pretty big item, and I secured as many as possible. Talking to other "Kriegies", my roommates and I learned many useful hints. We broke our stove down so that we would receive its full benefits for cooking facilities. Our next problem was to make utensils for cooking. We took empty "klim" (powdered milk) cans and cut these into strips. After getting four strips, we coupled them together with a flange. Then by bending the corners up and attaching two wire holders, our pan was complete. We divided the room into two compounds for eating purposes and chose cooks for the job. One boy volunteered and another said he would help. I don't think they knew what they were getting into. Under the prevailing conditions, I think they did a wonderful job. They turned out some pretty fancy dinners. We also made up a dish-washing schedule which occurred once in four days per two men.

"As the days rolled by, we became more and more accustomed to our new home. We tried to make living as pleasant as could be expected. The C.O. for my compound was Colonel Gabreski, well known fighter ace. He had quite a way in handling the Jerries. He managed to get us whatever privileges they were handing out. The rules and regulations were simple, and it didn't take a great deal of effort to obey them, but as time went by, and the compound filled, the enforcement of the rules had to be observed more keenly. The most important rule was to be in the barracks during an air raid. If anyone was seen outside during this time, the penalty was death.

"We were granted one shower per week. It was a short, fast one with forty men under half as many sprays. Keeping clean was very difficult and the problem of washing clothes arose frequently. Wash tubs were provided, and two bars of soap came in the joy box. I made a weekly habit to do my washing so that it wouldn't pile up.

"When I first arrived, the weather was pretty nice, and much of the time was spent playing football. A nippy wind blew in from the Baltic Sea, and it was invigorating to get out and run around. Another good reason for violent exercise was to tire myself out so that I could sleep, in spite of the knots in my mattress. By this time, it seemed as if the mice were making themselves as much at home in my beautiful "sack" as I was.

"Just before Christmas, the weather turned for the worse, and we were confined to our quarters most of the time. Cards then became my everyday pastime, and it didn't take long for me to learn to play bridge. A roommate and I entered a round-robin bridge tournament, and we did all right for a couple of beginners. At this stage, I tried smoking a pipe, but every morning my tongue felt like a raw piece of steak. So I gave it up as a bad habit. In my spare moments, I would do a little reading. Two books that I enjoyed were, "How Green was my Valley" and "The Robe".

"The Christmas holiday was a happy time for the "kriegies". The Red Cross donated Christmas parcels in which canned turkey and plum pudding were the main items. We had a huge feast, and quite a few boys had a little too much to eat. I went to mid-night Mass, and it was a beautiful ceremony. An English chaplain preached a wonderful sermon. He was very distinguished looking and spoke nobly. A variety show was put on by volunteers from the kriegies, and the performers really put on a good show for us. We were given inter compound privileges so we could visit old friends. I met two fellows with whom I had gone through training, and we really had a time of it. They had been there for a good number of months. New Year's Day was a duplicate of Christmas, and we listened to the prison band play.

"The thing everybody was interested in was the Pow Wow. It was the daily bulletin of the war news. The English who had been prisoner for four and five years bribed the guards to give them various parts so they could construct a radio. Jerry persistently tried to find the set or to catch us reading the paper but never succeeded. In January, "Uncle Joe" was making a forced drive to the Elbe River, which was ninety miles to the east. We could hear the big guns, and at night the camp would echo and re-echo with the prisoners' chant of, "Come on Joe!" Maps were drawn, and the front lines were traced on them. The guards would not believe them and listened only to the German propaganda. Our guard maintained that it was just the tides of war. In spring, The Germans would drive us back to the sea. They were bold in speaking against us, but when asked about the Russians, they would refuse to say anything.

"Towards the end of January, the Red Cross supply of food ran out. We started living on Jerry rations, which consisted of half a bowl of soup and a sixth loaf of bread per day. The stew was concocted, primarily, of potatoes, rutabagas, with a little horse meat thrown in occasionally. About once every nine days, we would get a small portion of cheese, margarine, and sugar. Maybe once in every two weeks, five or six heads of cabbage were distributed to a room. Slowly, but surely, everybody was becoming weaker, and some of the men would black out during the course of the day.

"The bad weather didn't help matters. We had to wade through the swamp area to receive our daily bucket of stew. In some spots, it was ankle deep. As day after day passed, we steadily deteriorated. We looked like the "walking dead". During the Lenten season, I attended Mass and Communion every morning. My daily offering was for a let up from this famine. The Germans told us that the Red Cross parcels were on the way, but that they could not transport them due to lack of fuel. The only thing for which we lived was to hear the news each night. I think it was the main reason we kept on living. In March, General Patton started his trek across Germany, and this time, Stalag I reverberated with the cry of, "Come on, George!". Rumours commenced to fly thick and fast, and it became a matter of days before we were going to be released.

"There was great rejoicing on Easter Eve. Ten thousand Red Cross parcels came into the camp, and we really celebrated the end of a true Lenten fast. We had an enormous feast which included a full bowl of spuds, two slices of Spam, dehydrated vegetables, and raisin pie for dessert. The pies were made by the two boys who had been chosen as permanent cooks.

"However, before long, other evils appeared. Decease struck the camp, and there was much pain and suffering. Diarrhoea and dysentery spread quickly due to overeating. It became quite a problem for the men to relieve themselves because of the lack of toilets. There were only two latrines, with twenty toilets to a latrine, to accommodate approximately two thousand men. At night we were locked in our respective barracks, and only two stools were available for two hundred men.

"A baseball league was started, and I played center field for our barracks. We had a good team and were in second place at the time of our liberation. The way the compound would turn out for the games reminded me of the big games at home.

"Towards the end of April, the fighting grew more and more intense. We could hear the big guns very clearly. We had daily air raid alarms. At night, the RAF would come over and contribute their bit to the damage. As the Russians approached Straslund, a seaport town about twenty miles away, the German personnel decided to leave the surrounding country. However, before they left, they blew up all of their important buildings and left little military matter to be found.

"The following morning, the camp was ours. We posted guards in the town and our ranking officers took command, but we were still behind barbed wire, and the sight of it infuriated us. On the following morning, we sent out a scouting patrol to locate the Russian army. Our scouts met three Russians in a jeep and had a hard time convincing them that the camp was in our hands. When the C.O. of the Russians found us imprisoned, he ordered us to tear the place apart. We complied with a vengeance. We pulled the barbed wire down and rocked the sentinel towers until they collapsed. We headed for the warehouses and found more clothing and equipment than we knew what to do with. I had a clean set of clothes every day for the next two weeks. All sorts of cooking utensils were brought back to the room. Next, we wandered into town, and took whatever we could lay our hands on. The Russians didn't pay much attention to this small town and left it for the hungry Yanks.

"After three or four days, we were getting on edge. We were free, yet we were not free. We wanted to get out of that God-forsaken place. Some of the men took matters in their own hands and left. This displeased the Russians, and they posted guards in a ten mile radius around the camp. We were informed that the Eighth Air Force had been notified, and that measures were being taken for our evacuation. The first step was to clear the airfield of mines. The English won this job. The Russians ordered a passport to be made out for each man as a precaution against Germans trying to sneak through the lines.

"On the 13th of May, Mothers' Day, flight upon flight of B-17s swarmed over the airfield. What a gorgeous sight they were! The cheering must have been heard in Paris. One by one they landed, received a load of men, and took off. Being in the newest compound, I didn't leave until afternoon. Once again, I passed through that town. This time the people look dejected and were asking for mercy. The airfield was three miles from the camp. I wore my newly acquired flying boots, and by the time I had reached the airfield, my feet were a mass of blisters. We had to wait for a few minutes for the planes to land and while waiting, we got our first glimpse of real American beauty.

"A flight of transports came in to evacuate the sick. There were six nurses on board, and man, were they easy on the eyes!

"My name was called, and I passed through the gate and out to the runway. I boarded the plane, and as we took off, I thanked God that I was alive, and was leaving that No Man's Land. As we left Stalag Luft, I looked far below us and knew it was one place to which I hoped never to return.

NOT HOME FOR CHRISTMAS

Pilot **Ralph J. Butler** recalls:

"On November 26, 1944, I was shot down five minutes away from Hannover by FW 190's. I was captured immediately. I bailed out at 18000 feet: My plane was on fire due to incendiary bullets from the FW 190's. On opening my chute five panels were blown. I landed rather hard in a freshly ploughed field. I was picked up by German soldiers and taken to a small town. I was questioned by a Luftwaffe pilot. I gave him rank, name and serial number.

"From there I marched to another small town where I was searched. I was held in a small room for about an hour. Then I helped load some wounded Germans on two trucks and then we were transported to a hospital about ten miles away. There we were searched again and medical attention was given although I did not get treated for the burns I had received. The right side of my forehead, right side of my nose, the entire right side of my face and my right ear was badly burnt."

1Lt. Ralph J. Butler

About navigator **Herman C. Bauer**, the author Jim Haas of Annapolis, Maryland wrote the following biography:

"Bob Schlesinger Among Five Area War Deaths" was the headline in a front-page story in the March 30, 1945 edition of the Hammond Times. In addition to Schlesinger, another man written about was 22-year-old Herman C. Bauer, a recently married 1st Lieutenant. Bauer had served in the Army Air Corps as navigator in the crew of a B-24 Liberator. Flying on its 19th mission, the plane was shot down on November 26th, 1944 during a bombing raid over the synthetic oil factory in the village of Misburg, Germany near Hanover.

"The youth was a former Boy Scout, becoming an Eagle Scout in Troop 9 of the Pokagon council. He served as an acolyte at St. Paul's Episcopal Church in Hammond for five years. He is a grandson of the late Herman Poppenhusen, well known region industrialist." the reporter wrote, but what could not have been known was the fascinating genealogical history of this very accomplished young man, and the irony associated with his death in the skies over Germany in 1944.

"Bauer's Poppenhusen lineage in the United States got its start with his great, great grandfather, Conrad Poppenhusen. Born in Hamburg, Germany in 1818, he came to America early in the 19th century landing in New York City on July 19, 1843. Recently married, Poppenhusen had travelled alone to the U.S. His wife Bertha, and one year-old son Adolph, joined him a year later. The family settled in the Borough of Brooklyn, and soon thereafter, a baby brother named Herman was born.

"By profession, Poppenhusen was an industrialist, and helped to manage a business that manufactured combs and corset stays from an ever-diminishing supply of whalebone. In the early 1850's a friendship with Charles Goodyear resulted in his acquiring limited sole rights for the use of Goodyear's invention, vulcanized rubber. From this product he manufactured and sold hard rubber combs. As a result over a twenty-year span, Conrad Poppenhusen amassed a large fortune, and was well known in the New York City area as a very generous philanthropist. An educational facility he founded in 1868 bore his name, and still functions today. Called the Poppenhusen Institute in College Point, NY, it was the site of the first free kindergarten in the United States. He was also very active in support of the emerging German-American community.

"Toward the end of the 1870's Poppenhusen was forced into bankruptcy due largely to the financial mismanagement of his fortune on the part of his son Herman. The elder Poppenhusen died in 1883, and shortly thereafter Herman moved his family from New York to Evanston, Illinois, where the family prospered. Herman served on the Evanston School Board, and schools closed in his honour on the day of his funeral in March 1891. One of his three sons, Conrad, was a founding member of a Chicago law firm, Gregory, Poppenhusen and McNab. The firm continues to function today under the name of Jenner & Block, and is among the nation's leading law firms.

"A second son, Paul, co-founded the Green Engineering Company in East Chicago with his brother Herman, who had earned an electrical engineering degree from M.I.T. late in the 19th century. In 1922 the Hammond Times reported the purchase of Green Engineering by the International Combustion Engineering Company.

Carl Bauer, an employee of Green Engineering, married Herman Poppenhusen's daughter Caroline in 1921. Bauer also had German ancestry.

A son, Herman C. Bauer, was born in 1922. In the years to follow his name appeared on occasion in the pages of the *Hammond Times*. He was active in Boy Scouts, and an accomplished musician. The "Dunes" yearbook for Hammond High School, Class of 1940, carried a graduation photo of Herman Bauer, he bearing a close resemblance to contemporary actor Ralph Fiennes. Additional photographs showed him preparing to dive as a member of the swim team, as a member of the German Club, (Elizabeth Mason, his sweetheart and future wife and widow, was the Secretary) and as a member of Hi-Y, part of the National Y.M.C.A. whose objectives were "to maintain a high standard of leadership and character and abide by the "Y" platform of clean speech, clean leadership, clean athletics and clean living." Upon graduation he, along with Elizabeth Mason, enrolled in Purdue. Two and a half years later he left the school. Bauer then enlisted in the Army Air Corps.

The couple married in South Carolina according to the Sunday, May 2, 1943 edition of the Hammond Times. Herman had been assigned to Erskine College for a course in aircrew training given there. After five months Bauer joined a B-24 flight crew at Peterson Air Field in Colorado Springs. Subsequently assigned to an air base in England, the newly formed crew took off for Lincoln, Nebraska then on to a stop over in Bangor, Maine. There, radioman Ed Kamarainen, a surviving crew member, recalled that Bauer had invited him to take part in a swim across a nearby lake, "surely more than a mile", he said. Kamarainen declined the offer, but remarked that Bauer had made mention of his love for swimming, and his participation in high school sports. During the same layover, Kamarainen recalled, Bauer had invited him to join him in a 30-mile bike ride. That offer too, was declined.

"Upon arrival at the base in North Pickenham, England, the 9-man crew of the B-24, affectionately nicknamed "Dorty Treek", was assigned to the 853rd Bomb Squadron of the 491st Bomber Group of the 8th Air Force. Having completed eighteen successful missions, pilot Ralph J. Butler lead his crew in an attack on the oil refinery at Misburg near Hanover. Flying to the target with 28 other B-24's, the formation encountered three new ME-262 jets of the Nazi Luftwaffe. The jets took no hostile action; they simply observed. Shortly thereafter the massive bomber formation, its size, course and speed known, was attacked by upwards of 200 German fighter aircraft.

"According to Allan Blue, author of Ringmasters - A History of the 491st Bomber Group, sixteen of the twenty-eight planes were shot down, and of the 84 men in the 853rd Squadron, 50 had died, and many of the rest were badly injured. Butler's "Dorty Treek" was shot to shambles in the air", he added. "The aircraft was covered by fire and all the engines shot out when I left the plane", said Ed Kamarainen, the Dorty Treek's radioman. "After he had landed safely he was beaten by civilians and made a prisoner of war. He lives today in the state of Washington.

"The body of Herman Bauer, who as navigator would have flown in the nose of the plane, was recovered. His remains, and those of other fallen crewmembers, were returned to the U.S. Government.

"The 853rd Bomber Squadron was awarded the Presidential Unit Citation and Bauer was posthumously awarded the Air Medal with Two Oak Leaf Clusters. At the close of the war he was buried in the Ardennes American Cemetery in Neuville-en-Condroz in Belgium.

"Elizabeth, widowed and pregnant with a child Herman had known was on the way, but never got to see, remained at Purdue. A son was born in mid-December and given the name William Herman. He lives today in Massachusetts. His mother Elizabeth remarried and currently resides in Indiana.

In the early 1950's the War Memorial at City Hall was built to honour all of Hammond's soldiers, sailors and marines who perished in all wars fought. As the 60th anniversary of the new article's appearance nears, it is worthwhile to recall the loss of Herman C. Bauer and all the other men and women of our nation's "greatest generations", especially during these times when newspapers across our country print banner headlines of deaths of military personnel in Iraq and other places around the world.

Bombardier **Stanley A. Yergey** had attended Omaha Central High School, Nebraska. More than half a century later Scott Wilson, a history teacher at CHS wrote the following biography:

"Stanley Allan Yergey was born February 23, 1923, in Omaha, to parents John and Charlotte. Stan's five siblings were brothers, Jack, Arthur and Robert and sisters, Bonnie and Betty. They all lived in a large, old house at 4919 Davenport Street.

"Stan entered Central High School in 1937. While at Central, Stan was involved in many activities, most notably in Student Council. He was also a Home Room Representative, helped with Road Show advertising, and was a member of the Omaha Intercity Student Council. Stan was also Student Council President his senior year. Stan had good grades (particularly in his math and mechanical drawing classes) and was thought of highly by his teachers. He missed only eight days in his four years of high school. He was graduated in June 1941.

"The most important thing to happen to Stan while at Central High was meeting a beautiful, young classmate by the name of Virginia Gantz. She met Stan while he was working as an usher at the Dundee Theatre, just around the corner from his house. They began dating immediately and formed a relationship that would last the rest of his short life.

"Virginia said Stan was a "handsome guy" and was a "people person". Apparently he was an avid golfer too. Her mother really liked Stan and he and Mrs. Gantz developed a strong bond. Both Virginia and Stan were fond of their days at Central High. She said, "It was wonderful. I did not want to leave, because I loved every minute of it. Those were some of the happiest days of our lives."

"After graduation, Stan attended the University of Omaha and also went to work as a draftsman for a local company called Henningson Engineering. Virginia went to UNO as well where she joined the Sigmy Chi Omicron sorority. After a year in college, Stan joined the military by enlisting into the Army Air Corps in the summer of 1942. He was called into the service in March of 1943 and then left for cadet training in San Antonio, Texas and speciality training in various other locations.

"Stan and Virginia were married in March, 1944. Virginia's father gave her away. Her dress was a "bittersweet red wool suit". She also wore a small hat of white flowers and a shoulder corsage of white roses. Three days later, Stan left for Colorado Springs where his unit was training. Virginia joined him there shortly.

"Stan was now part of the 491st Bomb Group. After completing stateside training, the group was sent to England to join the 8th USAAF's bombing campaign just in time for the invasion of Normandy. Their mission was to reduce Germany's capacity to wage war by destroying their industrial and military installations with high-altitude, precise, daylight bombing. The 8th Air Force suffered some of the highest casualty rates for any group from any branch of the U.S. military in WW II, even higher than the Marines in the Pacific Theatre.

"The crew flew its first mission on September 13, 1944, in the bomber called "Eight Ball". They were bombing the airfield at Schwabisch in Germany when they were shot up by flak. The pilots managed to nurse "Eight Ball" back to England where they crash landed at Woodbridge Air Base. On their seventh mission, they were so badly shot up that they had to "dead stick" land their new plane at a closed British airbase.

"On Sunday, November 26, 1944, 8th USAAF mounted a massive bombing raid on various major targets in northwest Germany. The 491st was tasked with destroying the synthetic fuel refinery in Misburg, an suburb of Hannover.

"As the Group reached the IP (initial point, or start of the bomb run) around 12:26 pm, about 400 German fighter planes appeared from the southeast. The fighter escort, comprised of P-51 Mustangs and P-47 Thunderbolts, went in after them and engaged in a large scale air battle while the bombers plodded along alone on the bomb run. Over Misburg, the bombers released their payload on the target. Lieutenant Stanley Yergey, sitting in the nose of their third plane, "Dorty Treek" called out, "Bombs Away". These were likely the last words anyone ever heard him say.

"Over Misburg, the German flak guns near the target opened up on the formation with devastating effect. The formation split into an upper and a lower group to avoid the bursts of exploding metal being hurled at them from the ground. This left the bombers vulnerable to fighter attack because the mutual firepower afforded by tight formation flying had been greatly reduced.

"As if on cue, the flak stopped and about a hundred German FW-190 fighters rolled in from above. The bombers were alone.

"The crew of "Dorty Treek" were now fighting for their lives. Two waves of fighters hit her from the front. The plane was riddled with canon and machine gun fire and was badly crippled. Pilot Ralph Butler ordered, "Bail Out" as the plane began to roll and was now burning badly. Ralph Butler called for his men to check in. There was only silence from the nose. Stan Yergey and the navigator Herman Bauer were obviously killed during the initial wave of fighters that hit the "Dorty Treek".

"The rest of the crew struggled towards the various escape hatches. Gordon Fuller, the right waist gunner, was hit by enemy fire. He was last seen lying motionless on the floor of the plane. He was gone. Victor Callicrate, co-pilot Robert Ostrander, Ed Kamarainen, Elmer Jones, Robert Trombly, and pilot Ralph Butler managed to bail out and parachute into German territory. They would soon be POW's. "Dorty Treek" crashed on a railway track near Sarstedt.

"Back in Omaha, Virginia and Stan's parents were notified that he was missing. Virginia knew already that something was very wrong. Stan had written letters to her nearly everyday but then the letters had suddenly stopped coming.

"In April 1945, the War Department delivered the terrible news that Stan was dead. Ralph Butler and Robert Ostrander, who had been liberated from their POW camp, met Virginia in Chicago in June 1945 to try to explain to her what had happened.

"Stan Yergey was buried at Santa Fe National Cemetery in New Mexico in 1950. He shares a grave and headstone with Gordon Fuller. The remains of these two men could not be separately identified and hence they were buried together in New Mexico, about half-way between their California and Nebraska homes.

"Virginia left Omaha shortly after Stan's death. She said she did not want to be in Omaha when old friends began to come home from the war and Stan was not one of them. She attended to the University of Colorado and studied Fine Arts and Interior Design and graduated in 1949. She moved to Dallas, Texas later that year to be with her family who had also moved from Omaha.

"In 1952, she married Don Thompson. They had a son, Scott and still live in Dallas.

"The 491st Bomb Group flew its last mission on April 25, 1945. The war in Europe was over less than two weeks later. They had done their job and would soon be going home. The airfield and related buildings are almost all gone now. A beautiful memorial in the area marks their time there. A go-kart company used part of the old runway, and a wind farm occupies much of the North Pickenham site today.

"For his service First Lieutenant Stanley Allan Yergey was awarded the WW II Victory Medal, Honourable Service Lapel Button, a Purple Heart, and the European-African-Middle East Campaign medal with one Bronze Service Star. His name is on Omaha's War Memorial in Memorial Park. His name is also forever inscribed on the Central High School Memorial to students lost in WW II.

Tail-gunner **Robert V. Trombly** wrote in 2005:

"After graduation from high school in June 1942, I was enlisted in what then was the Army Air Corps. Part of my training was at gunnery school and eventually, I was assigned to an air crew. After some brief training together, we were sent to our posting in North Pickenham, England.

"On our nineteenth mission, to Misburg, we encountered heavy flak and were attacked by German fighter planes. The bombardier, the navigator and one of the waist-gunners were killed. The pilot ordered us to bail out as the plane was on fire and no longer flyable. During the attack, I was wounded in the right hand. I believe it was shrapnel from an exploded 20 mm cannon shell fired from one of the fighter planes. I had some difficulty with my parachute. It was the type that attaches to straps on the chest and couldn't be worn while seated in the turret. My wound was hindering my efforts. I realized that Sgt. Fuller, the right waist-gunner, was dead. The other gunner had already jumped. I went out through the camera hatch. We had been warned that the Germans might shoot at us as we were floating down. I delayed pulling the rip cord for some time because of this fear.

"I landed in a farmer's field. I didn't see any of my crew. Capture came soon after by some locals that I assumed were part of the Volksturm. They took me to a farm house. There followed a much heated discussion among them. However not knowing more than a word of German, I didn't know what it was about. I recall they were fascinated by my escape kit which contained some money, maps and other items. They took that and my watch. The lady of the house was friendly and seemed concerned about my wound.

"After the discussion, the armed men marched me to a small village. A large crowd gathered and I received some kicks and shoves, but the guards protected me rather well. They put me in a building that looked like the local jail. I was quite frightened about what their plans were. The next morning they gave me some bread and a cup of water. I was taken to what I would describe as a trolley car or tram. There were other people on it. They placed me in a seat and the guards stayed near the back. No one paid much attention to me until it was time to collect the fare. Then the guards had to explain how I came to be there. We arrived at a larger town where they took me to the train station where I saw other prisoners and Ed Kamarainen, our radio man.

"We were taken to an interrogation center. After a couple of days, I had my turn being asked questions but they knew nearly all about me: the name of my Group, where I was from, etc. After they decided I didn't know anything of interest, they sent me to a hospital. There were some British doctors there as well as a nurse who was later repatriated. My hand didn't heal properly and they had to re-break it and reset it. I don't recall how long I was there except I do remember seeing prisoners arrive from the "Battle of the Bulge".

"I recall being taken to a new camp in a town called Obermasfeld. We went there in a small bus-like vehicle that had been converted to run on charcoal. The large room I was in had tiered bunks and one night the town was bombed by the British. The next day a large unexploded bomb was found just a few yards from the building. Food was scarce at this time and I was losing weight. The purpose of this camp was for recuperating from injury.

"The next move was to a Stalag in Nurenberg. It was a very large camp

NOT HOME FOR CHRISTMAS

with prisoners from many countries. As Allied forces got closer, the camp was evacuated and we were force-marched to Mooseburg on the outskirts of München. On April 29, 1945, we were freed by forces under the command of General Patton. The General greeted us in person, standing in his jeep wearing his famous pearl handled pistols.

"Rather than wait for official transport, some of us made our way back to France on our own by hitching rides with military units. We had orders to arrive at Le Havre, France and in early June returned to the United States by way of ship.

"Back in the States we were given a ninety days leave during which I decided to re-enlist for three more years. On the Tenth of November 1945, my girlfriend Rosemary and I were married and after several months at bases in Massachusetts and New Hampshire, I returned to flying status and was sent to Nebraska at a base for B-29's. Our son, David, was born there and we were transferred to Roswell, New Mexico, a Strategic Air Command base. My job on the crew was assistant flight engineer. There were B-29's in the air 24 hours a day. This was a critical period of the "cold war" and we always had the "A" bomb on board.

"When my three years enlistment ended, we returned to Vermont. I worked for a granite company as a draftsman. Rosemary worked there as well. The company closed about three years later and I was hired by the Vermont Highway Department. Eventually after various promotions, I became a licensed highway engineer and worked until retirement at the end of 1982.

"After retirement we travelled in the States and Europe. We spend four winter months in Florida. We enjoy walking, golf and read a lot. Rosemary has done some painting, is an accomplished seamstress and does volunteer work.

From radio-operator **Edwin E. Kamarainen**'s book "From Parachute to Barbed Wire".

Sunday, November 26, 1944:

The Squadron, the 853rd, was ready to fly again. In formation they rose to the skies, ready for more action. Ed Kamarainen felt the thrill again as the squadron soared to meet the clouds above. Each man had his job and their goals to hit the target. As the bombs fell they could see that they had made a hit, which brought thumbs up and cheers among the crew.

Thirty aircraft left England for the mission, but two aborted the mis-

491st Bomb Group, 853rd Bomb Squadron

sion because of mechanical problems. They had just completed the bomb run when suddenly there came the roar of German planes. To their dismay, the rest of the squadron was shot down. Sixteen aircraft had been shot down in their Group. They were now alone, being attacked by ME-109's. Ed saw the oncoming planes and thought; "What chance do we have to make it now?" They were sitting ducks for the fighters. Somebody yelled, "They got Fuller." Gordon Fuller had been killed.

"Pilot Ralph Butler tried to catch up with the squadron ahead when a ME-109 appeared and started to fire. The nose of their plane was hit and burst into flames. There wasn't any response on intercom from the nose. Butler gave instructions, "Bail out, bail out."

"The men scrambled to bail out. Ed was wearing his parachute, a chest type, underneath his flak vest. Two sections on the flak vest snapped together at the shoulders. A cord ran from the shoulders and out a hole in the lower front. Jerking the cord would release the snaps and drop the flak vest. Ed jerked the cord but nothing happened. He began to panic. The others were getting out and he was having trouble with his parachute. Ed stood in front of the catwalk and looked down to see that the bomb bay doors were still partway open. There wasn't much time left. It was now or never. Feeling someone in back of him, Ed rolled forward and bailed out.

"Once clear of the aircraft, Ed was still rolling forward and his fall was increasing at the rate of thirty-two feet per second. He straightened himself out and began a normal free fall. The plane went down taking Gordon Fuller with it.

"Ed's flak vest was still on him. Soaring down in the air, Ed trying to save his life managed to slide his hands next to his body and pushed upward. With all the adrenaline he could muster, Ed was able to push the flak vest over his head along with his headgear. Now, free of the obstacles he pulled the rip cord. The most beautiful sight above him was the opening parachute as he glided downward towards the earth. Relief was replaced with fear as to what was ahead of him. The Germans could shoot as he glided down.

"Ed hit the ground hard. He unsnapped the chute and then looked around the area for an escape route. It was a stubble field between two villages, one north and one south, with a canal about a hundred feet wide to the east. Ed looked to the west and saw a man coming towards him, appearing to be carrying a firearm. He was not alone. A number of people came after him armed with different weapons.

"What am I in for?" were his thoughts as the man came close. Ed put his hands up. Everything went black as Ed collapsed on the ground after being hit with something. He didn't know how long he laid there but when he revived the first thing he saw were a pair of black shiny boots. Ed looked up to see a German officer with a pistol in his hands. Some of the men in the crowd standing by had been threatening Ed with a pitchfork. The German began shouting at the people that had gathered about, waving his pistol to keep them back. Some of the men had stabbed Ed.

"A man bundled up his chute and pushed it to Ed to carry: then shoved him ahead to march. The crowd followed them as they reached a small village ahead. People came out from their houses to stand on the sidewalks to watch the captured American. Others hung out from second and third floor windows. Everyone was yelling. Ed knew they were shouting obscenities against him, their enemy. It was a victory for them and a holiday to see a captured American. Ed was marched down the middle of the street for all to see, while the proud German followed with a pointed gun. Ed had no idea where he was or where he was going.

"When the reached the outskirts of the town they came to a building and stopped. The German motioned for Ed to go inside where he was taken to a small room, pushed inside and the door was closed. Looking around, Ed could see that there weren't any windows. The room was barren except for a small cot.

"At least he was still alive. Ed felt relief and some security being alone at last. He took off his flight suit and boots, which were over his shoes. Ed began examining himself for bruises and pitchfork punctures feeling lucky that he got away as well as he did, so far.

"There was a knock on the door. Ed stood still in fear of what was coming. It was a young man that came into the room who looked to be about seventeen years old. He kept looking at Ed's boots on the floor near the cot and was gesturing. Ed realized that the boy wanted something, perhaps a souvenir. Then he pointed at the boots. Ed figured that he would lose them anyway so he handed the boots to the boy. The boy was excited and smiled, muttering something in German as he thanked Ed. Then he left with his prize.

"Ed settles down on the cot, exhausted from this trying day and near death experience. He realized he hadn't had anything to eat all day, but he wasn't hungry. All the excitement and stress only made him want to lay down and sleep. All night he was restless and woke up at every sound. Ed wasn't able to relax not knowing what any minute might bring to him.

"Morning came and to Ed's surprise a man brought him a bowl of oatmeal and a cup with coffee. Or so he thought it was coffee. The Germans brewed a horrible tasting beverage called ersatz. After eating the oatmeal and a couple of sips of the bitter liquid, an armed guard came into the room. Ed stood up and his parachute was shoved to him to carry. Then he was led out of the building. Everything was quiet and they walked quickly to a town along a narrow road that was lined with threes on both sides. After about a kilometre the German mentioned Ed to go into a driveway. They walked up on a porch of a house ad knocked on the door. When the door opened, a young fraulein stood there and talked with the German. He turned to Ed and took the parachute and handed it to the girl. Her eyes brightened and she smiled happily to have the pure silk of a parachute. It could have become a wedding dress for her.

"Ed was glad to see the parachute gone, his load lightened. It was another kilometre to a railroad station where they entered into a deserted waiting room. Another German joined with Ed's guard so the two of them became his escorts. They started to argue with the station agent. There wasn't any scheduled passenger train due for awhile.

"Ed began to feel hungry. A small bowl of oatmeal had been his last meal. He noticed that the empty station room now had another occupant, a middle aged lady. She walked over and sat down on a bench across from Ed, and kept staring at him.

"Ed was looking around and the only escape would be through the front door, where he knew he couldn't get very far. Suddenly, the lady stood up and walked towards him. Ed stiffened in response. The lady was carrying a bag. Ed thought, "What if she had a gun in the bag?" All kinds of thoughts wandered and the guard may have thought the same as he came closer to watch. The woman put her hand in the bag and took out a beautiful apple and handed it to Ed. Ed took it as gracefully as he could and tried to show his appreciation for this kind act. He did not want to show how desperate his hunger was so he put the apple in his pocket.

"A steam locomotive stopped and a few moments later the German motioned for him to follow. Ed couldn't believe it but they put him in the locomotive. One of the guards boarded first and then Ed came up and finally the other guard. They all knew where they were going, except Ed. He was being well guarded and there wasn't any chance to escape.

Ed was amused at the thought of what he was costing the Germans with two guards and a locomotive along with the engineer and the fireman: first class capture.

"They travelled an estimated twenty mph, for a half-hour to another location where Ed was taken off the train into another waiting room. It was crowded. Ed looked around and with surprise and joy he saw his tail-gunner Robert Trombly. The room was crowded and there were other men that had been taken as POWs. The civilians were loud and began shouting at the prisoners but the guards managed to keep them in a separate corner.

"When the train came, Ed and the other prisoners boarded all in one end of it. They all had seats which gave them a chance to sit down and reflect on recent events. Ed was mostly thankful that he was still alive, even though he had been stripped of all rights and was under the mercy of his captors.

"Ed remembered the apple in his pocket and reached in to take it out. He ate it, core and all. That was his last memory of fruit for a long time to come. After exchanging stories, they settled down to a rest they mostly needed. They were all exhausted and confused. It was quiet and the sound of the train soon lulled them to sleep.

"In the interrogation center about a hundred prisoners were brought into a stockade. The name of the town was Oberursel. They would be registered as prisoners of war.

"The rest of Ed's crew was also there. They were surprised to see each other. They would have their own story of capture to tell. Ostrander had his head wrapped up because of burns. Ed bore results of mugging and had a gash over his left eye. This is war. We were prisoners of the enemy.

"Shortly Ed and Bob Trombly were put into confinement. They were taken to a place where they walked down into an underground cell. Once inside the 6 by 8-foot concrete building they could see bunks on each side. There was a single light bulb in the ceiling. It was cold in there without any ventilation and the dirt floor gave off a nasty smell.

"It could have been worse; being in there alone. But thankfully Ed and Bob had each other to compare histories. They did some speculation about what would happen next. They correctly assumed that their captors would interrogate the officers first. As non-commissioned officers they would get the treatment last.

"There was a pounding on the door and a German brought in a cup of ersatz. By this time they welcomed any kind of food and pretended it was really coffee. There was also a piece of black bread, which was not all flour and they couldn't tell what it was made with.

"Three days and three nights went by and on the third day Ed was escorted to the office and seated in front of a German officer. Ed promptly gave his name, rank and serial number. The German then read off information about Ed that he couldn't believe they knew. The German stated that Ed was from a farm in Northern Wisconsin and was of Finnish descent. That he was the radioman in Butler's crew. He gave Ed the bad news that the navigator, bombardier and waist-gunner went down with the plane. He had only known about Fuller.

"It was the last night in the dungeon. That evening was the first time they got anything that could be called a meal. It consisted of the same black bread, the bitter ersatz coffee and what looked like potato soup.

"The next morning Ed was escorted to a formation of "Kriegies" and loaded into a railroad car. In the afternoon they reached their destination to be processed. They were issued POW dog tags, a shirt, eating utensils and a safety razor.

"Ed, with a large group of POW's was marched to four boxcars that are described as 8x40 (8 horses or 40 men). The prisoners were astonished to see where they were being loaded into. There was only standing room with so many men shoved inside a boxcar. This was for three days.

"Cracks in the walls were big enough to see through so Ed could see a little as to where they were travelling. There were buckets inside the cars where they could relieve themselves and once a day the train would stop. The doors were unlocked and the men jumped out into the snow. Any civilians who happened to be there at the time saw many men dropping their pants and leaving a mark in the snow.

"The train pulled into a station and the prisoners were unloaded and lined up four abreast. The guards waiting for their arrival stood with fixed bayonets and guard dogs on leashes. Manned machine guns were in the trees next to the road. Ed was scared as were all the other men. This was a nightmare come true. A German yelled, "Raus", commanding them to move on. The dogs came into the prisoners but were held back far enough not to bite, but to terrorize the men. It was a warning.

"The prisoners did double time for about two miles. The guards were belligerent without any respect to human kind or the rules of the Geneva Convention. Ahead was a gate that opened to a prison camp. This was their new home for the duration of the war.

"In February 1945, the Russians were heading west and the Germans made plans to evacuate all of the eastern prison camps, forcing the prisoners to march hundreds of miles across Germany. The march had already started from other camps in January and they were picking up additional marchers on the way. Ed's POW buddies were told to prepare for a forced march. They had no idea they would be marching through snow and cold for how long and to where. When the order came, the prisoners formed columns of four abreast. Each was handed a Red Cross parcel to carry, not realizing that the Germans weren't planning to feed them. The marchers kept up a fast pace for about an hour until they were given a ten-minute

NOT HOME FOR CHRISTMAS

break. The men opened their parcels and took out what they didn't need, to make it a lighter load. All the items for bartering and food to survive were kept. They walked all day into the night. They crossed the Oder river and into Schweinemünde in the dark as it started to rain. The formation was ordered to tighten up. Towards morning they stopped at an open field to catch some sleep.

"Ed doubled up with a fellow named Ben. They doubled their blankets and huddled under them. Tired as the men were, they didn't sleep well. Before long, daylight came and they picked up their belongings to be on the way again, wet, cold and miserable. The rain had stopped but the ground was wet and damp. They had ten-minute breaks each hour but mostly because the Germans wanted it for themselves.

"The next stop was a huge barn. This time the Germans managed to find potatoes and cook them. That was the meal, along with black bread.

"The march continued and this time without any night stops. Two days without rest was tough on everyone, even the Germans. Some of the POW's fell out, to weak to walk any further and their fate was unknown. Others lagged behind but were helped by their marching buddies.

"On the third day they settled into a routine, walking and walking. They travelled mostly on secondary roads around larger towns. The smaller towns had cobbled stone streets that were uneven to walk on, causing more misery to the marchers. They were herded like animals and slept like animals. There never was a chance to wash up. If there was a barn to sleep in, they considered themselves lucky. These days dragged into weeks and then months.

"One day the guards let everyone stop for a day's rest. The men stripped their clothes and spent hours picking the lice from their bodies.

"April 1945. The winter was now over and spring brought about a fresh growth of grass and warmer days. The column arrived at Fallingbastel to Stalag XIB, located near Celle and Hannover. Ed noticed that he was near Misburg which had been the target the day he was shot down.

"The camp contained about 6.500 British POWs. Ed's group of about two hundred men were placed in a separate compound that had large tents. They settled in as best as they could, sleeping on the ground.

"A couple of days later the POWs were ordered out for a head count and advised that they were marching again. The German officer announced that if anyone felt he couldn't continue he could fall out. But when examined by the doctor and it wasn't necessary, he would then be shot. Ed had varicose veins in both of his legs. He decided to take the chance and fall out. His friend pleaded with him to come with them, but

Ed had made his decision. About seven men fell out and were sent back to their tents. Ed prayed that he wouldn't be shot. The others who had fallen out were also scared and everyone was quiet. They sat and waited for the doctor to come in.

The day ended with all the anxiety of waiting for the doctor who never showed up. Three days later there wasn't any doctor coming in. On the fourth day Ed and the other prisoners realized that there weren't any German guards around the camp. A group of the men with Ed jumped the fence and went into town, which was deserted.

It was early morning of April 16, 1945 and the men heard a commotion outside their tent. British tanks were pulling up. They were finally free.

The next day a British lieutenant came in and distributed ID's to all the men. Then the liberated POW's were driven to a field were a DC-3 was waiting for them. They flew to Brussels where they were put trough the de-lousing process. They had hot showers and shaves and were issued new uniforms. Each man was given one hundred dollars in advance pay. A good meal fed them well and they even had a beer or two. They were turned over to the US forces and subsequently shipped to Camp Lucky Strike at Le Havre in France. There they waited for the rotation to the good old USA – Home.

***

Acknowledgments:
Edwin E. Kamarainen's book: "From Parachute to Barbed Wire".
Gini Giddiens, daughter of pilot Ralph J. Butler
Jim Haas for navigator Herman C. Bauer, www.jimhaasbooks.com
Scott Wilson , Social Studies Department, Omaha Central High School for bombardier Stanley A. Yergey
Robber V. Trombly

CHAPTER 21

491ST BOMB GROUP 853RD BOMB SQUADRON

Aircraft Type: B-24J, Serial # 42-110167,
"Firebird", MACR 10768
Airbase: North Pickenham

"Morale low, you can't keep plowing through this "black stuff" without getting hurt, sooner or later."

—From Daniel Budd's diary about meeting flak during his mission to Misburg on September 12, 1944

Pilot: 1Lt Daniel C. Budd (KIA) Falls Church VA

Co-Pilot: 2Lt Noel A. Oury (KIA) Richmond VA

Navigator: 1Lt Norman F. Hirsch (KIA) Brooklyn, NY

Bombardier: 1Lt William F. Phelps (KIA) Noank CT

Top-Turret: T/Sgt Vernon R. Brock (KIA) Albion MI

Radio-Operator: T/Sgt Elmer H. Bemis (KIA) Marlboro MA

Left- Waist: S/Sgt Thaddeus C. Jarosz (POW) Lawrence MA

Right-Waist: S/Sgt Frank Verbovsky (POW) North Bergen NJ

Tailgunner: S/Sgt Thomas R. Crane (KIA) Salem NJ

Navigator: 2Lt Floyd A. Walker Jr. (KIA) Des Moines IA

Total: 8 KIA, 2 POW

Target: Misburg

Crash Site: Bredenbeck near Bennigsen, 23 km SW of Misburg

NOT HOME FOR CHRISTMAS

For pilot **Daniel C. Budd**, his sister Alice Kleyman wrote the following biography:

"Daniel Budd was born in Morristown, New Jersey in 1921. His father, Daniel Spencer Budd, was an engineer, who served overseas in the Bobcat Regiment in WW I. Dan's mother was a high school teacher of English, Latin and German. He had one younger sister, Alice, who married Maxwell I. Klayman. They had two daughters, Judith and Naomi, and a son, Daniel Budd Klayman. Alice is now a widow living in Amherst, Mass.

"As a young child, Dan was sensitive and even fearful at times. He outgrew this, but I realised later that courage is a mental attitude that has to be acquired. The lack of fear in a young child may be due to the fact that he/she is, to a certain extend, unaware of danger. At elementary school in Morristown, Dan was somewhat shy and didn't make friends easily. He was bullied at times. Later, I realized that there were tough boys at that school – and Dan had been taught that it was wrong to fight.

"The depression hit Dan's father in 1931 when his engineering job ended. The family moved to a large family house in near-by Chester, which was a village of 1000 people. This was a good environment for kids and Dan developed into a fun-loving boy (who was also a fearless tree climber and athlete). He was a caring older brother, who helped me to learn how to play baseball and touch football and always beat me at table tennis. We had a tennis court and a croquet lawn. Our mother taught us to play both games: our father was into hunting and fishing; but neither Dan nor I had the patience for those sports. Dan liked the big bands and the jazz music of his time. He also had a good voice and was sometimes asked to sing at picnics and get-togethers.

"We had great parents who, for those times, were progressive. In Morristown, when Dan was about ten, he thought he had been denied something unfairly. The year was 1931 and "sit down" protests were first starting. So Dan organized the local kids and got about ten of us, on various strikes, bikes and scooters, to parade around our house, chanting "We want children's rights". Our mother came to the porch to see what the hullabaloo was – and laughed heartily even as she called him in and lectured him. That was not the answer Dan had hoped for.

"As a teen-ager, Dan attended three different schools. Dan was smart, but he was not a student. However he learned to write easily and well. He also developed a good tennis game and played on the team that unofficially represented the village of Chester.

491st Bomb Group, 853rd Bomb Squadron

Pilot Daniel C. Budd

"Before volunteering for the Air Force, Dan worked as a secretary in a technical organization. While in training to become a pilot, studying hard for he first time in his life, he kept up a heavy correspondence with family members, and also corresponded with many friends. On one day, he wrote that his incoming mail had comprised over half the mail received by his unit.

"After he became an officer, he wrote a very appreciative letter to his mother and father, thanking them for being such wonderful parents. He added; "I fully realized, for the first time, that I had been the problem in the family and you were always loving and tolerant". (His only real problem was his academic record.) His parents were very happy when he wrote, from England, that he was planning to go to college when he returned. He added that he might try to major in psychology because he might be successful at, and enjoy, some job in Personnel. Since the whole family thought Dan's personality, which included an ability to charm people, was one of his strongest points, his parents wrote back that they thought his plan was great.

"During his last year of high school, he wrote a theme in which he described Hitler as a menace to the U.S. and wrote that the United States might have to come to the aid of England. On his last visit with the family, Dan told us that he had to volunteer many times to be accepted for overseas duty. (His father guessed that he was held back because his superiors thought he had a high value as an excellent stateside flying instructor.) On his last "home" visit, after enjoining me to take great care of our parents, he told me; "If the world doesn't adopt some sort of League of Nations after this war, it might not survive".

Navigator **Norman F. Hirsch**. From the book *Passing the Baton* by his brother Bill, an attorney-at-law in Wayne, PA:

"At the headquarters, 8th USAAF, message clerks pounded out their teletype messages starting around 03.40 a.m., Sunday, November 26. 1944.

NOT HOME FOR CHRISTMAS

Crew members who participated in the November 26, 1944 mission.
Back row: 1st from left: Co-Pilot Noel A Oury; 2nd from Left: Bombardier William Phelps
Front Row: 2nd from left: Engineer Vernon R. Brock; 3rd from left: Radio-Operator Elmer H. Bemis; 1st from right: Waist-Gunner Thaddeus C. Jarosz

The baton was passed, from topside down to each bomb group. Around 03.40 a.m. hours, the 491st received its instructions, and around 04.00 Norm could hear the squeal of bike wheels outside the hut's door. Buds Nissen hut got his wake-up call. "Briefing at five." That allowed an hour for putting on your clothes, latrine, breakfast, equipment room, briefing and loading.

"Like all preceding mission mornings, Norm jumped out of the sack and was off to the mess hall. All the crew members moved fast, even when they would rather have sacked in for just a few more minutes. One incentive was that lateness could cost you a two-day pass.

"Norm would be wearing his dog tags with the "H" for Hebrew stamped out in the "Religion" area. He did this routinely, just as other Jewish flyers did. It was a way of simply ignoring the known fierce anti-Semitism awaiting any Allied combatant ending up in enemy hands. Norm thought twice about the bulky standard issue .45 calibre automatic pistol. Finally he decided against carrying it.

491st Bomb Group, 853rd Bomb Squadron

"At the equipment shed, Norm picked up his electric flying suit, flak vest, parachute chest harness and parachute. He put on the harness, but not the silky chute. It would end up in a corner of the navigator's station near *Firebird*'s nose. It was too bulky to wear, and could be clipped on when needed.

"Out in the cold dreary flight line area, the ground crew loaded *Firebird* and the other flying elephants. Each plane had a specified area called a *hardstand*. The bomb load consisted of twelve 500 pounders. At the same time, about 2800 gallons of fuel and ammo for the .50 calibre machine guns were added. Switches, gauges, indicators, warning lights, and other instruments were checked out, with boxes marked on the handy checklist.

"Briefing began at 05.30 for the 491st. Before long, the target announcement was made. *"Misburg oil refineries"*, which was no stranger to the 491st. This was a target that was partially destroyed twice before. On the first raid, on September 12th, two crews of the 491st were shot down and all crewmen were either missing or killed in action. All the eyes were on the long, red thin ribbon that led from North Pick to the target. Also, the Colonel pointed to a chart on the side wall, for each crew to quickly study. It contained the flying positions for each crew of the flying squadrons. It also gave the time to start engines, taxi and take-off.

"As with prior missions, the rendezvous point was identified. That was the point in the air where the group was formed, at the usual 7.000 to 10.000 feet level for group assembly. That point would be directly over Felixstowe, in East Anglia, on the English east coast. Each plane would go through its traffic pattern, circling until it got together with the other eight planes in the squadron. For *Firebird* it was 853rd Bomb Squadron. The other squadrons in the group flying that day were the 854th and the 855th. Then the planes in each squadron would reach altitude, would circle, and continue to circle, until the planes in the three squadrons would join in the 491st Bomb Group formation.

"There would be a planned shield of three escorting fighter groups. They would consist of a total of 197 P-51 Mustangs and 48 P-47 Thunderbirds. Once over enemy territory, the bombers of the two Air Divisions would be spread over a distance of up to forty miles. The P-51's always had long distance capability and at this point the P-47 were carrying extra tanks which greatly increased their distance capability..

"The weather was stinko at North Pick. It had been raining all night and the runway showed it. *Firebird* was covered with ice and frost. Hey, you couldn't see out the windows and turrets. So, Norm, Budd, Phelps

NOT HOME FOR CHRISTMAS

and Oury did double duty. They climbed up and washed the plane with de-icer fluid. They knew that the cleaning would be an improvement, and it was. But, still, the de-icer fluid left a scummy surface, interfering with visibility.

"The green flare went up at 09.04. Planes from the 853rd started to taxi out, and form up as a line of noisy, grey monsters. When the squadron reached the runway, the throttles were moved to high and the labouring elephants took off in thirty seconds intervals.

"You can just imagine *Firebird*, building up power, with its pent-up horses held in tight rein like a big aluminium prairie schooner. Then, at the signal, the brakes would be loosened and Budd would accelerate *Firebird* down the runway, splashing through puddles and tossing up wide sprays of water. There would even be the chaplain at the end of the runway, giving off with his blessings.

"The group left the English coast at 10.12 hours and the flight path was north-east over de Zuider Zee. An hour later, as the planes of the 853rd Squadron crossed into the enemy coast, Lt. Greaser in another bomber had to feather the malfunctioning number one engine. And then the number two went out, and Greaser had to turn back. He dropped his bomb load off the Dutch coast, and had to return to the base.

"The other nine planes of the 853rd went on. The pilots of these crews were Stewart, Moore, Ecklund, Cloughly, Butler, Bennett, Stevens, Hite and, you guessed it, Budd. You can bet that all the pilots in the 853rd and 854th Squadrons were jockeying their controls, at 24.000 feet, to be sure to be in contact with each other, in a semblance of a formation behind the planes of the leading 855th Squadron of the 491st Bomb Group.

"Droning along, another B-24 got lucky. It's engines started to sputter. It couldn't go on, but instead turned back, leaving a total of twenty-eight aircraft heading into Germany, forward, into flak and enemy fighters, toward the target. The irony was that for the moment, the sky was as benign and beckoning as a bright beach day. But the beauty and quiet were illusions, and all the crewmen knew it.

"The scene was pregnant with unexpected encounters that might suddenly mount up to something more than anyone had expected. Here was one unintended event: the B-17's in the 1st Division would be arriving at Misburg about six minutes earlier than the planned arrival time. The time spread between the two divisions, the 1st and 2nd, had grown to twenty minutes, whereas the briefing had planned on a twelve minutes spread. And there was a sky distance spread among the aircraft as well. Spread is the opposite of compact. And compact is what you want.

491st Bomb Group, 853rd Bomb Squadron

"The B-17 and B-24 heavies were lumbering onward. But the fighter escort had too great a distance to cover. The planned shield of escort fighters was thin and thinning. The shield started with the B-17 Flying Fortresses up front, but hardly reached back to the B-24 Liberators flying behind them.

"At around 11.55 hours, the B-24 crewmen spotted three Me 262 jct fighters flying parallel to them and about 2.000yards to the left. Bur the enemy jets did not attack. Their mission, probably, was just to chart the direction, altitude, speed and strength of the B-24's as they approached the Initial Point.

"Throughout this time, the flak had been heavy and constant. The planes of the 491st were now in tight formation, rocking from the bursts, and the shells were coming closer. The 491st was, as I said, flying tail-end-charley in a formation of three squadrons, lead, low and high. To repeat, the 855th was flying lead, with the 854th flying low. That left the 853rd Squadron, which was Norm's. It was flying in the high location. All of them, the entire group, were like exposed elephants lumbering across the sky.

"As the Liberators began to reach the I.P., and make a turn for the target, the flak suddenly ceased. I'll bet Norm and the other crewmen in the 853rd Squadron were both relieved and baffled. But those two feelings couldn't have lasted long. Suddenly the air was filled with previously unseen enemy fighters, mostly FW-190's. They raced in, all guns blazing, with the sun at their backs. They cut into the high formation like sharply clawed leopards pouncing on unsuspecting deer.

"The high formation was the first on the list of the FW-190's. It all happened fast, almost in an instant. *Firebird* was hit with a fusillade of 20mm shells. The bomb bay was ablaze. Shells ripped through it. Communications were dead. The controls were snapped. Norm, and Budd's crew, was going down! *Firebird* was dropping like a rock. Then, moments later, three more planes were cut down. Then two more.

"Eight of the planes in the 853rd were ablaze, and going down. Bennett's *Ark Angel*, the ninth, was still aloft, but not for long. Here and there a few chutes were seen. But there weren't many. Every plane, all nine of the 853rd that had come so far, were knocked out!

"Who knows what was going on in these planes? Was the crew still alive? Were they burning? Was Norm hit? Was he bleeding? Was he trying to get out?

"There might have been a chute or two coming out of *Firebird*; it just wasn't clear. Was it all over of almost all over? Would some of them land

NOT HOME FOR CHRISTMAS

safely, only to be met by German pitchforks? Would some lucky ones, maybe Norm, survive and end up as a prisoner in a Stalag?

"Sure, lots of enemy fighters were shot down. The Luftwaffe paid a price too. A top-turret gunner named Burbank, flying with the low squadron, 854th, had tracked an FW-190. The enemy fighter came in from 4 o'clock., and Burbank opened fire at 700 yards. His .50 calibre rounds were on target, into the cabin of the FW-190. All of a sudden the FW-190 veered, its guns were silent, smoke poured from its cabin, its nose pointed down, and the FW-190 spiralled to earth.

"Yet along the way, the FW-190's left their mark. Twenty-eight Liberators of the 491st Bomb Group reached the target area, and twelve returned to the base.

About bombardier **William F. Phelps** his sister Helen McGuire wrote:

"Our dad use to spend a lot of time with Bill and my brother Don, building boats, flying kites, observing the planets through my dad's telescopes, fishing, and swimming. We lived in a small town that was considered to be a peninsula. Our home was right near the ocean. My sister Linda lives there now. I have loving thoughts and memories of Billy.

"He used to give me lots of hugs and kisses. There were six of us; two boys and four girls. My dad was a carpenter and my Mom was a stay-at-home housewife. Bill went to a small elementary school in Noank. He went to Robert E. Fitch High School after. He did not attend college. He sure would have liked: he did very well academically in school. He was one of the top students. in all his classes.

"He was small framed. He had a head full of blond curly hair. He was a quiet boy: he only spoke when he had a good word to say.

His niece Joan Russell added:

"I was at the house when the boy brought the telegram that said he was "lost in action". I told my Grandfather a man was at the door with a letter. He took the letter, then called up the stairs to Billy's mother: "Helen there is a telegram!" She screamed, "No.. no . . .". He looked at me and said: ""go home kid".. I was visiting with grandmother a few houses away. I went there and told her: "A boy brought a letter and Aunt Helen screamed".

"Grandmother quickly took off her apron and said "stay here" and went running down there to their house.

"I also remember Billy's bedroom. From the ceiling hung many airplanes made with balsam wood. It was a small room but I can still see them. It was a fascinating sight.

About top-turret gunner **Vernon R. Brock** his sister Mary Damron wrote:

"I remember my Mother had hopes that one day my brother would come home. The government never gave her a definite feeling of certainty about what happened. In May of 1949 she went to the funeral services at Arlington Cemetery and knew that the grave was supposed to be of the five crew members, but since there was not proof positive of the individual identity of the men, she never gave up hope he would somehow appear on our doorstep. She would not move from the neighbourhood where we lived and the bus station use to be a block from our house and I can remember watching people get off the bus and looking for a soldier who might seem confused and looking for someone.

"To my knowledge my Mother never knew exactly where the plane went down or where Vernon was buried before the ceremony in Arlington. His dog tags were never recovered and returned, so that is one reason she never gave up hoping he would return. The government just listed him missing in action and then a year later declared him to be legally dead.

"When they had the funeral service in Arlington. they just told her they were reasonably sure that his was one of the five bodies.

About radio-operator **Elmer H. Bemis,** the family historian Curtis Bemis wrote:

"Elmer was born in August 1924 in Chesham, NH, at the large Bemis family home of his grandparents. Chesham was often referred to as "Bemisville" for obvious reasons. His father, also born in Chesham in the same house in 1878, was railroad station worker.

"Elmer's father died during the winter of 1937 of pneumonia. Some time later, Elmer's mother moved her family to Marlborough, Massachusetts, her family home.

"After High School, and at the beginning of WW II, Elmer left Marlborough and became a welder in one of the many shipyards, in Providence, Rhode Island.

NOT HOME FOR CHRISTMAS

Left waist-gunner **Thaddeus "Teddy" C. Jarosz**, whose parents had come from Poland in the early 1900's, was born in Lawrence, MA on October 20th, 1924 and graduated from Lawrence High School in 1943. Upon graduation, Teddy enlisted in the Air Corps at the age of eighteen. Prior to his enlistment, he worked part-time evenings and summers at a local market called Mohican Market and also, in the Pacific Mills of Lawrence.

He was on his twenty-fourth mission when he was shot down. He and the other waist-gunner, Frank Verbovsky, bailed out. Teddy however was badly wounded and died as a POW on December 17th.

Teddy's brother Bill, who was with the 3rd Armoured Division, was wounded in France on August 15th, 1944. As a result, he was sent to a hospital in England to recuperate that was located not far from the 491st BG base and he and Teddy met regularly during Bill's recovery. He was on the base when Teddy's complete squadron failed to return after the Misburg mission.

Only the two waist-gunners, Frank Verbovsky and Teddy Jarosz, bailed out of *Firebird*. Teddy was heavily wounded and it was a miracle that he managed to open his parachute. Frank reported after the war:

> "We were shot down by fighters about five minutes after we dropped our bombs over Misburg, near Hannover, Germany. After we hit the ground the Germans gave us first aid. We were then brought to a hospital where we were operated on. Thaddeus Jarosz was hit in the right leg and left arm. The Germans amputated his left arm above the elbow. We were at this hospital for about four days. We were than brought to Frankfurt, Germany.
>
> "The last time I saw Jarosz was December 2, 1944. He was in good condition. We were then sent to different hospitals. About a fortnight later, a Pole was brought to my hospital and he told me that Thaddeus died on December 17, 1944. He claimed that the sulphur from the bullets got into his system. Everything possible was done to him but it was too late.

The Chief Surgeon of the Luftwaffe Hospital in Frankfurt stated after the war:

> "I remember an American flyer whose right arm was blown off at the shoulder in an air battle. Gangrene had already set in and the patient was

in a critical condition. The nature of the wound indicated that it was probably caused by a phosphoric shell. Although he received several blood transfusions, he died after a few says.

Four years after the end of the war with Germany, the remains of Thaddeus Jarosz were returned to Lawrence, Mass, where he was buried on June 25, 1949.

Right-waist Gunner **Frank Verbovsky** was born on November 18, 1923 in North Bergen. NJ. He was the second of five kids with Joseph and Sophie as parents. Joseph was a WW I veteran.

Frank graduated Union Hill High School in June of 1942. On April 13, 1943, he entered the Air Corps and received his bombardier wings at Tyndall Field, Florida.

On November 26, 1944 he bailed out with leg wounds and fractures of the jaw and fingers. He underwent four operations in a German hospital. He was then transferred to a German POW camp. On May 9 1945 he was liberated and on October 27, 1945 he was discharged from the army while earning two purple hearts.

After the Army he was employed by Folger Embroidery of Union City, NJ. In July 1949, Frank married Madelyn Ghibisi of Jersey City N.J. They had three sons Frank, Micheal and Steven. In 1985 his wife passed away. He retired in 1987 and passed away in 1995. In 1995 he was survived by his 3 sons and 6 grandkids. Today in 2008 it would be 8 grandkids and 1 great grandkid.

***

Acknowledgements:
Alice Kleyman for pilot Daniel C. Budd
Bill Hirsch, with the book "Passing the Baton".
Helen McGuire and Joan Russell for bombardier William F. Phelps
Curtis E. Bemis Jr. for radio-operator Elmer H. Bemis
Steven Verbovsky for his father waist-gunner Frank Verbovsky

CHAPTER 22

491ST BOMB GROUP
853RD BOMB SQUADRON

Aircraft Type: B-24J, Serial # 44-10534,
MACR 10761
Airbase: North Pickenham

"I landed near a village and it appeared as if all the residents came out to welcome me"

—Pilot Charles J. Ecklund after arriving on German soil

Pilot: 1Lt Charles J. Ecklund (POW) Harveyville KS

Co-Pilot: 2Lt Marvin E. Strohl (POW) Detroit MI

Navigator: 2Lt George K. Voseipka (POW) North Platte NE

Bombardier: 2 Lt Horace R. Simms Jr. (POW) Oakland CA

Top-Turret: T/Sgt Edward C. Guerry (POW) Imperial CA

Radio-Operator: T/Sgt John N. Heib (KIA) Seattle WA

Left-Waist: S/Sgt Burton A. Johns (POW) Los Angeles CA

Right-Waist: S/Sgt Samuel S. Rosenfield (POW) New York NY

Tail Gunner: S/Sgt Dennis C. Cole (POW) Westby WI

Total: 1 KIA, 8 POW

Target: Misburg

Crash Site: Rieste District of Bersenbrück, along the railroad from Rieste to Neuenkirchen, Germany

Time of Crash: 13.16

NOT HOME FOR CHRISTMAS

Pilot **Charles J. Ecklund** was born on February 4, 1922 in Burdick, Kansas and grew up in a rural community near Harveyville, also in Kansas. He graduated from Harveyville Rural High School in 1941.

He enlisted in the Army Air Corps in November 1942. On September 20, 1944, Charles and his crew flew to England.

There were three Ecklund brothers flying combat missions during World War II; Lt. Charles D. who flew B-24 over France and Germany, Lt. Robert D. who was a P-38 fighter pilot over North Africa and Italy and Lt. Lee E. who flew B-17 over Europe.

In January 2002, Charles wrote about his last flight in WW II:

"I was shot down during a mission over Hannover, Germany. The target was the synthetic fuel plant at Misburg, a suburb of Hannover.

"To recap the mission: the 8th USAAF dispatched 1.137 B-17 and B-24 bombers into Germany. The final count of losses was staggering. The 8th Air Force lost thirty-four bombers whereas the Germans lost ninety-eight fighter planes.

"As we left the target – the strike had fair results – we were struck from behind by an estimated 200 FW-190 and ME-109.

"After leaving the target area, all action ceased – undoubtedly no ammunition was left. Our crew immediately went into survival mode attempting to get to allied controlled Belgium. The tail-gunner was badly wounded. The plane was riddled with bullet holes. There were no communications, no radio, no intercom and I had no rudder control.

1Lt. Charles J. Ecklund

"Initially, our B-24 had four working engines. Soon, they began to fail . . . . almost in order. Number one failed but could be feathered. Then number four failed. By this time we were a plane by itself and, of course losing altitude rapidly. Then, number two failed so all we could do was to increase to max super charge power on number three to extend our glide.

"When the time came for bail out, I gave the order by hand signals as there was no intercom. My crew pushed the wounded tail-gunner Dennis Cole through the escape hatch and pulled his rip cord.

"Now, it is time for me to evacuate the plane. The engineer Edward

491st Bomb Group, 853rd Bomb Squadron

Guerry had manually – no power – cranked one bomb bay door partly open before I gave the order to bail out. I left my pilot position, ran to the bomb bay and tried to squeeze my one-hundred-forty pound body plus parachute through the partially open door

"Unfortunately, I found myself half way in half way out of the plane – caught in the middle so to speak. This action resulted in becoming the most memorable seconds for me as I relived my entire life, twenty-two years, in that time. As the aircraft started to roll, evidently due to the change in air flow, I was released from my trapped position, pulled the rip cord and found myself floating down.

"I landed near a village and it appeared as if all the residents came out to welcome me. At this point there were no German troops, only civilians, some carrying guns that resembled our .22 rifle. The group took me, limping, to a barn. I was wet and cold but not unduly alarmed so it came as no surprise when a teen age girl approached me and asked; "Are you married?" My reply; "No, are you?" resulted in a blushing young lady and much laughter.

"With my crew we were picked up by German troops and transported by truck, train and boxcar to Nürnberg for interrogation, and a short stay in hospital to mend my broken ankle. I was transported to Stalag Luft 3 at Sagan, Germany. This was an English compound near the Russian border. There were no more vacancies in American prison camps. My crew was sent to Stalag Luft 1 in Barth, Germany where they met my brother, Robert, who had been interned there over two years.

"Prison camp was not unbearable as the British had been there for years and had established a community like atmosphere with shows and holiday events. Every prisoner received one-half of a Red Cross parcel every month. The package contents were varied and some things more useful to one than another. An exchange program was set up where a person could deposit unwanted merchandise – in turn, he was awarded points. For example, I did not smoke; hence, the much sought after cigarettes allowed me to "buy" the dehydrated chocolate bar and Spam. This item exchange system worked very well.

"Life in the POW camp had its good days and bad days. The morale was always lifted upon receiving letters from home that supported our mission. Our primary concern was following the progress of the war. The British solved the problem as over the years they managed to smuggle in enough radio parts to assemble a receiver. The current information was then passed from one to another in our daily exercise around the compound.

NOT HOME FOR CHRISTMAS

"The food was somewhat scarce. The menu for most days was boiled barley laced with weevils and bread made from part flour and sawdust.

"During the month of February we began hearing heavy artillery fire coming from the east. Each day it would become closer and closer as the Russians were driving towards Berlin. About the middle of the month when it was bitterly cold and the ground snow covered, we were awakened at midnight, told to pack and move out. You can imagine the array of back packs, make shift sleds and any container that would hold our gear assembled in the compound.

"So, off we go in a very loose formation heading west into the interior of Germany. We walked, rode in box cars, walked and walked some more. This routine was repeated over and over, not knowing what would be our final destination: however, we were greatly comforted that our movements were being monitored by United States and British fighter aircraft.

"Final destination was a POW camp near Nürnberg. On 4 April 1945 we were liberated by General Patton's armoured division. I shall always remember the day he rode into camp standing in his jeep wearing pearl handled pistols with his dog beside him. Waving to us all he announced; "The city of Nürnberg is secure to the river and the gate is open!!!."

"On April 30 I was sent to Camp Lucky Strike, Le Havre, France for processing and ticket to the United States. I chose to "hang around" after I was booked to depart for the States as my brother, Robert, had not been liberated. There were thousands of military milling around awaiting stateside transportation. One day I was nearing the Red Cross tent to get an eggnog, I looked to my left and noticed an airman looking to his right. I said; "Hi, Bob". He replied; "Hello Bossy" . . . . my family's nickname for me. We sailed back to the States on the same ship.

"After my 1945 discharge from the United States Air Corps I bought a farm near Harveyville, Kansas. I fell in love with the Mayor's daughter. We married and had a son. We later moved to Portland, Oregon, where I became active in the 403rd Troop Carrier National Guard.

"In 1951, during the Korean conflict, our unit was recalled to active duty. We were then sent to Brady, Japan, to fly missions into Korea. Our orders were to be therefor a six months tour; however, we were there over a year as there were no replacements.

"I returned to the States where I met my nine month old daughter for the first time. There was no problem . . . . it was love at first sight.

"In 1959, with my family, we flew to Japan. During the next four years I was chief of the 315th Air Division Transport Movement Control at Tachikawa. While stationed in Japan I spent six months in Saigon, Vietnam, setting up airlift schedules between Japan, Philippines, Thailand and other countries.

"In 1953 we returned stateside to Stewart Air Force Base, Smyrna, Tennessee. For the next few years I was involved with missions to Vietnam.

"On 1 April 1970 I retired after nearly thirty years of military service to my country.

Charles John E. Ecklund passed away on August 17, 2002. His wife Jeanne wrote about him:

"Charles retired from the military in 1970 and immediately began working for a rental agency as chief of maintenance. Throughout our marriage of 56 plus years, I referred to him as my "live in handyman". He was an electrician, plumber, carpenter, mechanic, garden/landscape artist, etc. etc. He possessed the innate quality of finding the source of most problems. Of course, the past two years as his health declined, we had to have help but the service people listened with respect to Charles' diagnosis – the mind was clear.

"At age 65 Charles retired for the second time. We immediately joined a spa where we met a group of young men and women who adopted us. We continued to play golf and bridge with friends of our age while embracing our new found young people. Four of the group were attempting to enter into the country music business. Charles and I attended every performance – night clubs, fan fanes, grand openings – wherever. Two of the bunch were upscale restaurant managers and we found ourselves as guests and treated as royalty throughout the past fifteen years. Charles dubbed the group "The Outlaws" (not relatives, hence, they could not be in-laws.

"When Charles retired from the Air Force in 1970 our plans were to return to the west; however, we were reluctant to leave Nashville as we had a year old grandson. As it developed Marshall came to live with us. On his first grade report card his teacher noted "A born leader". After studying the life of General Mac Arthur in grade four, Marshall announced he was going to West Point. From that time every decision he made was with that goal in mind. You can imagine how proud Charles was to commission his grandson into the army upon graduation!

NOT HOME FOR CHRISTMAS

Back row, left to right: Pilot Charles J. Ecklund, co-pilot Marvin E. Strohl, navigator George K. Voseipka, Bombardier Horace R. Simms
Front row, from left to right: Engineer Edward C. Guerry, radio-operator John N. Heib, Waist-gunner Burton A. Johns, Nose-gunner Knight (not on the 11.26.44 mission), Gunner Cullicrate (not on the 11.26.44 mission), Tail-Gunner Dennis C. Cole.

Navigator **George K. Voseipka** passed away in January, 2008 at the age of 83. His daughter wrote about him:

"George was born in 1922 in North Platte, Nebraska. George's paternal grandfather was the first in that family to come to the US, sometime before 1872 (that is when the marriage certificate shows him being married in Iowa), and he was naturalized in 1876. They came from Bohemia, part of what was formerly Czechoslovakia. In all the papers I have on them, the last name is spelled several different ways: Woseipka, Voseipka, Vosipka, Wasepka. His father was born on April 16, 1883 in Iowa City, Iowa.

"After graduation from North Platte High School and before enlisting in the Air Corps, George was employed by Union Pacific Railroad (his father was an engineer, and he was a telegrapher) in Cheyenne, Wyoming. After five months in a German POW camp, George returned home, finished college and graduated from law school at the University of Denver in March 1948. He became a lawyer for a short time but re-enlisted then in the Air Force.

"He made a tour of 3½ years in Sembach, Germany and graduated from the USAF Command and Staff School at Maxwell Air Force Base in Montgomery, Alabama. After Maxwell, he was stationed in Hamilton AFB (San Francisco area of California) for not quite a year, followed by less than a year on Long Island, New York, at a base whose name I don't remember. Next assignment was Robins AFB in Warner Robins, Georgia, for about 3½ years, followed by a year in Saigon, Vietnam ('63-'64). He saw no action, as Saigon was quiet at that time. Upon return to the States, he was reassigned to Kelly AFB in San Antonio, Texas, in the Security section for his final 3+ years, until he retired December 1, 1968, as a Lt. Col., and returned to Perry, Georgia, where the family has stayed since moving there in 1961.

Bombardier **Horace R. Simms Jr.** from his self-published book *Indelibly Etched*:

"26 November, 1944.
 "Quiet voice wakes me in darkness, "Lt. Simms?"
 "Mff"
 "Breakfast at 0300. Briefing at 0400"
 "OK".
 "Lights come on. Crew members start ritual of dressing for the mission. We use "buddy system" to make sure we forget nothing. Navigator George Voseipka is my buddy, using checklist. First don silk longjohns to conserve body heat, then regular army shirt and trousers. Next, electrically heated suit followed by heavy flight pants and jacket. Wool stocking cap. Heavy wool socks. Flight boots. Thus attired, crew shuffles off to mess hall. Today is Sunday so cooks prepare meal with extra care. Scrambled eggs and good English bread. Strawberry jam.
 "We proceed to briefing room for details on target of the day. Whole crews are assembled now, both officers and enlisted men. Target is to be the oil refineries at Misburg - Hannover. We get more information on I.P., winds aloft, pressure altitudes, etc.
 "Today I am to be "B-Lead" and will have a bombsight for the first time since joining the 491st Bombardment Group (H) based in North

NOT HOME FOR CHRISTMAS

Pickenham, England. Final words came from Group Commander and chaplains. Watches are hacked (set) so all are on same time. After stop at Quartermaster to deposit personal items and identification and to receive earphones and oxygen masks, we take perimeter trucks to our B-24 bomber. Now our only I.D. is on the metal dog tags hanging from a chain around the neck. Weather very bad today: Freezing conditions have deposited thin coating of ice over everything. We enter plane and begin final check-up, left-waist Gunner Burton Johns and I paying special attention to the bomb loading.

"Engines start and warm up. Green Very lights appear and we begin slow approach to the runway. Pilot Charley Ecklund revs the four Pratt and Whitney engines while holding breaks. When brakes are released, plane starts forward, gaining speed until finally we are airborne. After making the left turn familiar to all pilots we break through overcast to brilliant sunshine.

"Long flight finally brings us to I.P. ca. 1300 hours. This will be another pattern bombing with bombs to be toggled off. Some flak encountered during bomb run. I see one bomber disabled and going down. We release our bombs with rest of group. Hit target squarely, destroying it. As we turn off and close bomb bay doors I see huge column of smoke from ruined refinery. There is something else to be seen out on horizon. Smoke trails coming from unusual aircraft executing loops. Our fighter cover drawn off in pursuit. Intercom warns of "bandits" in the area.

Soon we see them by the dozen. I remember ME 109's. We are being shot up severely by 20 mm cannon projectiles. The carnage could have been worse, but many of the Nazi pilots get in too close, resulting in "overshoot". As it is, we lose almost half of our group. Now we have essentially only one functional engine, another "windmilling" and running away.

"I hear Charley calling the waist and tail positions and getting no answer. Since my guns are hopelessly jammed I volunteer to go back and man the waist guns if necessary. I connect to a portable oxygen bottle and head aft, encountering top-turret gunner Eddy Guerry amidships. His entire Sperry Upper Local Turret has been blown away, but he does not appear to be badly injured. He has his chest pack on and helps me buckle mine to the harness. We proceed to the waist. Both John Heib the radio-operator and waist-gunner Samuel Rosenfeld are O.K. Dennis Cole lying on catwalk, left leg severely injured. Heib's chute pack had shrapnel hole in it but he buckles it on, anyway.

"The co-pilot Marvin Strohl and I help others to exit through the camera hatch. I am next to last to go out, catching flight boot on jagged part of airplane and cutting gash in my heel. I delay pulling ripcord but nothing happens until I free the pilot chute. Then I'm floating down but oscillating. Hit ground on back swing, injuring lower back.

People running towards me from the fields and village, many wearing wooden shoes. I think, "ah, Holland!" But then another figure approaches, waving a pistol. I see the Nazi insignia on his uniform. Truck arrives. Other American soldiers in it, including Ed Guerry and Burton Johns. We drive to place where we can see Dennis Cole lying on the ground in shock. I take off my flight jacket for use as a temporary splint. They take him away. Now we are taken to a nearby airstrip and separated from each other. I can hear Ed in the next room. They are threatening him and hurting him in some way. I call out to him, "Give them only name, rank, and serial number, Eddy!" Nazi Major rushes into my room. He is furious. Punches, slaps, and kicks me. Calls soldier with rifle. I am forced to run around airfield perimeter on injured foot, being prodded in the back by rifle. Now we are all put in cell with bars. Marvin Strohl has joined us. Later we were given ersatz coffee and schwarzbrot. German fighter pilot comes to view us, probably some of the same ones who had shot us down. Fitful sleep comes later.

The end of the war left many thousands of people, including me, unemployed and vainly searching for work. America was once again in a recession.

I eventually landed a night job in Oakland, driving a tow truck. This was a good job, interesting work, and well paid. Eventually I became restless and moved to Albuquerque where my cousin was living. My ambition was to finish college on the G.I. Bill. After a semester at the University of New Mexico, the old restlessness reasserted itself and I began taking flying lessons at Cutter Carr Airport in Albuquerque. But it soon became apparent that I was never going to be a really accomplished pilot. For one thing, I was becoming too reckless, preferring to "sideslip" in to land, for example, a perfectly valid manoeuvre except when performed at excessive speed.

Chastened after a couple of near disasters, I finally decided to leave the flying to others. When I met Kay, I was a psychological mess, again working a night job and trying to build up a Spanish Colonial furniture business. Kay was employed by Albuquerque Public Schools. She saw me through many of my bouts of depression and despair. Finally, after almost two years, we decided to tie the knot. Then another difficulty arose: my church would not marry us because of our previous divorces. I could neither understand nor accept this, and I left the Episcopal Church. We were married in the First Presbyterian in Albuquerque and have recently celebrated our fifty-sixth anniversary.

"We moved from New Mexico to Colorado in 1961, so that I could complete my Ph.D. at the University of Colorado, Boulder. I took a teaching job at Eastern Washington University as a Professor of Biology. I did teaching and research there during the next sixteen years, retiring in 1983. EWU was not Kay's cup of tea, so we lived mostly apart for ten years or so: she, in our Colorado Mountain cabin, and I in the Cheney house. During that time I was also wrestling with John Barleycorn. Finally, with the help of Alcoholics Anonymous, I got sober and have remained so for over twenty years now. It is a sad fact that most of my friends of previous years have had trouble with alcohol.

"Kay and I now live in Boulder. Margaret, my daughter, is happily married to David Brigham, and Sean, our grandson, now 15 is a delight.

Radio-operator **John N. Heib.**

Horace Simms writes: "We proceed to the waist. Both John Heib the radio-operator and waist-gunner Samuel Rosenfeld are Okay. Dennis Cole lying on catwalk, left leg severely injured. Heib's chute pack had shrapnel hole in it but he buckles it on, anyway."

John Heib did not survive the jump so we can safely assume that his parachute did not open correctly. The Individual Deceased Personnel File concerning Heib mentions that he was initially buried in Damme about 20 miles NE of the crash site of his bomber."

Tail-gunner **Dennis C. Cole** was born in July 1920 in Clinton Township, Vernon County, Wisconsin. His wife wrote the following bio.

"He grew up on a dairy farm which also raised tobacco in the summer for a cash crop. He and his brothers would often buy an older ewe in the fall hoping for a lamb the following year for extra spending money.

"Dennis along with his brothers, sister and cousins attended a one room school that could be seen from his home. The children would cut through the fields to attend this school on foot or sled since it was half de distance this way, rather than following the road which was a round about way. The name of this school was *Sugargrove* so named after the maple trees that grew in this area. He attended this school for seven years graduating with an eighth grade diploma. He was the only student in second grade and doing so well that the teacher promoted him to third grade.

"Although Dennis's mother wanted him to attend high school, his father, who did not believe it necessary to continue on the high school, overruled the idea and Dennis started working at various other farms doing everything from raising crops to milking cows by hand. Milking cows was one thing he would later in life never do even for his father in law. He would do anything else that his father in law needed done, but would not milk a cow. He eventually started on a crew building silos for farmers all over the area.

"In April of 1943 Dennis enlisted in the Army Air corps. While in military training Dennis met Carolyn Gertrude Iftner in St. Louis, Missouri. Dennis met Carolyn at a local dance hall by the name of Toon Town. They dated from 1943 until he went overseas in 1944. Prior to going overseas Dennis met his future in-laws Mr. And Mrs. Andrew Iftner, who thought the world of him. In fact any time that Dennis was to visit them his mother-in-law would be sure to bake him an apple pie even if it meant his father in law going all over Pike County Illinois for apples.

"On November 26, 1944, Thanksgiving, when his plane was shot down, he and fellow crew members parachuted to the ground where they were captured by the Germans. Dennis was wounded during the fighter attack and spent some time at the POW hospital in Osnabrück-Haste. The prisoners in the hospital lived on bread and water. The baking pans were lined with sawdust. Following his release Dennis would never eat whole wheat bread again.

"Johnny Heib was another member of the crew. Being Jewish, he made it known to others in his plane that he would never be captured by the Germans. He was known to carrying a hand gun on all missions. While Dennis hit the ground, he heard a shot and decided that it was Johnny shooting himself.

"The Allies liberated Dennis in the spring of 1945, Easter Sunday. He told me that one day the prisoners could hear the sound of fighting in the distance. The senior PW officers were seen talking to a prison guard, who was an American who was in Germany at the beginning of the war and was conscripted into the German Army. The following morning the guard was nowhere to be found and that afternoon the Allies rolled in liberating the prison camp.

"When Dennis was shot down, the war department sent his parents a telegram stating that he was reported missing. When Dennis' brother, Ray, returned from the Pacific, he was shown the telegram and told his parents that Dennis was probably dead. It wasn't until Dennis had re-

NOT HOME FOR CHRISTMAS

turned to the States that they learned he was alive. In 1945 telephone communication in the rural areas was not dependable, so when Dennis arrived on American soil with other POW's his first phone call was to Carolyn. He then contacted his parents while he was recuperating at a hospital in Chicago.

"Dennis married Carolyn on December 30, 1945 in Barry, Illinois. They were married for forty-four years. They had three daughters, Denise, Andrea and Melissa. With education being a priority in both parents minds, all have at least one college degree. Dennis also has four Grandchildren, Christina, Christofer, Alystra and Catherine.

"Following the war Dennis attended auto mechanic school and was an auto mechanic throughout his life.

"Dennis was an avid baseball fan (St. Louis Cardinals) and a fan of football. He was also active in Parent Teacher Organisations, any activities his daughters were involved in and in Square Dancing. For seven years he managed a girls' fastpitch softball team. This team won the Missouri-Illinois Championship two times.

"Following the war Dennis would suffer from a bone inflammation. Square Dancing would become the tool that we used to tell how he was feeling. If he did not want to go square dancing, all knew he was feeling very bad.

"In May 0f 1989 he was diagnosed with Colon Cancer. Dennis died April 17, 1990 in St. Louis, Missouri.

***

Acknowledgements:
Kay Voseipka Stocking for George K. Voseipka
Horace R. Simms
Carolyn and Denise Cole for Dennis C. Cole

CHAPTER 23

491ST BOMB GROUP
854TH BOMB SQUADRON

Aircraft Type: B-24J, Serial # 44-40172, "Grease Ball", MACR 11157, Airbase: North Pickenham

---

"A chance mishap occurred in the lead aircraft of the low squadron—the nose gunner brushed against the bomb toggle switch with his shoulder. (At this stage of the war most Lead aircraft carried an extra navigator. This put four people in the nose compartment of a B-24 which was overcrowded with three.) The entire squadron, as briefed, dropped on their leader and 30 tons went down into open fields 15 miles short of the target."

—491st Bomb Group's historian Al Blue about the 854th Bomb Squadron

---

Pilot: Lt. Robert W. Simons (POW) Algonac MI
Co-Pilot: 2Lt Charles M. Scott (POW) Huntington WV
Navigator: Lt. William H. Mooney (POW) Washington DC
Nose-Turret: S/Sgt Theodore Raybould (KIA) Stanton KY
Bombardier: 2LT. Thomas S. Tolin (KIA) Tyrone NM
Top-Turret: T/SGT Johnnie H. Martin Jr. (KIA) Belton TX
Radio-Operator: S/Sgt Donald U. Romberger (KIA) Pinegrove PA
Left-Waist: S/Sgt Harvey B. Duncan (KIA) Marion IN
Right-Waist: S/Sgt Robert Richards (KIA) South Whitley IN
Tail-Gunner: S/Sgt Robert J. Burnett (KIA) Washington Court House, OH

Total: 7 KIA, 3 POW
Target: Misburg
Crash Site: Northern Dankersen, E. of Minden, 57 Km W of Misburg
Time of Crash: 13.30

NOT HOME FOR CHRISTMAS

Jan Hey, in his summary of the Missing Air Crew Report pertaining to the crew of "Grease Ball":

"After bombing, 75 – 100 FW190s and Me109s attacked the formation. The intercom and alarm bell were shot out. It was impossible to move in the B-24 due to an uncontrollable fire raging in the bomb bay. Only three men could bail out. Radio-operator Donald Romberger and waist-gunner Harvey Duncan were killed during the fighter attack. Others in the rear were either also killed during the attack or when the plane exploded in mid-air.

"The bomber crashed in the northern part of the village of Dankersen, about forty miles west of the target Misburg, Germany. The wreckage was strewn over a large area.

The seven killed airmen of "Grease Ball" were buried in the civil cemetery of Dankersen. Their grave was marked with a cross "Here rest 7 American Soldiers". The local priest said that two men could not be identified. These must have been Richards and Duncan as the others were identified by name.

In 2007, pilot **Robert W. Simons** wrote about his November 26, 1944 mission:

"We completed our training at the end of July 1944 and were sent to England where we joined the 854th Bomb Squadron of the 491st Bomb Group.

"Our Co-Pilot Lt. Charles M. Scott ("Scotty") was a single engine trainee who was not needed so they sent him to be a co-pilot on four engine equipment. He was a quick learner and a very competent man in the right seat.

"We flew about fourteen or fifteen missions through flak areas but were never troubled by enemy fighters.

"On Sunday, November 26, 1944, at about three a.m. we were shaken awake to make another run over Nazi Germany. This seemed to be their favourite wake up time. Out we went to the unheated latrine to wash up and shave and then to the mess hall for breakfast. All had to be done at half trot as briefing session waited on no one.

"We were on the bomb run and about three or four minutes to the bomb zone - bomb bay doors open and heading for a sky full of nasty black flak then suddenly all bombs in our flight dropped. Who made this error I will probably never know.

491st Bomb Group, 854th Bomb Squadron

From left to right: Bombardier Thomas S. Tolin, pilot Robert W. Simons, co-pilot Charles M. Scott.

The following explanation is given by Al Bleu, the official historian of the 491st.

"..... A chance mishap occurred in the lead aircraft of the low squadron -- the nose gunner brushed against the bomb toggle switch with his shoulder. (At this stage of the war most Lead and Deputy Lead aircraft carried an extra, or pilotage, navigator who normally occupied the nose turret. This put four people in the nose compartment of a B-24 which was considered overcrowded with three. The entire squadron, as briefed, dropped on their leader and 30 tons went down into open fields 15 miles short of the target. In order to avoid further exposure to flak, which had become heavy since the IP, the low squadron veered away from the formation and angled for the rally point south of Hanover, bypassing the target."

Robert Simons continues:

"The pilot in the lead ship made a turn to the right, leaving the main groups to presumably avoid the flak field we were facing. This seemed a sensible thing to do and I was happy to be on our way home when I heard from my tail gunner that a fighter was closing in from the rear. My quick response was to feel free to shoot at him but I was very chagrined when he responded; "I can't - my guns are frozen." About then the hail hit us and bullets were sailing thru the cockpit area and through the instrument panel.

"This was just enough to damage two engines and cause run away props on both. Our electrical system was knocked out. This meant that we could not feather the props nor did we have any means to communicate with other areas of the ship.

"I must digress briefly here to introduce our navigator Lt. William "Bill" Mooney who was flying his last three missions with me. How he survived the first attack I do not know. I heard him yell that we had a bad fire in the bomb bay area and that he was leaving the ship. He bailed out at that time.

"Things were happening quite fast. We were hit again and this was unbelievable: no guns fired from my ship permitting the attacker taking his time and really socking it to us. Lead was literally flying thru the cockpit again and a small cannon shell hit the instrument panel - it now looked like a scrap heap. Scott and I were protected by armour plating to our rear and sides. If not for that we would never have survived.

"At this point it was just a question as to when the fire would catch the fuel tanks and blow us up with the plane. We were completely helpless and sitting there waiting for the inevitable. I motioned to Scott to go. When I left my seat my foot caught between the seat and the control pedestal and I was trapped. Off oxygen I lost consciousness. How I got out of that plane I will never know. The cold air revived me when I hit it. A short time later I pulled the rip cord and I was floating into enemy territory. It was only a matter of seconds after leaving the ship that I heard a loud "whoosh" when she finally blew up.

"I landed in the middle of a farmer's field. It was a little muddy. "Halt" seems to be a universal term. I saw a person with a gun aimed at me so I complied and walked out of the field. He was a local police man I guess and he made me go back and get my chute from the field. By that time I had quite an audience of women and children ogling this creature that had just dropped out of the sky. It was obvious to them that I was no threat as I was in a somewhat dazed condition. I had been badly burned on my left hand and slight burns around my face. The guard seemed to be aware of this and let me rest for a period of time before ushering me into town and the local jail. He did let me rest the chute on his bike during our procession into a small town called Bittburg.

"Scott came in from the other side of town. It was great to see him alive even though he had a black eye. Some civilian punched him. I had been lucky.

"We were put in separate rooms on the second floor of this building. There was a brick chimney and what was meant to be a bed next to it for some warmth. Not much. I was taken to a medic who cut my ring off a swollen finger then treated and bandaged my hand and face and sent me back to the room. It was a rather sleepless night as I had so much on my mind. A couple of times during the night someone came in and gave me a drink of delicious cold water served in a sardine can. Most welcome and appreciated.

"The following day they sent Scott and me on the road guarded by a young Austrian soldier: armed of course. We walked all day except for a mile or so we where taken on a farmer's hay wagon. The owner was not pleased but the guard was persuasive. Al this way I was carrying my parachute until mid afternoon the guard left it at some building. We were heading for the nearest train station it seemed. We boarded the train full of civilians and travelled thru the night. After dark the young soldier shared a cake with us.

"We arrived at some station of a large city: could have been Hanover? Red Cross ladies gave us coffee and a doughnut. Bless the Red Cross organization .We were then joined with a group like ourselves, and walked thru the very bombed out streets. A very old and bent lady with a cane hobbled by us and called us "Swinehunds". We were out of the city that night and were put in a hay barn to sleep.

"We were guarded there by about three young German soldiers. One of them spoke excellent English and we talked quite a bit during the evening He did ask at one point why we were fighting them and not the Russians. He was sure that we would soon be joining hands to campaign against the army from the east.

"We arrived at the interrogation centre Oberursel not far from Frankfort where we were put in solitary confinement. The room was about 6 by 8 feet. There was a cot as the only furniture. There also was a window and a light bulb that was turned off at about 7 p.m. There was no heat but fighting fleas kept me busy. The walls were like soft wallboard and a thumb nail indentation was my means of keeping track of days. Soup for dinner and ersatz bread with jam for breakfast. They did serve warm ersatz coffee.

They did go for a bit of interrogating twice but it was very low key and half hearted. I was in the office of the interrogator and his radio was giv-

NOT HOME FOR CHRISTMAS

ing a news update that he seemed to be very interested in. He then asked me if I knew what it was about and of course I didn't. He then told me that Von Rundstedt had just started an offensive that we call "The Battle of the Bulge". His next remark was: "I wonder why he did that?"

"A very kind young doctor or medic took care of my burned hand about once a week. He was very gentle and careful and seemed to be completely capable of handling burn problems. After treatment my hand would be bandaged in a paper like bandage that looked like our crepe paper we used to decorate with.

"Time passes so slowly when you have no one to talk to or even hear a human voice. At about seven p.m. they closed the shutters outside the window, barred it and the light went out indicating that another day had passed. I often thought: "When and how will this ever going to end?"

"It finally did end and I was sent to a staging area where there were many POWs waiting to be sent to their final permanent camp. Scott was also there and I had my first shower and shave since leaving England. We were also given small suitcases with clean trousers and a shirt, shaving equipment and a pipe and tobacco. That was in Wezlar.

"A couple days later we boarded the train for someplace. We were on a rail yard when the sirens started. The guards ran for cover but told us if we left the train we would be shot.

"My hand had been treated before we boarded the train and they had given us a box of medical supplies when we left. The next day I was getting rather sharp pains up my arm. I knew that an infection had set in so I opened the box. I found a bottle of antiseptic and soaked my bandaged hand with it and leaned back to see what happened. It worked.

"December 25th.we spent the night in the outskirts of Berlin. Dec. 27 we arrived in Barth, Germany and were marched through the snow to Stalag Luft 1.

"After the war I joined a close relative in the construction and real estate business, but I am not sure if that it was one of my smarter decisions. I did meet Barbara thru this venture and that was well worth everything. We raised three lovely daughters and have been married 56 years.

"After the construction venture I managed properties for about forty years. Half of this time was spent in Atlanta, Ga. I retired in 1986 and we returned to Florida to be nearer to the children. Not too close however. We now live in 55 and older community that is as near perfect as one could find and have everything we need here to be comfortable and a great social life.

491st Bomb Group, 854th Bomb Squadron

Back row, left to right: Pilot Robert W. Simons, Co-pilot Charles M. Scott, Bombardier Thomas Tolin, *John Fulmer
Front row, left to right: Top-turret gunner Johnnie H. Martin, Radio-operator Donald U. Romberger, Waist-gunner Robert Richards, Waist-gunner Harvey B. Duncan, Nose-turret gunner Theodore Raybould, Tail-gunner Robert J. Burnett.
*Did not participate in the November 26, 1944 mission.

The son of nose-turret gunner **Theodore Raybould's** brother wrote about his uncle:

"My grandfather, William John Raybould, was the son of a Methodist minister originally from Birmingham, England who immigrated to the United States in the 1880's. My grandmother, Margaret Raybould, was born on the family farm near Stanton in the 1880's to John and Amanda Johnson. Her family was also part of the original settlers in this part of Kentucky. My grandmother first married a young man by the last name of Vance. He was killed in a train accident shortly after his second daughter was born. A few years after his death my grandmother met the reportedly very engaging young travelling salesman, William J. Raybould, fell in love and married him. They had two son's together, my father William Raybould (no middle name) in 1921 followed by Teddy in 1925.

NOT HOME FOR CHRISTMAS

"My Raybould grandparents had a modern marriage before their time. He lived in Lexington running numerous business enterprises including a prosperous butcher shop and also as a successful thoroughbred horse trainer. He only visited my grandmother and her two sons for short stays. My grandmother lived with her brother, the local physician. Because of this my father related more to Dr. Ishmael Johnson (my great uncle) as his father than to his own father and I must assume Teddy did as well. When the war broke out my father was studying pre-medicine hoping to be a doctor like the man he grew up to admire. This turbulent time changed millions of lives, including his, as he did the patriotic duty and joined the Army Air Corp in the spring of 1942. He became a pilot and flew a PBY doing air rescue in North Africa in 1943. He returned to the States in 1944 to serve as a pilot instructor.

"Teddy, eager to be like his older brother enlisted in the Army Air Corp to be a pilot. He was disappointed not get his first choice of pilot training due to his age. He was gung ho to do his duty and went on to be a gunner on the "Grease Ball."

"My grandmother never got over the death of her baby boy. Some of my enduring memories of her were her re-reading the letters he had sent her that she kept next to her bible in her living room next to the fireplace. A large oil painting of Teddy hung over the fireplace (the painting had been done from a military photograph). This photograph now hangs over the fireplace at my parent's home. My grandmother also had a photograph of Teddy and his crew in front of the Grease Ball hanging in her bedroom. My father gave me this photograph along with his Air Medal, Purple Heart and citations and other memorabilia that I have displayed in my study at home.

"My grandfather Raybould died a year after Teddy was killed in action. My grandmother Raybould died in March 1969 while we were living in Wiesbaden, Germany just before my father retired from the Air Force. As I told you in my first correspondence, my father died in 1997 at the age of 76. His half sisters have also passed on so that generation on that side of the family has all passed on. They are dead but not forgotten, thanks to people like you. I and my two older brothers Ron and Roger and my mother are honoured to help us keep Teddy's memory alive. Our gut response when we heard about your interest in Teddy was to tell my father, but sadly he is gone too, but it brightens our memories to know he is in a sense being brought back to life.

491st Bomb Group, 854th Bomb Squadron

About bombardier **Thomas S. Tolin** we only have a page of his Individual Deceased Personnel File:

Statement

about the crash of an American plane in the northern part of the village Dankersen on the 26th of November 1944.

On Sunday, the 26th of November 1944 at ohne o'clock in the afternoon, the village of Dankersen had flyer-alarm for 2nd time. Big formations were flying over us in direction West, so we went into cellar of the priest's house.

After a short time (about half past one) we heard the falling of heavy pieces and thought, it must be bombs, but no detonation occured. Some hours later on, I was told by children, that a 4 motored bomber had crashed in many parts in the northern part of the village. Still long time I saw the remains lying in a space of 1000 m. Children told to me, that some soldiers had come to ground without parachut in Dankersen likely 2 or 3.

Next day I heard, that in the plane also some dead fliers were found. I myself did not go to the place, unless to make a curious impression; furthermore I was refused by the Party, which was responsible for the salvage.

In the Month of Obtober a plane had com to ground in our vicinity, in Wietersheim, and therfore I knew, that a priest must be present at a burial and I waited to be informed, at what time these dead soldiers would be buried. On Monday, in the afternoon, I was told, that the burial already had occured on Monday-noon; during the night the bodies lay in the fire-station. About details of the burial I heard nothing. Unfortunately our caretaker of the cemetery was murdered by some Polish on the 11th of April. Who else has been present at the burial, I cannot say. Then I took care, that the grave of the dead soldiers were marked with a cross.

As the names and personalities of the deceased, I had inquired without result at Minden, Lahde and the Burgermeister of Dankersen; then I got an answer from Gütersloh (Fl.Pl.Kdo.Detmold, Flugleitung); 5 names with identification tags were indicated to me; moreover the remark: Names and rank of other 3 dead members of the crew could not be established, as these 3 already had been buried at the arrival of the taking-over-command. Besides those dead soldiers had "according to the information of the Burgermeister Piepenbrink, no legetimations and identification tags.

I remark to this, that the number 3 is not certain; it is possib that it were only 2 soldiers.

Das evangl.luth.Pfarramt Dankersen
G l u e r , Pastor.

Certified true copy

JOHN S H A N N O N , 2nd Lt.Inf.
46th QM.G.R.CO.,Disinterring Officer.

NOT HOME FOR CHRISTMAS

About top-turret gunner **Johnnie H. Martin Jr**. his daughter Kay Martin Sandhoff wrote:

"Johnnie was born on October 31, 1916, near Temple, Texas. He was the son of John H. Martin, Sr., a Baptist minister, and his wife, Emma Gorden Martin, a homemaker, and was the youngest of 3 children. He attended Temple public elementary and high schools.

"Johnnie married Martha Mae Sandlin Martin in October, 1939. He worked for Lone Star Gas Company when he volunteered for the Army Air Corps on November 9, 1944, at Ft. Sam Houston, San Antonio, Texas. He was sent to Blackland Army Air Field in Waco, Texas, where he served as a mechanic for the airplanes used by the cadets stationed there. His only child, Margaret Kay Martin, was born in Waco, Texas in 1943.

Johnnie H. Martin Jr.

"He could have stayed at Blackland as an airplane mechanic for the duration of the war, but Johnnie volunteered for overseas duty because, "I don't want someone else doing my fighting for me."

"Johnnie took overseas training at Tonopah Army Air Field in Tonopah, Nevada, from March, 1944, to August, 1944. He arrived in Europe around September 1, 1944. Johnnie was stationed at North Pickenham in England and flew with the Simons crew as flight engineer and top-turret Gunner. He was on his 15th mission when the 491st Bomb Group, 854th Squadron, was attacked by German fighters.

Waist-gunner **Robert Richards** was probably an orphan boy.

Robert lived with Effie Belle Hays Mink. Her granddaughter wrote about her:

My grandmother was widowed and lived alone on a farm a few miles from the small town of South Whitley in Indiana. She was small of stature, five feet tall. She raised leg horn chickens and gathered and crated the eggs to sell for her livelihood. Being in advanced years and needing help, she "took in" Robert Richards to give him a home and to have help

Robert Richards with his two nieces

with the hard work on the farm. He loved her dearly, as she was a very positive person who lived her Christian faith and values daily. They had a great relationship. When he was killed, his life insurance policy was made out to my grandmother, and that was a financial help the rest of her life. Otherwise, she would have had very little money. A beautiful story.

***

Acknowledgements:
Robert W. Simons
Jan Hey of the Netherlands
Ted Raybould for nose-turret gunner Theodore Raybould
Jo Ellen Adams for waist-gunner Robert Richards

CHAPTER 24

491ST BOMB GROUP
854TH BOMB SQUADRON

Aircraft Type: B-24J, Serial # 44-40271,
"House of Rumor", MACR 10766
Airbase: North Pickenham

"I found the gunners Yuzwa, Caruso, and Byrnes completely ignoring the order to bail out. Yuzwa absolutely refused to stop firing and to put on his parachute."

—Bombardier Harry W. Sonntag when going through the plane to make sure all crew members had heard the bail out bell

---

Pilot: 1Lt George A. Meuse (POW), Brookline MA

Co-Pilot: 2Lt Richard G. Lipinski (POW) Milwaukee WI

Navigator: 2Lt Fred V. Willis Jr. (POW)*

Bombardier: 1Lt Harry W. Sonntag (POW)*

Flight Engineer: T/Sgt John W. Eldridge (KIA) Elmira NY

Radio: T/Sgt Russell D. Dennis (POW), Manalapan NJ

Nose Gunner: S/Sgt Samuel Yuzwa (KIA)*

Right W. Gunner: S/Sgt Michael A. Gallo (POW) Binghamton NY

Left W. Gunner: S/Sgt Joseph R. Caruso (KIA)*

Tail Gunner: S/Sgt Hartwell P. Byrnes (KIA)*

* Hometown not available

Total: 4 KIA, 6 POW

Target: Misburg (Hannover)

Crash Site: North of the railway line from Hannover to Minden, near Stone 24.3 at Nordsehl. This is 15 km NE of Minden

Time of Crash: 13.00 h.

NOT HOME FOR CHRISTMAS

The Dutchman **Jan Hey**, writes about this bomber:

"Shortly after bombing the # 3 engine was set afire by 20 mm shells from German fighters and the bail-out order was given. Apparently the gunners in the waist did not hear the alarm bell as they were still firing at the German fighters when there was an explosion in the waist, probably by a flak shell because the 22nd Flak division claimed this aircraft.

"The sergeants Caruso, Byrnes and Yuzwa were buried in the civil cemetery at Meerbeck.

"In 5 films M1217 (Nat. Archives) with the "War Crimes Trials in Dachau" is case 12-1534 against five Germans who got two years imprisonment when they beat and kicked Lts. Lipinski and Willis after capture at Lauenau.

Pilot **George Meuse** wrote the following story about his experiences on that Sunday in November 1944.

"Our mission was Misburg, Germany, an oil refinery just outside Hannover, located in the north central part of the country. It was my twelfth mission and I felt much more confident about my flying abilities than on my first mission. The weather was clear and sunny, but very cold at our bombing altitude; about 25000 feet.

"After an early wake-up, about 04.30, thirty B-24's of the 491st Bomb Group took off and formed over England for the mission to Misburg. En route two aircraft aborted and returned to base, leaving twenty-eight bombers to continue. Due to various errors, almost thirty minutes separated the 1st Division of B-17's from our 2nd Division of B-24's, probably the primary cause for the losses suffered by the 491st Bombardment Group. Luftwaffe fighters shot down four of the B-17's ahead of us, spreading our fighter forces even more.

"We were flying "tail end charley" in the 854th Bomb Squadron formation as we turned at the Initial Point for the bomb run. Heavy flak bursts ahead indicated the target area as we came under attack from over a hundred enemy fighters. Out of sixteen, we were the fourth B-24 shot down; lost in a little over fifteen minutes of very intense enemy attacks. Our number thee engine was of fire and our electrical system was damaged, causing all the turbochargers to fail. At over 25'000 feet this was like shutting off all engines. We fell like a large rock.

"My co-pilot Dick Lipinski was unable to extinguish the engine fire and flames were passing the rear gunners hatch. I gave the bail out order,

491st Bomb Group, 854th Bomb Squadron

turned on the alarm bell and announcing "Bail out" over the intercom. After I saw the nose-gunner pass by, I got up to jump. At that moment we were rammed in the rear by an out-of-control fighter. I dove thru the bomb bay and fell until I could see buildings before pulling my rip cord. Six crew members got out of the front and one from the rear of "House of Rumor".

Back row, left to right: Waist-Gunner Michael Caruso, Co-Pilot Dick Lipinski, Engineer John Eldridge, Pilot George Meuse, Navigator Fred Willis, Waist-Gunner Michael Gallo
Front row, left to right: Tail-Gunner Hartwell Byrnes, Radio-Operator Russell Dennis, Nose-Gunner Samuel Yuzwa

Here I interrupt George Meuse's story to include what bombardier Harry Sonntag reported after the war:

"As the pilot rang the bailout bell, I went through the plane making sure that everyone had the word. I found Nose-Gunner Samuel Yuzwa, Waist-Gunner Joseph Caruso and Tail-Gunner Hartwell Byrnes completely ignoring the order to bail out. Yuzwa absolutely refused to stop firing and to put on his parachute.

Sonntag was blown out while checking the rear escape hatch and the three gunners went down with the plane.

NOT HOME FOR CHRISTMAS

George Meuse continues:

"I landed in some trees on the side of a hill and ended up suspended about thirty feet in the air, hanging in my parachute harness, between three trees. By swinging back and forth, I was able to wrap my legs around one tree trunk and I planned on sliding down to the ground below. However, when I hit my parachute quick release, I was unable to grab the tree with my hands, so I slid upside down and knocked myself out when I hit the ground.

"After several minutes, I recovered and crawled away from the tree and hid in some bushes while I assessed the situation. The temperature was about 40° with some snow in gullies. I was wounded in the right ankle, had only one boot and was obviously dressed differently than a German. I did not speak or understand German. I could hear people searching thru the woods. I made the decision to bury my .45 pistol as there was no way to avoid being captured.

"I saw a German nearby with a young boy helping him. Occasionally he would fire his rifle into a large chump of bushes too big to search. After he fired nearby, I crawled out and surrendered. The young boy ran off, which I thought was unusual. Later, as I was being beaten and set up for execution against a wall, the young boy came back with his father, August Hausser, a forester, who fired his pistol in the air to stop the civilians from beating me.

"August helped me to his home where his wife bandaged me and gave me some bread and ersatz coffee. August spoke a little English and explained that he saved me because his son, in the Afrika Korps, was captured in North Africa and was then a prisoner of war in Nebraska, USA. I read a letter from his son that told of his good treatment by the Americans. August turned me over to his friend, the chief of police of Reinsdorf über Haske. The chief protected me from the angry mob and turned me over to the Luftwaffe in Wunsdorf, near Hannover the next day.

"Hausser wrote me in 1949 asking for help with the British Authorities who had been told by the local people that he was a Nazi. Because I had recently completed Atom Bomb School in Albuquerqeu, I was not permitted to correspond with Hausser who was a foreign national. However, I was able to write a letter thru the State Department vouching for his help in saving my life.

About his life after WW II, George wrote;

"Flo and I married in July 1945 and I remained in military service after my release from various hospitals in 1946. I regained flying status and flew numerous aircraft, at least fifteen different types including the B-29 I flew sixty missions in over Korea.

"I was in Strategic Air Command and B-29's for about seven years flying all over the world while attending Atom Bomb School. I was in aircraft maintenance on KC97's, which was interrupted by a tour in Vietnam as an adviser to the Viet Nam Air force flying F8F Bearcats: a very exciting assignment. Along the way Flo raised four daughters, which was one reason for me to retire after all these tours away from home. I said farewell to the Air Force as a Lieutenant Colonel early 1965.

"We moved to NE to enable me to complete my degree at UNO and to look for employment, which I found flying to the owner of Brandeis Department Stores in his Lear Jet. He taught me retailing and for twelve years I loved my work. I retired (again) in 1977 as Vice-President of the company.

"We moved to our summer house in MO at The Lake of the Ozarks, where a partner and I operated an airport, offering flight instruction, maintenance, charters and air ambulance until 1982 when I sold my interest. I kept a few customers to fly for, since they wanted to fly with me only. In 1989 I put my license away and haven't flown since.

Co-pilot **Richard "Dick" G. Lipinski** told the following story to his granddaughter Courtney Lynn :

"It was Sunday, November 26, 1944. That day began in the usual manner; early wake up call, breakfast, briefings, equipment and a ride to the hard stand for a crew meeting prior to take off. From the moment my B-24 bomber, "The House of Rumor," left the ground, my life changed drastically for six months. My name is Richard Lipinski. Here is my story.

"I woke up at 7:00 p.m. on the last Sunday in November. That very day, everyone in the 491st Bomb Group, including myself, slumped out of bed, quickly dressed, and made the way down to the mess hall for breakfast. After breakfast we proceeded to the briefing room, where we learned our target for the day was the Misburg synthetic fuel plant in Germany. From there, everyone headed toward the equipment room where we gathered our necessary accessories and appliances for that day's quest. In the midst of all this equipments, we withdrew our electrically-heated flying suits, our fleece-lined outer suits, oxygen masks, and other important gear needed for the bombing mission.

NOT HOME FOR CHRISTMAS

"My crew and I set out to prepare our plane "The House of Rumor" for take off. We were excited for the mission because we had recently installed new windshield side armor and coffin seats in our bomber. The weather was not too good for take off that day. It had been raining most of the night and puddles had formed everywhere, including on the runway.

"When the time came for take off, I climbed into the passenger seat, taking my role as the co-pilot. The pilot of my plane and my best friend in the squadron, George Meuse, climbed in the left hand seat shortly after me. The seven other crew members of "The House of Rumor", crawled into the back of the plane, attending to their duties prior to take off. Prepared, we waited for the green flare to signal us out onto the runway. Before long, the green flare blinked brightly, and we made our way toward the runway. Every plane took off with 30-second intervals.

"When our turn came, George stepped on the brakes and built up engine power. As the final signal came, George took his foot off the brakes and the plane accelerated down the runway, splashing through puddles and throwing up big sprays of water. Out the corner of my eye, I saw the chaplain giving blessings to all the planes leaving on the mission. George had no difficulty climbing into formation altitude once we had left the ground. I did not know it at the time, but from the moment I left the ground in "The House of Rumor," on that late November morning, I would not return for six months. Sadly, I was unable to receive a proper goodbye from my sweetheart, Isabel, who would remain alone in North Pickenham, England.

"The flight to Misburg was pleasantly short, but immensely cold. By the time we had reached twenty-thousand feet, the air was piercing, temperatures as low as twenty-five degrees centigrade. Even with our electrically-heated flying suits, I was cold. When we were nearing Misburg, we were informed that our squadron was thirty minutes late.

"Apparently, the storm clouds that had been stationed over North-West Germany a week ago had long since moved on, for the sky over Misburg was cloudless. Even though the cloudless sky made our vision relatively good, the Germans were given a clear visibility range of our planes. Even from the sky, it wasn't hard to miss the vapor trails our planes were setting off. The German air defense fighters were able to set up their attack in good time. A force of fifty to eighty German fighters went into action against the 855th Squadron ahead of us. At our altitude, the sky was clear and we could see the flak ahead over the target as we approached Misburg. Unknowing the outcome of the first squadron at the time, we continued on toward the flak and were suddenly attacked by German FW

190s. Our own fighters had been turned away to help protect some B-17 ahead of us.

"Abruptly, we became an independent plane fighting for survival. I will admit that at this time, I had tingling nerves spreading throughout my body. I was excited, anxious, nervous, and terrified all at the same time! The clear sky had suddenly become filled with the sound of machine-gun fire. Before long we had a German FW 190 attempting to shoot us down. George struggled to escape the German FW 190's machine guns, but we were hit within a matter of time. We had been badly struck by the enemy fighters, causing our third engine to catch fire. The flames were creeping down along the right side, entering the tail compartment. We tried to stay in formation but we were hit again. This time, we lost our electrical system, making the turbo supercharges in the engines inoperative. At this time we dropped our bombs, and shortly after our plane began to fall straight down at a rapid speed. I had a terribly dizzy sensation of downward pulling as the plane dropped into lower and lower altitudes. Suddenly, there was an explosion in the rear of the plane. At once, George commanded it was time to bail out. I rang the alarm bell for the eight other crew members to hear in the back.

"Before turning to open the door, I took one last glance at George, not knowing if I would ever see him again. Aware that I was running out of time, I turned and opened the door. I jumped and after a few seconds of falling I pulled the rip cord. My parachute opened. Coming closer and closer to making contact with the ground, I somehow managed to crash into a small gathering of pine trees. I was tangled on one of the trees and attempted to break free by swinging myself back and forth. Looking back at this situation many years later, I realize that it was a stupid idea. I ended up falling backward, knocking myself against one of the trees, and becoming unconscious. I regained consciousness as I was entangled from the trees by German soldiers and then beaten by them with the butts of their rifles. I was captured and became a prisoner of war.

"The German soldiers took me to Wetzlar. I stayed there for ten days, getting very little to eat and waiting for whatever was next. I hadn't seen any crew members until our pilot George Meuse showed up who told me had landed near Reinsdorf. He too was beaten by German soldiers but was rescued by a man called August Hauser. He stayed with Hauser for a week but was then turned over to the Luftwaffe. George arrived just in time for us to leave on December 10, 1944, for Stalag Luft One in Barth, Germany. Before we left, we were both given a Red Cross parcel containing underwear, towels, nylon socks, chewing gum, cigarettes and a little food.

NOT HOME FOR CHRISTMAS

"When George, twenty-four other prisoners, and myself arrived at Stalag Luft One, we were taken to our rooms immediately after roll call. George and I shared a double bunk bed. Each bed was made of six wooden slats. The mattress was a potato sack which contained a cushion of mixed wood chips and sawdust. All of the prisoners were given one small blanket, hardly enough to cover a man from his shoulders to his feet. The first night was bitterly cold and I remember not sleeping much because the cold kept my teeth shattering and my eyes open and alert. The following night, George and I decided to sleep on the bottom bunk together. Covering ourselves with two blankets, we snuggled together. This made the night somewhat warmer than the night before. George and I continued sleeping this way for the next six months. However, the nights were still chilly because most of the time there was no heat. To make thing worse, it was one of the coldest and longest winters that Germany had experienced in years.

"Throughout the entire six months, the Germans fed us poorly and I lost weight to the point were I was unhealthily thin. Electricity rarely worked, and throughout the entire six months I only had one shower. The stove in our room was made of powdered milk cans and it heated the room poorly.

"To pass the time, many of us wrote poetry. Some others painted or drew pictures of the camp surroundings. Overall, it was a very harsh and tiresome time at Stalag Luft One. The days slowly passed by, and the nights were even longer.

"On May 1, 1945, we were liberated by Russian soldiers. The Russians drove their tanks through the barbed wire fences around Stalag Luft One. The Russian officers drove in cattle, which they shot and fed to us. They also brought horse-drawn wagons filled with loads of potatoes for us to eat. After celebrating for many days, all prisoners were flown out in B-17s. We were flown to France on May 17, were deloused, shaved and given new uniforms. From there we went by train to Camp Lucky Strike where a great many ex-prisoners were waiting for ships to take them back to America again. I went back to England and to Isabel.

"In mid June, I hitched a ride to North Pickenham. I was excited to see Isabel again and to start our lives together! I dreamed about sweeping her off her feet and giving her a big kiss as compensation for all those months. The war was over and I was a happy man.

"When I arrived, I found myself on Isabel's doorstep with a bouquet of white lilies in my hand. I rang the bell, and a few seconds later Isabel appeared in the doorway. From the sight of me she jumped back in shock and her breath stirred in amazement. Suddenly, she wrapped her arms and held me tightly. When I let her go, she was trembling and tears were melting down her face. She invited me in for tea and showed me all the articles she had saved on the Misburg mission. There was a particular one that had listed the planes that had crashed on November 26, 1944. "The House of Rumor" was listed and she told me she thought I had died in the crash. She explained that through her grieving she had met someone else and he had proposed. She was going to get married in two weeks. I was devastated, shocked, angry, and heartbroken. We had a long farewell and then I left her forever. I did not want to be in town for the wedding, so I returned home to the States on a hospital ship. When I arrived at New York City, I went back to Milwaukee, Wisconsin, where I started my life as a city clerk for the government. Years later, I married and had three beautiful children.

The fate of engineer **John W. Eldridge** was unclear for quite some time. German authorities mentioned the capture of the six airmen who had saved themselves by parachute and the burial of three crew members Caruso, Byrnes and Yuzwa who were found in the wreck of the bomber. That left John Eldridge as unaccounted for.

After the war, co-pilot Richard Lipinski made the following statement about him:

> "I saw him preparing to bail out. When I finally was ready to bail out myself and proceeded towards the bomb bay he was no longer on the flight deck. I sincerely believe he bailed out before I did. I also believe he might have been beaten to death by the Volksturm as I nearly was.

Early 1949, Clyde Fanning, a U.S. military investigator went to Nordsehl in Germany where "House of Rumor" had crashed to collect details of John Eldridge. He reports:

> "Eldridge was a crew member of a B-24 J, which crashed on 26 November 1944 next to an embankment in the area of the domain Brandenburg, community Nordsehl. Three remains have been recovered and reburied in U.S. They were exhumed from Meerbeck, this is the competent parish for Nordsehl. Records lists three dead and six captured but also the name of Eldridge is mentioned. However no further information is given. The six captured crew members have returned to Military Control. The only

NOT HOME FOR CHRISTMAS

unaccounted for casualty is T/Sgt. Eldridge. It was revealed from other statements that the aircraft crashed near Wunstorf, Germany. Subject deceased was last seen preparing to bail out.

"Upon my arrival I went to the Police-Station of Lauenhagen, where I was told that there were no other bodies nor parts of bodies found in the plane wreckage, except the three deceased mentioned above. The plane came from the East or North-East. No parachutists were sighted in this area.

"I then contacted the Community Director of Meerbeck, where the three deceased had been buried. He gave a statement to that fact and also that nobody has any knowledge about the fate of the rest of the crew, no parachutists were seen there.

"Then I obtained a statement from the gravedigger Mr. Watermann. He states that there were only three deceased buried in the cemetery. The son of the local priest in Meerbeck, Mr. Hans-Martin Sturhan states, that he saw three bodies in the wreckage the day after the crash, who were buried later in Meerbeck.

"I then checked with police stations, town mayors, and other authorities to locate the area where the six parachutists were taken prisoner. I checked an area of about 80 square miles but with negative result.

"The plane crashed against a railroad track bed in the area of Brandenburg near Meerbeck, Germany. One wing of the plane landed on the railroad tracks and the other wing landed out in the field. The plane was burning prior to the time it crashed and continued to burn after it crashed. The local police stated that the plane did not cause a crater. Wreckage of the plane has since been removed.

So it remained unclear what had happened to Eldridge until the connection was made with an unknown airman found not far from where one of the surviving crew members was captured. The Individual Deceased Personnel File pertaining to Eldridge says:

"X-6428 was found in the woods near Reinsdorf and buried in the cemetery of Apelern. Tooth chart, height and colour of hair, date and place of death for x-6428 are in agreement with comparable points for T/Sgt. Eldridge.

In January 1950, John W. Eldridge was buried in his home town Elmira, NY.

***

Acknowledgements:
George Meuse
Individual Deceased Personnel File pertaining to engineer John W. Eldridge
Courtney Lynn for co-pilot Dick Lipinski

CHAPTER 25

491ST BOMB GROUP
854TH BOMB SQUADRON

Aircraft Type: B-24J, Serial # 42-51253,
MACR 11108
Airbase: North Pickenham

"My top-turret dome was blown off, my left .50 caliber machine gun was gone, my computer sight right in front of me was gone, my steel helmet was gone, my oxygen mask was knocked loose and I had to grab it so I could keep breathing."

—Top-turret gunner Dale Allan after having been attacked by German fighters

---

Pilot: Lt John S. Warczak Jr. (KIA) Chicago IL
Co-Pilot: 2Lt Charles D. Miller (POW) Hemet CA
Bombardier: 2Lt Robert J. Brennan (KIA) Hingham MA
Nose Turret: S/Sgt William R. Boling (KIA) Canton GA
Top-Turret: T/Sgt Dale E. Allan (POW) Craig MO
Radio-Operator: S/Sgt Earl R. Hoppe Jr. (POW) Abilene TX
Left-Waist: S/Sgt Harold E. Henley (POW) Bristol VA
Right-Waist: S/Sgt Walker E. Conrad (POW) Jonesboro AR
Tail-Gunner: S/Sgt Carl W. Groshell (POW)*

* Hometown not available

Total: 3 KIA, 6 POW
Target: Misburg
Crash Site: Bledeln, 15 km N of Hildesheim
Time od Crash: 12.40

NOT HOME FOR CHRISTMAS

It was a patched up crew.

On September 9, 1944 Pilot John Warczak had technical problems just after take-off. One engine caught fire at 400 feet followed by a second engine at 900 feet. Warczak was unable to maintain altitude and to drop his bomb load. The pilot crash landed the plane but the fully loaded bomber caught fire immediately. The pilots could evacuate the plane through the broken windshield and also the two waist gunners escaped uninjured. The bombardier and the engineer bailed out but because of the low altitude their parachutes did not open.

*Standing, left to right: Co-pilot Charles D. Miller, * navigator Robert C. Bacher, *pilot Loren W. Meyer, bombardier Robert J. Brennan*
*Sitting, left to right:Waist-gunner Harold E. Henley, *waist-Gunner Joseph E. DeBrule,*radio-operator Albert T. McMillian, * tail-gunner Jesus Brisino, *waist-gunner Richard Wallace, top-turret gunner Dale E. Allan*
*did not fly with Pilot Warczak on the November 26, 1944 mission

Co-pilot **Charles D. Miller** was born on April 5, 1924, in Des Moines, Iowa.

Charles moved to Hemet, CA, with his family in or about 1925 and attended school in Hemet for 13 years until his graduation in 1942. He joined the Army Air Corp in 1942 or 1943. He was shot down over France and made it back to his base before being shot down again in Germany on Sunday, November 26, 1944.

He returned home and worked in the Los Angeles area for a while before moving to New Mexico where he worked as a Security Guard at the Los Alamos Atomic plant. Went to work for the State police and was stationed in Santa Fe, New Mexico where he married his 2nd wife Wanda. He returned to Hemet in the late 1950's where he worked with his father H.L. Miller as a partner in the Valley Paving Company until his retirement.

He passed away in 1988 and found his final place of rest at the Riverside National Cemetery, a military facility about thirty miles from Hernet.

Not many airmen could claim having bailed out of a stricken bomber three times in WW II but this happened to Top-turret gunner **Dale E. Allan.** He wrote in 1987:

"Our crew picked up our new B-24 in Topeka Kansas in July 1944. We left Topeka Kansas on 16 July 1944 - I can remember this date as it was my 22nd birthday. We flew to Bangor Maine and were detained there a few days because of bad weather. We left Bangor, and I believe we made a stop in Labrador and then a trip to Greenland. I know we flew up between the mountains and had to make a quick turn to the right to hit the runway at sea level. We stayed there a few days and flew on to Iceland and made a stop and then on to Wales. We left our B-24 there as it had to go through modifications. In Bangor Maine we had a pretty girl picture painted on her right front with the name - "The Travelling Bag".

"After a little training somewhere in England we were sent by train to 491st Bomb Group, 854 Bomb Squadron at North Pickenham.

"On our 5th mission (this was on 13th of September 1944) we were bombing Schwabische Hall and we were hit in the bomb bay by flak. The control cables were cut going to the tail section but we managed to make it back to the front line and were advised there was a storm over the Channel. We knew that in our condition we could not fly through a storm

NOT HOME FOR CHRISTMAS

or even bad weather. I was helping the pilot to control the tail section by pulling cables from the bomb bay.

We all bailed out and were picked up by the French underground who got us back into American hands, after we proved we were Americans. We walked and hitch-hiked back to Paris where we checked into a special hotel and from there we were flown back to England to rejoin our Group. At this time we were given a ten day flak leave. Then back to flying again.

"On our 7th mission we had a very close burst of flak under our left wing that really rocked the B-24 but we could not see any damage However, when we got back to our base our left

Dale E. Allen

landing gear would not lock down. We were advised to fly to Woodbridge, an airstrip for damaged planes that were expected to crash. The pilot and co-pilot kept wobbling the B-24 and at about the time of landing our left landing gear locked down and we made a safe landing at the time. Next day back to the 491st again.

"On our 8th mission, 9 October 1944 our target was Koblenz. Just after we had dropped our bombs we had a very near burst of flak and you could hear the schrapnel rattling the plane. Our gas lines were hit and gas was leaking badly. The waist-gunners and tail-gunner were soaked with gas. The gas fumes were going out the bomb bay and out the tail section. Other planes advised us to bail out before the plane brew up. We were not too eager to bail out again so with the consent of the pilot we choose to stay with the plane as long as possible. We all put our chutes on exept pilot and co-pilot and their chutes were right close so they could grab if necessary.

"We kept flying towards home until the engines started cutting out from lack of fuel. We were above clouds just at the time and not sure where we were. I went back to the waist and also got soaked in gas and told the pilot to order bail out and that I would count the chutes. I told the pilot from the waist every one was out except himself, the co-pilot and myself and as soon as I quit talking I would go through the back hatch and wait for him and the co-pilot to jump. The bomber was quickly losing altitude.

491st Bomb Group, 854th Bomb Squadron

"This time I pulled the rip cord as soon as I went out the back hatch and this gave me an awful jolt but I sure felt good that the chute had opened. Again we landed in France and again the French underground helped us back to American controlled territory. Again we walked and hitch-hiked back to Paris and checked into the designated hotel. I was put in a French hospital the day after we bailed out as I was caughing and spitting up blood. I stayed in hospital a couple of days and the bleeding stopped. I do not know what the matter was. Again we were flown back to England and to the 491st Bomb Group. We were again given a ten days flak leave.

"The navigator Lt. Backer was put on a lead plane. The rest of the crew still wanted to fly. We were given a pilot by the name of John Warczak who had crashed back in England a short time before and a gunner by the name of Conrad and a gunner by the name of Sgt. Croshell.

"My 11th and last mission was on November 26, 1944 with as target Misburg.

After briefing we went out to the airplane and I found that it was covered with ice and frost. Impossible to see out of the windshield or turrets. We washed the airplane with de-ice fluid to help clean off the ice.

"We were told that the glass would clean up when we got to altitude but even when we joined the formation we still could not see properly. We had a hard time getting into formation as the windshield did not clear up. The co-pilot Lt. Miller was doing a lot of the flying looking out the right cockpit window to stay in formation. I finally got up in the top-turret and could not see out of it either. I kept a hole cleaned up on the right side of my turret with my glove so I could see a little of the outside world.

"At some time around Initial Pount our fighter escort left us.. We were getting heavy flak at this time. Suddenly the flak stopped and we knew that we were going to be in trouble. I was slowly moving my turret around clockwise looking out the hole in the right side of the turret that I was keeping clear with my glove. Suddenly with my guns pointed over the left wing and me looking through the front of plane thru my hole I saw this bunch of FW 190's heading straight at us. I hollered at the pilot and about that time it looked like the wings of the FW 190's were on fire and about that instant later I knew what this fire meant.

"My top-turret dome was blown off, my left .50 caliber machine gun was gone, my computer sight right in front of me was gone, my steel helmet was gone, my oxygen mask was knocked loose and I had to grap it so I could keep breathing. My turret was dead. I dropped the seat and got out to see if I could help the pilot and co-pilot. My flak vest just fell in pieces. The back of my turret seat was reddish. I could feel pain in my right left leg. It felt like a burning.

"I got between the pilot and co-pilot and could see that the windshield was shattered. I looked at the pilot and his face was bloody. I reached for the throttles to open them up. We were heading down. The right inboard engine was on fire. The co-pilot called me to bail out as we were done for. I got my chute on and helped the radio-operator with his. The radio-operator went ahead of me and when I went through the bomb doors I also got burned on the forehead.

"I waited a few seconds before I opened my chute and saw the plane blow up. I did not know who all got out. The sky was full of planes going down and I could see other parachutes in the air. On the way down a German fighter headed for me and I thought this was the end but he turned off and just circled me. Closer to the ground I could hear gun shots and saw someone running in my direction. I hit the ground pretty hard, the wind was blowing and I had a hard time to spilling the wind out of my chute. I finally got the chute off and by this time the German was pretty close and yelling for me to put my hands up. Thank god that I was not wearing my .45 pistol that day. I lost it on the 2nd bail-out and had not been issued another. It was a German civilian who captured me and as soon as he found out that I was not armed he beat the hell out of me. Both legs were hurting me and the burn on the forehead also.

"Finally a German soldier came to my rescue and made him quit the beating. I was forced to pick up my parachute and carry it about a mile to an old barn. There were about a dozen other prisoners ahead in there, we were not allowed to talk. In just a little while I saw them bring our co-pilot in. He got close to me and whispered he thought the pilot John Warczak was killed and that the bombardier Robert Brennen was blown out off the plane.

"I was taken to a hospital in Hildesheim, Germany, and I stayed there for about a month. Also in hospital was waist-gunner Harold Henley. His face was badly burned . His eyelids were burned off and when he closed his eyes he would only roll them up in his head. The hands of the other waist-gunner Carl Croshell were badly burned: you could almost see the bones. The only treatment we got was powder sprinkled on our wounds and wrapping in paper bandages.

"I was taken from the hospital to Oberursel near Frankfort for interrogation and then to Wetzlar to be assigned to a camp. I was goaded in a box car and headed for Barth at the Baltic Sea. The English were bombing the railroad by night and the Americans during the day. We never made it to Barth. We were locked in a box car in Berlin for eight days and nights before they finally put me in a camp thirty miles South of Berlin in a town called Luckenwalde. We were liberated by the Russians in the early part of May.

"I was married in 1942 to my present wife Jane and we just celebrated my 65 birthday and also one of my grandsons' birthday. I have three children. One boy who was born in February 1945 while I was a prisoner and didn't even know whether the baby was a boy or girl or anything until in June 1945 and two daughters, six grandchildren and one step son. All living here in Wichita, so that is a lot to be thankful for.

"I always said I wouldn't take a million dollars for my experience, but wouldn't give a penny to go through war again.

About left-waist Gunner **Harold E. Henley**, his sister Elizabeth Henley wrote the following bio:

"During his first mission his B-24 was hit but the pilot could keep the plane in the air until they were over friendly territory: France. Harold came down by parachute and was picked up by a farmer who brought them over the front line and into American controlled territory. However, Harold had broken a bone in an ankle and had to wait until the ankle healed before going on another raid. When he was able to go, that raid proved to be the fateful one.

"Their fighter escort was called away and the enemy downed his plane. The gasoline line burst and Harold's face and hand were badly burned. He dived down through the bomb bay doors.

"On the ground they were greeted by elderly men and boys with clubs, or anything they could hit the young men with. Fortunately, they did not beat up Harold. Possibly, the thought Harold was in a too bad condition with his burned face.

"He was taken to a hospital where a doctor treated his face. Every day the doctor picked off all the scabs. Harold was blind. One night the doctor asked him if he could see after picking the scabs. The doctor was pleased, after Harold told him he could indeed see again..

"One day, a Canadian soldier, who also was a patient in the hospital, told the others there that he was trying to escape. They tried to convince him it would be foolish to try but the Canadian jumped out of the window anyway. That made the Germans afraid that the others would try to escape too. So, they took all the others out of the hospital and took them to the rail road and put them in box cars and took them to a prison camp which was located about thirty miles from Berlin. Harold said there were many raids on Berlin. He was afraid that the camp would be hit.

"When the German guards heard that the Russians were attacking near their camp, they released their prisoners.

"Believe it or not, Harold had perfect vision, even though he had been burned

"After Harold came home he was given his old job as an announcer to a radio station WOPI. Later he moved to a radio station in Elizabeth, Tennessee. He commuted to the station in Elizabeth for it is about 25 miles from Bristol.

"He met a young lady and they married. Harold did well and bought a house. Everything was going well with him until he became ill. He had no children.

""He died at the age of forty-one years. He developed blood clots in his leg and they travelled upward to the valve between the heart and lungs. He went to the hospital in Charlotteville, VA. The doctors there tried what they could but the damage had already been done. He died at that hospital on the second trip there.

Tail-Gunner **Carl W. Groshell** was on his 30th mission.

The first he knew they were hit was when he heard bullets coming through the front to the back of the bomber. He put on his parachute and began to go through the plane to bail out but the smoke was so black in the plane he passed out. He came to in the air and he opened his parachute. He, Dale Allen, Henley, and Miller all landed very near each other. Miller was the only one not injured. The Germans took them to a barn. The military came and took Miller "straight to prison camp" because he was not injured. The other three were taken to a hospital. Carl was in the hospital for 30 days. Henley was badly injured - worse than any of them. None of them ever saw Mr. Conrad. He was not in the barn with them and they never saw him in the hospital.

***

Acknowledgements:
Engineer Dale E Allen
Elizabeth Henley, sister of waist-gunner Harold Henley

CHAPTER 26

491ST BOMB GROUP
854TH BOMB SQUADRON

Aircraft Type: B-24H, Serial # 44-95007,
"Scarface", MACR 11159
Airbase: North Pickenham

> *"I looked behind me and saw that both waist gunners were lying on the floor. They were obviously badly wounded or dead."*
>
> —Sole survivor Kenneth Peiffer just before he bailed out

Pilot: 1Lt. James J. Wynn (KIA) Hercules CA
Co-Pilot: 2Lt. Michael Krivonak (KIA) Central City PA
Navigator: 2Lt. Herman E. Roberts Jr. (KIA) Murray KY
Bombardier: 2Lt. Paul C. Odell (KIA) Los Angeles CA
Top-Turret: T/Sgt. Joseph Di Filippo (KIA) Trenton NJ
Radio-Operator: T/Sgt. Dewey A. Deweber (KIA) Post Oak TX
Ball-Turret: Sgt. Lawrence H. Carmichael (KIA) Indianapolis IN
Left-Waist Gunner: S/Sgt. Glenn T. Swanby (KIA) Los Angeles CA
Right-Waist Gunner: S/Sgt. Fred M. Wakeman (KIA) Redding CA
Tail-Gunner: S/Sgt. Kenneth M. Peiffer (POW) Mount Gretna PA

Total: 9 KIA, 1 POW
Target: Misburg
Crash Site: N of Deckbergen, Schaumburg District, 6.5 km ENE of Rinteln, 45 SW from Hannover.
Time of Crash: 13.00

NOT HOME FOR CHRISTMAS

Jan Hey's summary of the Missing Air Crew Report:

"The formation was attacked by 75 – 100 German fighters after bombing and this bomber was shot down. The only survivor was the tail-gunner who reported that the intercom was shot out and the tail section was on fire. Due to his isolated position in the tail-turret he didn't know what happened in the fuselage and front part, so he bailed out. It is believed that controls were lost or that it exploded in mid-air because the dead crew members were buried in three different cemeteries.

Six crew members could after the war not be individually identified and received a Group Burial in Fort McPhersen National Cemetery in Maxwell, Nebraska.

The only survivor was the tail-gunner **Kenneth M. Peiffer.** He wrote after the war the following story:

"This was our crew's eleventh mission and became our last. I was the tail-gunner and we had ten men aboard. I have been told that you can sense when things were not right and this day everything started out wrong. Our bombardier, Paul Odell was sick after arriving at the hard stand and we were having trouble with our 50 Cal Machine Guns. As we went over the English Channel, we still had trouble with the guns and I had to fix the nose turret gun as well. We felt we were in for troubles.

"We were well on our way and shortly after noon we were hit by over 200 ME 109's and FW 190's. I heard the bombardier say: "My GOD, there goes the plane on our left" and then "My GOD, there goes the plane on our right down." Then he said that he wondered if we could make it. Well, we were finally hit by ME 109,s and I heard a terrible explosion. The plane shook and I new we were hit.

"I was busy trying to locate the enemy and before I could see any enemy planes in my firing range, I felt something warm running down my face and goggles. I was hit in the head and bleeding heavily. I wiped off my face and then my gloves got sticky. I finally was able to fire some good hits into two ME 109's. Both planes were smoking and I did damage them. I then tried to talk over the intercom, but couldn't reach anyone. I looked behind me and saw that both waist-gunners were lying on the floor. They were obviously badly wounded or dead. I then saw more ME 109's about 5 o'clock but could not reach them with the tail guns.

"I went towards the waist-gunners position but when I got out of my turret and had released my flak suit, there was another big explosion that knocked me to the floor. Fortunately, I regained my senses and was right in front of an oxygen outlet so I stuck a hose in my mouth and turned it up to 100 %. Looking back, I could see that the tail section was on fire. Then another explosion came in the bomb bays that set that area on fire. I put on my chute, could not see the flight deck crew at all so I bailed out from the rear hatch.

"I made a delayed action jump and think I pulled the ripcord at about 3'000 feet. There was a hard jerk and I lost both my boots. It was cold. After hitting the ground, I figured that I was wounded in at least four places. I saw a wooded area and tried to run for it but every time I stood up I fell over. I think I was weak from loss of blood. Then a German farmer with a gun and a Frenchman approached me. The German stuck the gun in my eye and was going to kill me but the Frenchman talked him out of it. They threw me onto a wheeled cart and took me to a hospital in Minden, Germany. The trip took five hours. I spent nine weeks in the hospital and they removed the schrapnel with not even an aspirin.

"After healing the Germans sent me to Wetzlar, Frankfurt, Nurenburg and Moosburg. I was liberated from POW camp by General Patton's Army on April 29, 1945.

Margaret Bender, the sister of co-pilot **Michael Krivonak** wrote in October 2003 the following story about her brother and the rest of her family:

"Michael Krivonak was born May 10, 1922, graduated from high school in May 1940, worked at Vought Sikorsky Corsair Plant making airplanes and loved it, enlisted in the Air Force in February 11, 1943, and died on November 26, 1944. Michael was listed missing in action at first, and we were not sure that he was dead until the war in Europe had ended.

"I remember when the druggist (he delivered the telegrams from the War Department) brought that piece of paper to our door that said he was missing and in no time we got the second that said his brother John had been killed in the Pacific. So the blue stars that were hanging in our front window to indicate we had boys in the service were changed to silver and gold. I can remember wondering why the stars got prettier as you lost the people they symbolized.

"Michael was my mother's prize. He was her first boy after four daughters and I can still see her adoring gaze as she looked at him in his dress uniform the last summer he came home. I wished that I knew what

NOT HOME FOR CHRISTMAS

Co-Pilot Michael Krivonak's grave. Ardennes American Cemetery and Memorial

I could do to have her look at me that way. And even the memory of the sadness in my mother's eyes every time she looked at Michael's pictures still brings a desire to weep. I was the last of eleven children and probably had the best luck in getting to know my parents so very well.

In a letter from San Antonio, Michael wrote:

"I am sending this from the Army Air Force Classification Center here at San Antonio, Texas, where I arrived today. I was met on arrival and am now here with the rest of the future Army Air Crews

"I've registered and assigned to Squadron 102 where I expect to remain until I am ready to enter a Pre-flight School. During this time I will have my physical examinations and tests which will determine whether I become a Bombardier, Navigator, or Pilot. If I am classified as a bombardier, navigator, or pilot, I will be appointed an Aviator Cadet and will receive free a $10,000 National Service Life Insurance Policy. After being classified and transferred to Pre-flight School, I will commence my actual pre-flight training, which will last about nine weeks.

"You will, no doubt, think it strange receiving this type of letter from me instead of a personal note, but here is why: Our Commanding Officer knows that during the process of setting during the next few days, some of us will be apt to forget to write to the folks at home. This is his way of letting you know where I am and that I am well"

About engineer **Joseph Di Filippo,** the following article appeared in *The Times* of Trenton:

"On Sunday, November 26, 1944, Joe was 21 years old, the eldest of six children born to Italian immigrants. He was living in Chambersburg and was a 1942 graduate of Trenton Central high School.

"When word came that he was missing, and later that he was dead, it crushed his family, particularly his mother, Teresa. And it blackened the month of November and the Thanksgiving holiday in the Di Filippo home for years to come. Joe had not only died at Thanksgiving time but also on his parents' wedding anniversary.

"My mother would never want to celebrate it," Joe's brother, Thomas Jr., recalls about Thanksgiving as a boy. "It was not a good month," said the 66-year-old retired engineer and Hamilton resident who was seven when his brother died. He believes his mother had a nervous breakdown, though nobody called it that.

"There was something else to worry about too. Dan Di Filippo, a year younger than Joe, was in the South Pacific in the Marine Corps. The family didn't know it then, but Dan was preparing for the invasion of Okinawa.

"It was traumatic . . . . We were living in a bad state," recalled Joe's little sister, Frances Di Filippo Fluhr, now living in Ocean Township.

"Compounding the grief was the absence of a funeral. Joe Di Filippo's body did not come home until 1949. The family knew only scant details of how he died – his bomber went down over Europe – and they searched for more in an era void of instant news reports or available public records.

"Joe's personal effects were shipped home, and his medals came later. *The Times* of Trenton wrote a brief story when they were presented to his parents, accompanied by a photo of the ashen-faced couple, with Teresa wearing her son's Purple Heart.

"Life went on. Dan made it home and the brothers and sisters grew up, went to work or college and had families of their own."

***

Acknowledgements:
Jan Hey for the summary of the MACR
Kenneth Peiffer story: from the "Ringmasters' History" and authorized by
    Nelson Leggette, Editor, Ringmasters' Log
Maggie Bender, sister of Michael Krivonak
The Times of Trenton, Nov. 27, 2003 edition. Reporter Kevin Shea for
    Joseph Di Filippo.

CHAPTER 27

491ST BOMB GROUP
854TH BOMB SQUADRON

Aircraft Type: B-24J, Serial # 44-40117,
"Hare Power", MACR 11156
Airbase: North Pickenham

"I knew that Francis was gone even before the telegram. I talked to the Western Union man one day when we were walking to work. (I worked in a grocery store). I told him he was gone and not to bring the telegram to the store. Two days later he walked in the door at the store. I knew I had been right."

—Francis Reffner's widow

Pilot: 2Lt Floyd I. Weitz (POW) Winona WA
Co-Pilot: 2Lt Chester Adkins (KIA) Holly Oak DE
Navigator: FO Frank C. Roe (KIA) Springfield TN
Bombardier: FO James W. Cook (KIA) Post TX
Top-Turret: S/Sgt William B. Bigham (POW) McCalla AL
Radio-Operator: Sgt Melvin L. McDaniel (KIA) Xenia OH
Left-Waist: Sgt Francis M. Reffner (KIA) McPherson KS
Right-Waist: Sgt Walter O. Schatzel (KIA) Town Line NY
Tail-Gunner: Sgt Frank B. Rivera (KIA) Egypt MA

Total: KIA 7, POW 2
Target: Misburg
Crash Site: N of Deckbergen, 6.5 km ENE of Rinteln, 45 km SW of Hannover
Time of Crash: 13.00

NOT HOME FOR CHRISTMAS

Jan Hey's summary of the Missing Air Crew Report:

"Shot down by a mass of German fighters.

"Roe and McDaniel reported buried in the cemetery of Deckbergen, Adkins in the cemetery of Rehren where also an Unknown Airman was buried.

"The other dead of the crew could be individually identified and received a Group Burial in Arlington National Cemetery, Fort Myer, VA, U.S.A.

"Bigham was captured at Lauenau, 17 km S of Wunstorf.

About navigator **Frank C. Roe** his sister Jean Ardis Sory wrote the following bio:

"Frank Clifford Roe was born September 22, 1921. His parents were Frank Cephus Roe and Addie Elizabeth Krisle Roe. We lived on a farm in Robertson County, Tennessee on Route #5. Our father grew tobacco and wheat as his main crops.

"One day when Clifford was about 5 years old he just disappeared. Mama and the rest of us were looking for him. I finally found him under the house asleep. He found a nice shady spot and went to sleep.

Living in a rural environment, Clifford attended Bell School, a one room schoolhouse for Grades 1-8. Although he was in the Greensboro High School district, his mom and dad rented an apartment in Springfield so he and his sisters could attend Springfield High School. Both Clifford and Sue graduated from SHS in 1939.

"He studied accounting at Tennessee Technological University in Cookeville, Tennessee for two years. He had to hitch hike to get back to school and once he got robbed. My mother always sent him money for food, books, and room rent.

"After that he married Rebecca "Sue" Smith and they had two children, Clifford Leroy Roe and Suzanne Smith Roe Maynard. He was

Navigator Frank Clifford Roe with future wife Rebecca

working at Vultee Aircraft, a defense plant in Nashville, Tennessee when he was drafted. Roy was one year old and Suzanne was on the way, but they took him anyway.

"Clifford trained at the San Marcos Air Field in Texas graduating with the Class of 9/02/44. Then he was sent to England. He started out in the Army, but soon asked to be transferred to the Air Force. He loved that. He came home on his last visit and told me all he had learned about radar and all the newest equipment on the airplanes. When he left home for the last time, he told his wife and mother that he felt he would never be back home again and asked them to see that his body was brought back to America.

"When Sue was notified that he was MIA (Missing In Action), it was almost time for Suzanne to be born. They lived in Springfield, but her doctor was about 30 miles away in Nashville, where I lived. She came there to stay with me for a few days before the baby was due. The night after she arrived, her labor pains started. My husband was a traveling salesman and was away. He had to travel by train because of the gas shortage. I called my neighbor to stay with my three children and Sue's son, Roy, while I drove her to the hospital. I grabbed a wheel chair and took her up to delivery and came back to check her in. The baby (Suzanne) was born within one hour. Clifford never saw her, but had told Sue if the baby was a girl he would like for her to have a name with Sue in it.

"The doctor came out and said "Where is this child's father"? I said "I wish I knew". He said "Who are you"? I said "I am his sister and my brother is "Missing In Action" and I think you know that". He said "I forgot", so I said "He is over there fighting for you and me and you make a smart statement like that. I do not appreciate it"!

"The way Clifford got home is awesome. Our cousin, Paul Maddox, was a chaplain in the Navy. He lived in California as did many of our relatives, but he came to see my mother and told her he was going to England and asked if there was anything he could do for her. She said "Yes! Find my son and bring him back alive or dead. That was his last request".

"Paul found the place in Germany where the plane was shot down and talked to some of the people who remembered it. They said they buried the dead in that area first and then they were transferred to a cemetery in France, where Paul later found them. The five dead men had to stay together as two of them were so mangled they could not separate them.

"Paul contacted all five families and told them what he had learned and asked where they wanted to bury them that would be fairly close to all five families. They decided on Arlington in Washington, D.C. All our family went to the funeral. Roy and Suzanne were about seven and six years old, but they went too.

Clifford had three older sisters, Ann born in 1911, Audrey born in 1914, Jean born in 1916 and one younger sister, Rubye born in 1924. Rubye said he was the best brother anyone could have as he was patient and always in a good humor - plus when they were older, he let her double date with him and Sue.

The most frequent comments of cousins and friends were that they remembered Clifford for being handsome with a flirtatious smile, having a wonderful personality and for being lots of fun. Sue always commented he was the kindest person she ever knew.

About waist-gunner **Francis Merle Reffner** his widow Ann Rawson wrote:

"Merle had three sisters Martha, Rita and Judy and two brothers Morris and Charles. Morris has passed away as Rita has also. His folks Cecile and Margaret are also gone. Martha and I are very close. She lives 65 miles away in Colwech but we still talk every day even after all these years.

"Merle and I went together all through High School. He graduated in 1940 and worked in Dillons grocery store. When I graduated May 28th 1941 we were married June 1st. I wouldn't be 18 until November 29th so my dad had to sign the papers. I am glad we did this because we didn't have too much time together as it was.

"We moved to St. John, KS, when Merle got sent to a bigger Dillons store. He had worked in their store in McPherson until we got married. Denny was born 18 months after we were married. He was drafted when Denny was two. Denny and I lived with my folks. He was stationed in Denver, Colorado, Amorilla, Texas and Boise Idaho.

"Martha went with me on a trip to see Merle. We got to meet the crew. In these days of course there was no T.V. We listened to the radio and read Merle's letters. He got home twice for a few days and I went where I could be with him in Colorado, Texs and Boise.

"I knew that Merle was gone even before the telegramm. I talked to the Western Union man one day when we were walking to work. (I worked in a grocery store). I told him he was gone and not to bring the telegramm to the store. Two days later he walked in the door at the store. I knew I had been right."

About waist-gunner **Walter O. Schatzel** his niece Martha Kalinowski wrote in 2003:

"I was only four years old when I last saw my uncle, but I have wonderful memories of him.

"He was born in June 1918 in the city of Buffalo, New York.

"When Walter was a little boy, his father died. His mother raised him on her own, along with his older sister, Alice (Schatzel) Kwitowski, my mother. In 1934 when my Grandmother married Albert Pries, they moved to the small hamlet of Town Line, NY.

Back row, left to right: Walter's sister Alice, Walter, Walter's mother Martha
Front: Martha A. Kaloniwski, Alice's daughter

"Uncle Walter had a very caring, outgoing and warm personality. He quickly made many friends including William Kwitowski, who he introduced to his sister. They soon married.

"Our family was very close and when I was baptised, Walter became my Godfather.

"When he came home on leave, he used to call me his "Little Soldier Girl". I used to like to wear his soldier's cap. Walter was single. He had girlfriends, but he used to say I was his best girl. I was told he carried my picture in his vest pocket when he was stationed in England. When he left on his last mission, he put the picture in his duffle bag for safe keeping. I still have the picture and the duffle back.

"My brother Bill was born in 1950. His middle name is Walter.

***

Acknowledgements:
Jean Ardis Sory for F/O Frank C. Roe
Ann Rawson for waist-gunner Francis Merle Reffner
Martha Kalinowski for waist-gunner Walter O. Schatzel

CHAPTER 28

491ST BOMB GROUP
854TH BOMB SQUADRON

Aircraft Type: B-24J, Serial # 44-40108,
"Blue Circle", MACR 11155
Airbase: North Pickenham

"Vukovich's B-24 fell off in a vicious spin that trapped everyone inside."

—Allan G. Blue in *The Ringmasters*

Pilot: 2Lt Matthew Vukovich Jr. (KIA) Pittsburgh PA

Co-Pilot: 2Lt Carl L. Geppert (KIA) Wilmette IL

Navigator: 2Lt Warren K. Simmons (KIA) Rochester NY

Bombardier: 2Lt Donald T. Burke (KIA) Charlotte IA

Top-Turret: S/Sgt William H. Fulkerson (KIA) Marion KS

Radio-Operator: Sgt Edward F. Sloane (KIA) Long Island City NY

Left -Waist: S/Sgt Mitchell H. Moore (KIA) Ray City GA

Right-Waist: Sgt Richard F. Yergey (KIA) Pottstown PA

Tail-Gunner: Sgt Sheldon P. Markham (KIA) Waterford PA

Total: 9 KIA

Target: Misburg

Crash Site: Annaturm a.d. Deister, 1.5 mile N of Springe, 18 miles SW of Hannover

NOT HOME FOR CHRISTMAS

About bombardier **Donald T. Burke his** sister wrote:

"Don was born August 16, 1922 on a farm near Charlotte where our parents farmed. He was second in a family of eleven, seven brothers and four sisters. When he was eight, the family moved west to South Dakota. As fate would have it, it was not a good move. The 1930 decade was disastrous for Midwest farmers. The whole nation suffered a severe economic depression and the Midwest had a devastating drought and grasshopper infestation.

"In 1943 they returned to Iowa in the same Charlotte area where they had lived before. Don attended grades 1-8 in small rural schools and High School in a small town five miles from our farm. He was first in the family to attend high school.

"He would ride a horse to school, turn the horse loose and the horse would return home. Don would hitch hike a ride home when school let out. He usually caught a ride with neighbours or friends. Occasionally, but not often he would have to walk home. Since his only venture into the athletic programs offered at school was running the two-mile race, so his occasional five mile walk just improved his endurance.

"He never considered the alternative, to drop out of school. He was always a good serious student, well aware of the advantages of education.

"He was a good example of the American genetic composite of citizens. His father was Irish, his mother was Scotch, English, French and American Indian of the Sioux tribe.

"He enlisted in the Army Air Force just as soon as he became eighteen, just a few months after he graduated from High School. He received most of his training at Randolph Army Air Base in Texas and at several other bases for special training. He hoped to become a pilot but because of an eye problem he didn't qualify for that and was trained as a navigator-bombardier. He received his commission as Second Lieutenant in July or August of 1944. His family was very proud of him.

"He had met and courted a girl in Texas and they planned to marry after the war.

"He was assigned overseas duty in October, 1944. He wrote home frequently, keeping us informed about his activities. We think he had been on only one or two missions before the ill-fated November 26 one. While he well recognized the risks he was anxious to get into the fray. He was a good God fearing Christian, wanted to do his duty and help his country. We are very proud of him and all the young men who sacrificed so much while serving our country in so many ways. But we still miss him.

Top-turret gunner **William Harold Fulkerson** was born on December 2, 1916, to William James Fulkerson and Mabel Louella (King) Fulkerson in El Dorado, Kansas. His sister, Edna Marie Fulkerson, had been born two years earlier on July 19, 1914 in Drumright, Oklahoma.

At the time, William was working as an oil driller for Harry Sinclair, a wellknown oilman. When oil was discovered in El Dorado, he moved the family there. The newly discovered oil field was located three miles west of town. It was called the Stapleton # 1, which was part of the El Dorado field. This particular field provided much of the oil needed for WW I. A community named Oil Hill had been built by Cities Service Oil Company for the workers to live in. However, since William was working for Harry Sinclair, he did not live there but in El Dorado. It was there that Bill was born.

The 1918 Flu Epidemy became a real concern. William stayed at the oil rig to insure that he would not carry any germs to the family. However, a neighbor who had been infected came to the house and Mabel contracted the disease and died. She was buried at the El Dorado cemetery. William took the two children to live with their grandmother Mary Ellen King, in Wichita, Kansas, while he continued to work in the oil fields. However, this was not a good situation for the children.

William married Clara Ann Mehl on October 20, 1920. He and the children went to live on the Mehl farm, 3 miles east of Marion, Kansas. The Mehls had been early settlers in Marion County and owned a sizable amount of land on the edge of the Flint Hills of Kansas where they did farming and ranching.

Bill and Marie attended the Bixler Country School for eight grades. When they reached the eighth grade, they were expected to quit school to work on the farm. This was all right with Bill since he did not care for school anyway, but for Marie it was a big disappointment and something she has regretted her whole life.

It was very difficult work for both of them. Bill did not like farming with horses and convinced his father to get a tractor. He farmed about 200 acres of wheat land and the rest of the land was rented out. Marie had the job of milking and feeding the cows, taking care of the other lifestock, and helping with household chores.

NOT HOME FOR CHRISTMAS

William developped lung problems around 1936 and needed to leave the cold Kansas winters. He and Clara went to Tucson, Arizona, for that winter and the next three. The children took care of the farm in their absence. When Marie married Joseph Scott Mason and left the farm in 1939, Bill was left to take care of everything by himself. He developed pneumonia and Marie, who had been living in Eureka, Kansas, came home to help him. When Bill enlisted in 1942, it was necessary to sell the farm machinery and livestock and to rent out all the land.

There was time for pleasure. It mostly revolved around the church and the school. They would have community meetings at the school where they would also hold cake walks. At church, they were involved in pageants. William bought a car for the two of them in 1932. When they were older, they went to dances at Pilsen, Kansas, a Czechoslovakian community close to Marion. Marie liked to play baseball. Bill hunted, fished, and did things with his friends. Sometimes they would go to Wichity, Kansas, to hear big bands such as the Gene Krupa Band.

On the day Pearl Harbour was bombed, Bill and Scott were hunting. They had the radio on and heard what happened. Bill made an immediate decision to enlist and did so in January 1942.

He went to Kansas City to begin with. He was then sent to Randolph Field in San Antonio, Texas, where he worked with the ground crew. He wanted to be a pilot and went to a crash course offered by Texas A & M at College Station, Texas. He took the test and was accepted to become a pilot. However, his buddy did not pass so he went to gunnery school with him in Laredo, Texas. He came home on furlough several times. The last time he came home, Marie and Scott drove him to Topeka, Kansas, where he was to fly to Seattle, Washington.

During October of 1944, he was sent to North Pickenham, England. He was killed in action on a bombing raid over Hannover, Germany, on November 26, 1944. He was initially buried in Eimbeckhausen, Germany, but exhumed after the war and reinterred in the American Military Cemetery near Liège, Belgium.

In 1944 Scott enlisted in the army. He went to fort Hood at Temple, Texas, for basic training. He was sent to Europe at about the same time Bill went to England. He served in the Third Army 377th Infantry Regiment, 95th Division. He fought with General Patton at the Battle of the Bulge and received the Purple Heart and the Bronze Star. He wrote letters to Bill but they were returned, stamped «missing». He came home in June 1945 for a furlough and then was sent to Camp Shelby at Hattiesburg, Mississippi. He was discharged in December 1945, and returned to civilian life in El Dorado, Kansas.

Top-turret gunner William H. Fulkerson

When Scott was sent to war, Marie and her daughter, June Ann, moved to the farm. Rationing had been imposed and it was difficult to get tires and gasoline. Other staples were difficult to get without coupons but those living on the farm were self-sufficient so they were not severely affected by any shortages. Marie worked at a grocery store in Marion and helped town people by giving them coupons they did not need.

When the telegram came to the family notifying them that Bill was missing in action, everyone was devastated. William was unable to go to town for supplies for quite some while. It was left up to Marie to deal with the reponsibilities of keeping up the farm.

There is a letter from the Army Air Forces dated 1 March 1945 explaining what had happened. There was some communication with the Sloane and Simmons family but no letters remain. The War Department sent a letter on 8 August 1946 to notify the family that Bill's remains had been taken to the cemetery in Liège. Then on 15 January 1948, the family was given an option to have the remains return to them or left in the Belgium cemetery. They chose to leave him there.

They were then notified on 19 August 1949 that Bill's remains had been permanently interred at Plot A, Row 20, Grave 15 at Neuville-en-Condroz. On 18 March 1963, they received an invitation to attend the dedication of the Americam Memorial Room of the Cen-

NOT HOME FOR CHRISTMAS

tral Library at Norwich, England. There is a Book of Remembrance with the names of all the members of the 2nd Air Division who lost their lives in World War II.

Bill never married. His father died in 1951 of lung cancer. His stepmother died in 1966. Marie is still alive and living in Marion. She has three children, June Ann (Mason) Rasmussen who lives in Tulsa, Oklahoma; William Scott Mason, who lives in Kansas City, Missouri: and Jerry Lee Mason, who lives in Houston, Texas. Marie's boys never had the opportunity to know their uncle.

***

Acknowledgements:
Mary & Don Wendel for Donald T. Burke
June Rasmussen for top-turret gunner William Harold Fulkerson

CHAPTER 29

445ᵀᴴ BOMB GROUP 701ˢᵀ BOMB SQUADRON

Aircraft Type: B-24H, Serial # 42-94940,
MACR 10754
Airbase: Tibenham

"Dad returned from the war (and his imprisonment) quite a different man my mom told me."

—Cheryl Martin, daughter of radio-operator Donald N. Welch

Pilot: 2Lt William L. Boykin Jr. (KIA) Philadelphia PA
Co-Pilot: 2Lt Gary V. Tubergen Jr. (KIA) Plymouth MI
Navigator: 2Lt Herbert E. Bailey (KIA) New Haven CT
Nose-Turret: S/Sgt Joe A. Gutowsky (KIA) Racine WI
Top-Turret: T/Sgt Junius C. Price (POW) Florence SC
Radio-Operator: T/Sgt Donald N. Welch (POW) Lima OH
Left-Waist: S/Sgt Americo A. Crespolini (KIA) Old Forge PA
Right-Waist: S/Sgt Walter C. McFadden (POW) Grove City PA
Tail-Gunner: S/Sgt Otis D. Craig (KIA) Wilmington DE

Total: 6 KIA, 3 POW
Target: Misburg (Hannover)
Crash site: 1 km SW of Sorsum, 6 km SW of Hildesheim
Time of Crash: 12.15

NOT HOME FOR CHRISTMAS

Jan Hey of the Netherlands about this bomber:

"After having bombed the target this B-24 was attacked by German fighters and shot down. Crashed 1 km. SW of Sorsum, 6 km. SW of Hildesheim, Germany"

About top-turret gunner **Junius C. Price** of Florence SC, the following article appeared in the December 23, 2005 issue of what was then called the *Florence Morning News*:

"It was just seven years ago that Junius Price, as an aerial engineer, was winging his way across Germany, part of the crew of a B-24.Then came the German Luftwaffe. Even the mighty bomber was no match for the ME's. Bullets screamed everywhere. Price stopped several of them before the big ship went down and crashed.

"Price spent almost a month in the hospital. Then on December 24, Christmas Eve, 1944 he was sent to a prisoner of war camp near Frankfurt. "Some Christmas present", he recalls.

"We didn't have much to do in that camp. We had our two meals a day and answered roll call. That call came pretty often. They wanted to keep counting us to make sure we were all there.

"Christmas Day wasn't any holiday where we were concerned. We got up in the morning and then just walked around all day, trying to keep warm and trying not to think it was Christmas. I recall that it was as cold as the dickens and that the snow outside was knee deep.

"There wasn't any celebration that day – and there sure wasn't any Christmas turkey. Know what we got to eat? About the middle of the morning we had some sort of toast and jam. Then late in the evening the Germans served us a meal of potatoes mashed together with salmon and some of that ersatz bread. Brother; that bread was out of this world and should be. It seemed like combination of everything from sawdust to old tin cans.

The coming of the Russians to the area brought liberation for Price. He was returned to the United States and then was flown from Miami to San Antonio, Texas for discharge. "that was the last flying for me. And from there I intended to keep these two feet firmly on the ground."

About radio-operator **Donald N. Welch** his daughter Cheryl Martin wrote the following bio:

"Dad returned from the war (and his imprisonment) quite a different man my mom told me. When Dad and I talked years later, it was never a subject he wanted to discuss; but once he did share with me how terrible it was to have been captured, ridiculed and treated so badly. He mentioned a boy offering what looked to be a piece of candy and then how he got so sick from whatever it really was.

"Dad and my mom divorced when I was two. Six years later he married Barbara Jean Woolley. Dad played clarinet in the local American Legion band, and the director, Gail Woolley, introduced him to his daughter, Barbara.

"Dad was an accountant by trade. He worked for Superior Coach Corporation in Lima, Ohio; but in 1968 he was transferred to Kosciusko, Mississippi where they lived for quite a few years but his job was abolished just before he was scheduled to retire--a cruel turn of events. Dad wasn't the only one in America who suffered that indignity, but it was a tough blow for them.

"I remember my dad as a very strict disciplinarian in my very young years. He was probably a tormented man after the war, but back then there was no name for what soldiers experienced. Today we have all sorts of "syndromes" attached to the various experiences people endure. In 1968 my dad gave his life to Christ and became a Christian. I can tell you that totally changed him. He and I weren't very close in the early days. After my husband I were married in 1968, my dad struggled with me being married to someone who just didn't quite measure up to his expectations. I suppose most fathers are that way. Anyway, a couple of years later Dad and my husband, Tim, started to become friends and actually became very close over the years.

"Dad was a teacher in his church's adult education classes (called Sunday School); he directed their choir; and he and Barb were very involved in other activities at their church. His faith pretty much defined who my dad was from 1968 until his death on April 4, 2000. Dad had both a bad heart and cancer. I think he knew of the cancer, but the actual diagnosis came on Jan. 29 of 2000, so he didn't last long after that.

About navigator **Herbert E. Bailey** the following obituary appeared in *The Haven Register*:

"2lt. Herbert E. Bailey, son of Marion T. Bailey and Meyer E. Bailey of 105 Laurel Road who has been missing in action since November

26, 1944, is now listed as dead according to word received by his parents. Lt. Bailey, a navigator with the Eighth Air Force, was shot down by enemy fighter planes while on a bombing mission over Germany and was officially carried as missing until war department authorities completed an investigation of his case. At the time of his death he had completed fifteen missions and wore the air medal. His parents have since received a posthumous award of the purple heart.

Navigator Herbert E. Bailey

"A graduate of the Susan Sheriden Junior High School, and the Millford Prep School, he spent one year each at Virginia University and at Pennsylvania Military College before enlisting in the air force in April 1943. Before going overseas he was graduated from the Air Force Navigation school at Selman Field, Monroe, LA. Besides his parents he leaves a younger brother, Alan Bailey.

David Bailey, the son of Allan Bailey, wrote about his uncle:

"While I was growing up, my dad never spoke about his brother. My mom and dad are extremely close and my mom told me also that dad would never talk to her about his brother. Many of my parents' friends today were also friends of theirs back when they were in high school so I have been able to ask them about my uncle Herbert over the years trying to get information about him. What I gathered was that he was the golden boy, and that when he died my grandparents were never the same. They never got over it. I always felt that my dad has somewhat been abandoned by his parents as a result of the loss of their eldest son.

About ten years ago I went to Neuville-en-Condroz in Belgium to visit the grave of my uncle Herbert to help me to experience my dad's pain and suffering. Upon returning, I told my dad about my trip to visit his brother's grave asked him if he wanted the information that I had been given about his brother. His response was that he didn't want it.

***

Acknowledgements:
Florence Morning News for Junius Price
New Haven Register for Herbert Bailey
Cheryl Martin for Donald Welch
David Bailey for Herbert Bailey

CHAPTER 30

445™ BOMB GROUP 701ˢᵀ BOMB SQUADRON

Aircraft Type: B-24J, Serial # 42-50467, MACR 11214
Airbase: Tibenham

"Chubby now rests beside my Dad and Mom and his maternal grandparents and two uncles are on the same plot."

—Dorothy Holt about her brother William "Chubby" Vance

Pilot: 1Lt John D. Barringer Jr. (KIA) Nashville TN
Co-Pilot: 2Lt Robert D. Levy (KIA) Philadelphia PA
Navigator: F/O Paul J. Juliano (KIA) Niagara Falls NY
Bombardier: 2Lt Norman F. Brunswig (KIA) Rock Island IL
Top-Turret: S/Sgt Joseph F. Black (KIA) Fort Smith AR
Radio-Operator: S/Sgt Eugene J. Sullivan (KIA) North Cambridge MA
Left-Waist: Sgt Eldon R. Personette (KIA) Minneapolis MN
Right-Waist: Sgt Roland C. Lyons Jr. (KIA) Portsmouth VA
Tail-Gunner: Sgt William L. Vance Jr. (KIA) Asheville NC

Total: 9 KIA
Target: Misburg (Hannover)
Crash site: western corner of Hämelerwald, 6 km W of Peine, 12 km E of target
Time of Crash: 12.55

NOT HOME FOR CHRISTMAS

German boy, Heinz Redecke, had his fourteenth birthday on November 22, 1944. Four days later, on Sunday, November 26, 1944 he watched high flying bomber formations passing through the air direction east. After having left Hannover behind them, they turned sharply south and dropped their bombs on the synthetic oil plant in Misburg. Even at a distance of fifteen miles he could hear the detonations and saw the dark clouds of burning oil.

He saw a four-engined bomber with one engine burning that flew under the formations and was rapidly loosing altitude. She was still being escorted by fighters but her situation was hopeless. Heinz was happy that she passed over his village Sievershausen. The crash was followed by a terrifying explosion.

Together with three friends Heinz went on his bicycle in the direction of the black smoke that could be seen from far away. About six hundred yards from the crash site, in the middle of the forest, they saw a couple of people standing near a dead aviator who seemed to have tried to bail-out at the very last moment. His parachute had caught a tree and he hang about three yards above the ground. He was dead but without visible injuries. A picture was passed around that showed him with his young family.

At the crash site they saw a house-deep crater. They wondered; "Why did one of them jumped too late and why did others not bail out in due time".

We can assume that this airman was the Tail-Gunner William L. Vance. He was the only married crew member,

The bodies or parts of the bodies of eight dead aviators were spread over an area of about thirty yards.

Another German boy, Willi Sander, also saw the B-24 come down. He remembers:

> "I was born in 1934 so I was ten years old when the plane crashed. November 26, 1944 was a clear day under a blue sky. I stood in the garden of my parents' house in Hämelerwald and watched the planes that came from the east and flew direction west. Altitude about 8000 meter. Behind the planes condense stripes could be seen.
>
> "All of a sudden German fighters appeared and fired on the bomber formation. At the same time the formation drew fire from a flak battery stationed in the neighbourhood. It can be assumed that flak hit the

bomber. We saw a huge fireball in the sky and from the center of the formation the bomber, turning as a screw, crashed on the ground with an enormous roar. Still in the air the tail broke off and came down at a different location.

"After the "all clear" we and some other boys ran to the crash site. The bomber had come down in a wood. It was a terrible sight. We saw dead and totally burned airmen. The bomber had completely disintegrated while it had come down with a full load of bombs. A few bomb craters had appeared in the surrounding area, meaning that the plane had lost its bombs already before coming down.

"The airmen were interred by German inhabitants of Hämelerwald under supervision of Mr. Hermann Lichtenberg. He was also present when later an American unit exhumed the bodies at the crash site and transported them home.

For bombardier **Norman F. Brunswig** his brother Ray wrote the following biography:

"My brother Norman was born in rural Illinois In 1918. At about the age of four the family moved to Rock Island, Illinois and he attended school in the public system there. Our mother was confined to a special care hospital when Norm was twelve. Our Dad and Grandfather raised us boys. I am seven years younger than Norm.

"In the early 1930s in an effort to survive the deep depression our country was going thru, my dad moved us back to a farm near Taylor Ridge, Ill. My dad and Norm worked day and night to make a living. Norman left school to make the whole thing work. It took sun up till well after sun down to make it go on a farm in those days but we still found time to fish and hunt.

"He had been an excellent student. Although he never complained I was always sure he resented the fact that he was deprived of the education he would like to have continued.

Even with just a High School education he was able to get in the Army Air Force when they were only taking people with college educations. He was a great brother.

"Norm joined the Army in 1940. In the days of "Good bye dear I'll be back in a year" a nice song but as we all know those guys where gone for many years…some for ever.

"Norm made corporal in an infantry unit but applied to the Air Corps and made it. He was trained in Texas and California and became a bombardier and a 2nd lieutenant. You could not have found a more proud father and young brother for that matter.

Dorothy Holt tells about her brother tail-gunner Sgt. **William "Chubby" L. Vance Jr.:**

"The news that Chubby was missing in action came the day after Christmas 1944 and was delivered by a messenger from Western Union. My mother had become so despondent and worried about Chubby that we became concerned and the doctor recommended that she get some diversion away from the home. She took a job in a very small handmade rug operation (she was a wonderful seamstress, quilt maker, embroiderer, etc.) and was at that location the morning the message came in. My Dad worked for the railroad and his hours were 7:00 a.m. sto 3:00 p.m., so he too was not at home. Only my sister Louise and Chubby's wife Vera along with 14-month old Judy were in the home at the time.

"They immediately called me at my office, and it became my duty to take the sad news to my Mom and then to my Dad. That is an experience indelibly imprinted in my mind.

"My Mom never recovered from the loss of her beloved son. During the year before Chubby was declared dead and the almost two years before we were notified that his body had been recovered, she became suicidal and this was an anxious time for all of us. In 1946 my Dad got up from the dinner table saying, "I don't believe I can stand it much longer if we don't hear something from my boy." He walked into another room still talking, and suddenly we noticed his speech was slurred, and he had suffered a stroke. He recovered sufficiently to return to work for awhile, but his health continued to deteriorate and he died in 1947 before we received the word that my brother's body had been found in Germany and was interred in Belgium. Chubby now rests beside my Dad and Mom and his maternal grandparents and two uncles are on the same plot.

"Mom kept her promise to Chubby that she would take care of Vera and Judy for him. Chubby had met Vera through a cousin's girl friend and they became a foursome. She was a native Ashevillian too but had attended school in a different district from the one Chubby attended. Vera was a pretty, petite, and sweet girl - always pleasant and a lot of fun. They were very much in love. She was 17, he was 21 when they eloped with the other couple to Clayton, Georgia and were married. This was in October, 1941. Vera continued to live with our family during the time Chubby attended aircraft school in Nashville, Tennessee.

In 1984, Judy Garren, Chubby's daughter, received the following letter:

"Judy, I knew your father from the time we "crewed up" in Westover, Mass. until he was lost with the rest of the crew near Brunswick, Germany in November, 1944.

"Please allow me to introduce myself. I am Ford P. Tracey (then a Captain in the Air Corp) the original pilot of your father's crew. We trained together at Charleston Air Base, S.C. and Langley Field, VA., flew the Atlantic Ocean to England and flew 8 combat missions together in the months of October and November 1944. The crew was then transferred to Lt. Barringer to become a "lead" crew, and I took an assignment as Operations Officer in the 701st Squadron. Being a lead crew meant an extra promotion for all hands on the crew. The pilots could go up to the grade of Captain and all grades go up an extra grade promotion. This was an excellent team, and they were recognized as such prior to being selected as lead crew.

"The crew members flew two or three missions with Lt. Barringer after they left me.

"Where were we in 1944 and what did we do? Some of the information is from memory, some from my flight records, and letters which I sent my wife from England.

"The crew all came together at Westover Field, Mass. about the 2nd week in May. There we went through the "prepare for overseas movement" type of things, such as getting teeth filled or pulled as was required; lectures on do's and don'ts in foreign lands, and in general waste time until our transfer by troop train to Charleston, SC. We started flying on the 24th of May and flew our 100 training mission hours by the 25th of July 1944. It was so hot in Charleston that summer that we had to fly from daylight to 0900 and from 4 o'clock in the afternoon until 9 o'clock at night.

"We arrived at the briefing rooms at 0330 in the a.m. There wasn't much of an urge for a social life in that stage of training. I do remember our two boxers, Vance and Zimmer, would get out under the wing of the B-24 and box with open hands. The rest of the crew, not being boxers, thought they were a bit rough but they loved it. They assured us, "it was just getting the circulation going." Charleston was not a good base in those days. Tar paper shacks for barracks and we had to sleep under netting to guard against malaria, and the heat was unbearable. The town of Charleston ripped off the GIs any place they could. (Charleston Air Base 20 May to 9 August, 1944.)

NOT HOME FOR CHRISTMAS

"We were all happy to receive our orders to Mitchell Field, New York on the 25th of July 1944 to pick up our aircraft for the flight across the Atlantic to Europe. However, the bombardier, Lt. Brunswig, became ill and was hospitalized, so the rest of the crew was given a leave and we all went home for two weeks. On the 9th of August 44 we were assigned to Langley Field, VA for radar training for the navigator and bombardier (Juliano and Brunswig). Most of the training missions at Langley Field were conducted by the crew of pilot, copilot, navigator, bombardier, engineer, and radio operator, so the gunners spent the time enjoying life – most took another short leave. I must admit only Juliano and Brunswig had to go to ground school so the rest of us enjoyed barracks life in the "Sand Banks." Our area was out by the base farm and dairy complex and consisted of temporary buildings as you see in the group pictures. These were much better than those at Charleston (barracks).

"I remember your father was the champion horseshoe pitcher on the crew. In fact, he was better than most around. We pitched a lot of horseshoes and played a lot of volleyball during our stay. The food at Langley was better than at most bases, both in quality and quantity. At least at Langley we were not awakened by the wild pigs that would root beneath the barracks at night.

"Another memory was the trip to North Carolina made by one member of the crew, I don't remember who, on a three-day pass. The return trip was what was memorable because he brought back two paper suitcases (cardboard) full of quart mason jars containing white lightning moonshine. It was the first I had ever seen or tasted…pure white in color. The whole crew sat on the beds of my room in the barracks and drank the "best in the world" according to the provider of the libation. Whoever it was said that he had made his first fifty cents watching for revenuers on the North Carolina- Tennessee border when the pack mules were transporting the moonshine.

"En route to England. 1 September 1944 to 26 September 1944.

"We picked up our brand new B24J at Langley. Although they didn't have to fly the initial checkout of the aircraft, they all went, the whole crew. The navigator and pilot did the final compass "swing" and calibrated the other necessary instruments including the radar equipment. The temporary name of the aircraft was "Banana Wagon" – someone said that's all they would be good for after the war "to haul bananas from South America."

445th Bomb Group, 701st Bomb Squadron

"We departed Langley on the 3rd of September for Bangor, Maine, and after a short flight on the 5th proceeded to Newfoundland on the 7th. Weather – the biggest enemy of the Air Corp in WWII – held us on the ground several days on the way over, as well as during combat mission days. After five days of waiting in Newfoundland, on the 12th of September we proceeded to Blue West 3 in Greenland. (*inserted: this was Chub's 24th birthday*) This base was located at the end of a long fjord about 30 miles inland. The main feature was a large glacier which ended about a hundred yards from the end of the aircraft runway. We landed toward it and took off away from it. Being September, the sun rose about 10 o'clock in the morning and set about 2 o'clock in the afternoon. There wasn't one earthly thing to do in Greenland except eat, sleep, go to the clubs and drink or gamble, or walk to the end of the glacier. (I had my 25th birthday there.)

"Finally on the 18th of September, we departed Greenland for Kevlavik, Iceland. After 4 hours, 45 minutes across the ice fields of Greenland and the ice flows of the north Atlantic Ocean, we arrived at the airfield near the capital of Reykjavic. The next morning, the 19th, we were briefed and took off at "first light" for Valley, Wales. That flight of 6 hours and 30 minutes was on instrument practically all the way. The complete trip across the Atlantic was without incident.

"At Valley, Wales, we turned in our "Banana Wagon" for modification (took out the ball turret) and installation of the new VHF radios (still used in civil aviation today). After a night of rest (confined to the base) we were taken by bus and train to Hadley, Stone on Trent, England, for redeployment. This then, on the 20th of September, was our first contact with the English people – we were given a pass but had to make the curfew at 11 o'clock. Oh, well, we found out what a pub and English beer were all about. Oh, yes, the English people didn't care too much for us at the time. I look back on it, we were so wild, so brash, and so young, one could not blame them for resenting the invasion by the "Yanks."

"26th September 1944.

"Assignment 445th Bomb Group (H), 701st Bomb Squadron

"On the 26th of September the Tracey crew made the shipping list and were escorted to the railway station in Hadley and put on a train for Tibbenham via London. My memory of the trip was that of the crew gathered in one compartment and playing poker using the English money as

NOT HOME FOR CHRISTMAS

chips. It didn't take too long to understand the "new" system, especially if we lost a pot. A couple of Englishmen probably helped us more with the explanation of the coinage.

"The night of the 26th we arrived at Tivitshall station about a mile from the base at Tibbenham. The "liberty" truck met us at the station and literally dumped us out at the Headquarters Building where no one knew what to do with the new crew. We were told to go to the mess hall, but it was 8 o'clock (PM) and they probably would not feed us. We did – and they did feed us…steak and fresh eggs. We didn't see fresh eggs and steak again for weeks and weeks. That meal must have been a mistake because although unknown to us, we were starting on an enforced diet of powdered eggs, brussel sprouts, spam, mutton, fish (not good), etc. We ate a lot of jelly and jam, catsup and mustard on everything. Bread and cheese were our staple.

"We were assigned to Nissen Huts, the officers to one and the airmen to another in a different area. They were all alike: a group of huts around a central latrine which supplied the only water. No showers. The water for washing, either clothes or your person, was heated in an old fashion hog slop cooker used on the farms in the States. No bath tub. The toilets were separated from the wash room, but there was always a line-up for the use of each.

"Our first morning in the 445th came early as the operations Duty Sergeant made the wake-up calls for the combat crews. After they cleared the huts, it was a couple of hours sleep till the mission took off. Then the noise of the aircraft got you out of bed. The crew got together after breakfast and was told that training and checkout would start the next day because there were no aircraft available today. We helped gather wood for the stove (one) in the hut and walked over to the base facilities such as PX and clubs. These base facilities were separated by large fields of winter crops including sugar beet and Brussel sprouts. (After a while we threatened to bomb these fields with any we had left from a mission because we got so sick of eating Brussel sprouts.)

"The combat mission aircraft were due back at about 2:30 p.m., so as was the custom when not flying on the mission, we went down to the flight line to watch the return of the planes. To the dismay of all, only three aircraft returned to the base and one of those crash landed in the traffic pattern off the base. (28 aircraft out of 37 dispatched were lost according to Roger A. Freeman <u>Mighty Eighth War Diary</u>.) Thus was the introduction of combat missions to the crew. There were many thoughts running through our heads after this great loss to the group. Many ques-

445th Bomb Group, 701st Bomb Squadron

tions were asked, but very few answers were known or given. What do the next few months have in store for us was our biggest question now.

"After two full crew practice missions and an evaluation mission we were declared operational. Our first mission on October 7, 1944 was back to Kassel, Germany where they had been wiped out on September 27. We flew missions regularly through the 19th of October. After that mission, the whole crew took a 72-hour pass to London, staying in the Rainbow Red Cross Club. We were all excited about this trip until we got there and saw all the devastation we had not seen in the blackout of changing trains when passing through London to Tibbenham. A few of the V1, flying bombs, were still hitting their mark in the town so London was not the "liberty town" we had all expected. All of us agreed we didn't want to end it in a London hotel at wrong end of a "Buzz Bomb."

"We saw the people that came every night to the subways to sleep. We passed within a foot of them. We tried to find some steak (even black market) in a restaurant but could not. The same fare we had at the base was available in the eating places in London. We were limited to the number of drinks we could buy – usually one per establishment and room temperature beer never did come into favor. It was my only trip to London on pass, but the crew went back at least once more I knew about – perhaps more.

"After the 10th of November and the Hanau, Germany mission, the transfer of pilots was made. I don't know the exact number of combat missions they flew with Lt. Barringer, as I have said, but I know he was a good pilot because I flew several practice missions with him and the crew after the transfer.

"After the Misburg mission I talked to the pilot who had been flying the wing of Lt. Barringer and he said that plane, after being attacked by German fighter aircraft, went slowly in a level flight glide into the cloud formation about 3 or 4 thousand feet below them (about 17,000' or so). At the time we were all confident they would get out of the aircraft, although be captured and made prisoners of war, and would have a good chance of survival. My letter to my wife although cryptic suggested that "we should be hearing about them in about a month or two" or "no news on the December POW List – still a little soon".

"About your father – I called him Bill Vance. Judy, as you know, forty years dims a great number of details of the close interactions that two people had. You don't remember the things he said, but you can remember how he said them and that was with a big grin or smile on his face. He was a happy person with a face that radiated enjoyment. While the rest of the crew hated the early morning briefings, he was always trying to get us going with funny jokes and comments. He was a "ball of energy" always on the go, always wanting to do something – pitch horseshoes, play catch with a baseball, shoot baskets, etc., and he was good at most everything he did. He was a fine, warm energetic person with a heart of gold – he was a "man's man" enjoyable and fun to be around.

"Judy, I hope this sheds a little light on what your father was like. I knew him only a year and that year put us on a pretty fast track. We were a superior crew and William L. Vance, Jr., a part of that crew, was also a part of me that was lost on November 26, 1944.

Yours truly, (signed) Ford P. Tracey.

***

Acknowledgements:
Heinz Redecke and Willi Sander, witnesses of the crash
Ray Brunswig for his brother bombardier Norman F. Brunswig
Dorothy Holt and Judy Garren and Ford P. Tracey, for tail-gunner William "Chubby" L. Vance

CHAPTER 31

445TH BOMB GROUP
703RD BOMB SQUADRON

Aircraft Type: B-24J, Serial # 42-51549,
MACR 11218
Airbase: Tibenham

Pilot: 2Lt Clarence W. Harris (POW)*
Co-Pilot: 1Lt Benjamin W. Long (POW)*
Navigator: 2Lt Harold L. Anderson (POW)*
Bombardier: 2Lt Ashley J. Carswell (POW)*
Top-Turret: Sgt Warren H. Voelz (POW)*
Radio-Operator: Sgt Francis E. Welter (POW)*
Left-Waist: Sgt Gene S. Trumpower (POW)*
Right-Waist: Sgt John F. Conboy (POW)*
Tail-Gunner: Sgt Charles E. Stoetzer (POW)*

* Hometown not available

Total: 9 POW
Target: Misburg (Hannover)
Crash Site: Near Fischbek/Weser, 6 km NW of Hameln
Time of Crash: 12.40

NOT HOME FOR CHRISTMAS

Jan Hey, Hengelo (Netherlands) summarized the MACR:

"The aircraft caught fire after German fighter attacks and was abandoned by the crew.

"On this day a number of aircraft was shot down in the area of Hameln and many airmen bailed out. As most prisoners refused to give information about the composition of their crew, it was difficult for the Germans to link the POWs to specific crashed aircraft. They reported that this crew belonged to a B-24 crashed at Rehren, 12 km ENE of Rinteln/Weser, but in MACR 11217 (for B-24J 42-50576 of the same squadron) they stated that 42-51549 crashed near Fischbeck."

No further details available.

***

CHAPTER 32

445ᵀᴴ BOMB GROUP 703ᴿᴰ BOMB SQUADRON

Aircraft Type: B-24J, Serial # 42-50756,
MACR 11217
Airbase: Tibenham

"While dropping down over enemy territory under my chute, I saw the red tracer lines of shots coming at me from the guns of a FW 109 fighter. The shells were ripping at the pants of my flight suit.

—Waist-Gunner Stanley Moronski, after bail out

Pilot: 2Lt Daniel W. Snow (POW) Silver City NM
Co-Pilot: 2Lt Harvey Spiegel (POW) Brooklyn NY
Navigator: 2Lt Robert F. Hudson (POW) Rochester NY
Nose-Turret: Sgt Biaggio R. Valore (POW) Cleveland OH
Top-Turret: T/Sgt Joseph W. Barbieri Jr. (POW) Jamaica NY
Radio-Operator: T/Sgt Ernest M. McKim (POW) Glen Cove NY
Left-Waist Gunner: S/Sgt J.B. Rogers (POW) Wheeler TX
Right-Waist Gunner: Sgt Stanley J. Maronski (POW) Angola NY
Tail-Gunner: Sgt Robert Jordan (POW) Upper Montclair NJ

Total: 9 POW
Target: Misburg (Hannover)
Crash site: Rehren, Germany
Time of Crash: 12.40

NOT HOME FOR CHRISTMAS

Mr. Jan Hey of Hengelo in the Netherlands who has summarized the Missing Air Crew Reports (MACR), says about this bomber:

"The aircraft was lost after attacks by German fighters. All of the crew bailed out and .were captured. The Germans linked the crew to B-24J, serial # 42-51549 (*also of the .445th BG, Pilot Harris – John Meurs*) of the same squadron that crashed near .Fischbeck/Weser, 6 km nw of Hameln, but this refers to MACR 11218. The crew of # 42-51549 was initially recorded in connection with a B-24 that crashed at Rehren, .12 km. ENE of Rinteln.The distance between Fischbeck and Rehren is only 10 km. .Moreover, airmen of both crews were captured at Holtensen near Hameln. It seems .that # 42-50576 did not crash at Rehren, but much more to the west, as Lt. Snow and .Sgt. McKim were captured in the vicinity of Osnabrück, according to German reports attached to the MACR.

Evelyn Snow:

The reason that Sgt McKim and my husband (Lt. Snow) were captured in a different location was because my husband's parachute caught on the aircraft as he was bailing out. For some reason, Sgt. McKim was still there and he helped pull him back into the plane. At that point, the plane stopped spinning and regained level flight, so they flew another 30 miles or so before they were hit with anti-aircraft fire and went down. They were then captured at nightfall, by soldiers, I believe.

For Pilot **Daniel W. Snow** his sister Vivian Derrick wrote in 2004 the following story:

"Daniel was named after our father, Dan W. Snow, who was born in Alabama. He and my mother met in San Francisco, and were married. They moved to Colorado where all three of us were born, my sister Cecelia, myself, and Dan. When Dan was still a baby my father was told to move to a warmer climate, so they sold everything, bought a Ford sedan and started south, ending up in Fort Worth Texas.

"My father was a barber, and since it was during the end of the depression, he couldn't make any money, so he decided to go to California. We were on our way when we met a man coming from California who said not to go there, the roads were terrible, washboard roads, and we would probably die from the heat through the desert. My dad didn't know what to do, so he tossed a coin, and it came up for us to go back to Colorado.

All this time during our travels we slept in a tent, which my dad had to put up every night. No such thing as motels like today.

"Our Dad was 6 feet 2 inches tall and a very strong man. He had some Indian blood, but he was very white and had blue eyes. When we came to Santa Fe, New Mexico, my dad found a job as a barber - the depression hadn't hit Santa Fe, and there were lots of people there that had money (from back east). Quite a few people there had come there for their health (tb was prevalent then). We went on fishing trips every chance our dad had time off, or prospecting, or hunting. We all had a wonderful time doing this, and our mom always had the best lunches for us. Sometimes we would stop on the way home and build a fire and my mom would cook the fish my dad caught. We had a happy childhood.

"When we were coming into Santa Fe for the first time we had to come up La Bajada hill, which was a very scary narrow road at that time, and my mother had to get out and put rocks behind the car to keep it from rolling backwards. When Dan was a little boy, probably about 3 and a half years old, he would pull on my mother's skirt, and say he was going to go over the mountains to the fat man's school and fly a plane. He would say this about fifteen times a day, and my mother would tell him it was ok if that was what he wanted to do.

"Dan was as nice a brother as one would ever want. He was quiet and a very sweet person. My sister and I were always afraid something would happen to him. One time when we were out fishing, our dad said "Look at Dan, he will never be a fisherman," and Dan was sitting on a rock, and dabbling his pole in the water. (probably thinking about the fat man over the mountain where he was going to learn to fly a plane). Our father died when he was 47 years old from a gall bladder surgery after a week of suffering. I was married in 1937, the year he died, and my mom and brother were the only ones left at home.

"Dan became an eagle scout. He went on any hikes up in the Sangria de Christo range of mountains that border Santa Fe on the east. My mother was working for the governor of New Mexico, and since it was a political job, she decided to get transferred to Civil Service. She transferred to Washington, D.C. and then to Albuquerque, and then back to Santa Fe. So I stayed at her house to watch after Dan.

"Dan was no trouble at all. I remember one time he asked me if I would drive my car around the plaza for an upcoming football game that he played in, and I said sure, and then about ten boys were hanging on my car shouting for Santa Fe High Demons. I had fun doing that. Dan had a couple of friends that he went to games, etc., with. One of his friends and

NOT HOME FOR CHRISTMAS

he manufactured a belt made of little wooden squares with sayings on them held together with leather strips. He told me he needed some equipment for them, and I gladly bought a kit with things to work with wood and leather, and he was forever grateful for that. He and his friend spent many hours on our back porch, which he concerted into a little workshop, sometimes not speaking to any one for hours.

"When Dan was just a little guy there was a boy that was a bully, and he pushed Dan down a hill by our house and Dan had a bloody nose and was crying, so I saw this bully at the top of the hill laughing, and I ran up the hill and hit him right on the nose: that is satisfaction. I have never been sorry I did that!

"I forgot to tell you our mother was French. She didn't teach us French because she said the neighbours would call us "foreigners". My mother was training to be a nun, but she met my dad, and that ended that.

"When my mother came back to Santa Fe, Dan received his Eagle Scout award. He had gone on so many hikes, he had huge muscles in his legs and arms. As soon as he was old enough, he enlisted, and when he was leaving the Army man in charge said was there anyone there who was an eagle scout, and my brother said he was. So he was put in charge of the bus. I didn't see him very many times after this. One time he came home and was a lieutenant and most of the men in town were in the service. I was so proud of Dan because the men saluted him!! When we received word that Dan was missing in action, I gave up and thought him dead, and I was devastated. But my mother told me he had told her if he was ever missing in action, he would come home and she believed it.

"When he went to war, I took a page in the back of my bible, wrote Dan's name, and drew a square around it, and asked the Lord to take care of him. I am sure that is one of the reasons Dan got out of the POW camp.

"After the war he told us how his plane was shot down - he got all of the men out of the plane, then jumped himself and his parachute caught on the opening in the plane. He said that you don't know your own strength when you're going to

Daniel W. Snow

die. He climbed up the shrouds of the parachute and pulled the metal loose from the opening to get loose.

"Dan was such an angel when he went into the air force, but when I saw him after his time in the POW camp, he had a grim, hard look I had never seen before. When the Germans caught Dan they made him march on two broken arches which were caused by his feet getting buried up to his ankles in the earth because his parachute hadn't opened properly. I don't know how long he was in the prisoner of war camp. He was liberated by the Russians.

"Dan died when he was only 56 years old. We drove two full days to go to his funeral.

*From left to right: Navigator Robert F. Hudson, Pilot Daniel W. Snow, * F.O. Smith (* not on the 11.26.1944 mission)*

Radio-Operator **Ernest M. McKim** wrote in 2002:

"In the beginning of the year 1942, I attempted to join the United States Marines, but was turned down. The reason given was that I was not an American citizen. I was born in Scotland and came to this country at the age of 4 ½ years with my parents. I was raised in Glen Cove, Long Island, NY and always considered myself to be an American. I was disappointed and annoyed. Taking my cue from some friends, another friend and I went to Canada and joined the Royal Canadian Air Force. While

NOT HOME FOR CHRISTMAS

there, I received experience in pilot training and familiarization with the construction and workings of aircraft. After a year, I resigned from the Royal Canadian Air Force and returned to the United States. I joined the U.S. Army Air Force as they would accept non-citizens. I then took the necessary steps to becoming an American citizen before going overseas.

"After training as a radio-operator/machine gunner, I was sent to Massachusetts and was assigned to my crew. On a training mission over Massachusetts, the pilot asked all members of the crew to come to the pilot's area and be tested to see who was the best qualified of the crew to fly the plane in the event the pilot or co-pilot were injured and unable to fly the plane. I was appointed as second co-pilot which moved the engineer up to the top-turret if we were in combat. Due to unforeseen circumstances, I was also assigned as second engineer. This placed me in the position of physically standing between the pilot and the co-pilot in the plane.

"We went overseas to England in October 1944 and joined the 445th Bomb Group of the 8th Air Force flying B-24's. On our 5th and last mission, our P-51 escort left us to go the right side of the formation. The P-51 escort on the right side was supposed to come to our left side. The reason for this being escorting fighters on the left side looked over their left shoulders to protect their backs. The fighters on the right side looked over their right shoulders. After 4 hours or so, this causes a strain on their necks. This switch should take no more than one or two minutes.

"The new fighter escort for us did not show up and I wondered where they were. A B-24 with multiple colors dropped in and flew along side of us. I tried calling them on the radio and received no answer. I tried signaling them with a signal lamp and received no answer. I determined that they were not an allied plane, but a German spy plane. I ordered Barbieri, top turret gunner, to turn his guns toward the plane and shoot it down. As soon as Barbieri turned his gun, the plane dropped out of formation. Before he could turn his guns back to position, we were attacked by German fighters from the front.

"At this point, I called the P-51 fighters on the radio. I said, "May Day", "May Day" Come in fighters, we are being attacked by enemy fighters on the left flank". I called this twice. The German fighters came in six waves of six planes in each wave. Each wave having three Messerschmitts and three Focke Wolf fighters. I was admiring the way the planes looked and their formation. I then realized when the second wave was coming

"The Me's had a cannon in their nose. When they fired, I ducked. The shell came right between the pilot and co-pilot over my head and knocked

498

the seat right out from under Barbieri. All the controls that operate that turret were in that seat and were now inoperable, but Barbieri was not hurt. A small fire broke out behind the radio transmitters which I put out with a fire extinguisher. Then the third wave of German fighters hit us and knocked out one engine on the right side and half of the engine on the left side. We immediately went into a death spiral in which everyone could have been killed.

"No one could have bailed out during the spiral, but luckily, Lt. Snow managed to pull the plane out of the spiral after dropping 5000 feet. Now we were alone and could only fly in a straight line with the right wing tilted 6 degrees. At this point, Lt. Snow, the pilot, ordered everyone to get ready to bail out. The engineer and the co-pilot went to the rear of the plane where they could bail out. We were low and started flying through flak batteries. Lt. Snow ordered a bail out, but there was no communication in the rear or the nose of the plane. I climbed through the bomb bay and signaled (thumbs down) to the crew to bail out. I returned to the pilot area and climbed through the tunnel and signaled the bombardier and nose gunner to bail out. I then crawled back to the pilot area.

"Snow was having trouble putting on his parachute or his harness possibly was jammed in his seat area. He told me to take control of the plane which I did. I flew the plane for about 5 minutes with the right wing tipped until Snow could free himself. Lt. Snow then said "Let's Go". I crawled through the tunnel to the nose wheel opening where we would have to bail out. At this altitude, we were sitting ducks for the next few flak batteries that we were running into. I straddled the nose wheel opening, waiting to see if Snow was coming up behind me, or if he was wounded. When I saw him coming toward me, I let go and bailed out.

"I counted to ten and then opened my chute. Lt. Snow was the last one to leave the plane. I soon realized that all the crawling through the plane had dislodged one of my chute buckles causing me to descend with only one chute strap in the crouch area. This caused my descent to be much faster than normal. It looked like I was going to crash into a red tile roof. I then realized I was going to miss the roof, but not the chimney. I pulled my legs up to miss the chimney and landed hard on the ground injuring both ankles. I must have been knocked unconscious for a while. When I awoke, I found myself surrounded by about 50 German civilians and one of them had a small pistol, which to me, at that time, looked like a cannon. He said "Arms". So I raised my hands over my shoulders. He said "Árms" again, and I raised my hands higher. He said "Arms" again, so I raised my hands as high as I possibly could.

NOT HOME FOR CHRISTMAS

"About this time, a German Air Force soldier arrived, who was about 6 ft. 3, weighing about 225 lbs. He asked me if I had a pistol. I said "no" and he said "Lower your arms and follow me". He started barking orders to the civilians. One little old lady ran back to her house and brought back my parachute. I was unaware how she had obtained the chute. The German soldier took the chute and stuffed it into my arms and marched me off to a German interrogation center.

"Upon arriving there, I was placed in a small room by myself. After a few hours, I was interrogated by a German officer. He asked to see my dog tags (GI Identification), but unfortunately, I had left them hanging on the end of my bed back in England. When he received this information, he began asking me questions about my bomb group and my position of the plane. Upon receiving my answer of name, rank, and serial number and because I had no identification, he stated I could be shot in the morning as a spy.

"I was then escorted back to the small room. I remained there until the next morning. I was then taken back to the interrogation room and asked the same questions. He received the same answers. He then informed me that I was the radio operator on the plane. He also quoted the six radio frequencies used by our group and they were all correct with the exception of one. That particular one had been changed that morning shortly before take off. I did not acknowledge his error. He dismissed me again and as I was returning to my room, I met Dan Snow, the pilot, coming from the other direction. I stopped him and asked if and when he was interrogated, he would identify me as his radio operator and part of his crew thereby removing me from the possibility of being shot as a spy. He said Okay.

"That afternoon, two other airmen, who I did not know, and myself were marched down and put in a box car. We were given a loaf of German black bread and were locked in the car. The train started to move and we rode for three days. Since we had not eaten before taking off from England the previous morning around 4 AM, we were pretty hungry. We divided up the bread and ate it. The box car door was not opened again until we reached the prison camp. We were hungry and asked for food and water. A German soldier who spoke English asked what we had done with the loaf of bread. He informed us that the loaf of bread was to have lasted us for three days. We arrived at Stalag Luft IV in Gross Tychow in northeastern Poland, a short distance from the Russian border.

"After arrival at the camp, we were assigned to a barracks approximately around noon. They came around serving everyone in the barracks a watered down soup which we were glad to get. We were not physically abused at the camp, but food supply was meager. We did receive Red Cross parcels that arrived approximately every two weeks. However, all the chocolate was removed before we received the parcels. The balance of the parcel was split between 4 men. In addition to the parcel, we received watered down soup daily that was made from potatoes or barley or something unknown. We also received half loaf of German black bread to be divided between two men who had become buddies. The bread was divided as evenly as possible. The man who did not divide the bread got first choice of what piece he wanted, usually the heel. Therefore, great care was given to be sure the pieces were divided evenly as possible.

"We were constantly on the look out for some way to get more food. In one corner of the compound, there was a small stream of water. Outside the compound, about 20 or 30 feet away, some women prisoners, who looked like Polish or Slavic civilians (probably cooks for the Germans), came to the stream to wash and slice potatoes and carrots. They also washed clothing in the stream with soap. Some of the scrapings would come under the fence into our compound. We would gather them up and take them back to our rooms and make soup to supplement our meager diet. We made soup on small stoves that we built out of empty powder milk cans.

"The compound was surrounded by a tall fence with barbed wire on top. German shepherd attack dogs were outside the fence guarding the prison camp. We had permission to walk around inside the compound between the barracks and the barbed wire fence for exercise. We passed the time sleeping and playing checkers or cards supplied by the Red Cross. We all got along well together as everyone was too weak and tired for bickering. We observed no medical facilities at this camp. Eventually, my ankles that were injured, healed without any medical attention. While at this camp, I never saw any of my crew with the exception my brief encounter with Dan Snow at the interrogation center. Dan would have been transferred to another camp for officers. After about a week, we were given flimsy paper postcards to send back home. My future wife, Mary, was the first in my family to receive a card. My parents received their card immediately after.

"Every evening at the end of a long barracks hall, away from the front doors, Sgt. Willliam J. Knightly would have a prayer service for the Catholics or anyone else who wished to attend. Therefore, we all called him "The Padre". His attempts to raise our morale was a great consolation to us. On Christmas Eve, there was a small barrack near the front gate that was entirely empty. There were two windows on each side of this

NOT HOME FOR CHRISTMAS

barracks and double doors in the front. The guards told us we could have Christmas Eve services there, if we wished to do so. The religious leaders of each barracks joined together to have a service and to sing Christmas carols. The barracks was too small to hold everyone. There were more men standing outside in the snow than were inside the barrack, who were trying to see what was happening. They were singing along with everyone else. It was a very touching scene and everyone was emotionally moved. On Christmas Day, the Red Cross surprised us with a Christmas dinner of turkey, dressing and plum pudding.

"Rumors began circulating that we would be marching out of the camp. We began doing more walking in order to strengthen our legs. Sometime around the first week in January, 1945, the Germans started breaking up the camp and marching us out in groups of about 200 men per group.

"Before we left the camp and started on the march, we were marched past a big vat, approximately 5 feet wide and 2 feet deep, that was full of all the small chocolate bars that were stolen out of the Red Cross parcels. As we passed the vat in single file, the guards told us to grab a handful. They marched us south, away from the Russian border in a lot of different directions so we would not know where we were going. We were also completely separated from any other group. This was in the middle of winter and conditions were bad. Between the snow, mud, freezing rain and freezing temperatures, we were pretty miserable.

"We marched about 20 miles per day and slept in barns when we could find one. Otherwise, we slept outdoors in fields and gullies. Three men would buddy together, sharing blankets and food and cuddling together at night for warmth. The worst day I can remember was Valentine's Day. We had walked all day in drizzling rain, and we had to sleep that night in a wet field in the freezing rain.

"Sometime around the middle of April, we marched within 10 miles of the Elbe River south of Berlin. We stayed in a large barracks type camp. We stayed there about a week and slept in regular bunk beds. Stories began circulating in the barracks that all men who were not ill would be marched west, away from the Elbe River. A German airman came in with about 4 or 5 other airmen and began taking temperatures with a thermometer. Not wishing to be marched out again, when the guard was taking my temperature and briefly turned his back, I cupped a lit cigarette in my hand and raised the temperature of the thermometer. As a result, I stayed and did not have to march out.

"On the following day, there were no guards about. An American GI with a rifle over his shoulder came in and yelled, "Get dressed and ready to move out". A few more armed GI's came in and lined us up to go out the main doors. Outside, there were quite a few GI trucks with tarpaulin covers. We were loaded into the trucks and driven across the Elbe River on a bridge into American territory. The nearest battalion was a field artillery unit. Upon arriving home, I learned that particular unit was my brother's artillery unit. They had been waiting there for a few days negotiating with the Germans to get us out.

"We were driven to an Army base where we received medical attention and plenty of food. When I was taken prisoner, I weighed 170 lbs. I now weighed around 120. We stayed there about 30 days. We received three meals a day and milk shakes in between meals. The Red Cross and Salvation Army were also giving us donuts and coffee. By the time I left there, I had gained a lot of weight. We were sent home by boat and taken to an American hospital for evaluation. We were then given a 30 day furlough. I got married during this furlough on July 4, 1945, and after a honeymoon trip, I was transferred to Mitchell Field, Long Island, New York. I received an Honorable Discharge on November 3, 1945.

In 2002, when he was 83 years old, waist-gunner **Stanley J. Maronski** remembered about his last flight in WW II:

"Our bomber that day was brand new and had just been delivered from the United States to our base in England. It had no "nose-art" to identify it. Our assigned plane would have carried the nose-art of "Snow Ball from Hell and Eight little Snow Flakes", but it was in for engine replacement, so on this mission we were given the new plane. Our ground mechanic had asked us, when we were preparing to leave, "please bring it back with no holes in it. It's brand new."

"Normal flight crews on a B-24 Liberator numbered 10 men. We only carried nine because Bob Hudson, our bombardier, was also a navigator. As one of the other crews had lost their navigator, our regular navigator (Robert Conrad) was transferred to that crew - leaving us with nine men aboard. After capture, the Germans did not believe that we had only nine men in our crew and insisted we identify the tenth man.

"Over our target, the oil refinery in Misburg, Germany, we met heavy flak, and saw German fighters everywhere. The plane next to us blew up and for a long time my friends from other planes in the formation thought it was our plane. I do not know the identity of the plane that was next to us. (A few years ago, at an air show, by chance, I ran into Bob Conrad and he also told me everyone thought our plane had exploded. As assistant

NOT HOME FOR CHRISTMAS

engineer, I armed the bombs in the bomb bay and all bombs were dropped before our plane was hit.

"The German FW 109 fighters attacked our formation. The first hit knocked out the number three engine which controlled the electronics on the plane. Because this engine was hit first, there were no sparks to ignite the fuel aboard and the plane continued to fly. The next engine to get hit was number 4 and was followed by the loss of engine 2. This heavy bomber was now left to struggle home on one engine.

"No one in the crew was wounded during this attack. As pilot Dan Snow tried valiantly to keep the plane aloft, he told us to get everybody out and said "I'll see you guys in the funny papers". While the rest of the crew prepared to bail out, I assisted Sgt. Biaggio Valore out of the ball turret position so he could bail out. A shell had damaged the doors at the tail gunner position and I forced the doors open so Sgt. Bob Jordan could also bail out. I retrieved and put on my chest pack parachute from under the window where my 50-caliber gun was mounted and I was the last of the crew (outside of the pilot and radio-operator) to jump from the faltering plane. Pilot Snow and radio-operator McKim told me they were going make every effort to try to fly the plane to safety. They almost made it.

"While dropping down over enemy territory under my chute, I saw the red tracer lines of shots coming at me from the guns of another FW 109. The shells were ripping at the pants of my flight suit. The sky was overcast as I looked up and sent a fervent prayer to our Creator saying that I could use "help" down here. Out of the clouds came three American P-51 fighters who chased and shot down the FW 109. They were so close I could almost touch their wingtips. The nearest fighter pilot saluted as he turned away and I drifted down to land in a farmer's field. The farmer caught me after I landed and aimed a pitchfork at me until the German soldiers arrived to take me away. The farmer's wife asked if she could have my white silk parachute to make a dress for her daughter. The German soldiers would not let me give it to her. I was to carry it to the base where they took me.

"In the barracks where I was held, a German soldier spoke to me in Polish. I thought I had found a possible friend, but he reported to his commanding officer that I spoke Polish. The Germans wanted to know if I had escaped from the Polish army and how did I end up in the American air force. They did not believe that an American would speak Polish. All I have told the German officers, was the standard reply of "name", "rank", and "serial number". This made them angry and I was put in solitary confinement in a cellar room that was like a dungeon with only a straw bed to

445th Bomb Group, 703rd Bomb Squadron

sleep on. All I received for 14 days was water to drink. After the 14 days were over the Germans put me on a train (a cattle car) with other captives and sent us over to Stalag Luft IV.

"I stayed at Stalag Luft IV until January, 1945. While we were kept in that POW camp, the Germans would turn loose guard dogs that would go under the raised barracks. I was told by other prisoners that several dogs were killed by the prisoners by choking them. The dogs were lured to holes in the floor under the beds, where a loop would be dropped around their necks and pulled until the dog was near to death. They were released just before death so they would run from the barracks and die near the fence. When we left Stalag Luft IV, there were only four guard dogs left.

"On January 3, 1945, when the Russians came too close, the Germans moved us out of Stalag IV and walked us 25 kilometers a day until the 26t^h of April. On the 26th of April we crossed the Elbe River to rejoin the American forces.

"On the march we were guarded by the German Home Guard which was made up of old men who were in their 50's and 60's. Because the Germans worried about the fact that I spoke Polish, they assigned one of the guards to watch me. I remember his name only as "Schwarz" or "Schultz". For the purposes of this narrative, I will call him "Schwartz". He was about sixty years old at that time. Food was scarce for everyone, including the old guards. The food the guards received from the German Army consisted of a small loaf of bread made with sawdust and some sausage. Schwartz started trusting me to hunt for food and return to our group of prisoners (about 5 or 6 men in each small group looking out for each other). Schwartz knew I was a butcher by trade before the war. He would say to me, "If I turn my back, you will come back?" And I would run off in the night and search for food.

"We marched mostly on small side roads. We never saw a city while we were walking. If we passed Polish forced labourers, they would tell me in Polish where any food could be found. After dark, I would go back to the places where I thought food might be taken. Sometimes it was a chicken from a farmer's yard, or vegetables hidden under the ground near the road, or an old bone that had been left for a dog to chew on. To pluck the chickens we took, we would hide them under our coats and pull the feathers off as we walked, letting the feathers fall along the roadside. Once it was a large hog tied in the woods, that sadly we had to beat to death. We ate whatever we could find and cooked it the best we could with what we had and shared what we found with the Guards. Washing one's self was done at rain barrels even though it was so very cold. Lice were always a difficult problem and killing them at night became a prisoner pastime.

"At night we were kept in barns if they were available. If not, we had to sleep in the fields. One night we were put into a big barn which housed sheep. Many of us spent the night in the hayloft above. We were hungry and the sheep were below. Fifteen sheep were killed and eaten that night. The most difficult part was burying the fleece. We dug up the dirt floor and buried the remains of the sheep and kept the rest of the sheep moving until they packed the floor down again. In the morning the owner came back to count his sheep. Becoming very angry, he told the soldiers fifteen sheep were missing. We were lined up against the wall with machine guns on us as they searched our clothes for any remnants of the sheep. Nothing was found so no one was shot that day.

"On April 25, 1945, my last night as a prisoner of war, we were housed in an old barn. Early on the morning of April 26, Schwartz came up to me and whispered to me that I was going home this morning. He said the Americans are across the Elbe River. Schwartz and I left the barn and he handed me his gun (I still have the gun) and said to me, "I be your prisoner" and started walking with his hands up in the air. I told him to put his hands down again and we walked across the river together. An American GI threw me his carbine and told me to "get rid of the German". I told him that he was only an old Home Guard and had treated us decently.

"Schwartz was placed with a group of other Home Guards now held as allied prisoners. I returned the carbine to the GI, and asked him for a couple of cigarettes: he gave me a few and I took them over to Schwartz and the other Home Guards. With shaking hands, Schwartz thanked me for them.

***

Acknowledgements:
Evelyn Snow for Pilot Daniel Snow
Radio-Operator Ernest McKim
Waist-Gunner Stanley Moronski

CHAPTER 33

445TH BOMB GROUP 703RD BOMB SQUADRON

Aircraft Type: B-24J, Serial # 42-50729,
MACR 11216
Airbase: Tibenham

Question: "Do you remember the murder of an American airman who parachuted from a burning bomber?"
Answer: "Yes, I do remember very well."

—7708 War Crimes Group: testimony by German doctor Wilhelm Bause on February 1947

Pilot: 2Lt Lee E. McPartland (KIA) Cicero IL
Co-pilot: 1Lt Carl J. Hert (KIA) Chicago IL
Navigator: 2Lt Joseph J. Hanzook (POW) Brooklyn MD
Nose-Turret: Sgt George E. Diamond (POW) Winnsboro LA
Top-Turret: T/Sgt Walter O. Grotz (POW) Delano MN
Radio-Operator: S/Sgt Donald B. Dykstra (POW) Buffalo NY
Left-Waist: S/Sgt Cletus A. Sisley (POW) Lancaster WI
Right-Waist: Sgt Gordon L. Benson (POW) Cherry Valley MA
Tail-Gunner: Sgt William R. Foster (POW) Waterville KS

Total: 2 KIA, 7 POW
Target: Misburg (Hannover)
Crash Site: Near Springe a.d. Deister, about 30 km SW of target
Time of Crash: 12.50

NOT HOME FOR CHRISTMAS

In August 1946, Top-Turret Gunner Walter Grotz and his brother paid a visit to Gladys Hert, the widow of co-pilot **Carl J. Hert**. She wrote:

"Walter Grotz, one of the boys who were on the ship that Carl was flying on that fatal day of November 26, 1944, and his brother are touring the country visiting the homes of the other boys of Carl's crew.

"Before "bombs away" the plane was attacked by the Germans. Waist-gunner Gordon Benson was the first to see the bullets enter the wing and causing a fire. He notified the pilots and dropped through the bomb bay before "bombs away". The warning was given and the other boys bailed out. During this catastrophe the pilot held the ship steadily, enabling the boys to jump. The interior of the plane was alive with flames.

Co-Pilot Carl J. Hert

Carl Hert had also bailed out and landed safely on German soil but his legs were hurt either during the attack by German fighters or possibly by a hard landing. Shortly after his capture he was shot by his sole German guard. In 1947 the War Crimes Office launched a thorough investigation.

The accused was the German soldier Heinrich R., who on that fateful Sunday in November 1944 was an inmate of a nearby military hospital. Three other people played a role in this drama: the forester Ringelhan who had seen the airman come down and who was armed with a hunting rifle, the police officer Schoenemeier and the medical doctor Bause.

When Schoenemeier arrived on the scene he found Ringelman, the accused Heinrich R. who was wearing the blue-white uniform of the hospital and Carl Hert, who was sitting near a tree.

Schoenemeier motioned Carl Hert to get up but Carl pointed at his legs. Schoenemeier then gave Carl two sticks of wood to support himself. Carl managed to cover about thirty meters and sat down again.

Schoenemeier told Ringelhan that he would have to go over to the crash site of the plane and asked him to remain with the airman as he had a loaded rifle. Heinrich R. then volunteered to remain with Carl Hert, received the rifle from Ringelham and was told to bring the airman to the nearby hospital.

About what then happened Heinrich R. made the following statement:

"I was walking with a comrade in the park. Over Hannover was a big air battle. Then a plane came down very deep and crashed in the Sau Park. Then we saw several parachutists coming down, one went down in the park. Then I took a bicycle from the forester and drove there. I arrived at this spot together with the forester and a policeman. I cannot say exactly which of both gave me the rifle. Then the policeman said to me: "can you bring the man to the hospital" and they drove to the place where the airplane had crashed.

"Until we came to the road the flyer went in an ordinary walk, then he pointed to a club and I gave him one. Then he said to me; "Machine". I said to him that we would not meet a car on this way. Then he still went further and pointed to the grass. I said to him yes, he could have a seat. I sat down close to him and all of a sudden he took the club and held it before my face. I gave him to understand that he should not do this, but he did not hear that. I said it again to him, then he came towards me, I jumped on the side and then shot him. Where the bullet had gone I cannot remember anymore."

Testimony made by Dr. Wilhelm Bause on February 1947:

Question: "Do you remember the murder of an American airman who parachuted from a burning bomber?"

Answer: "Yes, I do remember very well."

Question: "I understand that you had an investigation ordered concerning this case?"

Answer: "Yes, I did."

Question: "Tell me in your own words what took place and what action you undertook."

Answer: "The November 26, 1944 was on a Sunday. I was chief medical doctor for the military hospital in Bad Muender and had several emergency hospitals under me, among them the hospital 'Huntinglodge' near Springe. During the week following the Sunday in question I made a tour of inspection and arrived at Springe towards the end of the week.

"I immediately was informed that one of the lighter wounded patients had killed an American airman. The name of the soldier was Heinrich R. I at once instructed my assistant, Captain Schultze, who was a lawyer in civilian life, to investigate the case, so I could forward my report to higher headquarters which at that time was in Hameln. I personally did not investigate the said Heinrich R. but when I stepped into the room where Captain Schultze conducted the investigation I saw the soldier and as the report was finished I read it. In this report R. pleaded self defence, said he had to shoot the American because he attacked him with a club. I had heard that the bullet wound was in the back of the American's head which made the self defence plea not very plausible. As I was not powerful enough to make a decision in this case, I forwarded the report to higher headquarters in Hameln, recommending a court martial for R."

Question: "Did you not question R. to what actually happened?"

Answer: "Yes, I did. He told me that the flier was injured on his leg and used a stick for support. He ordered the flier to walk towards the hospital. After a short walk the flier sat down on a mile stone to rest. When R. ordered the flier to proceed on his way, he refused and presumably threatened R. with his stick, whereupon R. shot the flier."

Question: "Did you believe his story?"

Answer: "No, I don't."

On December 4, 1947, Heinrich R. was sentenced to death by hanging. A year later this sentence was commuted to life imprisonment.

Carl Hert was born on September 22, 1915 in Chicago, Illinois, the son of Joseph and Irene Hert. After graduating from Lakeview High School in Chicago, he went to work as a mechanic for his father who owned a garage and trucking business. In August, 1941, he married Gladys Marzullo and they had a son David who was born on October 22, 1942. Carl entered active duty in the air Corps in February, 1943 and trained as an aviation cadet at the San Antonio Texas Aviation Cadet Center. He also had a younger brother, Norman. Today, his descendants include not only his son, but two grandchildren and one great grandchild. He was 29 when he was murdered.

About Navigator **Joseph J. Hanzook** his son Joseph recalls:

"Dad was always reluctant to share his war time experiences. We had to really pry to get him to speak on the subject.

"Just before Dad bailed out he saw pilot Lee McPartland "engulfed in fuel and flames". Dad exited by the bomb bay doors that at first he could not open. Only by jumping up and down was he able to get the jammed doors open. Immediately after exiting the bomber there was an explosion that initially knocked Dad out. When he regained his senses, he was in mid-air.

"When Dad pulled his rip cord he immediately remembered he had failed to tighten the crotch harness straps. As a result, when the canopy opened, the crotch straps felt like they had ripped his body in half.

"He landed in a tree and was knocked unconscious. When he awakened, Dad was surrounded by Home Guard members who cut him down and took him to a small town. Having arrived there, an elderly lady approached him and put a pistol to his head. After all that had just happened, my Dad thought this was a lousy way to die. However, a German officer appeared and hit her in the end with the butt end of his weapon.

From a letter of Joe Hanzook to the POW Camp Reunion in 1993:

"From Kriegie Camp to Paris then back to the States in June 1945, yours truly was discharged at Fort George G. Meade which is about 25 miles from my boyhood home and where I was instructed into the service. That summer was spent in Rest & Recreation in Miami Beach, Florida and in renewing old acquaintances, especially with the girl, Lee, whom I have known since 5th grade and with whom I was corresponding before being shot down. In December, 1945 we were married and here we are 50 years and 4 children later, ready to celebrate 50 years of marriage.

"September 1945 found me as a freshman at John Hopkins University along with hundreds of other ex-GI's. I majored in Industrial Engineering and graduated with a B.E. in June 1949. It was tough settling in as a student after my experience overseas.

"After graduation my jobs were diverse and of short span until I started with Minneapolis Honeywell in 1950 as a sales engineer. This remained my field through Tate Engineering and Diebold, from which I retired.

"My interests over the years developed into building boats, garages and houses. Since May 1986 we've been living in the last house I worked on.

NOT HOME FOR CHRISTMAS

It is a remodelled summer home on the Magothy River near Annapolis, MD. Before Parkinson disease hit me I enjoyed boating, both sail and motor, as well as fishing, crabbing and travelling in our Winnebago motor home.

"It's been a good life. Until ten years ago my health was excellent. There are no complaints.

In August 2004, Top-Turret Gunner **Walter O. Grotz**, wrote the following:

"On the morning of November 26, 1944, we flew from Tibenham Airfield outside or Norwich and headed for Germany to bomb the synthetic oil plant in Misburg, east of Hannover.

"At about 26000 feet we started descending towards the target when we were intercepted by Focke Wulf 190's. We took a number of hits on their first pass, which started a fire in the vicinity of number 2 engine. It is believed that the main fuel lines in the leading edge of the wing were severed. This burning gasoline rand down the wing and started a fire in the bomb bay area that created a lot of smoke in the rear of the airplane where two other crew men and myself were stationed at our gun positions. I was the flight engineer on the plane but also acted as gunner. I tried to call the people on the flight deck but the intercom was apparently damaged.

"The next thing I heard was the bail out alarm bell so I put on my chute, opened the rear hatch and bailed out. I estimated that we were on 22.000 feet, so I delayed pulling the rip cord. When I did I experienced quite a jolt throughout my body. A Focke Wulf 190 circled me several times and I was afraid he would either strafe me with his machine guns or dive on my blossomed parachute. We had been briefed that this was happening rather often but in my case it didn't happen.

"It was about noon at the time of bail out and it took me almost half an hour to float down before reaching the ground. The weather was clear and I could see a number of people streaming from a small village to the field I was heading for. I landed into a dead furrow against my left leg, injuring it.

"I was pulled to my feet by two youths who I later learned were members of the Hitler Youth. Then a man in a green uniform came and started beating me with the butt of his gun. Then a tall man in a blue uniform came and pulled him away and said to me in English: "You'll be all right now. I'll take care of you." I later learned that he was an officer in the German Luftwaffe.

"The two Hitler Youths led me down the street of the village. I had to walk with a limp because of my injury. The people were lined up along the street and were yelling and jeering. The youth brought me to a building which apparently was a military office. An officer was sitting behind a big desk. Behind his back was a huge picture of Hitler. The two youths put me in front of this officer, saluted and clicked their boots saying; "Heil Hitler". They then searched me and found in one of my pockets my rosary which they kept for one reason or the other. A few minutes later two crew members were brought in; the tail-gunner William Foster and the nose-turret gunner George Diamond.

"Foster was bleeding under his chin and later told me that he had bailed out without buckling his leg straps. The main buckle had slipped from his chest to under his chin and so he floated down.

"I could see that George Diamond was in great pain. He also had bailed out with his leg straps unbuckled, wrenching his back pretty bad. The three of us were loaded in a small car and driven about twenty miles to an air field where they put us in single cells with a barred window high up. In the room was a wooden bed, no mattress and one cotton blanket. In about an hour, fear finally struck me. I began to tremble and my heart began a pretty fast beat. I didn't sleep at all during that first night in Germany. In the morning they gave me one piece of very dark bread with margarine, nothing at noon and then a repeat of the same for the evening meal.

"After two days they moved me to another cell and already there was Gordon Benson, the right-waist gunner of our crew. When he saw me he was shocked because he was sure I was dead. I had taken two parachutes with me as instructed at a briefing the night before and had put one of these in the front of the plane and the other in the back.

Benson told me that he had tapped the pilot Lee McPartland on the shoulder as well as the radio-operator Donald Dykstra, had pointed to the fire in the bomb bay and had bailed out.

"A few days later, Benson and I were taken from our cell, put on a bus and brought to the rail road station in Hannover. On the station our guard told us to face the wall at all times because the people of Hannover were angered with all allied airmen because of the recent bombing of their city. Our group of 34 men were put on several trains before reaching at the interrogation centre in Oberursel. One of the men in our group was badly burnt and was not able to walk. The smell from his burnt flesh was almost unbearable. Donald Dykstra and I carried him from the train depot to the interrogation center: a distance of half a mile. His face and head were badly burnt and so was one hand and one foot.

NOT HOME FOR CHRISTMAS

He said it was caused by a direct hit in the bomb bay. The first thing the Germans at the interrogation center was to take care of the wounded so that was the last we saw of him.

"We were taken into the basement of the building and we were called out one by one. I was the last one to be called. They took me upstairs and asked me questions. I only gave them my name, rank and service number. I was also told that I could be treated as a spy and shot or they could turn me over to the Gestapo with all their tactics. The next step found me in solitary confinement for about a week and I was then sent to Stalag Luft IV. That camp housed 8000 POW's, most of them were American but there was a section that held British and Australian airmen.

"In late January 1945, rumours began to spread throughout the camp that the Russians were on the move to the west and we would soon have to vacate the camp. We could see large groups of people moving on the roads just outside the camp. We did not know if they were refugees or POW's. Early February, the word came that we would be moving out the next day. I gathered all I could into a pack that I could carry on my back.

"On February 6, as we left camp we were each given one Red Cross parcel. We marched out past the rail road station and onto the open road. All trough the march we were watched over by armed German guards. There were four columns that marched out of the camp and each of them had their own guards. At the end of each column was a guard with two shepherd police dogs. Anyone who lagged behind was attacked by these dogs. After the war our dog guard was detained for war crimes.

"On the 10th of February, my 20th birthday I met one of our crew, Donald Dykstra and we decided to stick together. We marched all that day and late into the night. At the end of the day, we were turned into an open field and told that this was where we would spend the night. Dykstra and I spent the night sitting in an upright position. I asked Dykstra if he had anything to eat as I had finished my Red Cross parcel. "One cold boiled potato" he said which we shared. The next morning we were put on barges and crossed the river Elbe.

"All during February and most of March this march continued. Since it was wintertime, it often snowed or rained and the sun rarely shone. The last week in March we were put on a train in box cars packed in so tight that all we could do was stand. After a one hour ride we were taken to Stalag XI B, just outside Fallingbostel where we stayed about a week. On April 3, 1945 we were told to get ready to march again. While we were in line ready to march, one of the guards told us that we were going to Lübeck on the Baltic Sea to be put on a ship and to sail to Norway. In the mid-morning we marched out heading north. We now had different guards; members of the German Home Guard.

"On the night of April 15, we had been in a barn for several hours I heard a low flying airplane go over. The next thing I heard were bobs exploding. Then I heard machine gun fire as the plane strafed the barn we occupied. A fire started in the roof of our barn. I was near to the door and I grabbed my shoes and gear and hurried out of the barn.

"We were marched a short distance and told to stay in a ditch. It was then that I learned that there were a number of wounded caused by the air attack. After an hour, they marched us back to another barn adjacent to the one that was still burning. The next morning we could see two bomb craters in the yard from the previous night's bombing, a hundred feet from the barn we had been in.

"I also learned in the morning hat one POW had been killed and twenty-six were wounded. That afternoon we buried our dead comrade who was British and attended the memorial service at the cemetery where he was buried. A local minister gave the eulogy in German. The next days on the march were similar to the days before.

"On the morning of May 1st the weather was cold and snowy. We marched a long time along the muddy roads before a break. It was there and then that my morale had hit its lowest point. I told Dykstra that I just couldn't go on anymore but he encouraged me to keep on going and I did.

"We came to a small city called Wittenburg where we were put in a barn. Each of us received a cupful of boiled potatoes, none exceeding one inch in diameter. A fellow POW from Idaho said; "Back home we wouldn't even pick these up when we harvested". Later that evening the guards came and told us; "To-morrow you're comrades will come". We could hear artillery being fired and that continued the whole night.

"The next morning two British soldiers on motorcycles came through, stopped for a short time and said that they were going to meet up with the Russians. Shortly after, a fleet of British tanks rumbled through and never stopped. Then a few British jeeps with some high ranking Germans as prisoners stopped and told us that we were liberated. Our guards had smashed their weapons and had taken off over the fields.

"I stayed around the farm that day. Some of the other POW's had gone to Wittenburg on a looting spree. On May the 3rd, early in the morning someone had lined up a farmer with horse drawn wagon to take us to Laurenberg, where a POW receiving station had been set up by the British. After riding the wagon for about two hours, we came upon some abandoned German vehicles. We stopped to investigate and saw that these trucks were loaded with medical and office supplies. Amongst the vehicles was a Dutch school bus. The key was left in the bus so I got in, started it and all POW's in the horse drawn wagon climbed aboard. We asked British soldiers along the way how to get to Laurenburg.

"Having arrived at the main highway we saw miles and miles of refugees on both sides of the road in every kind of vehicle you could imagine: from horse drawn to hand drawn carts all with people trying to get away from the Russians. The night before the Germans had blown up the bridge over the Elbe but the British had constructed a pontoon bridge open only for the Allied military and POW traffic. We crossed the river and found our way to the POW receiving camp.

"There we were given a good meal of all we could eat and a change of clothes and shoes of British issue. We were told that we could take a shower but only with ice cold water as the Germans had blown up the hot water system. The whole complex appeared to have been a school for the military. I took a cold shower and that night became very ill, because of overeating and having taken the cold shower.

"The next morning they loaded us up on big trucks and took us to the outskirts of an air field where we were told that we would be airlifted to American controlled territory. We were flown to Liege in Belgium and turned over to an American hospital where they found I still had a fever. While in hospital I was debriefed and went by train to Camp Lucky Strike in France where I stayed about a week. From there I was taken by truck to the port of Le Havre where I boarded the "Admiral Mayo", a Liberty ship bound for the United States

Don Dykstra, the son of radio-operator **Donald B. Dykstra**, wrote in 2005:

"Donald Benjamin Dykstra was born December 30, 1917 in Buffalo, New York. He was the first-born of Rose (McCue) and Benjamin Dykstra. While Rose was born in this country, Benjamin was an immigrant from Friesland, Holland. Rose and Benjamin did have one other child, a daughter named Janet. Unfortunately, Janet was born with birth defects and was institutionalized at a young age.

"Donald attended public schools on the north side of the City of Buffalo, including Bennett High School where he was an assistant football coach in the late 1940s. He was a rather big teenager and, while in high school, played semi-pro football under various assumed names each week. He came to the attention of the varsity football coach at Canisius

College, a Jesuit college located in Buffalo which, at that time, played a Division 1 schedule.

"He attended Canisius for about 2 years before dropping out and continuing to work in his father's large (for that time) grocery store.

"In July, 1941 Donald married Eileen Elizabeth Kelly and on May 5, 1942 they had their first-born, a daughter named Kathleen Elizabeth. He continued to work at the family business as a butcher until he was drafted in 1943.

"My father always believed that the pilot and co-pilot refused to bail out of the burning plane. You have found that not to be the case. He said that Gordon Benson, the waist-gunner, lost his gloves so my dad gave Benson his gloves. When my dad jumped out the bomb bay door, he knew he was not supposed to pull his ripcord immediately due to other planes which could rip up his parachute. He pulled it anyway because he was afraid his hands might freeze. He landed in a freshly-plowed field injuring his knee. He hobbled over toward a creek to look for others who might have landed nearby and that was when he was captured by some young boys with long knives."

"My dad never went into detail about much. He said he was sent to Stalag Luft 4. He said he was interrogated within his first week and that the German interrogators knew his wife's name, his daughter's name, and that he had worked in the family store in Buffalo. He said he had heard that German Intelligence was very good but he was really impressed with them after his interrogation.

"I met a man a couple of years ago who was also at Stalag Luft 4. That former prisoner said that the camp held up to 10,000 airmen (do not know if that was true) and that he and 1,000 others were put on trains and transferred to Stalag Luft 1. He was very grateful after he learned that the others, like my dad, were put on the road in what became known as "The German Death March".

"One day there was a new prisoner in the column and, although his uniform was not in the greatest shape, he was healthy. Dad said the new prisoner told them that he had recently been shot down, that the war was going very well, and that they should be liberated soon. This new prisoner was only in the column for three or four days, then he was gone.

"In 1948 my dad went by train from Buffalo to Chicago for a trade convention (he did not fly again until 1965 or 1966) and the train got in late. He said he went to the hotel bar for a beer and no one was there except the bartender and one man seated at the far end of the bar. While sipping his beer, he thought he recognized the man so he moved to the

NOT HOME FOR CHRISTMAS

middle of the bar for a better look. After a few seconds he walked over to the man, told him that he believed he knew him but was having trouble placing him. The man responded, "Try Germany". Then my dad remembered - - - it was the new prisoner.

"In May, 1945, the column was liberated by the British. The emaciated POWs were taken to "Camp Lucky Strike" which my Dad thought was in Belgium. Upon arriving, the POWs were directed to throw their clothing onto an outdoor fire and step into the first tent. It was time for a very long shower.

"When they emerged from the first tent, they were met by a barber who cut off any body hair they had. Then, into the second tent for, you guessed it, another long shower. There was a sergeant in that shower who would not let anyone out until he felt that they were extremely clean. He said the water was scalding hot but admitted that may not have been true because this was his first shower since the Death March began and because he was so thin.

"When that sergeant said they could leave the second tent, he directed the POWs to "walk into the white sheet". Behind that white sheet was a Sister of Charity. They learned later that the U.S. Army had hired these Belgian Sisters to assist. All of the Sisters were nurses. The Sisters examined each POW's skin for anything unusual and if it was found, it was back to the second tent and that Army Sergeant again.

"My dad said he passed the nurses' inspection and was directed into the third tent for a clothing (i.e. new uniforms and underwear) issue. The distributing personnel had to ask each POW what he used to weigh and what the waist size was before they became prisoner so that there was a chance the POW could grow into the clothes.

"When they were outfitted, they were directed to a mess tent but were warned by a mess sergeant at the door to only take a little bit of food now, then come back in two hours and take a little bit more. My dad asked him how long the mess tent would be open and the sergeant replied "Oh, we never close! Not when we know you guys will be coming in every two hours or so!" My dad said he took the sergeant's advice and only ate some fruit and a little bit of bread. In 10 minutes, he vomited "all" of that food. Two hours later he came back and tried it again. This time with success. After a long sleep, he went back to that mess hall and tried a real meal. Three pieces of lamb stayed down. He then knew he would be just fine.

"After the war Dad worked in the family grocery shop until 1964 when it closed, then worked at J.C. Penny, Bethlehem Steel, and finally as a let-

Left-waist gunner **Cletus A. Sisley** wrote in January 2003:

"We had made our final turn to start on our bomb run over the target which was the oil refinery at Misburg, Germany. I had opened the bomb bay doors from my nose turret position prior to the bomb run. My position was nose gunner and there we had a toggle switch mounted in the turret to use at a precise time to salvo the whole load of bombs.

"After our 2nd mission over Germany they decided to remove the ball turret from all our B-24's to eliminate the drag and give us more air speed. I was originally the ball-turret or belly-gunner, but due to the fact that I had gone thru Armourer Gunnery School, I knew how to operate and repair all the turrets, plus the operation of the bomb racks, bomb sights, etc.

"I had armed the bombs and we were on our bomb run when I saw German fighters coming in out of the sun. They came in on 11:00 position in order to hit our engines, gas tanks and pilots compartment. I had dropped the bombs before we got hit by the fighters. On the first pass thru our deputy lead plane blew up. We were in the number three position in the formation so we were one of the first planes to be hit.

"Our right wing was hit and on fire after the first pass thru the formation. Shortly after this our radio-operator gave the bail-out signal over the interphone. Apparently our pilot was seriously hit, but was still handling the controls at that time. I was wounded in the right arm when the fighters went thru the formation again. Our navigator shouted that he was bailing out and I told him I would follow him.

"When I left the plane it had started into a power dive, so I felt I was the last one to bail out. When I was going down I noticed some of our escort planes were showing up, but it was too late to help us. I think I floated across a canal and landed in a field not far from a hay stack. I could see that the Home Guard was all around me, so I hid my bill fold under the hay stack and waited in the field until an angry farmer knocked me down with the but end of his shotgun.

"Shortly after this a German soldier came by and took me into a small town jail where they kept me until the next day, when I was put on a train and taken to Frankfort, Germany. I was put in a dark room with another prisoner for two days, and then interrogated by a German officer for about an hour. The Germans then put several of us on a train and took us to a transient camp called Dulag Luft at Wetzlar, Germany. We were issued

U.S. army winter clothes, shoes, socks, a knife, spoon and mess kit that was furnished thru our Red Cross.

"On the third day we were shipped out of there by train to our permanent prison camp (Stalag-Luft 4) at Grostychow in East Prussia near the Baltic Sea. We were held there until the Russians forced them to evacuate our camp on Feb. 6, 1945.

"We were put on a 84 day march which covered over 700 miles across Germany. This was known as the Black Death March, because of the severe cold, lack of food, water, medicine, and a decent place to sleep. We were crowded into barns, old schools, warehouses, and we often slept in a field or in a forest. A lot of the prisoners got pneumonia, trench foot, pellagra and dysentery which was often acquired by drinking contaminated water. We did a lot of back tracking over certain areas because of the different advancing troops. The Germans didn't want to give us up because they thought it would help them in their negotiations with the allied forces.

Jody Benson Bagdis, the daughter of waist-gunner **Gordon Benson** wrote the following eulogy:

". . . . As a kid he was the one to lead the charge across the thin coat of ice after the first freeze and was usually the first one to fall through. He was the boy who had to lead the "damn cow" down McCarty Avenue in Cherry Valley each day so it could graze. Dad hated that cow so much that even in his 80's he continued to curse it. All in all Dad was the boy next door who hung out with his friends and got into mischief just like every other boy his age.

"As a young man Dad became known as Sgt. Benson, Air Force Gunner. His fellow soldiers knew him as a man who wanted to be a pilot but couldn't because of a heart murmur. He was the airman shot down over Germany who saw two of his crewmen never make it out of the plane. He was the man who was unconscious when he was captured because he did not understand the German commands being shouted at him. He was herded into a boxcar and travelled to Poland where he became a close friend to many POW's. He was the story of an 86 day, 488 miles forced march through Germany and through the dead of winter. The ordeal involved 9500 American airmen many of whom did not survive this infamous march and later received a purple heart and three bronze stars. This was a very private part of his life that he held deep inside himself."

Gordon Benson passed away in September, 2003.

About nose-turret gunner **George Eugene Diamond** his sister June Girlinghouse wrote:

"George Diamond was born in 1923 and grew up on his parents farm in Franklin Parish near Winnsboro, Louisiana. Since this was rich delta farming land, the main crop was cotton. Farming is a life of hard physical work and George learned hard work at an early age.

"George was called "Gene" by his parents George and Alma Diamond and he was known by that name throughout his life. His parents soon added a sister Roma to the family followed by a son Louis and then another sister June.

"George loved football and as soon as he entered high school he tried out and made the team. After football practice, he had to walk five miles home and usually arrived after dark. June was always waiting for his arrival to get her hug from her big brother and hero.

Nose-turret gunner George E. Diamond

"During the summer months, community baseball was the popular recreation. Naturally, George became involved playing various positions and his Dad frequently umpired. It was a fun time for the family.

"After graduating from Winnsboro High School, he needed a job and joined the Civilian Conservation Corp where he worked on the Hoover Dam for two years and then enlisted in the USAAF during World War II. He was transferred to the 445th Bomber Group, Squadron 703, in England. He achieved the rank of sergeant as a gunner on a B-24. George had a total of 150 combat hours before he was declared missing on his 8th combat mission on November 26, 1944.

"His sister June, who was only 8 years old, says she will never forget the telegram delivered by the War Department with the news that George's plane had been shot down and he was missing in action. The family knew the odds of survival were not good. There were many days of anxiously waiting for news which came primarily by radio. The fam-

NOT HOME FOR CHRISTMAS

ily did not have a telephone in those days. Many encouraging letters and telegrams started arriving from distant family and friends as soon as the news was known. All the neighbors came calling in person. After a few months another telegram came from the War Dept. saying he was a POW. Oh, what joy!

"George's mother corresponded with several of the mothers and wives of the crew of his bomber each offering sympathy and encouragement to each other.

"George's account through the years of the Nov. 24, 1944 date and POW months and days came little by little. He told of bailing out so quickly he did not get his parachute properly fastened and his back was injured as he came down in an open field. He could see young German soldiers with guns pointing at him but, miraculously, he was not shot as were one or more of the crew. He eventually was taken to a prison where he joined a few of his crew. He thinks he may have been in Stalag #4. He told of not having enough food and hiding potato peelings to eat after dark to keep from starving.

"After a few months his prison group was forced to retreat from the approaching Allied armies. He was in what was known as the "death march" in winter and no one had enough clothes. Many suffered frostbite and some fell by the way who were not strong enough to keep marching. He and a fellow POW escaped during the march and hid out in haystacks and barns and lived on the stored raw produce of the German farmers. He was recaptured but George's wife Mamie tells that by escaping he was liberated a few weeks earlier by the Allied Forces.

"When liberated he was hospitalized in England weighing under 100 pounds and had to be fed small meals for awhile. By the time he returned home he was looking healthy and well-fed.

"What a "Happy Day" it was to see him walk in the front door and surprise the family. George was discharged in November 1945. His decorations included: two bronze stars, a distinguished unit badge, an American Theater Metal, Good Conduct Metal, and a POW Badge.

"Soon after having been discharged and returned to his home near Winnsboro, LA, he discovered a good looking 18 year old brunette named Mamie Barefield had moved to a farm near his home. The courting quickly became quite intense and soon there was a marriage. During the remainder of his life he and Mamie lived in Winnsboro, Baton Rouge and Monroe while he worked in different jobs; first in insurance, then construction and his final job was with the U. S. Postal System for several years. During those years four healthy, energetic boys were born to them. To quote their mother Mamie, she was blessed with wonderful boys.

"As his boys were growing up, George enjoyed playing and coaching them in sports. The family loved the outdoors and included camping in their activities. During the years he enjoyed writing as a hobby and sent articles to Readers Digest and other magazines, but none were ever published. He and Mamie joined a square dance group and spent many fun hours square dancing.

"George lived to see his sons become adults, then marry and bless him with six grandchildren before his death at the age of 56 due to a heart attack. Three of his sons served in different branches of the U. S. Military and one became a minister.

"Among the family's cherished memories of George were hearing his entertaining stories and jokes while his blue eyes twinkled. He had many friends who enjoyed visiting with him and listening to his stories.

"George (Gene) Diamond leaves a legacy of being a part of liberating Europe and ending WW11 and is one of those written about in the book "The Greatest Generation." His legacy also includes four boys, eleven grandchildren and 20 great grandchildren, family and friends who loved him.

***

Acknowledgements:
David Hert for co-pilot Carl J. Hert
National Archives and Records Administration for Carl Hert
Joseph Hanzook for his father navigator Joe J. Hanzook
Veteran Walter O. Grotz
Don Dykstra, the son of radio-operator Donald B. Dykstra
Judy Benson Bagdis for waist-gunner Gordon Benson
June Girlinghouse for nose-turret gunner George Diamond

CHAPTER 34

389TH BOMB GROUP 566TH BOMB SQUADRON

Aircraft Type: B-24J, Serial # 44-10579, "Pugnacious Princess Pat", MACR: 11208
Airbase: Hethel

"Red was knocked unconscious when he was blown from the plane and came to while plummeting toward the earth. He was on his back and he said it was very quiet and he thought he'd gone to heaven. Then he rolled over and saw the earth rushing up. He pulled his rip cord and landed safely".

—Navigator Wayne "Red" Buhrmann as told by his widow Jo Buhrmann

---

Pilot: 1Lt Robert A. Hicks (POW) Beaumont TX
Co-Pilot: 1Lt Harry N. Alexander (KIA) San Rafael CA
Navigator: 2Lt Wayne H. Buhrmann (POW) Princeton NE
Nose-Turret: S/Sgt Henry M. McCormack Jr. (KIA) Kingsville TX
Top-Turret: T/Sgt Eugene A. LaLanze (KIA) New Eagle PA
Radio: S/Sgt Kenneth C. Wylie (KIA) Lowell MA
Left-Waist Gunner: S/Sgt John T. Fithen (POW) Amelia OH
Right-Waist Gunner: S/Sgt Alfred H. Fromm (POW) Pentwater MI
Tail-Gunner: T/Sgt Richard M. Sagers (KIA) Hood River OR
Observer: Major Paull C. Garrett (KIA) San Antonio TX

Total: 6 KIA, 4 POW
Target: Misburg
Crash Site: 1 km NW of Altwarmbüchen, District Burgdorf, 8 km N of Misburg
Time of Crash: 13.00

NOT HOME FOR CHRISTMAS

Jan Hey of the Netherlands summarizing the Missing Air Crew Report:

"This B-24 received two direct flak hits on the bomb run. The bail out order was given but no response came. The right wing and part of the tail were cut off. Both waist-gunners managed to bail out; the navigator was blown clear when the aircraft exploded.

About pilot **Robert A. Hicks**, his widow Carolee Hicks Pierce and his daughter Pat wrote:

"Robert Auston Hicks was born to Gertrude and William Herbert Hicks in Humble, Texas on October 28, 1922. He had an older brother, W.H. Their father was killed in an oil rig accident when Robert was 3 years old. Robert was known as "Buddy" to his family. It was when he joined the service that he was known as "Tex". Gertrude and the boys lived with her mother until he was seven when Gertrude married James T. Claxton. James worked for Sun Oil Company and they moved around a lot in Texas working in the oil fields.

"Buddy was promoted from Junior High School to Senior High School from Crocked Jr. High School, Beaumont, Texas in May, 1941.

"A friend of Buddy had gotten his draft notice and he talked Buddy into joining the service with him, although I think Buddy was too young. They were sent to Kessler Field in Biloxi, Mississippi on October 28, 1941 for basic training. Both of the boys tried out for pilot training, but the friend's eyesight was not good so he did not make it and they parted ways. Around December of 1943 Buddy was sent to Liberal Air Force Base in Liberal, Kansas. for his B-24 bomber training. The base was built solely for this purpose and was closed when the war was over.

"I graduated from Liberal High School in May of 1943 and went to work at the base in the Quartermaster Corp. I met Buddy on a blind date and we "hit it off" and fell in love. We spent our free time together until he was sent to Casper, Wyoming and eventually overseas. Buddy was an excellent dancer and we spent our nights dancing at the Liberal Country Club dancing to the "Big Band Music". He was so good at dancing that people would get off the dance floor to watch us. That all changed when he came back with his leg injury and we had to give up dancing. We took up bowling and Buddy became an avid fisherman.

"Buddy returned to the States on the U.S. Army Hospital ship "Blanche F. Sigman" at Charleston, S.C. on July 30, 1945. He was sent to a hospital in Massachusetts where they reset his leg. He was on crutches for 2 years. We married on November 8, 1945 and he was sent to Brooks Army Hospital in San Antonio, Texas. We enjoyed San Antonio.

"Buddy decided not to stay in the service because he would not be able to fly. He went to work for National Supply Company as a salesman in the oil field. We lived in Hebronville, Texas, Corpus Christi, Texas and Victoria, Texas. We had 3 children, James Auston, Patricia Carol, and Jacque Ellen. In 1960 we moved to Houston, Texas and he worked for Standco Oil Company. He enjoyed being a salesman in the oil field and he covered Texas, Louisiana, and Mississippi.

"His health deteriorated and he was "in and out" of the hospital. He had to give up traveling because of his health and he was not happy working in the office.

"When we were in Corpus Christi and Victoria, Buddy enjoyed fishing every weekend. He had his own small boat and went with friends in their

Back Row, left to right: Henry McCormack, Alfred Fromm, Eugene LaLanze, John Fithen, Kenneth Wylie, *Claude Kershner
Front Row, left to right: *Bernard Cheerer, Wayne Buhrmann, Harry Alexander, Robert Hicks
(* not on the November 26, 1944 mission)

larger boats. He would even go as a crew member on a chartered boat out of Rockport, Texas just to fish and be with his friends. I always encouraged him to "do his thing" because he deserved it.

"Robert Auston Hicks (Buddy) passed away in Memorial Hospital on September 6, 1981 at the age of 58.

About co-pilot **Harry Noel Alexander** his nephew wrote the following bio:

"Harry was born May 21, 1920 in Miller, Nebraska as the second child of William Warren Alexander and Ethel Velma (Tingley) Alexander with seven siblings all born in Nebraska.

"Harry, who was known to the family as "Dutch" attended school in Halsey, Nebraska. Dutch got his nick name for two reasons. His Uncle Harry Alexander was living at the house and of course had the same first name and the family wanted to avoid confusion. He was a little boy at the time and had a bit of a funny way of saying some of his words which the family decided made him sound like he was speaking "Dutch" so they began calling him the "Little Dutchman". With time it was simply shortened to "Dutch" and it stuck.

"In 1938 Harry drove the family from Nebraska to Ukiah, California, following his father who had gone to California seeking work.

"On July 31 1940 Harry enlisted in the Army at Hamilton Field in Marin County near San Rafael and was assigned as a fireman with the Fire Department.

"On April 5, 1941, he married Alice Lucille Haas of Ukiah in San Rafael, California. Daughter Harriet Lucille Alexander was born August 10, 1943 in San Rafael, California.

"In 1944 I remember Uncle "Dutch" coming home and visiting us and I remember all the activity going on at my grandparent's home during his visit. I clearly remember that it was a very happy time. I did not know that it was his last leave after receiving his commission as an officer in the Army Air Corps and I had no way of knowing that would be the last time I would see him. Being the first grandchild there was a

1Lt. Harry N. Alexander

528

389th Bomb Group, 566th Bomb Squadron

great deal of attention paid to me which is probably why I can remember that day so vividly even though I was only two.

"My next recollection was my grandmother hanging a small "flag" in the window facing the road and crying. At two and a half years old I was too young to understand.

"Pugnacious Princess Pat" nose art

Harry is buried at: Plot H Row 18 Grave 27 in the Netherlands American Cemetery, Margraten, Netherlands

Original art

Navigator **Wayne "Red" Buhrmann** as told by his widow Jo Buhrmann:

"He joined the Army Air Cadet Corp in 1942 but was deferred until February of 1943. At that time he was in his last year of college. He would have graduated in May. The military in their infinite wisdom sent him to pilot's training even though his tests had shown he would make a better navigator. However he flunked out of pilots training and then was given a chance at navigation.

"Eventually the crew was assembled in Casper, WY and sent to England. They flew over on July 4th, 1944. Their first landing was in Ireland and the crew promptly came down with food poisoning and ended up in the hospital. Strangely enough when Goodyear sent him to Ireland many years later we lived very near the landing strip (now a place for flea markets) and the hospital where he had been. Talk about life coming full circle.

NOT HOME FOR CHRISTMAS

"When they flew on to Hethel their plane was given to an old seasoned crew and they flew in someone else's bomber. The fateful day they were shot down they were not scheduled to fly but were awakened and told they were replacing someone else. Major Paull Garrett who flew with them was unknown to them as he had arrived very recently to take over the command of the 389th.

"That morning as he boarded the plane was the first time any of them had met the major. They proceeded to their target and flak hit them and they went down. Red was knocked unconscious when he was blown from the plane and came to while plummeting toward the earth. He was on his back and he said it was very quiet and he thought he'd gone to heaven. Then he rolled over and saw the earth rushing up. He pulled his rip cord and landed safely.

"Thinking a mile a minute and remembering his instructions on what to do, he bundled his parachute up and tried to hide it under a rock. About this time two old German farmers came up to him and one said, "For you der var is ofer." He was taken to a small shed and put in it and the door was locked from the outside. About this time shock set in. He had received a head wound (a piece of his skull was missing) and had a couple of teeth knocked out. To control the shaking he wrapped his arms around his knees. About this time the latch on the door was lifted and in came a little girl of about five or six with a cup of water (the cup had the handle missing) that she shakily extended toward him. Her little brother was peeking out behind her. About this time the girl's mother descended letting her daughter know clearly that this was not acceptable practice.

"Red said he didn't understand the words but he sure understood the tone as mothers are the same the world over.

"In later years like the 80's Red tried to find that little girl to thank her but the effort came to naught.

"Shortly the military came and took him away. He was reunited with his pilot, Tex Hicks, who had a broken leg. Tex kept asking Red for a cigarette, taking two puffs and then throwing it away. The old German that was driving them on a horse drawn wagon, would stop the wagon and hop out and get the cigarette. Red finally told Tex he didn't have any more cigarettes as he knew he would not be getting any more and he wanted to save some for himself.

"When they got to the interrogation center the two men were separated and didn't get back together until several years after the war.

"Somewhere along the line when he was captured his wound of the head was treated. A German doctor cleaned it up, poured sulfa into it, wound a crepe paper like bandage around it and made the statement, "Keep it clean."

"At the interrogation center Red was placed in a small cell that he could not stand up in or lie down and stretch out. There was no window. A small opening in the door was opened twice a day and food was shoved through. Not having anything else to do Red said he slept 20 hours out of 24. This was probably a good thing. It allowed him to regain energy and recoup from his wounds and trauma of being shot down. The food he was given was not very good but he knew he was a Prisoner of War so didn't expect much. He also knew the Germans must be short on many things and they were certainly not going to coddle prisoners.

"While being interrogated, he only told them what was required by the Geneva Convention, his name, rank and serial number, he was shown files about him that included where he had gone to college, where he had gotten his training, and other facts that probably came from the newspapers that his parents subscribed to. Red was amazed at the details they had on his life. The interrogator, a man who had attended college in the USA and spoke very good English, told him about whom his commanding officer, a married man, was dating among the Red Cross girls.

"After he had been interrogated for a while he was allowed to look out the window. The two surviving gunners were marched across the compound and disappeared behind a wall. Red was told that unless he talked, those two men would be shot. Red repeated his name, rank, and serial number. The next sounds he heard were rifles being fired. At that time he did not know what had happened. Afterwards he learned that the shots were a ploy to get him to talk. He didn't. Because he wouldn't tell the Germans what they wanted to know they shipped him out to Stalag Luft 1. So many planes were being shot down that there were more prisoners coming in at a great rate and they might be easier to break down so he was sent on his way.

"He rode on an old train with many other prisoners of war. One story to come out of that ride was of John Fitzgerald who was small enough to fit in the baggage rack to sleep. The train either rounded a curve or stopped abruptly and he came down on Red who, of course, still had the bandage on. Much later Fitz told me that he thought he had killed him.

"Eventually they reached Stalag Luft 1 and they were assigned to the North Compound. I forget the room number. There were 24 men in a room 24 X 24. As I remember him telling me there were tiers of bunks. He said Bill Blue was in the upper one and would hang his head down over the

NOT HOME FOR CHRISTMAS

side to talk to him. Food was a constant source of talk and the elaborate menus concocted were to dream for. That was where Red learned about "Pigs in a Blanket" which are sausages rolled up in biscuit dough. Red made up his mind that never again would he be without food. He would always have a candy bar, orange, apple, or something else in his pocket. However, when he returned home and food was everywhere he quickly got rid of that resolve.

"In the compound next to his Red found a college friend. They would get together on Sunday when the religious services were held. Those services were held in a common meeting area. When the Catholics would go the friend would go to that service but instead of returning to his compound he would go to Red's. When the next service was held, he would go to that one and return to his own compound. The fellow's name was Don Lienemann.

"One time Don was going through the garbage on his side of the fence and Red was going to the garbage on his side. They acknowledged each other's presence. A few years later the two men were traveling together from Nebraska to Iowa to see a common friend. Red reminded Don of that incident. Don immediately pulled the car over to the side and said he did not want Red to ever speak of that again. Naturally my husband couldn't wait to tell how touchy Don was about that subject and it was a favorite joke of his on Don whenever Red had an audience who knew them both.

"Once or twice Red Cross parcels were allowed in. Red volunteered to go through the parcels with a German guard. The Guard was expected to confiscate the pepper as it could throw dogs off in case of an escape. Red bribed the guard to let him have some of the pepper in exchange for cigarettes. Pepper was needed to give the food some flavor. Mostly they ate rutabagas. The men in this room had divided into small groups to do the cooking. Because Red was a math whiz his group of seven people chose him because they felt he could divide more fairly. Much as cigarettes were prized Red said he wished the Red Cross had put food in their place and since he was a smoker at that time in his life, you know how much food meant to them.

"Back to America.

"The radio news broadcast had reported 35 heavy bombers down over Germany. For the first time since WWII had begun Red's mother Lydia noted this on the kitchen calendar. The date was November 26, 1944. After all, her second son was a navigator on a B-24 and stationed in England. Weeks passed and there was no word from Wayne also known as Red. At first this was not particularly worrisome. Red had never been one to write frequently. Still as Christmas approached and there was no word worry began to creep in around the edges of her consciousness. As best she could she hid it from her husband Hermann whose health was not the best

"With son Chester on a minesweeper and son-in-law Alfred Bogle serving in the Seabees, deep concern was never far from their minds. The days dragged nearer to Christmas but no letter or card from Wayne turned up in the mail. Christmas came and went with no word. Why hadn't he written? What had happened? When would they know? All they could do was go about their daily lives as though everything was all right. But it wasn't all right. With no Christmas communication they were certain something had occurred that they didn't know about.

"Sleep at night was always accompanied by fervent prayers, which also included their son Chet, and son-in-law Alfred. Daytimes frequent silent prayers went up for their son's safety. Was he all right? When would they know? Who could they turn to? Knots in the stomach were a daily occurrence. The mailbox was at once their best friend and worst enemy. Every morning they were ever so hopeful that there would be a communication from Wayne. But once the mailman passed and there was nothing despair set in.

"On December 27, 1944, a strange car came up the driveway. The man got out and asked Herman to step outside. He then told him of the telegram he was delivering announcing that Wayne had been shot down on November 26, 1944, the very day his mother had noted on the calendar that the Germans had downed 35 heavy bombers. At last the anguish of not knowing what had happened was settled. Now the anguish of wondering if Wayne was alive was to settle in. Herman returned to the house and told his wife and youngest daughter. One can only imagine the pain this family went through of not knowing where their son and brother was.

"Now came the difficult task of notifying their eldest daughter and eldest son. Herman and Lydia sent a telegram to Eunice Bogle. It was delivered to her mailbox at the post office in Pleasanton, CA where she and Alfred were living while Alfred served in the Seabees. The post office was right on her walking route to the Pleasanton Public School where she taught. Unsuspecting she picked up the mail on her way to work. Reading it was a shock but in the true tradition of the time she carried on throughout the day, never letting on to anyone the tragedy that had befallen her family. After school she returned home. It was only when she saw her sister-in-law, Dorothy Bogle that she burst into tears.

NOT HOME FOR CHRISTMAS

"Her nephew, Tommy Bogle, 4, asked, "Aunt Eunice, where does it hurt?"

"On Dec. 28, 1944, a telephone call came from the Princeton, NE, postmaster. He told Lydia that there was a telegram being delivered to her mail box that she would want to see. Even though it was after 5 p.m. when the call came, and it was getting dark, Lydia bundled up and trudged half a mile to the mailbox through the snow. Because of Herman's health problems with rheumatoid arthritis he could not do the fetching.

"In the mailbox was the telegram from the government saying they had picked up a broadcast from the enemy saying 2nd Lt. Wayne H. Buhrmann was in their hands. Again the tears flowed, but this time they were tears of joy. Wayne was alive. However, this was an unofficial announcement but nevertheless a very welcome one. In time to come an authentic notice was issued and later there would be official word from Wayne in which he wished them a Merry Christmas and a Happy New Year and that he was fine. For his parents it was a belated Christmas gift that was more joyous than any they could have imagined.

"As time marched on more telegrams reached their household. Ones announcing Wayne's freedom from captivity, his impending journey home, his arrival in the United States and when they could expect him. Now my husband, Wayne "Red" Buhrmann, was something of a prankster. He told them he'd be home a day later than he planned. So when he arrived they did not have the fatted calf ready for him. His sister was washing her hair. I don't think she ever forgave him for that. My mother-in-law always lamented that all she had to serve him was tomato soup. That was what the family was having for supper that evening so there wouldn't be a lot of dirty dishes in preparation for the grand homecoming the next day. But never mind, everyone was glad he was back safe and sound.

"Oh yes, they had expected him to totter in all thin and emaciated from his six months in a POW camp. But Red topped the scale at 212 pounds, heavier than he had ever been. How had that happened? Well, as soon as they could the POWs were fed quite well by their liberating forces and they never passed up a chance to eat.

About Observer Major **Paull C. Garrett** his son Paull Burnett recalls:

"Paull Cather Garrett was born in Martinsburg, West Virginia, on 25 Jan 1915. He graduated from Syracuse University and was employed as an assistant bank manager in Martinsburg when he joined the Army Air Corps on 21 December 1940 at the age of 25 (quite old for a pilot). He went to pilot training at Randolph Air Force Base, San Antonio, Texas.

"My father was actually the first commanding officer of the 319th Women's Flying Training Detachment. He arrived to take command on 16 Nov 1942 in Houston. Apparently, the women of the WFTD did not like Capt Garrett primarily because he hated the training job and did not care about or support the program. All he wanted to do was to fly in combat.

Sunday, November 26, 1944. As the incoming squadron commander of the 566 Bomb Squadron, 389th Bomb Group he was on his first mission (theater orientation ride) and was occupying the jump seat as an extra crew member with an already experienced crew.

Major Paull C. Garrett

He was initially buried in the civilian cemetery of Altwarmbuchen, Germany not far from the crash site. After the war my father was re-interred in the Ardennes American Cemetery, Plot A, Row 41, Grave 17, Neuville-en-Condroz, Leige, Belgium.

My Mother, then Martha D. Garrett, received the ill-fated telegram at her parent's home in San Antonio, Texas, while just five months pregnant with me. She still vividly recalls the numbing pain she felt when she read the words that her husband was MIA.

"I have grown up wondering what my Father was like and wishing I could have known him. I was named after him (his name was spelled with two Ls instead of one) and grew up as Paull Cather Garrett until I was adopted and my last name was changed to Burnett. In my younger years much to my dismay, everyone (including my teachers) always wanted to correct the spelling to Paul.

Since then I completed a very rewarding career in the United States Air Force where I flew fighter aircraft for 24 years before retiring. My Father was my inspiration.

***

NOT HOME FOR CHRISTMAS

Acknowledgements:
Carolee Hicks Pierce and daughter Pat for pilot Robert A. Hicks
Lewis Ruddick for co-pilot Harry N. Alexander
Jo Buhrmann for navigator Wayne "Red" Buhrmann
Paull Burnett for observer Major Paull Garrett

EPILOGUE

The Kyle Smith Monument

On Monday, November 26, 2007, John Meurs and his wife Carien attended the unveiling of a monument dedicated to the pilot of "Little Guy," the B-17 bomber that had crashed just outside his hometown of Apeldoorn, Netherlands, on Sunday, November, 26, 1944. The rest of the crew had bailed out over the village, but pilot Kyle Smith had remained behind the controls so that his plane—with some bombs still on board—would avoid in the village. He lost his life in this endeavour.

Having witnessed the crash as a nine year old schoolboy, Meurs played an integral role in getting the monument erected. A few years before the dedication he wrote the local Apeldoorn newspaper about the monument, but did not get a positive reaction. Some time later he contacted a retired Brigadier General of the Royal Dutch Army who lives in Apeldoorn about a mile from the crash site and told him about "Little Guy".

Brigadier General Jelle Reitsma began to work on the project and on Monday, November 26, 2007—exactly 63 years after the crash of "Little Guy"— the simple monument was unveiled by Ann Trout and her son Aaron of Albany, Ohio, family of Kyle Smith. Also present were the Mayor of Apeldoorn, representatives of the US Ambassador to the Court of The Hague, and more than 100 residents of the village. A band from the Royal Dutch Air Force provided the music and a fighter of the Air Force made a "fly over".

Quite a few people who, like John, had watched the bomber go down were also present and it was nice for him to exchange memories about what happened on that same date so long ago.

His primary school, located about half a mile from the crash site, adopted the monument and a group of kids sang the American

NOT HOME FOR CHRISTMAS

national anthem when the two flags (American and Dutch) were raised. He had tears in his eyes when he saw these kids: he had been their age and attended their school when "Little Guy" came down. Life had come full circle.

The location of the monument is very important. Smith crashed "Little Guy" smack in the municipal outdoor swimming complex of Apeldoorn (which was vacant at that time in November) where every year thousands of young people come for a swim, a flirt and a bite. It is an excellent spot for a monument that reminds them that their freedom has been heavily paid for by men like Kyle Smith.

***

The opening of the ceremony.

Epilogue

Playing of the Last Post by the Royal Dutch Air Force Band. Members of the Royal Dutch Army (right) guard the two national flags.

The students of the Berg en Bos School sing the American Anthem.

NOT HOME FOR CHRISTMAS

The monument.

"On November 26, 1944, an American B-17 bomber crashed on this spot. The damaged plane was on its way back to base after a mission to the marshalling yard of Osnabrück. Still on board were two heavy bombs.

The plane was about to crash over Apeldoorn when the pilot, 24-year-old Lieutenant Smith, ordered the crew to bail out. He continued to fly the plane to avoid crashing in the center of the village. The aircraft crashed where we stand. Kyle Scott Smith died in the crash but because of his courage he avoided a disaster in Apeldoorn."

ABOUT THE AUTHOR

John Meurs was born in Nijmegen in the Netherlands in 1935. When he was a nine-year-old schoolboy living in the Nazi-occupied village of Apeldoorn, a B-17 crashed behind his house. The date was November 26, 1944. He never forgot it.

After primary and secondary school Meurs attended the State College of Tropical Agriculture in Deventer (Holland). Why "tropical?" Because his parents had spent a long time in the Dutch East Indies, what is now called Indonesia, and had planted a desire to go and live in the tropics.

John Meurs

Instead of becoming a planter on one of the big plantations in Indonesia after having finished his studies, Meurs went to Cameroun in West Africa to work for a Dutch international trading house with subsidiaries all over the African west coast. There he had all the things he could not get at that time in Holland: a large apartment, an interesting job, and quite a bit of money in his pocket. He witnessed the transition of the French colony Cameroun into the independent République du Cameroun—a very interesting period.

After four years in Cameroun, Meurs spent another five years in Zaire, also in West Africa, and also in the importing-exporting business. Then he left Africa to settle again in Europe. There he joined the giant electronic company Philips in 1967 and worked at their headquarters in Eindhoven (Holland). He had some trouble, after his wild African years, adapting himself to the regular life in Holland.

About the Author

In 1968 Meurs met his future wife Carien, who had grown up about ten miles from his hometown. She's the sister of one of his Dutch colleagues in Zaire.

Early 1970 Meurs joined the American GTE and worked in the export department of their European HQ in Geneva, Switzerland. He and Carien married on May 5, 1970—Liberation Day in Holland. It is celebrated each year to mark the end of the Nazi occupation during World War II.

In 1979 the Meurs left Geneva and moved to Rüti, a small town in the German-speaking part of the country where they live today.

Both John and Carien are now retired.

Note: Meurs uses both terms Holland and Netherlands in his book. This is because the country is officially called the Kingdom of the Netherlands of which the provinces of North and South Holland are only a small part, but as they were historically very important. Foreigners (and almost all the Dutch) call the whole country Holland.

***

Order Form

NOT HOME FOR CHRISTMAS

A Day in the Life of the Mighty Eighth

by John Meurs

Quantity: _____ x $16.00 each = $ _____

Shipping: $4.00 (for any number of books ordered) $ $4.00

TOTAL $ _____

Name _____

Address _____

City _____ State _____ Zip _____

Phone _____ Email _____

❏ Check OR Credit card:

❏ Visa ❏ Mastercard ❏ Amex ❏ Discover

Card # _____ Exp. _____

Name on card _____ CDC# _____

Mail or fax order form to: **QUAIL RIDGE PRESS**
P. O. Box 123 • Brandon, MS 39043
fax: 1-800-864-1082

To order by phone, call **1-800-343-1583**.

To order online, visit **www.quailridge.com**.